Salt Water Neighbors

Salt Water Neighbors

International Ocean Law Relations Between the United States and Canada

TED L. MCDORMAN

OXFORD
UNIVERSITY PRESS

OXFORD
UNIVERSITY PRESS

Oxford University Press, Inc., publishes works that further Oxford University's objective of excellence in research, scholarship, and education.

Oxford New York
Auckland Cape Town Dar es Salaam Hong Kong Karachi Kuala Lumpur Madrid Melbourne
Mexico City Nairobi New Delhi Shanghai Taipei Toronto

With offices in
Argentina Austria Brazil Chile Czech Republic France Greece Guatemala Hungary Italy
Japan Poland Portugal Singapore South Korea Switzerland Thailand Turkey Ukraine
Vietnam

Published by Oxford University Press, Inc.
198 Madison Avenue, New York, New York 10016

Library of Congress Cataloging-in-Publication Data
McDorman, Ted L.
Salt water neighbours : international ocean law relations between the United States and Canada / Ted L. McDorman.
p. cm.
Includes bibliographical references and index.
ISBN 978-0-19-538360-7 (hardback : alk. paper) 1. Territorial waters—United States.
2. Territorial waters—Canada. 3. Economic zones (Law of the sea)
4. United States—Boundaries—Canada.
5. Canada—Boundaries—United States. I. Title.
KZA1450.M33 2009
341.4'48—dc22
2008036036

1 2 3 4 5 6 7 8 9

Printed in the United States of America on acid-free paper

Note to Readers
This publication is designed to provide accurate and authoritative information in regard to the subject matter covered. It is based upon sources believed to be accurate and reliable and is intended to be current as of the time it was written. It is sold with the understanding that the publisher is not engaged in rendering legal, accounting, or other professional services. If legal advice or other expert assistance is required, the services of a competent professional person should be sought. Also, to confirm that the information has not been affected or changed by recent developments, traditional legal research techniques should be used, including checking primary sources where appropriate.

(Based on the Declaration of Principles jointly adopted by a Committee of the American Bar Association and a Committee of Publishers and Associations.)

To Allana

Contents

Preface

Canada and the United States are inextricably intertwined geographically, culturally, politically, linguistically, economically, and in numerous other ways. Being intertwined, however, does not make these countries the same. Nor does it mean either that Canada has a latent desire to become legally and politically part of the United States or that the United States is intent on annexing Canada. The complex interrelationship does, however, play a large role in how the two States interact on international legal and political matters, particularly those pertaining to Canada and the United States as salt water neighbors, which is the subject of this book-the Canada–United States (U.S.) relationship respecting maritime boundary, navigational rights, and fisheries issues that have arisen as a result of modern international ocean law. What emerges is that, although significant international legal dispute exists on a host of these matters, the two States have usually found ways to prevent the legal disagreements from unduly interfering in the reaching of a comfortable *modus vivendi* regarding the disputed issues.

A good example is the August 2007 joint press conference of U.S. President George W. Bush and Canadian Prime Minister Stephen Harper. The two acknowledged each other's differing views regarding the international legal status of the Northwest Passage, but stressed that the issue had been managed for a number of years and that they expected the matter to continue to be managed to the benefit of both States into the future.

Given the nature of its content, this monograph is the antithesis of most academic work. No crisis is exposed or identified. Nor is there a clarion call for action. While a number of the Canada-U.S. ocean disputes are potentially problematic and, for example, clearly more needs to be accomplished regarding cross-border cooperative management of fisheries, overall the two States are cooperating to their mutual advantage on existing salt water disputes. The purpose of this manuscript is to document and explain both the legal nature of the salt water disputes, but more important, the ways in which Canada and the United States are cooperating and managing most of these disputes.

The writing of this manuscript was hugely facilitated by five months as the 2007 Fulbright Chair in Canada-U.S. Relations at the Canada Institute of the Woodrow Wilson International Center for Scholars in Washington, D.C. The Wilson Center is an extraordinary environment for research and writing. Among many others at the Wilson Center, I am grateful to David Biette, Lindsay Collins, and Janet Spikes. I also wish to thank the Canada-U.S. Fulbright Programme for providing the opportunity to spend time at the Wilson Center.

From 2002 to 2004, I was the academic-in-residence at the Legal Bureau of the Canadian Department of Foreign Affairs and International Trade (DFAIT) in Ottawa. While at DFAIT, I was not involved in any of the principal disputes or issues discussed in this book. Nevertheless, colleagues at DFAIT, including Colleen Swords, Robert Hage, Louis Simard, Wendell Sanford, and Hugh Adsett, helped me to understand the operational realities (both the opportunities and limitations) of the practice of international law from a government perspective.

On the U.S. side, I am grateful to J. Ashley Roach, Robert Smith, and David Colson, all of whom have been or are still with the U.S. Department of State, for sharing their insights and perspectives on many of the matters addressed in this book.

At the University of Victoria, I received invaluable assistance from, among others, Rosemary Garton; Stella Chan; two student research assistants, Paul Hearnden and Michael James; and the outstanding law library staff, including Professor Neil Campbell, Caron Rollins, Serena Ableson, and Irene Godfry.

My thanks to a number of friends who were helpful in various ways: John Gamble (Penn State University, Erie); Rob Huebert (University of Calgary); Chris Joyner (Georgetown University); Susan Karamanian (George Washington University); Suzanne Lalonde (University of Montreal); Don McRae (University of Ottawa); Justin Nankivell (PhD candidate, University of British Columbia); Clive Schofield (University of Wollongong, Australia); and Mike Shepard (Victoria).

I also wish to acknowledge funding support from ArcticNet which allowed me to engage a student to assist with the research and preparation of those parts of this book that address Arctic matters.

Some sections of this book draw on my previously published work and papers. The following are acknowledged for permission to reproduce, in modified form, paragraphs from these works:

- *San Diego Law Review*, Vol. 25, 1988, "Will Canada Ratify the Law of the Sea Convention?"

- *Canadian Yearbook of International Law* (University of British Columbia Press), Vol. 43, 2005, "A Canadian Perspective on the Continued Non-Ratification of the Convention on the Law of the Sea by the United States;"
- *Marine Policy* (Butterworths), Vol. 9, 1985, coauthored with P.M. Saunders and D.L. VanderZwaag, "The Gulf of Maine Boundary: Dropping Anchor or Setting a Course?"
- *Willamette Journal of International Law and Dispute Resolution*, Vol. 6, 1998, "A Canadian View of the Canada–United States Pacific Salmon Treaty: The International Law Context (I);" and
- *Loyola of Los Angeles International and Comparative Law Journal*, Vol. 17, 1995, "The West Coast Salmon Dispute: A Canadian View of the Breakdown of the 1985 Treaty and the Transit License Measure."

The following are acknowledge for permission to reproduce maps:

- David H. Gray;
- *Loyola of Los Angeles International and Comparative Law Journal*, Vol. 17, 1995, "The West Coast Salmon Dispute: A Canadian View of the Breakdown of the 1985 Treaty and the Transit License Measure;"
- International Boundaries Research Unit, University of Durham, and David H. Gray, *Boundary and Security Bulletin*, Vol. 5, No. 3, 1997, "Canada's Unresolved Maritime Boundaries;" and
- Larry Herman, *Dalhousie Law Journal*, Vol. 7, 1982, "Proof of Offshore Territorial Claims in Canada."

Three friends and colleagues deserve special mention. My thanks to Jennifer Bond, a former student at the University of Victoria, currently clerking with the Supreme Court of Canada, and with whom I prepared a paper on West Coast fisheries from which I have drawn, with modification, several sections in Chapter Seven. Also, my thanks to David Gray for his close reading of parts of the manuscript, permission to reproduce some of his maps, and his assistance on a number of matters over the years. Thanks also to John Duff for providing insight on several technical U.S. legal matters and not putting the car in a snowbank.

Dr. Allana C. Lindgren, Theatre Department, University of Victoria, provided support at home, including patience throughout the many evenings and weekends of my research and writing. She listened to almost every sentence, paragraph, and footnote of this book. For this, and many other reasons, this book is dedicated to her.

Finally, in May 2006, my friend and colleague Douglas M. Johnston passed away. He was an outstanding scholar, possessor of a brilliant and original mind, a baseball fan, and a wit. His agreeing in the late 1970s, to hire me as a research assistant at the Dalhousie Ocean Studies Programme (DOSP) and our subsequent adventures (Fenway Park, SEAPOL, Singapore, Victoria, etc.) made all the difference.

Ted L. McDorman
June 2008

Abbreviations

AJIL	American Journal of International Law
AWPPA	Arctic Waters Pollution Prevention Act (Canada)
Bevans, *US Treaties*	*Treaties and Other International Agreements of the United States of America, 1776–1949* (ed CI Bevans)
BISD	General Agreement on Tariffs and Trade, Basic Instruments and Selected Documents
BTS	British Treaty Series
Can Gaz	Canada Gazette
CBD	Convention on Biological Diversity
COPs	Conference of the parties
CRC	Consolidated Regulations of Canada
CTS	Canada Treaty Series
Con. TS	*The Consolidated Treaty Series* (ed. C. Parry)
CYIL	Canadian Yearbook of International Law
DFO	Department of Fisheries and Oceans (Canada)
FAO	Food and Agricultural Organization of the United Nations
Fed Reg	Federal Register (United States)
FERC	Federal Energy Regulatory Commission (United States)
GATT	General Agreement on Tariffs and Trade
GPA	Global Plan of Action for the Protection of the Marine Environment from Land-Based Activities
Gulf of Maine Pleadings	*Case Concerning Delimitation of the Maritime Boundary in the Gulf of Maine Area (Canada/United States), ICJ Pleadings, Oral Arguments, Documents*
Haskell, *US Treaties*	*United States Treaties and Conventions, 1776-1889* (US Government Printing Office, 1889)
HC	House of Commons (Canada)
IATTC	Inter-American Tropical Tuna Commission
IBC	International Boundary Commission

ICCAT	International Commission for the Conservation of Atlantic Tunas
ICJ Rep.	International Court of Justice Reports
IJC	International Joint Commission
IJMCL	International Journal of Marine and Coastal Law
ILM	International Legal Materials
ILR	International Law Reports
IMCO	Inter-Governmental Maritime Consultative Organization
IMO	International Maritime Organization
Intl J	International Journal
IPHC	International Pacific Halibut Commission
ISA	International Seabed Authority
ISPS Code	International Ship and Port Facility Security Code
ITLOS	International Tribunal for the Law of the Sea
IUU	Illegal, unreported and unregulated fishing
JMLC	Journal of Maritime Law and Commerce
LOSB	Law of the Sea Bulletin
LOS Convention	United Nations Convention of the Law of the Sea (1982)
LNG	Liquefied natural gas
LNTS	League of Nations Treaty Series
MARPOL	International Convention for the Prevention of Pollution from Ships
Mar Pol	Marine Policy
Moore, *International Arbitrations*	*History and Digest of the International Arbitrations to Which the United States has been a Party* (US Government Printing Office, 6 vols., 1898)
MOPs	Meeting of the parties
NAFO	Northwest Atlantic Fisheries Organization
NASCO	North Atlantic Salmon Conservation Organization
NATO	North Atlantic Treaty Organization
NIEO	New International Economic Order
NORAD	North American Aerospace Defense Command
NPAFC	North Pacific Anadromous Fish Commission
ODIL	Ocean Development and International Law Journal
OYb	Ocean Yearbook
PCA	Permanent Court of Arbitration
PSC	Pacific Salmon Commission

PSI	Proliferation Security Initiative
Pub L.	Public Law (United States)
RECIEL	Review of European Community and International Environmental Law
RIAA	United Nations, Reports of International Arbitral Awards
RSC	Revised Statutes of Canada
SEAFAC	Southeast Alaska Submarine Noise Measurement Facility
SOLAS	Safety of Life at Sea Convention
SPLOS	State Parties to the Law of the Sea Convention
St Can	Statutes of Canada
SUA	Convention for the Suppression of Unlawful Acts against the Safety of Maritime Navigation
TAC	Total allowable catch
TSCZC	1958 Territorial Sea and Contiguous Zone Convention
TIAS	United States Treaties and Other International Acts Series
UNCLOS I	First United Nations Conference on the Law of the Sea (1958)
UNCLOS II	Second United Nations Conference on the Law of the Sea (1960)
UNCLOS III	Third United Nations Conference on the Law of the Sea (1973-1982)
UNEP	United Nations Environment Programme
UNTS	United Nations Treaty Series
UNYB	Yearbook of the United Nations
USC	United States Code
US Stat.	United States Statutes
UST	United States Treaties
USTS	United States Treaty Series
WCPFC	Western and Central Pacific Fisheries Commission

Table of Treaties

1783	Great Britain/US: Definitive Treaty of Peace, Paris, 3 September 1783, entered into force 9 April 1794; 48 Con. TS 487
1794	Great Britain/US: Treaty of Amity, Commerce and Navigation, London, 19 November 1794, entered into force 28 October 1795; 52 Con. TS 245
1814	Great Britain/US: Treaty of Peace, Ghent, 24 December 1814, entered into force 17 February 1815; 63 Con. TS 422
1818	Great Britain/US: Convention of Commerce, London, 20 October 1818, entered into force 30 January 1819; 69 Con. TS 294
1825	Great Britain/Russia: Limits of their Respective Possessions on the North-West Coast of America and the Navigation of the Pacific Ocean, St. Petersburg, 16 February 1825; 75 Con. TS 95
1827	Great Britain/US: Convention Continuing In Force Article 3 of the Convention of October 20, 1818, London, 6 August 1827, entered into force 15 May 1828; 77 Con. TS 366
1846	Great Britain/US: Treaty Establishing the Boundary in the Territory on the Northwest Coast of America Lying Westward of the Rocky Mountains, Washington, 15 June 1846, entered into force 5 August 1846; 100 Con. TS 39
1854	Great Britain/US: Treaty on North Atlantic Fisheries, Commercial Reciprocity, etc., Washington, 5 June 1854, entered into force 9 September 1854; 112 Con. TS 31
1867	Russia/US: Alaska Treaty, Washington, 30 March 1867, entered into force 20 June 1867; Con. TS 331
1871	Great Britain/US: Treaty for the Amicable Settlement of All Causes of Difference, Washington, 8 May 1871, entered into force 17 June 1871; 143 Con. TS 145
1873	Great Britain/US: Protocol defining the Boundary Line through the Canal de Haro, Washington, 10 March 1873, entered into force 10 March 1873; 146 Con. TS 35

1892 Great Britain/US: Treaty for submitting to Arbitration the Questions relating to the Seal Fisheries in the Behring Sea, Washington, 29 February 1892, entered into force 7 May 1892; 176 Con. TS 447

Great Britain/US: Boundary Convention, Washington, 22 July 1892, entered into force 23 August 1892; 177 Con. TS 246

1903 Great Britain/US: Convention for the Adjustment of the Alaska Boundary, Washington, 24 January 1903, entered into force 3 March 1903; 192 Con. TS 336

1908 Great Britain/US: Treaty respecting the Demarcation of the International Boundary with Canada, Washington, 11 April 1908, entered into force 4 June 1908; 206 Con. TS 377

1909 Great Britain/US: Boundary Waters Treaty, Washington, 11 January 1909, entered into force 11 January 1909; BTS 1910/23

1910 Great Britain/US: Treaty Fixing the Boundary Line in Passamaquoddy Bay, Washington, 21 May 1910, entered into force 20 August 1910; USTS 551

1911 North Pacific Fur Seals Convention, Washington, 7 July 1911, entered into force 12 December 1911; Con. TS 80

1912 Great Britain/US: North Atlantic Fisheries Agreement, Washington, 20 July 1912, entered into force 15 November 1912; 216 Con. TS 314

1923 Canada/US: Halibut Fisheries Convention, Washington, 2 March 1923, entered into force 21 October 1924; 32 LNTS 93

1925 Canada/US: Demarcation of the Boundary Treaty, Washington, 24 February 1925, 17 July 1925; 43 LNTS 239

1930 Canada/US: Fraser River Sockeye Salmon Convention, Washington, 26 May 1930, entered into force 28 July 1937; 184 LNTS 305

1935 Canada/US: Convention Relating to Certain Complaints arising from the Operation of the Smelter at Trail, Ottawa, 15 April 1935, entered into force 3 August 1935; 162 LNTS 73, CTS 1935/20

1946 International Whaling Convention, Washington, 2 December 1946, entered into force 10 November 1948; 161 UNTS 72

1948 Inter-Governmental Maritime Consultative Organization Convention, Geneva, 6 March 1948, entered into force 17 March 1958; 289 UNTS 3

1949 North Atlantic Treaty, Washington, 4 April 1949, entered into force 24 August 1949; 34 UNTS 243

Inter-American Tropical Tuna Convention, Washington, 31 May 1949, entered into force 3 March 1950; 126 UNTS 3

1952 North Pacific Fisheries Convention, Tokyo, 9 May 1952, entered into force 12 June 1953; 205 UNTS 65

1953 Canada/US Halibut Fishery Convention, Ottawa, 2 March 1953, entered into force 2 March 1953; 222 UNTS 77, CTS 1953/14, 5 UST 5, TIAS 2900

United Nations Convention on the Law of the Sea, Montego Bay, 10 December 1982, entered into force 16 November 1994; 1833 UNTS 397

1984 Provisional Understanding Regarding Deep Seabed Matters, Geneva, 3 August 1984, entered into force 2 September 1984; 23 ILM 1354

1985 Canada/US: Pacific Salmon Treaty, Ottawa, 28 January 1985, entered into force 18 March 1985; 1469 UNTS 357, CTS 1985/7, T.I.A.S. 11091

1987 Canada/US: Exchange of Notes on Resolution of Practical Problems with Respect to Deep Seabed Mining Areas, Ottawa, 14 August 1987, entered into force 14 August 1987; TIAS 11438

Agreement on the Resolution of Practical Problems with Respect to Deep Seabed Mining Areas, New York, 14 August 1997, entered into force 14 August 1987; 26 ILM 1502

1988 Canada/US: Arctic Cooperation Agreement, Ottawa, 11 January 1988, entered into force 11 January 1988; CTS 1988/29, TIAS 11565

Convention for the Suppression of Unlawful Acts Against the Safety of Maritime Navigation (SUA), London, 10 March 1988, entered into force 1 March 1992; 1678 UNTS 221

1990 US/USSR: Maritime Boundary Agreement, Washington, 1 June 1990, provisionally in force 15 June 1990; 29 ILM 941

Canada/US: Fisheries Enforcement Agreement, Ottawa, 26 September 1990, entered into force 16 December 1991; CTS 1991/36, TIAS 11753

1992 North Pacific Anadromous Stocks Convention, Moscow, 11 February 1992, entered into force 16 February 1993; CTS 1993/16

Biological Diversity Convention, Rio de Janeiro, 5 June 1992, entered into force 29 December 1993; 1760 UNTS 79

1994 Bering Sea Pollock Convention, Washington, 16 June 1994, entered into force 8 December 1995; 34 ILM 67

Agreement Relating to the Implementation of Part XI of the United Nations Convention on the Law of the Sea, New York, 28 July 1994, entered into force 28 July 1996; 33 ILM 1309

Canada/France: Mutual Fishing Relations Agreement, Paris, 2 December 1994, entered into force 14 April 1995

1995 Canada/EC: Agreed Minute, Brussels, 20 April 1995; 34 ILM 1262

Straddling and Highly Migratory Fish Stocks Agreement, New York, 4 August 1995, entered into force 11 December 2001; 2167 UNTS 3

Canada/US: Agreement on the Establishment of a Mediation Procedure regarding the Pacific Salmon Treaty, Montreal, 11 September 1995, entered into force 11 September 1995; 2029 UNTS 307, CTS 1995/13, TIAS 12689

Canada/US: Interim Agreement Concerning Pacific Salmon, 3 December 1995; CTS 1995/39

1996 Canada/US: Agreement to Extend the North American Aerospace Defence Command (NORAD) Agreement, Washington, 28 March 1996, entered into force 28 March 1996; 2030 UNTS 111, CTS 1996/36 (renewed in 2000 and amended in 2004)

1999 Canada/US: Agreement relating to the Pacific Salmon Treaty, Washington, 30 June 1999, entered into force 30 June 1999; CTS 1999/58

2000 Mexico/US: Delimitation of the Continental Shelf in the Western Gulf of Mexico Agreement, Washington, 9 June 2000, entered into force 17 January 2001; TIAS 2143

Western and Central Pacific Ocean Fisheries Agreement, Honolulu, 5 September 2000, entered into force 19 June 2004; 40 ILM 278

2001 Underwater Cultural Heritage Convention, Paris, 6 November 2001; 41 ILM 40

2002 Canada/US: Exchange of Notes Amending the Albacore Tuna Treaty, entered into force 28 May 2004; CTS 2004/12

Canada/US: Agreement under the Pacific Salmon Treaty (Yukon River Agreement), Washington, 4 December 2002, entered into force 4 December 2002; CTS 2002/27

2003 Canada/US: Pacific Hake/Whiting Agreement, Seattle, 21 November 2003, entered into force 25 June 2008; available at:<wwwcomm.pac.dfompo.gc.ca/pages/release/bckgrnd/2003/HakeAgreement_e.htm> (accessed on 5 December 2006)

2004 Ships' Ballast Water Convention, IMO Doc. BWM/Conf./36, 16 February 2000, in Michael Tsimplis, "Alien Species Stay Home: The International Convention for the Control and Management of Ships' Ballast Water and Sediments 2004" (2004), 19 International Journal of Marine and Coastal Law 411, 446–482

2006 Canada/US: Agreement on the North American Aerospace Defence Command (NORAD), Ottawa, 28 April 2006, entered into force 12 May 2006; available at < www.treaty-accord.gc.ca/ViewTreaty.asp?Treaty_ID=105060> (accessed on 2 August 2007)

Table of International Cases and Awards

St. Pierre and Miquelon Arbitration (Canada/France) (10 June 1992) 31 ILM 1149

San Juan Island Arbitration (21 October 1872) Haskell, US Treaties, 494

Trail Smelter Arbitration (Canada/US) (16 April 1938 and 11 March 1941) iii RIAA 1911

Tunisia-Libya Continental Shelf Case [1982] ICJ Rep. 18

Tuna Case (Canada/US) (22 February 1982) GATT BISD (29th Supp.) 91

Washington Award (1854) Moore, International Arbitrations, iv, 4342

Table of Legislation

Canada

Arctic Waters Pollution Prevention Act
Arctic Waters Pollution Prevent Regulations
Arctic Shipping Pollution Prevention Regulations
Canada–Nova Scotia Offshore Petroleum Resources Accord Implementation Act
Canada Shipping Act
Coastal Fisheries Protection Act
Coastal Fisheries Protection Regulations
Fishery (General) Regulations, amendment
Fishing Zones of Canada (Zone 1, 2 and 3) Order
Fishing Zones of Canada (Zones 4 and 5) Order
Fishing Zones of Canada (Zone 6) Order
Oceans Act
Oil Carriage Limitation Regulations
Oil and Gas Production and Conservation Act
Order Exempting the U.S. C.G. Icebreaker Healy from the Application of the Arctic Shipping Pollution Prevention Regulations
Public Lands Grant Act
Territorial Sea and Fishing Zones Act
Territorial Sea and Fishing Zones Geographical Coordinates (Areas 1, 2 and 3) Order
Territorial Sea and Fishing Zones Geographical Coordinates (Areas 4 and 5) Order
Territorial Sea Geographical Coordinates (Area 7) Order
U.S.C.G.C. Polar Sea Exemption Order
United States Waters Fisheries Regulation

United States

Act Establishing a Fisheries Zone Contiguous to the Territorial Sea
Contiguous Zone of the United States Proclamation
Exclusive Economic Zone and Maritime Boundaries (Public Notice)

List of Maps

ONE

Introduction

CANADA AND THE UNITED STATES (U.S.) are immediate salt water neighbors on the Atlantic Ocean (New Brunswick and Nova Scotia, and Maine), the Pacific Ocean (British Columbia and Washington to the south, and British Columbia and Alaska to the north), and the Arctic Ocean (Yukon and Alaska).

The geography of the Canada-U.S. ocean relationship has over time undergone an important change—the area requiring neighborliness has expanded dramatically. Historically, fishing was the principal maritime issue between Canada and the United States with the 1800s populated with numerous agreements and disputes over access to fishing grounds. Delineating ocean spaces for purposes of fishing and more general national authority was also historically important. The oldest Canada-U.S. maritime boundary is in the Juan de Fuca Strait between British Columbia and Washington state, which was completed in 1846.[1] The ocean areas involved in the fisheries and maritime boundary matters of the 1800s were near the coasts. Maritime issues between Canada and the United States in recent years have continued to involve fisheries and maritime boundaries in waters near shore, supplemented by issues respecting navigational rights in near-shore waters. However, as a result of significant changes in international ocean law commencing in the second half of the Twentieth Century and set out in the 1982 United Nations (U. N.) Convention on the Law of the Sea (LOS Convention)[2] involving exclusive national authority over the resources within 200-nautical-mile zones and continental shelves that extend beyond 200 nautical miles, Canada-U.S. neighborly maritime issues now engage ocean areas well beyond the near shore.

---

1 Treaty Establishing the Boundary in the Territory on the Northwest Coast of America Lying Westward of the Rocky Mountains, Washington 15 June 1846, entered into force 5 August 1846, 100 Con. TS 39.

2 U. N. Convention on the Law of the Sea, Montego Bay, Jamaica, 10 December 1982, entered into force 16 November 1994, 1833 UNTS 397.

The focus of this work is the *ocean relationship* between Canada and the United States that directly involves or arises from modern international ocean law. The best known and most important of the Canada-U.S. international ocean law disputes are:

- The controversy over the international legal status of and navigational rights that exist within the Northwest Passage that first arose as a high-profile bilateral issue in 1969 to 1970 and, despite efforts to manage the dispute, resurfaced in 1985 and, more recently, as part of the concern over the effect of global climate change on ice conditions in the Arctic;
- The fisheries and maritime boundary dispute in the Gulf of Maine region between Maine and, Nova Scotia and New Brunswick that arose in the 1970s as a consequence of the adoption by Canada and the United States of 200-nautical-mile fishing zones and which resulted in the 1984 International Court *Gulf of Maine Case*[3] demarcating the maritime boundary and the subsequent efforts by the two States to agree upon cooperative fisheries management in the area; and
- The difficulties between Canada and the United States in reaching agreement and management arrangements respecting Pacific salmon that has a negotiating history back to the 1930s but, as a result of 200-nautical-mile zones and differing assessments of national interests and interpretation of treaty wording, caused serious difficulties in the 1980s and 1990s and may emerge again as an issue at the end of this decade.

The above big three issues have been paramount in the bilateral international ocean law relationship over the last few decades. Of equal importance, but albeit increasingly only of historical interest, is the different perspectives that Canada and the United States had regarding the 1982 LOS Convention in the 1970s and 1980s during the negotiation and adoption of the Convention and the immediate aftermath of its conclusion.

There is an important reality to the Canada-U.S. salt water relationship that will become evident throughout this work. Despite the number of disputes and differences of perception that exist between the neighbors as regards maritime boundaries, fisheries, and navigational matters, few of the discords create significant turbulence on a regular basis between the States. Canada and the United States have frequently found ways to "agree to disagree"

3 *Delimitation of the Maritime Boundary in the Gulf of Maine Area (Canada v. United States)*, [1984] ICJ Rep. 246.

respecting international ocean law matters and have been able to proceed pragmatically to overlook legal disputes. The classic example is the 1988 Agreement whereby Canada and the United States accept to cooperate respecting U.S. Coast Guard vessel traffic through the Northwest Passage while making it clear that each State was maintaining its position on the international legal status of the Passage.[4]

Cooperation, coordination, and a healthy amount of benign neglect of disputes are fundamental characteristics of the bilateral ocean relationship. The two States are almost always interested in defusing a problem rather than inflaming a controversy. Nevertheless, there have been ocean matters of high public and political profile between the two States, for example, the already-mentioned Pacific salmon negotiations in the 1980s and again in the 1990s; the Arctic sovereignty questions in the 1970 and 1980s; and the Gulf of Maine fisheries and maritime boundary dispute of the late 1970s and early 1980s. As long as there are underlying international legal disputes, the possibility remains that there could be flare-ups that will bring a given matter to the attention of the public and the highest levels of the governments of either or both States.

One of the reasons for the pragmatism of the two States in avoiding legal and political confrontation is the fear of resolving a dispute. Most of the issues in dispute discussed in this work involve assertions by one or both countries of sovereignty over ocean areas or international legal rights opposed by the other. Negotiations involving sovereignty matters that may lead to resolution "tend to be heavily laden with emotional freight" and negotiators, mindful of "symbolic significance," are often "required to negotiate with relatively little flexibility."[5] The resolution of many of the Canada-U.S. international ocean law disputes would almost certainly involve compromise and/or a perceived backing down on sovereignty. The public face of a resolution, therefore, is highly likely to be problematic for any government and most acutely for Canada. The only significant international legal dispute that can be said to have been resolved between Canada and the United States in the modern law of the sea era (since 1970) is the maritime boundary in the Gulf of Maine, which was settled by the International Court in 1984. The differences between Canada and the United States, for example, respecting

4 Agreement on Arctic Cooperation, Ottawa 11 January 1988, entered into force 11 January 1988, CTS 1988/29, TIAS 11565.

5 D. M. Johnston, The Theory and History of Ocean Boundary-Making (McGill-Queen's University Press, Montreal 1988) 27.

Pacific salmon were not resolved in the 1985 Pacific Salmon Treaty[6] or in the 1999 Agreement.[7] Rather, in both cases, the two sides agreed to suspend their disagreement in order to provide temporary stability for the fishing interests of both States.

This reluctance to seek to resolve international legal disputes is not unique to Canada and the United States. The nature of the relationship (a large partner and a small partner) and, in particular, the domestic politics of Canada, where sovereignty is often referenced regarding ocean matters either directly by the government, the media, or participants, makes compromise to reach resolution of a sovereignty dispute difficult and, in most cases, unlikely. Moreover, some of the issues in dispute are not easily open to compromise. For example, a navigation right for foreign vessels either does or does not exist within the Northwest Passage; there is little wriggle room. Fear of resolution is better understood as being the fear of the political repercussions of a resolution of an ocean dispute that involves a compromise of sovereignty.

One of the goals of this study is to document and explain the international legal disputes that have and continue to exist between Canada and the United States arising from modern international ocean law. An equally important goal is to detail that the two States have been good neighbors and have worked cooperatively and even inventively to manage the disputes in order to prevent them from becoming difficult issues in the bilateral relationship.

The organizational structure of the manuscript is to provide in Chapter Two, "Context and Background," Part A, an overview of the ocean relationship looking at the ocean profiles of the two States, the broader bilateral relationship, and Canada's peculiar political history with the United States. Chapter Two, Parts B and C, designed for non-ocean law experts, contains background material respecting international law, the LOS Convention, the ocean jurisdiction exercised by both Canada and the United States, and a brief review of ocean topics that extend beyond the LOS Convention.

Chapter Three, "1970: The Landmark Year," focuses on 1970 in the development of the Canada-U.S. international ocean law relationship. In 1970, the

---

6 Pacific Salmon Treaty, Ottawa, 28 January 1985, entered into force 18 March 1985, CTS 1985/7, TIAS 11091, 1469 UNTS 357.

7 Exchange of Notes constituting an Agreement relating to the Pacific Salmon Treaty, Washington 30 June 1999, entered into force 30 June 1999, CTS 1999/58, Pacific Salmon Commission (PSC), 1999/2000 Fifteenth Annual Report, 111–114 and 120–169.

United Nations agreed to convene the Third U. N. Conference on the Law of the Sea (UNCLOS III), the outcome of which was the 1982 U. N. Convention on the Law of the Sea (1982 LOS Convention). Hence, 1970 can be seen as the beginning of the modernization of the international law of the sea. In 1970, Canada adopted laws and measures respecting the continental shelf, territorial sea, fisheries, and the Arctic, all of which had implications for the ocean relationship with the United States. The most important of these Canadian measures was the enactment of the Arctic Waters Pollution Prevention Act (AWPPA),[8] which led to a sharp diplomatic exchange with the United States. The Canadian measures and the policy statements made by the United States in 1970 indicated the positions that both countries would take during the UNCLOS III process.

The 1970 chapter is followed by one on UNCLOS III and the LOS Convention, which outlines the Canadian and U.S. approaches to the key issues under discussion and the subsequent relationship of the two States regarding the LOS Convention. In the 1970s, both States supported the need for the development of a modern law of the sea treaty, but their approaches to the negotiations and the issues were significantly different. On issues such as the width of the territorial sea, environmental protection of Arctic waters, and national control over offshore resources, Canada took action and sought legal justification for its actions through the LOS Convention. The United States approached the LOS Convention negotiations looking for international consensus before taking national action. This general posture of the two States was and is at odds with the popularly accepted images of Canada as measured and internationalist, and the United States as the unilateralist belatedly expecting the international community to accept its actions. The positions of the two States realigned with the popularly accepted images in the 1980s when Canada was seen as embracing the LOS Convention and the United States rejected the Treaty as not meeting its needs. Despite this 1980s image, Canada only became a party to the LOS Convention in 2003. The United States still is not a party to the LOS Convention since, while it was endorsed by both the Clinton and Bush II administrations, the U.S. Senate has not provided the necessary approval for the United States to become a party.[9]

---

8 St Can 1969–1970 c 47.

9 President Clinton, Message from the President of the United States transmitting United Nations Convention on the Law of the Sea, with Annexes, done at Montego Bay, 10 December 1982 (the Convention) and the Agreement Relating to the Implementation of Part XI of the

The bulk of this study (Chapters Five, "Canada-United States Maritime Boundaries;" Six, "Status of Waters and Navigation Rights;" and Seven, "Fisheries") is an examination of the issues that have arisen between Canada and the United States that directly involve or arise from modern international law of the sea and the cooperative arrangements taken by the two States to minimize the potential disruption of the legal disputes:

- Overlapping claims by the two neighboring States to offshore ocean areas (maritime boundaries) and the management of ocean boundary areas;
- Differences between the two States regarding the existence of rights of navigation through specific ocean areas; and
- Fisheries matters that have arisen primarily because of extended national fisheries zones.

Maritime Boundaries

Overlapping offshore claims of States are inherently issues or disputes. Since 1925, with the exception of the 1984 Canada-U.S. *Gulf of Maine* adjudication which, as noted, resulted in a maritime boundary being drawn by the International Court, Canada and the United States have not entered into any resolutive ocean boundary agreements.[10]

Both countries have made claims to 12-nautical-mile territorial seas, contiguous zones, 200-nautical-mile exclusive economic zones (EEZs), and continental shelves beyond 200 nautical miles. As a result, there are overlapping claims in every geographic area where the two States are direct ocean neighbors, albeit a number of the overlapping offshore claim disputes predate modern

---

United Nations Convention on the Law of the Sea of 10 December 1982, adopted at New York, 28 July 1994 (the Agreement) and signed by the United States, subject to ratification, on 29 July 1994, U.S. Senate, Treaty Document 39, 103d Congress, 2d Session IV (1994), 34 ILM 1393.

President Bush, Statement on Advancing U.S. Interests in the World's Oceans, 15 May 2007, 46 ILM 890.

> I urge the Senate to act favorably on U.S. accession to the United Nations Convention on the Law of the Sea . . . Joining will serve the national security interests of the United States, including the maritime mobility of our armed forces worldwide. . . . Accession will promote U.S. interests in the environmental health of the oceans.

10 Treaty regarding the Demarcation of the Boundary between the United States and Canada, Washington, 24 February 1925, entered into force 17 July 1925, 43 LNTS 239. This agreement extended the existing maritime boundary 2,383 meters within the Grand Manan Channel (between Maine and the New Brunswick Island of Grand Manan).

international law of the sea. On the Atlantic, overlapping claims exist in the inner Gulf of Maine as a result of the disputed ownership of Machias Seal Island and North Rock. These tiny islets, with an inhabited lighthouse on Machias Seal Island, are the only pieces of land that are in dispute between Canada and the United States, but a consequence is that the ocean area around the Islands is also disputed. Seaward of the maritime boundary constructed by the International Court in the *Gulf of Maine Case*, there is a small, anomalous area of the Canadian 200-nautical-mile zone that is seaward of the United States 200-nautical-mile zone, and there is an area of common continental shelf beyond the 200-nautical-mile limit of both States. In the Arctic Ocean, the neighbors have overlapping offshore claims in the Beaufort Sea adjacent to the Yukon Territory-Alaska land boundary. On the Pacific, there is an area of overlapping claims seaward of the Juan de Fuca Strait. Between British Columbia and Alaska, the overlapping areas are, first, within the Dixon Entrance (located between the Queen Charlotte Islands of British Columbia and the southern Alaska islands), which dates back to the 1903 *Alaska Boundary Arbitration*;[11] and second, involving 200-nautical-mile zones seaward of the Dixon Entrance.

The existence of a maritime boundary between States usually solves the legal question of national jurisdiction, but does not end the maritime issues that can arise for adjoining States. The cross-boundary management of resources can be a significant source of dispute. Canada and the United States have a number of cross-boundary arrangements respecting fisheries, navigation, and hydrocarbon exploration that seek to minimize boundary-related problems. Overall, however, this is an area of incompleteness for the two States.

Rights of Navigation Disputes

There are Canada-U.S. issues and disputes regarding the existence of navigational rights through specific Canadian waters. These issues exist on every coast and involve: the Northwest Passage in the Arctic; the Head Harbour Passage/Passamaquoddy Bay on the Atlantic Coast; and the Hecate Strait and other waters on the Pacific Coast. In all of these cases, the United States does not contest that the waters are Canadian; rather, the issue is, "How Canadian are they?" The pattern is for Canada to take the view that the

11 *Decision of the Alaska Boundary Tribunal under the Treaty of 24 January 1903 between the United States and Great Britain*, 20 October 1903, *Proceedings of the Alaska Boundary Tribunal*, U.S. Senate, 58th Cong., 2nd Session, Document 162, Vol. I, 29–97.

waters in question are historic internal waters such that no navigation rights exist, whereas the United States asserts that the waters are not historic waters and that innocent or transit passage exists through the waterway on the basis that the waterway is a strait used for international navigation.

Fisheries

Although both countries accept each other's national 200-nautical-mile fishing zones, although not necessarily the precise location of the zones, fisheries matters remain as a subject of dispute. First, overlapping claims create fishing areas of dispute. It was the fishery that was the key provocateur leading to the 1984 *Gulf of Maine Case*, and it remains an issue on both East and West Coasts where maritime boundaries have not been resolved. Second, fish cross into the national waters of each State leading to disputes about overharvesting and mismanagement. The most complex and high profile of this type of dispute concerns Pacific salmon.

Chapter Eight, "Reviewing the Past and Looking to the Future," makes the case that, irrespective of the various international ocean law disputes, generally speaking, Canada and the United States ocean law relations are on an "even keel." There is no relationship crisis on ocean matters between the neighbors. There is an ethos of cooperation between the two States on ocean matters. Despite the numerous bilateral international ocean law disputes, the two States have found ways to cooperate and agree on many operational ocean matters. In some cases, this has involved "agreeing to disagree" respecting an international ocean law matter and proceeding in a pragmatic way to overlook the international legal dispute.

Although new challenges will most certainly arise as a result of increased concerns over security, access to energy resources and the effects of global climate change both in the Arctic and elsewhere, the fundamental characteristics of the Canada-U.S. salt water relationship in the last few decades—cooperation, coordination and a healthy amount of benign neglect of disputed matters—will ensure that the two States continue to pursue their ocean relationship in a constructive and neighborly manner.

TWO

Context and Background

1.0 Introduction

Part A of this chapter deals with the context of the Canada-United States (U.S.) ocean relationship. Elements of this context include the ocean profiles of both States and the peculiar history of Canada whereby, until into the 1920s, it was the Great Britain government in London that directly addressed the United States on matters of importance to Canada. While few topics captivate the press, citizens and foreign policy wonks in Canada more, and those in the United States less, than the state of Canada-U.S relations, nevertheless, the nature and dynamics of the overall relationship is an important context for understanding the bilateral ocean relationship.

Part B first provides a brief introduction to international law (treaties, customary law, and adjudication) in the context of the 1982 United Nations (U. N.) Law of the Sea Convention (LOS Convention)[1] and the practices of Canada and the United States. Second, it sets out the basic international law respecting national offshore zones, including internal waters, territorial sea, the 200-nautical-mile exclusive economic zone (EEZ), and the continental shelf beyond 200 nautical miles) that are of most relevance to Canada and the United States. Part B is designed primarily for non-experts in international law of the sea. Part C provides a few words on international ocean matters that extend beyond the strictly bilateral Canada-U.S. ocean law relationship and the LOS Convention. Again, this is intended for the non-law of the sea experts.

1 U. N. Convention on the Law of the Sea, Montego Bay, Jamaica, 10 December 1982, entered into force 16 November 1994, 1833 UNTS 397.

PART A

2.0 Context of the Canada-U.S. Ocean Relationship

2.1 Perceptions and Interests

The ocean profiles of Canada and the United States are remarkably similar. Both States have extensive coastlines; have benefited greatly from 200-nautical-miles zones; and have areas where the continental shelf extends beyond 200 nautical miles. Each State has an active fishing industry that is nevertheless declining in overall economic importance. Both States are engaged in off-shore oil and gas development. The focus of this activity for the United States is in the Gulf of Mexico far away from its northern borders; in Canada, the activity is adjacent to Newfoundland far away from its southern borders. Major seaports in each State handle large volumes of trade but, as a result of containerization, pay little heed to national boundaries. Both States have taken significant measures to reduce marine environmental pollution from all sources (vessel-source, land, and dumping) in their ocean waters. The United States, of course, has a much larger navy and military capacity than Canada and has responsibilities and expectations—some sought, others thrust upon it—at the global level. Canada, along with the United States, is a member of the North Atlantic Treaty Organization (NATO)[2] and as a result has similar, albeit more limited, naval interests and responsibilities. The military defense of North America rests more heavily on U.S. shoulders than those of Canada, with Canada (its citizens, if not its leaders) tending not to see a need for significant military defense spending.

In recent years, maritime security in national waters has taken on a greater importance for both the United States and Canada. In conjunction with expanded mandates for the U.S. Navy and U.S. Coast Guard to protect the sea approaches to the United States as a result of the events of 9/11,[3] Canada announced an enhancement of resources and a redesign of internal command structures to address the sea approaches to Canada.[4] A more concrete

---

2 North Atlantic Treaty, Washington, 4 April 1949, entered into force 24 August 1949, 34 UNTS 243.

3 *See* United States, *The National Strategy for Maritime Security* (September 2005) and *National Plan to Achieve Maritime Domain Awareness* (October 2005). One of the most significant changes was the placing of the U.S. Coast Guard within the newly created Department of Homeland Security.

4 Canada, *Securing an Open Society: Canada's National Security Policy*, 37-39 (Ottawa 2004).

indication of cross-border ocean security cooperation was the 2006 expansion of the decades-old North American Aerospace Defense Command (NORAD) Agreement to include maritime warning.[5] The two countries have formally agreed to a sharing of information, although not to joint or collective responsibilities, regarding maritime surveillance and control.[6] Beyond adjacent waters, in recent years, the Canadian Navy has been engaged in boarding and inspection operations in conjunction with the U.S. Navy (and others) as a consequence of the first Gulf War and through Operation Apollo as regards Afghanistan. Canada is also a participant in the Proliferation Security Initiative (PSI) promoted by the United States in 2003 as a means to curtail the international movement of weapons of mass destruction, their delivery systems, and related materials between "states and non-state actors of proliferation concern."[7]

Despite what appears to be a matching oceans profile, including more recently on ocean security matters, it is still the "military security factor" that has led to significant differences in the actions of Canada and the United States regarding many ocean issues which, in turn, has led to differing perceptions within each State of the other's ocean policies and measures. On ocean matters, the United States has generally based its actions and reactions on security considerations, which has often meant strong support for freedom of navigation, and concerns about and opposition to measures and international efforts that might undermine navigational freedoms. Canada, though not unmindful of naval security and vessel mobility concerns,[8] has

---

5 Agreement on the North American Aerospace Defence Command, Ottawa, 28 April 2006, entered into force 12 May 2006, Art 1, at < www.treaty-accord.gc.ca/ViewTreaty.asp?Treaty_ID=105060> (accessed on 2 August 2007).

The 2006 Agreement supersedes the 1996 NORAD Agreement (Exchange of Notes constituting an Agreement to Extend the North American Aerospace Defence Command (NORAD) Agreement for a Further Five-Year Period, Washington, 28 March 1996, entered into force 28 March 1996, CTS 1996/36, 2030 UNTS 111 which had been renewed in 2000 and amended in 2004), which had superseded the original 1958 NORAD Agreement (Agreement concerning the Organization and Operation of the North American Air Defence Command (NORAD), Washington, 12 May 1958, entered into force 12 May 1958, CTS 1958/9, 316 UNTS 151).

6 J. T. Jockel and J. J. Sokolsky, *Renewing NORAD – Now If Not Forever* (July/August, 2006) Vol. 27, No. 6 POLICY OPTIONS 53, 57.

7 *See* Department of State website respecting the Proliferation Security Initiative, at www.state.gov/t/np/c10390/htm and the Canadian Department of Foreign Affairs website, at www.dfait-maeci.gc.ca/arms/psioverview-en.asp (accessed on 19 July 2007).

8 B. H. Oxman, *The Territorial Imperative: A Siren Song at Sea* (2006) 100 AJIL 830, 840 comments:

> The interest in global mobility [of vessels] seeks to avoid impediments to the deployment of forces by sea anywhere in the world. This interest is ordinarily associated with naval powers. In fact, the security of almost every State depends in some measure upon the mobility of the forces of naval powers for the maintenance of stability in its region.

more often based its actions and reactions on attaining or asserting greater exclusive national control over adjacent waters, both as regards resources but also as regards passing foreign flagged vessels.

The military security factor also plays a role in the priority given by each State to most ocean issues. As one author has suggested, Canada tends to give a high priority to law of the sea matters, such as fishing rights and environmental protection; whereas the United States tends to see these matters as secondary to its global geopolitical considerations and politics.[9]

In the bilateral sphere, Canada tends to see and argue ocean matters with the United States in localized terms focusing on the specifics of an ocean space (for example, the unique environmental characteristics of the Arctic). Conversely, the United States tends to see and argue ocean matters with Canada by referring to the global context of precedents being set and taken up elsewhere. This is not always the case, of course; it depends on the issue. On many of the Canada-U.S. maritime boundary and fisheries matters, both sides see and argue the issues concentrating on the local. The Pacific salmon debates are a case in point.

2.2 Broader Bilateral Relationship

A recent book argues that, although the border marks the distinct national polities of Canada and the United States, the cultures, societies, and economies are "intertwined as a shared, transnational whole."[10] At a later point, it is commented that Canada and the United States "share the most intertwined, intimate, interdependent, and profitable binational relationship in the world."[11] The author ends the work with the sentence: "[A]nyone who believes that Canadian-American relations are just about presidents and prime ministers has missed 98 per cent of what goes on."[12] The point made is that the interrelationship of the citizens of Canada and the United States goes well beyond the formal interaction of the governments in Washington and Ottawa

9 C. F. Doran, Forgotten Partnership: U.S.-Canadian Relations Today (The Johns Hopkins University Press, Baltimore 1984) 186 uses the phraseology low politics and high politics.

10 R. C. Stuart, Dispersed Relations: Americans and Canadians in Upper North America (The Johns Hopkins University Press, Baltimore 2007) 1.

11 *Id.* 216.

12 *Id.* 293.

and that it is a misdirection of attention to assess the bilateral relationship solely by looking at the engagement of the governments and political leaders.

Nevertheless, it is the political realm of the relationship[13] that attracts most of the attention with the issues that are within the political realm involving borders, boundaries, foreign policy matters, security, transboundary resource allocation, and formal treaties, such as those respecting trade and military cooperation. Unlike other realms of Canada-U.S. interaction, in which it is primarily the actions of individuals or corporations that define the relationship, in the political realm the relationship is defined by the two governments and politicians. As such, it is in the political realm that the constitutional, historic, and political differences between the two States are most often evident, though at the same time, the two States are aware of having shared responsibilities for upper North America.[14] It can also be suggested that while Canadian citizens are interlinked with their U.S. neighbors in countless ways, they do not expect or encourage the Canadian government to emulate fully this practice.

Within the Canadian government, chattering class, academia, and the public, much attention is given to Canada's political relationship with the United States. There is no question that the cross-border relationship is the most important foreign policy concern for Canada,[15] leaving most of the chatter to be about how the relationship is to be characterized (Is Canada the best friend of or in a special relationship with the United States?); how to manage the relationship (as if that were possible); and how Canada can influence decision making within the United States on matters of importance to Canada.[16]

For the United States, the situation is different: Its relationship with Canada is not a top priority. Little attention is given to Canada by the U.S. government, public, academia, or chattering class. An oft-heard Canadian

---

13 *See id.* 5, 215–219 and 285–286.

14 *See id.* 291.

15 I. L. HEAD AND P. E. TRUDEAU, THE CANADIAN WAY: SHAPING CANADA'S FOREIGN POLICY 1968–1984 (McClelland and Stewart, Toronto 1995) 17 comment:

> The most dominant factor in Canadian foreign policy is the ponderous presence of the United States. With its overwhelming influence on the economy and culture of Canada, the United States had been for more than a century the single most important consideration in the design of successive Canadian foreign policies.

16 For example, J. WELSH, AT HOME IN THE WORLD: CANADA'S GLOBAL VISION FOR THE 21ST CENTURY (Harper Collins, Toronto 2005) 24–25, 32–86, 245–246; B. Bow, *Out of Ideas? Models and Strategies for Canadian—U.S. Relations* (2006–2007) 57 INTERNATIONAL JOURNAL (INTL J) 123–142.

complaint is that attracting official Washington's attention to a matter Canada considers to be of importance is usually very difficult; whereas the United States has little difficulty getting a hearing by Canada on a matter it believes is important. Canadians often perceive this as a slight. The reality is that there is intense competition among numerous matters, both foreign and domestic, for official Washington's attention.[17] Canada's situation is not unique. Fortunately, there is an extensive network of Canadian-U.S. official and unofficial interactions that are deeply entrenched, intertwined, and most often routine. It has been summarized that:

> The bulk of governmental interaction between Canada and the US occurs through highly specialized and functional channels that have evolved over decades. For the most part, these channels operate "under the radar," supporting the work of ministers but receiving limited public visibility.[18]

Of course, it is the difficult matters that receive the most public exposure and demand engagement at the highest levels.

Since the relationship with the United States is a Canadian preoccupation, in Canada almost every dispute and issue with the United States is seen in political and national terms. As an observer has recently commented: "Canadians have tended to freight . . . disputes [with the United States] with symbolic meaning" such that "anything short of US capitulation . . . will . . . lead to crises of outrage and accusations of American bullying."[19] For the United States, the situation is inverted. Most bilateral issues with Canada are

---

17 Stuart, *supra* note 10, at 276.

18 J. Higginbotham and J. Heynen, *Managing Through Networks: The State of Canada-US Relations,* in D. Carment, F. O. Hampson and N. Hillmer (eds.) Canada Among Nations, 2004: Setting Priorities Straight (McGill-Queen's University Press, Montreal 2005) 133.

19 C. Sands, *The Rising Importance of Third-Country Issues in Canada's Relations with the United States,* in A. F. Cooper and D. Rowlands (eds.) Canada Among Nations, 2006: Minorities and Priorities (McGill-Queen's University Press, Montreal 2006) 128. Sands goes on to comment:

> Governments in Canada play on these emotional responses to portray Ottawa as either bravely standing up to Washington's vested interests and power brokers, or forthrightly lecturing forgetful and even willful purblind American counterparts about the importance of Canada as a trading partner.
>
> This type of response makes for good politics in Canada . . . Yet in Washington it appears part of a familiar script. . . . As an expression of the long-standing . . . pastime of "running against Washington."

not seen in national terms, rather are seen as technical or local matters not freighted with political significance.

Ocean matters are within the political realm of Canada-U.S. relations. The issues of maritime boundaries, navigation rights, and fisheries all involve allocation decisions, formal treaties, and foreign policy. The questions are primarily addressed by the national governments of both States. All three of the ocean matters involve directly or are seen as engaging questions of national "sovereignty." As compared to many other bilateral issues, what is involved in ocean matters is not a question of the harmonization of Canadian-U.S. laws or practices. Where harmonization or joint approaches are involved, the inevitable result is Canadian adoption of the U.S. norm. The ocean issues are about the sharing of space (maritime boundaries and rights of navigation) and resources (fisheries). Neighborliness as a means to accommodation is important, but it is not the situation that harmonization (Canadian adoption of the U.S. position) is the inevitable result. On maritime boundaries, navigation rights, and fisheries, Canada and the United States are essentially co-equals. This makes the relationship on these matters somewhat different than that which exists regarding a large number of other bilateral matters, for example, trade, in which Canada's economic dependency on the U.S. market far outweighs the portion of the U.S. economy that is tied to the Canadian market. This may partly explain why, in Canada, many of the ocean issues are freighted with the sovereignty rhetoric; their status is as close to a co-equal as is possible between the two States.

The place of ocean matters in recent Canada-U.S. relations is best described as episodic. Only rarely have specific maritime issues found there way onto the formal Ottawa-Washington agenda. This has not always been the case. Historians of the Canada-U.S. relationship refer frequently to fisheries matters and maritime boundaries as being major concerns, well into the early 1900s.[20] In the 1970s, ocean matters figured prominently in the relationship primarily as a result of action taken by Canada regarding fisheries and the Arctic, and during the negotiation of the LOS Convention. In the 1980s, fisheries (the Pacific salmon and East Coast fisheries that led to the *Gulf of Maine Case*) and the passage of the U.S. Coast Guard vessel *Polar Sea* through the Canadian Arctic ensured that maritime issues would continue to have a place on the Canada-U.S. political agenda.

---

20 For example, J. L. GRANATSTEIN AND N. HILLMER, FOR BETTER OF FOR WORSE: CANADA AND THE UNITED STATES IN THE 1990s (Copp Clark Pitman, Toronto 1991) 10–13, 15, 22–24.

The absence of ocean issues on the current bilateral relations agenda is the result of two realities. First, other matters have crowded out ocean issues; most recently, security has become the primary concern, while trade was the biggest preoccupation over the last three decades. The other reality is that the last decade has been one of comparative calm on bilateral ocean matters. One exception is Arctic concerns, specifically the Northwest Passage, that was raised in talks between the U.S. President and Canada's Prime Minister during the 2007,[21] although it does not appear that the conversation went beyond position posturing.

2.3 History

An incidental part of the current Canada-U.S. ocean relationship is one particular aspect of Canada's international story that has been described as "perplexing to those engaged in the practice of foreign relations."[22] Reference has already been made to the fisheries and maritime boundary issues that frequent the history of Canada-U.S. ocean relations. It is to be noted, however, that throughout the 1800s and into the 1900s, on formal foreign relations matters, Canada did not deal directly with the United States; rather the government of Great Britain dealt with the United States. The 1846 Oregon Treaty[23] which constitutes, among other things, the first maritime boundary between Canada and the United States, predates by almost twenty years the formation of the entity called Canada that would eventually become the State independent from Great Britain. At its birth in 1867, Canada was essentially a colony of Great Britain and the power to conduct foreign relations was in the hands of Great Britain.[24] As a matter of law, the colonial relationship ended in 1931,[25] although as a matter of practice, it had ended before

---

21 News Conference—President Bush, Prime Minister Harper and President Calderon, Montebello, Quebec, 21 August 2007, WEEKLY COMPILATION OF PRESIDENTIAL DOCUMENTS, 2007, 1091.

22 Head and Trudeau, *supra* note 15, at 17.

23 Treaty Establishing the Boundary in the Territory on the Northwest Coast of America Lying Westward of the Rocky Mountains, Washington, 15 June 1846, entered into force 5 August 1846, 100 Con. TS 39.

24 *See generally* P. W. HOGG, CONSTITUTIONAL LAW OF CANADA (5th ed., supplemented) (Thomson-Carswell, Scarborough, Ontario (loose-leaf) 2007) 1–3.

25 The legal disconnect was accomplished through a 1931 British enactment, the Statute of Westminster, 22 Geo V c 4, RSC 1985 Appendix II, no. 27.

1931. The first international agreement entered into by Canada without the engagement of Great Britain was a fisheries agreement with the United States: the Pacific Halibut Treaty of 1923.[26] It has been observed that during the nearly sixty-year period (1867 to 1923) of British conduct of relations, "Canada realized on many occasions how indifferent to Canadian interests the colonial power could be."[27] The 1903 *Alaska Boundary Arbitration*,[28] for example, is often seen in Canada as Great Britain trading Canada's interests for the good of the broader Anglo-American relationship.[29]

There are two British-U.S. treaties that are of special note since they created processes for addressing Canada-U.S. neighborhood matters that continue to exist. For the most part, the two processes do not directly engage Canada-U.S. salt water concerns, but the existence of the processes demonstrates the underlying relationship between the two States on neighborhood issues. First, in 1908, Great Britain and the United States created the International Boundary Commission, charging it with the technical task of demarcating and maintaining the agreed boundary (land and sea) between the two countries.[30] This temporary body was made permanent in 1925.[31] Second, through the 1909 Boundary Waters Treaty the International Joint Commission (IJC or the Commission) was established.[32] The IJC has three members

---

26 Convention for the Preservation of the Halibut Fisheries of the Northern Pacific Ocean, Washington, 2 March 1923, entered into force 21 October 1924, 32 LNTS 93.

The 1923 Convention was negotiated and signed by the Canadian Minister of Marine and Fisheries as a representative of the British Crown. C. L. Wiktor, Canadian Treaty Calendar, 1928–1978, Vol I (Oceana Publication, New York 1982) xii.

27 Head and Trudeau, *supra* note 15, at 18.

28 *Decision of the Alaska Boundary Tribunal under the Treaty of 24 January 1903 between the United States and Great Britain*, 20 October 1903, *Proceedings of the Alaska Boundary Tribunal*, U.S. Senate, 58th Cong., 2nd Session, Document 162, Vol. I, 29–97.

29 Stuart, *supra* note 10, at 269. *See also* Chapter Five, section 2.3.

30 Treaty respecting the Demarcation of the International Boundary with Canada, Washington, 11 April 1908, entered into force 4 June 1908, 206 Con. TS 377–391.

31 Treaty regarding the Demarcation of the Boundary between the United States and Canada, Washington 23 February 1925, entered into force 17 July 1925, 43 LNTS 239, Art 4. *See* H. G. Classen, Thrust and Counterthrust: The Genesis of the Canada-United States Boundary (Longmans Canada, Don Mills, Ontario 1965) 355–367.

32 Treaty relating to Boundary Waters and Questions Arising between the United States and Canada, Washington, 11 January 1909, entered into force 13 May 1910, BTS 1910, No. 23, USTS 548, Bevans, *US Treaties*, xii, 319–327.

See generally M. Cohen, *The Regime of Boundary Waters—The Canadian-United States Experience* (1975) Vol. III Recueil des Cours 219–339; F. J. E. Jordan, *The International Joint Commission and Canada—United States Boundary Relations*, in R. St. J. Macdonald, G. L., Morris and D. M. Johnston (eds.) Canadian Perspectives on International Law appointed from each State. Articles III and IV provide that the approval of the Commission is required before either State can undertake projects that would affect the flow or level of boundary waters. Article IX indicates that that either State can refer matters to the Commission "involving the rights, obligations, or interests of either in relation to the other or to the inhabitants of the other, along the common frontier." The results of the Commission investigations under Article IX are not are not binding on the parties. The 1909 Treaty applies to fresh water, not salt water,[33] with the result that the IJC is not directly engaged in bilateral ocean issues. Although there are significant limitations on the IJC and the use that has been made of it by Canada and the United States, it has been hailed as having an "impressive record of accomplishment"[34] and being an important part of the Canada-U.S. institutional relationship.

2.4 The Other Neighbors

Although not a direct influence on the Canada-U.S. ocean relationship, both States are mindful that they have other maritime neighbors and neighborhood issues.

In the case of the United States, the ocean neighbors are numerous in part because of U.S. dependencies and territories in the Pacific Ocean and Caribbean Sea. Focusing on the forty-nine North American states, the United States is a direct ocean neighbor with Mexico on the Pacific Coast and within the Gulf of Mexico; the Russian Federation opposite to Alaska; and Cuba and the Bahamas in the Atlantic Ocean. The United States has entered into maritime boundary arrangements with all of these States,[35] except for

---

AND ORGANIZATION (University of Toronto Press, Toronto 1974) 522–543; and the succinct overview provided by P. K. Wouters, *Allocation of the Non-Navigational Use of International Watercourses: Efforts at Codification and the Experience of Canada and the United States* (1992) 30 CANADIAN YEARBOOK OF INTERNATIONAL LAW (CYIL) 43, 52–55.

33 L. M. BLOOMFIELD AND G. F. FITZGERALD, BOUNDARY WATERS PROBLEMS OF CANADA AND THE UNITED STATES (Carswell, Toronto 1958) 17.

34 Jordan, *supra* note 32, at 525.

35 Agreement between the United States and the Union of Soviet Socialist Republics on the Maritime Boundary, Washington, 1 June 1990, provisionally in force 15 June 1990, 29 ILM 941–945.

Maritime Boundary Agreement between the United States and Cuba, Washington, 16 December 1977, provisionally in force 1 January 1978, 17 ILM 110–112. The Agreement was to be provisionally in force for two years. By exchange of notes, the provisional application of the agreement has been extended every two years. *See* J. A. Roach, R. W. Smith, and the Bahamas.[36] Fisheries is a neighborhood issue in the Gulf of Alaska beyond the 200-nautical-mile zone of both the United States and the Russian Federation in the so-called doughnut hole[37] and as regards tuna on both the Atlantic and Pacific Coasts.[38] The illicit movement of migrants and drugs by sea is also a major neighborhood issue for the United States.[39]

In the case of Canada, there are only two ocean neighbors in addition to the United States, namely, Denmark/Greenland, and France/St. Pierre and Miquelon.[40] These Canadian neighbors (Greenland, and St. Pierre and Miquelon) are far distant from their home metropolitan States. After considerable acrimony and an international adjudication, Canada and France resolved the maritime boundary within Canada's 200-nautical-mile zone for French/St. Pierre and Miquelon waters.[41] In 2005, Canada and France

---

T. Malionek, *Cuba - United States*, in D. A. COLSON AND R. W. SMITH (EDS.) INTERNATIONAL MARITIME BOUNDARIES, Vol. V (Martinus Nijhoff, Leiden 2005) 3555–3557.

Treaty to Resolve Pending Boundary Differences and Maintain the Rio Grande and Colorado River as the International Boundary between the United States and Mexico, Mexico City, 23 November 1970, entered into force 28 April 1972, (1972) 23 UST 373, TIAS 7313. Treaty of Maritime Boundaries between the United States and Mexico, Mexico City, 4 May 1978, entered into force 13 November 1997, 28 UST 5256, TIAS 8625. Treaty between the United States and Mexico on the Delimitation of the Continental Shelf in the Western Gulf of Mexico beyond 200 nautical miles, Washington, 9 June 2000, entered into force 17 January 2001, TIAS 2143, 44 LOSB 71–75.

36 It is reported that no serious discussions have taken place between the United States and the Bahamas on a maritime boundary. The Editors, *North American Maritime Boundaries*, in Colson and Smith, *supra* note 35, at 3402.

37 *See* Convention on the Conservation and Management of Pollock Resources in the Central Bering Sea, Washington, 16 June 1994, entered into force 8 December 1995, 34 ILM 67–77 and D. A. Balton, *The Bering Sea Doughnut Hole Convention: Regional Solution, Global Implications*, in O. S. STOKKE (ed.) GOVERNING HIGH SEAS FISHERIES: THE INTERPLAY OF GLOBAL AND REGIONAL REGIMES (Oxford University Press, Oxford 2001) 143–177.

38 *See* the Convention for the Establishment of the Inter-American Tropical Tuna Commission, Washington, 31 May 1949, entered into force 3 March 1950, 126 UNTS 3 and the International Convention for Conservation of Atlantic Tunas, Rio de Janeiro, 14 May 1966, entered into force 21 March 1969, 673 UNTS 63.

39 *See generally* U.S. Coast Guard, Office on Law Enforcement at <www.uscg.mil/hq/g-o/g-opl/Welcome.htm> (accessed on 13 July 2007) and E. Feege and S. C. Turver, *Homeland Security: Implications for the Coast Guard*, in S. J. TANGREDI (ed.) GLOBALIZATION AND MARITIME POWER (National Defense University Press, Washington 2002) 447–450.

40 It is possible that Canada and the Russian Federation are neighbors in the Arctic Ocean as a result of their continental shelves extending beyond 200 nautical miles from each State. *See* T.L. McDorman, *The Continental Shelf Beyond 200 nm: Law and Politics in the Arctic Ocean* (paper presented in Oslo at the International Conference, The World Ocean in Globalization, 23 August 2008).

41 *Case Concerning the Delimitation of the Maritime Areas between Canada and France*, 10 June 1992, 31 ILM 1149–1219.

announced a cross-boundary hydrocarbon agreement,[42] and earlier a fisheries arrangement was achieved.[43] Canada and Denmark agreed on a maritime boundary for the continental shelf in 1973 that leads from Baffin Bay to the Arctic Ocean and the Lincoln Sea.[44] In the Lincoln Sea itself, there is not yet a maritime boundary agreement between Canada and Denmark.[45] The 1973 Agreement left unresolved the ownership of the barren islet Hans Island located in the High North. Despite the emergence of the Hans Island dispute in the public consciousness in 2005, this is much ado about very little.[46]

The neighborhood issue of political importance to Canada concerns foreign fishing activities in the waters immediately adjacent to Canada's 200-nautical-mile zone in the Atlantic. It is European fishing interests that are of most concern, not U.S. fishing activities. The government of Canada has been under significant pressure to deal effectively with alleged overfishing activities beyond 200 nautical miles through the assertion of national authority, most recently, under the rubric of custodial management.[47] Canada has

---

42 Department of Foreign Affairs, Canada and France to Work Together in Atlantic Waters, 17 May 2005.

43 Process-Verbal Applying the 27 March 1972 between Canada and France on their Mutual Fishing Relations, Paris 2 December 1994, entered into force 14 April 1995, and Agreement between Canada and France on their Mutual Fishing Relations, Ottawa, 27 March 1972, entered into force 27 March 1972, CTS 1979/37.

44 Agreement between Canada and Denmark relating to the Delimitation of the Continental Shelf between Greenland and Canada, Ottawa, 17 December 1973, entered into force 13 March 1974, CTS 1974/9.

45 *See* D. H. Gray, *Canada's Unresolved Maritime Boundaries* (1994) 48 No. 2 GEOMATICA 131, 137–138. This paper is reprinted in (1997) Vol. 5, No. 3 BOUNDARY AND SECURITY BULLETIN (University of Durham, International Boundaries Research Unit) 60–69.

46 *See* R. Huebert, *The Return of the Vikings: The Canadian—Danish Dispute over Hans Island —New Challenges for the Control of the Canadian North*, in F. BERKES, R. HUEBERT, H. FAST, M. MANSEAU, AND A. DIDUCK (EDS.) BREAKING ICE: RENEWABLE RESOURCES AND OCEAN MANAGEMENT IN THE CANADIAN NORTH (University of Calgary Press, Calgary 2005) 319–336.

47 Report of the Advisory Panel on Straddling Stocks, *Breaking New Ground: An Action Plan for Rebuilding The Grand Banks Fisheries* (June 2005), noted at 60–61 that while custodial management has widespread support in Newfoundland and Labrador, and in other parts of Canada, it is not a well-defined nor understood notion. Its interpretation varies with its various proponents, including federal and provincial representatives, a variety of public and private institutions, industry participants, and members of the public.

The Report notes at 70–71 that:

> Any form of a custodial management regime, as proposed to date, involves Canada exercising the same types of management rights on the adjacent high seas as it exercises in its EEZ. The idea that Canada would enforce these decisions outside its own 200 mile EEZ is particularly difficult to envisage, given the jealously guarded principle of flag State enforcement. In any case, the international community and international law do not accept any of these types of expanded coastal State rights.

invested heavily in multilateral efforts to curtail alleged illicit foreign fishing activities in this area through the Northwest Atlantic Fisheries Organization (NAFO)[48] and the negotiation of the 1995 United Nations Agreement on Straddling Fish Stocks and Highly Migratory Fish Stocks (1995 Fish Stocks Agreement).[49] The United States has clearly endorsed the multilateral approach by joining NAFO in 1995 and by being one of the first States to become a party to the 1995 Fish Stocks Agreement.

PART B

3.0 LOS Convention, International Law, and National Offshore Zones

The 1982 LOS Convention is the foundational document of modern international ocean law. The Convention, referred to as the "constitution of the oceans"[50] and seen as one of the major achievements of the United Nations, sets out, among other things, the legal regimes for the 12-nautical-mile territorial sea; the 200-nautical-mile EEZs; international straits; freedom of navigation; and national authority over the continental shelf beyond 200 nautical miles. These are all matters of importance for both Canada and the United States. Moreover, the differences and commonalities between Canada and the United States during the negotiation of the LOS Convention and

---

Short of unilateral action (which would be hotly disputed), the adoption of a custodial management approach to straddling stocks is not possible unless advances in international law either reduce the extent of the high seas or remove flag State authority over a country's vessels when they are fishing in the regulatory area of an RFMO [regional fisheries management organizations]. Neither of these changes is in the immediate offing.

48 NAFO is established by the Convention on the Future Multilateral Cooperation in the Northwest Atlantic Fisheries, Ottawa 24 October 1978, entered into force 1 January 1979, CTS 1979/11.

49 Agreement for the Implementation of the Provisions of the United Nations Convention on the Law of the Sea of 10 December 1982, to the Conservation and Management of Straddling Fish Stocks and Highly Migratory Fish Stocks, New York, 4 August 1995, entered into force 11 December 2001, 2167 UNTS 3.

50 *See* T. T. B. Koh, *A Constitution for the Oceans*, in M. H. Nordquist (ed.) United Nations Convention on the Law of the Sea, 1982: A Commentary, Vol. I (Martinus Nijhoff, Dordrecht 1985) 11–16 and S. V. Scott, *The LOS Convention as a Constitutional Regime for the Oceans*, in A. G. Oude Elferink (ed.) Stability and Change in the Law of the Sea: The Role of the LOS Convention (Martinus Nijhoff, Leiden 2005) 9–38.

subsequent to the completion of the Treaty are a significant context for the bilateral ocean relationship.

Although the LOS Convention looms large in the Canada-U.S. ocean relationship, the Treaty provides little guidance:

- On how States are to delimit maritime boundaries where claimed ocean areas overlap;
- In determining when a waterway is an international strait; and
- No guidance respecting when national waters are historic internal waters.

It is these matters that are at the core of many of the ocean relationship issues between Canada and the United States.

3.1 International Law: Treaties, Custom, and Adjudication

3.1.1 Treaties

An international treaty does not have the effect of legislation and, therefore, an international treaty is not automatically binding on all States. It is a fundamental rule of international law that only treaties to which a State has consented to be bound are legally binding on that State. In the case of the LOS Convention, the process of finalizing and becoming a party to the Convention involved three steps. Step one was the adoption of the finalized text through a formal vote in 1982 that was requested by the United States.[51] Step two involved States signing the LOS Convention,[52] and step three required States to ratify or accede to the Convention.[53] The LOS Convention entered into force for State parties in November 1994, one year after receipt of the sixtieth instrument of ratification or accession.[54] It is only the third step that has the legal result of a State becoming a party to and bound by the LOS Convention. Moreover, the last step is independent of the posture of a

---

51 James L. Malone, Statement, 30 April 1982, UNCLOS III, Official Records, Vol XVI, 154–156.

52 LOS Convention, *supra* note 1, Art 305.

53 *Id.* Arts 306 and 307.

54 *Id.* Art 308.

State regarding the first two steps. Thus, even though the United States voted against the adoption of the LOS Convention and elected not to sign the Treaty, by completing step three, the United States will become a party to the LOS Convention.

The United States and Canada have different domestic processes for becoming a party to an international treaty. The U.S. Constitution provides that the President has the authority to negotiate international agreements subject to the "advice and consent" of the U.S. Senate regarding the United States becoming a party to an international treaty. This constitutional division between the powers of the Presidency and the Congress is a major feature of the U.S. constitutional system. The U.S. treaty ratification process requires two-thirds majority approval by the Senate.[55] The process is for the U.S. President to send to the Senate treaties for ratification with the treaty referred to the Senate Foreign Relations Committee. The chair of the Foreign Relations Committee employs significant discretion in determining if and when the committee will consider a treaty. Upon consideration of a treaty, the committee can recommend that the full Senate grant its "advice and consent" to the treaty. Upon receipt of such a recommendation, the treaty is placed on the Senate calendar, but will not be considered until the Senate leadership brings the treaty to a vote.[56] The system places significant authority for U.S. treaty action within the Senate and in the hands of the chair of the Senate Foreign Relations Committee and senior members of the Senate leadership.

On paper, there is no equivalent process in Canada. In fact, there is no legally mandated process at all. Under Canadian constitutional law and practice, the executive (the cabinet of the federal government) has the exclusive decision-making authority respecting negotiation and ratification of an international treaty.[57] There is no legal requirement for approval from or discussion within the House of Commons.[58] However, in January 2008 it was announced that treaties would be tabled in the House of Commons prior to

---

55 U.S. Constitution Art II, s 2, cl 2.

56 *Standing Rules of the Senate* in TREATIES AND OTHER INTERNATIONAL AGREEMENTS: THE ROLE OF THE UNITED STATES SENATE, Senate Part 103–53, (November, 1993), Rule XXX—Proceedings on Treaties, 89.

57 *See* G. VAN ERT, USING INTERNATIONAL LAW IN CANADIAN COURTS (Kluwer Law International, The Hague 2002) 66–74.

58 *See* Department of Foreign Affairs, *Memorandum—Canada Ratification Practice*, April 2002, in (2002) 40 CYIL 490–492. *See also* J. Harrington, *The Role for Parliament in Treaty-Making*, in O. E. FITZGERALD (ED.), THE GLOBALIZED RULE OF LAW: RELATIONSHIPS BETWEEN INTERNATIONAL AND DOMESTIC LAW (Irwin Law, Toronto 2006) 178–187.

Canada's ratification so that the House of Commons can, if it wishes, have a role in reviewing international agreements.[59] It is the Canadian practice not to ratify an international treaty that requires legislative implementation until the necessary legislation is enacted.

3.1.2 Customary International Law

Despite the rule that treaties are only binding for their States parties, treaties can, in whole or in part, be internationally legally binding on States as a result of customary international law. Customary international law is best understood as being legal obligations on a State that arise from the wide-scale practice of States. Unlike treaty law, in which there is a text and clear rules of its application to a State party, customary international law is flexible and amorphous, yet is accepted as a source of obligations and rights by States, international courts, and international lawyers. The difficulty is the determination of particular rules of customary international law. As noted by Birnie and Boyle:

> [I]t is often difficult to determine whether or not a new custom has crystallized into international law, and, if so, at what point. Thus, identification of customary law always has been, and remains, particularly problematical, requiring the exercise of skill, judgment, and considerable research.[60]

Customary international law is of importance in Canada-U.S. relations since Canada is a party to the LOS Convention and the United States is not. However, the United States has asserted that much of the LOS Convention is customary international law and, in particular, that the navigational rights provisions in the Treaty represent customary international law. The U.S. assertion was made in the March 1983 Oceans Policy Statement of President Reagan, in which it was declared that the United States "is prepared to accept and act in accordance with the balance of interests relating to traditional uses of the oceans–such as navigation" in the LOS Convention and that "the United States will exercise and assert its navigation . . . rights and freedoms

---

59 Department of Foreign Affiars, Canada Announces Policy to Table International Treaties in House of Commons, 25 January 2008.

60 P. Birnie and A. E. Boyle, International Law and the Environment (Oxford University Press, 2nd ed., Oxford 2002) 16.

on a worldwide basis in a manner consistent with the balance of interests in the [LOS] convention."[61] Moreover, in 2004, the Legal Advisor to the U.S. Department of State commented:

> . . . the United States has actively sought to achieve global acceptance of, and adherence to, the Convention's provisions, particularly in relation to freedom of navigation. President Reagan's 1983 Oceans Policy Statement directed the United States to abide by, and enjoy the rights accorded by, the non-deep seabed provisions of the Convention. Abroad, the United States has worked both diplomatically and operationally to promote the provisions of the Convention as reflective of customary international law.[62]

It is important to note that Canada's party status to the LOS Convention does not mean that Canada accepts that specific provisions of the LOS Convention are customary international law or that the provisions of the Convention are opposable as between Canada (a party) and the United States (a non-party). Moreover, an assertion by the United States that a provision of the LOS Convention is customary international law does not *ipso facto* make it so such that Canada would have to or does accept the assertion.

3.1.3 Adjudication

International adjudication (State *versus* State) has played a limited but important role in both advancing and clarifying international ocean law and in resolving disputes that arise respecting the existence or application of international ocean law. In some respects, the paucity of cases has ensured that they are carefully picked over by lawyers for every possible nuance and nugget. The overwhelming majority of the ocean adjudications have involved resolution of overlapping claims to ocean spaces - maritime boundary delimitation. The most recent of these cases are the 2007 *Guyana and Suriname Arbitration*[63]

---

61 President Reagan, Statement - U.S. Oceans Policy, 10 March 1983, 22 ILM 464–465.

62 William H. Taft IV, Legal Adviser, U.S. Department of State, before the Senate Armed Services Committee on 8 April 2004, at www.globalsecurity.org/military/library/congress/2004_hr/040408-taft.pdf (accessed on 7 October 2006).

63 *In the Matter of the Arbitration between Guyana and Suriname*, 17 September 2007, on the website of the Permanent Court of Arbitration, available at www.pca-cpa.org (accessed on 29 September 2007).

and *Nicaragua- Honduras Case* before the International Court.[64] The Canada-U.S. 1984 *Gulf of Maine Case*,[65] before a panel of the International Court, will be referred to frequently in this work. The 1949 *Corfu Channel Case*, between the United Kingdom and Albania, remains as the only international adjudication that addresses the sensitive issue of navigation rights and international straits.[66] The International Tribunal for the Law of the Sea (ITLOS), created by the LOS Convention,[67] has had a number of cases involved interpretation of the provisions of the LOS Convention respecting the obligation to promptly release arrested fishing vessels on the payment of reasonable bond.[68] ITLOS has also had a case dealing with the authority of a coastal State to engage in hot pursuit and vessel seizure.[69]

All State *versus* State adjudicative dispute settlement is based on the consent of the States. Not surprisingly, States are reluctant to pursue international adjudication since with adjudication, unlike with negotiation, the participating States lose control over and accountability respecting the outcome. The United States and Canada fit the profile of reluctant States. Canada maintains a robust image respecting acceptance of the possibility of international adjudication having long accepted the compulsory jurisdiction of the International Court. However, Canada has had a marked propensity to exercise its right of exception when a serious possibility of adjudication exists. In 1970, when Canada took action respecting Arctic waters, Canada withdrew its acceptance of the Court's compulsory jurisdiction for that matter.[70] In 1993, Canada was careful to exempt its adventurist legislation and subsequent action in seizing, on the high seas, the Spanish trawler *Estai* from the scrutiny of the International Court and, when challenged by Spain, successful argued before the Court that its exemption was valid.[71] On the

---

64 *Case Concerning Territorial and Maritime Dispute between Nicaragua and Honduras in the Caribbean Sea*, 8 October 2007, 46 ILM 1053.

65 *Delimitation of the Maritime Boundary in the Gulf of Maine Area (Canada v. United States)*, [1984] ICJ Rep. 246.

66 *The Corfu Channel Case (Albania/United Kingdom)*, [1949] ICJ Rep. 4.

67 LOS Convention, *supra* note 1, Annex VI.

68 *See* T.L. McDorman, *An Overview of International Fisheries Disputes and the International Tribunal for the Law of the Sea* (*ITLOS*) (2002) 40 CYIL 119–149 and *see* the website of ITLOS at www.itlos.org (accessed on 4 August 2007).

69 *The M/V Saiga (No. 2) Case (St. Vincent and the Grenadines v. Guinea)*, 38 ILM 1323–1442.

70 Declaration Recognizing as Compulsory the Jurisdiction of the Court, 7 April 1970, in International Court, YEARBOOK 1969–1970 (The Hague, 1970) 55–56, 9 ILM 598–599.

71 *Fisheries Jurisdiction Case (Spain v. Canada)*, [1998] ICJ Rep. 342.

plus side, Canada has, in recent decades, engaged in adjudicative dispute resolution on oceans matters twice with France.[72] For reasons unrelated to Canada or the oceans, in 1985, the United States formally withdrew its acceptance of the compulsory jurisdiction of the International Court.[73] It is regularly noted that the United States has become very shy about international adjudication.[74] The Canada-U.S. *Gulf of Maine Case* only arose as a last resort after a tortuous decade of discussions and disappointment.

When ratifying the LOS Convention, Canada took advantage of all the possible exemptions to compulsory adjudication offered within the Treaty, including exempting disputes regarding ocean boundary delimitation, historic bays or title, military activities, and law enforcement activities regarding fisheries and marine scientific research within 200 nautical miles.[75] It appears that the United States, when it becomes a party to the Convention, will also take advantage of all the possible exemptions to compulsory adjudication.[76] Thus, even if the United States and Canada are both parties to the LOS Convention, few of the ocean matters in dispute bilaterally will be subject to the compulsory dispute settlement regime of the LOS Convention.

International third-party adjudication or quasi-adjudication, however, has had a role to play in the Canada-U.S. ocean relationship. In addition to the *Gulf of Maine Case*, there have been a number of other cases of importance, although all of these involved Great Britain directly rather than Canada and the most recent of these was in 1910.[77]

---

72 *Case Concerning Filleting within the Gulf of St. Lawrence between Canada and France*, 17 July 1986, xix RIAA 225 (in French) and *Case between Canada and France, (St. Pierre and Miquelon), supra* note 41.

73 Letter to the Secretary-General of the United Nations from Secretary of State George P. Shultz, 7 October 1985, 24 ILM 1742–1745 and *see* Department of State, CUMULATIVE DIGEST OF THE UNITED STATES PRACTICE IN INTERNATIONAL LAW, 1981–1988 (Washington, 1995) 3329–3338.

74 J. F. MURPHY, THE UNITED STATES AND THE RULE OF LAW IN INTERNATIONAL AFFAIRS (Cambridge University Press, Cambridge 2004) 350–351.

75 Declaration Made Upon Ratification, 7 November 2003, 53 LAW OF THE SEA BULLETIN (LOSB) 15 and *see* T. L. McDorman, *Canada Ratifies the 1982 United Nations Convention on the Law of the Sea: At Last*, (2004) 35 OCEAN DEVELOPMENT AND INTERNATIONAL LAW (ODIL) 103, 106.

76 In December 2007, the U.S. Senate Foreign Relations Committee voted to recommend U.S. accession to the LOS Convention and reported this to the full Senate for consideration. Attached to the Advice and Consent Resolution before the Senate was a declaration (section 2) outlining the exemptions that were proposed to be attached by the United States to its instrument of accession. U.S. Senate, Executive Report 110–9, Part VIII–Text of Resolution of Advice and Consent to Ratification, 19–24 (2007).

77 *Award of the Tribunal of Arbitration in the Question Relating to the North Atlantic Coast Fisheries*, 7 September 1910, xi RIAA 173.

3.2 Offshore Zones

What follows is an explanation of the national offshore zones that exist under the LOS Convention that are of most relevance to Canada and the United States. The Appendix to this chapter provides an overview of the claims by Canada and the United States respecting these zones.

3.2.1 Internal Waters

As a matter of international law, a coastal State enjoys full territorial sovereignty over its internal waters. In general, this means that within a coastal State's internal waters, there is no right of passage for foreign vessels with the result that foreign vessels have no right of access to a coastal State's internal waters.[78]

Internal waters are defined as being those waters landward of baselines that exist for the purpose of determining the location of the territorial sea.[79] Baselines are either straight baselines used to address geographically complex coastlines or normal baselines based upon the low-water mark with account being taken for river mouths, bays, and similar physical anomalies.[80] The use of baselines employing the low-water mark, while not free of controversy, involves considerations of a physical nature and the amount of ocean area that can be enclosed as internal waters using low-water-mark baselines is limited. The same cannot be said for internal waters created using straight baselines where considerable offshore spaces can be enclosed as internal waters.

In addition to the existence of internal waters noted above, there are also historic internal waters, which will be discussed in detail below.[81]

The United States has longstanding policy of not utilizing straight baselines, thus it relies on normal baselines based upon the low-water mark.[82] Canada established straight baselines around most of its Arctic archipelago

---

78 R. R. CHURCHILL AND A. V. LOWE, THE LAW OF THE SEA (Manchester University Press, 3rd edition, Manchester 1999) 61.

79 LOS Convention, *supra* note 1, Art 8(1).

80 *Id.* Arts 5, 6, 7, 9–13.

81 *See* Chapter Six, section 2.1.

82 L. M. Alexander, *The Nature of Offshore Boundaries*, in L. M. ALEXANDER AND R. S. HAWKINS (eds.) CANADIAN—U.S. MARITIME PROBLEMS (Law of the Sea Institute, Kingston, R.I. 1972) 56.

in 1985,[83] along the coasts of Newfoundland and Nova Scotia on the East Coast in 1967,[84] and along Vancouver Island and the Queen Charlotte Islands on the West Coast in 1969.[85]

3.2.2 Territorial Sea

The territorial sea is the ocean area up to 12 nautical miles from the baselines.[86] Within the territorial sea, the coastal State has jurisdiction over all the living and non-living resources and over vessel traffic, subject to a foreign vessel's right of innocent passage.[87]

Regarding innocent passage, Article 19(1) of the LOS Convention provides that:

> Passage is innocent so long as it is not prejudicial to the peace, good order or security of the coastal State. Such passage shall take place in conformity with this Convention and with other rules of international law.

Article 19(2) provides a listing of activities which, if engaged in by a passing vessel, leads to the passage not being innocent.[88] Many questions exist regarding innocent passage. For example, is the Article 19(2) listing exhaustive of what constitutes non-innocence? Is it only the "activities" of a passing foreign vessel that can make it non-innocent? Can other things be considered in determining whether a vessel's passage is non-innocent, such as the type of the vessel or the cargo being carried?[89]

---

83 Territorial Sea Geographical Coordinates (Area 7) Order, Can Gaz Part II, Vol. 119, SOR/85-872, 10 September 1985, 3996–4002.

84 Territorial Sea and Fishing Zones Geographical Coordinates (Areas 1, 2 and 3) Order, Can Gaz Part II, Vol. 101, SOR/67-543, 26 October 1967, 1700–1704, replaced by Territorial Sea Geographical Coordinates Order, Consolidated Regulations of Canada (CRC) (1978), Vol. XVIII, c 1550, 13751–13758.

85 Territorial Sea and Fishing Zones Geographical Coordinates (Areas 4 and 5) Order, Can Gaz Part II, Vol. 103, SOR/69–278, 29 May 1969, 792–795, replaced by Territorial Sea Geographical Coordinates Order, CRC (1978), Vol. XVIII, c 1550, 13751–13758.

86 LOS Convention, *supra* note 1, Art 3.

87 *Id.* Arts 2, 17.

88 *Id.* Art 19(2).

89 *See* Chapter Six, section 4.2.3.

Where vessel passage is non-innocent, a coastal State "may take the necessary steps" to prevent the vessel passage.[90] Even where vessel passage is innocent, a coastal State can enact laws regarding a vessel engaged in innocent passage[91] and can, in some cases, enforce that law against a vessel engaged in innocent passage. A coastal State, however, is not to "hamper" the innocent passage of foreign ships.[92] More specifically, coastal States are not to "impose requirements on foreign ships which have the practical effect of denying or impairing the right of innocent passage."[93]

In 1989, the President proclaimed that the U.S. territorial sea would move from three to 12 nautical miles in width.[94] One of Canada's 1970 measures was establishing a 12-nautical-mile territorial sea.[95]

3.2.3 Contiguous Zone

The 12-nautical-mile contiguous zone, if claimed by a State, exists seaward of the territorial sea.[96] Within the contiguous zone, the adjacent coastal State can exercise "the control necessary" to prevent and punish infringement of its customs, fiscal, immigration, and sanitary laws and regulations that apply within its territorial sea.[97] The coastal State authority within the contiguous zone is understood by most States to be an enforcement jurisdiction and not a legislative or prescriptive jurisdiction.[98] There is some question about whether a coastal State within the contiguous zone can take action for security reasons.[99] Finally, Article 303(2) of the LOS Convention provides that

---

90 LOS Convention, *supra* note 1, Art 25(1).

91 *Id.* Art 21(1).

92 *Id.* Art 24(1).

93 *Id.* Art 24(1)(a).

94 Territorial Sea of the United States, Proclamation 5928 of 27 December 1988, 54 Federal Register (Fed Reg) 777, 28 ILM 284.

95 Act to amend the Territorial Sea and Fishing Zones Act, St Can 1969–1970, c 68, s 1. In 1996 the Territorial Sea and Fishing Zones Act was repealed and replaced by the Oceans Act, St Can 1996, c 31 with the 12-nautical-mile territorial sea set out in s 4.

96 LOS Convention, *supra* note 1, Art 33(2).

97 *Id.* Art 33(1).

98 Churchill and Lowe, *supra* note 78, at 138.

99 *Id.*

a coastal State has authority over archaeological and historical objects on the seafloor of its contiguous zone.[100]

In 1999, President Clinton proclaimed the existence of a U.S. contiguous zone tracking the wording on the contiguous zone in the LOS Convention.[101] In 1996, Canada created its contiguous zone in the Oceans Act.[102]

3.2.4 200-Nautical-Mile Exclusive Economic Zone

The 200-nautical-mile exclusive economic zone (EEZ), constructed from the baselines employed to delineate the territorial sea,[103] originally was only to be available to those countries which ratified the LOS Convention. However, only a few years after the arrival of the concept, a coastal State's entitlement to a 200-nautical-mile zone became part of customary international law.[104]

The legal status of the EEZ is of a *sui generis* character "situated between the territorial sea and high seas."[105] Within its EEZ, a coastal State has national jurisdiction respecting exploration and exploitation of living and non-living resources[106] and marine scientific research.[107] As regards marine pollution prevention and environmental protection, there is a delicate balance in the LOS Convention between the authority of the coastal State and the navigational freedoms of vessels.[108] Non-coastal States have rights within the 200-nautical-mile zone respecting navigation, overflight, and the laying of submarine cables and pipelines.[109] These rights are to be exercised with "due

---

100 LOS Convention, *supra* note 1, Art 303(2). *See also* Convention on the Protection of the Underwater Cultural Heritage, done at Paris, 6 November 2001, not yet in force, 41 ILM 40–56.

101 Contiguous Zone of the United States, Proclamation 7219 of 2 August 1999, 64 Fed Reg 48701–49702.

102 Oceans Act, *supra* note 95, s 10.

103 LOS Convention, *supra* note 1, Art 57.

104 In 1985, the International Court stated that it was "incontestable that . . . the institution of the exclusive economic zone . . . is shown by the practice of States to have become a part of customary law." *Case Concerning the Continental Shelf (Libya/Malta)*, [1985] ICJ Rep. 13, para 34.

105 Churchill and Lowe, *supra* note 78, at 166.

106 LOS Convention, *supra* note 1, Art 56 (1)(a).

107 *Id.* Arts 56 (1)(b)(ii), 246(1–2).

108 *Id.* Arts 56 (1)(b)(iii), 210(5), 211(5), 216, 220(3)(5–7).

109 *Id.* Art 58(1).

regard" to the rights of the coastal State.[110] For rights or jurisdiction regarding activities not explicitly allocated, each situation has to be evaluated on a case-by-case basis with the LOS Convention providing "no presumption in favour of either the coastal State or other States."[111]

In 1976, the United States adopted a 200-nautical-mile fishing zone[112] and, in 1983, proclaimed a 200-nautical-mile EEZ.[113] Canada also put in place its 200-nautical-mile fishing zone in 1977[114] and, through legislation in 1996, adopted its 200-nautical-mile EEZ.[115]

3.2.5 Continental Shelf Beyond 200 Nautical Miles

Where the physical continental margin (shelf, slope, and rise) extends beyond 200 nautical miles, the adjacent coastal State has exclusive jurisdiction over the living and non-living resources of the continental shelf, *i.e.*, sedentary fish species and hydrocarbon resources.[116] Coastal State jurisdiction over its adjacent continental shelf area beyond 200 nautical miles is linked to a required sharing with the international community of revenues derived from non-living resources exploited beyond the 200-nautical-mile limit,[117] and with the application of detailed criteria and a process to assist States in the establishment of the outer limit of their continental margin. The detailed criteria involves determination of the thickness of sediment, the foot of the continental slope, the 2,500-meter isobath, and distinguishing among submarine ridges, oceanic ridges, and submarine elevations.[118] The process involves the

110 *Id.* Art 58(3).

111 Churchill and Lowe, *supra* note 78, at 176 and LOS Convention, *supra* note 1, Art 59.

112 Fishery Conservation and Management Act (renamed the Magnuson Fishery Conservation and Management Act), 90 US Stat. 331, Pub L. 94–265, codified at 16 USC 1801–1882, effective 1 March 1977.

113 Exclusive Economic Zone of the United States, Proclamation 5030 of 10 March 1983, 48 Fed Reg 10605, 22 ILM 464–465.

114 Fishing Zones of Canada (Zones 4 and 5) Order, Can Gaz Part II, Vol. 111, SOR/77-62, 1 January 1977, 115–120 replaced by Fishing Zones of Canada (Zones 4 and 5) Order, CRC (1978), Vol. XVIII, c 1548, 13741–13746 and Fishing Zones of Canada (Zone 6) Order, Can Gaz Part II, Vol. 111, SOR/77-173, 24 February 1977, 652–655, replaced by Fishing Zones of Canada (Zone 6) Order, CRC (1978), c 1549, 13747–13750. Zones 4 and 5 were on the east and west coasts and zone 6 was the Arctic.

115 Oceans Act, *supra* note 95, s 13.

116 LOS Convention, *supra* note 1, Arts 77(1), 76(1).

117 *Id.* Art 82.

118 *Id.* Art 76(1–6).

Commission on the Limits of the Continental Shelf (Commission on Limits) to which States are to submit information on their proposed outer limit calculations.[119] Although the Commission on Limits cannot impose its views on a coastal State, in order for a coastal State's outer limit to be considered final and binding, the outer limit is to be made "on the basis" of the recommendations of the Commission.[120]

In 1945, through the Truman Proclamation on the Continental Shelf (Truman Proclamation), the United States asserted that it had the exclusive authority to address the natural resources of its adjacent continental shelf.[121] In 1953, the United States enacted the Outer Continental Shelf Lands Act, which defined the outer continental shelf as all submerged lands "of which the subsoil and seabed appertain to the United States."[122] In the 1960s, Canada issued oil and gas permits and licenses covering large areas of its adjacent continental shelf[123] and, in 1970, amended the Oil and Gas Production and Conservation Act to provide a definition of the continental shelf adjacent to Canada.[124] The current Canadian definition of its adjacent continental shelf is in the Oceans Act.[125] Both the United States and Canada have physical continental margin areas beyond 200 nautical miles. The most important such area for the United States is in the Gulf of Mexico[126] and for Canada is adjacent to Newfoundland.[127] Seaward of the Gulf of Maine and in the

---

119 *Id.* Art 76(8) and Annex II—Commission on the Limits of the Continental Shelf.

120 *Id.* Art 76(8). See T.L. McDorman, *The Role of the Commission on the Limits of the Continental Shelf: A Technical Body in a Political World* (2002) 17 INTERNATIONAL JOURNAL OF MARINE AND COASTAL LAW (IJMCL) 301–324.

121 Executive Order 9633 of September 28, 1945—Reserving and Placing Certain Resources of the Continental Shelf Under the Control and Jurisdiction of the Secretary of the Interior, 10 Fed Reg 12303, 59 US Stat. 884.

122 Outer Continental Shelf Lands Act, 67 US Stat. 462, Pub L. 95–372, codified at 43 USC 1301–1356, s 1331(a).

123 B. G. Buzan and D. W. Middlemiss, *Canadian Foreign Policy and the Exploitation of the Seabed*, in B. JOHNSON and M. W. ZACHER (eds.) CANADIAN FOREIGN POLICY AND THE LAW OF THE SEA (University of British Columbia Press, Vancouver 1977) 5, 17–18.

124 Act to amend the Oil and Gas Production and Conservation Act, St Can 1969–1970, c 43, s 3.

125 Oceans Act, *supra* note 95, s 17.

126 *See* United States—Mexico Agreement on Delimitation of the Continental Shelf beyond 200 Nautical Miles, *supra* note 35.

127 *See* D. G. Crosby, *The UNCLOS III Definition of the Continental Shelf: Application to the Canadian Offshore*, in D. M. JOHNSTON AND N. G. LETALIK (eds.) THE LAW OF THE SEA AND OCEAN INDUSTRY: NEW OPPORTUNITIES AND RESTRAINTS (Law of the Sea Institute, Honolulu 1984) 473–486.

Beaufort Sea are areas where the continental shelf extends beyond 200 nautical miles, which will require some type of Canada-U.S. maritime boundary or cooperation agreement.[128]

PART C

4.0 A Few Words on Other Treaties and Ocean Governance

Beyond the LOS Convention, a large number of multilateral agreements and instruments are part of international ocean law and are often more important operationally than the LOS Convention. Although there are differences between Canada and the United States on various issues that arise in these agreements and bodies, the three matters focused on in this work involve issues regarding the legal authority of the coastal State respecting either an ocean space or activities (*i.e.*, navigation) within an ocean area. As a result, it is the international ocean law framework agreement, the LOS Convention, which is the most directly relevant. Nevertheless, a tour of the horizon of the other ocean treaties and activities is important.

4.1 Ocean Fora

There is not a single focal point at the multilateral level where States meet to discuss, negotiate, and mediate international ocean matters. As Johnston has noted "the global arena consists of highly disparate components."[129]

The LOS Convention did not provide for a regularized institution or process in which State parties could meet and discuss issues of implementation of the Convention or emerging issues. The LOS Convention predates the now widely accepted institutionalization of regular meetings of convention State parties referred to as either conferences of the parties (COPs) or meetings of

---

128 *See* Chapter Five, sections 5.3.2 and 5.4.

129 D. M. Johnston, *The Challenge of International Ocean Governance: Institutional, Ethical and Conceptual Dilemmas*, in D. R. Rothwell and D. L. VanderZwaag (eds.) Towards Principled Oceans Governance: Australian and Canadian Approaches and Challenges (Routledge, New York 2006) 381.

the parties (MOPs).[130] Moreover, unlike many of the treaties to be noted below, the LOS Convention did not emerge from an international organization that provides an ongoing venue for discussion. The United Nations (U. N.) Secretary-General, using authority provided for in the LOS Convention,[131] however, has convened annual meetings of the State Parties to the LOS Convention (SPLOS) that address administrative matters such as the election of judges for ITLOS and members of the Commission on the Limits of the Continental Shelf.[132] Whether SPLOS will develop into a body in which States can discuss issues of concern, raise new matters, and assist in implementation matters is yet to be determined.[133]

The LOS Convention was the product of a conference convened as a result of a resolution passed by the U. N. General Assembly.[134] The United Nations and its General Assembly has remained engaged with law of the sea matters ever since.[135] In recent years, there has been an annual debate in and resolutions adopted by the General Assembly on "Oceans and Law of the Sea"[136] and "Sustainable Fisheries,"[137] which have been informed by the yearly report of the Secretary-General on oceans matters[138] and the annual meetings entitled the United Nations Open-ended Informal Consultative Process on Oceans and the Law of the Sea.[139] As a technical legal matter, General

---

130 *See generally* R. R. Churchill and G. Ulfstein, *Autonomous Institutional Arrangements in Multilateral Environmental Agreements: A Little-Noticed Phenomenon in International Law* (2000) 94 AJIL 623–659.

131 LOS Convention, *supra* note 1, Art 319(2)(e).

132 *See generally* the website for SPLOS, at www.un.org/Depts/los/meeting_states_parties/meeting_states_parties.htm (accessed on 4 August 2007).

133 *See* T. Treves, *The General Assembly and the Meeting of States Parties in the Implementation of the LOS Convention*, in Oude Elferink, *supra* note 50, at 55–58, 62–65, 68–74.

134 General Assembly Resolution 2750C (XXV), adopted 17 December 1970, recorded vote of 108 to 7, with 6 abstentions, (1970) UNYB 82–83.

135 *See generally* Treves, *supra* note 133, at 58–61, 66–68 and L. de La Fayette, *The Role of the United Nations in International Ocean*, in D. Freestone, R. Barnes, and D. M. Ong (eds.) The Law of the Sea: Progress and Prospects (Oxford University Press, Oxford 2006) 63–74.

136 For example, General Assembly Resolution 61/222, adopted 20 December 2006, 157 in favor, one against and three abstentions.

137 For example, General Assembly Resolution 61/105, adopted 8 December 2006, without a vote.

138 For example, U. N. Secretary-General Report: Oceans and the Law of the Sea, UN Doc A/62/66, 12 March 2007.

139 *See generally* the website for the U. N. Open-Ended Informal Process, at www.un.org/Depts/los/consultative_process/consultative_process.htm (accessed on 4 August 2007).

Assembly resolutions are almost never legally binding, although they can be politically important.[140] Ocean-related General Assembly resolutions that are exceptional in this regard are those from 1989 and 1991 calling for the cessation of high seas driftnet fishing and a moratorium on this method of harvesting.[141]

4.2 Deep Seabed Mining

The principal institution created by the LOS Convention is the International Seabed Authority (ISA).[142] The ISA is mandated to "organize and control activities" in the Area, designated as the deep seabed area beyond national jurisdiction, "with a view to administering the resources of the Area."[143] The importance of the ISA was made clear at the end of UNCLOS III when the States created the Preparatory Commission in order to ensure that, when the LOS Convention came into force, the ISA would be able to commence operations without delay.[144] As a result of the 1994 Agreement Relating to the Implementation of Part XI of the United Nations Convention on the Law of the Sea of 10 December 1994,[145] changes were made to the workings of the ISA as had been set out in the 1982 LOS Convention. The ISA is located in Kingston, Jamaica.[146]

---

140 *See generally* O. SCHACHTER, INTERNATIONAL LAW IN THEORY AND PRACTICE (Martinus Nijhoff, Dordrecht 1991) 85–94.

141 General Assembly Resolution 46/125, 20 December 1991, adopted without vote, (1991) UNYB 503–504; General Assembly Resolution 45/197, 21 December 1990, adopted without vote, (1990) UNYB 631–632; and General Assembly Resolution 44/225, 22 December 1989, adopted without vote, (1989) UNYB 447–448.

142 LOS Convention, *supra* note 1, Art 156.

143 *Id.* Art 157(1).

144 Final Act of the Third United Nations Conference on the Law of the Sea, U. N. Doc A/Conf.62/121, 27 October 1982, Annex I, Resolution I, Establishment of the Preparatory Commission for the International Sea-Bed Authority and for the International Tribunal on the Law of the Sea, UNCLOS III, OFFICIAL RECORDS, Vol XVII, 145–146.

145 Agreement relating to the Implementation of Part XI of the United Nations Convention on the Law of the Sea, New York, 28 July 1994, entered into force 28 July 1996, 33 ILM 1309–1327.

146 *See* the website for International Seabed Authority (ISA), at www.isa.org.jm (accessed on 4 August 2007). For a recent overview of the work of the ISA, *see* S. Nandan, *Administering the Mineral Resources of the Deep Seabed*, in Freestone, Barnes and Ong, *supra* note 135, 75–92.

4.3 Ship Safety and Vessel-Source Pollution

The International Maritime Organization (IMO) is the organ of the United Nations with the mandate to address the safety of vessels and vessel-source marine environmental pollution.[147] On ship safety, the first-among-equals of the number of treaties in this area adopted under the auspices of IMO is the 1974 Safety of Life at Sea Convention (SOLAS).[148] Through the numerous chapters of the SOLAS Convention and regular updating done through amendments, standards are set for commercial vessels on a large variety of safety-related items.[149]

The principal vessel marine pollution convention is the 1973 International Convention for the Prevention of Pollution from Ships (MARPOL) and its 1978 Protocol of Amendment[150] which establishes regulations aimed at preventing and minimizing pollution from ships whether accidental or resulting from the routine operation of vessels.[151] There is also the London Ocean Dumping Convention,[152] which addresses ocean pollution by the intentional dumping from ships or ship-like structures. The newest of the IMO marine pollution treaties is the 2004 International Convention for the Control and Management of Ships' Ballast Water and Sediments,[153] which is designed to

---

147 *See generally* the website for the IMO, available at www.imo.org (accessed 4 August 2007).

148 International Convention for the Safety of Life at Sea (SOLAS), London, 1 November 1974, entered into force 25 May 1980, 1184 UNTS 2. Both Canada and the United States are Parties to SOLAS.

149 Respecting the work of the IMO in this area, *see generally* P. BOISSON, SAFETY AT SEA: POLICIES, REGULATIONS AND INTERNATIONAL LAW (Bureau Veritas, Paris 1999) 195–371.

150 International Convention for the Prevention of Pollution from Ships (MARPOL), London, 2 November 1973, and the Protocol of Amendment, London, 1 June 1978. The Protocol absorbed the earlier Convention with the combined document entering into force 2 October 1983, 1340 UNTS 61. Both Canada and the United States are Parties to MARPOL 1973/1978.

151 *See generally* A.K-J. TAN, VESSEL-SOURCE MARINE POLLUTION: THE LAW AND POLITICS OF INTERNATIONAL REGULATION (Cambridge University Press, Cambridge 2006) 126–155, 184–192.

152 Convention on the Prevention of Marine Pollution by Dumping of Wastes and Other Matters, London, 29 December 1972, entered into force 30 August 1972, 1046 UNTS 120. Both Canada and the United States are Parties to the London Dumping Convention.

153 International Convention for the Control and Management of Ships' Ballast Water and Sediments, IMO Doc BWM/Conf./36, 16 February 2000, reprinted in M. Tsimplis, *Alien Species Stay Home: The International Convention for the Control and Management of Ships' Ballast Water and Sediments* 2004 (2005) 20 IJMCL 411, 446–482. *See generally* Tsimplis, at 411–445 and Tan, *supra* note 151, at 172–174.

combat the unwanted introduction of alien species into coastal waters through the release of ballast water by visiting vessels.

Facilitating the enforcement of the numerous vessel standard-setting conventions is the global network of Port State Control Understandings through which port authorities within specific regions agree to inspect visiting vessels for their compliance with the international standards and, if necessary, detain a vessel pending attainment of compliance.[154]

4.4 Land-Based Sources of Marine Pollution

It is estimated that 80 percent of marine pollution has its origins on land, reaching the oceans through rivers and runoff. There is no global instrument that addresses explicitly with this source of marine pollution. However, in 1995, under the auspices of the U. N. Environment Programme (UNEP), States adopted the Global Programme of Action for the Protection of the Marine Environment and Land-Based Activities (GPA)[155] to coordinate and direct specific attention to land-based sources of marine environmental pollution. The GPA is a continuing process within UNEP.[156]

4.5 Fisheries

The most significant recent addition to international fisheries law is the 1995 U. N. Fish Stocks Agreement.[157] This Agreement, which is directly tied to the LOS Convention, is an attempt to fill gaps in the LOS Convention as regards the management of straddling fish stocks (stocks that migrate between the waters within and beyond a coastal State's 200-nautical-mile zone) and highly migratory species (such as tuna which have migration patterns that involve the waters of one of more coastal States and the high seas).

---

154 *See generally* Z. O. OZCAYIR, PORT STATE CONTROL (Lloyd's of London Press, London 2001) 61–233, 277–321, 379–401.

155 Global Programme of Action for the Protection of the Marine Environment and Land-Based Activities, adopted by the Intergovernmental Conference, Washington, 1995, UN Doc UNEP(OCA)/LBA/IG.2/7, 5 December 1995, on the website of the GPA at www.gpa.unep.org (accessed on 4 August 2007).

156 *See generally* the website for the GPA at www.gpa.unep.org (accessed 4 August 2007).

157 Fish Stocks Agreement, *supra* note 49. Both Canada and the United States are Parties to the Fish Stocks Agreement.

The origins of this Treaty were the 1992 U. N. Conference on Environment and Development held in Rio de Janeiro, which called for a conference to deal with straddling and highly migratory fish stocks[158] and the subsequent General Assembly Resolution that convened the conference.[159] The 1995 Agreement is designed to strengthen the existing, or lead to the creation of new, regional fisheries management organizations which have the task of managing either highly migratory stocks or straddling fish stocks. As already noted, the most important regional fisheries management organization for Canada is the NAFO,[160] which addresses the waters adjacent Canada's east coast 200-nautical-mile zone. It is the tuna organizations that are of most importance for the United States: the Inter-American Tropical Tuna Commission (IATTC);[161] the International Commission for the Conservation of Atlantic Tunas (ICCAT);[162] and the Western and Central Pacific Fisheries Commission (WCPFC).[163]

In recent years, attention has been focused on "illegal, unreported and unregulated" (IUU) fishing activity on the high seas. The Food and Agricultural Organization of the United Nations (FAO) has been the principal organization developing strategies on this issue. In 2001, the member States of the FAO adopted the International Plan of Action to Prevent, Deter and Eliminate Illegal, Unreported and Unregulated Fishing (IOPA-IUU).[164] Although not legally binding, the IOPA-IUU commits countries to undertake actions and report on efforts taken to reduce IUU fishing.

---

158 *Report of the United Nations Conference on Environment and Development*, U. N. Doc A/Conf.151/26, 12 August 1992, Annex II, Agenda 21, para 17.49.

159 General Assembly Resolution 47/192, 22 December 1992, adopted without vote, (1992) UNYB 688–689.

160 NAFO Convention, *supra* note 48. Both Canada and the United States are members of NAFO.

161 The IATTC was created by the IATTC Convention, *supra* note 38. Both Canada and the United States are members of the IATTC.

162 The ICCAT was created by the ICCAT Convention, *supra* note 38. Both Canada and the United States are members of the ICCAT.

163 The WCPFC was established by the Convention on the Conservation and Management of Highly Migratory Fish Stocks in the Western and Central Pacific Ocean, Honolulu, 5 September 2000, entered into force 19 June 2004, 40 ILM 278–309. Both Canada and the United States are members of the WCPFC.

164 International Plan of Action to Prevent, Deter and Eliminate Illegal, Unreported and Unregulated Fishing, adopted by the FAO Council on 23 June 2001, (Rome, 2001) at www.fao.org/DOCREP/003/y1224e/y1224e00.htm (accessed on 4 August 2007). *See generally* W. Edeson, *The International Plan of Action on Illegal, Unreported and Unregulated Fishing: The Legal Context of a Non-Legally Binding Instrument* (2001) 16 IJMCL 603–623.

4.6 Whaling

The 1946 International Whaling Convention (the Whaling Convention),[165] which established the International Whaling Commission, addresses the emotive issue of marine mammals and the harvesting of whales. The United States is a party to the Whaling Convention. Canada is not, having withdrawn in 1982 over the efficacy of the Whaling Commission adoption of a moratorium on the commercial harvesting of whales.[166] Whaling was an issue between Canada and the United States in the 1990s when the United States threatened trade sanctions against Canada because of permits given for Inuit harvesting of whales in northern Canada.[167]

4.7 Biodiversity

The Framework Convention on Biological Diversity (CBD)[168] has firmly placed genetic resources and ecosystem diversity on the world agenda. One of the first priorities for action under the Convention was marine and coastal biodiversity. In 1995, the Jakarta Mandate on Marine and Coastal Biological Diversity was adopted,[169] followed in 1998 by a program of work[170] which was reviewed and updated in 2004.[171] The five principal areas covered by the work program are: the implementation of integrated marine and coastal area

---

165 International Convention for the Regulation of Whaling, Washington, 2 December 1946, entered into force 10 November 1948, 161 UNTS 72.

166 *See* S. L. Waters, *Non-Consumptive Utilisation of Marine Mammals in Canada: International and National Regulation*, in D. VanderZwaag (ed.) Canadian Ocean Law and Policy (Butterworths, Toronto, 1992) 148 and T. L. McDorman, *Canada and Whaling: An Analysis of Article 65 of the Law of the Sea Convention* (1998) 29 ODIL 179, 180.

167 *See* McDorman, *supra* note 166, at 179–180.

168 Framework Convention on Biological Diversity, Rio de Janeiro 5 June 1992, entered into force 29 December 1993, 1760 UNTS 79. Canada is a party to the Convention. The United States is a signatory to the Convention. Regarding the United States and the CBD, *see* Murphy, *supra* note 74, at 341–344.

169 Second CBD COP, (1995), Decision II/105—Conservation and Sustainable Use of Marine and Coastal Biological Diversity.

170 Fourth CBD COP, (1998), Decision IV/5—Conservation and Sustainable Use of Marine and Coastal Biological Diversity, Including a Programme of Work.

171 Seventh CBD COP, (2004), Decision VII/5—Marine and Coastal Biological Diversity.

management; sustainable use of marine and coastal living resources; marine and coastal area protected areas; mariculture; and alien species.[172]

One issue within the CBD that has attracted significant attention concerns provisions on the access and benefit sharing and their application to marine genetic resources.[173] Although genetic resources within a State are subject to the exclusive control by that State,[174] and this includes marine genetic resources within territorial waters and the exclusive economic zone of a State,[175] one of the stated objectives of the CBD is "the fair and equitable sharing of benefits arising from the use of genetic resources."[176] The sharing is understood as being States (countries of origin) allowing access to genetic resources to non-nationals and those granted access (user countries) sharing the benefits of the genetic resources with the countries of origin. Article 1 of the CBD indicates three means by which "sharing of benefits" may take place through appropriate access to genetic resources; through the appropriate transfer of relevant technologies; and through appropriate funding. In 2002, the Bonn Guidelines on Access to Genetic Resources and Fair and Equitable Sharing of the Benefits Arising out of Their Utilization[177] were adopted to provide detail regarding the mechanics of genetic resource access and benefit

---

172 *See* M. Vierros and C. Salpin, *Evaluating and Enhancing the Implementation of the Marine and Coastal Programme of Work of the Convention in Biological Diversity* (2005) 19 OCEAN YEARBOOK (OYb) 232, 232–233 and at 249 where they conclude that:

> [A]lthough . . . the status of implementation of the programme of work is still inadequate for many programme elements, it is evident that actions have been undertaken on the national level towards the conservation and sustainable use of marine and coastal biological diversity. . . . However, despite such progress, much more needs to be done in order to halt the global decline in marine and coastal biological diversity.

173 *See, for example,* D. GREER AND B. HARVEY, BLUE GENES: SHARING AND CONSERVING THE WORLD'S AQUATIC BIODIVERSITY (Earthscan, London 2004) and R. J. McLaughlin, *Foreign Access to Shared Marine Genetic Materials: Management Options for a Quasi-Fugacious Resource* (2003) 34 ODIL 297–348.

See also M. Gorina-Ysern and J. H. Jones, *International Law of the Sea, Access and Benefit Sharing Agreements, and the Use of Biotechnology in the Development, Patenting and Commercialization of Marine Natural Products as Therapeutic Agents* (2006) 20 OYb 221–281, who argue, among other things, that the LOS Convention has similar affects to those sought by the CBD on access and benefit sharing and, at 280, conclude that the LOS Convention "is a much neater system of access when compared to the ABS mechanism of the CBD."

174 CBD, *supra* note 168, Arts 3, 4.

175 McLaughlin, *supra* note 173, at 309.

176 CBD, *supra* note 168, Art 1.

177 Sixth CBD COP, (2002), Decision VI/24—Access and Benefit-Sharing as Related to Genetic Resources.

sharing. An *Ad Hoc* Open-Ended Working Group has been established with the mandate to "negotiate the international regime on access and benefit sharing" regarding all genetic resources and to complete work of a possible draft instrument by 2010.[178]

In 2004, the U. N. General Assembly established a different *ad hoc* Open-Ended Informal Working Group "to study issues relating to the conservation and sustainable use of marine biological diversity beyond the areas of national jurisdiction."[179] A key international legal and policy issue is whether marine genetic resources beyond national jurisdiction should be considered as part of the common heritage of humankind and, therefore, come within the jurisdiction of the International Seabed Authority or whether these resources are already sufficiently covered by the high seas provisions of the LOS Convention.[180] In the "Summary of Trends prepared by the Co-Chairpersons" of the Informal Working Group, the co-chairs indicate that there is "a need to study and determine whether there is a governance gap in marine areas beyond national jurisdiction" and, if so, "how it should be addressed."[181] The most recent full meeting of the Working Group was in April-May 2008.[182]

---

178 *See* Seventh CBD COP, (2004), Decision VII/5—Access and Benefit Sharing, Part D, para 1 and Eighth CBD COP, (2007), Decision VIII/4—Access and Benefit-Sharing, para 7.

179 General Assembly Resolution 59/24, adopted 17 November 2004, 141 in favor, one against, and two abstentions, para 73.

180 *See* Report of the Ad Hoc Open-Ended Informal Working Group to Study Issues Relating to the Conservation and Sustainable Use of Marine Biological Diversity Beyond Areas of National Jurisdiction, UN Doc A/61/65, 20 March 2006, paras 29–30.

See generally C. Salpin and V. Germani, *Patenting of Research Results Related to Genetic Resources from Areas beyond National Jurisdiction: The Crossroads of the Law of the Sea and Intellectual Property Law* (2007) 16 Review of European Community and International Environmental Law (RECIEL) 12–23; D. K. Leary, International Law and the Genetic Resources of the Deep Sea (Martinus Nijhoff, Leiden 2006); and S. Arico and C. Salpin, Bioprospecting of Genetic Resources in the Deep Seabed: Scientific, Legal and Policy Aspects (United Nations University, Yokohama: 2005).

181 *Summary of Trends Prepared by the Co-Chairpersons*, Appendix I to Report of the Ad Hoc Working, *supra* note 180, para 11.

182 *See* Letter dated 15 May 2008 from the co-chairpersons of the Ad Hoc Open-Ended Informal Working Group to Study Issues Relating to the Conservation and Sustainable Use of Marine Biological Diversity Beyond Areas of National Jurisdiction, addressed to the President of the General Assembly, UN Doc A/63/79, 16 May 2008.

4.8 Port Security and Terrorism at Sea[183]

The forum for multilateral discussions of international legal developments concerning maritime terrorism has been the IMO. The work of the IMO on maritime terrorism has yielded two major products. The first came in 2002 with the adoption of amendments to the 1974 Safety of Life at Sea Convention,[184] which included the addition of a new chapter to SOLAS, namely, the International Ship and Port Facility Security Code (ISPS Code).[185] The SOLAS amendments and the ISPS Code deal with vessel and port security requirements.

The second IMO product came in October 2005 with the adoption of Amendments to the Convention for the Suppression of Unlawful Acts (SUA) Against the Safety of Maritime Navigation, 1988 (2005 SUA Amendments).[186] The 2005 SUA Amendments substantially expand the scope of the original 1988 Rome Convention for the Suppression of Unlawful Acts Against the Safety of Maritime Navigation (1988 SUA Convention).[187] The 1988 SUA Convention addressed the apprehension, conviction, and punishment of those who committed acts on board a vessel that were likely to endanger the safe navigation of the ship; these included seizing control of a vessel by force or threats; acts of violence against a person on a vessel; destroying or damaging a vessel; or placing a device on a vessel likely to destroy the vessel.[188]

---

183 This section is drawn, with modification, from T. L. McDorman, *Maritime Terrorism and International Law of Boarding of Vessels at Sea: A Brief Assessment of the New Developments* (manuscript, 2006).

184 SOLAS, *supra* note 148.

185 The 2002 Amendments to the 1974 SOLAS and the ISPS Code entered into force on 1 July 2004. *See* IMO adopts comprehensive maritime security matters, at www.imo.org/Safety/mainframe.asp?topic_id=583&doc_id=2689 and SOLAS amendments and ISPS Code enter into force on 1 July 2004, at www.imo.org/Safety/mainframe.asp?topic_id=848&doc_id=3692 (accessed on 4 August 2007). *See generally* H. Hesse and N. L. Charalambous, *New Security Measures for the International Shipping Community* (2004) 3 World Maritime University (WMU) J Maritime Affairs 123–138.

186 IMO Doc, Leg/Conf.15/DC/1, 13 October 2005, adopted by the Diplomatic Conference on the Revision of the SUA Treaties, 10-14 October 2005, held in London. The text is on the website of Intertanko, at www.intertanko.com/pdf/pt/marnavigation.pdf (accessed on 14 July 2006). *See* Revised treaties to address unlawful acts at sea adopted at international conference, 17 October 2005, at <www.imo.org/Newsroom/mainframe.asp?topic_id=1018&doc_id=5334> (accessed on 4 August 2007).

187 Convention for the Suppression of Unlawful Acts Against the Safety of Maritime Navigation, London 10 March 1988, entered into force 1 March 1992, 1678 UNTS 221.

188 *Id.* Art 3.

There was no requirement for an explicit "terrorist" motive for the offence. The 2005 SUA Amendments considerably broaden the covered offenses beyond concerns of vessel and navigation safety to deal directly with:

- The use of a vessel as an instrument of or platform for terrorist activity;
- The transport of certain suspect materials or biological, chemical, or nuclear weapons (BCN weapons); and
- The transport of a person who has committed an act that is an offense under any of nine terrorist conventions.[189]

The 1988 SUA Convention obligated State parties to establish the listed offenses as offenses in national laws such that, if an individual alleged to have committed one of the offenses was in the territory of a State party, that State was either to prosecute the individual or extradite the individual to a State party that would or could prosecute the individual. The 1988 SUA Convention was designed to eliminate the situation where a State could not prosecute or extradite an alleged SUA offender because the incident was not an offense under that State's national law. With minor wording adjustments, these core obligations are the same in the 2005 SUA Amendments. An addition is Article 11*bis*, which indicates that for the purposes of extradition none of the listed offenses are to be regarded as "a political offence" or "as an offence inspired by political motives" such that extradition can be denied on this basis.

The 1988 SUA Convention was silent respecting the possibility of a State party boarding a vessel of another State party to prevent a SUA offense or after the occurrence of a SUA offense. The presumption was that, on the high seas, the traditional law of the sea prevailed such that a vessel was subject to the sole jurisdictional authority of the flag State. Through the 2005 SUA Amendments, the possibility has been created for the boarding of State party vessels on the high seas to prevent a terrorist action or to intercept the transport of terrorists or materials related to terrorism.[190] These provisions respect the necessity for flag State consent for boarding and provide a number of modalities for the giving of flag State consent. Moreover, the 2005 SUA Amendments creates an operational presumption that SUA States will provide consent for the boarding of its vessels by other SUA States where there are reasonable grounds to suspect that a listed offense is involved.

---

189 2005 SUA Amendments, *supra* note 186, Arts 3*bis*, 3*ter* and the annex.

190 *Id.* Art 8*bis*.

Appendix One

Canada and United States Claimed Offshore Zones—2007

A. 200-nautical-mile Exclusive Economic Zone/ Fishing Zone

Canada

Fishing Zone:

- Atlantic and Pacific coasts: Fishing Zones of Canada (Zones 4 and 5) Order, CRC (1978), Vol. XVIII, c 1548, 13741-13746.
- Arctic Coast: Fishing Zones of Canada (Zone 6) Order, CRC (1978), c 1549, 13747-13750.

Exclusive Economic Zone:

- Canada, Oceans Act, St Can 1996, c 31, as amended, s 13.

United States

Fishing Zone:

- Magnuson Fishery Conservation and Management Act, 90 US Stat. 331, Pub L. 265 (1976), as amended, codified at 16 USC. 1801-1882.

Exclusive Economic Zone:

- Exclusive Economic Zone of the United States, Proclamation 5030 of 10 March 1983, 48 Fed Reg 10605.
- Exclusive Economic Zone and Maritime Boundaries, Public Notice 2237, 23 August 1995, 60 Fed Reg 43825-43829.

B. Continental shelf beyond 200 nautical miles

Canada

- Oceans Act, St Can 1996, c 31, as amended, s 17.

United States

- Outer Continental Shelf Lands Act, 67 US Stat. 462, Pub L. 95-372, as amended, codified at 43 USC 1301-1356, s 1331(a).

C. 100-nautical-mile Arctic Waters Pollution Protection Zone[1]

Canada

- Arctic Waters Pollution Prevention Act, RSC 1985, c A-12, as amended.

D. Contiguous Zone

Canada

- Oceans Act, St Can 1996, c 31, as amended, s 10.

United States

- Contiguous Zone of the United States, Proclamation 7219 of 2 August 1999, 64 Fed Reg 49801-48702.

E. Territorial Sea

Canada

Straight Baselines:

- Arctic: Territorial Sea Geographical Coordinates (Area 7) Order, Can Gaz Part II, Vol. 119, SOR/85-872, 10 September 1985, 3996-4002.

---

1 In August 2008, Canada announced that the Arctic Waters Pollution Prevention Act would be amended to extend its coverage to 200 nautical miles. Canada, PM Announces Government of Canada Will Extend Jurisdiction over Arctic Waters, 27 August 2008.

- Nova Scotia and Newfoundland: Territorial Sea Geographical Coordinates Order, CRC (1978), Vol. XVIII, c 1550, 13751-13758.
- Vancouver Island and Queen Charlotte Islands: Territorial Sea Geographical Coordinates Order, CRC (1978), Vol. XVIII, c 1550, 13751-13758.

Outer Limit:

- Oceans Act, St Can 1996, c 31, as amended, s 4.

United States

- Territorial Sea of the United States, Proclamation 5928 of 27 December 1988, 54 Fed Reg 777.

F. Fisheries Closing Lines

Canada

- Fishing Zones of Canada (Zone 1, 2 and 3) Order, CRC (1978), Vol. XVIII, c 1547, 13739-13740.

THREE

1970: The Landmark Year

1.0 Introduction

Hollick has observed that: "The United States and Canada emerged from the year [1970] with law of the sea attitudes and policies pointing in different directions."[1] In light of subsequent events, 1970 is indeed the year that the Canada-United States (U.S.) salt water relationship both set off in different directions and moved into the modern era. Almost forty years later, 1970 can be seen as informing the attitudes and perceptions of Canada and the United States respecting many aspects of their salt water relationship. This chapter will examine the key 1970 events that shaped and continue to shape the Canada-U.S. ocean relationship. The events to be looked at are:

- Canada's defining of its offshore continental shelf for the purposes of regulating the production and conservation of oil and gas development[2] and Canada's ratification of the 1958 Convention on the Continental Shelf (Continental Shelf Convention);[3]
- Canada's expansion of its territorial sea from three to 12 nautical miles;[4]
- The announcement by Canada of its intention to establish fishing zones in the Gulf of St. Lawrence, Bay of Fundy, and along the coast of British Columbia by putting in place fisheries closing lines;[5] and

1 A. L. Hollick, *Canadian-American Relations: Law of the Sea*, in A. B. Fox, A. O. Hero, Jr., and J. S. Nye, Jr., (eds.) Canada and the United States: Transnational and Transgovernmental Relations (Columbia University Press, New York 1976) 172.

2 Act to amend the Oil and Gas Production and Conservation Act, St Can 1969–1970, c 43, s 3.

3 Convention on the Continental Shelf, Geneva 29 April 1958, entered into force 10 June 1964, 499 UNTS 311. The Convention entered into force for Canada on 8 March 1970.

4 Act to amend the Territorial Sea and Fishing Zones Act, St Can 1969–1970, c 68, s 1.

5 Jack Davis, Minister of Fisheries and Forestry, House of Commons (HC), *Debates*, 18 December 1970, 2189–2190. *See* Fishing Zones of Canada (Zone 1, 2 and 3) Order, Can Gaz Part II, Vol. 105, SOR/71-81, 25 February 1971, 363–364, came into effect on 10 March 1971.

- Canada's enactment of the Arctic Waters Pollution Prevention Act,[6] which created a 100-nautical-mile pollution prevention zone adjacent to Canada's Arctic islands.

The global context for the above events was that 1970 was the beginning of the transition from traditional international ocean law to modern international law of the sea. The above Canadian events and the U.S. reaction to these events reflected the transition that was beginning to take place. The transitional global event was the adoption by the United Nations (U.N.) General Assembly of Resolution 2750C, which called for the convening of an international diplomatic conference in 1973 to deal with a broad range of law of the sea issues.[7] The Third U. N. Conference on the Law of the Sea (UNCLOS III) would meet until 1982 and ended with the adoption of the U. N. Convention on the Law of the Sea (the LOS Convention).[8]

2.0 1970: The Year of Transition in International Ocean Law

The December 1970 U. N. General Assembly Resolution calling for the convening of a diplomatic conference on law of the sea was the culmination of several years of discussions within the United Nations of ocean law matters.[9] The impetus to again look at international ocean law was the 1967 speech of Malta's Ambassador Arvid Pardo,[10] described by one commentator as "perhaps one of the most remarkable speeches ever given in the United Nations

6 Arctic Waters Pollution Prevention Act, St Can 1969–1970, c 47.

7 General Assembly Resolution 2750C (XXV), adopted 17 December 1970, recorded vote of 108 to 7, with six abstentions, (1970) UNYB 82–83.

8 U. N. Convention on the Law of the Sea, Montego Bay 10 December 1982, entered into force 16 November 1994, 1833 UNTS 397.

9 In December 1967, the General Assembly unanimously adopted Resolution 2340(XXII), which created the *Ad Hoc* Committee on the Peaceful Uses of the Seabed and Ocean Floor beyond the Limits of National Jurisdiction, (1967) UNYB 48–49. As a result of General Assembly Resolution 2467A(XXIII), adopted 21 December 1968, recorded vote of 112 to 0, with seven abstentions, the *Ad Hoc* Committee became the Committee on the Peaceful Uses of the Seabed and Ocean Floor beyond the Limits of National Jurisdiction, (1968) UNYB 80–81. General Assembly Resolution 2750C, *supra* note 7, turned the Committee into a preparatory committee for the Third United Nations Conference on the Law of the Sea (UNCLOS III).

10 *General Assembly Official Records*, First Committee, 1515th meeting, UN Doc A/C.1/PV.1515, 1 November 1967, 1015 and 1516th meeting, UN Doc A/C.1/PV.1516, 1 November 1967, 1–3.

General Assembly,"[11] while in the background the United States and Soviet Union were collaborating on the need to revisit international ocean law.[12] The 1970 Resolution was the beginning of a fundamental readjustment of the traditional international law of the sea.

Until the 1950s, international law of the sea had been principally focused on navigation and fishing with customary international law favoring limited coastal State rights and maximal freedoms of navigation and fishing. Indicative of the limited coastal State authority and the pressure for change was the 1951 International Court case between Norway and the United Kingdom respecting the assertion by Norway of exclusive national authority over the waters connecting its near-shore islands.[13] Also in the 1950s, there was the so-called cod war between Iceland and the United Kingdom over Iceland's assertion of a 12-nautical-mile exclusive fishing zone.[14] Although both situations ended favorably for the State asserting greater national authority in its adjacent offshore waters (Norway and Iceland) and, therefore, presaged the coming shift in balance between coastal and high seas interests, the disputes indicated the uncertainty and tension that existed regarding coastal State authority expansion respecting navigational and fishing rights in the water column.

It was as regards the continental shelf that coastal States were almost immediately successful in acquiring exclusive national rights over adjacent offshore areas and the resources therein. The commencement of the erosion of high seas freedoms or, put another way, the beginning of the expansion of coastal State jurisdiction, came in 1945 with the Truman Proclamation on the Continental Shelf (Truman Proclamation).[15] Through the Truman Proclamation, the United States asserted that it had exclusive authority over the natural resources of its adjacent continental shelf. Other States, particularly

---

11 L. JUDA, INTERNATIONAL LAW AND OCEAN USE MANAGEMENT: THE EVOLUTION OF OCEAN GOVERNANCE (Routledge, New York 1996) 189.

12 *See* E. L. MILES, GLOBAL OCEAN POLITICS: THE DECISION PROCESS AT THE THIRD UNITED NATIONS CONFERENCE ON THE LAW OF THE SEA 1973–1982 (Martinus Nijhoff, The Hague 1998) 35–36 and B. H. Oxman, *From Cooperation to Conflict: The Soviet Union & the United States at the Third U. N. Conference on the Law of the Sea*, 1984 Donald L. McKernan Lecture in Marine Affairs (University of Washington Press, Seattle 1985) 4–9.

13 *Fisheries Case (United Kingdom v. Norway)*, [1951] ICJ Rep. 116.

14 R. R. CHURCHILL AND A. V. LOWE, THE LAW OF THE SEA (Manchester University Press, 3rd edition, Manchester 1999) 284.

15 Executive Order 9633 of September 28, 1945 – Reserving and Placing Certain Resources of the Continental Shelf Under the Control and Jurisdiction of the Secretary of the Interior, 10 Fed Reg 12303, 59 US Stat. 884.

in Latin America, made similar types of claims.[16] The continental shelf had the benefit of being new and not encumbered unduly by freedom of the seas considerations which had attached historically to activities (fisheries and navigation) in and on the water column.

In light of the pressures on the traditional freedom of the seas and the new issue of continental shelf resource development, in 1958 the First U. N. Conference on the Law of the Sea (UNCLOS I) sought to achieve international agreement on rules and guidelines for orderly relations in the oceans respecting the balance between coastal State offshore authority and freedom of the seas. The result of UNCLOS I was the adoption of four multilateral treaties:

- The Convention on the Territorial Sea and Contiguous Zone;[17]
- The Convention on the High Seas;[18]
- The Convention on Fishing and Conservation of the Living Resources of the High Seas;[19] and
- The Convention on the Continental Shelf.[20]

Although the 1958 Treaties embraced exclusive coastal State authority over the resources of the adjacent continental shelf, this was done without providing a clear definition of the outer limit of a coastal State's continental shelf. Article 1 of the Continental Shelf Convention reads:

> For the purposes of these articles, the term "continental shelf" is used as referring . . . to the seabed and subsoil of the submarine areas adjacent to the coast but outside the area of the territorial sea, to a depth of 200 metres or, beyond that limit, to where the depth of the superjacent waters admits of the exploitation of the natural resources of the said areas . . .

Moreover, there was no agreement in 1958 on the permissible width of a coastal State's territorial sea within which the State could exercise full sovereignty

16 *See* Juda, *supra* note 11, at 97 and Churchill and Lowe, *supra* note 14, at 144.

17 Convention on the Territorial Sea and Contiguous Zone (TSCZC), Geneva 29 April 1958, entered into force 22 September 1964, 516 UNTS 205.

18 Convention on the High Seas, Geneva April 29, 1958, entered into force 3 January 1963, 450 UNTS 11.

19 Convention on Fishing and Conservation of the Living Resources of the High Seas, Geneva 29 April 1958, entered into force 20 March 1966, 559 UNTS 285.

20 Continental Shelf Convention, *supra* note 3.

subject to the right of foreign vessels to innocent passage. The 1960 Second U. N. Conference on the Law of the Sea (UNCLOS II) also failed to reach agreement on the width of the territorial sea. In addition, the traditional freedom to fish remained largely unaffected despite attempts, supported by Canada and the United States, to expand national fishing zones from the then-recognized three nautical miles to 12 nautical miles.[21] The ocean's water column, beyond an undefined but narrow territorial sea, remained subject to the traditional high-seas freedoms, while the resources of the continental shelf adjacent to a coastal State were seen as being under exclusive national authority.

Although agreement on the outer limits of national jurisdictional zones was not accomplished in the 1958 Treaties, there was agreement on the nature of the legal rights of a coastal State over its adjacent territorial sea and continental shelf. In the territorial sea, the coastal State had authority over all natural resources and, subject to the right of innocent passage, over all vessels within the territorial sea.[22] Passage was defined as being "innocent so long as it is not prejudicial to the peace, good order or security of the coastal State."[23] The territorial sea was identified as being seaward of baselines, either normal (the low-water line along a coast)[24] or straight (lines adjoining selected points),[25] with the water landward of baselines "part of the internal waters of States."[26] As regards the legal continental shelf, Article 2(1) of the Continental Shelf Convention noted that coastal States had "sovereign rights" over the shelf "for the purposes of exploring and exploiting its natural resources." Article 3 made it clear that there was a disconnect between the rights of coastal State respecting the continental shelf and the rights of the coastal State respecting the water column:

> The rights of the coastal State over the continental shelf do not affect the legal status of the superjacent waters as high seas . . .

The above matters remain among the major achievements of the 1958 Conventions.

---

21 *See* D. M. Johnston, The International Law of Fisheries (Yale University Press, New Haven 1965) 241–244.

22 TSCZC, *supra* note 17, Arts 1 and 2.

23 *Id.* Art 14(4).

24 *Id.* Art 3.

25 *Id.* Art 4.

26 *Id.* Art 5.

Canada and the United States overcame differences between them on the nature and extent of national fishing zones in evidence in 1958 at UNCLOS I,[27] to work together in 1960 at UNCLOS II to support a proposed six-nautical mile territorial sea and a six-nautical mile exclusive fishing zone.[28] However, as noted above, this proposal was not accepted by the Conference. In the end, the United States ratified all four Geneva Conventions in 1961, thus indicating its support for the Treaties. Canada, however, despite signing each of the 1958 Conventions, only ratified one of them, the 1958 Continental Shelf Convention, in 1970.[29] No reason for Canadian non-ratification was publicly given. One writer has reported that Canada's concern was that the Convention on the Territorial Sea and Contiguous Zone and the Convention on the High Seas "could be construed to mean that the unilateral declaration by a State of extended fishing jurisdiction would be illegal."[30] This writer commented that the issue of ratification of the Geneva Law of the Sea Conventions "seems never to have been discussed in cabinet and was left to fade away."[31]

The 1958 Conventions stalled but did not prevent coastal States from seeking to expand their offshore jurisdiction. Moreover, by the late 1960s, new ocean issues were emerging, including vessel-source marine pollution; declining fish stocks; and calls for internationalization of the mineral resources of deep ocean floor under the rubric of the Common Heritage of Mankind.[32] Note also must be made of the decolonization that led to the emergence of a number of new States with a different agenda as regards ocean matters.

It was the possibility of "untold riches from the oceans" in the form of mineral wealth on the deep ocean floor that seized the attention of many States in the late 1960s.[33] In 1968 and 1969, discussions in the United Nations focused principally on the need for a legal regime and machinery respecting the deep ocean floor and the practical realities of defining the area in question. In 1969, the General Assembly adopted a Resolution declaring that States

---

27 *See* Alvin Hamilton, Minister of Northern Affairs and Natural Resources, HC, *Debates*, 25 July 1958, 2682–2683; Juda, *supra* note 11, at 139–142; and B. Johnson, *Canadian Foreign Policy and Fisheries*, in B. JOHNSON AND M. W. ZACHER (eds.) CANADIAN FOREIGN POLICY AND THE LAW OF THE SEA (University of British Columbia Press, Vancouver 1977) 61–62.

28 *See* Juda, *supra* note 11, at 160–162 and Johnson, *supra* note 27, at 64.

29 *See* Chapter Three, section 3.1.

30 Johnson, *supra* note 27, at 64.

31 *Id.*

32 *See* the speech by Ambassador Pardo, *supra* note 10.

33 Juda, *supra* note 11, at 189–190.

"are to refrain from all activities of exploitation of the resources" of the seafloor beyond the limits of national jurisdiction and that, "No claim to any part of that area or its resources shall be recognized."[34] Both Canada and the United States opposed the Resolution. In the case of the United States, the concern was not *per se* the moratorium, rather it was the view that the Resolution would lead States to make extended claims of national jurisdiction in order to avoid the moratorium.[35] Canada shared this concern but, given the lack of clarity regarding the outer limit of a coastal State's continental shelf, Canada was also motivated by the possible "adverse effects" of the Resolution on resource activities taking place on what it claimed as being its shelf.[36]

In May 1970, the U.S. Oceans Policy Statement[37] was announced, followed by issuance of a draft convention.[38] These documents demonstrated that on the high-profile issue of the mineral resources of the deep ocean floor, the United States was willing to enter into negotiations to develop a governing treaty.[39] There is a direct line between the U.S. Statement and the General Assembly December 1970 Resolution to convene UNCLOS III.

The U.S. Policy Statement was inventive respecting deep seabed minerals. It called for a treaty to recognize the natural resources of the seabed beyond the 200-meter water depth as "the common heritage of mankind."[40] For the continental shelf area beyond the water depth of 200 meters to the physical outer limit of the continental shelf, a trusteeship zone was proposed with the adjacent coastal States acting as trustees for the international community. It was proposed that the benefits of the resources from this area of the shelf be

---

34 General Assembly Resolution 2574D (XXIV), adopted 15 December 1969, recorded vote of 62 to 28, with 28 abstentions, (1969) UNYB 69–70.

35 L. JUDA, OCEAN SPACE RIGHTS: DEVELOPING U.S. POLICY (Praeger Publishers, New York 1975) 104 and A. L. HOLLICK, U.S. FOREIGN POLICY AND THE LAW OF THE SEA (Princeton University Press, Princeton 1981) 225.

36 G. W. Alexandrowicz, *Canadian Approaches to the Seabed Regime*, in R. ST. J. MACDONALD, G. L. MORRIS, AND D. M. JOHNSTON (eds.) CANADIAN PERSPECTIVES ON INTERNATIONAL LAW AND ORGANIZATION (University of Toronto Press, Toronto 1974) 417–418.

37 President Nixon, Statement—United States Policy for the Seabed, 23 May 1970, in S. H. LAY, R. CHURCHILL, AND M. NORDQUIST (eds.) NEW DIRECTIONS IN THE LAW OF THE SEA, Vol. II (Oceana Publications, Dobbs Ferry, N.Y. 1973) 751–752.

38 *See* Summary of Provisions of Draft United Nations Convention on the International Seabed Area, prepared by John R. Stevenson, Legal Adviser, 3 August 1970, in *id.* 753–768.

39 On the background to the 1970 U.S. Policy Statement, *see* Juda, *supra* note 35, at 82–102; Hollick, *supra* note 35, at 208–234 and L. S. Ratiner, *United Nations Ocean Policy: An Analysis* (1971) 2 JOURNAL OF MARITIME LAW AND COMMERCE (JMLC) 225, 227–244.

40 1970 Policy Statement, *supra* note 37, para 4.

shared between the international community and the adjacent coastal State. Beyond the outer limit of the physical continental shelf, the U.S. Statement proposed creation of "international machinery" to authorize and regulate the resources of the deep ocean floor.[41] The U.S. Statement called for a treaty that:

> [S]hould provide for the collection of substantial mineral royalties to be used for international community purposes, particularly economic assistance to developing countries. It should also establish general rules to prevent unreasonable interference with other uses of the ocean, to protect the ocean from pollution, . . . and to provide for peaceful settlement of disputes.[42]

The principal aim of the Policy Statement, and the subsequent draft convention prepared by the United States, was to constrain coastal State jurisdictional expansion.[43] The Statement called on States to renounce "all national claims over the natural resources of the seabed" beyond the 200-meter depth line.[44] Moreover, the Statement alluded to navigational and fishing matters in the following terms: "It is equally important to assure unfettered and harmonious use of the oceans as an avenue of commerce and transportation and as a source of food."[45] The Presidential Statement indicated clearly the U.S. preference for an international approach to ocean claims through multilateral negotiations as opposed to unilateral offshore claims by coastal States.

Within the United Nations, the U.S. Presidential Statement and draft treaty provided a focal point for dissenting views with concerns expressed over the trusteeship zone concept and the absence of fisheries provisions.[46] One author has summarized:

> Aside from the specific criticisms of the American draft treaty, an analysis of the observations of foreign diplomats on the proposal indicates that it was regarded as too refined and too definitive a plan for the period of

---

41 *Id.* para 8.

42 *Id.* para 5.

43 Ratiner, *supra* note 39, at 239 and Juda, *supra* note 35, at 104.

44 1970 Policy Statement, *supra* note 37, para 4.

45 *Id.* para 13.

46 *See* Juda, *supra* note 35, at 119–121 and B. Buzan, Seabed Politics (Praeger Publishers, New York 1976) 105–106.

negotiations at which it was introduced. It seemed to reflect the belief that wide consensus already existed or was close to achievement.[47]

Canada and the United States both supported the 1970 General Assembly Resolution convening UNCLOS III.[48] Moreover, both countries supported, over the objections of the Soviet Union, an agenda for the conference that was broad and not confined to a limited number of matters.[49] In the case of the United States, this support was more a product of having read the tea leaves than conviction, since, as one analyst has written: "[T]he Latin Americans had convinced both the Africans and the Asians that a new conference should not have a restricted agenda and that the entire Law of the Sea should be reopened."[50]

3.0 Canadian Actions in 1970

The 1970 U.S. Ocean Policy Statement was clear that the United States supported an international approach to multilateral ocean issues and opposed States unilaterally determining national authority over adjacent ocean areas and that freedom of navigation, both for military security and economic reasons, was the number one concern for the United States. The United States was not opposed to a transition of international ocean law but wanted it to be orderly, rather than haphazard, and sought to protect its interests.

Canada also supported the transition of international ocean law but, contrary to the U.S. view, in 1970, clearly staked out its position on matters of key concern through direct legislative action. Moreover, in contrast to U.S. interests, the Canadian position was on the side of accretion of coastal State authority over adjacent offshore areas.

As noted above, traditional ocean law addressed uses of the water column (fisheries and navigation) and only in the mid 1900s did the resources of the continental shelf and seafloor of the oceans become of concern to States. The practice in the 1950s and 1960s was acceptance of exclusive national authority over adjacent continental shelves, but there was uncertainty

47 Juda, *supra* note 35, at 120.

48 General Assembly Resolution 2750C (XXV), *supra* note 7.

49 *See Promoting the Peaceful Uses of the Sea-Bed* (1970) UNYB 72.

50 Miles, *supra* note 12, at 37.

respecting national authority over the water column. This distinction existed as regards the actions of Canada in 1970. Canada's measures regarding the territorial sea, fisheries closing lines, and the Arctic, although evolving from different histories and detailed in separate sections below, all involved fisheries and navigational matters and were seen as being part of a single package of action.[51] Moreover, the three measures were addressed together in April 1970 in the principal U.S. public statement made about the Canadian measures[52] and the U.S. diplomatic notes presented to Canada.[53] Canada's actions regarding the continental shelf, however, were not seen as being related directly to the other measures.

3.1 Continental Shelf

1970 was the culmination of a period of Canadian measures and thinking regarding its adjacent continental shelf and Canada's position on the delineation of the area of national jurisdiction from the area of the deep seabed. As already noted, Canada had opposed the 1969 General Assembly Resolution calling for a moratorium on deep seabed activities,[54] since the ambiguities on delineating the national area from the international area might have interfered with Canadian activities on its adjacent continental shelf.[55] However, Canada supported the 1970 General Assembly resolution on the declaration of principles for the deep ocean floor, which included the common heritage of mankind wording.[56]

Canada had not joined other countries in making continental shelf claims in the immediate post-Truman Proclamation period. In the 1960s, however,

---

51 I. L. Head and P. E. Trudeau, The Canadian Way: Shaping Canada's Foreign Policy 1968–1984 (McClelland and Stewart, Toronto 1995) 56.

52 Department of State, Statement on Government of Canada's Bills on Limits of the Territorial Sea, Fisheries and Pollution, 15 April 1970, 9 ILM 605–606.

53 Note from the Secretary of State to Embassy of Canada, 14 April 1970, and Note from the Secretary of State to Embassy of Canada, 5 May 1970, in *Case Concerning Delimitation of the Maritime Boundary in the Gulf of Maine Area (Canada/United States), ICJ Pleadings, Oral Arguments, Documents (Gulf of Maine Pleadings)*, Vol. 5, Annex 8 to Reply of the United States, 529–530 and 535–537.

54 General Assembly Resolution 2574D (XXIV), *supra* note 34.

55 Alexandrowicz, *supra* note 36, at 417–418 and B. G. Buzan and D. W. Middlemiss, *Canadian Foreign Policy and the Exploitation of the Seabed*, in Johnson and Zacher, *supra* note 27, 19.

56 General Assembly Resolution 2749 (XXV), adopted 17 December 1970, recorded vote of 108 to 0, with 14 abstentions, (1970) UNYB 78–79.

Canada granted oil and gas permits and licenses covering large areas of its adjacent continental shelf based on the maximal view of the wording of Article 1 of the 1958 Continental Shelf Convention[57] that the 200-meter water depth criteria was not a limitation, that "exploitability" was the key, and that the legal continental shelf extended to the deep ocean floor.[58] The introduction of natural prolongation of the adjacent coastal State as a basis of title over the continental shelf, as set out by the International Court in the 1969 *North Sea Continental Shelf Cases*,[59] provided additional support for the Canadian view that coastal States could exercise exclusive national authority over the resources of the adjacent continental shelf far distant from shore.

In February 1970, Canada ratified the 1958 Geneva Convention on the Continental Shelf[60] and, in May 1970, amended the Oil and Gas Production and Conservation Act by explicitly incorporating into the legislation the wording of Article 1 of the Convention.[61] This legislation was directed at issues arising from the production of oil and gas, while the granting of permits and licenses was done pursuant to the Public Lands Grant Act.[62] Nevertheless, the Minister of Energy, Mines and Resources claimed that the 1970 legislative amendments:

> will have the effect of confirming Canada's assertion of rights to offshore mineral resources in areas extending far beyond either our territorial limits or the 200-metre water depth.[63]

Moreover, the Minister noted that: "Canada is probably the most aggressive nation in the world in asserting her rights to offshore mineral resources."[64]

Buzan and Middlemiss take the view that, given the international discussion taking place on the extent of the area to be subject to the common heritage of mankind, Canada's strategy was to be in the best position possible to argue in favor of Canada already possessing exclusive rights over its broad

57 Continental Shelf Convention, *supra* note 3.

58 *See* Buzan and Middlemiss, *supra* note 55, at 5, 17–18.

59 *North Sea Continental Shelf Cases (Denmark/The Netherlands v. Germany)*, [1969] ICJ Rep. 3.

60 Continental Shelf Convention, *supra* note 3.

61 Amendment of the Oil and Gas Production and Conservation Act, *supra* note 2.

62 Public Lands Grant Act, RSC 1970, c P–29.

63 J. J. Greene, Minister of Energy, Mines and Natural Resources, HC, *Debates*, 9 March 1970, 4570.

64 *Id.* 4569.

adjacent continental margin based on the existing international law.[65] They note that, by 1970, "the Canadian case for the legal right of the coastal State to the resources of the margin was complete" and that:

> The case had sufficient weight to serve as both the basis of a campaign and as a possible fallback position because it gave the government a very credible unilateral position.[66]

The aggressive Canadian position on asserting its legal rights to resources of the adjacent the continental shelf beyond the 200-meter water depth to the full extent of the geological margin was in direct opposition to the proposal made in the 1970 U.S. Presidential Statement that States should not make shelf claims beyond 200-meter water depth.[67] The position of the two States on this issue has been characterized as a significant parting of ways.[68] However, unlike regarding other Canadian actions in 1970, there is no record of the United States formally taking issue with Canada over its continental shelf legislation or position, albeit in 1969, the United States protested Canada's oil and gas permits and leases granted in the Gulf of Maine region as possible encroachment on U.S. continental shelf claims in the area.[69]

3.2 Territorial Sea and Fishing Zones

In 1964, Canada enacted legislation establishing a three-nautical-mile territorial sea and, beyond this, a nine-nautical-mile exclusive fishing zone.[70] The legislation also allowed for the establishment of straight baselines along the Canadian coast, which would have the dual purpose of being used to delineate the outer limits of the three- and 12-mile zones and bring within the regime of internal waters those waters landward of the straight baselines.[71]

---

65 Buzan and Middlemiss, *supra* note 55, at 17–21.

66 *Id.* 21.

67 *See* 1970 Policy Statement, *supra* note 37, para 4.

68 Hollick, *supra* note 1, at 182.

69 Note from the Department of State to the Canadian Embassy, 5 November 1969, in *Gulf of Maine Pleadings*, Vol. 2, Annex 56 to Memorial of the United States, 356–357 and, *see generally*, *Delimitation of the Maritime Boundary in the Gulf of Maine Area (Canada v. United States)*, [1984] ICJ Rep. 246, at paras 132–138.

70 Territorial Sea and Fishing Zone Act, St Can 1964–1965, c 22, ss 3, 4.

71 *Id.* s 5.

Although the United States initially protested the creation of the nine-mile fishing zone,[72] in 1966, the United States created its own nine-nautical mile fishing zone.[73] Moreover, Canada explicitly exempted fishers from the United States (and a number of other States) from the 1964 legislation.[74] Though no such exemption existed under the 1966 U.S. legislation, there was a reciprocal exemption arrangement regarding Canadian fishing activities in U.S. waters.[75]

The focus of U.S. attention, however, was on Canada's potential use of straight baselines to enclose areas, seen by the United States as high seas or territorial waters, as Canadian internal waters. In 1963, Prime Minister Pearson announced, in the House of Commons, Canada's intention to establish straight baselines,[76] it being understood that these lines would extend around the Arctic islands, across the mouths of the Gulf of St. Lawrence and Bay of Fundy and across Queen Charlotte Sound (which would effectively enclose the Hecate Strait).[77] Hollick reports that the Hecate Strait (between the Queen Charlotte Islands and the mainland of British Columbia) was a waterway of particular concern to the United States.[78] In 1967 and 1969, Canada announced straight baselines along the coast of Labrador, Newfoundland, Nova Scotia, Vancouver Island, and the Queen Charlotte Islands,[79] but did not announce straight baselines to enclose as internal

72 Hollick, *supra* note 35, at 172.

73 Act Establishing a Fisheries Zone Contiguous to the Territorial Sea, 80 US Stat. 908, Pub L. 89–658, codified at 16 USC 1091–1094.

74 Coastal Fisheries Protection Regulation, amendment, Can Gaz Part II, Vol. 98, SOR/64-275, 17 July 1964, 723, s 1. *See* L. H. J. Legault, *Maritime Claims*, in Macdonald, Morris and Johnston, *supra* note 36, 383 and L. S. PARSONS, MANAGEMENT OF MARINE FISHERIES IN CANADA (National Research Council of Canada, Ottawa 1993) 227.

75 *See* Note from the Department of State to the Embassy of Canada, 29 November 1966, in *Gulf of Maine Pleadings*, Vol. 4, Annex 34 to Counter-Memorial of the United States, 472. *See also* R. M. LOGAN, CANADA, THE UNITED STATES, AND THE THIRD LAW OF THE SEA CONFERENCE (Canadian-American Committee, Montreal and Washington 1974) 34.

76 Lester B. Pearson, Prime Minister, HC, *Debates*, 4 June 1963, 621.

77 Hollick, *supra* note 35, at 172 and A. Gotlieb and C. Dalfen, *National Jurisdiction and International Responsibility: New Canadian Approaches to International Law* (1973) 67 AJIL 229, 234. *See* Department of State, FOREIGN RELATIONS OF THE UNITED STATES (Johnson Administration, 1964–1968), (Washington, 2001), Vol. XII, Document 321, Memorandum of Conversation, (Ottawa, 6 July 1964) 684–686 and Document 325, Telegram from the Department of State to the Mission to the United Nations (Washington, 9 December 1964) 693–694.

78 Hollick, *supra* note 35, at 172.

79 Territorial Sea and Fishing Zones Geographical Coordinates (Areas 1, 2 and 3) Order, Can Gaz Part II, Vol. 101, SOR/67-543, 26 October 1967, 1700–1704 and Territorial Sea and Fishing Zones Geographical Coordinates (Areas 4 and 5) Order, Can Gaz Part II, Vol. 103, SOR/69-278, 29 May 1969, 792–795.

waters any of the above-noted controversial ocean areas. Nevertheless, the 1967 and 1969, Canadian straight baselines were protested by the United States as being "contrary to established principles of international Law of the Sea,"[80] which would have been Article 5 of the Territorial Sea and Contiguous Zone Convention[81] and the 1951 *Anglo-Norwegian Fisheries Case*.[82]

In 1970, Canada extended its territorial sea from three to 12 nautical miles and enacted legislation to allow for the creation of fishing zones in waters adjacent to Canada through the use of "fisheries closing lines."[83] The extension of the territorial sea was tied both to Canada's interest in fishing and in the capturing of key waters within the Northwest Passage.[84]

The fishing zones eventually established in 1971 by the fisheries closing lines were the Gulf of St. Lawrence; Bay of Fundy; and the waters of the Dixon Entrance, Hecate Strait and Queen Charlotte Sound on the west coast.[85] U.S. fishing interests were largely unaffected by the Canadian measures since a bilateral fisheries agreement was concluded in February 1970 that continued most U.S. fishing rights in newly created Canadian fishing zones.[86] However, the United States reportedly "formally disregarded the fishery closing lines in Dixon Entrance ... and continued its trawl fisheries there and to the south of Queen Charlotte Sound."[87] The character of the fishing zones changed as a consequence of amendments proposed to the Canada Shipping Act in 1970 and passed in 1971, which applied vessel-source pollution laws and regulations to foreign vessels within the newly created fishing zones.[88] As noted by commentators, "[T]he government [of Canada] had unilaterally proclaimed

80 Note from the United States Department of State to the Embassy of Canada, 1 November 1967, in *Gulf of Maine Pleadings*, Vol. 4, Annex 34 to Counter-Memorial of the United States, 473–474 and Note from the Secretary of State to Embassy of Canada, 25 April 1969, in *Gulf of Maine Pleadings*, Vol. 5, Annex 4 to Reply of the United States, 503–504.

81 TSCZC, *supra* note 17.

82 *Anglo-Norwegian Fisheries Case*, *supra* note 13.

83 Amendment of the Territorial Sea and Fishing Zones Act, *supra* note 4, ss 1, 4.

84 *See* Head and Trudeau, *supra* note 51, at 38 and J. Kirton and D. Munton, *The Manhattan Voyages and Their Aftermath*, in F. Griffiths (ed.) Politics of the Northwest Passage (McGill-Queen's University Press, Montreal 1987) 87.

85 Fishing Zones of Canada (Zone 1, 2 and 3) Order, *supra* note 79.

86 Agreement on Reciprocal Fishing Privileges in Certain Areas off the Coast, Ottawa, 24 April 1970, entered into force 24 April 1970, CTS 1970/11, UST 1283, TIAS 6879.

87 Johnson, *supra* note 27, at 68.

88 Amendment of the Canada Shipping Act, St Can 1970–71–72, c 27, s 2. *See* Legault, *supra* note 74, at 384.

WEST COAST BASELINES

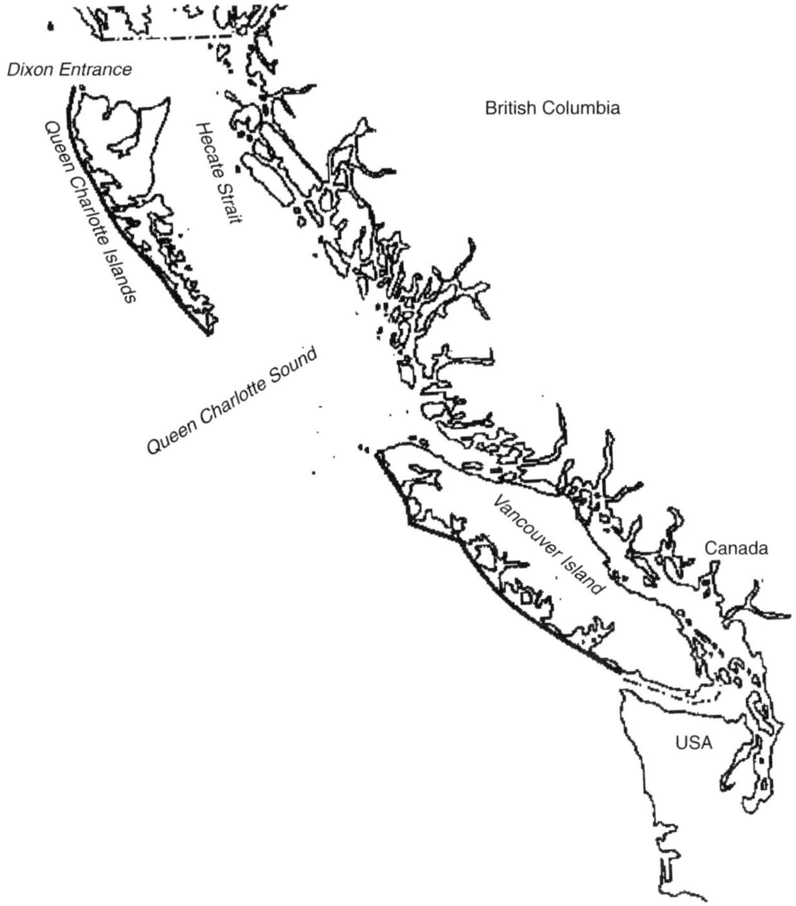

Source: LL Herman, 'Proof of Territorial Claims in Canada' (1982) 7 Dalhousie LJ 1, 36.

its authority to set whatever [pollution] measures [respecting foreign vessels] it wished in the fishing zones as well as in the territorial sea."[89]

The U.S. reaction to the extension of the territorial sea by Canada from three to 12 nautical miles was one of concern over process rather than substance. The 1970 U.S. Ocean Policy Statement and the "U.S. Statement on

89 R. M. M'Gonigle and M. W. Zacher, *Canadian Foreign Policy and the Control of Marine Pollution*, in Johnson and Zacher, *supra* note 27, 122 and generally 120–122.

WEST COAST FISHERIES CLOSING LINES

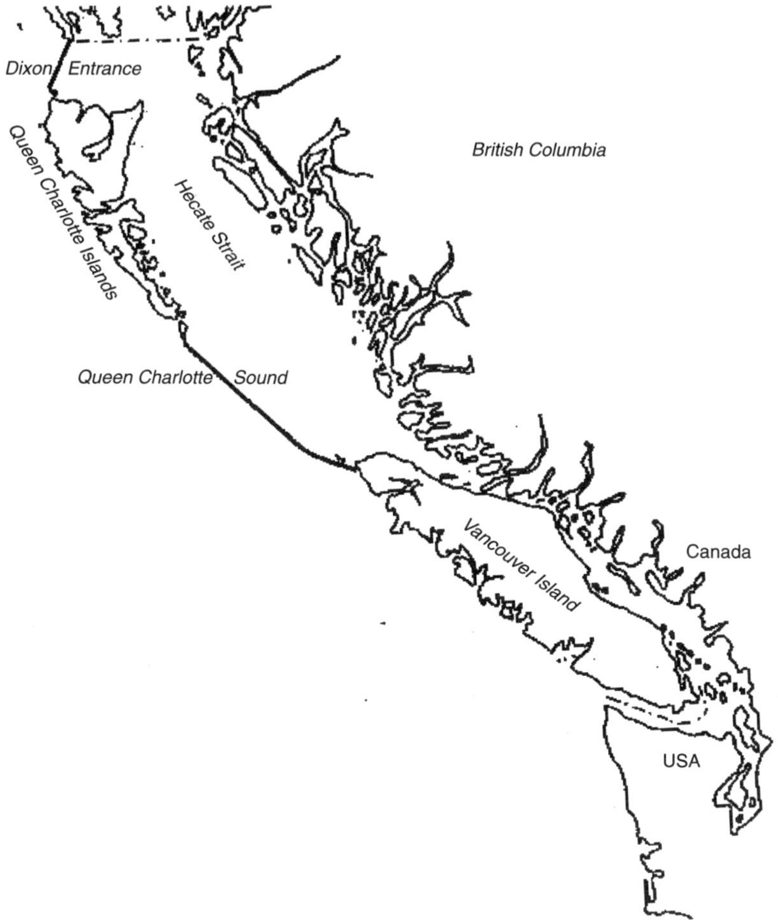

Source: LL Herman, 'Proof of Territorial Claims in Canada' (1982) 7 Dalhousie LJ 1, 34.

Canada's Proposed Legislation" both made it clear that the United States was willing to accept such a change to the breadth of the territorial sea, "but only as part of an agreed international treaty . . ."[90] For the United States, it was the

90 1970 Policy Statement, *supra* note 37, para 13 and Statement on 15 April 1970, *supra* note 52, para 10. The formal U.S. communication to Canada expressed regret that Canada had extended its territorial sea in advance of international agreement and that the United States continued to regard the waters beyond 3-n. miles as high seas. Note to Canada 14 April 1970, *supra* note 53, para 5.

EAST COASTAL FISHERIES CLOSING LINES

Source: LL Herman, 'Proof of Territorial Claims in Canada' (1982) 7 Dalhousie LJ 1, 33.

unilateral nature of Canada's assertion of a 12-mile territorial sea that was problematic.[91]

The announcement of the intention to establish fisheries closing lines which would bring waters beyond 12 nautical miles under a high degree of Canadian authority received special U.S. attention. In April 1969, the United States had formally expressed concern about the possibility of fisheries

91 Statement on 15 April 1970, *supra* note 52, para 3 and Note to Canada, 14 April 1970, *supra* note 53, para 3.

closing lines.[92] As noted in March 1970, the U.S. "opposition to the establishment of fishery closing lines . . . has been restated many times and is well known to the government of Canada."[93] Thus, when the fisheries closing lines were announced in December 1970, there was no surprise that the U.S. State Department issued a Statement specifically on the fisheries closing lines which referred to the Canadian measure as a "unilateral act . . . totally without foundation in international law."[94] The Statement also noted that the fisheries closing lines announcement was "*only one day*" after Canada had supported the convening of UNCLOS III, which was designed to deal with a broad range of law of the sea issues.[95] In diplomat-speak, this was a reference to alleged Canadian hypocrisy and a questioning of Canadian sincerity and was seen by some in Canada as a "stinging–and justified" statement.[96]

In anticipation of a possible adjudicative legal challenge by the United States, or any other State, to Canada's new fishing zones, in April 1970, Canada altered its acceptance of the compulsory jurisdiction of the International Court to exempt from the Court's authority disputes concerning fisheries or marine environmental pollution.[97] This had the effect of insulating the Canadian fisheries zones (including the application of the Shipping Act therein) from international adjudicative assault.[98] As early as 1964, in discussion with the United States, Canadian Ambassador Marcel Cadieux reportedly made it clear that "Canada . . . will not appear before the [International] Court in any circumstances" as regards the waters subsequently established in 1971 as fisheries zones.[99]

---

92 Note to Canada, 25 April 1969, *supra* note 80.

93 Department of State, FOREIGN RELATIONS OF THE UNITED STATES (Nixon-Ford Administrations, 1969–1976), Vol. E-1, Document 367, Information Memorandum for Mr. Kissinger—The White House: Subject—Imminent Canadian Legislation on the Arctic, from T.L. Eliot, Jr., (Washington, 12 March 1970), at www.state.gov/r/pa/ho/frus/nixon/e1/53180.htm (accessed on 7 August 2007).

94 Statement on Canadian Fisheries Closing Lines Announcement, 18 December 1970, in S. H. LAY, R. CHURCHILL, AND M. NORDQUIST (eds.) NEW DIRECTIONS IN THE LAW OF THE SEA, Vol I (Oceana Publications, Dobbs Ferry, NY, 1973) 74, para 2.

95 *Id.* para 4, emphasis in original.

96 Head and Trudeau, *supra* note 51, at 61.

97 Declaration Recognizing as Compulsory the Jurisdiction of the Court, 7 April 1970, International Court, YEARBOOK 1969–1970 (The Hague, 1970) 55–56, 9 ILM 598–599. Regarding this decision of Canada to make this reservation, *see* Head and Trudeau, *supra* note 51, at 53 and Kirton and Munton, *supra* note 84, at 88–90.

98 Head and Trudeau, *supra* note 51, at 53.

99 Memorandum of Conversation, 6 July 1964, *supra* note 77, at 686.

3.3 Arctic Waters Pollution Prevention Act

It is the 100-nautical-mile pollution zone of the 1970 Arctic Waters Pollution Prevention Act (AWPPA)[100] that is most identified with the shifting of the Canada-U.S. international ocean law relationship. A Canadian participant at the time noted that the enactment of AWPPA, together with the amendments to the Territorial Sea and Fishing Zones Act, "led to what may be one of the most acerbic exchanges in the history of diplomatic communications between the two countries."[101]

Two key features of the legislation need to be noted. First, although several States had proclaimed 200-nautical-mile national zones before 1970, these were largely confined to Latin American States.[102] The 100-nautical-mile pollution zone was the first extended water-column claim beyond a narrow territorial sea made outside of Latin America. Second, the Arctic legislation involved a pollution zone and the extension of national marine environmental pollution prevention laws, primarily in regards to vessels, into what were high-seas areas. As a result, the legislation raised the possibility of a new concept in the law of the sea, namely, national pollution zones.[103]

Though Arctic waters had been part of the Canada-U.S. dialog regarding the 1964 Canadian legislation, specifically as regards straight baselines,[104] the arrival of Arctic waters as a high-profile issue between Canada and the United States in 1968 to 1970 was the result of the discovery of oil at Prudhoe Bay in Alaska and the decision by Humble Oil to test the viability of transporting oil through the Northwest Passage using the refitted tanker *Manhattan*.[105] Aware of the uncertainty over the international legal status of the waters of the Northwest Passage, what Canada sought, but did not receive from either Humble Oil or the U.S. government, was a request for

---

100 AWPPA, *supra* note 6.

101 Legault, *supra* note 74, at 385.

102 *See generally* F. V. GARCIA AMADOR, LATIN AMERICA AND THE LAW OF THE SEA (Law of the Sea Institute, Kingston, R.I. 1972) 1–5.

103 R. B. Bilder, *The Canadian Arctic Waters Pollution Prevention Act*, in L. M. ALEXANDER (ed.) THE LAW OF THE SEA: THE UNITED NATIONS AND OCEAN MANAGEMENT (Law of the Sea Institute, Kingston, R.I. 1971) 212 noted: "There appear to be no precedents in terms of practice by other States directly supporting the Canadian assertion of a 100-mile contiguous zone for pollution control purposes."

104 *See* Memorandum of Conversation, 6 July 1964, *supra* note 77, at 685.

105 *See* Head and Trudeau, *supra* note 51, at 27–28 and Kirton and Munton, *supra* note 84, at 70–71.

permission to navigate through the Passage.[106] This was, and remains, the legal core of the Northwest Passage dispute: whether Canada has the legal right to control foreign vessel access to the waters of the Passage by requiring that permission be requested and granted to navigate. The United States was adamant that vessels utilizing the Northwest Passage did not require the permission of Canada.[107] Even though no request for permission was forthcoming respecting the *Manhattan*, Canada, Humble Oil, and the U.S. government did engage in what has been described as "practical co-operation" respecting the proposed and actual 1969 passage of the *Manhattan*.[108]

The practical co-operation approach, which involved Canadian assertions of authority over the Northwest Passage short of the permission request threshold, was derailed in 1969 when the Canadian public became preoccupied with the question of Canadian sovereignty in the North.

> The Arctic became front-page news as long-dormant Canadian nationalism found cause and focus. Before the sequence of events concluded, the Northwest Passage was destined to arouse within Canada an unprecedented volume of popular outcry... An unsavoury, and altogether uncharacteristic, jingoism swept across Canada.[109]

Much of this nationalistic passion had "a distinct anti-American bias."[110] The public call was for the government of Canada to firmly and unequivocally proclaim and assert national sovereignty over all Arctic waters.

After much internal discussion and some engagement with the United States, Canada opted to put in place both a 12-nautical-mile territorial sea which provided Canada with exclusive authority, subject to innocent passage, over several of the key waterways within the Northwest Passage and, through AWWPA, a 100-nautical-mile pollution zone north of 60 degrees.

---

106 Kirton and Munton, *supra* note 84, at 71 and *see also* E. FRANCKX, MARITIME CLAIMS IN THE ARCTIC: CANADIAN AND RUSSIAN PERSPECTIVES (Martinus Nijhoff, Dordrecht 1993) 78, footnote 127.

107 Franckx, *supra* note 106, at 78 refers to this as U.S. "stubbornness" and notes that "the United States . . . was prepared to let the status of the Arctic waters become an issue of direct confrontation."

108 Kirton and Munton, *supra* note 84, at 73 and *see* 71–73. The "practical cooperation" involved, amongst other things, Canadian Coast Guard escort for and Canadian government representatives on board the *Manhattan*.

109 Head and Trudeau, *supra* note 51, at 28.

110 *Id.* 32.

It appears that the establishment of straight baselines around the Arctic archipelago to enclose the waters of the Northwest Passage as internal waters was dropped at the last minute.[111] Apparently respecting this, the Minister of External Affairs explained in the House of Commons:

> It is quite clear that, whether or not the Canadian Government chooses to establish . . . its claim to the whole of the waters of the Arctic archipelago by drawing straight baselines from island to island so as to enclose the

---

111 Information Memorandum for Mr. Kissinger, 12 March 1970, *supra* note 93, is the report of a meeting held on 11 March 1970, between State Department officials and the Canadian Ambassador to the United States Marcel Cadieux; Alan Beesley, Legal Advisor to the Department of External Affairs; and Ivan Head from the Prime Minister's Office. Ambassador Cadieux is reported to have set out the following:

> The Ambassador said that no Canadian Government could take a position inconsistent with Canadian sovereignty over the waters of the Canadian archipelago.
>
> . . .
>
> Canada then said that three courses of action were now under active consideration by the Government:
>
> A. Drawing straight baselines around the outer perimeter of the Arctic islands. . . .
> B. Establishment of a 100-mile Arctic pollution zone. . . .
> C. Establishment of fisheries closing lines across the Gulf of St. Lawrence, Bay of Fundy and other areas presently outside of Canadian territorial waters and beyond 12 miles of the Canadian coast.
>
> . . .
>
> During the discussion it became clear that the Canadians were not interested in having out comments, suggestions, modifications, or alternatives. . . . It is equally clear that the Canadian presentation was in fact only notification and that they did not anticipate real bilateral consultations before legislation is a fait accompli.

This meeting is described in Head and Trudeau, *supra* note 51, at 46–48.

Department of State, FOREIGN RELATIONS OF THE UNITED STATES (Nixon-Ford Administrations, 1969–1976), Vol. E-1, Document 369, Memorandum for the President, prepared by U.A. Johnson (21 March 1970), at www.state.gov/r/pa/ho/frus/nixon/e1/53185.htmat (accessed on 7 August 2007), is the summary of a meeting held in between U.S. and Canadian officials (including the Minister of External Affairs) in Ottawa on 20 March 1970. The memorandum states:

> In summary, I believe we have caused the Canadians to rethink, and undoubtedly to make some revisions in the proposals they are committed to make to Parliament next week.

While this does not explicitly reference application of straight baselines to the Arctic, of the "three courses of action" outlined the week before, it is Arctic straight baselines that were not pursued by Canada.

See also R. HUEBERT, STEEL, ICE AND DECISION-MAKING: THE VOYAGE OF THE POLAR SEA AND ITS AFTERMATH—THE MAKING OF CANADIAN NORTHERN FOREIGN POLICY (Dalhousie University, Ph.D. thesis, Halifax 1994) 319–320, on file with the author.

> waters, the facts that this Government does not draw such baselines, . . ., do not thereby weaken our sovereignty claim.
>
> I have made it clear, . . ., that we shall not back down one inch from our basic position on sovereignty, but there is no interest on the part of the Canadian Government in the exercise of chauvinism.[112]

Canada adopted measures that did not assert complete sovereignty over all Arctic waters, preferring instead a more nuanced and functional approach premised on the unique environmental considerations of the Canadian Arctic.[113] Moreover, perhaps to ease U.S. concerns, AWPPA provided that foreign government vessels (e.g., military and coast guard vessels) could be excluded from its application where the vessels substantially met the Canadian standards.[114] The public furor over Arctic sovereignty in Canada was largely calmed by the legislation.[115]

The United States was not unsympathetic to Canada's environmental concerns respecting the Arctic[116] and was aware of the intense political pressure on the government of Canada respecting Arctic sovereignty.[117] Prior to the tabling in the Canadian Parliament of AWPPA, the United States had proposed an interim bilateral commission to regulate U.S. vessels operating in the Arctic, in particular, the impending 1970 voyage of the *Manhattan*, pending an international solution.[118] The non-acceptance of this proposal by Canada was explained in an internal U.S. memorandum as follows:

> [T]he Canadian representatives felt that the political pressures they faced were such that they could not accept a solution which would appear to

---

112 Mitchell Sharp, Minister of External Affairs, HC, *Debates*, 17 April 1970, 6014–6015.

113 Mitchell Sharp, Minister of External Affairs, HC, *Debates*, 16 April 1970, 5951.

114 AWPPA, *supra* note 6, s 12(2) and *see* Note No. 105 from the Embassy of Canada to the United States Department of State, 16 April 1970, in *Gulf of Maine Pleadings*, Vol. 5, Annex 8 to Reply of the United States, 534 and Summary of Canadian Note of 16 April Tabled by the Secretary of State for External Affairs in the House 17 April, 9 ILM 613.

115 Head and Trudeau, *supra* note 51, at 56.

116 Statement on 15 April 1970, *supra* note 52, para 7 and Note to Canada 14 April 1970, *supra* note 53, para 7 which states: ". . . the United States is acutely aware of the peculiar ecological nature of the Arctic region, and the operational dangers of oil pollution in that area. . .".

117 *See* Head and Trudeau, *supra* note 51, at 48; Information Memorandum for Mr. Kissinger, 12 March 1970, *supra* note 93; Memorandum for the President, 21 March 1970, *supra* note 111; and L. Ratiner, *Commentary*, in Alexander, *supra* note 103, 307–309.

118 Head and Trudeau, *supra* note 51, at 52 and Memorandum for the President, 21 March 1970, *supra* note 111.

> give the "big and powerful" U.S. such a strong voice in how they handle their Arctic waters.[119]

The United States also suggested an international conference on Arctic matters,[120] a proposal that the United States pursued subsequent to enactment of AWPPA. However, the U.S. proposal encountered lukewarm interest from other States, including the Soviet Union, and was eventually dropped.[121]

The U.S. opinion that the Canadian Arctic legislation and the amendments to the Territorial Sea and Fishing Zones Act were inconsistent with international law[122] and inconsistent with U.S. naval security interests was well known prior to the tabling of the proposed legislation by the government of Canada.[123] Thus, Canada was well aware that the United States would feel compelled to respond.

The U.S. response to the Arctic, territorial seas, and fisheries zone legislation came in April 1970 through a diplomatic note[124] and a public statement.[125] A key paragraph in the diplomatic note stated:

> It is the view of the United States that these assertions of claims to unilateral extension of jurisdiction of sovereignty on the high seas are without foundation in international law. The United States will neither accept nor acquiesce in the assertion of such jurisdiction. Accordingly, *the United States will be required to take lawful and appropriate steps to protect the integrity of its position on these matters.*[126] (emphasis added)

The last sentence, that was not part of the U.S. public statement,[127] was uncharacteristically strong wording and essentially warned Canada that U.S. action challenging Canada ". . . will be required..". Reportedly, threats of such

---

119 Memorandum for the President, 21 March 1970, *supra* note 111.

120 *See* Head and Trudeau, *supra* note 51, at 52; Statement on 15 April 1970, *supra* note 52, para 7; and Note to Canada, 5 May 1970, *supra* note 53, para 7.

121 *See* Kirton and Munton, *supra* note 84, at 93–95.

122 Statement on 15 April 1970, *supra* note 52, para 3 and Note to Canada, 14 April 1970, *supra* note 53, para 3.

123 Head and Trudeau, *supra* note 51, at 53 and Kirton and Munton, *supra* note 84, at 94.

124 Note to Canada, 14 April 1970, *supra* note 53.

125 Statement on 15 April 1970, *supra* note 52.

126 Note to Canada, 14 April 1970, *supra* note 53, para 3.

127 *See* Statement on 15 April 1970, *supra* note 52, para 3.

action (e.g., defying the Canadian position by using a submarine to pass through the Northwest Passage) had previously been made by the U.S. Secretary of State.[128] In the end, no direct confrontation was initiated by the United States to assert its navigational rights in Arctic waters.

One avenue of confrontation that Canada foreclosed was recourse to the International Court. As already noted, Canada removed the authority of the International Court to deal with disputes involving marine environmental pollution.[129] This insulated AWPPA from direct legal attack. Nevertheless, the United States called on Canada to voluntarily submit the disputes over the Arctic waters, fisheries zones, and territorial sea to the International Court.[130]

The U.S. concern respecting the Canadian Arctic, territorial sea, and fisheries measures was focused primarily on the precedent involved. As explained in the 14 April 1970 U.S. diplomatic note:

> If Canada had the right to claim and exercise exclusive pollution and resources jurisdiction on the high seas, other countries could assert the right to exercise jurisdiction for other purposes, some reasonable and some frivolous, but all equally invalid according to international law. The result would be anarchy on the seas. Merchant shipping would be severely restricted and naval mobility would be seriously jeopardized. The potential for international dispute is obvious.[131]

More particularly, the concern was that the precedent setting was being undertaken by Canada. That this was clearly a major concern was noted in an internal U.S. memorandum:

> [O]ur efforts to limit extensions of coastal State sovereignty over the high seas worldwide will be damaged when other nations see that a country—physically, politically and economically—as close to the United States as

128 Head and Trudeau, *supra* note 51, at 55.

129 Declaration Recognizing as Compulsory the Jurisdiction of the Court, *supra* note 97; Head and Trudeau, *supra* note 51, at 53; and Kirton and Munton, *supra* note 84, at 88–90.

130 Note to Canada 14 April 1970, *supra* note 53, para 8 and Statement on 15 April 1970, *supra* note 52, para 9.

131 Note to Canada 14 April 1970, *supra* note 53, para 4. The wording of the publicly released U.S. statement was slightly different. *See* Statement on 15 April 1970, *supra* note 52, para 4.

> Canada, feels it can undertake such action in the face of United States opposition.[132]

The United States was of the view that changes to the high seas legal regime could only be accomplished by multilateral agreement.[133]

Canada responded in a fulsome manner to the U.S. Statement and diplomatic communication expressing regret that the United States was not able to accept or acquiesce to the Canadian measures and explaining at length the rationale for the Canadian measures and noting the inconsistency of the U.S. position.[134] The Canadian response articulated:

- That the waters of the Arctic archipelago had "always been.. regarded as Canadian;"[135]
- That the Northwest Passage "had not attained the status of an international strait;"[136]
- The "unique characteristics of the Arctic;"[137]
- The "inadequacies" of existing international law respecting protection of the marine environment and conservation of fisheries resources;[138]
- Canada's unwillingness to await the "gradual development of international law" in these areas,[139] that customary international law is developed by State practice,[140] and that the United States had itself made use of unilateral action to develop international law;[141]

---

132 Information Memorandum for Mr. Kissinger, 12 March 1970, *supra* note 93.

133 Note to Canada, 14 April 1970, *supra* note 53, para 6.

134 Note No. 105, 16 April 1970, *supra* note 114 and Summary of Canadian Note of 16 April *supra* note 114.

135 Note No. 105, 16 April 1970, *supra* note 114, para 10 and Summary of Canadian Note of 16 April, *supra* note 114, para 10.

136 Note No. 105, 16 April 1970, *supra* note 114, para 8 and Summary of Canadian Note of 16 April, *supra* note 114, para 7.

137 Note No. 105, 16 April 1970, *supra* note 114, para 7 and Summary of Canadian Note of 16 April, *supra* note 114, para 5.

138 Note No. 105, 16 April 1970, *supra* note 114, para 7 and Summary of Canadian Note of 16 April, *supra* note 114, para 5.

139 Note No. 105, 16 April 1970, *supra* note 114, para 7 and Summary of Canadian Note of 16 April, *supra* note 114, para 6.

140 Note No. 105, 16 April 1970, *supra* note 114, para 4 and Summary of Canadian Note of 16 April, *supra* note 114, para 2.

141 Note No. 105, 16 April 1970, *supra* note 114, para 4 and Summary of Canadian Note of 16 April, *supra* note 114, para 2.

- That "a danger to the environment of a State constitutes a threat to its security" and Canada "reserves to itself . . . how best to protect . . . its vital interests, including in particular its national security,"[142] and that the Arctic legislation "is based on the overriding right of self-defence of coastal States to protect themselves against grave threats to their environment;"[143] and
- That Canada was determined "to fulfill its responsibilities to its own peoples and to the international community to preserve the ecological balance of Canada."[144]

Although the 100-nautical-mile pollution zone was enacted in 1970, the Act only came into legal effect in August 1972.[145] Moreover, it was known, in 1970, that the operational aspects of the legislation were to be the standards to be applied to vessels navigating within the zone. Canada had made it clear that such standards would involve consultation with other States, including the United States.[146] In 1972, following detailed discussions primarily with shipping interests and States,[147] the vessel standards and other regulations for the Arctic pollution zone were adopted by Canada.[148] This was largely unnoticed and attracted no known protest from the United States.

It is worth noting that Canada had made it clear that the purpose of the Arctic measures was not to close the Northwest Passage. Canada expressed its determination to "open up the Northwest Passage" to vessel traffic "subject, however, to the necessary conditions required to protect the delicate ecological balance of the Canadian Arctic."[149]

---

142 Note No. 105, 16 April 1970, *supra* note 114, para 3 and Summary of Canadian Note of 16 April, *supra* note 114, para 5.

143 Note No. 105, 16 April 1970, *supra* note 114, para 7 and Summary of Canadian Note of 16 April, *supra* note 114, para 5.

144 Note No. 105, 16 April 1970, *supra* note 114, para 12 and Summary of Canadian Note of 16 April, *supra* note 114, para 12.

145 AWPPA, Proclaimed in Force 2 August 1972, Can Gaz Part II, Vol. 106, SI/72-76, 2 August 1972, 1453.

146 Note No. 105, 16 April 1970, *supra* note 114, para 9 and Summary of Canadian Note of 16 April, *supra* note 114, para 9.

147 M'Gonigle and Zacher, *supra* note 89, at 120.

148 Arctic Waters Pollution Prevent Regulations, Can Gaz Part II, Vol. 106, SOR/72-253, 11 July 1972, 1033–1037 and Arctic Shipping Pollution Prevention Regulations, Can Gaz Part II, Vol. 106, SOR/72-426, 5 October 1972, 1847–1881.

149 Summary of Canadian Note of 16 April, *supra* note 114, para 7.

3.4 Functionalism and Unilateralism

3.4.1 Functionalism

The Canadian mantra in 1970 was functionalism, the idea that the authority being exercised offshore by Canada was only that functionally necessary to achieve a particular goal and to interfere as little as possible with ocean activities unrelated to that goal.[150] The functional approach regarding national jurisdiction over adjacent ocean waters was to be contrasted with the territorial or spatial approach where a coastal State sought to exercise national authority over all ocean activities within a specific area.[151] In the case of the Arctic legislation, the functionalist goal was prevention of vessel-source pollution incidents within a 100-nautical-mile area adjacent to Canada's Arctic islands. In the case of the fisheries closing lines, the functionalist goal was "to manage coastal species and to have a preferential share in their harvest."[152] Given the existence of innocent passage within the territorial sea, Canada's assertion of a 12-nautical-mile territorial sea arguably also fit the functionalist approach to ocean authority, with Canada going further by adopting a policy of phasing out foreign fishing from the newly appropriated waters.[153] Finally, as regards the continental shelf, again arguably this also was a functional regime since, as set out in the 1958 Continental Shelf Convention, national authority only exists over the living and non-living resources of the shelf and not other shelf activities such as the laying of submarine cables or pipelines.[154]

Respecting the two issues that mattered most to the United States, namely, the Arctic legislation and the fisheries closing lines, the use by

---

150 Sharp, *supra* note 113, at 5951 explained:

> The Arctic waters bill represents a constructive and functional approach to environmental preservation. It asserts only the limited jurisdiction required to achieve a specific and vital purpose. It separates a limited pollution control jurisdiction from the total bundle of jurisdictions which together constitute sovereignty.

See also Gotlieb and Dalfen, *supra* note 77, at 246, 248–250, 254.

151 *See generally* D. M. Johnston, *Recent Canadian Marine Legislation: An Historical Perspective*, in L. M. ALEXANDER AND G. R. S. HAWKINS (eds.) CANADIAN—U.S. MARITIME PROBLEMS (Law of the Sea Institute, Kingston, R.I. 1972) 63–67 and D. M. McRae, *The Negotiation of Article 234*, in Griffiths, *supra* note 84, at 101.

152 Gotlieb and Dalfen, *supra* note 77, at 254.

153 *Id.* 249.

154 Continental Shelf Convention, *supra* note 3, Arts 2(1),(4), 4.

Canada of functionalist approaches rather than territorial-based approaches undoubtedly mitigated the U.S. reaction and response. The United States was not unsympathetic to Canada's marine environmental and fisheries concerns having the same concerns for its coastal areas.

The use of functionalist logic and language did not mask the creeping national jurisdiction into the high seas that resulted from Canada's 1970 Arctic legislation, the fisheries closing lines, and the claims regarding the continental shelf and the 12-nautical-mile territorial sea.[155] The clear coastal State expansionism of Canada's actions was what triggered the U.S. reaction and the Canada-U.S. divergence on many ocean law matters.

The functionalist logic and language regarding the Arctic and fisheries closing lines did no favor to Canada's later clearly stated legal claim that the waters within the fisheries closing lines and between the Arctic islands (e.g., the Northwest Passage) were historic internal waters over which Canada had absolute sovereignty.[156] Undoubtedly, in an attempt to rectify and explain this perceived situation, in 1970 External Affairs Minister Sharp in the House of Commons quoted from the 1910 *North Atlantic Coast Fisheries Arbitration*[157] to the effect that a State's claim cannot be undermined by not having vigorously asserting it since this "would discourage conciliatory diplomatic transactions and encourage the assertion of extreme claims to their fullest extent."[158]

3.4.2 Unilateralism

There is little question that Canada's 1970 fisheries and Arctic environment actions were unilateral measures inconsistent with then-existing international law.[159] Although it is the U.S. reaction that is focused upon, according

---

155 Over three decades later, a well-informed U.S. author commented that Canada's use of environmental language to justify the 1970 Arctic Waters legislation was the "origin" of the link between environmental rhetoric and attempts to nationalize the ocean. B. H. Oxman, *The Territorial Imperative: A Siren Song at Sea* (2006) 100 AJIL 830, 849.

156 Department of External Affairs, Letter, 17 December 1973, in (1974) 12 CYIL 277, 279.

157 *Award of the Tribunal of Arbitration in the Question Relating to the North Atlantic Coast Fisheries*, 7 September 1910, xi RIAA 173.

158 Sharp, *supra* note 112, at 6014–6015. The wording quoted is from *North Atlantic Coast Fisheries Arbitration*, *supra* note 157, at 197–198.

159 The inconsistency with international law of Canada's establishment of a 12-nautical-mile territorial sea and as regards the continental shelf is less certain.

For a well-argued legal defense of Canada's Arctic legislation, *see* L. Legault, *Canadian Arctic Waters Pollution Prevention Legislation*, in Alexander, *supra* note 103, 294–300 and to a Canadian government official "a drawer full of protests" was received, including one from the United Kingdom.[160] While arguing that international law was inadequate, Canada asserted that ecological self-defense provided a basis for its actions.[161] The U.S. view was that self-defense was considerably more limited.[162] More generally, Canada's taking care to ensure that compulsory international adjudication respecting its laws on these matters was not available,[163] leads to the supposition that Canada believed its legal arguments supporting its actions were "not . . . all that strong".[164]

Precedent and imitation by others rather than international legality and substantive disagreement were what primarily concerned the United States about Canada's 1970 fisheries and Arctic measures.[165] The U.S. concern about precedent needs to be understood against the backdrop that the preoccupying U.S. international and domestic ocean issue of the late 1960s were the seizures by several Latin American States of U.S. tuna vessels and their crews, which were being justified by the Latin American States on the basis of extended national jurisdiction.[166] Moreover, the timing of Canada's actions, while dictated more by domestic pressures than multilateral considerations, came during the transition in the international law of the sea signaled by the 1970 U. N. General Assembly Resolution convening UNCLOS III.[167]

Canada's unilateralism had its own context both internationally and domestically. Canada's principal justification for its 1970 actions was that, in the face of significant technological advances in the 1960s respecting the increased capacity of fishing vessels to harvest and the enlargement of vessels carrying potential environmentally catastrophic oil, the international legal regime was inadequate to ensure Canadian protection of its

---

D. Pharand, *The Implications of Canadian Marine and Arctic Legislation for the Development of International Law*, in Alexander and Hawkins, *supra* note 151, at 78–80.

160 Erik Wang, Director, Legal Operations Division, Department of External Affairs, HC, *Minutes of Proceedings and Evidence of the Standing Committee on External Affairs and National Defence*, 27 April 1978 (30th Parliament, 3rd Session, 1977–1978), Issue no. 16, 16.

161 Summary of Canadian Note of 16 April, *supra* note 114, para 5.

162 *See* T. A. Clingan, Jr., *Third-Party Imitations of Canadian Legislation and the Implications for International Law Development*, in Alexander and Hawkins, *supra* note 151, at 70–72.

163 Declaration Recognizing as Compulsory the Jurisdiction of the Court, *supra* note 97.

164 Gotlieb and Dalfen, *supra* note 77, at 245.

165 *See* Note to Canada 14 April 1970, *supra* note 53, para 4 and Information Memorandum for Mr. Kissinger, 12 March 1970, *supra* note 93.

166 *See* Hollick, *supra* note 35, at 162–166.

167 General Assembly Resolution 2750C, *supra* note 7.

national interests.[168] Canada argued that the unilateral approach was undertaken only after the multilateral route regarding fisheries and coastal State protection from vessel-source marine pollution had failed to yield adequate results.[169] Regarding this, a U.S. government official tartly noted that Canada had made no effort to engage the potential users of the Arctic waters before proceeding with its Arctic legislation.[170] Canada was not alone among States facing the above challenges and that these challenges were reasons for the overwhelming global support for the U. N. General Assembly Resolution convening UNCLOS III. Ultimately, what motivated Canada's 1970 ocean action creativity was pressure from fishing communities located primarily in economically challenged regions and the national sovereignty cacophony that arose regarding the *Manhattan*. Canada arranged with those States that would be affected by the fisheries measures to agree to phase out their activities.[171] As regards the Arctic, as already noted, the key vessel regulations arose following negotiations.[172] This consultation activity, combined with the functionalist nature of 1970 offshore measures, indicates a care respecting Canada's offshore actions. While the 1970 measures were unilateral, unlike the Canadian public perception of the measures, questions exist as to just how aggressive or unilateral the 1970 measures really were.[173]

---

168 *See* Note No. 105, 16 April 1970, *supra* note 114, para 7; Summary of Canadian Note of 16 April *supra* note 114, para 5; and Gotlieb and Dalfen, *supra* note 77, at 237, 240, 247.

169 Gotlieb and Dalfen, *supra* note 77, at 233, 241–242, 248–249. *See also* A. E. Gotlieb, *Canadian Diplomatic Initiatives: The Law of the Sea*, in M. G. FRY (ed.) FREEDOM AND CHANGE: ESSAYS IN HONOUR OF LESTER B. PEARSON (McClelland and Stewart, Toronto 1975) 147–151. Regarding Canada's efforts in the late 1960s respecting achieving adoption of vessel-source pollution measures at the Intergovernmental Maritime Consultative Organization (IMCO, renamed the International Maritime Organization (IMO) in 1982), *see* M'Gonigle and Zacher, *supra* note 89, at 106–117.

170 Ratiner, *supra* note 117, at 309.

171 Gotlieb and Dalfen, *supra* note 77, at 249.

172 Arctic Waters Pollution Prevent Regulations and Arctic Shipping Pollution Prevention Regulations, *supra* note 148. See M'Gonigle and Zacher, *supra* note 89, at 120.

173 *See* T. L. McDorman, *Will Canada Ratify the Law of the Sea Convention?* (1988) 25 SAN DIEGO LR 535, 549:

> . . . Canada's . . . reliance on unilateralism in ocean matters is largely mythical. To be successful, Canada, a middle State without the power of a major state, must proceed in step with international trends, although, of course, Canada can assist in developing new trends.

Nevertheless, Franckx, *supra* note 106, at 69 summarized that in 1970 Canada's "fundamental approaches to international law had changed drastically" and that Canada "appeared to be willing in certain areas where national self-interest was thought to require radical policies clearly at variance with international law, to further these goals without seeking a prior *fiat* from the world community or those sates thereof immediately involved."

4.0 The Canada-U.S. Ocean Relationship Emerging from 1970

The events of 1970 made two things respecting the Canada-U.S. ocean law relationship clear: The two States had different views on what constituted their national interests in the oceans and how to assert and protect these interests; and, despite these differences, "on the water" relations between the States involved avoidance of direct confrontation and a reasonable degree of accommodation of each others concerns.

4.1 Differing Ocean Interests and Approaches

4.1.1 Coastal *versus* Maritime State[174]

Canada's 1970 actions placed it firmly in the coastal State camp. Coastal States were ones with significant coastlines that saw their ocean interests as attaining exclusive national control over a significant portion of their offshore areas for purposes of resource exploitation and conservation; protection from marine pollution; and security concerns broadly defined. These States sought to ensure that the transition of traditional international ocean law to modern law of the sea strongly favored the interests of coastal States through the traditional area of high seas being constricted in favor of exclusive national zones and the traditional freedoms of navigation and fishing yielding to coastal State priorities.

The U.S. posture fit within the maritime State camp. Maritime States saw their ocean interests as being maintenance of existing high seas freedoms, in particular, the freedom of navigation. Navigational freedoms were important for security reasons both in terms of military security but also economic security. Maritime States were concerned both about vessels on international voyages being interfered with by coastal States and by those vessels encountering various coastal States applying differing laws and thus creating a patchwork effect detrimental to security and commerce.

The posture of each State was often more nuanced than the above stereotype paragraphs suggest. This was particularly so for the United States, which

---

174 The coastal—maritime State dichotomy is the traditional approach to categorizing and explaining State ocean law and policy actions. Oxman, *supra* note 155, provides a different approach essentially categorizing State actions into territorialists (extending national authority into the ocean) and internationalists (respecting freedom of navigation in the ocean).

has a lengthy coastline and, as a consequence, had many of the same concerns and priorities as coastal States. Nevertheless, as stated in the April 1970 U.S. diplomatic note to Canada: "The views of the United States and those of Canada differ with regard to the freedom of the high seas."[175] The stereotype characterization was the perception widely held of each State both by one another and by others.

4.1.2 Local *versus* Global

Inherent in the coastal versus maritime State dichotomy is the difference evident in 1970 between Canada and the United States respecting their scope of ocean interests. Canada's ocean interests were essentially local - its adjacent waters. Canadian policy was informed by domestic constituencies that saw themselves as being directly affected by activities in adjacent waters. This was most obviously the situation as regards fishing and offshore oil and gas development, but, as noted above, much of Canada got involved in the Arctic issue. Moreover, Canada argued in favor of its 1970s actions largely by stressing the special or unique characteristics of the local waters in question, most notably, the Arctic. Canada reached out to internationalize its oceans actions, again most noticeably as regards the Arctic, where phraseology such as trusteeship and Canada's responsibility to the international community to protect the Arctic were regularly utilized.[176]

U.S. ocean concerns such as navigation and security were more focused on the global picture. Canada's actions that interfered with high-seas freedoms were seen by the United States primarily in terms of the implications for the actions of States elsewhere and U.S. ocean interests elsewhere.[177] The global focus of U.S. ocean interests meant that it was less likely to be moved by the Canadian arguments about the special nature of specific waters or that the United States would be exempted in some manner from Canadian measures.

4.1.3 Politics of Sovereignty

Prior to 1970, Canada and the United States had been engaged in ocean issues that raised sovereignty concerns. The most obvious was the longstanding

---

175 Note to Canada, 14 April 1970, *supra* note 53, para 8.

176 Note No. 105, 16 April 1970, *supra* note 114, para 12 and Summary of Canadian Note of 16 April, *supra* note 114, para 12.

177 *See* Head and Trudeau, *supra* note 51, at 36.

bilateral dispute respecting the waters of the Dixon Entrance between Alaska and British Columbia that arose as a result of differing interpretations of the 1903 *Alaska Boundary Arbitration*.[178] However, within Canada, the 1968 to 1970 issues respecting the Arctic waters and the Northwest Passage engendered an unexpected nationalistic response that could not be ignored by the government. Sovereignty and the necessity to assert and protect it was the public demand and one that was an easy and highly emotive issue with which to challenge government action and/or inaction. The government of Canada had to consider carefully the politics of sovereignty as a consideration separate in its decision making from overall national interest calculations.

The United States, of course, was not immune from the politics of sovereignty playing a role in its ocean law and policy decision making and actions. However, not since the early 1900s had the sovereignty factor resulted in direct pressure on the U.S. government respecting its scope of action in dealing with Canada on ocean matters. While the United States aggressively pursued its interests and these involved ocean sovereignty concerns, the U.S. government was not directly confronted in its relations with Canada with the same politics of sovereignty as was the government of Canada.

The politics of sovereignty foreclosed certain resolutive options that might otherwise have been available. Most particularly, since the core of the U.S. concern with Canadian legislative action regarding the Arctic involved its international legality, an obvious option was recourse to international adjudication to assist in resolving the matter. It was the politics of sovereignty that led Canada to foreclose the possibility of international adjudication passing judgment on its 1970 ocean actions.[179]

4.2 Agreeing-to-Disagree

Despite the differences between Canada and the United States noted above, there was also reasonable accommodation made in 1970 by the two States respecting some of these differences. Canada was careful to promote and

178 *Decision of the Alaska Boundary Tribunal under the Treaty of 24 January 1903 between the United States and Great Britain*, 20 October 1903, *Proceedings of the Alaska Boundary Tribunal*, US Senate, 58th Cong., 2nd Session, Document 162, Vol. I, 29–97.

179 Declaration Recognizing as Compulsory the Jurisdiction of the Court, *supra* note 97; Head and Trudeau, *supra* note 51, at 53; and Kirton and Munton, *supra* note 84, at 88–90.

protect its ocean interests to avoid provoking the United States into taking directly confrontational action. The U.S. response to Canadian measures was principally to protect its international legal position through protests and statements, but not to engage in direct at-sea confrontation. There is a sense that the lawyers disagreed, but those directly involved in fishing and navigation worked to accommodate not confront. There was a willingness to agree-to-disagree on many matters.

On fisheries, U.S. fishing in the new Canadian fishing zones was addressed by a 1970 treaty that continued previous arrangements on fishing rights.[180] Respecting vessel traffic in Arctic waters, there was cooperation between Canada and the United States on the vessel standard regulations under AWPPA, the operational part of the legislation.[181] Although flexible on these matters, Canada was wary of calls by the United States to seek international negotiations on Arctic waters matters[182] and rebuffed the apparent willingness of the United States to adjudicate the legal disputes before the International Court.[183]

5.0 Continuing Echo of 1970

Almost forty years later, 1970 can still be seen as informing the attitudes and perceptions of Canada and the United States respecting many aspects of their salt water relationship. In particular, Canada's 1970 Arctic action set in place within the United States the widely held perception that Canada was and would be aggressive as regards coastal State authority over offshore areas and that this aggressiveness was inconsistent with U.S. concerns respecting freedom of navigation.[184] Indeed, Canada was aggressive in seeking to have the traditional law of the sea changed to the benefit of coastal States during UNCLOS III. Isolated events, such as the 1995 seizure by Canada of the Spanish trawler *Estai* on the high seas adjacent to Canadian

180 Agreement on Reciprocal Fishing Privileges of 1970, *supra* note 86.

181 Arctic Waters Pollution Prevent Regulations and Arctic Shipping Pollution Prevention Regulations, *supra* note 148. See M'Gonigle and Zacher, *supra* note 89, at 120.

182 *See* Kirton and Munton, *supra* note 84, at 93–95.

183 Note to Canada, 14 April 1970, *supra* note 53, para 8 and Statement on 15 April 1970, *supra* note 52, para 9.

184 For example, Oxman, *supra* note 155, at 849.

waters,[185] have served to reinforce the U.S. perception of Canadian jurisdictional aggressiveness. The United States, despite having started the cavalcade of coastal State expansion with the Truman Proclamation in 1945,[186] has always seen its interests as being more nuanced as regards both coastal State offshore authority, which the United States asserts, and the principle of navigational freedoms, which the United States sees as important for commerce and military purposes. The Canadian perception of the United States as regards ocean matters is that the United States is less committed to expansion of coastal State authority and that the United States is overly committed to freedom of navigation principles.

More directly, 1970 was a pivotal year for Canada and the United States in determining the approaches each country would take at UNCLOS III, where the modern law of the sea was to be developed and for which preparations began in 1971 and the Conference commenced in 1973.

As will be discussed in the next chapter, before the end of the 1970s, many of the specific issues that arose between Canada and the United States in 1970 had been rendered moot. The 200-nautical-mile zones adopted by both Canada and the United States in 1977[187] ended concerns about Canada's 1970 fisheries actions and the 12-nautical-mile sea. The 200-nautical-mile zone also rendered moot the U.S. concern about the breadth of national zones which had been part of its opposition to the Arctic Waters Pollution Prevention Zone. It appears that the United States calculated in the

---

185 For a colorful recitation of the seizing of the Spanish vessel *Estai*, *see* M. HARRIS, LAMENT FOR AN OCEAN (McClelland and Stewart, Toronto 1998) 1–38. More scholarly and insightful discussion are provided by P. M. Saunders, *Jurisdiction and Principle in the Implementation of the Law of the Sea: The Case of Straddling Stocks*, in C. CARMODY, Y. IWASAWA AND S. RHODES (eds.) TRILATERAL PERSPECTIVES ON INTERNATIONAL LEGAL ISSUES: CONFLICT AND COHERENCE (American Society of International Law, Washington, 2003) 382–393 and C. C. Joyner, *On the Borderline? Canadian Activism in the Grand Banks*, in O. S. STOKKE (ed.) GOVERNING HIGH SEAS FISHERIES: THE INTERPLAY OF GLOBAL AND REGIONAL REGIMES (Oxford University Press, Oxford 2001) 207–233. *Also see* Chapter Four, section 3.2.2, footnote 148.

186 Truman Proclamation, *supra* note 15.

187 In the United States, this was done through the Fishery Conservation and Management Act (renamed the Magnuson Fishery Conservation and Management Act), 90 US Stat. 331, Pub L. 94–265, codified at 16 USC 1801–1882.

Fishing Zones of Canada (Zones 4 and 5) Order, Can Gaz Part II, Vol. 111, SOR/77–62, 1 January 1977, 115–120 replaced by Fishing Zones of Canada (Zones 4 and 5) Order, CRC (1978), Vol. XVIII, c 1548, 13741–13746 and Fishing Zones of Canada (Zone 6) Order, Can Gaz Part II, Vol. 111, SOR/77-173, 24 February 1977, 652–655, replaced by Fishing Zones of Canada (Zone 6) Order, CRC (1978), c 1549, 13747–13750. Zones 4 and 5 are on the East and West Coasts and zone 6 is the Arctic.

early 1970s that there was "little likelihood of immediate imitation" of Canada's Arctic claim,[188] with the result that during UNCLOS III Canada, the Soviet Union, and the United States agreed on Article 234 of the LOS Convention which provides international justification for Canada's Arctic legislation.[189]

---

188 Clingan, *supra* note 162, at 69.

189 *See generally* McRae, *supra* note 151, at 98–114. *See* Chapter Four, section 2.2.2.

FOUR

UNCLOS III and the LOS Convention

1.0 Introduction

Emerging from 1970, Canada had clearly identified itself as having coastal State interests. During the Third United Nations Conference on the Law of the Sea (UNCLOS III) Canada pursued this agenda with vigor. One authority described Canada's image at UNCLOS III as being:

> that of an acquisitive, enormously capable, somewhat immodest, frequently aggressive, coastal state, willing to embrace fairly radical ideas and to forge new linkages and alignments with a wide range of friends, both old and new, if it served its immediate national interests to do so.[1]

At UNCLOS III, Canada was engaged in trying to attain international support for its 1970 actions, specifically, the enactment of the 12-nautical-mile territorial sea;[2] the Arctic Waters Pollution Protection Act (AWPPA);[3] and the broadest possible national continental margin. The latter two items in particular were priorities for Canada at UNCLOS III.[4] A third priority that emerged during the 1971 to1973 period prior to the formal commencement of UNCLOS III was the 200-nautical-mile exclusive economic zone (EEZ).[5]

---

1 D. M. Johnston, Canada and the New International Law of the Sea (University of Toronto Press, Toronto 1985) 65.

2 Act to amend the Territorial Sea and Fishing Zones Act, St Can 1969–1970, c 68, s 1.

3 Arctic Waters Pollution Prevention Act, St Can 1969–1970, c 47.

4 *See* Department of External Affairs, *The Third United Nations Conference on the Law of the Sea* (Ottawa, 1973) 13–15, 18, 22 and R. Hage, *Canada and the Law of the Sea* (1984) 8 Mar Pol 2, 3–4.

5 External Affairs, *supra* note 4, at 10–12.

The United States (U.S.) approach to UNCLOS III was seen primarily as that of a maritime State with the priority interest being navigational rights rather than expansion of national authority over adjacent waters.[6]

> The United States did not view the conference as a vehicle for expanding its own coastal-State jurisdiction. Quite to the contrary, the United States hoped to forestall the expansion of coastal State claims beyond the narrowest negotiable limits.
>
> The aspirations of many States, including Canada, were different.[7]

Unlike Canada, the United States was not seeking international support for action already taken. The U.S. position underwent significant change, however, from the U.S. Oceans Policy Statement of 1970[8] to the 1973 commencement of UNCLOS III. The United States came to recognize many of the coastal State jurisdictional concerns, such that the U.S. position at UNCLOS III was one of seeking to carefully balance navigational freedoms with its own coastal State aspirations.[9]

---

6 A. L. HOLLICK, U.S. FOREIGN POLICY AND THE LAW OF THE SEA (Princeton University Press, Princeton 1981) 253–254. G. V. GALDORISI AND K. R. VIENNA, BEYOND THE LAW OF THE SEA: NEW DIRECTIONS FOR U.S. OCEANS POLICY (Praeger, Westport, Connecticut 1997) 27 summarize that:

> In 1973 the paramount concern [of the United States] was preserving navigational and overflight freedoms against creeping jurisdiction of coastal States.

The security concerns, both strategic and commercial, that underlie the U.S. priority regarding navigational freedoms are discussed in R. E. Osgood, *U.S. Security Interests and the Law of the Sea*, in R. C. AMACHER AND R. J. SWEENEY (eds.) THE LAW OF THE SEA: U.S. INTERESTS AND ALTERNATIVES (American Enterprise Institute for Public Policy Research, Washington 1976) 11–35.

7 Reply of the United States, *Gulf of Maine Pleadings*, Vol. V, 386.

8 President Nixon, Statement—United States Policy for the Seabed, 23 May 1970, in S. H. LAY, R. CHURCHILL, AND M. NORDQUIST, (eds.) NEW DIRECTIONS IN THE LAW OF THE SEA, Vol. II (Oceana Publications, Dobbs Ferry, N.Y. 1973) 751–752.

9 T.A. Clingan, Jr., *The United States and the Law of the Sea Conference*, in G. PONTECORVO, (ed.) THE NEW ORDER OF THE OCEANS: THE ADVENT OF A MANAGED ENVIRONMENT (Columbia University Press, New York, 1986) 222 comments that the United States was "as interested as any State in protecting its access to fish, oil, and gas in broad zones adjacent to its coasts, while protecting to the maximum the freedoms associated with navigation and overflight." *See also* Hollick, *supra* note 6, at 240–241, 256–280. Galdorisi and Vienna, *supra* note 6, at 27 note that by 1973 U.S. priorities included conservation of fishery resources, protection of the marine environment, and national control over the hydrocarbon potential in the continental shelf adjacent to the United States.

Canada and the United States found themselves on opposite sides on a number of key issues during UNCLOS III, although on other issues there was a congruence of interests.

The result of UNCLOS III was the 1982 U. N. Convention on the Law of the Sea (the LOS Convention).[10] In the 1980s, the United States walked away from the Convention, going so far as to vote against the adoption of the Treaty,[11] and declaring that it would not sign the LOS Convention.[12] The principal stumbling block for the United States was the Convention's deep seabed mining regime.[13] Canada voted in favour of the adoption of the LOS Convention, publicly chastised the United States for its posture regarding the Treaty and appeared to warmly embrace the Convention. Nevertheless, only in 2003 did Canada become a party to the LOS Convention. While the United States remains as a non-party, both the Clinton and Bush II administrations have supported becoming a party with the U.S. Senate being the impediment.[14] The United States announced early on that it intended to comply with most of the LOS Convention beyond the deep seabed mining chapter.[15]

It is not the intention here to relive in detail the debates on all the agenda items at UNCLOS III or the machinations of Canada and the United States regarding the LOS Convention through the 1980s and 1990s. Nevertheless, a few brief comments on the Canadian and U.S. posture at UNCLOS III on coastal State authority over offshore resources, navigation, vessel-source pollution, and deep seabed mining, and more generally regarding the LOS

---

10 U. N. Convention on the Law of the Sea, Montego Bay, Jamaica, 10 December 1982, entered into force 16 November 1994, 1833 UNTS 397.

11 James L. Malone, Statement, 30 April 1982, UNCLOS III, Official Records, Vol. XVI, 154, 155–156.

12 President Reagan, Statement, 9 July 1982, in Department of State Bulletin, August 1982, Vol. 82, No. 2065, 71.

13 *See* Chapter Four, section 3.1.

14 President Clinton, Message from the President of the United States transmitting United Nations Convention on the Law of the Sea, with Annexes, done at Montego Bay, 10 December 1982 (the Convention) and the Agreement Relating to the Implementation of Part XI of the United Nations Convention on the Law of the Sea of 10 December 1982, adopted at New York, 28 July 1994 (the Agreement) and signed by the United States, subject to ratification, on 29 July 1994, U.S. Senate, Treaty Document 39, 103d Congress, 2d Session IV (1994), 34 ILM 1393–1447.

President Bush, Statement on Advancing U.S. Interests in the World's Oceans, 15 May 2007, 46 ILM 890. *See* Chapter Four, section 3.2.1.

15 *See* President Reagan, Statement—U.S. Oceans Policy, 10 March 1983, 22 ILM 464–465.

Convention, are important since this is part of the Canada-U.S. international ocean law relationship.

2.0 At UNCLOS III

2.1 Offshore Resources

2.1.1 The 200 Nautical Mile Zone

Although not on the Canada-U.S. horizon in 1970, in the pre-UNCLOS III negotiations, the idea of a 200-nautical-mile EEZ with national jurisdiction over living and non-living resources was advanced by developing States.[16] The proposed zone was seen as a compromise between those States advocating territorialism, an extension of the territorial sea to 200 nautical miles, and States with concerns about coastal State authority encroachment into the high seas and interference with high-seas freedoms such as navigation.[17]

Canada advocated and, through its 1970 actions, had practiced a functional approach to coastal State offshore authority, seen as being not total sovereignty over an offshore area but involving only the exercise of sufficient jurisdiction as required to protect specific interests.[18] Not surprisingly, therefore, Canada was one of the first developed States to be a proponent of the EEZ and cosponsored a set of draft articles in 1973 during the pre-UNCLOS negotiations[19] and again in 1974 at UNCLOS III.[20] The United States was less enamored with the EEZ concept but, by 1974, had accepted that there was no turning back the 200-nautical-mile tide.[21] In 1976, both the United States

---

16 R. R. Churchill and A. V. Lowe, The Law of the Sea (Manchester University Press, 3rd edition, Manchester 1999) 284.

17 *Id.* 284–285.

18 External Affairs, *supra* note 4, at 5.

19 Canada, India, Kenya, and Sri Lanka, Draft Articles on Fisheries, U. N. Doc A/AC.138/SC.II/L.38, 16 July 1973, in Report of the Committee on the Peaceful Uses of the Sea-Bed and the Ocean Floor Beyond the Limits of National Jurisdiction, Vol. III, 82–84.

20 Canada, Chile, Iceland, India, Indonesia, Mauritius, Mexico, New Zealand, and Norway, Working Paper, U. N. Doc A/Conf. 62/L.4, 26 July 1974, UNCLOS III, Official Records, Vol. III, 81–83.

21 Hollick, *supra* note 6, at 280.

and Canada enacted legislation claiming exclusive national authority over marine living resources out to 200 nautical miles.[22]

The fisheries issues and the 12-nautical-mile territorial sea that were contentious between Canada and the United States in 1970 were rendered moot by the adoption of the 200-nautical-mile zone, although new fisheries issues arose most particularly in the Gulf of Maine where the two States had overlapping 200-nautical-mile fishing zones.[23] Canada's quest for greater access to and control over marine living resources in its adjacent waters, the aims of the fishing zones action and of the territorial sea legislation in 1970, had unquestionably been met.

Two fisheries matters of importance to both Canada and the United States were not resolved by acceptance of the 200-nautical-mile zone at UNCLOS III. The more important of these concerned anadromous species (salmon). Anadromous species commence their life cycle in freshwater rivers, and then migrate to ocean waters before returning to freshwater rivers to die or recommence the cycle. Canada and the United States argued that anadromous species should be treated separately from other species of fish.[24] Canada's promotion of the salmon cause has been described as taking on "the appearance of a crusade."[25] The two States worked together, along with several other States, to have included in the LOS Convention a provision with two rules. First, the provision recognizes the special authority of the so-called State of origin regarding Atlantic and Pacific salmon wherever the species

---

22 In the United States, this was done through the Fishery Conservation and Management Act (renamed the Magnuson Fishery Conservation and Management Act), 90 US Stat. 331, Pub L. 94–265, codified at 16 USC 1801–1882.
Fishing Zones of Canada (Zones 4 and 5) Order, Can Gaz Part II, Vol. 111, SOR/77-62, 1 January 1977, 115–120 replaced by Fishing Zones of Canada (Zones 4 and 5) Order, CRC (1978), Vol. XVIII, c 1548, 13741–13746 and Fishing Zones of Canada (Zone 6) Order, Can Gaz Part II, Vol. 111, SOR/77-173, 24 February 1977, 652–655, replaced by Fishing Zones of Canada (Zone 6) Order, CRC (1978), c 1549, 13747–13750. Zones 4 and 5 are on the east and west coasts and zone 6 is the Arctic.

23 *See* Chapter Five, section 3.1.

24 *See* Working Paper on the Special Case of Salmon – The Most Important Anadromous Species, U. N. Doc A/Conf.62/C.2/L.81, 23 August 1974, UNCLOS III, OFFICIAL RECORDS, Vol. III, 240 and Special Considerations Regarding the Management of Anadromous Species and Highly Migratory Oceanic Fishes: Working Paper Submitted by the United States, U. N. Doc A/AC.138/SC.II/L.20, 2 April 1973.

25 B. Johnson, *Canadian Foreign Policy and Fisheries*, in B. JOHNSON AND M. W. ZACHER (eds.) CANADIAN FOREIGN POLICY AND THE LAW OF THE SEA (University of British Columbia Press, Vancouver 1977) 83. *See* A. L. C. de Mestral and L. H. J. Legault, *Multilateral Negotiation – Canada and the Law of the Sea Conference* (1979) 35 INTL J 47, 65.

migrates. Second, in waters beyond 200 nautical miles, the general rule is that salmon are not to be targeted for harvest (the abstention principle).[26]

The second fishery issue was of particular concern to the United States and that was regarding highly migratory species (e.g., tuna). The United States took the view, contrary to most other States including Canada, that highly migratory species were not subject to national authority within 200 nautical miles. Rather, the U.S. view was that highly migratory species were to be regulated by regional fisheries bodies such as the Inter-American Tropical Tuna Commission (IATTC)[27] and the International Commission for the Conservation of Atlantic Tunas (ICCAT).[28] Only in 1990 was U.S. legislation changed to accept that highly migratory species were not exempt from the national jurisdiction of other States within 200 nautical miles.[29]

2.1.2 Continental Shelf Beyond 200 Nautical Miles

Canada's view was that the continental shelf was unrelated to the 200-nautical-mile zone and that, if the geography of the shelf allowed, a coastal State had

---

26 LOS Convention, *supra* note 10, Art 66. *See generally* W. T. BURKE, THE NEW INTERNATIONAL LAW OF FISHERIES: UNCLOS 1982 AND BEYOND (Clarendon Press, Oxford 1994) 162–165; M. P. SHEPARD AND A. W. ARGUE, THE 1985 PACIFIC SALMON TREATY: SHARING CONSERVATION BURDENS AND BENEFITS (UBC Press, Vancouver 2005) 49–52; and T. L. McDorman, *The West Coast Salmon Dispute: A Canadian View of the Breakdown of the 1985 Treaty and the Transit License Measure* (1995) 17 LOYOLA OF LOS ANGELES INTL & COMP. LJ 477, 480–483. *See* Chapter Seven, section 2.1.

The origin of the abstention principle is the International Convention for the High Seas Fisheries of the North Pacific, Tokyo, 9 May 9, 1952, entered into force 12 June 1953, 205 UNTS 65, Annex, ss I, II. See the detailed explanation in D. M. JOHNSTON, THE INTERNATIONAL LAW OF FISHERIES (Yale University Press, New Haven 1965) 275–277.

27 The IATTC was created by the Convention for the Establishment of the Inter-American Tropical Tuna Commission, Washington, 31 May 1949, entered into force 3 March 1950, 126 UNTS 3.

28 The ICCAT was created by the International Convention for Conservation of Atlantic Tunas, Rio de Janeiro, 14 May 1966, entered into force 21 March 1969, 673 UNTS 63.

29 The U.S. position on highly migratory species is described in W. T. Burke, *Highly Migratory Species in the New Law of the Sea* (1984) 14 ODIL 273, 303–310. The U.S. position on tuna changed in 1990 through amendment to the Fishery Conservation and Management Act, 104 US Stat. 4436, Pub L. 101–627, codified at 16 USC 1812 with effect from 1992. *See* Aide-Memoire April 1991 from the U.S. Mission to the United Nations to the Secretary-General of the United Nations, in Department of State, DIGEST OF UNITED STATES PRACTICE IN INTERNATIONAL LAW, 1991–1999 (International Law Institute, Washington 2005) 1707–1708. *See also* C. J. Carr, *Transformations in the Law Governing Highly Migratory Species: 1970 to the Present*, in D. D. CARON and H. N. SCHEIBER (eds.) BRINGING NEW LAW TO OCEAN WATERS (Martinus Nijhoff, Leiden 2004) 65–69, 75–83.

jurisdiction over the resources of the shelf beyond 200 nautical miles.[30] The United States was at first willing to consider that the 200-nautical-mile limit could be applied to the seafloor as well as the water column,[31] but this changed in 1974[32] such that the United States, along with a handful of other States including Canada, banded together and successfully included in the LOS Convention that exclusive national authority existed over sedentary species and mineral resources on or in the continental shelf beyond 200 nautical miles, where geography allowed.[33] The compromise reached with those States seeking to limit coastal State continental shelf authority at 200 nautical miles included the adoption of a complex formula for determining the outer limit of a State's continental shelf beyond 200 nautical miles; creation of the Commission on the Limits of the Continental Shelf to assist a State in applying the complex formula; and revenue sharing with the international community in respecting of mineral resources exploited from the continental shelf area beyond 200 nautical miles.[34]

2.2 Navigation and Vessel-Source Pollution Issues

Oil tanker disasters such as the *Torrey Canyon* in 1967 off the coast of England had brought oil pollution of the marine environment to international attention.[35] For Canada, this attention was crystallized by the *Arrow* oil spill in Nova Scotia in 1970; the traversing of the Northwest Passage by the *Manhattan*;[36] and the possibility of tanker traffic delivering oil from Alaska to southern U.S. ports along

30 External Affairs, *supra* note 4, at 13–15.

31 Hollick, *supra* note 6, at 259–260 and R. M. LOGAN, CANADA, THE UNITED STATES, AND THE THIRD LAW OF THE SEA CONFERENCE (Canadian-American Committee, Montreal and Washington 1974) 21 referring to John R. Stevenson, *Some Likely Outcomes from the Next Law of the Sea Conference*, J. Seward Johnson Lectures in Marine Policy (Woods Hole Oceanographic Institution, 1973). *See also* Delegation Report from the Seabed Committee, Geneva, 2 July- 24 August 1973, in M. H. NORDQUIST AND C. PARK, (eds.) REPORTS OF THE UNITED STATES DELEGATION TO THE THIRD UNITED NATIONS CONFERENCE ON THE LAW OF THE SEA (Law of the Sea Institute, Honolulu 1983) 45–46.

32 Hollick, *supra* note 6, at 260.

33 LOS Convention, *supra* note 10, Art 76 (1).

34 *Id.* Arts 76 (2)–(6), (8), 82.

35 *See* M. M'Gonigle and M. W. Zacher, *Canadian Foreign Policy and the Control of Marine Pollution*, in Johnson and Zacher, *supra* note 25, 106.

36 Hage, *supra* note 4, at 3.

Canada's west coast.[37] At UNCLOS III, coastal States argued for national authority to prevent vessel-source marine environmental pollution in adjacent waters. Maritime States were concerned about interference with navigational freedoms and that coastal States would develop individualized national laws creating a patchwork-quilt of requirements.[38] Much of the negotiations at UNCLOS III on the balancing of navigation and national vessel-source pollution control concerned whether coastal State laws could or could not go beyond the internationally accepted standards respecting discharges, vessel operations, and requirements regarding a vessel.[39] The United States generally held to the view that coastal States could not go beyond internationally accepted standards.[40]

The "dominant objective" for Canada at UNCLOS III was acceptance of an Arctic waters regime[41] that would support the 1970 AWPPA[42] and provide Canada with international legal justification for the action taken to protect the Arctic marine and terrestrial environment from vessel-source pollution.[43] As a consequence, for Canada, all of the navigational and marine environmental issues on the UNCLOS III agenda were directly linked to the Arctic.

2.2.1 The 200 Nautical Mile Zone

The initial approach of Canada at UNCLOS III regarding national control over vessel-source pollution prevention in Arctic waters was to include in the developing 200-nautical-mile EEZ concept extensive coastal State

---

37 *See* W. R. D. Sewell and N. A. Swainson, *West Coast Oil Pollution Policies: Canadian Responses to Risk Assessment*, in O. P. DWIVEDI (ed.) RESOURCES AND THE ENVIRONMENT: POLICY PERSPECTIVES FOR CANADA (McClelland and Stewart, Toronto 1980) 216–229, 234–242 and J. E. CARROLL, ENVIRONMENTAL DIPLOMACY: AN EXAMINATION AND A PROSPECTIVE OF CANADIAN—U.S. TRANSBOUNDARY ENVIRONMENTAL RELATIONS (University of Michigan Press, Ann Arbor 1983) 72–79.

38 Churchill and Lowe, *supra* note 16, at 346.

39 Technical matters regarding vessel-source pollution are within the mandate of the International Maritime Organization (IMO). *See* the website of the IMO at www.imo.org.

40 Draft Articles for a Chapter on the Rights and Duties of States in the Coastal Sea-Bed Economic Area, U. N. Doc A/AC.138/SC.II/L.35, 16 July 1973, in Report of the Committee on the Sea-Bed, *supra* note 19, 75–77.

41 D. M. McRae, *The Negotiation of Article 234*, in F. GRIFFITHS (ed.) POLITICS OF THE NORTHWEST PASSAGE (McGill-Queen's University Press, Montreal 1987) 104.

42 AWPPA, *supra* note 3.

43 McRae, *supra* note 41, at 114. *See also* Rob Huebert, *Article 234 and Marine Pollution Jurisdiction in the Arctic*, in A. G. OUDE ELFERINK AND D. R. ROTHWELL (eds.) THE LAW OF THE SEA AND POLAR MARITIME DELIMITATION AND JURISDICTION (Martinus Nijhoff, The Hague 2001) 254–256.

control over vessel-source pollution.[44] This approach by Canada, and the other like-minded States, to intensify national authority within the EEZ beyond just resource jurisdiction, was regarded by the United States as "extreme."[45] Maritime States, including the United States, strongly countered the idea of extensive national control measures over vessel-source pollution in the 200-nautical-mile zone and were joined by many developing States in their concerns regarding interference with commercial navigation.[46] The resulting provisions of the LOS Convention, which tie national laws regarding vessel-source pollution within the EEZ to internationally accepted standards,[47] have been described as a "triumph of the maritime actors."[48]

It being clear that Canada's "radical stance" on national vessel-source control in the 200-nautical-mile zone was motivated by Arctic waters concerns,[49] there was an uncoupling by Canada of the Arctic from the 200-nautical-mile vessel-source pollution regime.

2.2.2 The Arctic Provision

The negotiation of what was to become Article 234, the "Ice-covered Areas" Article, was "one of the few provisions . . . the terms of which were directly negotiated by the States concerned . . . and incorporated without opposition"

---

44 External Affairs, *supra* note 4, at 22 and Canada, Fiji, Ghana, Guyana, Iceland, India, Iran, New Zealand, Philippines and Spain, Draft Articles on a Zonal Approach to the Preservation of the Marine Environment, UN Doc A/Conf.62/C.3/L.6, 31 July 1974, in UNCLOS III, OFFICIAL RECORDS, Vol. III, 249–251. *See also* M'Gonigle and Zacher, *supra* note 35, at 135–136, 138.

45 Hollick, *supra* note 6, at 309–310.

46 *Id.* 310 and E. L. MILES, GLOBAL OCEAN POLITICS: THE DECISION PROCESS AT THE THIRD UNITED NATIONS CONFERENCE ON THE LAW OF THE SEA 1973–1982 (Martinus Nijhoff, The Hague 1998) 129–132, 177–179, 212–213.

47 LOS Convention, *supra* note 10, Arts 211(5), 220(3) –(7). Art 211(5) states:

> Coastal States, . . ., may in respect of their exclusive economic zone adopt laws and regulations for the prevention, reduction and control of marine pollution from vessels conforming to and giving effect to generally accepted international rules and standards established through the competent international organization or general diplomatic conference.

See generally A. K-J. TAN, VESSEL-SOURCE MARINE POLLUTION: THE LAW AND POLITICS OF INTERNATIONAL REGULATION (Cambridge University Press, Cambridge 2006) 212–214 and, in particular, 195–197 regarding the interpretation of "generally accepted international rules and standards."

48 Tan, *supra* note 47, at 200.

49 Miles, *supra* note 46, at 53.

into what was to become the LOS Convention.[50] The countries involved were Canada, the Soviet Union,[51] and the United States. In the context of UNCLOS III, there was minimal concern or interest in Canada's Arctic waters quest since little international shipping was at stake and an Arctic exception would be limited to a specific and unique geography.[52]

Canada promoted a special regime for Arctic waters that would allow for national legislation respecting vessels. The United States was hesitant, favoring a regime that tied national legislation to review by an international body such as the International Maritime Organization (IMO).[53] Canada was able to prevail in that Article 234 is the only provision in the LOS Convention that permits a coastal State to adopt and enforce within its 200-nautical-mile zone national laws with more stringent standards than the existing internationally accepted rules.[54] The United States required, however, that warships and other government vessels be exempted; national laws be non-discriminatory; and that the dispute settlement regime of the LOS Convention applied.[55]

The United States has noted that:

> The purpose of article 234 . . . is to provide the basis for implementing the provisions applicable to commercial and private vessels found in

---

50 S. Rosenne and A. Yankov, United Nations Convention on the Law of the Sea 1982: A Commentary, Vol. IV (Martinus Nijhoff, Dordrecht 1991) 393. For a detailed review and analysis of the negotiation of Article 234, *see* McRae, *supra* note 41, 98–114. R. D. Brubaker, The Russian Arctic Straits (Martinus Nijhoff, Leiden 2005) 43–44 provides a brief review of the negotiation of Article 234 and comments: "It is difficult to know exactly what took place in the negotiation between the Soviet Union, the United States, and Canada over ice-covered areas."

51 Regarding Russian interests in the Arctic, *see* E. Franckx, Maritime Claims in the Arctic: Canadian and Russian Perspectives (Martinus Nijhoff, Dordrecht 1993) 137–228 and Brubaker, *supra* note 50, at 1–23, 33–40, 79–109.

52 *See* M'Gonigle and Zacher, *supra* note 35, at 142 and Tan, *supra* note 47, at 200.

53 McRae, *supra* note 41, at 108–109.

54 Rosenne and Yankov, *supra* note 50, at 393, 396.
LOS Convention, *supra* note 10, Art 234 states:

> Coastal States have the right to adopt and enforce non-discriminatory laws and regulations for the prevention, reduction and control of marine pollution from vessels in ice-covered areas within the limits of the exclusive economic zone, where particularly severe climatic conditions and the presence of ice covering such areas for most of the year create obstructions or exceptional hazards to navigation, and pollution of the marine environment could cause major harm to or irreversible disturbance of the ecological balance. Such laws and regulations shall have due regard to navigation and the protection and preservation of the marine environment based on the best available scientific evidence.

55 *Id.* 396.

> the 1970 Canadian Arctic Waters Pollution Prevention Act . . ., while protecting fundamental U.S. security interests in the exercise of navigational rights and freedom throughout the Arctic.[56]

Rosenne and Yankov make the same observation with the additional footnote that Canada's Arctic legislation "was widely regarded as being in violation of international law" when enacted.[57]

M'Gonigle and Zacher assert that once the Arctic exception was achieved, Canada's "advocacy of other coastal issues was reduced" at UNCLOS III.[58] Buzan explains that Canada moderated its environmental advocacy "in a spirit of reluctant realism."[59] That realism involved assessing, among other things, what could be accomplished in the face strong maritime State opposition and Canada not wanting to jeopardize a successful completion of the LOS Convention that included Article 234.[60]

2.2.3 The 12-Nautical-Mile Territorial Sea and Innocent Passage

The U.S. concern respecting the breadth of the territorial sea being 12 nautical miles melted in the face of the acceptance of the 200-nautical-mile zone. Canada and the United States disagreed, however, on one aspect of the contents of the right of innocent passage for foreign vessels navigating within the territorial sea. Essentially, Canada sought greater national authority to prevent and control the possibility of pollution from foreign vessels passing through its territorial sea;[61] whereas the United States was concerned about the subjective nature of the innocent passage wording in the 1958 Territorial Sea and Contiguous Zone Convention[62] which the United States felt left "to coastal State interpretation the question of what activities are innocent or

---

56 Commentary—The 1982 United Nations Convention on the Law of the Sea, *supra* note 14, 40.

57 Rosenne and Yankov, *supra* note 50, 398, footnote 7.

58 M'Gonigle and Zacher, *supra* note 35, at 142.

59 B. Buzan, *Canada and the Law of the Sea* (1982) 11 ODIL 149, 156.

60 *Id.*

61 External Affairs, *supra* note 4, at 16–17.

62 Convention on the Territorial Sea and Contiguous Zone, Geneva 29 April 1958, entered into force 22 September 1964, 516 UNTS205, Art 14(4):

> Passage is innocent so long as it is not prejudicial to the peace, good order or security of the coastal State. Such passage shall take place in conformity with these articles and with other rules of international law.

non-innocent."[63] The United States also had concerns regarding innocent passage rights that related to non-discriminatory coastal State action; the passage of nuclear-powered vessels and vessels carrying nuclear materials; warship immunities; submerged passage of submarines; and prior consent or notification for military vessels.[64]

The technical Canadian vessel-source pollution concerns with innocent passage at UNCLOS III were twofold. First, would vessel passage that threatened pollution make the passage non-innocent—the so-called leaky-tanker scenario?[65] Second, as regards national laws that are permitted regarding vessels engaged in innocent passage respecting the construction, design, equipment, and manning of foreign vessels in the territorial sea, must these national laws be consistent with existing international standards or could a coastal State have more rigorous national laws on these matters?[66] On both of these matters, Canada, and other coastal States, argued unsuccessfully; the position of the United States and other maritime States, favoring limitations on interference with foreign vessel passage within the territorial sea, prevailed.[67]

2.2.4 International Straits

Expanding the breadth of the territorial sea from three to 12 nautical miles would have the effect of bringing the waters of many narrow waterways that were once high seas within the territorial sea of adjacent States. Both the United States and Canada were concerned about the impact that this development might have on key international straits where unimpeded navigation was important both for strategic and economic reasons. For the United States, the protection of unimpeded navigation within international straits was a top priority. To attain this protection, the United States, along with other States, worked to have adopted in the LOS Convention the regime of transit passage, which is more favorable to navigable rights than innocent passage.[68]

---

63 E. L. Richardson, *Law of the Sea: Navigation and Other Traditional National Security Concerns* (1982) 19 San Diego LR 553, 560.

64 *See generally* Churchill and Lowe, *supra* note 16, at 88–92.

65 External Affairs, *supra* note 4, at 16–17 and Hage, *supra* note 4, at 6.

66 Hage, *supra* note 4, at 6.

67 *See* LOS Convention, *supra* note 10, Arts 19(2) (h), 20(2) and Tan, *supra* note 47, at 205–208.

68 LOS Convention, *supra* note 10, Arts 37–44.

Canada was not a significant participant in the international straits discussions at UNCLOS III,[69] although its focus on the Arctic and assertion that the Northwest Passage was not an international strait[70] were directly tied to the international straits issues.[71] Early on at UNCLOS III, Canada proposed wording to define international straits as being a natural passage between land formations which had "traditionally been used for international navigation."[72] This wording, in Canada's view, would have excluded the Northwest Passage. The proposal, however, was not accepted.

Once the resolution was achieved on the Arctic provision (Article 234), Canada supported the position of the maritime States, including the United States, on transit passage. A key part of what was achieved with Article 234 involved "a careful compromise on the question of the relationship of the Northwest Passage to the 'international straits' regime under the Convention," such that the LOS Convention international straits regime, which constrains the vessel-source pollution control laws that an adjacent State can adopt and enforce, "is not applicable to the Northwest Passage."[73] The importance of this is that the national laws permitted to be adopted pursuant to Article 234, such as the AWPPA,[74] can be applied to commercial vessels utilizing the Northwest Passage even if, despite Canada's objections,

---

69 R. McConchie and R. S. Reid, *Canadian Foreign Policy and International Straits*, in Johnson and Zacher, *supra* note 25, 186.

70 External Affairs, *supra* note 4, at 5 and 17–18 and *see* Hage, *supra* note 4, at 5.

71 *See* McRae, *supra* note 41, at 108–111.

72 Draft Article on a Definition of an International Strait, U. N. Doc A/Conf.62/C.2/L.83, 26 August 1974, in UNCLOS III, OFFICIAL RECORDS, Vol. III, 241. *See* McConchie and Reid, *supra* note 69, at 175–176.

73 McRae, *supra* note 41, at 110 who derives part of the argument from D. PHARAND, NORTHWEST PASSAGE: ARCTIC STRAITS (Martinus Nijhoff, Dordrecht 1984) 119–120. McRae, *supra* note 41, at 110 explains how this was achieved.

> The ice-covered waters provision [Article 234] is not included in the sections of . . . the Convention [on marine environmental pollution] that are subject to the international straits regime.[as per Article 233] Since the ice-covered waters provision clearly applies to the Northwest Passage, and since the ice-covered areas provision is not subject to the international straits regime, *ergo* the international straits regime is not applicable to the Northwtest Passage.

Brubaker, *supra* note 50, at 44, writes that the basics of the deal was that "the United States would allow unilaterally adopted coastal State environmental provisions for ice-covered areas, vaguely defined, in exchange for Canadian acquiescence to the . . . international straits regime advanced by Washington." At 133–135, he looks in detail at the relationship between Article 234 and the LOS Convention international straits regime summarizing that the relationship is arguable.

74 AWPPA, *supra* note 3.

the Northwest Passage is an international strait. In support of this view, the United States has acknowledged that U.S. commercial ships are subject to Canada's Arctic waters legislation.[75] It is to be noted that pursuant to Article 234 that a coastal State's Arctic legislation is to "have due regard to navigation."[76]

2.3 Common Heritage of Mankind and Deep Seabed Mining

In 1970, both Canada and the United States voted in favor of General Assembly Resolution 2749 on the Declaration of Principles Governing the Sea-Bed and Ocean Floor beyond the Limits of National Jurisdiction (Resolution 2749), which included the common heritage of mankind wording.[77] Developing States (the Group of 77) championed the common heritage concept and took the view that Resolution 2749 was legally binding and prohibited seabed mining outside of an international regime.[78] U.S. support for the common heritage concept was ambivalent since the wording of the Resolution was less than clear and the Resolution directed that deep seabed mining activities were to be governed by an international regime.[79] Canada shared some of the U.S. uncertainties about the common heritage wording in the 1970 Resolution, although it was more attuned to the strong support for the concept evidenced by developing States.[80] Canada's principal concern was that the location of the boundary between the outer limit of national jurisdiction and the area of high-seas deep ocean floor, to which the common heritage might attach, be favorable to Canada's

---

75 Department of State, *United States Responses to Excessive Maritime Claims*, LIMITS IN THE SEAS, No. 112 (Washington, 1992) 73, footnote 114 states: "[T]he United States considers U.S. commercial vessels subject to this law" [AWPPA], with no distinction made as regards the Northwest Passage.

76 *See* Article 234, *supra* note 54, last sentence.

77 General Assembly Resolution 2749 (XXV), adopted 17 December 1970, recorded vote of 108 to 0, with 14 abstentions, (1970) UNYB 78–79.

78 Churchill and Lowe, *supra* note 16, at 228.

79 Hollick, *supra* note 6, at 238.

80 *See* B. G. Buzan and D. W. Middlemiss, *Canadian Foreign Policy and the Exploitation of the Seabed*, in Johnson and Zacher, *supra* note 25, at 24.

continental shelf interests.[81] On the wording of the Resolution, Churchill and Lowe summarized that it:

> [A]dmitted of a wide range of interpretations, from that supporting open access to sea-bed resources under freedom of the high seas until such time as the "international regime" was established, to that supporting a moratorium on unilateral development of sea-bed resources pending the establishment of an international organization to govern the Area.[82]

The technical issues on deep seabed mining at UNCLOS III were primarily to do with the machinery of mineral resource exploration and exploitation. The Group of 77 sought an international seabed authority with significant independent powers. Developed States, in particular the United States, desired a weaker body with minimal powers of interference in deep seabed mining activities.[83] Behind the technical issues divide was the political and ideological gulf between industrialized States and the newly emerging Group of 77. In stark terms, developing countries "saw the potential of the seabed in danger of being captured solely for the benefit of the richest capitalist nations."[84] Industrialized States, particularly the United States, were concerned about the precedent of a strong international seabed authority since, first, it was antithetical to free market principles and, second, it was linked to New International Economic Order (NIEO) being promoted by developing States.[85] Deep seabed mining became the political and ideological polarizing

---

81 External Affairs, *supra* note 4, at 14.

82 Churchill and Lowe, *supra* note 16, at 228.

83 *See* the excellent summary by Churchill and Lowe, *supra* note 16, at 228. *See also* M. G. Schmidt, Common Heritage or Common Burden? The United States Position on the Development of a Regime for Deep Sea-Bed Mining in the Law of the Sea Convention (Clarendon Press, Oxford 1989) 103–105, 212. More generally and from a different perspective, *see* P. B. Payoyo, Cries of the Sea: World Inequality, Sustainable Development and the Common Heritage of Humanity (Martinus Nijhoff, The Hague 1997) 389–420.

84 C. L. Antrim, *Mineral Resources of Stateless Space: Lessons from the Deep Seabed* (2005) 59 No. 1 J Intl Affairs 55, 59.

85 Schmidt, *supra* note 83, at 105–109. The New International Economic Order (NIEO) was a proposal made by the developing countries to redress economic inferiority. Fundamental to the NIEO as part of a restructuring of economic power relations was a proposed redistribution of wealth from developed to developing countries. The NIEO was comprehensively articulated in a series of 1974 UN General Assembly Resolutions. See (1974) UNYB 305–332.

The literature regarding the NIEO and the law of sea is extensive. *See, for example*, E. M. Borgese, *The New International Economic Order and the Law of the Sea* (1977) 14 San Diego LR 584–596.

Antrim, *supra* note 84, at 59–60 notes that during the deep seabed mining discussions at UNCLOS III, the ideology of the NIEO was embraced by the Group of 77, particularly African States, since most developing States did not expect to otherwise derive any benefit from the deep seabed resources.

issue at UNCLOS III and the make-or-break issue regarding the successful completion of a comprehensive law of the sea treaty.

However polarizing deep seabed mining was, until the 1980s, the United States ascribed to the view that:

> If UNCLOS was to contribute to a more stable world order, concessions would have to be made on the scope of the sea-bed regime, which then would have to be balanced against gains concerning other ocean interests.[86]

The Canadian position was not that different. Deep seabed mining and the international seabed machinery were seen primarily in terms of requiring a result so as not to derail the successes in other parts of the negotiations.[87] However, Canada was more sympathetic to the developing country perspective regarding the NIEO, North-South relations, and equitable outcomes.[88] This was the case, in part, because many of Canada's concerns on deep seabed mining were being adequately expressed by other States[89] and, in part, because this allowed Canada to promote compromise.[90] The latter was the role primarily played by Canada during UNCLOS III on deep seabed mining.[91] One deep seabed mining issue that became identified with Canada

---

86 Schmidt, *supra* note 83, at 107, 211–212.

87 E. RIDDELL-DIXON, CANADA AND THE INTERNATIONAL SEABED: DOMESTIC DETERMINANTS AND EXTERNAL CONSTRAINTS (McGill-Queen's University Press, Montreal 1989) 36, 38.

88 *Id.* 75–77.
De Mestral and Legault, *supra* note 25, at 56–57 comment:

> [T]he Canadian delegation was profoundly aware of the political transformation the world . . . [had] undergone since the 1958 and 1960 conferences on the law of the sea, especially the emergence from colonialism of a great number of developing countries. The presence of these countries implied revolutionary changes in expectations, approaches and procedures, indeed the very process of making both customary and conventional international law. . . . Canada recognized that it shared many perceptions and interests with the developing countries . . . In the view of the Canadian delegation, these new relationships were necessary not only for the success of Canadian positions but also for the success of the conference itself and for the sake of a more equitable, more stable public order for the oceans.

89 Riddell-Dixon, *supra* note 87, at 37.

90 Hage, *supra* note 4, at 10 notes that:

> From the outset, Canada attempted to stay free from the controversy surrounding the regulatory machinery for seabed mining . . . This degree of independence on sea-bed mining questions permitted the Canadian delegation . . . to help resolve the differences between the developing countries and industrialized sea-bed mining states.

91 Riddell-Dixon, *supra* note 87, at 37–38 and Buzan and Middlemiss, *supra* note 80, at 34–35.

concerned production controls on deep seabed minerals that might compete with land-based sources of the minerals. This highly technical matter consumed significant energy during UNCLOS III and resulted in a provision with which Canada was not satisfied.[92]

3.0 The LOS Convention[93]

3.1 Adoption of the Convention and the 1980s

The posture of the United States respecting the product emerging from UNCLOS III took a dramatic shift following the election in late 1980 of President Ronald Reagan.[94] In January 1982, President Reagan announced that the United States had significant reservations about the draft LOS Convention that was emerging from UNCLOS III but that the United States remained committed to the multilateral process.[95] An internal U.S. policy review produced the so-called Green Book, which contained over one hundred proposed amendments to the draft LOS Convention and which was presented to UNCLOS III in early 1982.[96]

The primary goal of previous U.S. administrations had been ascertainment of navigational rights in an international treaty.[97] The Reagan administration, however, viewed navigational rights as sufficiently protected by the customary international law evolving from State action pursuant to UNCLOS III.[98] The goal of the Reagan administration switched to stressing security of

92 *See* Hage, *supra* note 4, at 10–11 and Riddell-Dixon, *supra* note 87, at 41–48

93 Parts of this section are drawn, with modification, from T. L. McDorman, *Will Canada Ratify the Law of the Sea Convention?* (1988) 25 SAN DIEGO LR 535, 539–541 and T. L. McDorman, *A Canadian Perspective on the Continued Non-Ratification of the Convention on the Law of the Sea by the United States* (2005) 43 CYIL 393, 394–401.

94 For a particularly insightful few pages on this shift, *see* Miles, *supra* note 46, at 348–350.

95 President Reagan, Statement and White House Fact Sheet, 29 January 1982, in DEPARTMENT OF STATE BULLETIN, March 1982, Vol. 82, No. 2060, 54–55. Note Schmidt, *supra* note 83, 240–242.

96 Changes Suggested by the Delegation of the United States, U. N. Doc A/Conf.62/WG.21/ Infrormal Paper 18, 10 March 1982, in R. PLATZODER (ed.) THIRD UNITED NATIONS CONFERENCE ON THE LAW OF THE SEA DOCUMENTS, Vol. VI (Oceana Publications, Dobbs Ferry, 1984) 278–303 and Vol. VIII (1985), 304–337. *See* Schmidt, *supra* note 83, at 214–242 and Miles, *supra* note 46, at 356–370.

97 The arguments in favor of a comprehensive treaty for protection of U.S. navigational interests can be found in Richardson, *supra* note 63, at 553–576.

98 L Ratiner, *The Law of the Sea: A Crossroads for American Foreign Policy* (1982) 60 FOREIGN AFFAIRS 1006, 1011.

supply of strategic minerals.[99] As a result, the United States focused on the deep seabed regime envisioned in the LOS Convention, especially the role that the International Seabed Authority (ISA) was to play with respect to the harvesting of and the access to minerals on the deep ocean floor.

The United States viewed the LOS Convention provisions regarding the deep seabed regime as "fatally flawed" and detrimental to its interests for the following reasons, among others: the decision making in the regime did not fairly reflect the political and economic interests or the financial contribution of the participating States; access to the seabed resources was not guaranteed to qualified entities; the regime was perceived as being detrimental to the development of deep seabed resources; and the regime would set an undesirable precedent for other international organizations.[100]

Despite the perceived problems with the LOS Convention, the real difficulty the United States had with the Convention was ideological. One commentator summarized:

> It cannot be over-emphasized that a new kind of political ideology had come to power with Reagan. It influenced every issue of domestic and foreign policy, and LOS was no exception. Officials made it clear that the Administration's problems with the Convention were based on ideology and precedential objections. The new Administration considered that the answer to the question of whether or not internationalist and non-free market structures should govern the development of ocean resources was a resounding "no"...[101]

---

99 *Id.* On the importance of access to strategic minerals, *see* White House, The Law of the Sea Convention, 15 April 1983, excerpts from an Office of Policy Information Paper, in (1983) 26 No. 2 OCEANUS 74–76.

One commentator has described the changing U.S. position on the LOS Convention as being the result of a perception that the United States and Soviet Union were about to engage in a resources war over strategic minerals and that the LOS Convention might inhibit U.S. access. L. Kimball, *Turning Points in the Future of Deep Seabed Mining* (1986) 17 ODIL 367, 377.

100 The reasons why the Treaty was rejected by the United States have been set out in numerous places, *for example, see* Malone, *supra* note 11, at 155–156; J. L. Malone, *Who Needs the Sea Treaty?* (1984) 54 FOREIGN POLICY 44–63; and D. Bandow, *UNCLOS III: A Flawed Treaty* (1982) 19 SAN DIEGO LR 475–492. For a detailed analysis of the U.S. concerns, *see* J. B. MORELL, THE LAW OF THE SEA: AN HISTORICAL ANALYSIS OF THE 1982 TREATY AND ITS REJECTION BY THE UNITED STATES (McFarland and Company, London 1992) 96–154.

101 Schmidt, *supra* note 83, at 259. *See also* W.S. Burke and F. S. Brokaw, *Ideology and the Law of the Sea*, in B. OXMAN, D. CARON, AND C. BUREDI (eds.) LAW OF THE SEA: U.S. POLICY DILEMMA (Institute for Contemporary Studies Press, San Francisco 1983) 43–58.

The deep seabed provisions of the LOS Convention were perceived to be anti-free market. Former United States law of the sea negotiator Leigh Ratiner explained the U.S. rejection of the Treaty as follows: "[The LOS Convention] established a mixed economic system for the regulation and production of deep seabed minerals and, as a matter of principle, the Reagan Administration could not, consistent with its free enterprise philosophy, have done otherwise [than reject the Treaty] when the time came to vote."[102]

The change of posture of the United States in the late stages of UNCLOS III respecting the carefully crafted draft LOS Convention, which contained many provisions already accepted by the United States, was not well received by most other delegations, including Canada.[103] Nevertheless, efforts were made to accommodate U.S. concerns. At the forefront of these accommodation attempts was Canadian Ambassador Alan Beesley.[104] In the end, however, the United States voted against adoption of the LOS Convention and a number of other industrialized States abstained from supporting the Convention.[105] In July 1982, President Reagan announced that the United States would not sign the LOS Convention.[106]

In contrast to the United States, Canada supported the adoption of the LOS Convention in 1982, taking the view that the Convention was very much in Canada's interests.[107] Although the U.S. decision not to support the Convention was unrelated to any specific Canada-U.S. matter, the U.S. deci-

---

102 Ratiner, *supra* note 98, at 1006.

103 Canada was one of the middle industrialized countries that joined the Group of 77 and Soviet bloc in dismissing the U.S. Green Book as a basis for negotiation since it involved so many extensive and fundamental changes to the existing draft LOS Convention. Assessment by the Canadian Delegation of the Eleventh Session of the United Nations Conference on the Law of the Sea held in New York from 8 March to 30 April 1982, (mimeo), 1, on file with the author.

More generally respecting the final stages of UNCLOS III, *see* Schmidt, *supra* note 83, at 240–260.

104 *See* Hage, *supra* note 4, at 12–13.

105 The abstaining industrialized States were Belgium, Germany, Italy, the Netherlands, Spain, the Soviet Union, and the United Kingdom. *See* UNCLOS III, OFFICIAL RECORDS, Vol. XVI, 155–156.

In Assessment by the Canadian Delegation of the 1982 Session, *supra* note 103, at 2 is the comment: "The United States did not believe, until it was too late, that the Group of 77 and other western States would adopt the Draft Convention over U.S. opposition."

106 Statement of President Reagan, 9 July 1982, *supra* note 12.

107 *See* A.J. MacEachen, Canadian Minister of External Affairs, Statement, 6 December 1982, UNCLOS III, OFFICIAL RECORDS, Vol. XVII, 14–16 and Hage, *supra* note 4, at 2–15.

sion was characterized by one commentator as a "direct menace to Canada."[108] Although the wording on the official record of the statement by Foreign Minister of Canada Allan J. MacEachen made at the 1982 signing ceremony was carefully measured,[109] the Canadian newspaper headlines noted that the speech was urging the United States to reverse its position of non-support of the LOS Convention.[110] As one commentator has well summarized:

> In sharp contrast to the Reagan administration's attempt to achieve security from international regulation, Canada large stake in the Law of the Sea lay precisely in achieving security *via* the reinforcement of international authority . . .[111] (*emphasis in original*)

Beyond the specifics of the LOS Convention, there was also the perception of the United States rejecting multilateralism and "one of the greatest accomplishments of the United Nations."[112]

Canada's frustration with, even hostility to the U.S. rejection of the LOS Convention dissipated as it became clear that the central concern of the United States with the LOS Convention, the alleged unworkability of the deep seabed mining regime (Part XI), was also of concern to other industrialized States, including Canada. Germany and the United Kingdom, while not overtly rejecting the LOS Convention, had abstained on the vote adopting the LOS Convention and were among the few States not to sign the Convention,[113]

---

108 S. Clarkson, Canada and the Reagan Challenge: Crisis and Adjustment, 1981–1985 (James Lorimer and Company, Toronto 1985) 216.

109 MacEachen, *supra* note 107.

110 *Canada calls for American reversal at Law of the Sea*, Halifax Mail-Star, 7 December 1982, 2 and *Sign Sea Pact, MacEachen Urges U.S.*, Toronto Globe and Mail, 7 December 1982, 17. *See also* J. A. Beesley, *International Political Context of the LOS Negotiations*, in L. Juda (ed.) The United States without the Law of the Sea Treaty: Opportunities and Costs (Times Press, Wakefield, R.I. 1983) 11–22.

111 Clarkson, *supra* note 108, at 216.

112 MacEachen, *supra* note 107, at 16.

113 On the first day that the LOS Convention was open for signature, 117 States signed the Convention. T. T. B. Koh, *A Constitution for the Oceans*, in M. H. Nordquist (ed.) United Nations Convention on the Law of the Sea, 1982: A Commentary, Vol. I (Martinus Nijhoff, Dordrecht 1985) 11 observed that:

> Never in the annals of international law had a Convention been signed by . . . [so many] . . . countries on the very first day on which it was open for signature. Not only was the number of signatories a remarkable fact, but just as important was the fact that the Convention had been signed by States from every region in the world.

primarily because of their concerns over deep seabed mining.[114] Many of the industrial States that did sign the LOS Convention "made it clear . . . that their ratification . . . would be subject to improvements to the Part XI regime . . ."[115] As one author notes, Canada came to consider the LOS Convention deep seabed mining regime as "unacceptable" in its original form and, like most other industrialized States, adopted a wait-and-see attitude regarding change.[116]

Also soothing Canada's concern with U.S. hostility to the LOS Convention was the removal from the bilateral ocean agenda of two high-profile matters. First, in 1984, the International Court muted the highly contentious Gulf of Maine fishing dispute by establishing a maritime boundary between Canada and the United States in the area.[117] This was followed in 1985 with Canada and the United States finalizing an agreement on conserving and sharing Pacific salmon.[118]

Finally, Canada was comforted by the emanations from the United States that it was going to operate on the basis that the LOS Convention, but for those provisions relating to deep seabed mining (Part XI), were either part of customary international law or evidence of customary international law.[119] This comfort was particularly important as regards Article 234, which a U.S. official confirmed in 1983 "reflects existing international law."[120]

---

114 *See* Malcolm Rifkind, Under-Secretary of State, Foreign and Commonwealth Office, House of Commons (UK), *Debates*, 2 December 1982, in (1982) 53 BRITISH YB INTL L 481 and R. Wolfrum, *Germany and the Law of the Sea*, in T. TREVES (ed.) THE LAW OF THE SEA: THE EUROPEAN UNION AND ITS MEMBER STATES (Martinus Nijhoff, The Hague 1997) 223.

115 P. Kirsch and D. Fraser, *The Law of the Sea Preparatory Commission after Six Years: Review and Prospects* (1988) 26 CYIL 119, 122.

116 Riddell-Dixon, *supra* note 87, at 180.

117 *Delimitation of the Maritime Boundary in the Gulf of Maine Area (Canada v. United States)*, [1984] ICJ Rep. 246.

118 Pacific Salmon Treaty, Ottawa 28 January 1985, entered into force 18 March 1985, CTS 1985/7, TIAS 11091, 1469 UNTS 357.

119 *See* Statement of President Reagan, 10 March 1983, *supra* note 15. *See also* the exchange between J. Alan Beesley and Brian Hoyle, Deputy Director, Office of Ocean Law and Policy, U.S. State Department in Juda, *supra* note 110, at 139–143.

120 B. Hoyle, *The United States Government Perspective*, in Juda, *supra* note 110, at 135. Ambassador Beesley in the question period following the above presentation, at 141, stated: "I would hesitate . . . to say that the Arctic exception . . . is already existing international law. However, I am relieved to hear others say it is, and I will take that into account." Hoyle commented, at 143, "I would have thought . . . that if Canada considered any provision to be customary law, it would be the ice-covered areas provision." To which Beesley responded, at 143, "I would not have given that opinion, but I was now reassured, by what you have said—and I now accept it [Article 234] as customary law."

3.2 Party Status

3.2.1 United States

Throughout the 1980s, the United States promoted an alternative regime for deep seabed mining.[121] Led by the United States, industrialized States entered into a series of controversial agreements regarding deep seabed mining that demonstrated their concerns with the LOS Convention regime.[122] Canada participated in three of these agreements primarily because of the involvement of two Canadian mining companies (INCO and Noranda) in deep seabed mining corporate consortia.[123] Though developing States decried the emerging reciprocating States regime, and serious questions about the international legality of the regime existed, the participating industrialized States asserted that their actions were not inconsistent with the deep seabed regime of the LOS Convention.[124] Essentially, the industrialized States, other than the United States, were preserving their options by remaining involved in both the LOS Convention regime and the reciprocating States regime.[125]

In 1990, with the magic number of sixty State parties for entry into force of the LOS Convention hovering into view, the U. N. Secretary-General initiated a process to find a means to accommodate the concerns of the United

---

Canada has asserted that Article 234 of the LOS Convention is part of customary international law. Department of External Affairs, *Paper*, 29 March 1988, in (1988) 26 CYIL 314. *See also* Pharand, *supra* note 73, at 120 who takes the view that Article 234 is part of customary international law. Brubaker, *supra* note 50, at 53–54 concludes that is "questionable" whether Article 234 has become part of customary international law.

On the impact of Article 234, *see* Huebert, *supra* note 43, at 256–258.

121 *See* Schmidt, *supra* note 83, at 277–306 and Morell, *supra* note 100, at 91–95.

122 Agreement concerning Interim Arrangements relating to Polymetallic Nodules of the Deep Sea Bed, (France, Germany, the United Kingdom, and the United States), Washington, 2 September 1982, entered into force 2 September 1982, 21 ILM 950–962; Provisional Understanding Regarding Deep Seabed Matters, (Belgium, France, Germany, Italy, Japan, the Netherlands, the United Kingdom, and the United States), Geneva, 3 August 1984, entered into force 2 September 1984, 23 ILM 1354–1365; and Agreement on the Resolution of Practical Problems with Respect to Deep Seabed Mining Areas, (Canada, Belgium, Italy, Netherlands, and the Soviet Union), New York, 14 August 1987, entered into force 14 August 1987, 26 ILM 1502–1507. There was also an Exchange of Notes between the United States and Canada on this matter, Ottawa, 14 August 1987, entered into force 14 August 1987, TIAS 11438, 26 ILM 1510–1512. *See generally* Churchill Lowe, *supra* note 16, at 232–234.

123 *See* Department of Foreign Affairs, *Memorandum*, 6 August 1987, in (1988) 26 CYIL 319, 320.

124 *See* Churchill and Lowe, *supra* note 16, at 232–235.

125 Antrim, *supra* note 84, at 62.

States and the other industrialized States respecting the deep seabed mining regime of the LOS Convention (Part XI). Oxman has identified four key factors that facilitated this re-evaluation:[126] there was a renewed desire on the part of many States to attain a uniform multilateral ocean law regime; "political, economic and intellectual developments" in the 1980s, including a waning of the attachment to the NIEO by the Group of 77 and the collapse of the Soviet Union, had made States more open to market approaches to resource development; it was clear that the hoped-for wealth from the minerals on the ocean floor was not going to materialize because of new sources of minerals and changes in mineral markets; and there was an acceptance that efficiency and costs mattered for international organizations. The process bore fruit with the adoption of the 1994 Agreement Relating to the Implementation of Part XI of the U. N. Convention on the Law of the Sea of 10 December 1994.[127] Within months, most industrialized States became party to the LOS Convention. The Clinton administration signaled U.S. contentment with the Convention by sending it to the U.S. Senate for advice and consent.[128]

The LOS Convention languished in the Senate until 2003 when it finally became the subject of consideration by the Senate Foreign Relations Committee, as well as a number of other Senate Committees.[129] In February 2004, the Senate Foreign Relations Committee voted unanimously to recommend U.S. accession to the LOS Convention and reported this to the full

---

126 B. H. Oxman, *The 1994 Agreement Relating to the Implementation of Part XI of the UN Convention on the Law of the Sea*, in D. Vidas and W. Ostreng (eds.) Order of the Oceans at the Turn of the Century (Kluwer Law International, The Hague 1999) 17.

127 Agreement relating to the Implementation of Part XI of the United Nations Convention on the Law of the Sea, New York, 28 July 1994, entered into force 28 July 1996, 33 ILM 1309–1327.
Regarding how the 1994 Agreement met the U.S. concerns expressed at UNCLOS III, *see* B. H. Oxman, *The 1994 Agreement and the Convention* (1994) 88 AJIL 687–696. Regarding the 1994 Agreement generally, *see* Oxman, *supra* note 126, at 22–35 and T. Treves, *The Agreement Completing the UN Law of the Sea Convention: Formal and Procedural Aspects*, in M. H. Nordquist and J. N. Moore (eds.) Entry into Force of the Law of the Sea Convention (Martinus Nijhoff, The Hague 1995) 99–118.

128 Message from the President, *supra* note 14.

129 *See generally* J. A. Duff, *A Note on the United States and the Law of the Sea: Looking Back and Moving Forward* (2004) 35 ODIL 195–219. *See also* M. A. Browne, *The U. N. Law of the Sea Convention and the United States: Developments Since October 2003*, 27 January 2006, (Congressional Research Service Report, Washington RS21890) and M. A. Browne, *The Law of the Sea Convention and U.S. Policy*, 12 May 2006, (Congressional Research Service Issue Brief, Washington IB95010).

Senate for consideration.[130] However, the U.S. Senate did not make a decision on U.S. accession prior to the expiration of the 108th Congress at the end of 2004.[131] The procedural consequence was that the Senate Foreign Relations Committee was required to reconsider the accession issue and make a new recommendation to the full U.S. Senate. In short, the Senate process regarding the LOS Convention had to start again from the beginning.[132]

In May 2007, President Bush directly called on the U.S. Senate "to act favorable on U.S. accession" to the LOS Convention.[133] President Bush indicated that:

> Joining [the LOS Convention] will serve the national security interests of the United States, including the maritime mobility of our armed forces worldwide. It will secure U.S. sovereign rights over extensive marine areas, including the valuable natural resources they contain. Accession will promote U.S. interests in the environmental health of the oceans. And it will give the United States a seat at the table when the rights that are vital to our interests are debated and interpreted.[134]

In June 2007, the U.S. Joint Chiefs of Staff also urged positive Senate action on the Convention.[135] Noteworthy also is the support for U.S. membership in the LOS Convention expressed by former Secretary of State George Shultz, who indicated that President Reagan supported the Convention subject to the deep seabed provisions and that these had now been fixed pursuant to the 1994 Agreement on the Implementation of Part XI.[136] In late October 2007, the Senate Foreign Relations Committee voted 17-4 in favor of recommending that the United States accede to the LOS Convention and, in December 2007 the Committee forward its recommendation to the full Senate.[137]

---

130 U.S. Senate, Executive Report 108–110, Part VII—Text of Resolution of Advice and Consent to Ratification, at 16–21 (2004) (Senate, Congressional Record S2712-S2716 (11 March 2004)). *See also* Duff, *supra* note 129, at 214–219.

131 *Note* J. A. Duff, *UNCLOS and the United States*, part of *From the Desk of the Editor-in-Chief* (2005) 36 ODIL 317–318.

132 *Id.*

133 President Bush, Statement on 15 May 2007, *supra* note 14.

134 *Id.*

135 Letter from the Joint Chiefs of Staff to Senator Joseph Biden, 26 June 2007, at <www.oceanlaw.org/downloads/JCSonLOS.pdf> (accessed on 7 October 2007).

136 George P. Shultz, Letter to Senator Lugar, 28 June 2007, at <www.oceanlaw.org/index.php?name=news&file=article&sid=25> (accessed on 7 October 2007).

137 U.S. Senate, Executive Report 110–9, (2007).

Attached to the advice and consent resolution before the Senate are twenty-four "declarations and understandings" proposed to be included by the United States in its instrument of accession.[138] Many of these "declarations and understandings" provide insight into how the United States views and interprets provisions of the LOS Convention.[139]

The non-party status to the LOS Convention by the United States is a product of an opposition that is based on ideology; the history of the U.S. opposition to the Convention; and fears regarding internationalization.[140] This opposition is reinforced by arguments that there is little to be gained by the United States in becoming a party. As noted by one author:

> Perhaps the most salient argument made by those opposing ratification is that the United States already enjoys the benefits the Convention would provide while avoiding the burdens being a party would entail. Specifically, the opponents argue, the United States already benefits from the navigational

---

138 *Id.* Part VIII—Text of Resolution of Advice and Consent to Ratification, 19–24. These "Declarations and Understandings" are identical to ones that accompanied the 2004 Senate Foreign Relations Committee Report to the full Senate, *supra* note 130.

LOS Convention, *supra* note 10, Art 310 allows States when signing, ratifying, or acceding to the Convention to make statements or declarations "provided that such declarations or statements do not purport to exclude or modify the legal effect of the provisions of this Convention in their application to that State."

139 For a review of some of the U.S. Senate Declarations and Undertakings, *see* Y. Song, *Declarations and Statements with Respect to the 1982 UNCLOS: Potential Legal Disputes between the United States and China after U.S. Accession to the Convention* (2005) 36 ODIL 261–289.

140 *See* Duff, *supra* note 129, at 205–206 and D. J. Bederman, *The Old Isolation and the New Law of the Sea: Reflections on Advice and Consent for UNCLOS* (2008) 49 HARVARD INTL LJ (ONLINE) 21, at <www.harvardilj.org/online/126> (accessed on 8 March 2008).

The detail of this opposition will not be discussed here. *See*, however D. Bandow, *Don't Resurrect the Law of the Sea Treaty*, No. 552 POLICY ANALYSIS, 13 October 2005, (Cato Institute, Washington) and Browne, *supra* note 129, at 9–13. P. M. LEITNER, REFORMING THE LAW OF THE SEA TREATY: OPPORTUNITIES MISSED, PRECEDENTS SET AND U.S. SOVEREIGNTY THREATENED (University Press of America, New York 1996) provides a critique of the deep seabed mining regime following the 1994 "fix" and concludes that the United States should still not become a party to the LOS Convention.

For a powerful rebuttal to the numerous points raised by opponents to the United States becoming a party to the LOS Convention, *see* W. L. Schachte, Jr., *The Unvarnished Truth: The Debate on the Law of the Sea Convention* (2008) Vol. 61 No. 2 NAVAL WAR COLLEGE REV 119–127.

As well, for an insightful analysis of U.S. attitudes to the LOS Convention, *see* J. E. Noyes, *U.S. Policy and the United Nations Convention on the Law of the Sea* (2007) 37 GEORGE WASHINGTON INTL LR 621–638.

and overflight provisions of the Convention because they have become part of the corpus of customary international law.

Similarly, the opponents contend, the United States currently benefits fully from the Convention's provisions on coastal state's control over natural resources, since the declarations on its territorial sea, contiguous zone, exclusive economic and continental shelf have gone unchallenged.[141]

3.2.2 Canada

As noted above, in the 1980s, it became clear that the central concern of the United States with the LOS Convention, the workability of the deep seabed mining regime, was also of concern to Canada. Canada was not a key participant in the development of the 1994 Agreement[142] that altered the deep seabed mining régime of the LOS Convention, although Canada was supportive of the changes.[143] Although the 1994 Agreement resulted in most industrialized States becoming party to the Convention and, reportedly, the Canadian cabinet "gave its approval to proceed" with ratification,[144] Canada remained a non-party.

For Canada, another law of the sea issue had emerged as a major public and political issue, namely, alleged uncontrolled foreign fishing outside the 200-nautical-mile zone along Canada's East Coast.[145] This was correlated with the collapse of East Coast cod stocks and the 1992 moratorium on domestic fishing of this once-important stock.[146] The LOS Convention was seen as not adequately addressing the matter and/or possibly being an impediment on Canadian actions to deal with the overfishing problem,

---

141 J. F. MURPHY, THE UNITED STATES AND THE RULE OF LAW IN INTERNATIONAL AFFAIRS (Cambridge University Press, Cambridge 2004) 241.

142 Agreement relating to the Implementation of Part XI, *supra* note 127.

143 R. Huebert, *Canada and the Law of the Sea Convention* (1996–97) 52 INTL J 69, 83.

144 *Id.* 82.

145 Respecting foreign fishing astride Canada's east coast 200-nautical-mile zone, *see* L. S. PARSONS, MANAGEMENT OF MARINE FISHERIES IN CANADA (National Research Council of Canada, Ottawa 1993) 263–283 and D. VanderZwaag, *The Management of Straddling Stocks: Stilling the Troubled Waters of the Grand Banks*, in D. VANDERZWAAG (ed.) CANADIAN OCEAN LAW AND POLICY (Butterworths, Toronto 1992) 115–139.

146 Regarding the collapse of the cod fishery, *see* G. D. Taylor, *The Collapse of the Northern Cod Fishery: A Historical Perspective* (1995) 18 DALHOUSIE LJ 13–22; A. T. Charles, *The Atlantic Groundfishery: Roots of Collapse* (1995) 18 DALHOUSIE LJ 65–83; and W. E. Schrank, *The Newfoundland Fishery: Ten Years After the Moratorium* (2005) 29 MAR POL 407–420.

particularly the possibility of unilateral action beyond 200 nautical miles.[147] The seizure of the Spanish trawler *Estai* outside of Canada's 200-nautical-mile zone in early 1995 for alleged breaches of regulations of the Northwest Atlantic Fisheries Organization (NAFO) was very popular in Canada.[148] Ratification of the LOS Convention was politically impossible without an acceptable fix to the issue of foreign fishing outside Canada's East Coast 200-nautical-mile zone. The answer was seen as being the 1995 Agreement Relating the Conservation and Management of Straddling Fish Stocks and High Migratory Fish Stocks.[149] In the fall of 2003, it became clear that the

---

147 T. L. McDorman, *Canada Ratifies the 1982 United Nations Convention on the Law of the Sea: At Last* (2004) 35 ODIL 103, 110.

148 In May 1994, Canada responded to the increasing evidence of fishing activity by non-NAFO members, internationally unregulated fishing activity, in waters adjacent to Canada's East Coast 200-nautical-mile zone with legislation and regulations designed to give Canada jurisdiction to address these alleged rogue fishers. Act to amend the Coastal Fisheries Protection Act, St Can 1994, c 14 and Coastal Fisheries Protection Regulations, amendment, Can Gaz Part II, Vol. 128, SOR/94-362, 25 May 1994, 2222–2227. Fisheries Minister Brian Tobin stated that the 1994 Canadian legislation was not designed to extend Canada's fisheries jurisdiction beyond 200 nautical miles; rather the action was necessary to prevent destruction of the fisheries in Canadian waters. Brian Tobin, HC, *Debates*, 11 May 1994, 4213–4214.

In March 1995, Canada modified its fishery regulations to allow for the arrest of Spanish and Portuguese vessels fishing outside of Canada's 200-nautical-mile zone. Coastal Fisheries Protection Regulations, amendment, Can Gaz Part II, Vol. 129, SOR/95-136, 3 March 1995, 650–654. The *Estai* was arrested outside 200 for allegedly harvesting turbot illegally. Canada justified its action on conservation grounds opining that the Spanish fleet was in the process of decimating the turbot stock and that aggressive Canadian action was necessary. The European Union protested the Canadian enforcement measures.

During the 1995 Easter weekend, Canada and the European Union reached an accord that ended the so-called turbot war. Canada—European Community: Agreed Minute, Brussels 20 April 1995, 34 ILM 1262–1272.

Spain, however, sought to bring Canada before the International Court. This was unsuccessful since Canada had altered its acceptance of the compulsory jurisdiction of the International Court to exempt fisheries actions outside of 200 nautical miles. *Fisheries Jurisdiction Case (Spain v. Canada)*, [1998] ICJ Rep. 342.

See P. M. Saunders, *Jurisdiction and Principle in the Implementation of the Law of the Sea: The Case of Straddling Stocks*, in C. CARMODY, Y. IWASAWA, AND S. RHODES, (eds.) TRILATERAL PERSPECTIVES ON INTERNATIONAL LEGAL ISSUES: CONFLICT AND COHERENCE (American Society of International Law, Washington 2003) 382–393; C. C. Joyner, *On the Borderline? Canadian Activism in the Grand Banks*, in O. S. STOKKE (ed.) GOVERNING HIGH SEAS FISHERIES: THE INTERPLAY OF GLOBAL AND REGIONAL REGIMES (Oxford University Press, Oxford 2001) 207–233; and T. L. McDorman, *Canada's Aggressive Fisheries Actions: Will They Improve the Climate For International Agreements* (1995) Vol. 2, No. 3 CANADIAN FOREIGN POLICY 5, 25–28.

149 Agreement for the Implementation of the Provisions of the United Nations Convention on the Law of the Sea Relating to the Conservation and Management of Straddling Fish Stocks and Highly Migratory Fish Stocks, New York, 4 August 1995, entered into force 11 December 2001, 2167 UNTS 3.

European Union and its member States, the principal fishing protagonists for Canada outside the East Coast 200-nautical-mile zone, were to become party to the Agreement.

Even with this fisheries fix, it was still not clear sailing for Canada's ratification. As noted above regarding the United States, and so too with Canada, the attainment of the most obvious benefits of the LOS Convention and the passage of time undermined any urgency for ratification and left promoters of ratification with only a scant few readily identifiable tangible benefits that would flow from ratification. For Canada, the case in favor of the LOS Convention was based ultimately on certainty, foreign policy, and closure, with the decision to ratify "seen as a necessary consequence and duty of being a responsible international citizen."[150]

4.0 Conclusion

In 1970, when the U. N. General Assembly called for the convening of UNCLOS III, Canada and the United States were diametrically opposed on a broad range of international ocean law issues. Canada was aggressively asserting offshore jurisdiction and the United States opposed the measures. Moreover, in 1970, Canada had acted unilaterally to pursue its ocean interests and the United States had objected strongly, preferring a more multilateral approach.

On substantive matters, during UNCLOS III, the differences between Canada and the United States either disappeared or were reconciled through conference compromises. Canada and the United States both supported and have benefited greatly from the 200- nautical-mile EEZ and the extension of exclusive national authority over the mineral resources and sedentary species of the continental margin where it extends beyond 200 nautical miles. Canada and the United States (with the Soviet Union) directly negotiated the Arctic exception, Article 234, that provides international support for Canada's AWPPA. On issues where the United States supported navigational rights and Canada sought greater coastal State pollution controls, the U.S. position usually prevailed. Canada, however, may not have been as concerned once the Arctic clause was accepted. On the politically divisive issues regarding deep seabed mining, Canada attempted to be a middle player between the

150 McDorman, *supra* note 147, at 111.

United States and other industrialized States and the developing States (Group of 77).

During UNCLOS III, Canada and the United States, even when in apparent cooperation, were not often approaching issues from the same direction. The United States tended to look at issues taking into account its global considerations and responsibilities, in addition to specific domestic interests. With regard to UNCLOS III, the United States was preoccupied with the possible implications for the U. N. system and multilateralism, geopolitical engagement with the Soviet Union, confrontation with the developing world, and concern about bad precedents that could infect other agendas, as much as the specifics issues in question. Canada, however, was focused on the specifics of issues and how immediate Canadian national ocean interests could be achieved. The dichotomy was one of global and local considerations and responsibilities.

In 1982, Canada saw the LOS Convention as a triumph. Canada had been able to achieve almost all of its negotiating objectives, in particular as regards Arctic waters and offshore resource acquisition. The usual narrative is that Canada's success at UNCLOS III vindicated its 1970 actions as being part of the process of the developing new international law. It has been questioned, however, whether the 1970 unilateral actions forced the expenditure of significant effort at UNCLOS III to "extract Canada from the embarrassment of falling out of line with international developments."[151] Either way, Canada was one of the big winners under the Convention. As a consequence, the decision by the United States in the 1980s to abandon the LOS Convention was not well received by Canada.

Beyond providing an important context and the general international legal architecture, in most cases, the LOS Convention has no direct application to the specific issues that exist in the Canada-U.S. international ocean law relationship. As regards maritime boundaries, the areas of overlapping claims exist because Canada and the United States assert rights to an adjacent 200-nautical-mile zone and continental shelf. Although the basis of the national claims may be the LOS Convention, the Treaty provides little guidance respecting how two States are to reconcile overlapping claims.[152]

151 Buzan, *supra* note 59, at 176–177.

152 *See* LOS Convention, *supra* note 10, Arts 74 and 83. Art 74(1) states:

> The delimitation of the exclusive economic zone between States with opposite or adjacent coasts shall be effected by on the basis of international law, as referred to in Article 38 of the Statute of the International Court, in order to achieve an equitable solution.

As regards the principal rights of navigation disputes between Canada and the United States, for example, as regards the Northwest Passage, the legal issues in question involve whether the waters are historic internal waters or a strait used for international navigation. The LOS Convention is silent on the definition of or requirements for waters to be considered historic or if a waterway is a strait used for international navigation. Moreover, for both of these types of issues, even if both Canada and the United States were parties to the LOS Convention, compulsory third-party adjudicative dispute settlement respecting maritime boundaries or those "involving historic bays or titles" can be avoided if a State exercises an option to this effect.[153] Canada has exercised this option[154] and most likely so too will the United States at the time of accession to the Treaty.[155] Finally, as regards fisheries issues between Canada and the United States, the problems tend to involve sharing a resource that exists in the 200-nautical-mile zones of both States. The LOS Convention, beyond encouraging cooperation,[156] provides little guidance. The compulsory dispute settlement provisions of the LOS Convention do not apply to the exercise by a coastal State of rights over marine living resources within its 200-nautical-mile zone.[157]

153 *Id.* Art 298(1)(a)(i).

154 Declaration Made Upon Ratification, 7 November 2003, para 2, 53 LOSB 15.

155 Declarations and Understandings, *supra* note 137, s 2(2).

156 *See* LOS Convention, *supra* note 10, Arts 63(1), 64(1), 66(4).

157 *Id.* Art 297(3)(a).

FIVE

Canada–United States Maritime Boundaries

1.0 Introduction

There have been maritime boundary issues between Canada and the United States going back to the 1800s. The boundary issues, then as now, are a product of the geographical relationship of the two States. The water areas in dispute have expanded from the near shore before 1970 to the situation today, of overlapping claims that extended to 200 nautical miles from shore and even beyond to the continental shelf. Moreover, Canada and the United States have overlapping maritime claims in all four of the geographic locations where the States are salt water neighbors.

The singular feature of the longstanding situation of maritime boundary disputes between the two States is that, with one exception, ever since the time Canada took over conducting its own foreign relations from Great Britain, there has been no agreed bilateral delimitation between the two States. The exception is the agreement reached in 1925 to extend the maritime boundary 2,383 meters within the Grand Manan Channel between Grand Manan Island, New Brunswick, and Maine.[1] This can be contrasted with the large number of bilateral maritime boundary agreements that exist worldwide[2] and the number of bilateral agreements on maritime boundaries entered into by both Canada and the United States with their other neighbors.[3] The only agreed maritime boundary between the two States in the

1 Treaty regarding the Demarcation of the Boundary between the United States and Canada, Washington, 24 February 1925, entered into force 17 July 1925, Art 3, 43 LNTS 239.

2 V. Prescott and C. Schofield, The Maritime Political Boundaries of the World (Martinus Nijhoff, 2nd edition, Leiden 2005) 217–218 estimate that of the 427 potential maritime boundary situations, approximately 168 boundaries have been agreed.

3 The United States has entered into maritime boundary agreements with its North American neighbors, Russia, Cuba, and Mexico: Agreement between the United States and the Union of Soviet Socialist Republics on the Maritime Boundary, Washington, 1 June 1990, provisionally in force 15 June 1990, 29 ILM 941–945; Maritime Boundary Agreement between the United

modern international law of the sea era arose as a result of the 1984 *Gulf of Maine Case*, where the International Court constructed the maritime boundary.[4]

A second feature of the Canada-U.S. maritime boundary relationship is that the underlying issue in many of the boundary disputes has been access to fisheries. Throughout the 1800s, there was bilateral disagreement whether certain East Coast bays were under exclusive Canadian or British control or were open to U.S. fishers. This was finally resolved in the 1910 *North Atlantic Coast Fisheries Arbitration*.[5] During the 1960s, there emerged a policy of reciprocal fishing rights such that fishers from one State could fish unhindered in the newly claimed waters of the other. When Canada expanded its authority over adjacent fisheries in 1964 by the creation of a nine-nautical-mile fisheries zone adjacent to the three-nautical-mile territorial sea, U.S. fishing activity was exempted from the new law.[6] When the United States followed with

---

States and Cuba, Washington, 16 December 1977, provisionally in force 1 January 1978, 17 ILM 110–112 (the Agreement was to be provisionally in force for two years, but by exchange of notes, the provisional application of the Agreement has been extended every two years) (*See* J. A. Roach, R. W. Smith, and T. Malionek, *Cuba-United States* in D. A. Colson and R. W. Smith (eds.) International Maritime Boundaries, Vol. V (Martinus Nijhoff, Leiden 2005) 3555–3557); Treaty to Resolve Pending Boundary Differences and Maintain the Rio Grande and Colorado River as the International Boundary, Mexico City, 23 November 1970, entered into force 18 April 1972, 23 UST 373, TIAS 7313; Treaty of Maritime Boundaries between the United States and Mexico, Mexico City, 4 May 1978, entered into force 13 November 1997, 28 UST 5256, TIAS 8625; and Treaty between the United States and Mexico on the Delimitation of the Continental Shelf in the Western Gulf of Mexico beyond 200 nautical miles, Washington, 9 June 2000, entered into force 17 January 2001, TIAS 2143, 44 Law of the Sea Bulletin (LOSB) 71–75.

By agreement, Canada has partially delimited its maritime boundaries with its neighbor Denmark. Agreement relating to the Delimitation of the Continental Shelf between Greenland and Canada, Ottawa, 17 December 1973, entered into force 13 March 1974, CTS 1974/9. With France, the maritime boundary has been fully delimited by an agreement and as a result of arbitration. Agreement between Canada and France on their Mutual Fishing Relations, Ottawa, 27 March 1972, entered into force 27 March 1972, CTS 1979/37 and *Case Concerning Delimitation of Maritime Areas between Canada and France, (St. Pierre and Miquelon)*, 10 June 1992, 31 ILM 1149–1219.

4 *Delimitation of the Maritime Boundary in the Gulf of Maine Area (Canada v. United States)*, [1984] ICJ Rep. 246.

5 *Award of the Tribunal of Arbitration in the Question Relating to the North Atlantic Coast Fisheries*, 7 September 1910, xi RIAA 173. *See generally* Chapter Seven, section 1.0.

6 *See* Territorial Sea and Fishing Zone Act, St Can 1964–1965, c 22, ss 3, 4 and Coastal Fisheries Protection Regulation, amendment, Can Gaz Part II, Vol. 98, SOR/64-275, 17 July 1964, 723, s 1. *See* L. H. J. Legault, *Maritime Claims*, in R. St. J. Macdonald, G. L. Morris, and D. M. Johnston (eds.) Canadian Perspectives on International Law and Organization (University of Toronto Press, Toronto 1974) 383 and L.S. Parsons, Management of Marine Fisheries in Canada (National Research Council of Canada, Ottawa 1993) 227.

similar legislation in 1966,[7] an arrangement exempted Canadian fishers.[8] The establishment by both Canada and the United States of 200-nautical-miles fishing zones in 1977 put significant pressure on the policy of reciprocal fishing rights, with the last general East Coast reciprocal fishing agreement expiring in December 1977[9] and on the West Coast in 1981.[10] Access to fishing resources was the unquestioned motivator behind Canada and the United States agreeing to utilize the International Court in the *Gulf of Maine Case.*[11] Fisheries issues are not now as interrelated with Canada-U.S. maritime boundary matters as in the *Gulf of Maine Case* or more generally in the past, although they remain important.

A third feature of the bilateral relationship is the wonderful inconsistency of the positions taken with respect to maritime boundary claims by the two States. In 1977, both Canada and the United States precisely delineated the extent of their offshore jurisdiction for the first time with both States indicating that their published boundaries were without prejudice to negotiations or subsequent adjustment.[12] Respecting the published boundaries, equidistance

---

7 Act Establishing a Fisheries Zone Contiguous to the Territorial Sea, 80 US Stat. 908, Pub L. 89–658, codified at 16 USC 1091–1094.

8 *See* Note from the Department of State to the Embassy of Canada, 29 November 1966, in *Gulf of Maine Pleadings*, Vol. 4, Annex 34 to Counter-Memorial of the United States, 472 and R. M. LOGAN, CANADA, THE UNITED STATES, AND THE THIRD LAW OF THE SEA CONFERENCE (Canadian-American Committee, Montreal and Washington 1974) 34.

9 Reciprocal Fisheries Agreement, Washington, 24 February 1977, entered into force 26 July 1977, Art XVIII(2), CTS 1977/23, 28 UST 5571, TIAS 8648.

There was an interim reciprocal fisheries agreement reached in 1978 that was not formally concluded. The implementation of the arrangements collapsed almost immediately which resulted in Canada discontinuing provisional implementation. *See* E. B. Wang, *Canada—United States Fisheries and Maritime Boundary Negotiations: Diplomacy in Deep Water* (1981) Vol. 38 No. 6 BEHIND THE HEADLINES, 10–13.

10 Preservation of the Halibut Fishery of the Northern Pacific Ocean and Bering Sea and Fishing Off the West Coast of Canada, agreement by an exchange of notes, Washington, 29 March 1979, entered into force 29 March 1979, para 2, CTS 1979/27, 30 UST 4067, TIAS 9448.

11 *See* Chapter Five, section 3.1.

12 Fishery Conservation and Management Act (renamed the Magnuson Fishery Conservation and Management Act), 90 US Stat. 331, Pub L. 94–265, codified at 16 USC 1801–1882. For the delineation of the U.S. 200-nautical-mile zone adjacent to Canada, *see* Department of State, Maritime Boundaries between the United States and Canada, Public Notice 506, 4 November 1976, 41 Fed Reg 48619–48620, 15 ILM 1435–1436, superseded by Department of State, Exclusive Economic Zone and Maritime Boundaries, Public Notice 2237, 23 August 1995, 60 Fed Reg 43825–43829.

Fishing Zones of Canada (Zones 4 and 5) Order, Can Gaz Part II, Vol. 111, SOR/77-62, 1 January 1977, 115–120 replaced by Fishing Zones of Canada (Zones 4 and 5) Order, CRC (1978), Vol. XVIII, c 1548, 13741–13746 and Fishing Zones of Canada (Zone 6) Order, Can Gaz Part II, Vol. 111, SOR/77–173, 24 February 1977, 652–655, replaced by Fishing Zones of was the methodology of choice for both States, except where it was not. For the United States, equidistance was utilized on the Pacific and Arctic coasts but not in the Georges Bank area of the Gulf of Maine. For Canada, fidelity to equidistance occurred in the Gulf of Maine and the 200-nautical-mile areas seaward of Dixon Entrance and the Juan de Fuca Strait, but not within Dixon Entrance or in the Beaufort Sea. The issue of consistency of delineation method used by the two States was seen as important in the Gulf of Maine context,[13] but in the *Gulf of Maine Case* and subsequent international boundary cases, this has proved not to be of consequence.[14]

The fourth feature of the Canada-U.S. maritime boundary relationship is that, following the *Gulf of Maine Case*, the existence of areas of overlapping claims has not caused significant difficulty between the two States. The two States have been adept at overlooking the disputes and, in most cases, finding ways to circumvent the "issue" and cooperate on a functional and operational level. Because of this, it appears that there have been few or no discussions between the two governments in the last three decades seeking resolution of any of the maritime boundary disputes.

The last comprehensive discussions of Canada–United States maritime boundary issues occurred in the late 1970s. In 1977, implementation of 200-nautical-mile zones by Canada and the United States coupled with several fruitless maritime boundary meetings during the early 1970s[15] occasioned

---

Canada (zone 6) Order, CRC (1978), c 1549, 13747–13750. Zones 4 and 5 are on the East and West Coasts and Zone 6 is the Arctic.

13 *See* Lorne Clark, Deputy Negotiator for Maritime Boundaries Canada/U.S., HC, *Minutes of Proceedings and Evidence of the Standing Committee on Fisheries and Forestry*, 11 April 1978 (30th Parliament, 3rd Session, 1977–1978), Issue no. 15, 21–22, and D. M. McRae, *Canada and the Delimitation of Maritime Boundaries*, in D. M. McRae and G. Munro (eds.) Canadian Oceans Policy: National Strategies and the New Law of the Sea (University of British Columbia Press, Vancouver 1989) 153.

14 In the *Case Concerning Maritime Delimitation in the Area between Greenland and Jan Mayen (Denmark v. Norway* [1993] ICJ Rep. 38, paras 82–86, the International Court rejected the relevance of the treaty practice of Norway and Denmark in other ocean boundary disputes in resolving the dispute before them. J. I. Charney, *Progress in International Maritime Boundary Delimitation Law* (1994) 84 AJIL 227, 252 summarized this aspect of the decision stating that:

> (T)he Court stressed the uniqueness of each maritime boundary delimitation, the freedom of States to use different methods for different boundaries, and the rights of States to take political considerations into account when reaching a maritime boundary settlement.

15 *See* Clark, *supra* note 13, at 6 and B. G. Buzan and D. Middlemiss, *Canadian Foreign Policy and the Exploitation of the Seabed*, in B. Johnson and M. W. Zacher (eds.) Canadian Foreign Policy and the Law of the Sea (University of British Columbia Press, Vancouver 1977) 41.

the two governments to appoint Special Negotiators with the mandate "to reach a comprehensive settlement of U.S.-Canadian maritime boundaries and related fishery and hydrocarbon issues."[16] The Special Negotiators submitted a Joint Report in October 1977 recommending for the areas where the two countries had overlapping claims to 200-nautical-mile zones that the countries concentrate on negotiating cooperative fisheries, including the retention of reciprocal fishing privileges and hydrocarbon arrangements, and leaving the delimitation of maritime boundaries to a later stage.[17] As a result, the October 1977 Joint Report contained detailed proposed principles respecting fisheries that involved joint management and a bilateral fisheries commission with an Atlantic and Pacific panel, and respecting hydrocarbon resources, that involved shared-access zones.[18] This was an innovative approach to addressing overlapping ocean claims with the potential fisheries and hydrocarbon arrangements designed to minimize the importance of the maritime boundary by dealing directly and cooperatively with the resources and their users.[19] As detailed below, the Special Negotiators were able to announce a transboundary fisheries agreement for the East Coast[20] that ultimately was not accepted by the United States and, reportedly, a West Coast agreement was also worked out but was unacceptable to Canadian fisheries advisors.[21]

---

16 United States—Canada Maritime Boundaries and related Resource Issues: Designation of Lloyd N. Cutler as the President's Special Representative for Negotiations, 27 July 1977, in PUBLIC PAPERS OF JIMMY CARTER 1977 (U,S. Government Printing Office, 1978) 1362. *See also* Wang, *supra* note 9, at 4.

17 Department of External Affairs, Joint Report by Chief Negotiators of Canada—U.S. Maritime Boundaries and Related Resource Issues, 21 October 1977, attached to the Department of External Affairs document is the Joint Report of Ambassador Cadieux and Ambassador Cutler to the Governments of Canada and the United States: Negotiations on Maritime Boundaries and Related Resource Issues, both are reprinted in *Minutes Committee on Fisheries*, *supra* note 13, appendix. *See also* Clark, *supra* note 13, at 6–7 and Wang, *supra* note 9, at 10.

18 Joint Report of Cadieux and Cutler, *supra* note 17.

19 Parsons, *supra* note 6, at 322 comments: "The approach was to design resource access and allocation arrangements which would be considered as fair no matter where the boundary was."

20 Agreement on East Coast Fishery Resources, Washington, 29 March 1979, U.S. Senate, Executive Document V, 96th Congress, 1st Session (1979), in M. NORDQUIST AND K. R. SIMMONDS (eds.) NEW DIRECTIONS IN THE LAW OF THE SEA, Vol. IX (Oceana Publications, Dobbs Ferry, 1980) 178–212. *See* Chapter Five, section 3.1.

21 D.R. Bollivar, Associate Director, International Fisheries Branch, Department of Fisheries and Environment, HC, *Minutes of Proceedings and Evidence of the Standing Committee on Fisheries and Forestry*, 23 February 1979, (30th Parliament, 4th Session, 1978–1979), Issue no. 6, at 5.

Despite the best efforts of the negotiators, in the end the overlapping maritime boundaries could not be ignored. First, "conflicting boundary claims gave rise to different perceptions of what was fair and reasonable in fisheries entitlements and shared access zones for hydrocarbon resources."[22] Second, ". . . maritime boundary claims . . . were charged with high political and indeed emotional content in the eyes of the constituencies affected on each side of the border."[23]

During the Special Negotiators' discussions in 1977 to 1978, the Canada-U.S. maritime disputed areas on the Atlantic, Pacific, and the Arctic Oceans were all on the table. The context of the boundary discussions was that they were part of a package with the fisheries and hydrocarbons initiatives. Although Canada provided assurances to its domestic constituencies that no tradeoffs of Atlantic-Pacific regions would be undertaken, some tradeoff of the Canadian position in the Beaufort Sea was seen as acceptable.[24] The discussions on maritime boundaries were described as being about "concepts, general principles, general directions of movements" rather than about precise proposals.[25] Canada's position was that equidistance was the appropriate methodology to be utilized, whereas the United States was less enamored with equidistance, particularly in the Gulf of Maine area.[26] British Columbia made clear its dissatisfaction with the position being taken by the government of Canada regarding the maritime boundaries in and beyond the Dixon Entrance and in the area seaward of the Juan de Fuca Strait, which stalled discussions.[27] In late 1978, the Special Negotiators were instructed to focus their attention on the East Coast and to disconnect the Atlantic from the Pacific and Arctic Ocean issues primarily because of the large area in dispute and the "greater potential for confrontation" that existed in the Gulf of Maine.[28] Ultimately, the negotiations led to the agreement to send the Gulf of Maine maritime boundary dispute to the International Court.

---

22 Parsons, *supra* note 6, at 322.

23 Wang, *supra* note 9, at 8–9.

24 Clark, *supra* note 13, at 8 stated: "In the Beaufort Sea the Canadian position is flexible in the context of an overall agreement, provided that balanced United States concessions are forthcoming elsewhere."

25 B. G. Hankey, Secretary, Negotiations for Maritime Boundaries Canada/U.S., House of Commons, *Minutes Committee on Fisheries, supra* note 13, at 18–19.

26 Clark, *supra* note 13, at 7–8 and M.B. Feldman and D. Colson, *The Maritime Boundaries of the United States* (1981) 75 AJIL 729, 750, 754–760.

27 Wang, *supra* note 9, at 25–26 and McRae, *supra* note 13, at 153. *See Submission of British Columbia on West Coast Maritime Boundaries between Canada and the United States* (1977), on file with the author.

28 Wang, *supra* note 9, at 15.

Following the *Gulf of Maine Case*, the United States broached the possibility with Canada of formal discussions on the remaining unsettled maritime boundaries.[29] The Canadian government found that there was little appetite on the West Coast for commencement of discussions[30] and no subsequent comprehensive formal talks have taken place.

Part A of this chapter looks at the agreed maritime boundaries that exist between Canada and the United States. Three of these boundaries date back a century or more with the most recent being as a result of the 1984 *Gulf of Maine Case*. A bilateral ocean boundary solves disputes respecting the geographic reach of national laws but the boundary area can still be one of dispute as a result of fish species (and fishers) crossing the borders and the impact that ocean activities on one side of the border can have on the other side. Some of these issues are explored as regards the Gulf of Maine boundary.

Part B of this chapter looks at the maritime boundary disputes that exist between Canada and the United States. Four of the five overlapping claims involve modest areas; three have strong historic elements; two primarily engage fisheries matters; and two others are principally about hydrocarbon resources. A large section of Part B is devoted to an exposition on the current international law as derived from adjudication on maritime boundary delimitation since this is the context for future negotiations and other options respecting the unresolved maritime boundaries.

PART A

2.0 Agreed Canada-U.S. Maritime Boundaries

2.1 Juan de Fuca Strait

A maritime boundary exists between Canada and the United States in the waters between Vancouver Island and the state of Washington that

---

29 J. D. Negroponte, *Current Developments in the U.S. Oceans Policy*, in DEPARTMENT OF STATE BULLETIN, September 1986, Vol. 84, No. 2114, 86 and Department of External Affairs, Some Examples of Current Issues of International Law of Particular Importance to Canada, (October, 1986), at 16, cited in D. Russell, *International Ocean Boundary Issues and Management Arrangements*, in D. VANDERZWAAG (ed.) CANADIAN OCEAN LAW AND POLICY (Butterworths, Toronto 1992) 494.

30 Some Examples of Current Issues, *supra* note 29, at 16 cited in Russell, *supra* note 29, at 494.

originates in the 1846 Oregon Treaty.[31] The Treaty provided that the maritime boundary in the Juan de Fuca Strait was to follow the middle of the channel and that navigation in the Strait was to "remain free and open to both parties."[32] Disagreement arose between Great Britain and the United States respecting the location of the channel through the San Juan Islands located east of Vancouver Island and west of Washington state. In 1871, the Emperor of Germany was asked to resolve the controversy[33] and, in 1872, the Emperor sided with the United States.[34] In 1873, Great Britain and the United States reached a final agreement on the implementation of the 1846 Oregon Treaty, and the 1872 *Arbitration Award* and the maritime boundary was demarcated.[35]

The 1846 Oregon Treaty was the completion of the 1818 Agreement between Great Britain and the United States, according to which the forty-ninth parallel was established as the land boundary from the Lake of the Woods to the Rocky Mountains.[36] Although the United States wanted to extend the forty-ninth parallel to the Pacific Ocean, Great Britain was unwilling to do so.[37] As a compromise, it was agreed to leave the area west of the Rocky Mountains, the Oregon Territory, "free and open" to the citizens and vessels of both States.[38] Intrigue, political machinations and perceived threats of armed conflict all played their role in the attainment of the 1846 Oregon Treaty.[39] Four key aspects of 1846 Treaty were the extension of the forty-ninth

---

31 Treaty Establishing the Boundary in the Territory on the Northwest Coast of America Lying Westward of the Rocky Mountains, Washington, 15 June 1846, entered into force 5 August 1846, 100 Con. TS 39.

32 *Id.* Art I.

33 Treaty for the Amicable Settlement of All Causes of Difference, Washington 8 May 1871, entered into force 17 June 1871, Art XXXIV, 143 Con. TS 145.

34 *Award of the Emperor of Germany Under the XXXIVth Article of the Treaty of May 8, 1871, Giving the Island of San Juan to the United States*, in J. H. Haskell (ed.) United States Treaties and Conventions, 1776–1889 (U.S. Government Printing Office, 1889) 494.

35 Protocol defining the Boundary Line through the Canal de Haro (Haro Strait), Washington, 10 March 1873, entered into force 10 March 1973, 146 Con. TS 35–39.

36 Convention of Commerce, London, 20 October 1818, entered into force 30 January 1819, Art II, 69 Con. TS 294.

37 *See* H. G. Classen, Thrust and Counterthrust: The Genesis of the Canada—United States Boundary (Longmans Canada, Don Mills, Ontario 1965) 112–122.

38 Convention of Commerce of 1818, *supra* note 36, Art III.

This aspect of the Agreement was to be for a ten-year period. In 1827, a further agreement was reached extending the Oregon Territory "free and open" provision until such time that agreement could be reached. Convention Continuing In Force Article 3 of the Convention of 20 October 1818, London, 6 August 1827, entered into force 15 May 1828, 77 Con. TS 366–367.

39 *See* Classen, *supra* note 37, at 161–208.

parallel to the Pacific Ocean; Vancouver Island being British; the maritime boundary being "the middle of the channel" of the waters between Vancouver Island and the United States; and those waters being "free and open" to the vessel traffic of both States. A major oversight with the hastily done Oregon Treaty was that no map was attached.

The difficulty that arose almost immediately between Great Britain and the United States was that, east of Vancouver Island, in the Strait of Georgia, there was not a single channel, rather there were two channels. One of the channels (Rosario Strait) is east of the San Juan Islands and the other (Haro Strait) put San Juan Island, Orcas Island, and Lopez Island on the U.S. side of the channel. Thus, the uncertain maritime boundary directly involved island ownership. It has been surmised that, in 1846, the geographic knowledge of the chief negotiators was "flagrantly incomplete," that both sides thought only one channel existed (albeit different channels), and that the existence of a more than one channel "seems never to have been understood."[40]

For the channel dispute and, in particular, the ownership of the San Juan Island, the period between the 1846 Oregon Treaty and the 1871 Agreement, which put the question of the "true meaning" of the 1846 Treaty wording to binding arbitration, was eventful. The most colorful event was the so-called "pig war" of 1859 that arose from the shooting by a U.S. citizen on San Juan Island of a pig owned by the Hudson's Bay Company.[41] Before cooler heads prevailed, the incident and its aftermath appeared to be leading to a war between British and U.S. forces. In 1860, a *modus vivendi* involving joint occupation, a British military outpost on the north of the Island, and a U.S. outpost on the south, calmed the situation.[42] Other activities involved: an unsuccessful joint boundary commission in 1856 to 1857;[43] an 1859 British proposed compromise that was rejected by the United States;[44] and an 1869 agreement to arbitrate that was not acted upon by the U.S. Senate.[45]

In 1870 to 1871, in order to attain better relations and avoid potential conflict, the United States and Great Britain sought to resolve all of their differences.

40 J. O. McCabe, The San Juan Boundary Question (University of Toronto Press, Toronto 1964) 4, 119–120.

41 *Id.* 37–38. *See also* Classen, *supra* note 37, at 217–270 and M. Vouri, The Pig War: Standoff at Griffin Bay (Griffin Bay Bookstore, Friday Harbour, Washington 1999).

42 *Id.* 53–56.

43 *Id.* 20–26.

44 *Id.* 27–35.

45 *Id.* 73–75 and see 63–65.

Many of these arose from actions taken during and in the aftermath of the U.S. Civil War, most prominently the claims for the British sinking of the *C.S.S. Alabama*.[46] Included in the list of matters was the San Juan maritime controversy. Although efforts were made to resolve the two channels issue,[47] ultimately what was agreed upon was arbitration on which of the two channels (Rosario Strait or Haro Strait) was "most in accordance with the true interpretation" of the 1846 Oregon Treaty.[48] The option of the arbitrator was narrowed to the emperors of Brazil or Germany, with the United States choosing the Emperor of Germany.[49]

The core of the British argument was that Rosario Strait was more readily navigable because it was less impeded by currents and that the intent of the 1846 Oregon Treaty, as evidenced in the preamble, was to resolve sovereignty issues in the area.[50] The U.S. view was that the Haro Strait was the wider, deeper, and shorter channel and, therefore, the navigable channel, and that the primary purpose of the 1846 Oregon Treaty was to have Vancouver Island be British.[51]

The Emperor of Germany submitted the dispute to three experts (a geographer and two lawyers), who delivered a majority and a minority report.[52] The German Emperor, in his binding decision, adopted the majority report, which agreed with the U.S. view respecting Haro Strait.[53]

---

46 The *C.S.S. Alabama* was one of several vessels built in Great Britain for the Confederacy, which inflicted serious damage on Union merchant shipping. The United States took the view that the construction and sale of the vessels by Great Britain was a violation of British neutrality in the U.S. Civil War. Pursuant to the 1871 Treaty for the Amicable Settlement of All Causes of Difference, *supra* note 33, Arts I-XVII, an arbitral tribunal was established, which eventually awarded the United States over $15 million. *See generally* A. COOK, THE ALABAMA CLAIMS: AMERICAN POLITICS AND ANGLO-AMERICAN RELATIONS, 1865–1872 (Cornell University Press, Ithaca 1975).

47 McCabe, *supra* note 40, at 86–102.

48 Treaty for the Amicable Settlement of All Causes of Difference, *supra* note 33, Arts XXXIV–XLII. A middle channel option (passing between San Juan Island and Lopez and Orcas Island) had been proposed by the British in the late 1850s, but the United States insisted, and the United Kingdom acquiesced, that the middle channel was not an option for the arbitration. McCabe, *supra* note 40, at 121 describes the decision by the United Kingdom to exclude the middle channel option as "inexplicable."

49 McCabe, *supra* note 40, at 102–103.

50 *Id.* 107 and see 108–119.

51 *Id.*

52 *Id.*

53 *Award of the Emperor of Germany*, *supra* note 34 and *see* McCabe, *supra* note 40, at 107.

In 1873, a final agreement was reached on the implementation of the 1846 Oregon Treaty, and the 1872 *Arbitration Award* and the maritime boundary was demarcated.[54] As a result of the boundary treaty reached between Great Britain and the United States in 1908,[55] the Canada-U.S. International Boundary Commission was given the task of re-examining the location of the maritime boundary established by the 1873 Agreement, which it completed in 1921.[56]

2.2 Passamaquoddy Bay

The Canada-U.S. maritime boundary from the mouth of the St. Croix River, through and beyond Passamaquoddy Bay, enclosed by the coasts of Maine and New Brunswick, is set out in three agreements: the 1908 boundary treaty between Great Britain and the United States;[57] the 1910 Treaty Fixing the Boundary Line in Passamaquoddy Bay, also reached between Great Britain and the United States;[58] and the 1925 United States and Canada Demarcation of the Boundary Treaty.[59]

There were two preliminary matters that had to be resolved before these agreements could be achieved. First, there was disagreement between the United States and Great Britain about whether the land boundary between Maine and New Brunswick should be the St. Croix River and related uncertainty about where the St. Croix River was located.[60] That the St. Croix River would be the boundary between the United States and the British colonies

54 Protocol defining the Boundary Line through the Canal de Haro, *supra* note 35.

55 Treaty respecting the Demarcation of the International Boundary with Canada, Washington, 11 April 1908, entered into force 4 June 1908, Art VIII, 206 Con. TS 377.

56 *See* International Boundary Commission (IBC), *Joint Report Upon the Survey and Demarcation of the Boundary Between the United States and Canada* (U.S. Government Printing Office, 1921) 28–42, 78–79.

57 Treaty respecting the Boundary with Canada, *supra* note 55, Art I.

58 Treaty Fixing the Boundary Line in Passamaquoddy Bay, Washington, 21 May 1910, entered into force 20 August 1910, Art I, USTS 551, C.I. Bevans, Treaties and Other International Agreements of the United States of America, 1776–1949, Vol. 12 (Department of State, 1974) 341.

59 Treaty regarding the Demarcation of the Boundary of 1925, *supra* note 1, Art III.

60 IBC, *Joint Report Upon the Survey and Demarcation of the Boundary between the United States and Canada from the Source of the St. Croix River to the Atlantic Ocean* (U.S. Government Printing Office, 1934), Appendix I, Historical Sketch of the International Boundary from the Source of the St. Croix River to the Atlantic Ocean, 135–142.

was set out in the 1783 Paris Treaty that concluded the U.S. Revolutionary War.[61] The location of the St. Croix River was not resolved until 1798 when the commissioners appointed by the two States pursuant to the 1794 Jay Treaty[62] issued their binding declaration.[63]

The second preliminary matter was the ownership of the islands in the Passamaquoddy Bay region. The key phraseology was from the 1783 Paris Treaty which indicated that all islands within twenty leagues of the U.S. coast were under U.S. sovereignty "excepting such islands as now are, or heretofore have been, within the limits of the . . . Province of Nova Scotia."[64] The division of the islands in the Passamaquoddy Bay region was decided by two commissioners appointed pursuant to the 1814 Treaty of Ghent[65] which concluded the War of 1812[66] with most of the islands in question going to the British colonies.

Concerns over the maritime boundary remained in abeyance until 1891, when a number of U.S. fishing vessels were seized by a Canadian fishery patrol vessel for allegedly fishing in Canadian waters within Passamaquoddy Bay.[67] Again, a joint commission was established.[68] Although they were able to agree on a maritime boundary for part of the area within Passamaquoddy Bay by relying on the principle "of giving equal water areas of the boundary waterways to each country,"[69] no agreement was ultimately concluded, in part because of an ownership dispute respecting Pope's Folly Island to the north of the channel between Maine and Campobello Island, New Brunswick.[70]

---

61 Definitive Treaty of Peace, Paris 3 September 1783, entered into force 9 April 1794, Art II, 48 Con. TS 487–489 and *see* Historical Sketch of the Boundary, *supra* note 60, at 142–143.

62 Treaty of Amity, Commerce and Navigation, London, 19 November 1794, entered into force 28 October 1795, Art V, 52 Con. TS 245–264.

63 Declaration of the Commissioners under the Fifth Article of the Treaty of 1794, October 25, 1798, Art V, 52 Con. TS 245–264. *See* Historical Sketch of the Boundary, *supra* note 60, at 143–146.

64 Paris Treaty, *supra* note 61, Art II. *See* further below: Chapter Five, section 5.5.1.

65 Treaty of Peace, Ghent, 24 December 1814, entered into force 17 February 1815, Art IV, 63 Con. TS 422–430.

66 Decision of the Commissioners under the Fourth Article of the Treaty of Ghent, 24 November 1817, in *Joint Report of the Boundary from the St. Croix River to the Atlantic Ocean*, *supra* note 60, Appendix II, Treaties and Conventions Pertaining to the Boundary Previous to the Treaty of 1908, 164. *See* Historical Sketch of the Boundary, *supra* note 60, at 146–150.

67 Historical Sketch of the Boundary, *supra* note 60, at 150.

68 Boundary Convention, Washington, 22 July 1892, entered into force 23 August 1892, Art II, 177 Con. TS 246–248.

69 Historical Sketch of the Boundary, *supra* note 60, at 151.

70 *Id.* 150–157.

PASSAMAQUODDY BAY MARITIME BOUNDARY

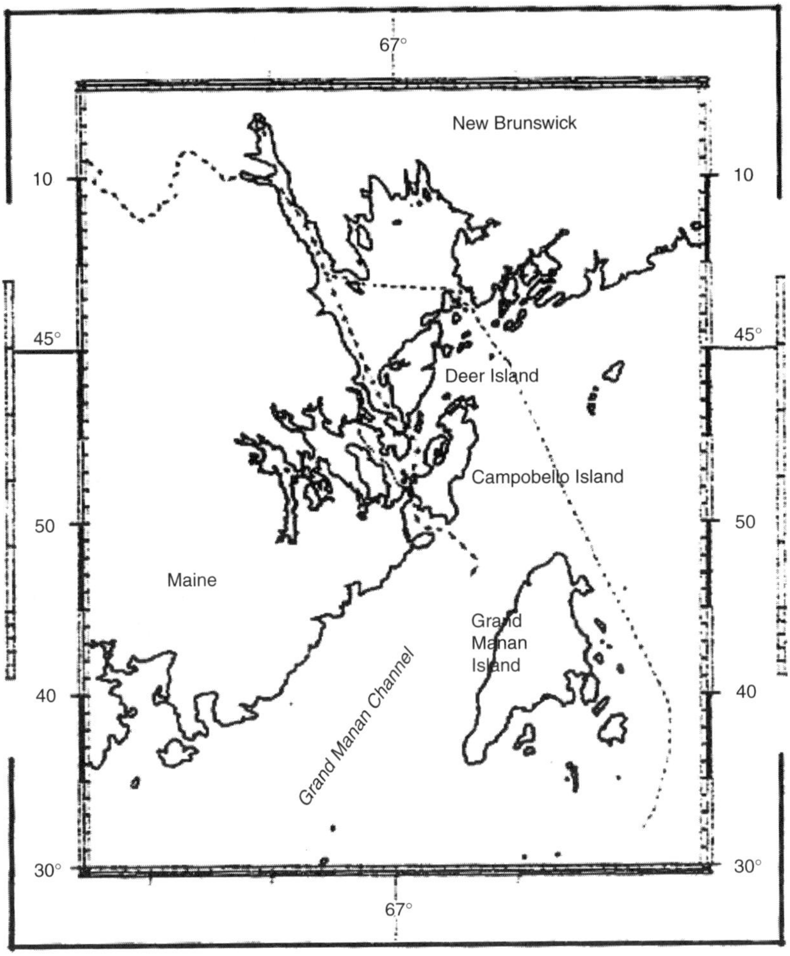

Source: DH Gray

The 1908 Boundary Treaty adopted the portions of the maritime boundary to which the above commissioners had agreed.[71] Another joint commission was to address the unresolved areas, with binding arbitration to be used if an accord was not attained.[72] In 1910, the commissioners agreed that Pope's Folly Island was part of the United States with a water area south of Lubec Channel, "Upper Middle Ground," being Canadian.[73] The 1910 Treaty

71 Treaty respecting the International Boundary with Canada, *supra* note 55, Art I.

72 *Id.*

73 Historical Sketch of the Boundary, *supra* note 60, at 157.

established the boundary through Lubec Channel (between Maine and Campobello Island) into the Grand Manan Channel.[74] The 1908 Boundary Treaty notes that, as regards the Lubec Narrows Channel, it "shall be equally free and open for the passage of ships, vessels, and boats of both parties."[75] Finally, it was discovered that the end point of the 1910 maritime boundary was less than three nautical miles from Grand Manan Island, New Brunswick, and the coast of Maine, thus leaving a territorial sea gap of 2,383 meters that was delineated in the 1925 Boundary Treaty.[76]

2.3 Portland Canal—The 1903 *Alaska Boundary Arbitration*

An often overlooked maritime boundary between Canada and the United States is the maritime boundary in the Portland Canal (Portland Channel), a lengthy fjord that reaches inland from the coast approximately 85 nautical miles to the Alaska-British Columbia land boundary terminus. In the 1825 Russia-Great Britain Boundary Treaty, the "line of demarcation between possessions" was described in the following terms: "the . . . line shall ascend to the north along the channel called the Portland Channel, as far as the point of the continent where it strikes the 56th degree of north latitude."[77] This wording was referred in the 1867 treaty transferring Alaska from Russia to the United States.[78] Because of islands at the mouth of the Portland Canal, it was uncertain precisely what channel was being referred to in the 1825 Treaty, and this became one of the major issues decided in the 1903 *Alaska Boundary Arbitration*.[79] It was the conclusion reached concerning the location of the Portland Channel through the islands, resulting in two Canadian/British

---

74 Treaty Fixing the Boundary in Passamaquoddy Bay, *supra* note 58, Art I.

75 Treaty respecting the International Boundary with Canada, *supra* note 55, Art I, para 6.

76 Historical Sketch of the Boundary, *supra* note 60, at 157–158 and Treaty regarding the Demarcation of the Boundary, *supra* note 1, Art III.

77 Convention between Great Britain and Russia Concerning the Limits of their Respective Possessions on the North-West Coast of America and the Navigation of the Pacific Ocean, St. Petersburg, 16 February 1825, Art III, 75 Con. TS 95–101.

78 Convention ceding Alaska between Russia and the United States, Washington 30 March 1867, entered into force, 20 June 1867, Art I, 134 Con. TS 331.

79 *Decision of the Alaska Boundary Tribunal under the Treaty of 24 January 1903 between the United States and Great Britain*, 20 October 1903, *Proceedings of the Alaska Boundary Tribunal*, U.S. Senate, 58th Cong., 2nd Session, Document 162, Vol. I, 29–97.

claimed islands being on the U.S. side, which created most of the furor in Canada that Great Britain had sold Canada out to the United States.[80] Implementation of the Arbitration decision was left to Canadian and U.S. boundary commissioners.[81]

The *Alaska Boundary Arbitration* was the culmination of three decades of disagreement involving Canada, Great Britain, and the United States respecting the boundary of the Alaska panhandle that arose out of the wording of the 1825 Treaty, in particular, the definition of the land boundary as following "the crest of the mountains situated parallel to the coast" and the uncertainty over the location of the Portland Canal.[82]

In 1903, Great Britain and the United States agreed to establish the Alaska Boundary Tribunal with the mandate to resolve these matters taking into consideration specific provisions of the 1825 Treaty between Great Britain and Russia.[83] The characterization of the tribunal as an arbitration and the number of members were both delicate issues. The United States was unwilling to adjudicate regarding U.S. territory; while Canada looked to adjudication as a way to save face in the event of a bad outcome.[84] It was agreed that the tribunal would be composed of six "impartial jurists of repute," three for each side, with a majority required for a decision.[85] As part of the process of obtaining U.S. Senate acceptance of the 1903 Treaty, the United States appointed to the tribunal three individuals who were "staunch defenders of American interests."[86] This was greeted by outrage in Canada and Great Britain. However, given the determination by the United States "to draw the boundary on essentially American terms,"[87] Great Britain accepted the appointees.[88]

---

80 *See generally* N. PENLINGTON, THE ALASKA BOUNDARY DISPUTE: A CRITICAL REAPPRAISAL (McGraw-Hill Ryerson, Toronto 1972) 103–108, 117–120.

81 *See* IBC, *Joint Report Upon the Survey and Demarcation of the Boundary between the United States and Canada from Tongass Passage to Mount St. Elias* (U.S. Government Printing Office, 1952) xiii–xiv.

82 *See generally* Penlington, *supra* note 80, at 17–47 and Classen, *supra* note 37, at 292–334.

83 Convention for the Adjustment of the Alaska Boundary, Washington, 24 January 1903, entered into force, 3 March 1903, 192 Con. TS 336–341.

84 Penlington, *supra* note 80, at 62–4, 70–71 and Classen, *supra* note 37, at 334–338.

85 Convention for the Adjustment of the Alaska Boundary, *supra* note 83, Art I.

86 Penlington, *supra* note 80, at 71–72.

87 *Id.* 75.

88 *Id.* 72–81 and Classen, *supra* note 37, at 338–339.

The Canadian-British appointments were all lawyers or judges, two from Canada and one, Lord Alverstone, from Great Britain.

Penlington's review of the creation and work of the tribunal, which includes reference to direct pressure from President Theodore Roosevelt on Great Britain, concludes that the tribunal was engaged in political compromise and not judicial discovery.[89] The three U.S. commissioners and two Canadian commissioners followed their national positions; Lord Alverstone was seen by the Canadians as the "umpire" between the competing claims.[90]

Regarding the mouth of the Portland Canal, the U.S. position was that the Canal followed the channel south of Kannaghunut Island, Sitklan Island, Wales Island, and Pearse Island. The Canadian-British view was that the channel was to the north of these islands. It appears that during the arbitration process, the United States and Great Britain agreed that the Portland Canal should split the islands, with the outer islands (Kannaghunut Island and Sitklan Island) being United States and the inner islands (Wales Island and Pearse Island) being Canadian-British. The British commissioner, Lord Alverstone, who had previously expressed the view that all the islands were Canadian-British, reversed himself and sided with the United States.[91]

The Arbitration identified the Portland Canal as commencing at 55 degrees 56 minutes north latitude and proceeding between Sitklan Island and Wales Island (Tongass Channel) and up the Portland Canal to the land terminus at the 56th degree of north latitude.[92] On a map, the Arbitration constructed a line from the center of the Canal point *B*, situated at the mouth of the Portland Canal, to point *C*, situated at the head of the Canal.[93] The Canadian-U.S. boundary commissioners determined the precise location of both points *B* and *C*[94] and delineated an equidistance line between these points through the Portland Canal, utilizing 28 boundary turning points.[95]

---

89 *Id.* 88–102.

90 *Id.* 93–94.

91 *Id.* 96–99 and Classen, *supra* note 37, at 346–347.

92 *Alaska Boundary Arbitration*, *supra* note 79, at 31.

93 *See Joint Report of the Boundary from Tongass Passage to Mount St. Elias*, *supra* note 81, at 31.

94 As regards Point *B*, *see* Agreements of the Commissioners as to the Manner in which the provisions of Article VI of the Convention of 1903, the Award of the Alaska Boundary Tribunal Appointed under that Convention, and the Exchange of Notes in 1905 between the Governments of the United States and Great Britain Should Be Carried Out, in *id.* 28–30, para IV. As regards Point *C*, *see id.* 43.

95 *Id.* xiv, 147.

PORTLAND CANAL BOUNDARY

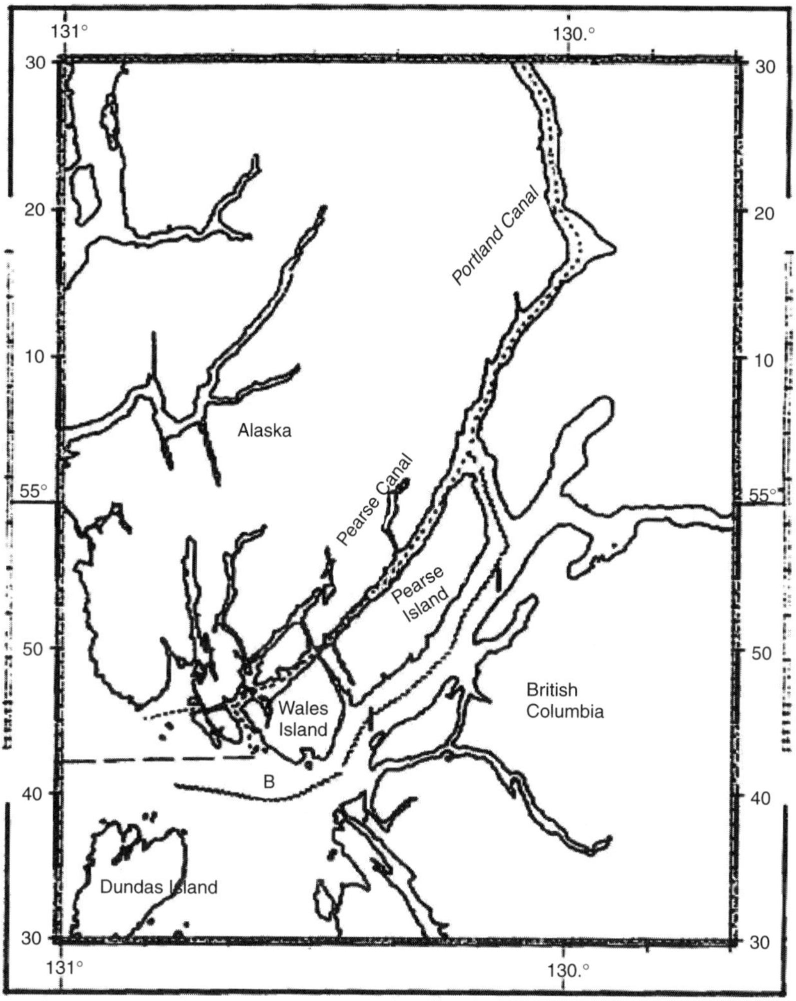

Source: DH Gray

3.0 The 1984 *Gulf of Maine Case*

The International Court, in 1984, established a final and binding maritime boundary between Canada and the United States in the Gulf of Maine.[96] The maritime boundary commences within the Gulf of Maine at a point that was mutually agreed by the States to be the starting point for the Court's line[97]

96 *Gulf of Maine Case, supra* note 4.

97 *Id.* para 20.

and proceeds in a southerly direction before turning in a southeasterly direction until it meets the U.S. 200-nautical-mile limit.[98] The *Gulf of Maine Case* is the only international adjudication to have taken place between Canada and the United States involving the International Court.[99]

The *Gulf of Maine Case* was novel for three other reasons. First, the case initiated use of the newly created chamber option of the International Court.[100] Second, the parties were for the first time requesting the Court to construct the maritime boundary between the States.[101] In the previous international adjudications, the International Court had been requested to give direction to the parties regarding the international legal rules and principles to be applied in the actual delineation. Third, and of most importance, the Court was requested by the parties to delimit a single maritime boundary for both the seabed and adjacent waters.[102] Previous cases had only involved the continental shelf, which had its origins in the 1940s; whereas

---

98 *Id.* para 228.

99 The other well-known Canada-U.S. international adjudication is the *Trail Smelter Arbitration*. Canada and the United States agreed on a three-member arbitral panel to answer questions respecting allegations of damage done in Washington state from emissions from a copper smelter in Trail, British Columbia. Convention relating to Certain Complaints arising from the Operation of the Smelter at Trail, British Columbia, Ottawa, 15 April 1935, entered into force 3 August 1935, Arts II, III, CTS 1935/20, USTS 893, 162 LNTS 73. In accordance with Article IV, the Arbitral Tribunal was required to "apply the law and practice followed in dealing with cognate questions in the United States of America as well as international law and practice." The Arbitral Tribunal delivered two decisions, one in 1938 and the other in 1941. *Trail Smelter Arbitral Tribunal- Decision*, 16 April 1938 and *Decision*, 11 March 1941, iii RIAA 1911.

K. Mickelson, *Rereading Trail Smelter* (1993) 31 CYIL 219, 219–220 commented that the *Arbitration*:

> has come to occupy a prominent but somewhat mysterious position in the legal canon. While it is one of the best known and most frequently cited international decisions, and is regarded by many scholars as the fountainhead of modern international environmental law, it is more an object of reverence that a subject of analysis.

100 States can request that a chamber of five judges rather than the full Court hear a case. *See generally* S. Rosenne, The Law and Practice of the International Court, 1920–2005 (Martinus Nijhoff, 4th edition, Leiden 2006) 410–414, 1342–1357 and E. Valencia-Ospina, *The Use of Chambers of the International Court of Justice*, in V. Lowe and M. Fitzmaurice (eds.) Fifty Years of the International Court: Essays in Honour of Sir Robert Jennings (Cambridge University Press, Cambridge 1996) 503–527.

101 Agreement to Submit to Binding Dispute Settlement the Delimitation of the Maritime Boundary in the Gulf of Maine, Annex A, Special Agreement to Submit to a Chamber of the International Court of Justice the Delimitation of the Maritime Boundary in the Gulf of Maine, Washington, 29 March 1979, entered into force 20 November 1981, Art II(2), CTS 1981/35, 33 UST 2797, TIAS 10204, 1288 UNTS 27. The Special Agreement (1979/1981) is reproduced in the *Gulf of Maine Case*, *supra* note 4, at para 5.

102 The Special Agreement (1979/1981), *supra* note 101, Art II(1).

the 200-nautical-mile zone had emerged in the late 1970s, with the result that there was little State practice regarding a maritime boundary for both the seafloor and water column.

The 1982 U.N. Convention on the Law of the Sea (LOS Convention)[103] had recently been finalized and, while neither Canada nor the United States were parties to the Convention in 1984, the provisions in the Convention relating to maritime boundary delimitation were important in the *Gulf of Maine Case*. The negotiation of the provisions on maritime boundary delimitation (Articles 74(1) and 83(1)) was one of the hard-core issues at the Third United Nations Conference on the Law of the Sea (UNCLOS III).[104] The 1958 Geneva Convention on the Continental Shelf had set out "equidistance" subject to "special circumstances" as the general approach to maritime boundary delimitation.[105] In 1969, the International Court, in the *North Sea Continental Shelf Cases*, determined that this wording in the 1958 Convention was not part of customary international law and that no special status existed for equidistance as a methodology.[106] The 1977 *Anglo-French Maritime Boundary Arbitration* similarly dismissed the legal application of equidistance preferring instead to rely on equitable principles, although the equidistance methodology figured prominently in the results of the Tribunal.[107] At UNCLOS III, States sided either for or against having equidistance included within the provisions. Canada was firmly in the equidistance camp.[108] The United States was not aligned with either group, although it did not favor equidistance preferring the so-called equitable principles.[109] As a result of compromise, Articles 74(1) and 83(1) are intentionally opaque. They do not provide a privileged position to any criteria or methodology to be used by States or

103 U. N. Convention on the Law of the Sea, Montego Bay, Jamaica, 10 December 1982, entered into force 16 November 1994, 1833 UNTS 397.

104 *See* S. N. Nandan and S. Rosenne (eds.) United Nations Convention on the Law of the Sea, 1982: A Commentary, Vol. II (Martinus Nijhoff, Dordrecht 1993) 796–816.

105 Convention on the Continental Shelf, Geneva 29 April 1958, entered into force 10 June 1964, 499 UNTS 311, Art 6.

106 *North Sea Continental Shelf Cases (Denmark/The Netherlands v. Germany)*, [1969] ICJ Rep. 3, paras 60–81, 39–56.

107 *Arbitration between the United Kingdom and France on the Delimitation of the Continental Shelf*, 30 June 1977, 18 ILM 397, para 97.

108 R. Hage, *Canada and the Law of the Sea* (1984) 8 Mar Pol 2, 9.

109 Feldman and Colson, *supra* note 26, at 738, 749.

third-party adjudicators in effecting delimitation. The only identifiable criterion is that the result is to be "an equitable solution." Article 74(1)[110] states:

> The delimitation of the exclusive economic zone between States with opposite or adjacent coasts shall be effected by agreement on the basis of international law, as referred to in Article 38 of the Statute of the International Court of Justice, in order to achieve an equitable solution.

3.1 Getting to Court

The most interesting feature of the twists and turns that ultimately resulted in Canada and the United States accepting independent third-party adjudication of the Gulf of Maine boundary issue was the effort made by the two States to minimize the importance to the fishing industries of both countries of a divisive line in the water. Ultimately, however, that effort was unsuccessful.

Although the fishery was the driving issue regarding the Gulf of Maine dispute, initially the differences between Canada and the United States in the Gulf of Maine related to the continental shelf. In the early 1960s, Canada and the United States issued hydrocarbon exploration permits in the Gulf of Maine area.[111] The International Court took the view that the maritime boundary dispute between the two States "became clearly established" in 1969 when the United States formally protested the location of Canadian oil and gas permits issued in 1964.[112] At the time, the United States suggested a moratorium on hydrocarbon exploration activity in the disputed area, but this was rejected by Canada.[113] The early 1970s witnessed further actions and reactions by both States regarding oil and gas leases and lobster fishing that

---

110 *See also* LOS Convention, *supra* note 103, Art 83.

111 *Gulf of Maine Case*, *supra* note 4, at para 61. *See also* Buzan and Middlemiss, *supra* note 15, at 39 and Wang, *supra* note 9, at 20–21.

112 *Gulf of Maine Case*, *supra* note 4, at para 64. *See* Note from the Department of State to the Embassy of Canada, 5 November 1969, in *Gulf of Maine Pleadings*, Vol. 2, Annex 56 to Memorial of the United States, 356–357. In early 1970, the United States publicly indicated that it did not acquiesce or recognize Canada's claims regarding Georges Bank. Department of State, Public Notice 320, 12 February 1970, 35 Fed Reg 3301.

113 *Gulf of Maine Case*, *supra* note 4, at para 64. *See* Note from the Department of State, 5 November 1969, *supra* note 112, at 357 and Canada, Diplomatic Note No. 366, 1 December 1969, in *Gulf of Maine Pleadings*, Vol. 1, Annex 44 to Memorial of Canada, at p. 390.

involved the continental shelf.[114] At no time prior to the Court case did either country engage in or permit drilling activity in the disputed area, with both sides adhering to "an unwritten moratorium on offshore drilling."[115]

The public face of the Gulf of Maine dispute changed in 1977 when both States enacted 200-nautical-mile fishing zone legislation and formally delineated the location of their exclusive fishing zones.[116] The Georges Bank in the outer Gulf of Maine was transformed from an area of the high seas where fishers from both Canada and the United States (and many other countries) had operated to waters under the exclusive authority of either Canada or the United States. In 1977, the U.S. view was that all of Georges Bank was within its exclusive authority. Canada claimed the northeastern portion of Georges Bank as being under its exclusive authority.[117]

In anticipation of the establishment of 200-nautical-mile zones, Canada and the United States agreed on interim fishery arrangements for 1977 that expressly called for the continuation of "existing patterns;" no expansion or initiation of new fisheries; and, in the areas where there were overlapping boundary claims, each State would enforce its regulations only against its own vessels (flag State enforcement).[118] Implementation of the 1977 Fisheries Agreement did not go smoothly and, although a 1978 Interim Agreement was concluded, by mid 1978, it was disowned by both States.[119] As one participant noted, however, "out of the wreckage of the [1978] agreement one element was salvaged," flag State enforcement for fisheries would continue in the disputed area.[120]

---

114 *Gulf of Maine Case*, *supra* note 4, at paras 66 and 67. The regime of the continental shelf applies both to minerals in the shelf and sedentary species on the shelf. *See* Continental Shelf Convention, *supra* note 105, Art 2(4). Lobster is generally understood to be a sedentary specie.

115 Wang, *supra* note 9, at 24–25.

116 Magnuson Fishery Conservation and Management Act, *supra* note 12 and Maritime Boundaries between the United States and Canada, *supra* note 12; and Fishing Zones of Canada (Zones 4 and 5) Order, *supra* note 12 and Fishing Zones of Canada (Zone 6) Order, *supra* note 12.

117 *See* Maritime Boundaries between the United States and Canada, *supra* note 12 and Fishing Zones of Canada (Zones 4 and 5) Order, *supra* note 12.

118 Reciprocal Fisheries Agreement of 1977, *supra* note 9, Art IX. *See* Wang, *supra* note 9, at 4 and Parsons, *supra* note 6, at 322.

119 Wang, *supra* note 9, at 10–14 and Parsons, *supra* note 6, at 322.

120 Wang, *supra* note 9, at 13–14.

1977 CLAIMED MARITIME BOUNDARIES IN THE GULF OF MAINE

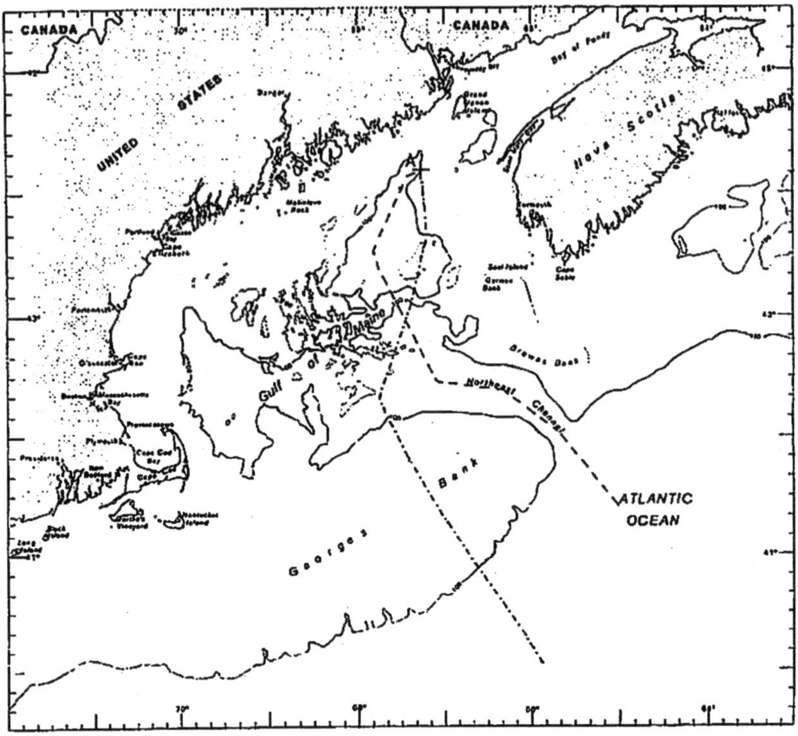

United States line - - - - - - -
Canadian line - · - · - · - ·

Source: Gulf of Maine Case, [1984] ICJ Rep. 246, 285.

Canada and the United States first formally discussed the Gulf of Maine dispute in 1970 and then again in 1975 to 1976.[121] More comprehensively, the Special Negotiators appointed in 1977 "to reach a comprehensive settlement of U.S.-Canadian maritime boundaries and related fishery and hydrocarbon issues,"[122] in addition to negotiating the 1978 Interim Fisheries Agreement, were engaged in seeking a long-term agreement respecting the Gulf of Maine and the other maritime boundary disputes. The Special Negotiators' Report

121 Clark, *supra* note 13, at 6; *Gulf of Maine Case*, *supra* note 4, at para 65; and Feldman and Colson, *supra* note 26, at 755–756.

122 Designation of Lloyd N. Cutler as the President's Special Representative for Negotiations, *supra* note 16. *See also* Wang, *supra* note 9, at 4.

of October 1977, endorsed by the two governments, contained proposed principles respecting fisheries, which involved joint management and a bilateral fisheries commission with an Atlantic and Pacific panel, and, respecting hydrocarbon resources, principles that involved shared-access zones.[123] The breakdown of the 1978 Interim Fisheries Agreement led the Special Negotiators to abandon discussions on hydrocarbon matters and to concentrate on fisheries, with a further refocusing taking place in late 1978 on the Gulf of Maine area rather than on Pacific and Arctic Coast issues.[124]

The outcome of the work of the Special Negotiators was two linked East Coast agreements: one on fisheries,[125] and the other to submit the maritime boundary question in the Gulf of Maine to binding international dispute settlement.[126] The East Coast Fisheries Agreement was a complex deal involving "an elaborate superstructure of entitlements, access areas, joint management authority and dispute settlement procedures."[127] The key feature of the Agreement was that:

> there was to be reciprocal access in perpetuity to all boundary stocks of interest to fishermen on both sides, *regardless* of where an agreed maritime boundary might eventually be drawn.[128] (*emphasis in original*)

This had been the negotiating goal of Canada–stability and certainty of access for fishermen, irrespective of the eventual location of the maritime boundary.[129] The linkage between the fisheries agreement and the Agreement to Adjudicate the Maritime Boundary was explicit in Article XXV(1) of the

---

123 Joint Report of Cadieux and Cutler, *supra* note 17.

124 Wang, *supra* note 9, at 14–15.

125 East Coast Fishery Agreement, *supra* note 20.

126 Agreement to Submit to Binding Dispute Settlement the Delimitation of the Maritime Boundary in the Gulf of Maine, Washington, 29 March 1979, U.S. Senate, Executive Document U, 96th Congress, 1st Session, (1979), in Nordquist and Simmonds, *supra* note 20, at 167–177.

127 Wang, *supra* note 9, at 17, and more generally regarding the 1979 East Coast Fisheries Agreement, at 17–20, and U.S. Senate, Executive Document U-V, 96th Congress, 1st Session, *Letter of Transmittal*, 18 April 1979, Secretary of State to the President, viii–xi. *See also* Parsons, *supra* note 6, at 324–327 and S-M. Rhee, *The Application of Equitable Principles to Resolve the United States—Canada Dispute Over East Coast Fishery* (1980) 21 HARVARD INTL LJ 667, 671–673.

128 Wang, *supra* note 9, at 17.

129 Parsons, *supra* note 6, at 327.

Fisheries Agreement, which provided that both Agreements were to enter into force at the same time.

The Agreement to Adjudicate the Maritime Boundary in the Gulf of Maine provided for the submission of the dispute to a chamber (as opposed to the full bench) of the International Court,[130] with Annex A spelling out the Special Agreement to Submit the Dispute to the International Court.[131] The Agreement also provided that, if within six months of its entry into force, the Chamber was not constituted or if a Chamber was constituted but a vacancy occurred and the vacancy could not be filled "in a manner acceptable" to Canada and the United States, either State could terminate the Agreement, whereupon the maritime boundary question would be submitted to a court of arbitration.[132] In either case, the maritime boundary to be constructed by the International Court or court of arbitration was to be "final and binding" on the two States.[133]

A significant portion of the fishing industry in New England was unimpressed with the insurance policy structure of the 1979 East Coast Fisheries Agreement. Opposition in the United States quickly formed and focused on the U.S. Senate that was constitutionally required to provide its consent in order for the United States to ratify the Agreement.[134] Canada was frustrated by the opposition, the delays in the Senate, the calls for renegotiation to placate U.S. concerns, and the aggressive fishing efforts by U.S. fishermen in the 1979 to 1980 period that were seen as undermining the Fisheries Agreement.[135] It became clear that without significant revision, which Canada opposed, the Senate would not consent to the East Coast Fisheries Agreement. As a result, in 1981, President Reagan withdrew the Agreement from the consideration

130 It appears that it was the United States that desired to utilize a Chamber of the International Court rather than the full Court. *See* D. R. Robinson, *The Convergence of Law and Diplomacy in United States—Canada Relations: The Precedent of the Gulf of Maine* Case (2000) 26 Canada—United States LJ 37, 43.

131 Agreement to Adjudicate the Maritime Boundary, *supra* note 126, Art I and Annex A, Special Agreement between Canada and the United States to Submit to a Chamber of the International Court of Justice the Delimitation of the Maritime Boundary in the Gulf of Maine.

132 Agreement to Adjudicate the Maritime Boundary, *supra* note 126, Arts II, III. *See* Annex B, Agreement between Canada and the United States to Submit to a Court of Arbitration the Delimitation of the Maritime Boundary in the Gulf of Maine.

133 Special Agreement to Submit to the International Court (1979), *supra* note 131, Art II(4) and Agreement to Submit to a Court of Arbitration, *supra* note 132, Art XII(1).

134 *See* Wang, *supra* note 9, at 30–33 and 41–44, and Parsons, *supra* note 6, at 327–328.

135 Wang, *supra* note 9, at 31–33.

of the Senate.[136] It is unnecessary to explore in detail why the 1979 East Coast Fisheries Agreement was opposed and ultimately failed,[137] except to note that, within the United States, the preference for the certainty of a maritime boundary played an important role, as did the willingness to gamble on the result of boundary adjudication.

At the same time the East Coast Fisheries Agreement was withdrawn from the U.S. Senate, the Reagan administration recommended proceeding with the Agreement to Adjudicate the Maritime Boundary in the Gulf of Maine.[138] The U.S. Senate approved, with several minor modifications, the Agreement to Adjudicate the Maritime Boundary in the Gulf of Maine in early 1981.[139] Though unhappy over the loss of the Fisheries Agreement, Canada accepted that east coast fisheries peace would only come with a maritime boundary. In November 1981, Canada and the United States exchanged instruments of ratification of the slightly amended version of the 1979 Agreement to Adjudicate the Maritime Boundary in the Gulf of Maine.[140]

Part of the boundary adjudication agreement process was careful negotiation on the composition of the five-member Chamber of the International Court. This raised concerns within the Court regarding independence and interference by litigants, but in the end the Court decided to proceed with the case.[141]

---

136 U.S. Senate, Executive Report No. 5, 97th Congress, 1st Session, Maritime Boundary Settlement with Canada (1981), 2.

137 *See* Parsons, *supra* note 6, at 328 and Maritime Boundary Settlement with Canada, *supra* note 136, 1–2. *See, more generally*, Rhee, *supra* note 127, at 673–680; D. L. VANDERZWAAG, THE FISH FEUD: THE U.S. AND CANADIAN BOUNDARY DISPUTE (Lexington Books, Toronto 1983) 89–94; and C. F. DORAN, FORGOTTEN PARTNERSHIP: U.S.–CANADIAN RELATIONS TODAY (The Johns Hopkins University Press, Baltimore 1984) 199–203.

138 Maritime Boundary Settlement with Canada, *supra* note 136, at 2.

139 Note Feldman and Colson, *supra* note 26, at 761 and Maritime Boundary Settlement with Canada, *supra* note 136, at 3–4.

The principal technical change occurred in Article I of the Special Agreement to Submit to the International Court, which dealt with the composition of the Chamber of the Court. The 1979 version indicated that the Chamber of the International Court was to be composed of three members of the Court and two *ad hoc* judges not nationals of their State (Art I(2)). The 1981 version of Article I indicated that the Chamber was to be composed of five members as provided for under the Statute of the International Court which meant four members of the Court (including the U.S. Judge on the Court) and an *ad hoc* Judge selected by Canada. *See* M. B. Feldman, *Testimony before the U.S. Senate Foreign Relations Committee,* 18 March 1981, in DEPARTMENT OF STATE BULLETIN, May 1981, Vol. 81, No. 2050, 23.

140 Agreement to Submit to Binding Dispute Settlement the Delimitation of the Maritime Boundary (1981), *supra* note 101. *See Gulf of Maine Case, supra* note 4, at para 5.

141 Note Robinson, *supra* note 130, at 43–44 and G. D. Nied, *International Adjudication: Settlement of the United States–Canada Maritime Boundary Dispute* (1982) 23 HARVARD INTL LJ 138, 141–142.

Unaddressed in the above narrative is why Canada and the United States accepted international adjudication to resolve the maritime boundary dispute in the Gulf of Maine given the prevailing, and subsequent, history of the two States avoiding adjudication on bilateral ocean matters. The following factors contributed to the acceptance by the two States of adjudication: the unwillingness of either the Canadian or U.S. governments to be tarred by the concerned domestic constituencies with having compromised the national position; an overwhelming necessity for the resource and the resource users to have a resolution regarding access; the understanding by the fishing communities in both countries of the gamble being taken by giving the decision on the boundary to third-party adjudicators; the belief on both sides of the strength of their legal positions; and the strong desire by the two governments to obtain a resolution of a significant irritant in the overall Canada-U.S. relationship.

3.2 Proposed Boundary Lines

From the earliest issuing of hydrocarbon permits in the 1960s, Canada took the view that the maritime boundary in the Gulf of Maine was a strict equidistance line.[142] The United States, however, took the view that the continental shelf boundary in the Gulf of Maine was the Northeast Channel as it constituted a break in the seafloor that separated Georges Bank from Browns Bank.[143] Originally these positions addressed the continental shelf, but both countries followed these positions in enacting and defining their 200-nautical-mile fishing zones in 1977.[144] The area in dispute was approximately 8,648 square nautical miles (29,663 square kilometers), most of which involved the fisheries-rich Georges Bank. The U.S. line deprived Canada of any access to Georges Bank, whereas the Canadian line placed about one-third of Georges Bank on the Canadian side. Although, as noted below, both

142 Diplomatic Note No. 626, 22 December 1976, in *Gulf of Maine Pleadings*, Vol. 1, Annex 46 to Memorial of Canada, 430–431. *See also* Wang, *supra* note 9, at 20 and *Gulf of Maine Case*, *supra* note 4, at para 61.

143 Note from the Department of State to the Embassy of Canada, 16 February 1977, in *Gulf of Maine Pleadings*, Vol. 2, Annex 66 to Memorial of the United States, 378. *See also* Feldman and Colson, *supra* note 26, at 755 and *Gulf of Maine Case*, *supra* note 4, at para 65.

144 *See* Magnuson Fishery Conservation and Management Act, *supra* note 12 and Maritime Boundaries between the United States and Canada, *supra* note 12; and Fishing Zones of Canada (Zones 4 and 5) Order, *supra* note 12.

countries subsequently proposed more expansive lines, it was the equidistance and the Northeast Channel lines that were the primary positions of the two countries. It is also to be noted that there is little indication during the bilateral negotiations in the 1970s that much flexibility was shown by either side as regards the conflicting claims in the Gulf of Maine.[145]

The 1958 Continental Shelf Convention, to which the United States became a party in 1961, provided some legal support for the primacy of equidistance in maritime boundary delimitation, subject to "special circumstances."[146] The United States took the view that the Northeast Channel constituted such a special circumstance and the use of equidistance created an inequitable result.[147] In 1970, Canada became a party to the Continental Shelf Convention, taking care to declare that the presence of "a depression or channel" was not to be considered as "an interruption" of the continental shelf.[148] The United States formally objected to the Canadian declaration.[149]

In the midst of the Special Negotiators discussions in 1977, Canada altered its claimed equidistance line in the light of the *Anglo-French Maritime Boundary Arbitration*, where the Tribunal had adjusted the equidistance line in the outer English Channel by giving only partial effect to the Scilly Islands.[150] Canada's claimed equidistance line was adjusted to the southwest by 14 nautical miles to reduce the effect of Cape Cod, Nantucket Island, and Martha's Vineyard on the construction of the line.[151] Not surprisingly, the United States rejected the revised Canadian claim.[152] In 1979, Canada

145 Clark, *supra* note 13, at 8 stated in 1978 that: "[I]n the Gulf of Maine, Canada is prepared to make only minimal concessions on the equidistance line."

146 Continental Shelf Convention, *supra* note 105, Art 6.

147 *Gulf of Maine Case, supra* note 4, at para 65 and Feldman and Colson, *supra* note 26, at 755.

148 *Gulf of Maine Case, supra* note 4, at para 65. *See also* Buzan and Middlemiss, *supra* note 15, at 40–41.

149 *Gulf of Maine Case, supra* note 4, at para 65.

150 *Anglo-French Arbitration, supra* note 107, at paras 243–251.

151 Diplomatic Note No. GNT-067, 3 November 1977, in *Gulf of Maine Pleadings*, Vol. 1, Annex 59 to Memorial of Canada, 452–454.

152 Note from the Department of State to the Embassy of Canada, 3 February 1978, in *Gulf of Maine Pleadings*, Vol. 2, Annex 70 to Memorial of the United States, 385–386. *See* Note from the Department of State to the Embassy of Canada, 20 September 1978 and Note from the Department of State to the Embassy of Canada, 15 February 1979, in *Gulf of Maine Pleadings*, Vol. 2, Annex 74 to Memorial of the United States, 396–398. *See also Gulf of Maine Case, supra* note 4, at paras 72, 74; Wang, *supra* note 9, at 22; and Feldman and Colson, *supra* note 26, at 758.

amended its legislation to reflect its revised equidistance claim,[153] although Canada indicated that it would not enforce its claim beyond the "strict" equidistance line.[154] It was this revised equidistance line that Canada put before the Chamber as the appropriate maritime boundary.[155]

At the beginning of the Court hearings, the United States indicated a correction in its proposed maritime boundary line. The new line put forward was one drawn perpendicular to the general direction of the New Hampshire and Maine coastline and then adjusted to avoid crossing Browns Bank and German Bank and dividing the "ecological unity" of these Canadian fishing grounds. The basis of the proposed line was the natural prolongation of the U.S. continental shelf.[156] This line, which started at the common point accepted by both parties, resulted in a proposed boundary to the northeast of the 1977 U.S. line using the Northeast Channel.[157]

The above dry recitation of the positions of the two States regarding maritime boundary lines overlooks the very real issue of the livelihoods of the fishermen of the region that were at stake. During the Court hearings, there was voluminous evidence presented on the socioeconomic aspects of the fishery relating to the various lines proposed by the States. In the end, the Court did not give much weight to these matters, despite the fact that it was the fishery that played the most significant role in the creation of the maritime dispute.

3.3 Judgment of the Court[158]

The decision of the Chamber was by a majority of four judges with one in dissent, and with one of the four majority judges (the U.S. Judge Stephen Schwebel) preferring a somewhat different line. The Chamber did not accept the lines proposed by either Canada or the United States.[159] Instead, the

153 Fishing Zones of Canada (Zones 4 and 5) Order, amendment, Can Gaz Part II, Vol. 113, SOR/79-107, 25 January 1979, 482–483. Wang, *supra* note 9, at 22–23 notes that this was done only when it became clear that negotiations on a Gulf of Maine boundary had been exhausted.

154 *Gulf of Maine Case*, *supra* note 4, at para 71.

155 *Id.* para 77.

156 *Id.* para 170 and Feldman and Colson, *supra* note 26, at 758–759.

157 *Id.* paras 73 and 77.

158 Parts of this section are drawn, with modification, from T. L. McDorman, P. M. Saunders, and D. L. VanderZwaag, *The Gulf of Maine Boundary: Dropping Anchor or Setting A Course?* (1985) 9 Mar Pol 90, 94, 96–99.

159 *Gulf of Maine Case*, *supra* note 4, at paras 164–189.

LINES PROPOSED BEFORE THE COURT

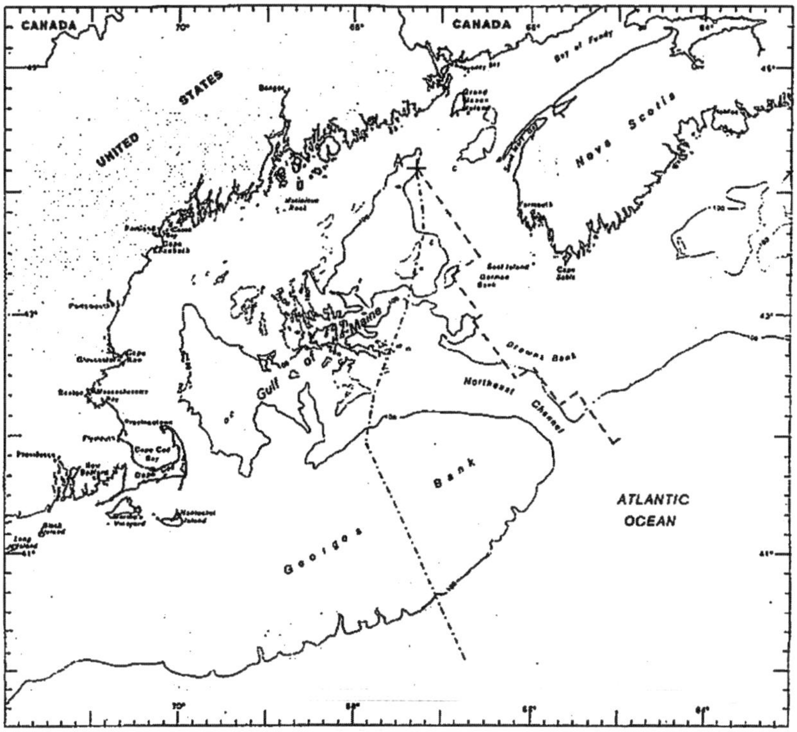

United States line - - - - - -

Canadian line - · - · - · -

Source: Gulf of Maine Case, [1984] ICJ Rep. 246, 289.

Court constructed a line that came close to an equal sharing of the principal area in dispute, with Canada attaining the northeast portion of Georges Bank.

Regarding the law to be applied, the Chamber noted that Canada and the United States were in substantial accord and that the agreed-upon "norm" was similar to that found by an analysis of the previous international cases and the conclusions reached at UNCLOS III.[160] The Court reformulated the international law with respect to maritime boundary delimitation as follows:

> What general international law prescribes in every maritime delimitation between neighbouring states . . . [can] . . . be defined as follows:
>
> (1) No maritime delimitation between States with opposite or adjacent coasts may be effected unilaterally by one of those States. Such delimitation

160 *Id.* paras 99–100.

> must be sought and effected by means of an agreement, following negotiations conducted in good faith and with the genuine intention of achieving a positive result. Where, however, such agreement cannot be achieved, delimitation should be effected by recourse to a third party possessing the necessary competence.
> (2) In either case, delimitation is to be effected by the application of equitable criteria and by the use of practical methods capable of ensuring, with regard to the geographic configuration of the area and other relevant circumstances, an equitable result.[161]

This statement of the law discarded earlier notions of equitable principles, special circumstances and equidistance, replacing them with equitable criteria, practical methods, and an emphasis upon "the geographic configuration of the area." What remained constant was the desire for an equitable result. Article 6 of the Continental Shelf Convention,[162] which provided that equidistance was the method to be used unless special circumstances dictated otherwise, was determined to be inapplicable since the Chamber was dealing not just with the continental shelf, but also the water column.[163]

The Court selected an equitable criterion which had not been suggested by either of the parties[164]—the equal division of those areas where the maritime projections of the States' coastal frontages overlapped. This approach was seen as being "intrinsically equitable" and appropriately simple,[165] as well as being a means for avoiding undue emphasis on either the continental shelf or the superjacent waters. The Chamber recognized the primacy accorded geography by the use of this criterion but justified this by stating that geography was of a "neutral character"[166] when applied in an equal division of coastal frontage projections.

Selection of the appropriate equitable criterion allowed the Court to proceed to the actual drawing of the line. This process required the choice of "practical methods" for implementing the equal division approach, a choice

---

161 *Id.* para 112.

162 Continental Shelf Convention, *supra* note 105, Art 6.

163 *Gulf of Maine Case, supra* note 4, at paras 115–125.

164 The criteria proposed by the parties are discussed, *id.* paras 164–189.

165 *Id.* para 197.

166 *Id.* para 194.

made more difficult by the fact that the Chamber found that no one method was adequate for all sections of the line. In the first part of the judgment, the Chamber visualizing the Gulf of Maine as a rectangle. The southern side was a line following the general direction of the coastline of Massachusetts from near Gloucester to Cape Cod. The first long side of the rectangle followed the coastline of Maine. The third side was the Canadian segment, drawn from the terminus of the U.S.-Canada land boundary across to the tip of Nova Scotia. The last long segment of the rectangle was an imaginary line joining the two most prominent seaward land points, Nantucket Island, Massachusetts, and Cape Sable, Nova Scotia. The parties agreed that this imaginary line constituted the "closing line" of the Gulf of Maine. The Court characterized this line as the boundary between the inner zone of the Gulf of Maine and the outer Atlantic Ocean zone.[167]

The decision sets out three distinct segments of the boundary line, the first two within the Gulf of Maine and the third involving the area beyond the closing line of the Gulf. The basic reasons for the definition of each section were geographic in nature. The first segment—the inner Gulf of Maine portion—was seen by the Chamber as delimiting an area where the coastlines of the two States were adjacent to each other. In the second part—the outer Gulf—the coastlines were characterized as opposite. Finally, the third portion would divide that area outside the Gulf of Maine.

In the inner Gulf of Maine, the Chamber had the agreed starting point (point *A*) and was left to set the direction of the line. Having rejected the use of equidistance because of the exaggerated effect accorded small rocks and low-tide elevations, as well as the fact that point *A* was not derived using equidistance,[168] the Chamber chose a geometrical method to effect the equal division of the inner Gulf of Maine. In essence, this method involved drawing two lines perpendicular to the respective relevant coastlines commencing at point *A*. The larger of the two angles formed by the intersection of these lines at point *A* (that is, the angle facing towards the Gulf) was bisected, with the bisector line determining the direction of the first segment of the boundary line.[169]

167 *Id.* paras 28–33.

168 Point *A* was chosen to avoid problems regarding the disputed sovereignty over Machias Seal Island and North Rock. Point *A* was the intersection of the Canada's equidistance line and the U.S. line that was based on the navigable channel. *See id.* paras 211, 20 and, *more generally*, Chapter Five, section 5.5.2.

169 *Id.* para 213.

LINE DRAWN BY THE COURT

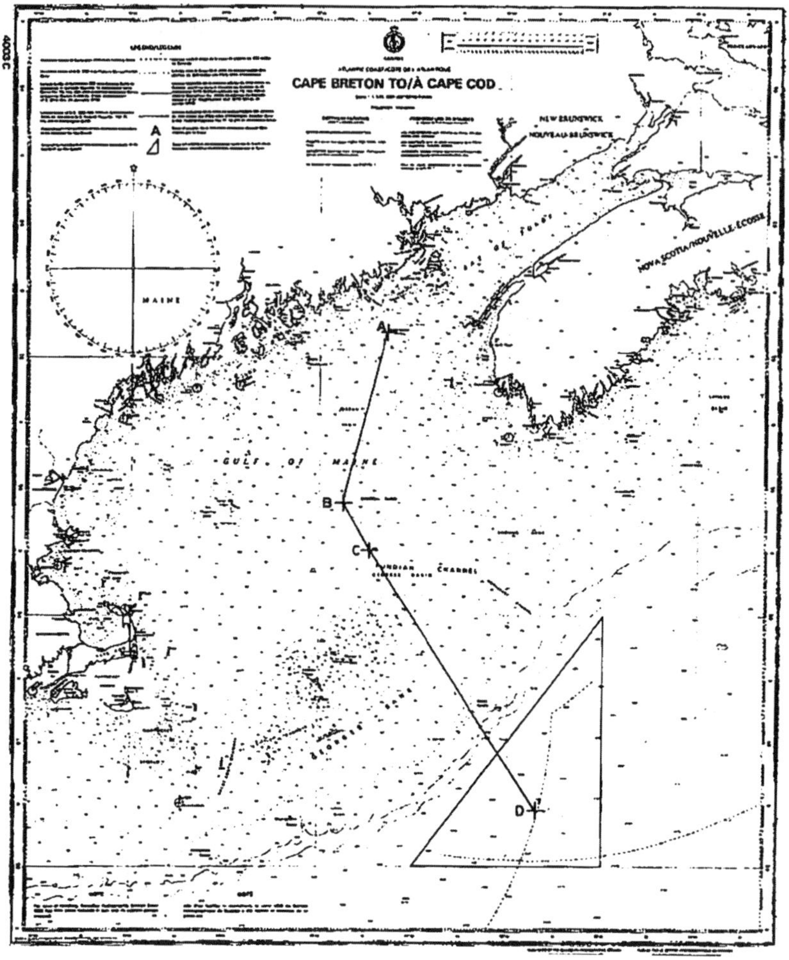

Source: Gulf of Maine Case, [1984] ICJ Rep. 246, 346.

In the outer Gulf section of the delimitation area, the Chamber viewed the relevant coastlines as opposite rather than adjacent. As a result, a different practical method was required. The opposition of the coastlines was used to justify the selection of an equidistance line parallel to the direction of the opposing coasts as the basic method of delimitation. As this line would ignore the significant differences in the lengths of the parties' coastlines bordering the affected area, the Court felt it necessary to correct or adjust the initial equidistance line through the use of an "auxiliary criterion," that of proportionality of coastline length to maritime area.[170] The use of proportionality was carefully defined as secondary to the concept of equal division, introduced only to "correct appropriately, on the basis of inequalities noted, the untoward consequences of applying a different main criterion."[171]

In calculating the proportionality ratio, the Court adopted a two-step approach. The Chamber first found the proportion of the relevant coastlines to be 1.38 to 1 in favor of the United States. As a second step, the Chamber adjusted the proportionality ratio to 1.32 to 1 by giving some effect to two small islands, Seal Island and Mud Island, off the coast of Nova Scotia.[172] The final coastline ratio of 1.32 to 1 was used to correct the initial equidistance line by the application of a simple practical method. First, the Chamber drew a line between the northeastern tip of Cape Cod and Chebogue Point in Nova Scotia (as the closest points on the opposite portions of the two coasts). The entire median line was then shifted southwest along the Cape Cod-Chebogue Point axis by a distance sufficient to reflect the 1.32 to 1 ratio.[173] The final result was a corrected equidistance line for the second segment of the boundary line extending to point *C* on the closing line of the Gulf. The intersection of this line and the first line drawn from point *A* was designated as the pivotal point (point *B*) for the change in direction of the boundary line within the Gulf of Maine.[174] Thus, the Court had established a line through points *A-B-C*, and it only remained to determine the direction and terminus of that segment of the line outside the Gulf.

The final segment of the boundary was drawn as a line perpendicular to the Gulf closing line, beginning at the point where the second segment intersected the closing line. The Chamber noted that this method produced a line of almost the same orientation (although not location) as the final-segment lines proposed by the parties, and saw "no reason for adopting a different orientation."[175] The terminus of this last portion of the line, which by the Special Agreement had to fall within the triangle defined by the parties, was set at the point where the third line intersected the outer limit of the overlapping 200-nautical-mile zone claims of the parties, in this case the 200-nautical-mile limit of the United States.[176]

---

170 *Id.* para 218 and note para 196.

171 *Id.* para 218.

172 *Id.* para 222.

173 *Id.* paras 222, 223.

174 *Id.* para 223.

175 *Id.* para 225.

176 *Id.* para 229.

Having determined the line utilizing equitable criteria, the Chamber tested whether the result was equitable. In making this determination the Chamber referred to the evidence presented regarding economic and human geography, indicating the importance of the area, particularly Georges Bank, to the States. These political and economic considerations, which encompassed fishing activities, hydrocarbon exploration, scientific research and defense, were not seen as legal considerations and hence were not considered as equitable criteria.[177]

Fishing was considered most important by the parties, but the Chamber dismissed the rival contentions of historic presence on Georges Bank and the relative importance of fishing in the economy of each country by noting that the key area, Georges Bank, had been high seas open to all prior to 1977, and that as a result no special rights could predate 1977.[178] In testing the equitableness of the line selected by the Court, recourse was had to the fisheries factor in that the Chamber asked itself whether the resulting delimitation would "unexpectedly be revealed as radically inequitable, that is to say, as likely to entail catastrophic repercussions for the livelihood and economic well-being of the population of the countries concerned."[179] No such dramatic result could be foreseen from the line as demarcated, and the Chamber went so far as to point out, in paragraph 238, that the line utilized gave each country the fisheries resources argued to be most important to its economy. Thus, the Chamber determined that its result was equitable.

3.4 Aftermath

3.4.1 Reaction

The Court decision came into effect in October 1984. The decision provided to Canada approximately one-sixth of Georges Bank. Some U.S. fishing interests were upset with the decision, with the result that the United States proposed both an interim arrangement to suspend implementation of the boundary for a year and a restoration of joint fishing activities.[180] Canadian fishing interests were generally pleased with the result, saw little need for

177 *Id.* paras 59, 232, 237.

178 *Id.* paras 233–236.

179 *Id.* para 237.

180 Parsons, *supra* note 6, at 333.

reciprocal fishing access and, thus, were cool to the U.S. overtures with the consequence that Canada rebuffed the United States.[181] This did not end U.S. pressure for a moratorium on the boundary. In 1985, the East Coast U.S. fishing community sought and eventually obtained countervailing duties against fish products from Canada, although this did not change Canada's position.[182] One Canadian commentator observed:

> Ironically, the U.S. fishermen who had scuttled the 1979 East Coast Fisheries Agreement were now attempting to ignore the Gulf of Maine boundary decision. These U.S. fishermen had gambled on winning all of Georges Bank and lost. Having made their bed, they would have to lie in it.[183]

3.4.2 Legal Precedent

The legal basis of the decision in the *Gulf of Maine Case* shunned equidistance as having any primacy or presumptive application. The Chamber put a premium on the physical facts and characteristics of the region in order to attain an "equitable result." One writer surveying the relevant case law up to 2003 indicates that the *Gulf of Maine Case* was the high point in autonomous equity and factualism with subsequent international cases, for the most part, more willing to adopt equidistance as a first step.[184] Another recent writer places the *Gulf of Maine Case* in the category of decisions using the result-oriented equity approach which is defined as rejecting any obligatory method for delimitation and stressing the equitable rights to be achieved; as opposed to the corrective equity approach which uses equidistance as a provisional step subject to correction.[185] The latter approach has dominated most of the recent international maritime boundary adjudications.[186]

---

181 *Id.* 333–334 and more generally 334–336.

182 *See* A. L. Springer, *Do Good Fences Make Good Neighbours? The Gulf of Maine Revisited* (1994) 6 Intl Environmental Affairs 223, 228.

183 Parsons, *supra* note 6, at 333.

184 R. Kolb, Case Law on Equitable Maritime Delimitation (Martinus Nijhoff, The Hague 2003) 537 and *see* 252–254.

185 Y. Tanaka, Predictability and Flexibility in the Law of Maritime Delimitation (Hart Publishing, Oxford 2006) 119–121.

186 *See* Chapter Five, section 4.2.

3.4.3 Fisheries Enforcement

In the years immediately following the *Gulf of Maine Case*, there was a high incidence of U.S. fishing vessels alleged to be crossing the line and a significant number charged by Canada with illegal fishing in its waters.[187] Canada increased the potential fines and armed its patrol vessels in order to reduce the incentive to fish in Canadian waters.[188] In order to calm the waters, the United States agreed to prosecute U.S. vessels for importing illegally caught fish, though the fines, if there was conviction, were small.[189] However, a 1989 incident in which Canadian-U.S. vessels collided and a cannon shot was fired across the bow of the fleeing U.S. vessel led to action by the two States.[190]

In 1990, Canada and the United States completed the Agreement on Fisheries Enforcement.[191] The 1990 Agreement obligated the two States to make it an offence under their national laws to fish in the waters of the other State without authorization,[192] an obligation that both States have implemented.[193] Article V of the 1990 Agreement specifically reaffirms the commitment of both States "to ensure full respect for the maritime boundaries between them delimited by mutual agreement or third-party dispute settlement, including by the International Court of Justice." Another part of the 1990 Agreement is the obligation to consult concerning its implementation,

---

187 Parsons, *supra* note 6, at 334; Springer, *supra* note 182, at 229; and G. J. Herbert, *Fisheries Relations in the Gulf of Maine: Implications of an Arbitrated Maritime Boundary* (1995) 19 Mar Pol 301, 311–313.

188 Parsons, *supra* note 6, at 334; Springer, *supra* note 182, at 229; and Herbert, *supra* note 187, at 314–315.

189 Springer, *supra* note 182, at 229.

190 *See Georges Bank Spawns Anger*, Calgary Herald, 13 December 1989, A-15 and *Deal signed to end U.S.-Canada fisheries war*, Toronto Globe and Mail, 27 September 1990, B-4. *See generally* Russell, supra note 29, at 480 and J. W. Lavers and I. S. Stewart, *Fisheries Surveillance and Enforcement*, in VanderZwaag, *supra* note 29, at 182–183.

191 Agreement on Fisheries Enforcement, Ottawa, 26 September 1990, entered into force 16 December 1991, CTS 1991/36, TIAS 11753.

192 *Id.* Art 1.

193 United States–Canada Fisheries Enforcement, implementation regulation of the Magnuson Fishery Conservation and Management Act, *supra* note 12, 50 Code of Federal Regulation 300.140–144.

United States Waters Fisheries Regulation, Can Gaz Part II, Vol. 125, SOR/91-660, 21 November 1991, 4241–4244, revoked in 1994 with the addition of provisions to the Fishery (General) Regulations, amendment, Can Gaz Part II, Vol. 128, SOR/94-296, 14 April 1994, 1818–1822.

including as regards "standard fisheries law enforcement practices in the vicinity of maritime boundaries."[194] This has resulted in yearly meetings of Canadian officials and the U.S. Coast Guard, which have enhanced cooperation and reduced the possibility of misunderstanding.[195]

The 1990 Agreement applies to both Atlantic and Pacific coasts. Unlike on the Atlantic coast, where U.S. vessels were allegedly illegally fishing in Canadian waters and scampering back to U.S. waters to evade prosecution, on the Pacific coast, Canadian fishers in the Juan de Fuca Strait area were using their home waters as a haven from U.S. prosecution.[196]

Since the early 1990s, there have been remarkably few instances of fishers of one State being arrested by the other in or near the Canada-U.S. maritime boundaries. This is seen as demonstrating the positive effect of the 1990 Agreement.[197]

3.4.4 Hydrocarbon Exploration Moratorium

As already noted, in the period leading to the *Gulf of Maine Case*, Canada and the United States adhered to "an unwritten moratorium on offshore drilling" on Georges Bank.[198] In the southern area of Georges Bank, however, the United States had permitted exploration drilling in the early 1980s.[199] This activity ended in 1982 with the United States adopting a series of one-year leasing moratoria for offshore drilling operations.[200]

The possible mixing of oil activities and fisheries on Georges Bank was a conflict issue domestically on both sides of the Gulf of Maine maritime boundary. Moreover, any offshore hydrocarbon operations on one side of the new boundary could have environmental consequences on the other side.

---

194 Fisheries Enforcement Agreement, *supra* note 191, Art II(c).

195 *See* U.S. Coast Guard, 17th Coast Guard District Enforcement Report, (Juneau, 2005), at <www.fakr.noaa.gov/npfmc/USCG/JUN05USCG.pdf> (accessed on 6 November 2006).

196 Springer, *supra* note 182, at 229.

197 D. Russell, D. VanderZwaag, E. Pudden, and T. Lowry, *Fisheries and Shellfish Sanitation*, in Department of Fisheries and Oceans, *Overview of Current Governance in the Bay of Fundy/Gulf of Maine: Transboundary Collaborative Arrangements and Initiatives* (May, 2006) 68.

198 Wang, *supra* note 9, at 24–25. *Note also* Herbert, *supra* note 187, at 315.

199 G. M. Edson, D. L. Olson, and A. J. Petty, *Georges Bank Petroleum Exploration: Atlantic Outer Continental Shelf* (OCS Report MMS 2000–031, May 2000) 1, at <www.gomr.mms.gov/PDFs/2000/2000-031.pdf> (accessed on 19 April 2007).

200 *Id.* 1–3.

Following the 1984 Court decision, a proposal was made for exploratory drilling on the Canadian side of the boundary[201] that apparently had some U.S. government support because a 1988 U.S. lease sale for Georges Bank was anticipated.[202] In 1988, however, Canada adopted a moratorium on drilling activity on Georges Bank to last until 2000.[203] In 1990, U.S. President Bush directed that no hydrocarbon leasing or development activity on Georges Bank would take place until after 2000.[204] As one writer notes, the Canadian and U.S. moratoria to 2000 were "not the result of direct U.S.—Canadian collaboration, but . . . [were] . . . not entirely coincidental."[205]

Under the Canadian legislation, a public review of the socioeconomic and environmental impacts of hydrocarbon development on Georges Bank was to be undertaken prior to a decision on the extension or removal of the moratorium in 2000.[206] The Georges Bank Review Panel reported in 1999 recommending against lifting the moratorium,[207] which was adopted by Canada such that the moratorium has been extended to 2012.[208] In 1998, U.S. President Clinton directed that the U.S. moratorium be extended to 2012.[209]

3.4.5 Cross-Boundary Fisheries Management

The failed 1979 East Coast Fisheries Agreement had identified a number of fish stocks on Georges Bank important to both Canadian and U.S. fishermen.

---

201 D. VanderZwaag, *Transbounday Challenges and Cooperation in the Gulf of Maine Region: Riding a Restless Sea Toward Misty Shores*, in H. N. SCHEIBER (ed.) LAW OF THE SEA: THE COMMON HERITAGE AND EMERGING CHALLENGES (Martinus Nijhoff, The Hague 2000) 267.

202 Springer, *supra* note 182, at 230.

203 Canada–Nova Scotia Offshore Petroleum Resources Accord Implementation Act, St Can 1988, c 28, s 141(1). *See* VanderZwaag, *supra* note 201, at 267.

204 Statement on Outer Continental Shelf Oil and Gas Development, 26 June 1990, in PUBLIC PAPERS OF GEORGE BUSH 1990 (U.S. Government Printing Office, 1991) 869–870.

205 Springer, *supra* note 182, at 230.

206 Canada–Nova Scotia Offshore Accord Implementation Act, *supra* note 203, s 141(2)–(7).

207 Department of Natural Resources and the Nova Scotia Petroleum Directorate, *Georges Bank Review Panel Report* (June 1999).

208 Department of Natural Resources, Georges Bank Moratorium Extended, 22 December 22, 1999, in Can Gaz Part I, Vol. 134, 29 January 2000, 274–276. *See* Canada–Nova Scotia Offshore Accord Implementation Act, *supra* note 203, s 141.

209 Memorandum on Withdrawal of Certain Areas of the United States Outer Continental Shelf from Leasing Deposition, 12 June 1998, in PUBLIC PAPERS OF WILLIAM J. CLINTON, 1998 (U.S. Government Printing Office, 1999) 945.

The 1984 maritime boundary artificially divided management responsibility for many of these stocks between Canada and the United States. The International Court noted, however, the long "tradition of friendly and fruitful co-operation in maritime matters" enjoyed by Canada and the United States and that this cooperation "now becomes all the more necessary . . . in the field of fisheries" and challenged the two States to once more join in such a common endeavor.[210] However, it is only in recent years that the two States have been able to attain cooperation and coordination of national management practices for a number of the transboundary Georges Banks stocks.

During the first decade after the *Gulf of Maine Case*, Canada and the United States "coordination of fisheries management strategies was virtually non-existent" respecting the transboundary fish stocks of Georges Banks, with the stocks suffering because of the lack of cooperation.[211] Both sides were aware of the need for some kind of cooperation respecting the key transboundary stocks but this produced only modest scientific information sharing.[212] One factor in the inertia was the recollection of the unhappy fate of the 1979 East Coast Fisheries Agreement, which had the effect of smothering any discussion of cooperative joint management.

Also identified as major a stumbling block was the different fishery management philosophies and structures within the two States.[213] Fisheries management in the United States, which for Georges Bank is under the authority of the New England Fisheries Management Council, has relied primarily on "input controls," meaning controls on fishing effort such as limited entry, mesh size restrictions, area and season closures, and restricted days-at-sea programs.[214] In Canada, fisheries management is under the authority of the Canadian Department of Fisheries and Oceans (DFO) and has relied

---

210 *Gulf of Maine Case*, *supra* note 4, at para 240.

211 Department of Fisheries and Oceans (DFO), Maritime Region, Transboundary Management Guidance Committee, *Development of a Sharing Allocation Proposal for Transboundary Resources of Cod, Haddock and Yellowtail Flounder on Georges Bank*, (Fisheries Management Regional Report 2002/01, January 2002) 3, at www.mar.dfo-mpo.gc.ca/science/tmgc/bacground/FMR%202002_01.pdf (accessed on 5 March 2007); Parsons, *supra* note 6, at 334–336; Springer, *supra* note 182, at 231–233; and Herbert, *supra* note 187, at 315–316.

212 Springer, *supra* note 182, at 234.

213 *Id.* 231–232 and Parsons, *supra* note 6, at 336. *See more generally*, VanderZwaag, *supra* note 137, at 37–87 and Herbert, *supra* note 187, at 310–311.

214 Transboundary Management Guidance Committee, *supra* note 211, at 7, Appendix 1, USA and Canadian Management Measures.

primarily on "output controls," meaning catch quotas, although many of the above-noted U.S. measures are also employed.[215]

Increased informal bilateral science and management contacts led to the creation in 1998 of the Transboundary Resource Assessment Committee, designed to coordinate and cooperate on stock evaluations and to ensure that the scientific advice used in management decisions by both States was "based on the best available combined information."[216] In 2000, the Transboundary Management Guidance Committee was formed, composed of six members (two from government and four from industry) from each State, "to provide non-binding guidance" respecting harvest levels and national catch allocations for cod, haddock and yellowtail flounder in the Gulf of Maine boundary area.[217]

Since 2003, the Transboundary Management Guidance Committee has been recommending the total allowable catch (TAC) for cod, haddock, and yellowtail flounder for the northeastern part of Georges Bank through which the maritime boundary passes and the sharing between Canada and the United States of the TAC and the two States have been implementing the recommendations.[218] For the 2007 fishing season, respecting cod, the TAC was set at 1,900 metric tons, with 74 percent for Canada and 26 percent for the United States; for haddock, the TAC was 19,000 metric tons, with 67 percent for Canada and 33 percent for the United States; and for yellowtail flounder, the TAC was 1,500 metric tons, with 28 percent for Canada and 72 percent for the United States.[219] Other commercial fisheries–herring, mackerel, halibut, dogfish and pollock–are either in process or under discussion

---

215 *Id.*

216 *Id.* 4. *See generally* Russell, *et al.*, *supra* note 197, at 57–59 and E. J. Pudden and D. L. VanderZwaag, *Canada–USA Bilateral Fisheries Management in the Gulf of Maine: Under the Radar Screen* (2007) 16 RECIEL 36, 37.

217 *Id.* 5–6. As stated at 6:

> The underlying motivation that fuelled the effort to reach an agreement was the recognition that each countries independent conservation actions could be compromised and that the full benefits of management actions were more likely to be realized if there was consistent management by the USA and Canada.

See generally Russell, *et al.*, *supra* note 197, at 59–62 and Pudden and VanderZwaag, *supra* note 216, at 37.

218 Pudden and VanderZwaag, *supra* note 216, at p. 38–40 and Russell, *et al.*, *supra* note 197, at 62–65.

219 DFO, Transboundary Management Guidance Committee, Guidance Document 2006/01, September 2006, at www.mar.dfo-mpo.gc.ca/science/tmgc/publications/GD2006_1_E.pdf (accessed on 5 March 2007).

for inclusion in the work of the Transboundary Management Guidance Committee.[220]

Although the work of the Canada–United States Transboundary Management Guidance Committee is not based on a bilateral treaty, and hence can be described as legally informal, the result is cross-border collaboration of fishing effort that, although a long time in coming, is welcomed.[221]

PART B

4.0 An Overview of Maritime Boundary Delimitation Law

4.1 State Practice

States are free to enter into agreements delimiting maritime boundaries of their liking with the result that States have entered into a large number of maritime boundary delimitation agreements.[222] There is, therefore, a significant State practice regarding maritime boundary delimitation. Moreover, on a number of occasions, States unable to reach delimitation agreements have engaged independent third-party adjudicative tribunals to either draw lines or provide assistance on the principles to be used to construct boundaries. The result is a body of adjudicative decisions that provide what is referred to as the international law of maritime boundary delimitation. Charney has commented:

> Even though there is no doctrine of *stare decisis* in international adjudication, it is not inaccurate to consider the impressive line of maritime boundary decisions as forming a common law in the classic sense. (footnotes deleted)[223]

---

220 Pudden and VanderZwaag, *supra* note 216, at 37.

221 *Id.* 41–43 applaud the informal process as being "positive on many fronts" but also criticize the bilateral arrangements for "falling short of modernization trends in ocean governance driven by sustainable development," noting in particular the "closed-shop" approach of the process.

222 *See* Prescott and Schofield, *supra* note 2, at 217–218.

223 Charney, *supra* note 14, at 228.

The international law of maritime boundary delimitation obviously plays an important role in adjudication with States arguing their cases by reference to it and tribunals required to apply it in reaching decisions. In bilateral negotiations, the international law of maritime boundary delimitation is also important. An assessment by a State of its legal position inevitably determines, or heavily influences, the position it will take in negotiations. Assessing the likelihood of success in adjudication based on maritime boundary delimitation law, even where such adjudication is highly unlikely, either strengthens or weakens a State's negotiating posture. Nevertheless, the practice of States is captured by this comment from a Canadian negotiator respecting discussions with the United States in the late 1970s: "The negotiations have . . . proceeded on the basis that strict legal principles should not stand in the way of an effort to seek a balanced, fair and equitable solution on the lines to be drawn."[224]

Before turning to the maritime boundary disputes that exist between Canada and the United States, a brief encapsulation of the existing international law on maritime boundary delimitation is provided.

4.2 The Law—The Two-Step Process[225]

Recent international adjudications have attained an impressive, but not totally uniform, consistency respecting the approach used by tribunals for maritime boundary delimitation involving a single maritime boundary for the exclusive economic zone (EEZ) and continental shelf. The Tribunal in the 2006 *Barbados-Trinidad and Tobago Arbitration* referred to the approach as the "equidistance/relevant circumstances" principle.[226] The Tribunal stated:

> The determination of the line of delimitation thus normally follows a two-step approach. First, a provisional line of equidistance is posited as a hypothesis and a practical starting point. While a convenient starting point, equidistance alone will in many circumstances not ensure an equitable result in the light of the peculiarities of each specific case. The second

---

224 Clark, *supra* note 13, at 8.

225 *See also* the Appendix to this Chapter, Questions and Detail Respecting the Application of the Two-Step Process.

226 *In the Matter of the Arbitration between Barbados and The Republic of Trinidad and Tobago*, 11 April 2006, 45 ILM 800, para 242.

> step accordingly requires the examination of this provisional line in the light of relevant circumstances, which are case specific, so as to determine whether it is necessary to adjust the provisional equidistance line in order to achieve an equitable result.[227]

This two-step approach has been explicitly utilized in: the 1993 *Case Concerning the Maritime Delimitation in the Area between Greenland and Jan Mayen (Denmark v. Norway)*;[228] the 1999 *Case of the Maritime Boundary Delimitation between Eritrea and Yemen*;[229] the 2001 *Qatar/Bahrain Case*;[230] the 2002 *Case Concerning the Land and Maritime Boundary between Cameroon and Nigeria*;[231] and the 2007 *Guyana and Suriname Arbitration*.[232]

The growing consistency of application of the two-step approach has not been affected by whether the States involved are or are not parties to the 1982 LOS Convention or the 1958 Continental Shelf Convention. Anderson, a former judge of the International Tribunal for the Law of the Sea (ITLOS), has commented: "The [International] Court and other tribunals have . . . found that the principles and methods are similar whether the applicable law was custom or convention (whether the Convention of 1958 or the 1982 Law of the Sea Convention) . . . "[233] The two-step process has similarly not

---

227 *Id.* para 242. This paragraph was cited with approval *In the Matter of the Arbitration between Guyana and Suriname*, 17 September 2007, para 340, on the website of the Permanent Court of Arbitration, at www.pca-cpa.org (accessed on 29 September 2007).

228 *Jan Mayen Case, supra* note 14, at para 51.

229 *Award of the Tribunal in the Second Stage of the Proceedings (Maritime Delimitation) (Eritrea and Yemen)*, 17 December 1999, 40 ILM 983, para 131.

230 *Case Concerning Maritime Delimitation and Territorial Questions between Qatar and Bahrain (Qatar v. Bahrain)*, [2001] ICJ Rep. 40, para 230.

231 *Case Concerning the Land and Maritime Boundary between Cameroon and Nigeria (Cameroon v. Nigeria: Equatorial Guinea intervening)*, [2002] ICJ Rep. 303, para 288.

232 *Guyana and Suriname Arbitration, supra* note 227, at para 342.

233 D. Anderson, *Development in Maritime Boundary Law and Practice*, in D. A. COLSON AND R. W. SMITH, (eds.) INTERNATIONAL MARITIME BOUNDARIES, Vol. V (Martinus Nijhoff, The Hague 2005) 3209.

See also Award of the Tribunal in the Second Phase of the Arbitration Between Newfoundland and Labrador and Nova Scotia, 26 March 2002, 128 ILR 504–581, a non-international maritime boundary arbitration, where, however, the Tribunal was requested to apply the relevant international law. The Tribunal stated, at para 2.28: "the use of a provisional equidistance line is now the starting point in most cases, whether the governing law is the 1958 Geneva Convention, the 1982 Law of the Sea Convention or customary international law" and at para 5.2: "The law governing maritime delimitation has thus attained a basic unity, while retaining the necessary flexibility to respond to the specific facts and features of each case."

been affected by whether the overlapping claims to be delimited involve the continental shelf, EEZ, a single maritime boundary for all purposes[234] or the territorial sea.[235]

The essential characteristic of the two-step approach is the prominence given to equidistance as the method for construction of a provisional line, combined with circumstances that can be invoked in order to justify an adjustment of the provisional equidistance line. The 2006 *Barbados-Trinidad and Tobago Arbitration* noted that ". . . the need to avoid subjective determinations requires that the method used to start with a measure of certainty that equidistance positively assures. . . . "[236]

It has long been recognized that equidistance often achieves equitable results where coasts are opposite (facing one another) and multiple points are used to construct a line, as opposed to the situation where coasts are adjacent (adjoining one another) and a single point can have a significant effect.[237] It was only in the 2001 *Qatar/Bahrain Case*, for one sector of the ultimate line, and in the 2002 *Cameroon/Nigeria Case*, that the equidistance method was used in international adjudication to construct a provisional line in the situation of adjacent States. Although the 2006 *Barbados-Trinidad and Tobago Arbitration* opined "that there is no justification to approach the process of delimitation from the perspective of a distinction between opposite and adjacent coasts . . . ," the Tribunal also noted the distinction between opposite and adjacent coasts may be relevant in enclosed geographic situations

---

234 *See* the discussion in the *Barbados-Trinidad and Tobago Arbitration*, *supra* note 226, at para 226–235. *See*, however, as regards overlapping claims to continental shelf areas beyond 200 nautical miles, D. A. Colson, *The Delimitation of the Outer Continental Shelf between Neighboring States* (2003) 97 AJIL 91, 102–104.

235 This is the outcome of Article 15 of the LOS Convention, *supra* note 103, and its predecessor the Convention on the Territorial Sea and Contiguous Zone, Geneva 29 April 1958, entered into force 22 September 1964, Art 12, 516 UNTS 205, which reads:

> Where the coasts of two States are opposite or adjacent to each other, neither of the two States is entitled, failing agreement between them to the contrary, to extend its territorial sea beyond the median line every point of which is equidistant from the nearest points on the baselines from which the breadth of the territorial seas of each of the two States is measured. The above provision does not apply, however, where it is necessary by reason of historic title or other circumstances to delimit the territorial seas of the two States in a way which is at variance therewith.

See Case Concerning Territorial and Maritime Dispute between Nicaragua and Honduras in the Caribbean Sea, 8 October 2007, 46 ILM 1053, paras 269, 280.

236 *Barbados-Trinidad and Tobago Arbitration*, *supra* note 226, at para 306.

237 *See* L. Legault and B. Hankey, *Method, Oppositeness and Adjacency, and Proportionality in Maritime Boundary Delimitation*, in J. I. Charney and L. M. Alexander (eds.) International Maritime Boundaries, Vol. I (Martinus Nijhoff, The Hague 1993) 216.

such as those that existed in the *Gulf of Maine Case*.[238] The 2007 *Guyana and Suriname Arbitration* summarized that the recent cases provided for a "presumption in favour of equidistance" regardless of whether the coastal configuration of the States is opposite or adjacent.[239] The 2002 *Newfoundland and Labrador-Nova Scotia Arbitration* expressed the matter well:

> In the context of opposite coasts and latterly of adjacent coasts as well, it has become normal to begin by considering the equidistance line and possible adjustments, and to adopt some other method of delimitation only if circumstances justify it.[240]

Although the trend in international adjudication is that a provisional equidistance line be constructed regardless of geographic or other considerations,[241] care is needed. The International Court in the 2007 *Nicaragua-Honduras Case* commented that while equidistance is widely used and "has a certain intrinsic value because of its scientific character and the relative ease with which it can be applied," that "the equidistance method does not automatically have priority over other methods of delimitation."[242] There are judicial precedents, for example, the 1982 *Libya/Tunisia Case*;[243] the 1984 *Gulf of Maine Case*,[244] and the 1992 *Case Concerning the Delimitation of Maritime Spaces between Canada and France*,[245] where equidistance was not a starting point. The 2007 *Guyana and Suriname Arbitration*, while accepting that as regards the territorial sea there was a primacy on the use of the median line,[246] did not utilize equidistance opting instead to base the first three nautical miles of the territorial sea boundary on the established practice of

---

238 *Barbados-Trinidad and Tobago Arbitration*, *supra* note 226, at paras 315, 316.

239 *Guyana and Suriname Arbitration*, *supra* note 227, at para 338.

240 *Newfoundland–Nova Scotia Second Phase Award*, *supra* note 233, at para 2.28, cited with approval in the *Barbados-Trinidad and Tobago Arbitration*, *supra* note 226, at para 306 and the *Guyana and Suriname Arbitration*, *supra* note 227, at para 339.

241 In the *Cameroon/Nigeria Case*, *supra* note 231, at para 288, the International Court appears to accept that a provisional equidistance line is mandatory. Based on the cases, Kolb, *supra* note 184, at 536, similarly notes that the use of equidistance for a provisional line has become mandatory in all situations.

242 *Nicaragua-Honduras Case*, *supra* note 235, at para 272.

243 *Case Concerning the Continental Shelf (Tunisia/Libya)*, [1982] ICJ Rep. 18.

244 *Gulf of Maine Case*, *supra* note 4.

245 *Canada/France Arbitration*, *supra* note 3.

246 *Guyana and Suriname Arbitration*, *supra* note 227, at para 295.

navigation between the two States,[247] with the subsequent nine miles of the territorial sea being a line to join the commencement of the maritime boundary adopted by the Tribunal for the single maritime boundary for the EEZ and the continental shelf.[248] However, for the single maritime boundary beyond the territorial sea, the 2007 *Guyana and Suriname Arbitration* rejected arguments that there existed "geographical peculiarities" that required the use of a methodology other than equidistance for the first step.[249] The manner of rejection indicated that in another situation such arguments could be successful to reverse what the Tribunal called "the presumption in favour of equidistance."[250] This occurred a scant few weeks later in the 2007 *Nicaragua-Honduras Case.* Neither State in this Case proposed a provisional equidistance line[251] and the Court determined that it was "impossible . . . to identify base points and construct a provisional equidistance line" because of the difficulty of identifying reliable base points in the River Coco area as a result of the shifting channel and islands and uncertainty over the title to the islands in river area.[252] Instead of equidistance, the Court adopted a bisector of an angle established by lines along the relevant coastlines of the two States where they met at an agreed end point of the land boundary.[253] The uncertainty over the title to islands in River Coco and the shifting channel and sands led the Court to commence the maritime boundary for the territorial sea three nautical miles seaward and to call on the parties to negotiate a boundary for this three nautical mile area.[254] The Court adopted the two-step process and a provisional equidistance line to separate the territorial seas adjacent to islands of the two States that were well beyond the 12 nautical miles from the coast,[255] reverting back to the use of a bisector beyond the territorial seas adjacent to the islands. Although both of the 2007 adjudications, the *Guyana and Suriname Arbitration* and the *Nicaragua-Honduras Case*, rejected use of a provisional equidistance line for the entirety of the

247 *Id.* para 306.

248 *Id.* para 323.

249 *Id.* para 372.

250 *Id.* para 338.

251 *See Nicaragua-Honduras Case, supra* note 235, at paras 229–258, 273–275.

252 *Id.* para 280 and see paras 277–279.

253 *Id.* paras 283–298.

254 *Id.* paras 311, 307–310.

255 *Id.* para 304.

maritime boundary, the Tribunals required that there be compelling reasons not to use equidistance and where no compelling reasons existed, the Tribunals adopted the two-step approach and constructed a provisional equidistance line.

The second step of the two-step process involves the circumstances that may lead to possible adjustments in a provisional equidistance line. The terminology of the circumstances as being special or relevant has been the subject of much discussion, with the difference often seen as being that special means a more limited set of circumstances as compared to relevant.[256] Moreover, there is often debate about whether the circumstances are to be seen as an exception to equidistance and, therefore, to be interpreted narrowly.[257] What can be identified is that, while the International Court in the 1969 *North Sea Continental Shelf Cases* talked in terms of there being "no legal limit" to the circumstances that may affect equitability,[258] subsequent maritime boundary adjudications have limited the factors that are considered, with the emphasis being on geographic circumstances.[259] The reason for a limitation on circumstances is the understanding that boundary delimitation needs to be anchored in objective considerations in the same way that the entitlement to offshore areas is anchored in the objective situation

---

256 R. R. CHURCHILL AND A. V LOWE, THE LAW OF THE SEA (Manchester University Press, 3rd edition, Manchester 1999) 187 describe the distinction between special and relevant circumstances as follows:

> "Special circumstances" have traditionally been regarded as being fairly narrow in scope: for example, the principal drafters of article 6, the International Law Commission, considered "special circumstances" as embracing (and apparently being limited to) exceptional configurations of the coast, and the presence of islands and navigable channels. "Relevant circumstances", on the other hand, have been regarded as being much wider in scope: indeed, in the *North Sea Continental Shelf* cases the International Court suggested that there was no limit to the kind of circumstances that might be taken into account in effecting an equitable delimitation. (footnotes deleted)

257 Kolb, *supra* note 184, at 551–552 noted:

> Until 2001, the Court adhered to the idea of an open category of circumstances capable of influencing the position of the line [provisional line], thus preserving to itself a considerable margin of discretion. . . . In *Qatar/Bahrein*, however, the Court abandoned this discretionary approach. It joined the special circumstances concept to the equidistance concept in accordance with the provisions of the 1958 Convention on the continental shelf. Equidistance was to be corrected only by strict qualified circumstances, particularly geographical ones, that would otherwise lead to inequity. . . . [S]pecial circumstances were conceived of as an exception to equidistance, and that exception was interpreted in a restricted way.

258 *North Sea Continental Shelf Cases*, *supra* note 106, at para 93.

259 Churchill and Lowe, *supra* note 256, at 188.

of coastal frontage.[260] Moreover, as the International Court commented in the 1993 *Jan Mayen Case*:

> The task of a tribunal is to define the boundary line . . . ; the sharing-out of the area is therefore the consequences of the delimitation, not vice versa.[261]

> The circumstances that have been considered in recent maritime boundary adjudications include:
>
> - the presence and effect of islands, rocks and other like features;
> - the configuration of the coasts in the area relevant to the delimitation;
> - the comparative proportionality of lengths of coasts in the area relevant to the delimitation;
> - the presence of ocean resources in the area to be delimited;
> - the conduct of the parties; and
> - agreements between Colonial powers.[262]

Although the above factors that may be determined by a court or tribunal as circumstances can be listed with confidence, "uncertainties . . . remain . . . as to the relevant criteria for deciding upon the existence of a need to adjust the provisional equidistance line."[263] Put a different way, adjudicative bodies have "a broad discretion to determine the relative weight of any particular circumstances, subject only to the need for some consistency with previous cases."[264] The uncertainty is not surprising. Whether a factor is relevant in adjusting a provisional line and how much might be the adjustment are

---

260 The connection between legal title, geography, and delimitation is well explained in the *Case Concerning the Continental Shelf (Libya v. Malta)*, [1985] ICJ Rep. 13, paras 27 and 61:

> The juridical link between the State's territorial sovereignty and its rights to certain adjacent maritime expanses is established by means of its coasts. . . . The legal basis of that which is to be delimited, and of entitlement to it, cannot be other that pertinent to that delimitation. . . . The criterion (of delimitation) is linked with the law relating to a State's title. . . .

261 *Jan Mayen Case*, *supra* note 14, at para 64.

262 Churchill and Lowe, *supra* note 256, at 189 note that security considerations may also be a circumstance.

Churchill and Lowe, at 190, also comment:

> Courts and tribunals have also been consistent in holding a variety of other factors to be irrelevant. These include socio-economic factors, such as disparities in the wealth and size of population of each party; differences in the area of land territory belonging to each party; and normally the natural resources and ecology of the delimitation area.

263 Anderson, *supra* note 233, at 3209.

264 Churchill and Lowe, *supra* note 256, at 188.

determined by whether the provisional line meets the criterion of being an equitable result or whether an equitable result is achieved by adjusting the provisional line taking into account one or more factors. Moreover, although maritime boundary adjudicative bodies rarely comment regarding burdens of proof or standards of proof, respecting adjusting a provisional equidistance line, the burden appears to lie on the party seeking to have an adjustment made,[265] with the standard required to be met being significant (e.g., "inequity," "disproportionate effect," "significant disparity").

5.0 Unresolved Maritime Boundaries

5.1 British Columbia/Alaska Maritime Boundary

The Canadian and United States overlapping claims adjacent to British Columbia and Alaska involve two distinct but adjoining areas. The first is within the Dixon Entrance (the waters separating the Queen Charlotte Islands of British Columbia and the Alexander Archipelago of Alaska), which is approximately 75 nautical miles in length and 30 nautical miles wide.[266] The second is seaward of the Dixon Entrance to the outer limit of the 200-nautical-mile zone. The dispute regarding the Dixon Entrance is based primarily in history and the notorious 1903 *United States-Great Britain Alaska Boundary Arbitration*.[267] The 200-nautical-mile dispute is one of technicality which, however, is connected to the Dixon Entrance issue.

5.1.1 The Dixon Entrance

As noted above, the *Alaska Boundary Arbitration* had the mandate to determine meaning to be given to the wording of Article III of the 1825 Russia-United Kingdom Treaty respecting:

> the line of demarcation between the possessions . . . : Commencing from the southernmost point of the island called Prince of Wales . . . the

265 While this appears to be inherent in the norm of international maritime boundary law, the International Court in the 2002 *Qatar/Bahrain Case, supra* note 230, at para 233 cited the following from the *Libya/Malta Case, supra* note 260, at para 63: "Thus, . . . it must be demonstrated that the equidistance method leads to an equitable result in the case in question."

266 D. H. Gray, *Canada's Unresolved Maritime Boundaries* (1994) 48 No. 2 GEOMATICA 131, 132. This paper is reprinted in (1997) Vol. 5 No. 3 BOUNDARY AND SECURITY BULLETIN (University of Durham, International Boundaries Research Unit) 60–69.

267 *Alaska Boundary Arbitration, supra* note 79.

> said line shall ascend to the north along the channel called Portland Channel. . . .[268]

The Arbitration was to answer two questions: First, what was the intended point of commencement of the line? Second, what was the course of the line from its commencement to the entrance of the Portland Channel?[269] The Arbitrators reached quick agreement on the first question. The commencement of the line was Cape Muzon, the southern point of Dall Island and not Cape Chacon, the southernmost point of the Prince of Wales Island.[270] The difference occurred since it was not realized in 1825 that Dall Island was separate from Prince of Wales Island.[271] Starting with Cape Muzon as point *A*, the Arbitration Panel constructed a line to join with point *B*, being at the entrance of the Portland Canal,[272] thereby creating the so-called A-B Line following 54 degrees 40 minutes north latitude.

Canada has long asserted that it was the intention of Russia and Great Britain in 1825 to create a maritime boundary line and, therefore, that the A-B Line is the ocean boundary within the Dixon Entrance. Canada's claim was first detailed in a 1909 Order-in-Council,[273] about which two law officers in the British government opined that Canada's position was not justified by international law.[274] The United States has long seen the A-B Line as one dividing the ownership of islands and not as a bilateral ocean boundary.[275]

An important feature of the A-B Line is that, if it is a maritime boundary, it would deprive the United States of any territorial waters within the Dixon Entrance adjacent to Cape Muzon on Dall Island, and severely restrict the

---

268 Convention between Great Britain and Russia Concerning the Limits of their Respective Possessions on the North-West Coast of America, *supra* note 77, Art III.

269 Convention for the Adjustment of the Alaska Boundary, *supra* note 83, Art IV and *Alaska Boundary Arbitration, supra* note 79, at 30.

270 *Alaska Boundary Arbitration, supra* note 79, at 31.

271 C. B. Bourne and D. M. McRae, *Maritime Jurisdiction in the Dixon Entrance: The Alaska Boundary Re-examined* (1976) 14 CYIL 175, 207, footnote 100.

272 *Alaska Boundary Arbitration, supra* note 79, at 32.

273 Order-in-Council, 6 July 1909, enclosed in letter from the Administrator to the Colonial Secretary, 13 July 1909, in *Documents of Canada's External Affairs*, Vol. I, 1909–1918 (Department of External Affairs, 1967) 400–405. See Bourne and McRae, *supra* note 271, at 213.

274 Summarized in a letter from the Colonial Secretary to the Governor General of Canada, 10 February 1910, in *Documents of Canada's External Affairs, supra* note 273, at 412–414. *See* Bourne and McRae, *supra* note 271, at 213–214.

275 *See generally* Bourne and McRae, *supra* note 271, at 178–179.

territorial sea area adjacent to Cape Chacon on Prince of Wales Island. Reportedly, the view of the United States "is that it is inconceivable that a determination of a maritime boundary would have been made in a way that deprived one party of a territorial sea."[276]

The U.S. position is that the ocean boundary in the Dixon Entrance is based upon equidistance, which produces a line generally favorable to the United States by moving the ocean boundary south of the A-B Line throughout most of its length.[277]

DIXON ENTRANCE

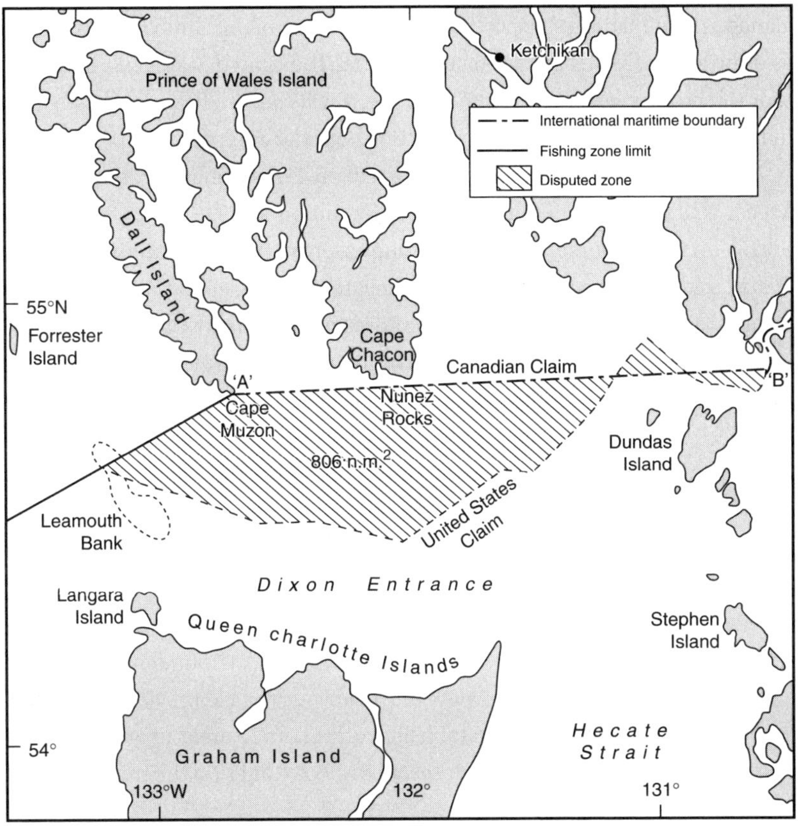

Source: DH Gray, 'Canada's Unresolved Maritime Boundaries' (1997) Vol 5 No 3 Boundary and Security Bulletin 60, 62.

---

276 D. M. McRae, *Delimitation Problems of Canada (First Part)*, in D. Pharand and U. Leanza (eds.) The Continental Shelf and the Exclusive Economic Zone: Delimitation and Legal Regime (Martinis Nijhoff, Dordrecht 1993) 165.

277 Note Feldman and Colson, *supra* note 26, at 750 and *see* Exclusive Economic Zone and Maritime Boundaries, *supra* note 12, at 43827.

The area in dispute in the Dixon Entrance is approximately 806 square nautical miles.[278] There are two anomalies associated with the overlapping area in the Dixon Entrance. First, point *B* of the A-B Line is located slightly south of the commencement of the maritime boundary in the Portland Canal leaving a small gap in the maritime boundary lines claimed by the two States.[279] Second, the claims of the two States in the Dixon Entrance create four distinct areas. The main overlapping area is in the middle of Dixon Entrance. Near point *B* is another area of overlapping claim. However, there are two small areas in the inner Dixon Entrance which neither State has officially claimed since the U.S.-claimed equidistance line goes north of the Canadian-claimed A-B Line.[280] These curious areas of unclaimed ocean add up to approximately 21.4 square nautical miles. The United States has indicated that, as the areas are north of the A-B Line, it will exercise fisheries jurisdiction in these unclaimed areas until a maritime boundary is established.[281]

The resources of importance in the Dixon Entrance are groundfish and access to salmon that are returning to Canadian and U.S. rivers. Based primarily on the A-B Line, Canada has long asserted that the waters within the Dixon Entrance and the adjacent Hecate Strait (separating the Queen Charlotte Islands from the British Columbia mainland) are Canadian internal waters, although through much of the twentieth-century, U.S. fishing has taken place beyond the three-nautical-mile limit in both areas.[282]

In 1976, Bourne and McRae published a detailed analysis of the A-B Line and the claims that it was or was not a maritime boundary. They looked at the intent of the negotiators in 1825; the conclusions reached by the 1903 *Alaska Boundary Arbitration*; and the practice of the two States. Bourne and McRae concluded:

> There is sufficient evidence to make both claims plausible, but insufficient evidence to make either claim conclusive. A tribunal might well be forced to conclude that, in view of the absence of clear evidence at least by 1903, neither State had established any claim to areas of water beyond three nautical miles from their respective coastlines on the mainland and

278 Gray, *supra* note 266, at 133.

279 *Id.* 132.

280 *Id.* 133.

281 Exclusive Economic Zone and Maritime Boundaries, *supra* note 12, at 43827, footnote 8.

282 Legault, *supra* note 6, at 380–381 and McRae, *supra* note 276, at 165–166.

the islands, a decision favourable to the United States, but reached by default rather than on the basis of any clear intention.[283]

In the 1985 *Guinea-Guinea-Bissau Arbitration*, a key question was whether the wording of the 1886 Convention on the Delimitation of French and Portuguese Possessions in West Africa established the maritime boundary in the ocean area adjacent to the two States.[284] Although the waters in question in the Arbitration were not enclosed as in the case of the Dixon Entrance, nevertheless the waters of the Dixon Entrance are greater than six nautical miles in width and this makes the findings of the 1985 Tribunal relevant. In examining the 1886 Treaty, the Tribunal noted that in the late 1800s international law only recognized narrow ocean areas as within coastal State control.[285] After noting numerous other bilateral arrangements from the same historical period that employed lines in the water, including the 1867 U.S.-Russia Alaska Treaty,[286] the 1985 Tribunal commented:

> To the knowledge of the Tribunal, it was never considered at the time that any of these treaties granted maritime sovereignty to any of the signatories over anything except the commonly recognized territorial waters.[287]

While not explicitly stated, the view of the *Guinea/Guinea-Bissau Tribunal* was that treaties which predated the development of extensive offshore jurisdiction must be carefully scrutinized where it is argued that such a treaty delimits modern offshore jurisdictional regimes.

As is clear from Bourne and McRae, academic opinion has not been favorable to Canada's claim respecting the A-B Line.[288] This same academic

283 Bourne and McRae, *supra* note 271, at 220.

284 *Delimitation of the Maritime Boundary between Guinea and Guinea-Bissau*, 14 February 1985, 25 ILM 251–307.

285 *Id.* para 80.

286 Convention ceding Alaska between Russia and the United States, *supra* note 78.

287 *Guinea–Guinea-Bissau Arbitration, supra* note 284, at para 81.

288 Bourne and McRae, *supra* note 271, at 217–220; McRae, *supra* note 276, at 165; and D. M. Johnston and M. J. Valencia, Pacific Ocean Boundary Problems: Status and Solutions (Martinus Nijhoff, Dordrecht 1991) 100. The latter comment:

> Unless one finds clear evidence of U.S. acquiescence to the formal boundary status of the line, as asserted by Canada, it is difficult, in the age of extended coastal State jurisdiction, to expect the United States to tolerate the anomaly of having no territorial sea off Cape Muzon ... Under the conditions of the new law of the sea, it is difficult to believe that any tribunal would use the "A-B line" as the basis of an "equitable solution" ...

opinion, however, does not accept that an unadjusted equidistance line is an inevitable solution and points out the inequality of comparative coastal lengths in the area[289] and that historic considerations respecting the A-B Line could be given some weight.[290]

5.1.2 Seaward of Dixon Entrance

In the ocean area seaward of the Dixon Entrance, the Canadian and U.S. 200-nautical-mile zones both utilize equidistance. As a result, the seaward lines are largely congruent, except that the Canadian starting point is Cape Muzon (point *A* of the A-B Line) and the U.S. starting point is the equidistance point between Cape Muzon and Langara Island (part of the Queen Charlotte Islands), which is consistent with the claims of each State in Dixon Entrance.[291]

5.1.3 Bilateral Discussions

In May 1914, Canada asked Great Britain to arbitrate the A-B Line question with the United States, but World War I interceded.[292] Negotiations apparently took place in the 1920s and 1930s.[293] Bourne and McRae relate that, as a result of discussions in the 1940s, Canada and the United States accepted to use equidistance to divide the Dixon Entrance with the added agreement that each State would have the right to fish and navigate on both sides of the equidistance line outside of three nautical miles.[294] British Columbia, however, reportedly rejected the arrangement.[295] In 1973, the United States suggested

---

289 McRae, *supra* note 276, at 166.

290 Johnston and Valencia, *supra* note 288, at 100.

291 Gray, *supra* note 266, at 134 and McRae, *supra* note 276, at 164–165. *See* Exclusive Economic Zone and Maritime Boundaries, *supra* note 12 and Fishing Zones of Canada (Zones 4 and 5) Order, *supra* note 12.

292 Bourne and McRae, *supra* note 271, at 213–214.

293 Noted in C. R. Symmons, Historic Waters in the Law of the Sea: A Modern Re-Appraisal (Martinus Nijhoff, Leiden 2008) 131, footnote 71, 138, footnote 115 where U.S. archival documents are referenced.

294 Bourne and McRae, *supra* note 271, at 215.
Symmons, *supra* note 293, at 138, footnote 115, relying on U.S. archival documents, notes that "it was agreed in a draft convention on the 'AB' line . . . that each party had the right to navigate (and fish) in the Dixon Entrance . . ."

295 *Id.* 215.

that the two countries agree to submit questions respecting the legal significance of the A-B Line to the International Court.[296] Canada declined to accept the suggestion but did indicate a willingness to enter into consultations.[297]

During the discussions of the Special Negotiators in 1977 to 1978, the United States sought a belt of water, three to six nautical miles wide, to the south of Cape Muzon and Cape Chacon, although no change to the A-B Line east of Cape Chacon to point *B*.[298] Thus, the United States would take possession of the two previously unclaimed areas north of the A-B Line and accept Canada assertion of the A-B Line in the eastern area. In exchange, the United States would consider moving the maritime boundary seaward of Dixon Entrance to the north of the equidistance line. In short, what was contemplated was a tradeoff of area inside Dixon Entrance for an area outside Dixon Entrance.[299] Seaward of the Dixon Entrance, Canada's objective was to have the line swing north of 54 degrees 40 minutes north latitude, while the United States suggested that the line seaward of the Dixon Entrance should follow 54 degrees 40 minutes north latitude, the A-B Line.[300] The U.S. proposal would amount to a gain of 9,000 square miles for Canada outside the Dixon Entrance, based on Canada's equidistance position, in exchange for 100 square miles for the United States in the Dixon Entrance.[301] In 1979, a Canadian negotiator indicated that Canada had been "able to ascertain from the Americans and receive assurances that" if an accommodation were made regarding the A-B Line in the Dixon Entrance that Canada could attach conditions "which would . . . in a practical sense not change anything in that area as far as Canada is concerned . . ."[302] What was noted was that the United States would

---

296 Department of State, DIGEST OF UNITED STATES PRACTICE IN INTERNATIONAL LAW, 1973 (Washington, 1974) 465–466 and DIGEST OF UNITED STATES PRACTICE IN INTERNATIONAL LAW, 1975 (Washington, 1976) 672–673.

297 Aide-Memoire from Embassy of Canada to the Department of State, 4 January 1974, in *Gulf of Maine Pleadings*, Vol. 5, Annex 18 to Reply of the United States, 552–553.

298 Hankey, *supra* note 25, at 19–20.

299 *Id.* 19–20.

300 *Id.* 20.

It appears that Canada also had this outcome in mind. *See* Extracts from the text of a Statement made by M. D. Copithorne, Leader of the Canadian team, at the Maritime Boundary Talks held in Washington on 23 July 1976, attached to Diplomatic Note No. 221, 26 May 1977, in *Gulf of Maine Pleadings*, Vol. 1, Annex 54 to Memorial of Canada, 448.

301 Hankey, *supra* note 25, at 19–20.

302 Lorne Clark, Deputy Negotiator for Maritime Boundaries Canada/U.S., HC, *Minutes of Proceedings and Evidence of the Standing Committee on Fisheries and Forestry*, 21 March 1979 (30th Parliament, 4th Session, 1978–1979), Issue no. 13, 11.

not expand fishing activities in the Dixon Entrance, First Nations rights would be preserved and oil tankers would not be free to use the area.[303]

Complicating the Dixon Entrance discussions was the view of British Columbia that there should be no deviation from the A-B Line.[304] This was enhanced by the "symbolic significance" of the A-B Line for the province "that almost precludes the political possibility of a concession by Canada."[305] Seaward of the Dixon Entrance, British Columbia was unhappy with Canada's announced equidistance line, taking the view that the Alaska Panhandle, being composed of small islands and a thin strip of coast, distorted the equidistance line and a maritime boundary discounting the panhandle was appropriate.[306]

Since the late 1970s, there has been no report of formal or informal discussions between the two States respecting the maritime boundary dispute in or seaward of the Dixon Entrance.

5.1.4 Submarine Passage in the Dixon Entrance

The United States maintains the Southeast Alaska Submarine Noise Measurement Facility (SEAFAC) in the Behm Canal in Alaska. Access to this facility by submarines is through the Dixon Entrance. In 1991, "in view of U.S.-Canadian mutual defence interests," the United States consulted with Canada regarding submarine passage in these waters.[307]

There may have been agreement in 1991 between Canada and the United States respecting the passage of the submarines in the Dixon Entrance. The Canadian Minister of External Affairs told the House of Commons:

> that we have discussed with them [the United States] and we have consent from them concerning their use of our sovereign waters and . . . we

---

303 *Id.*

304 *British Columbia Submission*, *supra* note 27, at 10. *See also* McRae, *supra* note 276, at 167.

305 Johnston and Valencia, *supra* note 288, at 100.

306 *British Columbia Submission*, *supra* note 27, at 15–18 and McRae, *supra* note 276, at 165.

307 Diplomatic Note to Canada, 24 December 1991, para 3, in Department of State, DIGEST OF UNITED STATES PRACTICE IN INTERNATIONAL LAW, 1991–1999 (Washington: International Law Institute, 2005) 1594. The full text of the Note is available at www.state.gov/s/l/c81883.htm (accessed on 4 November 2006), which is a documentary supplement to the *U.S. Digest, 1991–1999* and referred to therein at 1593.

have received from them assurances on how these waters will be passed through by . . . submarines to reach the acoustic testing facility.[308]

In 1992, the Minister referred to "an agreement that we signed with the Americans regarding their travel through Dixon Entrance."[309] A Parliamentary Secretary indicated that the submarine traffic in the Dixon Entrance "has to do with our agreements with the United States through NATO and NORAD."[310] A different minister indicated that the U.S. submarines "can only pass with advance notice and with the appropriate protection with respect to compensation if there should be an accident."[311] As regards advance notice, it appears that the U.S. Navy would give 72-hours advance notice "of the commencement and duration of operations" at SEAFAC that would be communicated to U.S. sources and to Canadian officials.[312] On the compensation point, in August 1991, the United States communicated with the Canadian Embassy on the general policies and procedures of the United States respecting their handling of claims or losses that might occur as a result of submarine transits.[313] In October 1991, an Order-in-Council was issued granting "Canada's prior consent for United States submarines to transit Dixon Entrance" on their way to SEAFAC.[314]

Depending on what, or whether an agreement exists between Canada and the United States, it is clear that, despite the comments above, the United States did not consent that the proposed passages of submarines through the Dixon Entrance involved Canadian waters. The United States made it clear in a diplomatic note in December 1991 that the intended navigation would be only in the claimed U.S. waters within the Dixon Entrance.[315] A Canadian diplomatic note in November 1991 had informed the United

308 Barbara McDougall, Minister of External Affairs, HC, *Debates*, 30 October 1991, 4212–3.

309 Barbara McDougall, Minister of External Affairs, HC, *Debates*, 10 March 1992, 7933.

310 Benno Friesen, Parliamentary Secretary for External Affairs, HC, *Debates*, 19 November 1991, 5062.

311 Mary Collins, Associate Minister of National Defence, HC, *Debates*, 6 November 1991, 4635.

312 Letter from Alan J. Kreczko, Deputy Legal Adviser, Department of State, to the Embassy of Canada, 2 August 1991, *U.S. Digest, 1991–1999*, *supra* note 307, at 1595.

313 *Id.* 1594–1595.

314 *See* Privy Council Order-in-Council 1991–2082, approved 30 October 1991, unpublished, available though the Library of Canada, copy on file with the author. The Order-in-Council is referred to by Jim Fulton, HC, *Debates*, 19 November 1991, 5061–5062.

315 Diplomatic Note to Canada 24 December 1991, *supra* note 307, at para 2, at 1594.

States that it was consenting "to the transit of Canadian internal waters in Dixon Entrance."[316] The U.S. response was clear:

> Consent of the Government of Canada was never sought for the transits of the submarines.... while ... the United States did consult Canada concerning the transits, the United States cannot accept that its authority to transit these waters is premised on Canada's consent to those transits.[317]

SEAFAC has been in operation since 1991. Submarine passage through the Dixon Entrance has taken place since then without incident, without much notice by the public, and without the necessity of Canada and the United States revisiting the apparent agreement-to-disagree.

5.1.5 Fisheries Enforcement Understanding

In all of the overlapping maritime boundary areas, Canada and the United States have an understanding that flag State enforcement will prevail. Paragraph 3 of the 1979 Preservation of the Halibut Fishery of the Northern Pacific Ocean and Bering Sea and Fishing Off the West Coast of Canada Agreement provided that "pending delimitation of maritime boundaries ... off the west coasts of the United States and Canada" the two States, as an interim measure, would exercise flag State enforcement. The Agreement addressed specific fishing matters up to 1981[318] and was not renewed, although the Agreement did not contain a specific termination clause. Specifically as regards the Dixon Entrance, Canada and the United States exchanged notes in August 1980 reaffirming that each side would continue to observe flag State enforcement respecting fisheries.[319]

5.2 British Columbia/Washington Maritime Boundary

Both Canada and the United States have utilized equidistance in the construction of their 200-nautical-mile ocean zones seaward of the Juan de Fuca Strait.

---

316 Diplomatic Note to the United States, 13 November 1991, reprinted in part in *U.S. Digest, 1991–1999*, *supra* note 307, at 1593 and *see* Diplomatic Note to Canada 24 December 1991, *supra* note 307, at para 1 (on the website).

317 Diplomatic Note to Canada 24 December 1991, *supra* note 307, at para 3, at 1594.

318 Halibut Fishery Agreement, *supra* note 10, para 2.

319 Referred to in Department of State, CUMULATIVE DIGEST OF UNITED STATES PRACTICE IN INTERNATIONAL LAW, 1981–1988 (Washington, 1994) 1930.

Despite commencing from the same starting point, the agreed endpoint of the maritime boundary at the mouth of the Juan de Fuca Strait,[320] the points relied upon by each State to construct their equidistance lines are different, hence the lines are not congruent and a small area of overlap exists.[321] The 1977 Canadian equidistance line uses base points along the U.S. coast and on the Canadian side uses points on the straight baselines that were established along Vancouver Island in 1969.[322] In 1969, the United States protested the use by Canada of straight baselines, including those along Vancouver Island, noting that the baselines were constructed "contrary to established principles of international Law of the Sea."[323] As a result, the U.S. 1977 equidistance line is constructed using base points along both the U.S. and Canadian coasts and ignores the Canadian territorial sea baselines.[324]

The difference between the Canada and U.S. equidistance lines is calculated as being 15.4 square nautical miles spread primarily over two areas, one near the mouth of the Juan de Fuca Strait and the other further seaward.[325] The area near the mouth of the Strait encompasses a small part of Swiftsure Bank.[326] Swiftsure Bank is an area for groundfish and there are other fishery resources in the disputed area including the presence of salmon heading into the Juan de Fuca Strait.[327]

An unusual dimension of the area seaward of the Juan de Fuca Strait is the presence of polymetallic sulfides in the Juan de Fuca and Gorda Ridges near

320 Protocol defining the Boundary Line through the Haro Strait, *supra* note 35, determined that the end-point of the Oregon Treaty line was "a point equidistant between Bonilla Point on Vancouver Island and Tatoosh Island lighthouse on the American shore." In the 1908 Treaty respecting the Demarcation of the International Boundary with Canada, *supra* note 55, the endpoint at the mouth of the Juan de Fuca Strait was described as "midway between Bonilla Point on Vancouver Island, and Tatoosh Island Lighthouse in the State of Washington" with coordinates provided.

321 Gray, *supra* note 266, at 132 and McRae, *supra* note 276, at 161.

322 Gray, *supra* note 266, at 132. See Fishing Zones of Canada (Zones 4 and 5) Order, *supra* note 12.

323 Note from the Department of State to the Embassy of Canada, 1 November 1967, in *Gulf of Maine Pleadings*, Vol. 4, Annex 34 to Counter-Memorial of the United States, 473–474 and Note from the Secretary of State to Embassy of Canada, 25 April 1969, in *Gulf of Maine Pleadings*, Vol. 5, Annex 4 to Reply of the United States, 503–504.

324 Gray, *supra* note 266, at 132 and Diplomatic Note No. 626, 22 December 1976, *supra* note 142, at 432. *See* Maritime Boundaries between the United States and Canada, *supra* note 12, superseded by Exclusive Economic Zone and Maritime Boundaries, *supra* note 12.

325 Gray, *supra* note 266, at 132.

326 *Id.*

327 McRae, *supra* note 276, at 160.

SEAWARD OF THE JUAN DE FUCA STRAIT

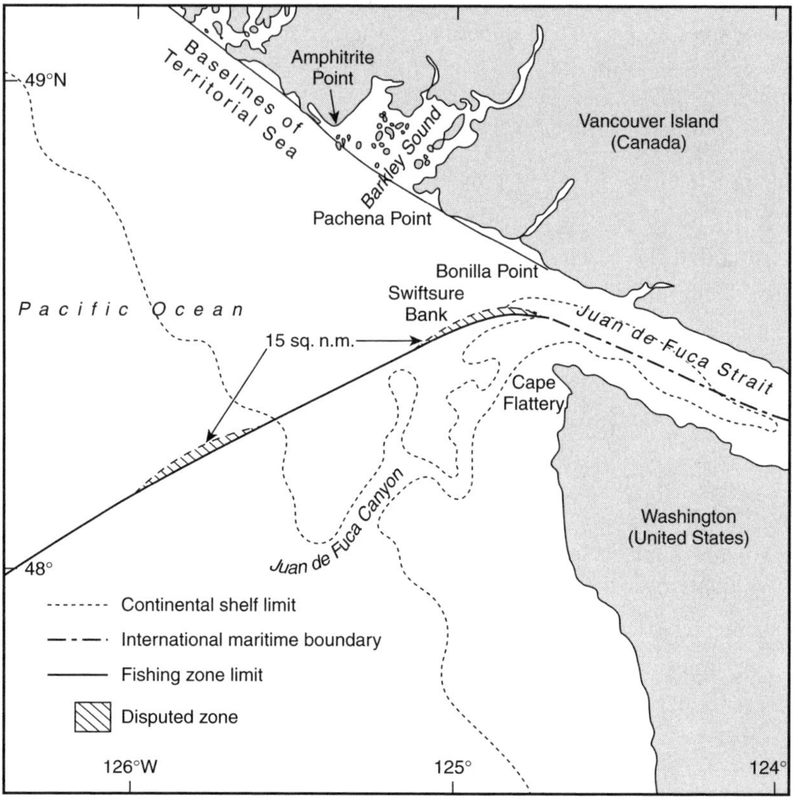

Source: DH Gray, 'Canada's Unresolved Maritime Boundaries' (1997) Vol 5 No 3 Boundary and Security Bulletin 60, 61.

the outer limit of the 200-nautical-mile zones of the two States.[328] A U.S. notice in the 1980s regarding its jurisdiction over the Juan de Fuca and Gorda Ridges was met with a Canadian communication that "the site of the recent discoveries of polymetallic sulfides on the Juan de Fuca Ridge . . . lies within the continental shelf of Canada."[329]

In the 1970s, British Columbia took the view that Canada's equidistance line seaward of the Juan de Fuca Strait did not serve the interests of the province. The province advocated a maritime boundary that followed

---

328 This is noted to varying degrees by Gray, *supra* note 266, at 132; McRae, *supra* note 276, at 161; and Johnston and Valencia, *supra* note 288, at 101–102.

329 Diplomatic Note No. 021, 17 January 1983, in *Gulf of Maine Pleadings*, Vol. 5, Annex 22 to Reply of Canada, 350–351. *See also* Diplomatic Note No. 49, 23 February 1983, in *Gulf of Maine Pleadings*, Vol. 5, Annex 22 to Reply of Canada, 351–352.

the seafloor depression known as the Juan de Fuca Canyon, which runs roughly parallel to the equidistance line but to the south and, thus, to the advantage of Canada.[330] The argument was primarily that the Juan de Fuca Canyon is a natural break in the seafloor and thus was congruent with the U.S. argument for the Northeast Channel as the "natural" maritime boundary in the Gulf of Maine.[331] The British Columbian posture was not well received by the government of Canada.[332] However, during the discussions of the Special Negotiators in 1977 to 1978, Canada sought an adjustment of the equidistance line southward in order to capture Swiftsure Bank.[333]

Since the Canada-U.S. maritime boundary discussions of the late 1970s, the small area of disputed waters seaward of the Juan de Fuca Strait has caused little concern and has not been the subject of Canada-U.S. discussions.

5.3 Seaward of the Gulf of Maine Boundary

The Chamber in the *Gulf of Maine Case* was directed to construct a single maritime boundary for the seafloor and water column[334] and, as such, was dealing with the 200-nautical-mile zone claims of Canada and the United States. Seaward of the Gulf of Maine, the physical continental shelf extends beyond 200 nautical miles, and Canada and the United States have overlapping continental shelf claims in this area. This situation was recognized by the two States in the Agreement to submit the *Gulf of Maine Case* to the International Court.[335]

It was known that the Court-drawn maritime boundary would not extend to the overlapping continental shelf claims since the Court was instructed to place the seaward end point of the maritime boundary within a specific area well short of the overlapping continental shelf area.[336] The two States agreed

330 *British Columbia Submission*, *supra* note 27, at 11–14, 19–21. *See also* McRae, *supra* note 276, at 161–162.

331 Feldman and Colson, *supra* note 26, at 755 and *see Gulf of Maine Case*, *supra* note 4, at para 65.

332 McRae, *supra* note 276, at 162.

333 Clark, *supra* note 13, at 14–15.

334 Special Agreement to Submit to the International Court (1981), *supra* note 101, Art II(1).

335 *Id.* Art VII and *see Letter of Transmittal*, *supra* note 127, at vii.

336 *Id.* Art II(1). Nevertheless, during the *Gulf of Maine* proceedings both States raised arguments about this area. These are well summarized in A. G. Oude Elferink, *Does Undisputed Title to a Maritime Zone Always Exclude its Delimitation: The Grey Area Issue* (1998) 13 ILMCL 143, 144, 160–161.

to a process to extend the maritime boundary seaward of the Gulf of Maine, whether the area in question was fisheries jurisdiction or continental shelf[337]—either State could request negotiations to extend the maritime boundary and, if no agreement on extension is reached a year after the request, either State may submit the question of seaward extension of the maritime boundary to binding third-party dispute settlement.[338] In the event that the States cannot agree on the "terms" for third-party dispute settlement, either State "may submit the question of the seaward extension of the maritime boundary to the Chamber of five judges" that heard the *Gulf of Maine Case*.[339] The agreement to adjudicate, if either Canada or the United States requests it, appears clear, although the default situation of using the Gulf of Maine Chamber may be, after over twenty years, stale.

The continental shelf area beyond 200 nautical miles seaward of the Gulf of Maine and the decision of the court in the *Gulf of Maine Case* create two interrelated maritime issues for Canada and the United States respecting the maritime boundary in the area.

5.3.1 Gray Area

The endpoint of the maritime boundary established in the *Gulf of Maine Case* is 200 nautical miles from the U.S. coast, but only 175.5 nautical miles from Canada.[340] Subsequent to the Case, Canada altered its 200-nautical-mile zone to respect the decision and also delineated its zone to include the 24.5 nautical miles beyond the Court's endpoint and to the point, to the southwest of the Court's endpoint, where the 200-nautical-mile zones of each State meet (the equidistance point).[341] The effect is a Canadian 200-nautical-mile zone of approximately 163 square nautical miles on the "wrong side" of an extension of the Court's line, all of which is beyond the U.S. 200-nautical-mile zone.[342] This area is referred to by the two States as

337 *Letter of Transmittal*, *supra* note 127, at vii.

338 Special Agreement to Submit to the International Court (1981), *supra* note 101, Art VII(1), (2).

339 *Id.* Art VII(3).

340 Gray, *supra* note 266, at 140.

341 Fishing Zones of Canada (Zones 4 and 5) Order, amendment, Can Gaz Part II, Vol. 119, SOR/85-229, 1529–1530 and *see* McRae, *supra* note 276, at 168 and Colson, *supra* note 234, at 104.

342 Gray, *supra* note 266, at 142.

the gray area.[343] Reportedly, the United States expressed concern that the 1985 Canadian action prejudged the extension of the maritime boundary.[344]

SEAWARD OF THE GULF OF MAINE BOUNDARY

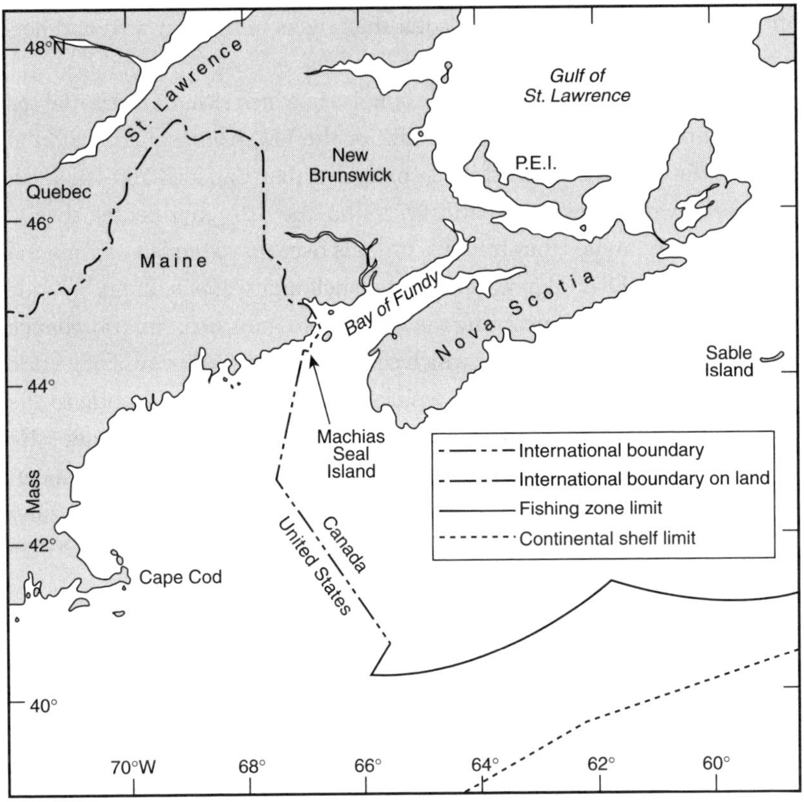

Source: DH Gray, 'Canada's Unresolved Maritime Boundaries' (1997) Vol 5 No 3 Boundary and Security Bulletin 60, 67.

The issue regarding the gray area involves a conflict between Canada's claimed 200-nautical-mile zone (EEZ) and the U.S. claimed continental shelf beyond 200 nautical miles. As explained by one commentator: "The question is whether, when a question of delimitation arises, the EEZ rights of one State take priority over the continental shelf claims of another State."[345] If the

343 McRae, *supra* note 276, at 168–169 and Colson, *supra* note 234, at 104.

344 *Id.* 169.

345 *Id.*

1984 Court's boundary were extended through the gray area, Canada would lose EEZ rights that could not be exercised by the United States since the area is beyond the U.S. 200-nautical-mile zone.[346] If Canada's zone were respected, there would be an "unnatural jog" in the boundary. The United States would have the Canadian EEZ just beyond its 200-nautical-mile zone and would be deprived of continental shelf rights in the gray area and perhaps beyond.[347]

One authority has noted several examples in which either a territorial sea has been truncated in favor of the EEZ or the EEZ has been truncated in favor of the continental shelf, and concluded that Canada's 200–nautical-mile zone would not automatically trump the U.S. continental shelf.[348] Another writer argues that the EEZ prevails over the extended continental shelf, since the EEZ addresses both the shelf and water column.[349] Oude Elferink asserts that, concerning the seabed of a gray area, "no precedence can be given either to the State which can claim . . . rights because of its title to an EEZ or to the State which can claim them because of its title to the continental shelf," since both have equal status under international law.[350] He goes on to suggest that, respecting the water column, the State having an EEZ right should be able to exercise it.[351] It is clear that there is uncertainty as to how a maritime boundary through the gray area should proceed.[352]

5.3.2 Continental Shelf Beyond the Gray Area

Canada and the United States each have continental shelf claims beyond the gray area, although the manner in which the gray area delimitation is resolved could affect the shelf areas that can be claimed. A delimitation line that extends the established Gulf of Maine boundary would be more favorable to the United States than a boundary that is based on equidistance.

The question of the maritime boundary in this area will become of some relevance in the near future because, in March 2005, Canada informed the

---

346 *Id.* Colson, *supra* note 234, at 104; and Gray, *supra* note 266, at 142.

347 *Id.* Colson, *supra* note 234, at 104; and Gray, *supra* note 266, at 142.

348 Colson, *supra* note 234, at 105.

349 I. Papanicolopulu, *A Note on Maritime Delimitation in a Multizonal Context: The Case of the Mediterranean* (2007) 38 ODIL 381, 386.

350 Oude Elferink, *supra* note 336, at 173.

351 *Id.*

352 Colson, *supra* note 234, at 105.

Commission on the Limits of the Continental Shelf (Commission) that its submission regarding the proposed outer limits of its shelf area would be in two parts, the first regarding the outer limit of the continental shelf for the Atlantic Ocean and then, at a later date, respecting other offshore areas.[353]

The Commission is a body established under the LOS Convention to which a State party is to submit information on its proposed outer limit of its continental shelf beyond 200 nautical miles.[354] It is critical to first note that a coastal State has exclusive jurisdiction over "the seabed and subsoil of the submarine areas that extend... to the outer edge of the continental margin"[355] and that this is not contingent in anyway on the submission of information to the Commission. Second, it is the coastal State, not the Commission, which has the legal capacity to establish the State's outer limit of the continental shelf.[356]

---

353 *See* Statement by the Chairman on the Commission, U. N. Doc CLCS/44, 3 May 2005, para 58, at www.un.org/Depts/los/clcs_new/clcs_home.htm (accessed on 25 July 2007).

354 LOS Convention, *supra* note 103, Art 76(8) and Annex II, Commission on the Limits of the Continental Shelf.

Pursuant to Article 4 of Annex II, coastal States which intend to establish outer limits of their continental shelf "shall submit particulars of such limits to the Commission along with supporting scientific and technical data as soon as possible but in any case within 10 years of the entry into force of this Convention for that State." Thus, for Canada the so-called ten-year rule is measured from 7 December 2003, meaning the necessary information is to be submitted by 7 December 2013. For the United States, the ten-year rule would commence when accession is completed.

355 *Id.* Art 76(1).

International Law Association, Committee on Legal Issues of the Outer Continental Shelf, *Report*, in REPORT OF THE SEVENTY-FIRST CONFERENCE HELD IN BERLIN, 2004 (London, 2004) 774–775 (footnotes deleted), commented:

> [A]rticle 76(1) of the Convention lays down that the basis of entitlement to the continental shelf is distance from the coast or natural prolongation of the land territory to the outer edge of the continental margin. An entitlement of a State exists by the sole fact that the basis of entitlement is present and does not require the establishment of outer limit lines.

356 The U.S. government, for example, has stated: "Ultimate responsibility for the delimitation [of the outer limit of the continental margin] lies with the coastal State itself." United States, Commentary–The 1982 United Nations Convention on the Law of the Sea, attached to Message from the President of the United States transmitting United Nations Convention on the Law of the Sea, with Annexes, done at Montego Bay, 10 December 1982 (the Convention) and the Agreement Relating to the Implementation of Part XI of the United Nations Convention on the Law of the Sea of 10 December 1982, adopted at New York, 28 July 1994 (the Agreement) and signed by the United States, subject to ratification, on 29 July 1994, U.S. Senate, Treaty Document 39, 103d Congress, 2d Session IV (1994) 57, 34 ILM 1393.

See also U. N. Division of Ocean Affairs and the Law of the Sea, *The Law of the Sea: Definition of the Continental Shelf* (New York, 1993) 29 and ILA Committee, *supra* note 355, at 785–786.

The information to be submitted to the Commission by a coastal State is to detail the coastal State's proposed outer limit of the shelf area beyond 200 nautical miles. Article 76(4)-(6) of the LOS Convention sets out the criteria to be used by a coastal State to determine the outer limit of its "legal" continental margin beyond 200 nautical miles. Article 76(2) notes that a coastal State's "continental shelf . . . shall not extend beyond the limits provided for in paragraphs 4 to 6." The following is a succinct summation of the Article 76 criteria:

> Pursuant to Article 76(4), the outer limit of a state's continental margin is to be either: (i) a line, connecting the outermost points where "the thickness of sedimentary rocks is at least one per cent of the shortest distance from such point to the foot of the continental slope", or (ii) a line connecting points "not more than 60 nautical miles from the foot of the continental slope". Lines created pursuant to 76(4) are not to extend beyond either 350 nautical miles from a state's baselines or 100 nautical miles from the 2,500 metre isobath. For submarine ridges the 350 nautical mile limit applies. For "submarine elevations that are natural components of the continental margin, such as its plateaux, rises, caps, banks and spurs," either the 350 nautical mile or the 100 nautical miles from the 2,500 metre isobath criterion is the limitation. A further general limitation is that the continental margin does not include the oceanic floor with its oceanic ridges. (footnotes deleted)[357]

The above criteria are not easily applicable in a specific instance because of the technical and definitional difficulties of determining thickness of sediment, foot of the continental slope, the 2,500-meter isobath, and distinguishing among submarine ridges, oceanic ridges, and submarine elevations that are natural components of the continental margin.

The role of the Commission is to consider the submitted material and make recommendations to the submitting State regarding the information received.[358]

---

357 T. L. McDorman, *The Role of the Commission on the Limits of the Continental Shelf: A Technical Body in a Political World* (2002) 17 ILMCL 301, 304–305.

358 LOS Convention, *supra* note 103, Art 76(8) and Art 3(1)(a) of Annex II. More generally on the role of the Commission, *see* McDorman, *supra* note 357.

The Commission, however, is not to address submissions respecting the outer limits of a continental shelf if the area in question is subject in any way to a dispute between States.[359] Article 76(10) of the LOS Convention notes that:

> The provisions of this article are without prejudice to the question of delimitation of the continental shelf between States with opposite or adjacent coasts.

Annex I to the Rules of Procedure of the Commission, paragraph 5(a) states:

> In cases where a land or maritime dispute exists, the Commission shall not consider . . . a submission made by any of the States concerned in the dispute.

For the purposes of Canada's submission to the Commission respecting the outer limit of the continental shelf in the area within and seaward of the gray area, Canada and the United States will either have to reach a maritime boundary agreement or, what is more likely, the two States will accept that either a designated area is not included within the submission or that, whatever is submitted and any comments by the Commission, are "without prejudice" to an eventual bilateral agreement. Without an arrangement of some type, the Commission cannot address that part of a Canadian proposed outer limit where the outer limit is subject to dispute with the United States.

5.4 Beaufort Sea

In the Beaufort Sea, defined by the coasts of Alaska and Yukon-Northwest Territories, Canada and the United States have their largest area of overlapping

---

359 *See generally* ILA Committee, *supra* note 355, at 809–813; C. R. Symmons, *The Irish Partial Submission to the Commission on the Limits of the Continental Shelf in 2005: A Precedent for Future Such Submissions in the Light of the "Disputed Areas" Procedures of the Commission* (2006) 37 ODIL 299–317; A. G. Oude Elferink, *Submissions of Coastal States to the CLCS in Cases of Unresolved Land or Maritime Disputes*, in M. H. Nordquist, J. N. Moore, and T. H. Heidar (eds.) Legal and Scientific Aspects of Continental Shelf Limits (Martinus Nijhoff, Leiden 2004) 263–285; and C. Johnson and A. G. Oude Elferink, *Submissions to the Commission on the Limits of the Continental Shelf in Cases of Unresolved Land and Maritime Disputes: The Significance of Article 76(10) of the Convention on the Law of the Sea*, in D. Freestone, R. Barnes, and D. M. Ong (eds.) The Law of the Sea: Progress and Prospects (Oxford University Press, Oxford 2006) 161–179.

claimed territorial sea and 200-nautical-mile zones, -6,250 square nautical miles.[360] The precise area in dispute as a result of overlapping 200–nautical-mile zone claims became known as a result of the articulation by each State of their 200-nautical-mile zones in 1977, with Canada using as its boundary the 141st west meridian[361] and the United States utilizing strict equidistance.[362]

Given the oil production at and near Prudhoe Bay in Alaska and the oil and gas finds in the Canadian Mackenzie Delta and Beaufort Sea,[363] it is reasonable to assume that there is a good potential for oil and gas in the Canada-U.S. overlapping claim area. The challenge is that large parts of the Beaufort Sea are ice covered for much of the year. There is little commercial fishing activity in the Beaufort Sea, but the harvesting of marine living resources, including whales, are important to the coastal inhabitants.[364]

The physical continental shelf extends beyond 200 nautical miles in the Beaufort Sea into the Canada Basin.[365] Both Canada and the United States are working independently and in cooperation[366] to assess fully the extent of the physical shelf in this area. As in the situation of the continental shelf seaward of the Gulf of Maine, the continental shelf area beyond the

---

360 Gray, *supra* note 266, at 135.

361 Fishing Zones of Canada (Zone 6) Order, *supra* note 12.

362 Maritime Boundaries between the United States and Canada, *supra* note 12, superseded by Exclusive Economic Zone and Maritime Boundaries, *supra* note 12.

363 National Energy Board, *Probabilistic Estimates of Hydrocarbon Volumes in the Mackenzie Delta and Beaufort Sea Discoveries* (Calgary, 1998) and Indian and Northern Affairs Canada, *Northern Oil and Gas Annual Report 2005* (Ottawa, 2006).

364 *See* G. B. Ayles, L. Amos, L. Bell, K. Bill, L. Harwood, and M. Papst, *Constraints and Opportunities for the Development of Commercial Fisheries in the Canadian Beaufort Sea*, powerpoint presentation prepared for the Coastal Zone Canada 2006 Conference, held in Tuktoyuktuk, August 2006, at www.czc06.ca/images/PDF/1-2-B%20Ayles.pdf (accessed on 16 August 2007) and *see* P. J. Usher, *Inivialuit Use of the Beaufort Sea and its Resources, 1960–2000* (2002) 55 Sup. 1 ARCTIC 18–28.

365 *See* J. Verhoef and D. MacDougall, *Delineating Canada's Continental Shelf according to the United Nations Convention on the Law of the Sea* (2008) 3 J OCEAN TECHNOLOGY 1, 4 and L. Mayer, M. Jakobsson, and A. Armstrong, *The Compilation and Analysis of Data Relevant to a U.S. Claim under United Nations Law of the Sea Article 76: A Preliminary Report* (Center for Coastal and Ocean Mapping and Joint Hydrographic Center, Durham, N.H. May 2002) Figures 5.10A and 5.10B.

366 *Canada, U.S. to team up on Arctic seabed mapping project*, CBC News, 30 June 2008, at www.cbc.ca/technology/story/2008/06/30/cda-mapping.html (accessed on 4 August 2008) and Department of State, Two Scientific Cruises to Map Arctic Seafloor, 11 August 2008, at www.state.gov/r/pa/prs/ps/2008/aug/108119.htm (access on 30 August 2008).

Beaufort Sea will involve bilateral discussion and Commission on the Limits of the Continental Shelf.[367]

5.4.1 141st Meridian

The 141st meridian is the land boundary between Alaska and the Yukon as set out in Article III of the 1825 Russia-Great Britain Treaty,[368] which is binding on the United States as a result of the U.S. acquisition of Alaska from Russia in 1867.[369] The Canadian position is that the 141st meridian is also the maritime boundary in the Beaufort Sea, based on the 1825 Treaty wording for a boundary along the meridian "in its prolongation as far as the Frozen Ocean" (*dans son prolongement jusqu'à la Mer Glaciale*, the authentic language of the Treaty, which is in French).[370]

Although the United States asserts that it has consistently rejected that either the 1825 or 1867 Treaties established an ocean boundary in the Beaufort Sea,[371] the United States did accept the 1867 Treaty line between Alaska and Russia in the Bering Sea, Chukchi Sea, and the North Pacific Ocean, as the maritime boundary.[372] In 1977, the United States and the Soviet Union exchanged notes which cited and accepted that the 1867 Treaty would be respected regarding delimiting the water column for the purposes 200-nautical-mile fishing zones.[373] This was confirmed in the 1990 U.S.-Russia maritime boundary Treaty.[374] As a result of the U.S. dealings with the Russians respecting the 1867 Treaty, it can be argued that the United States must

---

367 *See* Chapter Five, section 5.3.2 and T.L. McDorman, *The Continental Shelf beyond 200 nm: Law and Politics in the Arctic Ocean* (paper presented in Oslo at the International Conference, The World Ocean in Globalization, 23 August 2008).

368 Convention between Great Britain and Russia Concerning the Limits of their Respective Possessions on the North-West Coast of America, *supra* note 77, Art III.

369 Convention ceding Alaska between Russia and the United States, *supra* note 78.

370 Convention between Great Britain and Russia Concerning the Limits of their Respective Possessions on the North-West Coast of America, *supra* note 77, Art III. *See* Diplomatic Note No. 626, 22 December 1976, *supra* note 142, at 432 and Clark, *supra* note 13, at 7.

371 Feldman and Colson, *supra* note 26, at 750 and *see* K. L. Lawson, *Delimiting Continental Shelf Boundaries in the Arctic: The United States – Canada Beaufort Sea Boundary* (1981) 22 VIRGINIA JIL 222, 242.

372 Feldman and Colson, *supra* note 26, at 751–753.

373 *Id.* 752–753.

374 U.S.-Russia Maritime Boundary Agreement, *supra* note 3, Art 1.

accept that the 1867 Treaty also establishes an ocean boundary following the 141st meridian.[375]

Canada has used the 141st meridian as the boundary for oil and gas leases and permits issued going back to 1965.[376] In 1970, Canada utilized the 141st meridian as the western boundary of the 100-nautical-mile Arctic pollution prevention zone.[377] Although the United States objected strenuously to Canada's creation of the Arctic zone,[378] no specific comment was made as regards the use of the 141st meridian as the zone's western boundary. In 1977, Canada used the 141st meridian as the western limit in the Arctic of its 200-nautical-mile zone.[379] Only in 1976 did the United States officially protest the use by Canada of the 141st meridian for the issuing of oil and gas concessions and stated that it was "not aware of circumstances that would justify" the 141st meridian as a maritime boundary.[380] In 1977, the United States made clear its offshore claim in the Beaufort Sea.[381]

The 141st meridian is also the western segment of the so-called sector theory approach to Canadian Arctic jurisdiction, whereby the 141st meridian extends to the North Pole. It has been commented that Canada has had an "ambiguous position regarding the sector principle" and that Canada "maintains a position that neither claims nor disclaims the sector theory."[382] The argument that the sector theory provides a basis in international law for

---

375 One commentator has noted:

> The United States is virtually saying that the same treaty that delimits a maritime boundary in the west does not delimit a maritime boundary in the east, and it sets up an argument for equidistance in the east that does not recognize the 1867 Line as a special circumstance calling for deviation, partial or full, from an equidistance line.

C. M. Antinori, *The Bering Sea: A Maritime Delimitation Dispute between the United States and the Soviet Union* (1987) 18 ODIL 1, 34.

376 D. PHARAND, CANADA'S ARCTIC WATERS IN INTERNATIONAL LAW (Cambridge University Press, Cambridge 1988) 58.

377 Arctic Waters Pollution Protection Act, St Can 1969–1970, c 47, s 2.

378 *See* Department of State, Statement on Government of Canada's Bills on Limits of the Territorial Sea, Fisheries and Pollution, 15 April 1970, 9 ILM 605–606 and Note from the Secretary of State to Embassy of Canada, 14 April 1970, in *Gulf of Maine Pleadings*, Vol. 5, Annex 8 to Reply of the United States, 529–530.

379 Fishing Zones of Canada (Zone 6) Order, *supra* note 12.

380 Diplomatic Note No. 103, 20 May 1976, in *Gulf of Maine Pleadings*, Vol. 1, Annex 32 to Memorial of Canada, 410.

381 Maritime Boundaries between the United States and Canada, *supra* note 12, superseded by Exclusive Economic Zone and Maritime Boundaries, *supra* note 12.

382 K. M. Shusterich, *International Jurisdictional Issues in the Arctic Ocean*, in W. E. WESTERMEYER AND K. M. SHUSTERICH, (eds.) UNITED STATES ARCTIC INTERESTS: THE 1980s AND 1990s (Springer-Verlag, New York 1984) 253.

BEAUFORT SEA

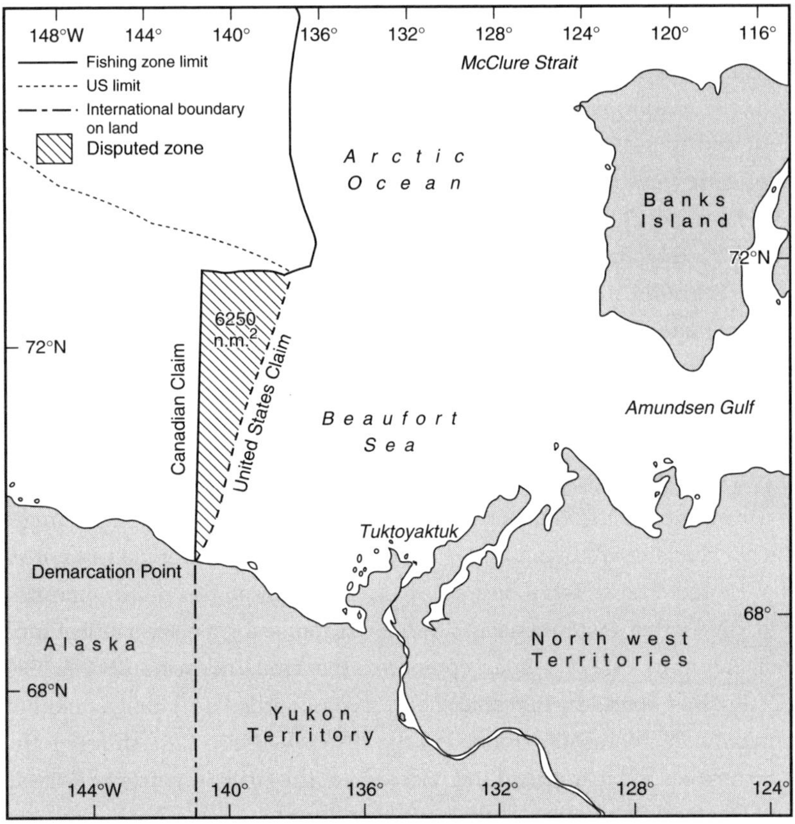

Source: DH Gray, 'Canada's Unresolved Maritime Boundaries' (1997) Vol 5 No 3 Boundary and Security Bulletin 60, 63.

offshore jurisdiction has been rejected by Pharand in a detailed study[383] and the theory is inconsistent with the modern international law of the sea of 200-nautical-mile zones and continental shelf jurisdiction beyond 200 nautical miles. The United States has explicitly and persistently objected to and not used the sector principle to claim offshore jurisdiction.[384]

Pharand, who has undertaken a detailed study of Article III of the 1825 Treaty, is of the opinion that the 141st meridian was to extend only to the

383 Pharand, *supra* note 376, at 3–87.

384 Diplomatic Note 103, 20 May 1976, *supra* note 380, at 411 states: "The United States must reiterate its longstanding position that the so-called 'sector' theory is not an accepted principle of international law." *See also* Pharand, *supra* note 376, at 68–69 and Lawson, *supra* note 371, at 233.

point of intersection of the land with "*la Mer Glaciale*, but not into the Arctic Ocean.[385] Further, in examining *la Mer Glaciale*, Pharand takes the view that this expression should be understood as a reference to a topographical feature and not to be understood in the sense of where the waters become frozen.[386] Finally, looking at the wording of Article III, which refers only to land and islands, he concludes that the 1825 Treaty addresses only land boundaries and does not create an ocean boundary in the Beaufort Sea.[387] This latter conclusion is consistent with the textual analysis of Article III by Bourne and McRae in which they determined that the line established in the Dixon Entrance was not an ocean boundary, but was "a line of allocation."[388] Note has already been made of the cautious treatment given historic treaties in the 1985 *Guinea-Guinea-Bissau Arbitration*.[389] According to these authorities, even if the 141st meridian extended into the Beaufort Sea, it would appear that it was a line demarcating land and island possessions and not an ocean boundary.

As regards the relationship between the U.S. treatment of the 1867 Treaty line *vis à vis* Russia as a maritime boundary and the 141st meridian, as noted, the United States has objected to the validity of the 141st meridian and, unlike the western line, utilized equidistance for its 200-nautical-mile delineation in 1977.[390] The acceptance of the 1867 Treaty line in the 1990 U.S.-Russian boundary agreement has been described as "strange" and not imperative.[391] Moreover, as noted in the 1993 *Jan Mayen Case*, in which the International Court rejected the relevance of the treaty practice of Norway and Denmark in another ocean boundary dispute in resolving the dispute before them, each ocean boundary dispute is unique, and though similar

---

385 Pharand, *supra* note 376, at 20.

386 *Id.* 20–21.

387 *Id.* 22.

388 Bourne and McRae, *supra* note 271, at 196.

389 *Guinea–Guinea-Bissau Arbitration*, *supra* note 284, at para 80.

390 *See* Diplomatic Note 103, 20 May 1976, *supra* note 380, at 410 and Maritime Boundaries between the United States and Canada, *supra* note 12, superseded by Exclusive Economic Zone and Maritime Boundaries, *supra* note 12.

391 A. Oude Elferink, *The 1990 USSR-USA Maritime Boundary Agreement* (1991) 6 IJMCL 41, 43:

> The boundary agreement concluded by both countries establishes that the maritime boundary in the Bering and Chukchi Seas is formed by the line of the 1867 Convention. The choice of this line, however, in no way seemed to be imperative. The line was originally intended to divide the islands belonging to the ceded territory from other Russian islands. It is strange that it has ipso facto evolved into a maritime boundary. (footnotes deleted)

political, legal, and geographic situations may be of influence, ultimately each dispute must be assessed independently.[392]

Nevertheless, it can be argued that U.S. acceptance of the meridian line with the Russians indicates what the United States might consider an equitable result. This argument may either displace equidistance as a first step in an adjudicated delimitation or be considered as a relevant/special circumstance in the adjustment of a preliminary equidistance line.

5.4.2 Hydrocarbon Activity Moratorium

Currently, there are two Canadian-issued exploration leases, dating from the mid 1980s, which encroach on the disputed area in the Beaufort Sea.[393] These leases are subject to work prohibition orders and are, therefore, not active.

Within the Beaufort Sea area, the U.S. federal government has exclusive authority over the hydrocarbon resources of the continental shelf beyond the three-nautical-mile territorial sea, while Alaska has authority within the three-nautical-mile limit.[394] The federal government of the United States has included the Beaufort Sea disputed area in lease sales since 1982, including in the 2007 lease sale 202.[395] However, any bids for leases received for tracts in the disputed area were to remain unopened until at least 2012.[396] As of January 2007, there were no existing U.S. federal leases in the disputed area.[397] Alaska has also made available tracts for lease within the disputed area, although it does not appear that any leases have been issued.[398]

---

392 *Jan Mayen Case*, *supra* note 14, at para 86 and *see* the comment of Charney, *supra* note 14, at 252.

393 *Northern Oil and Gas Annual Report 2005*, *supra* note 363, at 16 and Indian and Northern Affairs Canada, Map of Beaufort Sea Area, at www.ainc.inac.gc.ca/oil/pdf/bsmdnom2007ful.pdf (accessed on 9 April 2007).

394 Submerged Lands Act, 67 US Stat. 29, Pub L. 31 (1953), codified at 43 USC 1301 and Outer Continental Shelf Lands Act, 67 US Stat. 462, Pub L. 212 (1953), codified at 43 USC 1331.

395 Department of the Interior, Outer Continental Shelf (OCS) Beaufort Sea Alaska, Oil and Gas Lease Sale 202, Final Notice, 19 March 2007, 72 Fed Reg 12817, 12820.

396 *Id.*

397 Department of the Interior, Mineral Management Service, Beaufort Sea Existing Leases–January 2007, (map), at www.mms.gov/alaska/cproject/beaufortsale/sale202/bf_leases.pdf (accessed on 9 April 2007).

398 *See* Alaska, Department of Natural Resources, Division of Oil and Gas, Beaufort Sea Areawide 2006—Tract Map 8, at <www.dog.dnr.state.ak.us/oil/products/publications/beaufortsea/bsaw2006/bsmaps8.pdf> (accessed on 9 April 2007).

Both Canada and the United States have adopted a policy of preventing drilling or other hydrocarbon-related activity from taking place in the disputed area within the Beaufort Sea.[399]

5.4.3 Bilateral Discussions

In 1970, the United States suggested negotiation of all of the outstanding Canada-U.S. maritime boundaries, including in the Beaufort Sea. This implies that it was the U.S. view "that the boundary in the Beaufort Sea remained undelimited at that time,"[400] although it was only in 1976 that the U.S. protested Canadian oil and gas activities[401] and in 1977 that the United States formally indicated its equidistance claim in the Beaufort Sea.[402]

As already noted, during the discussions of the Special Negotiators in 1977 to 1978, Canada evinced a flexible position regarding the Beaufort Sea maritime boundary, it being clear that outcomes acceptable to Canada in the other boundary areas could be offset by compromise in the Beaufort.[403] There is no indication of a U.S. view.

The Beaufort Sea boundary dispute area has long been seen as a candidate for the development of some type of hydrocarbon joint development regime. Canada and the United States could either agree to set aside the boundary issue and share the exploration costs and development benefits of any hydrocarbon resources in the disputed area; or proceed with a maritime boundary but have a joint zone for hydrocarbon activity, the benefits of which would be shared by both States.[404] There are a significant number of both types of hydrocarbon joint development arrangements throughout the world that could be utilized as a model.[405]

---

399 Gray, *supra* note 266, at 135 refers to the two States having "established a moratorium on exploration" in the disputed area.

400 A. G. Oude Elferink, *Arctic Maritime Delimitations: The Preponderance of Similarities with Other Regions*, in A. G. OUDE ELFERINK D. R. ROTHWELL (eds.) THE LAW OF THE SEA AND POLAR MARITIME DELIMITATION AND JURISDICTION (Martinus Nijhoff, The Hague 2001) 192.

401 Diplomatic Note 103, 20 May 1976, *supra* note 380, at 410.

402 Maritime Boundaries between the United States and Canada, *supra* note 12, superseded by Exclusive Economic Zone and Maritime Boundaries, *supra* note 12.

403 Clark, *supra* note 13, at 8.

404 *See, for example*, Russell, *supra* note 29 at 496–498; McRae, *supra* note 13, at 159–160; and D. R. ROTHWELL, MARITIME BOUNDARIES AND RESOURCE DEVELOPMENT: OPTIONS FOR THE BEAUFORT SEA (Calgary: Canadian Institute of Resources Law, 1988) 45–57.

405 Note Tanaka, *supra* note 185, at 282–287 and regarding specific arrangements, *see* R. R. Churchill, *Maritime Delimitation in the Jan Mayen Area* (1985) 9 MAR POL 16–38; D. M. Ong,

The Special Negotiators, in 1977, reported on and received the approval of both States regarding a shared-access approach to hydrocarbon matters in overlapping disputed areas, specifically for the Gulf of Maine and the Beaufort Sea.[406] The idea was that shared-access zones would be created adjacent to a negotiated maritime boundary. Although each State would have exclusive authority over the hydrocarbon activities within the zone on its side of the maritime boundary, each State would have a right of purchase to obtain one-half of the volume of hydrocarbons produced within each shared-access zone.[407] Like the proposed fisheries principles in the 1977 Special Negotiators' Joint Report[408] and the subsequent 1979 East Coast Fisheries Agreement,[409] the proposed hydrocarbon shared-access zone concept was designed to make the location of a maritime boundary largely irrelevant. The significant differences in the legal regimes of Canada and the United States regarding oil and gas activities and the unwillingness of either State to contemplate legislative change removed the option of a "condominium system for oil and gas" and led to the shared-access zone concept.[410] The key to the concept was the location of the zones, but no agreement had been reached in 1977 "as regards the number, size or configuration of such zones."[411] Although some brief talks on the Beaufort Sea area in the late 1980s may have touched on joint development ideas, since the 1970s there has not been any significant discussion.

Joint hydrocarbon development agreements are never easily negotiated or implemented. Existing leases in a disputed area add a complexity. This concern is reduced by half since only Canada has leased tracts in the disputed area. Depending on the area in question, both the U.S. federal government and the state of Alaska would have a direct interest in a joint development regime. On the Canadian side, the overlapping international

---

The New Timor Sea Arrangement 2001: Is Joint Development of Common Oil and Gas Deposits Mandated under International Law? (2002) 17 IJMCL 79–122; and D. M. Ong, *The 1979 and 1990 Malaysia-Thailand Joint Development Agreements: A Model for International Legal Co-operation in Common Offshore Petroleum Deposits* (1999) 14 IJMCL 207–246.

406 Joint Report of Cadieux and Cutler, *supra* note 17, at 12.

407 *Id.* 3–4 and *see* 29–32, Proposed Principles for Offshore Hydrocarbon Shared-Access Zones.

408 *Id.* 14–28, Principles for A Joint Fisheries Commission to be Established by a Convention between Canada and the United States.

409 East Coast Fishery Agreement, *supra* note 20.

410 Clark, *supra* note 13, at 13.

411 Joint Report of Cadieux and Cutler, *supra* note 17, at 11.

maritime disputed area is within the Inuvialuit settlement region.[412] The Yukon Territory may also have an interest, although by legislation its boundaries do not extend into the Beaufort Sea.[413]

5.5 Machias Seal Island and North Rock

Machias Seal Island and North Rock, standing adjacent to Maine (9.2-nautical-miles distant) and Grand Manan Island, New Brunswick (10-nautical-miles distant)[414] in the inner Gulf of Maine, are the only non-submerged lands in dispute between Canada and the United States. Because of the disputed sovereignty over the islets, there is an area of overlapping maritime claims of approximately 210 square nautical miles.[415] Machias Seal Island has been home to one or more lighthouses maintained by the British and Canadians since 1832.[416] In 1944, the Island was designated by Canada as a migratory bird sanctuary.[417] The Island is part of the Maine Coastal Islands National Wildlife Refuge under the management of the U.S. Fish and Wildlife Service.[418] Beyond the lighthouse and visitors, there is no economic activity on the islands. In the waters adjacent to Machias Seal Island and North Rock,

---

412 Final Agreement, as Amended, (1984) at www.investnwt.com/aboriginal/inuvialuit_final_agreement.pdf (accessed on 9 April 2007).

413 Yukon Act, St Can 2002, c 7, sch 1. This Act provides that in a defined offshore "adjoining area," the Yukon Territory has administration and control of oil and gas resources. This area is near shore and not in the vicinity of the disputed area. *See* B. CALDERBANK, A. M. MACLEOD, T. L. MCDORMAN, AND D. H. GRAY, CANADA'S OFFSHORE: JURISDICTION, RIGHTS, AND MANAGEMENT (Trafford Publishing, 3rd edition, Victoria 2006) 178.

414 Gray, *supra* note 266, at 138.

415 *Id.* 140.

416 *Id.* 139–140.

417 *Id.* 138.

418 Fish and Wildlife Service, *Maine Coastal Islands National Wildlife Refuge: Final Comprehensive Conservation Plan* (April 2005), 3–76, at <library.fws.gov/CCPs/MaineIslands/ccp_final.pdf> (accessed on 6 December 2007).

Note is made that Machias Seal Island is "owned" by the Maine Department of Inland Fisheries and Wildlife and by a memorandum of understanding the management authority has been transferred to the U.S. Fish and Wildlife Service. It is also noted that by "verbal agreement with Canada, Canadian biologists manage the wildlife resources on the island." *See also US and Canada Collaborate on Bird Sanctuary Management despite Sovereignty Dispute* (Summer, 2007), Vol. 1, No. 2, Gulf of Maine Times, at www.gulfofmaine.org/times/summer97/index.html (accessed on 6 December 6, 2007).

the primary resource of interest is the lobster harvested by fishers from both Canada and the United States.[419]

5.5.1 Islands Ownership Dispute

In 1970, Canada announced that, in 1971, fisheries closing lines were to be employed to close the Bay of Fundy, and other waters on the East and West Coasts of Canada, to foreign fishing.[420] The Bay of Fundy fisheries closing line was constructed specifically utilizing points on Machias Seal Island and North Rock. Though the United States protested Canada's fisheries closing lines in 1970 as being a "unilateral act . . . without foundation in international law,"[421] no specific mention was made by the United States regarding Canada's clear assertion that Machias Seal Island and North Rock were under Canadian sovereignty. The U.S. view is that Canadian fisheries patrol vessels "first interfered with" U.S. fishermen within three nautical miles of Machias Seal Island only in August 1971[422] and that, at this time, the United States rejected the Canadian assertion of authority over Machias Seal Island and North Rock.[423] Baxter and Horwitz refer to discussions between Canada and the United States in 1938, when a Canadian representative reportedly noted that the islands were claimed as U.S. territory, but that the United States was prepared to relinquish all claims of sovereignty over the islets.[424]

In 1973, the United States formally proposed to Canada that the ownership of Machias Seal Island and North Rock be submitted to the International

---

419 *See* B. Cook, *Lobster Boat Diplomacy: The Canada—US Grey Zone* (2005) 29 MAR POL 385–390 and J. Marshall, *Defining Maritime Boundaries: "The Murky Hand of History's Oversight" in the Gulf of Maine* (2004) 48 THE CANADIAN GEOGRAPHER 266, 269–271, 277.

420 Jack Davis, Minister of Fisheries and Forestry, HC, *Debates*, 18 December 1970, 2189–2190. *See* Fishing Zones of Canada (Zone 1, 2 and 3) Order, Can Gaz Part II, Vol. 105, SOR/71-81, 25 February 25, 1971, 363–364, came into effect on 10 March 1971. *See* Chapter Three, section 3.2.

421 *See* Statement on Canadian Fisheries Closing Lines Announcement, 18 December 1970, in S. H. LAY, R. CHURCHILL, AND M. NORDQUIST (eds.) NEW DIRECTIONS IN THE LAW OF THE SEA, Vol. I (Oceana Publications, Dobbs Ferry, N.Y. 1973) 74, para 2.

422 R. R. Baxter and M. J. Horwitz, Opinion in Support of Sovereignty of the United States of America over Machias Seal Island and North Rock, submitted to the Marine Resources Commission, State of Maine, March 1, 1975, 24, on file with the author. It is unclear who requested this legal opinion.

423 *Id.* 30.

424 *Id.* 26–27.

Court for resolution.[425] Motivating this U.S. proposal were concerns over impeded oil and gas exploration and a number of violent incidents involving fishing vessels.[426] Canada rejected the U.S. proposal, stating that it "had long exercised undisputed sovereignty over the islands and that adjudication 'would of itself put Canada's longstanding unquestioned title into question.'"[427] The U.S. responded that the "unsettled issue of sovereignty over Machias Seal Island and North Rock has been noted by United States and Canadian officials for a number of years," and that the United States did not agree that no dispute existed and that title to the islands rested with Canada.[428]

To which country Machias Seal Island and North Rock belong is a question of interpretation of numerous historic documents. The 1783 Paris Treaty between the United States and Great Britain that ended the U.S. Revolutionary War provided that all islands within 20 leagues of the U.S. coast were under U.S. sovereignty "excepting such islands as now are, or heretofore have been, within the limits of the . . . Province of Nova Scotia."[429] The 1621 Letters Patent establishing the colonies of Nova Scotia and New Brunswick included all islands within six leagues of a line from St. Mary's Bay, Nova Scotia, to the mouth of the St Croix River.[430] Commissioners, looking at these documents in 1817 to determine British or U.S. ownership of islands in Passamaquoddy Bay, determined that Grand Manan Island, the closest island to Machias Seal Island and North Rock, was British, but had nothing to say about Machias Seal Island and North Rock themselves.[431]

5.5.2 Waters Around the Disputed Islands

The ocean area in dispute adjacent to Machias Seal Island and North Rock only became clear in 1977 when both Canada and the United States constructed

---

425 *Digest of United States Practice in International Law, 1973*, *supra* note 296, at 465–466.

426 *Id.* 466.

427 Aide-Memoire, 4 January 1974, *supra* note 297, at 552. *See also* Department of External Affairs, Letter, 9 June 1973, in (1974) 12 CYIL 279, 280: "The Canadian position is that the island belongs to Canada by virtue of possession stretching over a period exceeding one hundred years."

428 Department of State, Digest of United States Practice in International Law, 1974 (Washington, 1975) 673 citing from a U.S. aide-memoire to Canada, dated 22 April 1974.

429 Paris Treaty of 1783, *supra* note 61, Art II.

430 Gray, *supra* note 266, at 140.

431 Decision of the Commissioners under the Fourth Article of the Treaty of Ghent, *supra* note 66 and *see* Gray, *supra* note 266, at 140 and Baxter and Horwitz, *supra* note 422, at 1–5. Note above: Chapter Five, section 2.2.

their 200-nautical-mile zones. Consistent with Canada's position regarding the Gulf of Maine, Canada's line followed an equidistant line from the termination of the agreed maritime boundary in the Grand Manan Channel, to the west of the disputed islands, and seaward into the Gulf of Maine.[432] Consistent with the United States position regarding the Gulf of Maine, that the Northeast Channel was the delimitation line of the natural prolongation of Georges Bank,[433] the U.S. line does not follow equidistance; rather, it follows the deepest channel (the thalweg) to the east and south of the disputed islands and within the Grand Manan Channel.[434] The existing U.S. line is less favorable than would be an equidistance line giving full effect the Machias Seal Island and North Rock as being U.S. owned.

Canada and the United States agreed to exclude from the *Gulf of Maine Case* the question of the sovereignty over and the sea area adjacent to Machias Seal Island and North Rock. This was done by instructing the Chamber of the International Court to use Point *A* as the starting point for the maritime boundary to be constructed within the inner Gulf of Maine.[435] Point *A* corresponded with the point of crossing of the Canadian and U.S. claims south of Machias Seal Island.[436] An author has opined that the "apparent reason" for the exclusion of the Machias Seal Island and North Rock dispute from the *Gulf of Maine Case* was:

> That neither country wished the Chamber of the Court to rule one way for possession of the island and then feel obliged to rule against that country in the Georges Bank area. Both countries wanted the Georges Bank boundary to be decided on its own merits.[437]

Since the early 1970s, Canada and the United States have informally agreed upon and maintained a policy of flag State enforcement regarding fishing

---

432 Fishing Zones of Canada (Zones 4 and 5) Order, *supra* note 12. *See* Gray, *supra* note 266, at 140.

433 Feldman and Colson, *supra* note 26, at 755 and *see Gulf of Maine Case*, *supra* note 4, at para 65.

434 Maritime Boundaries between the United States and Canada, *supra* note 12, superseded by Exclusive Economic Zone and Maritime Boundaries, *supra* note 12. *See* Gray, *supra* note 266, at 140.
Regarding the Grand Manan Channel, note Diplomatic Note No. 626, 22 December 1976, *supra* note 142, at 431.

435 *Gulf of Maine Case*, *supra* note 4, at paras 20, 211.

436 Gray, *supra* note 266, at 140.

437 *Id.*

MACHIAS SEAL ISLAND

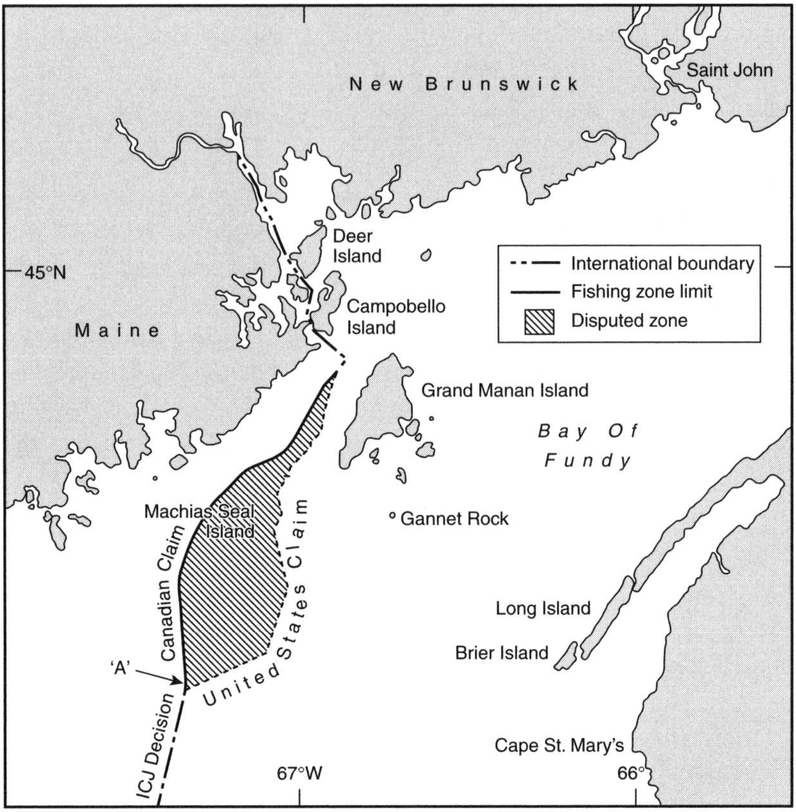

Source: DH Gray, 'Canada's Unresolved Maritime Boundaries' (1997) Vol 5 No 3 Boundary and Security Bulletin 60, 66.

activity within the disputed waters.[438] This has generally operated to avoid significant bilateral fisheries problems. However, in 2002, concerns within Canada of decreasing lobster catches and alleged increases in U.S. fishing effort in the disputed area put the lobster fishery within the disputed area on the bilateral agenda.[439] Moreover, management of the resource was made more difficult by differing management regimes in the two States.[440] In recent years, the increased availability of lobster and adjusted harvesting

---

438 See *Digest of United States Practice in International Law, 1973, supra* note 296, at 466. *See also* Russell, *et al., supra* note 197, at 70.

439 Marshall, *supra* note 419, at 277–278 and DFO, Backgrounder: The Machias Seal Island Lobster Fishery (LFA 38b), 30 June 2004, at <www.dfo-mpo.gc.ca/communications/maritimes/back04e/B-MAR-04-02E.html> (accessed on 16 April 2007). *See also* Russell, *et al., supra* note 197, at 65.

440 *See* Marshall, *supra* note 419, at 277–278 and Cook, *supra* note 419, at 387–388.

activities has resulted in a degree of calm on the Canada-U.S. lobster fishery adjacent to Machias Seal Island.

PART C

6.0 Conclusion

Canada and the United States earn very high marks for managing their bilateral maritime boundary disputes in such a way that they cause little ongoing friction between the two States. Formal and informal arrangements and *modus operandi* between the two States on fisheries and hydrocarbon activity, the usual culprits in maritime boundary disputes, have ensured calm in disputed waters. This has been helped by the fact that none of the remaining Canada-U.S. maritime boundary disputes involve large areas of waters in which there is significant fishing, as was the situation in the *Gulf of Maine Case.*

It can be challenged that the lack of immediate friction is an opportunity to address the underlying disputes, rather than the absence of heat being a reason not to be too concerned about the underlying disputes. Though it is hard to fault this perspective, the allocation of government resources, both human and political, inevitably flows to the immediate and urgent. Moreover, there are concerns about the political repercussions of negotiating maritime boundaries where compromise of long-held positions is inevitable. Account must also be taken of the *Gulf of Maine* fog that has shrouded the views of both governments on bilateral maritime boundary issues during the last two decades. Efforts to negotiate the Canada-U.S. maritime boundaries, in particular the Gulf of Maine boundary, were not successful because of an unwillingness or inability to reach compromise–essentially a failure of political will. Imaginative cross-boundary arrangements, such as the 1979 East Coast Fisheries Agreement,[441] were not supported by the very people they were designed to assist. The novelty in the 1970s of the 200-nautical-mile national fishing zone, an exclusive national zone for waters previously shared with foreign fishers, held an allure of sovereignty for those directly involved that undermined any desire to compromise. The Case itself, while establishing the maritime boundary and creating a degree of peace on the water, left neither side overly happy with the process or its results, and created a division of key fish stocks that left the resource subject to substandard management.

---

441 East Coast Fishery Agreement, *supra* note 20.

The *Gulf of Maine* fog has resulted in unwillingness in both countries to engage in formal resolutive discussions regarding maritime boundary delimitation.

The twenty-year *Gulf of Maine* fog may be lifting. There are two Canada-U.S. maritime boundaries that can be seen on the horizon: the area seaward of the Gulf of Maine and the Beaufort Sea. The former will need attention, if not resolution, when Canada makes its submission to the Commission on the Limits of the Continental Shelf regarding the outer limit of its continental margin beyond 200 nautical miles on the Atlantic Coast. Making the course of discussions easier is that there is little awareness of the existence of the dispute seaward of the Gulf of Maine maritime boundary, and there is unlikely to be much public or political concern on either side of the border over a compromise resolution provided that the hydrocarbon moratorium in each State is unaffected. The Beaufort Sea maritime boundary has long been seen as the one of most urgency, given the need for certainty in order to pursue the potential hydrocarbon resources in the area.[442] In the next few years, this should prove to be a sufficient incentive at least to allow for the initiation of serious discussions.

The maritime boundary disputes most entrenched in national history and sovereignty politics, this being mostly although not exclusively a problem for Canada—are the Dixon Entrance, and Machias Seal Island and North Rock. The conventional wisdom is that a resolution of these maritime boundaries and land disputes that does not involve a total U.S. capitulation is a political non-starter for Canada. Although the political fallout in Canada of compromise on the ownership of Machias Seal Island would be problematic, the same may not be the case regarding a compromise on the A-B Line in Dixon Entrance if the British Columbia government were fully involved.

The Dixon Entrance A-B Line dispute is the only one of the maritime disputes that might lend itself to adjudication. The issues are historic and involve the interpretation of texts. Such disputes are often decided by international arbitrations and courts.[443] Both countries have, at different times, sought the adjudication option respecting the A-B Line.[444] The area involved, though important, is not large and is contained (*i.e.*, not open ended). The tendency of adjudicators to find a middle ground would be an acceptable outcome for both States. Finally, an adjudicative approach and decision would likely satisfy the public in both States.

---

442 *See, for example*, McRae, *supra* note 276, at 159.

443 *See, for example, Frontier Dispute (Benin/Niger)*, [2005] ICJ Rep. 90.

444 *See* Bourne and McRae, *supra* note 271, at 213–214 and *Digest of United States Practice in International Law, 1973*, *supra* note 296, at 465–466.

Appendix Two

Questions and Detail Respecting the Application of Two-Step Process

I. Provisional Equidistance

Two questions that can arise regarding construction of a provisional equidistance line involve the use of islands and straight baselines as base points.

As regards islands and provisional equidistance, the International Court in the 2001 *Qatar/Bahrain Case* stated: "In accordance with Article 121, paragraph 2, of the 1982 Convention on the Law of the Sea, which reflects customary international law, islands, regardless of size, in this respect enjoy the same status, and therefore generate the same maritime rights, as other land territory."[1] The result is that islands are to be taken into account in constructing an equidistance line. However, two possible exceptions exist.

The first of the possible exceptions is the situation that arose in the 1977 *Anglo-French Arbitration* where the Tribunal took the view that the Channel Islands were on the "wrong side" of a notional equidistance line involving the opposite mainland coasts of France and the United Kingdom. The islands were given no effect by the Tribunal on that equidistance line. The Channel Islands were enclaved with their own offshore zones.[2] The outcome of the *Anglo-French Arbitration* was that the Channel Islands are surrounded by the ocean area of France and not connected by ocean area to the United Kingdom. A variation on this is partial enclaving where, for example, an island near a notional equidistance line between mainland coasts is given a 12-nautical-mile zone that creates a bulge in the delimitation line, but the island is given

---

1 *Case Concerning Maritime Delimitation and Territorial Questions between Qatar and Bahrain (Qatar v. Bahrain)*, [2001] ICJ Rep. 40, para 185.

2 *Arbitration between the United Kingdom and France on the Delimitation of the Continental Shelf*, 30 June 1977, 18 ILM 397, paras 201–203.

N. Marques Antunes, Towards the Conceptualisation of Maritime Delimitation (Martinus Nijhoff, Leiden 2003) 168–169, described enclaving as:

> The concept of "enclave" is defined in relation to equidistance. Typically, the method applies where islands are located either in the vicinity of the equidistance-line between mainland coasts, or on the "wrong side" thereof. . . . When combined with equidistance, it leads to discarding the basepoints of the islands to be enclaved.

no effect in the construction of an equidistance line.[3] The enclaving of inconvenient islands and disregard of their effect on equidistance, however, has not found favor in international adjudications. Tribunals have refrained from adopting the Channel Islands example. For example, although Canada argued in the 1992 *Canada-France Arbitration* that St. Pierre and Miquelon should be enclaved, the Tribunal did not accept the option.[4] In the 2001 *Qatar/Bahrain Case*, the International Court did not enclave the Hawar Islands of Bahrain (uninhabited except by a military garrison), even though the Hawar Islands were unquestionably "on the wrong side" of an equidistance line (essentially on the shore of Qatar) and again full (or in this case, partial) enclaving to avoid the effect of the islands on a mainland-to-mainland provisional equidistance line was a reasonable option.[5] The argument in the *Jan Mayen Case* was that Jan Mayen should not interfere with the 200-nautical-mile limit of Greenland (arguably a form of enclaving). This was not accepted by the International Court.[6] Regarding both Jan Mayen and Hawar Islands, the International Court used these islands in the construction of an equidistance line as a provisional line. The Arbitration Tribunal's approach to St. Pierre and Miquelon was different, but did not involve enclaving.[7]

The second possible exception involves islets or rocks, where it can be argued that if, as defined in Article 121(3) of the LOS Convention, a rock can only generate a territorial sea, then a rock should not be used as a base point for a provisional equidistance line extending beyond 12 nautical miles. This is countered by the argument that an equidistance line is to be based on

---

3 *See Dubai-Sharjah Border Arbitration*, 19 October 1981, 91 ILR 543, 677. The island in question was Abu Musa, an island inhabited by 800 people, with an area of 12 square kilometers and located 34 miles from Sharjah and 36 miles from Dubai. *Dubai/Sharjah Arbitration*, at 668.

4 *See Case Concerning Delimitation of Maritime Areas between Canada and France, (St. Pierre and Miquelon)*, 10 June 1992, 31 ILM 1149, paras 64–65, 68.

5 V. Prescott and G. Triggs, *Island and Rocks and their Role in Maritime Delimitation*, in D. A. Colson and R. W. Smith (eds.) International Maritime Boundaries, Vol. V (Martinus Nijhoff, Leiden 2005) 3272 note: "[I]t might have been expected that these islands would have been enclaved, as in the *Anglo/French* case, to take into account of their presence on the 'wrong side' of the equidistant line between the respective 'mainlands'."

6 *Case Concerning Maritime Delimitation in the Area between Greenland and Jan Mayen (Denmark v. Norway*, [1993] ICJ Rep. 38, paras 60, 70.

7 The Tribunal in the *Canada/France Arbitration, supra* note 4, did not adopt equidistance to construct a provisional line. Prescott and Triggs, *supra* note 5, at 3264 observe that the approach in the *Canada/France Arbitration* "stands in contrast to the Court of Arbitration's approach in the *Anglo/French* case where the Channel Islands were enclaved."

coastal base points usable for the territorial sea and, as such, would include near-shore rocks (and even low-tide elevations). Recent adjudications have used rocks or islets for generating provisional equidistance lines.[8] To the extent that a consistent approach can be said to exist, it is that rocks near shore are more apt to be used in determining a provisional equidistance line than rocks not near shore. However, attention must be heeded to the *Libya/Malta Case* example of a rock or islet that creates a "disproportionate effect" on an equidistance line.[9]

Regarding using non-land points located on straight baselines as base points for a provisional equidistance line, international maritime boundary adjudications have paid little attention to straight baselines asserted by States in constructing provisional equidistance lines. In no case has a tribunal used as a base point for an equidistance line a point not anchored on a land formation.[10] One commentator notes that: "Unless the parties agree that the straight baselines are to be given effect (or to be otherwise utilised), tribunals are bound not to consider them."[11] Although some questions can be raised about this statement,[12] given the existing adjudications and the

---

8 In the *Award of the Tribunal in the Second Stage of the Proceedings (Maritime Delimitation) (Eritrea and Yemen)*, 17 December 1999, 40 ILM 983, para 147, certain islands near-shore were considered as base points, whereas islands located far from the coast of Yemen and described as being "barren and inhospitable nature" were not. The Tribunal, however, did not dismiss them because they were "rocks," it being suggested that they were islands rather than rocks, but provided little indication as to why they were not taken into account. *See* R. Kolb, Case Law on Equitable Maritime Delimitation (Martinus Nijhoff, The Hague 2003) 538. In the 2001 *Qatar/Bahrain Case, supra* note 1, all offshore features appear to have been taken into account in the construction of the provisional equidistance line. Kolb, at 538.

9 In *Case Concerning the Continental Shelf (Libya v. Malta)*, [1985] ICJ Rep. 13, para 64, the International Court elected not to use the "uninhabited islet of Filfla" located 2.7 nautical miles from Malta's coast in constructing a provisional equidistance line.

More generally, in *Delimitation of the Maritime Boundary in the Gulf of Maine Area (Canada v. United States)*, [1984] ICJ Rep. 246, para 201, the Chamber warned of the "potential disadvantages inherent in any method which takes tiny islands, uninhabited rocks or low-tide elevations, sometimes lying at a considerable distance from *terra firma*, as base points for the drawing of a line . . . "

10 For a review of the relevant international cases, *see* Marques Antunes, *supra* note 2, at 300–301.

11 *Id.* 300.

12 The statement may be overly dismissive, particularly if the straight baselines in question are archipelagic straight baselines. This situation might have, but did not, arise in the *Qatar/Bahrain Case* since Bahrain had not declared itself as an archipelagic State and the Court determined that the straight baselines asserted by Bahrain did not meet the international legal criteria for straight baselines. *Qatar/Bahrain Case, supra* note 1, at paras 210–215. It is not clear, therefore, what the Court would have done with valid straight baselines.

undeniable creativity of straight baselines compared to land base points, straight baselines employed by a State are not likely to be considered by a tribunal in constructing a provisional equidistance line unless there is an explicit agreement to do so between the contesting parties.

II. Special Relevant Circumstances

(i) Islands, Rocks and Similar Features

Islands, rocks, or similar features are the quintessential circumstance that may lead the adjustment of a provisional equidistance line. What is usually looked at in addressing offshore islands or islets are:

- The physical aspects of the islands/islets (size, distance above surface at low-tide, composition (e.g., is it a rock?));
- The use of the islands/islets (population, lighthouses or similar uses);
- The location of the islands/islets in relation to the mainland coast; and
- The effect that the islands/islets have on a provisional equidistance line.

Though it is difficult to be definitive about islands and similar features, the maritime boundary cases provide some guidance. The *Eritrea/Yemen Arbitration* strongly suggests that the presence or effect of near-shore groups of islands or islands geographically integrated with the coast are unlikely to lead to an adjustment of a provisional equidistance line.[13] It is the outlier islands and features a significant distance from a coast that, either, because of specific attributes and/or because of their effect on a provisional equidistance line, attract the most attention. Tribunals have varied from giving such a feature no effect, partial effect, or half effect on an equidistance line.

In the Matter of the Arbitration between Barbados and The Republic of Trinidad and Tobago, 11 April 2006, 45 ILM 800, paras 246, 332, the provisional equidistance line was constructed without regard to the archipelagic straight baselines of Trinidad and Tobago.

13 Marques Antunes, *supra* note 2, at 293–294 talks in terms of whether base points on islands are geographically "representative" of the coast.

The following is a summary of the more significant outlier islands or features that have been addressed by tribunals in adjusting a provisional line:[14]

- Qit'at Jaradah, within 12 nautical miles of each parties' coast, less than 1 square kilometers, uninhabited, no vegetation, partial effect;[15]
- Fasht al Jarmin, within 12 nautical miles from Bahrain, minute part above high tide, no effect;[16]
- Al-Tayr and al-Zubayr, "well out to sea" from Yemen, "barren," "inhospitable," no effect;[17]
- Seal Island, 16 nautical miles from Nova Scotia, 2½ miles long, inhabited, half-effect;[18]
- Kerkennah Islands, 11 nautical miles from Tunisia, 180 square kilometers, partial effect;[19] and
- Scilly Islands, 21 nautical miles from the U.K. coast, 48 islands, 6 inhabited, half-effect.[20]

(ii) Coastal Configuration

The configuration of coasts may be a circumstance that may affect a provisional equidistance line. The most recognizable coastal configuration that might affect an equidistance line is where coastal concavity disadvantages a State. Coastal concavity was accepted as an important circumstance in the 1969 *North Sea Continental Shelf Cases*.[21] In the 2002 *Cameroon/Nigeria Case*,

---

14 As noted above, Filfla ("uninhabited islet," 2.7 nautical miles from Malta) was not used as base point in constructing an equidistance line. *Libya/Malta Case*, *supra* note 9, at para 64. Eddystone Rocks (lighthouse, most likely a low-tide elevation, near the U.K. coast) was given full effect on the equidistance line. *Anglo/French Arbitration*, *supra* note 2, at paras 139–141. In the *Dubai/Sharjah Arbitration*, *supra* note 3, at 543, Abu Musa, an inhabited islands, 12 square kilometers in area, located 34 miles from the coast, was given no effect on an equidistance line but was given a 12-nautical-mile territorial sea that did effect the equidistance line.

15 *Qatar/Bahrain Case*, *supra* note 1, at para 219.

16 *Id.* para 248.

17 *Eritrea/Yemen Arbitration*, *supra* note 8, at paras 147–148.

18 *Gulf of Maine Case*, *supra* note 9, at para 222.

19 *Case Concerning the Continental Shelf (Tunisia v. Libya)*, [1982] ICJ Rep. 18, para 129.

20 *Anglo/French Arbitration*, *supra* note 2, at para 251.

21 *North Sea Continental Shelf Cases (Denmark/The Netherlands v. Germany)*, [1969] ICJ Rep. 3, para 91. Note Kolb, *supra* note 8, at 20–21.

the Court looked a coastal concavity as a possible circumstance that would warrant adjustment of a provisional equidistance line, but found that the coastline showed "no particular concavity."[22]

The Tribunal in the 1992 *Canada/France Arbitration* took into account the encroachment on and the "cutoff" of the Newfoundland and Labrador Coast respecting the boundary for St. Pierre and Miquelon on the western side of the delimitation area,[23] although this was not a situation in which a provisional line was being adjusted. Artful attempts at claiming that certain coasts protrude or other coasts are somehow disadvantaged are usually seen as involving a refashioning of coastal geography, an exercise discouraged by adjudicative bodies.[24]

(iii) Comparative Proportionality of Coast Lengths

Almost all recent adjudications have examined comparative coast lengths as being a possible factor for the adjustment of a provisional delimitation line.[25] Reference can also be made to this use of coastline proportionality in the 1985 *Libya/Malta Case*[26] and the 1984 *Gulf of Maine Case.*[27]

Care is necessary respecting proportionality of coast lengths. Two Canadian authors have written:

---

22 *Case Concerning the Land and Maritime Boundary between Cameroon and Nigeria (Cameroon v. Nigeria: Equatorial Guinea intervening)*, [2002] ICJ Rep. 303, para 297.

23 *Canada/France Arbitration, supra* note 4, at para 67.

24 *North Sea Continental Shelf Cases, supra* note 21, at para 91.

> There can never be any question of completely refashioning nature, and equity does not require that a State without access to the sea should be allotted an area of continental shelf, any more than there could be a question of rendering the situation of a State with an extensive coastline similar to that of a State with a restricted coastline.

In the Matter of the Arbitration between Guyana and Suriname, 17 September 2007, para 374, on the website of the Permanent Court of Arbitration at www.pca-cpa.org (accessed on 29 September 2007), it was stated that "international courts and tribunals dealing with maritime delimitation should be mindful of not remaking or wholly refashioning nature, but should in a sense respect nature."

25 *See Guyana and Suriname Arbitration, supra* note 24, at para 392; *Barbados-Trinidad and Tobago Arbitration, supra* note 12, at paras 236–240, 327–328; *Cameroon/Nigeria Case, supra* note 22, at para 301; and *Qatar/Bahrain Case, supra* note 1, at paras 241–243.

26 *Libya/Malta Case, supra* note 9, at para 73.

27 *Gulf of Maine Case, supra* note 9, at paras 185, 221–222.

> Proportionality has a double role. In one role, a comparison of the coastal and area ratios is sometimes used as a test of the equity of a provisional delimitation. In the other role, an assessment of the relative lengths of the coastlines may be one of the factors taken into account in determining the method used to effect the delimitation.[28]

In light of the recent case law, both of these roles for proportionality are questionable. The role for coastline proportionality has primarily been confined to being a possible circumstance for adjusting a preliminary equidistance line. While coastline length disproportionality may reverse the presumption in favour of a provisional equidistance line, however, as noted in the *Libya/Malta Case*, "if proportionality [of coastal lengths] were the criterion for delimitation, it would exclude all other factors."[29]

Regarding the use of ratio of coastal lengths and offshore area as a test of equitableness, this was not addressed or applied in the 2002 *Cameroon/Nigeria Case* or the 2001 *Qatar/Bahrain Case*, although it was utilized in the 1999 *Eritrea/Yemen Arbitration*.[30] The Tribunal in the 2006 *Barbados-Trinidad and Tobago Arbitration* indicated that its delimitation line had to be examined in the light of proportionality, but indicated that this involved, not mathematical precision, but "a sense of proportionality."[31] One commentator has gone so far as indicate that the *ex post facto* proportionality test has been "renounced" by the International Court,[32] although, in fact, the Court has been silent. In the 2002 *Cameroon/Nigeria Case*, the Court looked to see whether there was a "significant difference" in coastal lengths and found none.[33] In the *Jan Mayen Case*,[34] the Court found the difference in coastal lengths "so significant" as to require an adjustment to the provisional line. The International Court in the *Libya/Malta Case* referenced "the great disparity in the lengths of the relevant coasts."[35] The 2006 *Barbados-Trinidad*

---

28 L. Legault and B. Hankey, *Method, Oppositeness and Adjacency, and Proportionality in Maritime Boundary Delimitation*, in J. I. CHARNEY AND L. M. ALEXANDER (eds.) INTERNATIONAL MARITIME BOUNDARIES, Vol. I (Martinus Nijhoff, The Hague 1993) 217.

29 *Libya/Malta Case*, *supra* note 9, at para 58.

30 *Eritrea/Yemen Arbitration*, *supra* note 8, at paras 165–168.

31 *Barbados-Trinidad and Tobago Arbitration*, *supra* note 12, at para 376.

32 Kolb, *supra* note 8, at 539.

33 *Cameroon/Nigeria Case*, *supra* note 22, at para 301.

34 *Jan Mayen Case*, *supra* note 6, at para 68.

35 *Libya/Malta Case*, *supra* note 9, at para 73.

and Tobago Arbitration noted the disparity in coastal lengths, but focused on the fact of "the significant coastal frontage" of Trinidad and Tobago on the relevant delimitation area as the circumstance that justified an adjustment to the provisional equidistance line.[36]

The next question is what coastal areas are relevant in determining lengths of coasts. The *Barbados-Trinidad and Tobago Arbitration* was confronted with the argument that the relevant coasts were only those that produced base points for a provisional equidistance line.[37] The Tribunal held, however, that:

> Relevant coasts are not strictly a function of the location of base points, because the influence of coastlines upon delimitation results not from the mathematical ratios discussed above [comparative coastal lengths] or from their contribution of base points to the drawing of an equidistance line, but from their significance in attaining an equitable and reasonable outcome, which is a much broader consideration.[38]

One commentator notes that, as there are different ways to measure coast lengths and significant subjectivity regarding the relevant area, arguments about coast length comparison are subject to "discourse manipulation."[39]

(iv) Presence of Ocean Resources

The 2006 *Barbados-Trinidad and Tobago Arbitration* stated that: "Resource-related criteria have been treated more cautiously by the decisions of international courts and tribunals, which have not generally applied this factor as a relevant circumstance."[40] The *Newfoundland and Labrador–Nova Scotia Arbitration* stated the concern as follows:

---

36 *Barbados-Trinidad and Tobago Arbitration*, *supra* note 12, at paras 334, 372–373, 378–379.

37 *Id.* para 325.

38 *Id.* para 329.

39 Marques Antunes, *supra* note 2, at 302 and, more generally regarding coastline measurement, at 171–173, 301–302.

40 *Barbados-Trinidad and Tobago Arbitration*, *supra* note 12, at para 241.

> to have regard to the location of potential resources stands in some tension with the often-repeated statement that a court engaged in maritime delimitation is not sharing out an undivided whole.[41]

The International Court in the *North Sea Continental Shelf Cases*,[42] the *Libya/Tunisia Case*,[43] and the *Jan Mayen Case* took the view that the presence of ocean resources could affect a delimitation line.[44] In the *Gulf of Maine Case*, the possibility of catastrophic results to the fishing industry resulting from a delimitation line was considered.[45] The 2006 *Barbados-Trinidad and Tobago Arbitration* noted that, in some situations, fisheries might be a circumstance to be considered in the adjustment of a provisional equidistance line.[46] However, only in the *Jan Mayen Case* was a provisional equidistance line adjusted to take into account an ocean resource, in this case the presence of capelin.[47] The cases demonstrate that a degree of certainty about the nature and extent of an ocean resource is necessary before the presence of ocean resources reaches a threshold at which it may become relevant as a factor in evaluating the equity of a provisional equidistance line and the possibility of adjustment. This approach discourages States from making claims after the location of a resource is reasonably clear and encourages resource development. Moreover, it discourages heightening bilateral tensions by having States engage in rival resource identification activity.

(v) Conduct of the Parties

Although tribunals have accepted that the conduct of the parties can be a circumstance that indicates that a provisional equidistance line is inequitable and in need of adjustment, tribunals have largely rejected the conduct argued before them as being adequate to demonstrate the inequity of a

---

41 *Award of the Tribunal in the Second Phase of the Arbitration between Newfoundland and Labrador and Nova Scotia*, 26 March 2002, 128 ILR 504, para 3.21.

42 *North Sea Continental Shelf Cases*, *supra* note 21, at paras 97, 101(D)(2).

43 *Libya/Tunisia Case*, *supra* note 19, at para 107 notes that the presence of oil wells may be an element to be taken into account in delimitation.

44 *Jan Mayen Case*, *supra* note 6, at para 76.

45 *Gulf of Maine Case*, *supra* note 9, at para 237.

46 *Barbados-Trinidad and Tobago Arbitration*, *supra* note 12, at para 241.

47 *Jan Mayen Case*, *supra* note 6, at para 76.

provisional line. For example, in the *Qatar/Bahrain Case*, the International Court did not find a 1947 British line addressing a division of the seabed as being relevant since the matter before them was a single line (continental shelf and EEZ).[48] The argument in the *Jan Mayen Case*, rejected by the Court, was that since Norway had entered into an agreement with Iceland regarding a maritime boundary, Denmark was entitled to equivalent treatment by Norway.[49] Conduct regarding oil concessions and oil wells was found by the International Court in the *Cameroon/Nigeria Case* not to be "circumstances justifying the adjustment or shifting of the provisional delimitation line" unless the practice was "based on express or tacit agreement."[50] The 2007 *Guyana and Suriname Arbitration* summarized that the cases "reveal a marked reluctance . . . to accord significance to the oil practices of the parties in the determination of the delimitation line" and that no evidence of an agreement between the parties existed.[51] As regards conduct as a circumstance that may lead to an adjustment of a provisional equidistance line, there is a very high threshold.

---

48 *Qatar/Bahrain Case, supra* note 1, at para 240.

49 *Jan Mayen Case, supra* note 6, at para 86:

> In the particular case of maritime delimitation, international law does not prescribe, with a view to reaching an equitable solution, the adoption of a single method for the delimitation of the maritime spaces of all sides of an island, or for the whole of the coastal front of a particular State, rather than, if desired, varying systems of delimitation for the various parts of the coast.

50 *Cameroon/Nigeria Case, supra* note 22, at para 304.

51 *Guyana and Suriname Arbitration, supra* note 24, at para 390.

SIX

Status of Waters and Navigation Rights

1.0 Introduction

The difference between Canada and the United States, viewed as a coastal State versus a maritime State, manifests itself most prominently regarding a number of near-shore salt water areas over which Canada claims exclusive jurisdiction, including the authority to prohibit foreign vessel navigation, and in which the United States claims that navigational rights exist. The best known of these navigation disputes involves the Northwest Passage. But there are other ocean areas that are subject to similar disagreement. On the Atlantic Coast, there is the Bay of Fundy, and more particularly, Head Harbour Passage, which is located between Canadian islands but is the principal navigation route in the Passamaquoddy Bay region into Eastport, Maine. On the Pacific Coast, the waters in question are Hecate Strait, between the mainland of British Columbia and the Queen Charlotte Islands; the Dixon Entrance; and Queen Charlotte Sound, the area between the southern end of the Queen Charlotte Islands and the northern tip of Vancouver Island.

All of the above waters have been enclosed by Canada either by straight baselines, in the case of the Arctic Islands that captures the Northwest Passage,[1] or by fisheries closing lines, in the case of the Bay of Fundy, the Hecate Strait and the Dixon Entrance, and Queen Charlotte Sound.[2] Canada has asserted that all of the above waters are historic internal waters.

> Canada . . . claims that the waters of the Canadian Arctic Archipelago are internal waters of Canada . . . Canada has similar historic claims to the

---

1 Territorial Sea Geographical Coordinates (Area 7) Order, Can Gaz Part II, Vol. 119, SOR/85-872, 10 September 1985, 3996–4002.

2 Fishing Zones of Canada (Zone 1, 2 and 3) Order, Can Gaz Part II, Vol. 105, SOR/71-81, 25 February 1971, 363–364, came into effect on 10 March 1971. *See* Chapter Three, section 3.2.

> waters of . . . the Bay of Fundy . . ., Dixon Entrance, Hecate Strait and Queen Charlotte Sound on the British Columbia coast.[3]

The United States has taken issue with the employment by Canada of the 1985 Arctic straight baselines[4] and the 1970 fisheries closing lines.[5] As regards the narrow waterways of the Northwest Passage and the Head Harbour Passage, the U.S. view is that they are straits used for international navigation with the consequence that there exists, within them, an unimpeded right of navigation.[6]

There is no debate that all of the above-noted waters are under the jurisdiction of Canada, as opposed to any other State, and that Canada has exclusive access to and control over all living and non-living resources within these waters. The question—How Canadian are the waters?—only arises as regards whether foreign flag vessels have a right of navigation through or within the waters, and whether Canada can require foreign vessels to obtain permission to utilize the waters. It is to be noted that the issue of Canadian authority only involves foreign vessels passing through the waterways if the vessel is not calling at a Canadian port. Foreign merchant vessels in port are subject to the law of the port State.[7] Moreover, absent an international treaty, international law does not provide to a

---

3 Department of External Affairs, Letter, 17 December 1973, in (1974) 12 CYIL 277, 279.

4 *See* Department of State, *Geographic Note*, No. 2, 31 January 1986, 6:

> Under international law, straight baselines may be drawn only in areas that are fringed with islands or deeply indented. The United States has not regarded the Arctic islands as meeting these criteria.

5 Statement on Canadian Fisheries Closing Lines Announcement, 18 December 1970, in S. H. LAY, R. CHURCHILL, AND M. NORDQUIST (eds.) NEW DIRECTIONS IN THE LAW OF THE SEA, Vol. I (Oceana Publications, Dobbs Ferry, N.Y. 1973) 74.

6 *See* Commentary–The 1982 United Nations Convention on the Law of the Sea and the Agreement on Implementation of Part XI, attached to Message from the President of the United States transmitting United Nations Convention on the Law of the Sea, with Annexes, Montego Bay, 10 December 1982 (the Convention) and the Agreement Relating to the Implementation of Part XI of the United Nations Convention on the Law of the Sea of 10 December 1982, adopted at New York, 28 July 1994 (the Agreement) and signed by the United States, subject to ratification, on 29 July 1994, U.S. Senate, Treaty Document 39, 103d Congress, 2d Session IV (1994) 18–19, 34 ILM 1393.

7 *See* R. R. CHURCHILL AND A. V. LOWE, THE LAW OF THE SEA (Manchester University Press, 3rd edition, Manchester 1999) 54–55; T. L. McDorman, *Port State Enforcement: A Comment on Article 218 of the 1982 Law of the Sea Convention* (1997) 28 JMLC 305, 308–310; and V. D. Degan, *Internal Waters* (1986) 17 NETHERLANDS YBK INTL L 3, 22–28.

foreign vessel a right of access to a port. Thus, a State can deny port access to foreign vessels.[8]

Canada encourages foreign vessels into its ports and other internal waters, provided the vessels meet Canada's safety and environmental regulations. There are few occasions in which a foreign vessel is denied entry to a Canadian port or other internal waters. However, as regards foreign fishing vessels, permission must be obtained to enter a Canadian port.[9] As a result of fisheries disputes, Canada has occasionally closed ports to fishing vessels from specific European States.[10]

Periodically, oil tanker and other vessel traffic has raised public concerns in Canada over the extent of national control over the vessels within Canadian waters. As in the case regarding the Northwest Passage, in 1969 to 1970 with the *Manhattan*, and in 1985, with the *Polar Sea*, the issue in Canada has been articulated as one of sovereignty and the apparent U.S. disregard for Canadian sovereignty. This rhetorical flourish often masks the real issues and the cooperative reality that usually exists between Canada and the United States on navigation matters, despite the legal disagreements.

The international legal architecture regarding Canada–U.S. salt water navigation disputes principally involves two elements: first, the international law respecting historic waters and, second, the straits used for international navigation. This legal architecture will be described in Part A of this chapter. Part B will look at the various navigation matters that have arisen between Canada and the United States respecting the Northwest Passage; the Head Harbour Passage; and the Canadian-claimed West Coast historic waters.

The Juan de Fuca Strait, which separates Vancouver Island from Washington state, will also be looked at in Part B. The 1979 Canada–U.S. Agreement on Vessel Traffic Management for the Juan de Fuca Region[11] has,

8 *Case Concerning Military and Paramilitary Activities in and Against Nicaragua (Nicaragua v. United States)*, [1986] ICJ Rep. 14, para 213 and *see generally* L. de La Fayette, *Access to Ports in International Law* (1996) 11 IJMCL 1–22.

9 Coastal Fisheries Protection Regulations, CRC (1978), c 413, s 5(1)(a).

10 *See* DFO, Canada Closes Ports to Fishing Vessels from the Faroe Islands, 21 March 2002, at www.dfo-mpo.gc.cca/media/newsrel/2002/hq-ac16_e.htm (accessed on 19 April 2007) and *see* de La Fayette, *supra* note 8, at 9, 20.

11 Exchange of Notes constituting an Agreement on Vessel Traffic Management for the Juan de Fuca Region, Ottawa, 19 December 1979, entered into force 19 December 1979, CTS 1979/28, 32 UST 377, TIAS 9706, 1221 UNTS 67.

for the most part, alleviated any concerns over navigation matters that might arise in international ocean law.

Overall, the Canadian and U.S. Coast Guards, the government agencies with the direct operational responsibilities regarding shipping, have a close relationship fostered through memoranda of understanding and regular meetings, regarding, for instance, search and rescue and oil spill response.[12] An important formal bilateral marine cooperative arrangement is the 1974 Agreement concerning the Establishment of a Joint Marine Pollution Contingency Plan[13] in which the two countries agreed to create and maintain a Joint Marine Contingency Plan to deal with spills of oil and other noxious substances from vessels.[14] The core of the plan is that, if incidents occur in the waters of one State that potentially threaten the other, the incident is to be reported to the other State and resources from both States are to be made available to address the incident.[15] The plan contains regional annexes (for the Atlantic and Pacific Coasts, the Beaufort Sea,[16] and the Dixon Entrance[17]), which define the jurisdiction, roles, response procedures, and other topics such as communications, reporting systems, and points of contact. The plan is tested every two years by joint Canada-U.S. exercises. In 2003, through a memorandum of understanding, the operational aspects of the Joint Marine Contingency Plan were updated.[18]

---

12 For a list of the agreements and arrangements between the Coast Guards of Canada and the United States, *see* Coast Guard, Canada–U.S. Relations, at www.ccc-gcc.ca/ia-ai/Canada_usa_e.htm (accessed on 14 May 2007).

Since 2005, there have been annual summits of the Canadian and U.S. Coast Guards. *See* DFO, Canada–U.S. Coast Guard Summit Meetings, September 2006, at www.dfo-mpo.gc.ca/media/backgroun/2006/hq-qc34c_e.htm (accessed on 14 May 2007).

13 Exchange of Notes constituting an Agreement concerning the Establishment of a Joint Marine Pollution Contingency Plan, Ottawa, 19 June 1974, entered into force 19 June 1974, CTS 1974/22, 25 UST 1280, TIAS 7861.

14 *See* Canada—U.S. Joint Marine Pollution Contingency Plan, at www.uscg.mil/d1/response/jrt/plans.html (accessed on 14 May 2007).

15 A. H. E. Popp, *Legal Aspects of International Oil Spills in the Canada/U.S. Context* (1992) 18 CANADA—UNITED STATES LJ 309, 322–323.

16 Added to the 1974 Joint Contingency Plan Agreement, *supra* note 13, by Exchange of Notes, Ottawa, 28 July 1977, entered into 30 August 1977, CTS 1977/25.

17 Added to the 1974 Joint Contingency Plan Agreement, *supra* note 13, by Exchange of Notes adding a further Annex (Annex V), Ottawa, 5 March 1982, entered into force 17 March 1982, CTS 1982/32.

18 *See* Letter of Promulgation between the Canadian and U.S. Coast Guards, 22 May 2003, Joint Marine Pollution Contingency Plan, *supra* note 14.

PART A

2.0 International Law Respecting Navigational Rights in National Waters

For the Northwest Passage, Head Harbour Passage, and the West Coast waters (the Dixon Entrance, the Hecate Strait, and the Queen Charlotte Sound), the issue between Canada and the United States is what, if any, navigational rights exist through these waters. The possibilities are:

- No navigational rights exist if the waters in question are:
  - Historic internal waters;
  - Landward of the low-water line;[19] or
  - Landward of straight baselines drawn pursuant to the 1958 Territorial Sea and Contiguous Zone Convention[20] or the 1982 U.N. Convention on the Law of the Sea (LOS Convention),[21] and were previously considered as being internal waters;[22]
- Innocent passage rights exist if the waters in question are:
  - Part of the 12-nautical-mile territorial sea;[23]
  - Landward of straight baselines drawn pursuant to the 1958 Territorial Sea and Contiguous Zone Convention or the 1982 LOS Convention and the waters were not previously considered as being internal waters;[24] or
  - A strait used for international navigation formed by an island and the mainland of the same State and a route of similar convenience exists seaward of the island;[25]

---

19 Convention on the Territorial Sea and Contiguous Zone (TSCZC), Geneva 29 April 1958, entered into force 22 September 1964, Arts 1, 5(1), 516 UNTS 205 and U. N. Convention on the Law of the Sea, Montego Bay, Jamaica, 10 December 1982, entered into force 16 November 1994, Arts 5, 8(1), 1833 UNTS 397.

20 TSCZC, *supra* note 19, Art 4.

21 LOS Convention, *supra* note 19, Art 7.

22 TSCZC, *supra* note 19, Art 5(2) and LOS Convention, *supra* note 19, Art 8(2).

23 TSCZC, *supra* note 19, Art 5(2) and LOS Convention, *supra* note 19, Art 17.

24 TSCZC, *supra* note 19, Art 5(2) and LOS Convention, *supra* note 19, Art 8(2).

25 LOS Convention, *supra* note 19, Arts 45(1)(a), 38(1).

- Non-suspendable innocent passage rights exist if the waters in question are:
  - A strait used for international navigation connecting part of the high seas or an exclusive economic zone (EEZ) and the territorial sea of a foreign State;[26]
- Transit passage rights exist where the waters in questions are:
  - A strait used for international navigation that connects one part of the high seas or EEZ with another part of the high seas or EEZ.[27]

The three types of passage rights, namely, transit, innocent, and non-suspendable innocent, entail different balances between the authority of the coastal State to regulate, manage, and engage with a passing vessel and the vessel's right to freedom of unimpeded navigation. Transit passage provides the highest degree of freedom for vessel passage from interference by the adjacent coast State.[28] Transit passage was an innovation of the LOS Convention, included because maritime States viewed innocent passage as too favorable to coastal States and, for certain international straits, a new, more navigation-friendly passage right was needed.[29] Innocent passage in the territorial sea has existed as a right in international law for a long time and is set out in both the 1958 Territorial Sea and Contiguous Zone Convention[30] and the LOS Convention.[31] A feature of innocent passage is that it can be temporarily suspended for all or part of a coastal State's territorial sea "if such suspension is essential for the protection of [the coastal State's] ... security."[32] Non-suspendable innocent passage removes this possibility but otherwise retains all of the other features of innocent passage. Only internal waters provides for the full control by the adjacent coastal State of all aspects of foreign-vessel navigation, including the right to deny access and to require a foreign vessel to obtain the permission of the coastal State for access.

---

26 TSCZC, *supra* note 19, Art 16(4) and LOS Convention, *supra* note 19, Art 45(1)(b), (2).

27 LOS Convention, *supra* note 19, Arts 37, 38 (1).

28 *Id.* Arts 38–44 and *see generally* Churchill and Lowe, *supra* note 7, at 107–110 and, in more detail, B. B. Jia, The Regime of Straits in International Law (Clarendon Press, Oxford 1998) 129–208.

29 *See* Chapter Four, section 2.2.4 and Chapter Six, section 2.2.

30 TSCZC, *supra* note 19, Arts 14–17.

31 LOS Convention, *supra* note 19, Arts 17–26. *See generally* Churchill and Lowe, *supra* note 7, at 81–92.

32 TSCZC, *supra* note 19, Art 16(3)(4) and LOS Convention, *supra* note 19, Art 25(3). Note Churchill and Lowe, *supra* note 7, at 87–88.

By definition, the 12-nautical-mile territorial sea is adjacent to the internal waters of a coastal State.[33] A strait used for international navigation essentially creates a special navigational regime for waters that are otherwise part of the territorial sea. A strait used for international navigation does not create a special navigational regime as regards waters that are internal, including those that are historic internal waters.

> If the waters are internal by reason of historic title, no right of passage applies and the strait would not be capable of becoming an international strait.[34]

Supporting this is Article 35(a) of the LOS Convention:

> Nothing in this Part ["Straits Used for International Navigation"] affects:
> (a) any areas of internal waters within a strait . . .[35]

This provision was promoted by Canada.[36] Although seen as meaning that internal waters within a strait used for international navigation retain their status of internal waters and are not subject to navigational rights,[37] the better view is that no strait used for international navigation exists through internal waters, including historic internal waters, where there is no accompanying territorial sea.[38] If all Article 35(a) did was protect the status of the waters within an international strait as internal waters, the provision would be unnecessary since Article 34 of the LOS Convention already accomplishes this: "The regime of passage through straits used for international navigation

---

33 LOS Convention, *supra* note 19, Arts 2(1), 3.

34 D. PHARAND, NORTHWEST PASSAGE: ARCTIC STRAITS (Martinus Nijhoff, Dordrecht 1984) 98 and D. PHARAND, CANADA'S ARCTIC WATERS IN INTERNATIONAL LAW (Cambridge University Press, Cambridge 1988) 223.

35 LOS Convention, *supra* note 19, Art 35(a).

36 *See* S. N. Nandan and D. H. Anderson, *Straits Used for International Navigation: A Commentary on Part III of the United Nations Convention on the Law of the Sea 1982* (1989) 60 BRITISH YB IL 159, 173.

37 S. N. NANDAN AND S. ROSENNE, UNITED NATIONS CONVENTION ON THE LAW OF THE SEA, 1982: A COMMENTARY, Vol. II (Martinus Nijhoff, Dordrecht 1993) 306 and *see* Nandan and Anderson, *supra* note 36, at 173.

38 Nandan and Rosenne, *supra* note 37, at 306, footnote 8, comment: "Part III [Straits Used for International Navigation] is not intended to apply in the case of internal waters or to waters outside the territorial sea."

established in this Part shall not . . . affect the legal status of the waters forming such straits. . ."[39]

Article 35(a) is linked to historic internal waters rather than internal waters created by straight baselines since the provision indicates that waters enclosed as internal by straight baselines "which had not previously been considered" as internal waters were still subject to being part of a strait used for international navigation for the purposes of rights of transit passage.[40]

Based on the above, the dichotomy of position between Canada and the United States as to whether the Northwest Passage and the Head Harbour Passage are historic internal waters or a strait used for international navigation is clear.

2.1 Historic Internal Waters

The 1962 U.N. Secretariat Study "Juridical Regime of Historic Waters Including Historic Bays," commented that:

> [T]he concept of "historic waters" has its root in the historic fact that States through the ages claimed and maintained sovereignty over maritime areas which they considered vital to them without paying much attention to divergent and changing opinions about what general international law might prescribe. . . .[41]

As international law of the sea evolved with three-nautical-mile territorial seas (and then 12-nautical-mile territorial seas) and baselines for measuring these waters, the historic waters concept was seen as "necessary in order to maintain a State's title to some areas of water which might escape the codification formula . . ."[42] This "safety-valve" approach[43] is evident in the manner with which historic bays are addressed the 1982 LOS Convention and the

---

39 LOS Convention, *supra* note 19, Art 34.

40 *Id.* Art 35(a).

41 *Juridical Regime of Historic Waters, Including Historic Bays*, Study prepared by the U.N. Secretariat, U. N. Doc A/CN.4/143, 9 March 1962, in YEARBOOK OF THE INTERNATIONAL LAW COMMISSION, 1962 Vol. II, 7, para 38.

42 D. P. O'CONNELL, THE INTERNATIONAL LAW OF THE SEA, Vol. I (edited by I.A. Shearer) (Clarendon Press, Oxford 1982) 425 referring to the U. N. Study, *supra* note 41.

43 U. N. Study, *supra* note 41, at 23, para 37 quoting from G. GIDEL, DROIT INTERNATIONAL PUBLIC DE LA MER, Vol. III (1934) 651.

1958 Territorial Sea and Contiguous Zone Convention. In virtually identical wording, these two Conventions indicate that the juridical bay provision, which sets out the possibility for making bays that meet selected geographic considerations internal waters, do not apply to historic bays.[44] These Conventions, however, provide no guidance respecting the definition or evaluation of historic water claims.[45] Although texts of draft provisions on historic waters were discussed during the negotiation of the 1982 LOS Convention, according to the U.S. delegation: "There was strong opposition to a general doctrine of historic waters . . ."[46] The result is that the international law respecting claims to historic waters is based on customary international law rather than reliance on multilateral treaties. The International Court, in the 1982 *Libya-Tunisia Case*, stated: "It is clearly the case that . . . the notion of historic rights or waters . . . are governed by . . . customary international law."[47]

Regarding what rights attach to historic waters, the International Court in the 1951 *Anglo-Norwegian Fisheries Case* provided:

> By "historic waters" are usually meant waters which are treated as internal waters but which would not have that character were it not for the existence of an historic title.[48]

The International Court in the 1982 *Tunisia-Libya Continental Shelf Case* noted, however, that:

> international law . . . does not provide for a single "regime" for "historic waters" or "historic bays," but only for a particular regime for each

---

44 TSCZC, *supra* note 19, Art 7(6) and LOS Convention, *supra* note 19, Art 10(6).

45 *Case Concerning the Continental Shelf (Tunisia/Libya)*, [1982] ICJ Rep. 18, para 100.

46 Delegation Report of Third Session, 1975 in REPORTS OF THE UNITED STATES DELEGATION TO THE THIRD UNITED NATIONS CONFERENCE ON THE LAW OF THE SEA (Law of the Sea Institute, Honolulu 1983) 94. More generally on the historic waters discussions during the negotiation of the LOS Convention, *see* L. F. E. Goldie, *Historic Bays in International Law–An Impressionistic Overview* (1984) 11 SYRACUSE J INTL L AND COMM 211, 265–267 and S. Rosenne, *Historic Waters in the Third United Nations Conference on the Law of the Sea*, in T. D. GILL AND W. P. HEERE (eds.) REFLECTIONS ON PRINCIPLES AND PRACTICE OF INTERNATIONAL LAW (Martinus Nijhoff, The Hague 2000) 195–197. Note also F. Francioni, *The Status of the Gulf of Sirte in International Law* (1984) 11 SYRACUSE J INTL L AND COMM 311, 321 who notes that the proposals were "quickly discarded."

47 *Libya-Tunisia Case*, *supra* note 45, at para 100,

48 *Fisheries Case (United Kingdom v. Norway)*, [1951] ICJ Rep. 116, 130.

> of the concrete, recognized cases of "historic waters" or "historic bays."[49]

In the 1992 *Gulf of Fonseca Case* before the International Court, El Salvador, Honduras, and Nicaragua agreed that the Gulf of Fonseca, on which all three States had coasts, was an historic bay and the Court found that a right of innocent passage existed noting that "rights of innocent passage are not inconsistent with a regime of historic waters . . ."[50] The 1962 U.N. Secretariat Study notes that "the scope of the historic title emerging from the continued exercise of sovereignty should not be wider in scope than the scope of the sovereignty actually exercised."[51] Thus, the legal effect of historic waters on navigation can depend on what was and is being asserted by the claiming State. Nevertheless, historic waters are usually associated with historic internal waters, with the claiming State asserting authority over foreign vessel navigation.

The 1962 U.N. Secretariat Study outlines three criteria for assessing the existence of historic waters.

> In determining whether or not a title to "historic waters" exists, there are three factors which have to be taken into consideration, namely,
>
> (i) The authority exercised over the area by the State claiming it as "historic waters;"
> (ii) The continuity of such exercise of authority;
> (iii) The attitude of foreign States.
>
> First, effective exercise of sovereignty over the area by the claiming State is a necessary requirement for title to the area as "historic waters" of that State. Secondly, such exercise of sovereignty must have continued during a considerable time so as to have developed into a usage. Thirdly, the attitude of foreign States to the activities of the claiming State in the area must have been such that it can be characterized as an attitude of general toleration.
>
> The burden of proof of title to "historic waters" is on the State claiming such title, in the sense that, if the State is unable to prove to the satisfaction

---

49 *Libya-Tunisia Case, supra* note 45, at para 100. This was cited with approval in *Case Concerning the Land, Island and Maritime Frontier Dispute (El Salvador/Honduras: Nicaragua Intervening)*, [1992] ICJ Rep. 351, 384 (the *Gulf of Fonseca Case*).

50 *Gulf of Fonseca Case, supra* note 49, at para 393.

51 U. N. Study, *supra* note 41, at 23, para 164.

of whoever has to decide the matter that the requirements necessary for the title have been fulfilled, its claim to title will be disallowed.[52]

The Study indicates that "there seems to be fairly general agreement" on the three criteria.[53] This continues to be the situation even though no international adjudication has pronounced definitively on the applicability of the above considerations for evaluating a claim of historic waters.[54]

There is a so-called fourth consideration referred to as "vital bays" or "vital interests." O'Connell argues that the "theory behind the doctrine of historic rights is that special situations crystallize as the result of historical evolution," and that arresting this process with an overly demanding deference to history is inconsistent with the purpose of the concept.[55] It is the view of O'Connell "that history will play a less prominent role . . ., and strategic and economic factors a much greater one . . ." such that a concept of "vital bays" will emerge.[56] Churchill and Lowe report that the United Kingdom and the United States have rejected the idea of vital bays as inconsistent with navigational interests.[57] Pharand notes that, "in addition to relying on the standard requirements . . . coastal States will usually buttress their claim of historic waters by invoking vital interests."[58] Bouchez refers to "the motives" that lead to a claim to historic waters (economic, security, political) and concludes that such interests "alone never justify" an historic waters claim.[59] Symmons refers to vital interests as "outdated"

52 *Id.* 25, paras 185, 186, 188.

53 *Id.* 13, para 80.

54 Churchill and Lowe, *supra* note 7, at 44 assert that the three criteria "were implicitly accepted by the International Court" in the *Gulf of Fonseca Case*, *supra* note 49.

The criteria have been applied in numerous U.S. Supreme Court cases involving claims by States to historic waters. *See, for example*, *United States v. Louisiana*, (1968), 394 U.S. 11; *United States v. Alaska*, (1975), 422 U.S. 184; *United States v. Louisiana (Mississippi/Alabama Boundary)*, (1985), 470 U.S. 93; and *Alaska v. United States*, (2005), 545 U.S. 75.

C. R. Symmons, Historic Waters in the Law of the Sea: A Modern Re-Appraisal (Martinus Nijhoff, Leiden 2008) 112 has commented that the three criteria set out in the U. N. Study, *supra* note 41, at 25, paras 185, 186, 188, "has had an authoritative standing with the U.S. courts–as elsewhere–as an accurate statement of the customary international legal rules."

55 O'Connell, *supra* note 42, at 425.

56 *Id.* 425 and see 435–438.

57 Churchill and Lowe, *supra* note 7, at 44. *See also* Symmons, *supra* note 54, at 256 discussing the U.S. view of Australian claims to certain waters as historic.

58 Pharand, Canada's Arctic Waters, *supra* note 34, at 102.

59 L. J. Bouchez, The Regime of Bays in International Law (A.Y. Sythoff, Leyden 1964) 282–297.

and an "anachronism."[60] O'Connell concludes that: "The correct view of the status of vital interests is that the notion has as yet no status in international law, but . . . it has a role to play in the evaluation of long usage."[61]

Two matters arise regarding the three criteria. First, although there is agreement on the elements relevant to evaluating a claim of historic waters, there is uncertainty regarding how the elements are to be understood and applied in a specific fact pattern.[62] Symmons explains at considerable length the difficulties, uncertainties, and "subrules" that are inherent in understanding and applying the deceptively simple three criteria.[63] Second, there is uncertainty about whether each of the three criteria must be met or whether what is involved is more of a balancing of the factors. On this matter, Pharand takes the view that the three criteria "must be met before a claim of historic waters is duly established."[64] O'Connell is of the view that what is involved is more of a balancing of the elements.[65] O'Connell's view appears to be consistent with the wording of the 1962 U.N. Secretariat Study which refers to "factors . . . to be taken into consideration."[66]

Regarding the first of these elements, Pharand writes:

> When a coastal State claims certain bodies of waters as historically forming part of its national territory, the type of jurisdiction it must exercise is the same as over its land areas, namely sovereign rights. More specifically, the exercise of jurisdiction must be exclusive and effective. Legislation and declarations, unaccompanied by enforcement, will not suffice. . . .
>
> It is of utmost importance that the claimant State be in a position to demonstrate that it took whatever action was necessary to exercise its exclusive and effective authority over the maritime area in question. The nature of the action will depend on the nature of the foreign challenge. If it is foreign fishing, the exclusion of foreign fishers must be effected. If it

---

60 Symmons, *supra* note 54, at 256 and *more generally* at 247–257.

61 O'Connell, *supra* note 42, at 438.

62 S. Kaye, *The South Australian Historic Bays: An Assessment* (1995) 17 ADELAIDE LR 269, 271 comments: "[I]t is possible to distil the elemental requirements of an historic bay claim, although it is by no means settled as to the exact nature of each."

63 Symmons, *supra* note 54, at 113–116, 285–287 summarizes some of the difficulties and subrules.

64 Pharand, CANADA'S ARCTIC WATERS, *supra* note 34, at 97.

65 O'Connell, *supra* note 42, at 433–434.

66 U. N. Study, *supra* note 41, at 25, para 185.

is navigation by foreign ships, their exclusion and subjection to special authorization would constitute the best proof of exclusive jurisdiction.[67]

Respecting the second element, duration, there is considerably more flexibility and each situation needs to be independently evaluated. Pharand comments: "How much passage of time must take place before a sufficiently long usage is attained cannot be determined in the abstract."[68]

The third element is "the attitude of foreign States to the activities of the claiming State in the area must have been such that it can be characterized as an attitude of general toleration."[69] Two situations can be distinguished. The first occurs if the waters in question are shared in that two or more States have coasts on the waters. The second is that the waters in question are not shared and are adjacent to a single State. If a historic waters claim arises regarding shared waters, the 1962 U.N. Secretariat Study states:

> the persistent opposition by one or more of the riparian States to the exercise of sovereignty over the bay by one or more of the other riparian States must naturally be of great if not decisive importance in evaluating whether or not the requirement of toleration had been fulfilled.[70]

At a later stage the Study notes that: "it would seem reasonable, in the case of a State (or States) claiming historic title to waters bordered by two or more States, to accord special importance to the attitude of the other riparian State (or States)."[71] Academic writers take the view that there is a strong

---

67 D. Pharand, *The Arctic Waters and The Northwest Passage: A Final Revisit* (2007) 38 ODIL 3, 7. *See also* Pharand, CANADA'S ARCTIC WATERS, *supra* note 34, at 97–98; O'Connell, *supra* note 42, at 423–433; Bouchez, *supra* note 59, at 238–250; and U. N. Study, *supra* note 41, at 13–15, paras 84–100.
For a detailed analysis, *see* Symmons, *supra* note 54, in c 10, "Exercise of Authority: The Need for a Formal, Clear and Consistent Claim," at 117–118, 120–121, 128–129 and c 13, "The Need for Effective Exercise of Jurisdiction," at 163–165, 170–176, 179–184, 190–199, 207–211.

68 Pharand, CANADA'S ARCTIC WATERS, *supra* note 34, at 98. *See also* Pharand, *The Arctic Waters*, *supra* note 67, at 7; O'Connell, *supra* note 42, at 432–433; Bouchez, *supra* note 59, at 250–257; and U. N. Study, *supra* note 41, at 15–16, paras 101–105.
For a detailed analysis, *see* Symmons, *supra* note 54, in c 12, "The Need for Continuity of Historic Claim and for the Satisfaction of the Time Factor," at 151–152, 156–158, 161–162.

69 U. N. Study, *supra* note 41, at 25, para 186.
For a detailed analysis, *see* Symmons, *supra* note 54, in c 11, "The Necessity for Publicity of Historic Claim: Publication/Notification of the Claim to Other States," at 139–140, 145–149 and c 14, "Knowledge of, and Acquiescence to, Historic Claims," at 213–220, 227, 230–245.

70 U. N. Study, *supra* note 41, at 21, para 148.

71 *Id.* 25, para 186.

presumption against a shared waterway being historic waters.[72] In the *Gulf of Fonseca Case*, the International Court accepted the claim by the three States (El Salvador, Honduras, and Nicaragua) that the shared waters were historic waters.[73] This suggests the existence of a very high threshold of explicit assent by the bordering States that shared waters are historic waters.

The more usual situation in assessing foreign State attitudes concerns a claim to historic waters adjacent to a single State. There has been debate regarding whether it is necessary for States with a direct interest in the claimed historic waters to consent or indicate recognition of the claim or whether it is sufficient for these same States to remain silent and therefore acquiesce to the claim.[74] It is the latter view that generally holds sway.[75] As the 1962 U.N. Secretariat Study notes: "there is substantial agreement that inaction on the part of foreign States is sufficient to permit an historic title to a maritime area to arise by effective and continued exercise of sovereignty over it by the coastal State during a considerable period of time . . ."[76] As a corollary, it is accepted that "effective" protests on the part of interested States of an historic waters claim will negate acquiescence and may defeat the claim.[77] Less clear is the number of such protests that are necessary and whether a single protest can undermine an historic waters claim.[78] O'Connell writes that "virtually total toleration of those nations whose interests are clearly affected" by an historic waters claim is required.[79] Thus, any protest

---

72 *See* Churchill and Lowe, *supra* note 7, at 45 and Y. Z. BLUM, HISTORIC TITLES IN INTERNATIONAL LAW (Martinus Nijhoff, The Hague 1965) 270.

73 *Gulf of Fonseca Case*, *supra* note 49, at para 394.

74 *See* Pharand, CANADA'S ARCTIC WATERS, *supra* note 34, at 99 and *see also* U. N. Study, *supra* note 41, at 16, paras 106–110.

75 U. N. Study, *supra* note 41, at 17, para 112; Pharand, CANADA'S ARCTIC WATERS, *supra* note 34, at 105; O'Connell, *supra* note 42, at 39; Pharand, *The Arctic Waters*, *supra* note 67, at 7; and Symmons, *supra* note 54, at 219–220.

76 U. N. Study, *supra* note 41, at 17, para 112.

77 Pharand, CANADA'S ARCTIC WATERS, *supra* note 34, at 105 and O'Connell, *supra* note 42, at 39.
In the historic waters context, both Bouchez, *supra* note 59, at 272–273 and Pharand, CANADA'S ARCTIC WATERS, *supra* note 34, at 100–102, place significant emphasis on the necessity of "effective protest" for which not just a paper protest but "more forceful steps" or "conduct in accordance with the protest" is necessary. The U. N. Study, *supra* note 41, at 17, paras 113–115 does not go this far. *See also* Symmons, *supra* note 54, at 230–231.

78 The inverse to this is the extent of acquiescence or non-acquiescence. The questions involved are well articulated in Symmons, *supra* note 54, at 236–241.

79 O'Connell, *supra* note 42, at 39.

from an interested State would defeat an historic waters claim.[80] The 1962 U.N. Secretariat Study is less categorical, commenting that "how wide-spread the opposition must be to preclude the emergence of historic title . . . is a matter of appreciation in light of the circumstances in each case."[81]

2.2 International Straits

The special situation of vessel passage rights in international straits was recognized in Article 16(4) of the 1958 Territorial Sea and Contiguous Zone Convention, which provided that in a strait used for international navigation, a non-suspendable innocent passage existed.[82] The expansion of territorial seas to 12 nautical miles and the possibilities to enclose ever-larger areas as internal waters through the use of straight baselines made the passage regime applicable to many international straits of utmost concern to maritime States during the negotiation of the LOS Convention.[83] A new package of navigation rights, referred to as the right of transit passage, applicable to many international straits, was the outcome of the negotiations.[84]

The LOS Convention creates five categories of international straits to which attach differing navigational rights. The LOS Convention directs that a transit passage applies to "straits which are used for international navigation between one part of the high seas or an exclusive economic zone and another part of the high seas or an economic zone."[85] However, two categories of straits used for international navigation are not subject to transit passage rights: those where within the strait there is a route of high seas or EEZ;[86] and those where a strait is formed by an island adjacent to the mainland of the same State and a route exists seaward of the island

---

80 Bouchez, *supra* note 59, at 273 appears to agree, at least in the context of historic bays: "An effective protest deprives claims to historic bays of one of its essential elements, namely the acquiescence of the community of States."

81 U. N. Study, *supra* note 41, at 18, para 130 and see 17–18, paras 116–120.

82 TSCZC, *supra* note 19, Art 16(4).

83 See Chapter Four, section 2.2.4.

84 LOS Convention, *supra* note 19, Art 38–44 and *see generally* Churchill and Lowe, *supra* note 7, at 107–110 and, in more detail, Jia, *supra* note 28, at 129–208.

85 *Id.* Art 37.

86 *Id.* Art 36.

of similar convenience.[87] In the latter situation, the right of innocent passage applies in the waters between the mainland and the offshore island.[88] Where a strait used for international navigation is between "a part of the high seas or an economic zone and the territorial sea of a foreign State," rather than transit passage applying the navigation regime is to be non-suspendable innocent passage.[89] Finally, note should be made that the provisions of the LOS Convention addressing international straits do not apply to straits "in which passage is regulated in whole or in part by longstanding international conventions."[90]

The term "strait used for international navigation" is not specifically defined in the LOS Convention[91] or the 1958 Territorial Sea and Contiguous Zone Convention. As a result, reference must be made to the 1949 *Corfu Channel Case* before the International Court and a particular passage in the Judgment, as follows:

> It may be asked whether the test [whether a waterway is an international strait] is to be found in the volume of traffic passing through the Strait or in its greater or lesser importance for international navigation. But in the opinion of the Court the decisive criterion is rather its geographical situation as connecting two parts of the high seas and the fact of its being used for international navigation. Nor can it be decisive that this Strait [Corfu Channel] is not a necessary route between two parts of the high seas, but only an alternative passage between the Aegean and Adriatic Seas. It has nevertheless been a useful route for maritime traffic.[92]

Based on this passage, two criteria are said to exist in determining whether a particular waterway is a strait used for international navigation:

- The geographic criterion; and
- The functional criterion.[93]

---

87 *Id.* Art 38(1).

88 *Id.* Arts 45(1)(a), 38(1).

89 *Id.* Art 45.

90 *Id.* Art 35(c).

91 J. N. Moore, *The Regime of Straits and the Third United Nations Conference on the Law of the Sea* (1980) 74 AJIL 77, 112.

92 *The Corfu Channel Case (Albania/United Kingdom)*, [1949] ICJ Rep. 4, 28.

93 *See generally* Jia, *supra* note 28, at 3–58; Pharand, NORTHWEST PASSAGE, *supra* note 34, at 89–95; and S. B. KAYE, THE TORRES STRAIT (Martinus Nijhoff, The Hague 1997) 78–79.

The geographical criterion set out in the *Corfu Channel Case*, that to be an international strait, a waterway must connect two parts of the high seas, has not been disturbed significantly by the LOS Convention. One modification is the addition of EEZ to the term high seas. Moreover, the LOS Convention and the 1958 Territorial Sea and Contiguous Zone Convention recognize, as an international strait, a waterway that connects "a part of the high seas or an economic zone and the territorial sea of a foreign State."[94] In the context of Canada-U.S. relations, the issue that arises in the geographic criterion is whether the Canadian waters are historic internal waters; if the answer is yes, the waters in question are not a strait used for international navigation.[95]

As regards the functional criterion, reliance is usually placed on the findings in the *Corfu Channel Case* and subsequent State practice to determine what is meant in customary international law by the term "used" for international navigation. The debating points concern, amongst other things, whether "used" means "actual use" or "potential use."[96] The latter view essentially bases "use" on geography, whereas the former view requires an examination of the sufficiency of actual use. The U.S. view is that "used for navigation" means capable of being used or potential for being used.[97] The U.S. claim has recently been articulated as follows:

> The definition of a strait used for international navigation is quite simple—a strait connects one part of the high seas or EEZ to another part of the high seas of EEZ. There is nothing in the Law of the Sea to suggest additional tests or requirements for recognition as an international strait, so there is no authority for the idea that a strait is only a strait if it meets a certain minimum threshold of shipping traffic, a specific number of transits,

---

94 LOS Convention, *supra* note 19, Art 45 and *see* TSCZC, *supra* note 19, Art 16(4).

95 *See* Pharand, NORTHWEST PASSAGE, *supra* note 34, at 91, 98; Pharand, CANADA'S ARCTIC WATERS, *supra* note 34, at 223; and *see* Chapter Six, section 2.0.

96 *See* Pharand, NORTHWEST PASSAGE, *supra* note 34, at 102.

97 In December 2007, the U.S. Senate Foreign Relations Committee voted to recommend U.S. accession to the LOS Convention and reported this to the full Senate for consideration. Attached to the Advice and Consent Resolution before the Senate was a declaration (section 2) outlining the exemptions that were proposed to be attached by the United States to its instrument of accession. U.S. Senate, Executive Report 110–9, Part VIII–Text of Resolution of Advice and Consent to Ratification, 19–24 (2007). Declaration 3(D) read:

> the term "used for international navigation" includes all straits capable of being used for international navigation.

See also R. J. Grunawalt, *United States Policy on International Straits* (1987) 18 ODIL 445, 456.

> a timetable or regularity of transits, transit by certain types of vessels, or whether the vessel is accompanied or not accompanied by icebreakers. The test is geographic, not function . . .[98]

The *Corfu Channel Case* does tip in favor of the geographic criterion being more important than the functional criterion.[99] However, the functional criterion is argued as having a role to play and many commentators examine in detail the actual use made of a waterway in determining whether a waterway is an international strait.[100]

There is no threshold of use (number of vessels, number of flag States, or tonnage that passes) that can be said to meet the "used" criterion. Moreover, the International Court in the *Corfu Channel Case* did not place significant weight on the importance of the waterway to international commerce, noting only that the Channel had been "a useful route for international maritime traffic."[101]

Pharand, after reviewing the *Corfu Channel Case* and much of the subsequent literature, concluded that the functional criterion requires that:

- "the strait must have a history as a useful route for international maritime traffic;"
- "the sufficiency of the use is determined mainly, although not exclusively, by reference to two factors, namely, the number of ships using the strait and the number of flags represented;" and
- "the number of ships and flags should normally reach the order of magnitude shown to exist in the Corfu Channel Case, but the location of the strait and other relevant circumstances might render lower numbers sufficient."[102]

---

98 J. Kraska, *The Law of the Sea Convention and the Northwest Passage (*2007) 22 IJMCL 257, 275.

99 Jia, *supra* note 28, at 39 comments that the Court "recognized the geographical situation as decisive" but that the Court went on to look at facts regarding the Channel having been used or useful for international navigation. S. C. Truver, The Strait of Gibraltar and the Mediterranean (Sijthoff and Noordhoff, Alphen aan den Rijn 1980) 151 notes that the Court included as international straits "those straits that have only rarely been used for international navigation."

100 *See* Pharand, Northwest Passage, *supra* note 34, at 91–95, 101–102 and Jia, *supra* note 28, at 34–58. O'Connell, *supra* note 42, at 314 states:

> The Corfu Channel Case established . . . that not all straits . . . are international straits, but only those which are important as communication links. The real significance of the Case is its treatment of the qualities that give a strait this importance. It is clear that it need not be the only or an indispensable or a necessary avenue, but equally clear that mere potential utility is insufficient.

101 *Corfu Channel Case, supra* note 92, at 28.

102 Pharand, Northwest Passage, *supra* note 34, at 95.

Part B

3.0 Northwest Passage

The Canada–U.S. disagreement regarding the international legal status of the Northwest Passage has been at the center of the bilateral salt water relationship for forty years. The Canadian view is that, as a matter of international ocean law, the waters within the Arctic archipelago (including the Northwest Passage) are historic internal waters.[103] The U.S. view is that the Northwest Passage is a strait used for international navigation through which there exists a right of transit passage.[104] The international legal difference comes down primarily to the extent of the authority that Canada has over vessels navigating through the Northwest Passage and, more sharply, whether Canada can require that passing foreign vessels obtain permission before using the Passage.

The nature of the international legal disagreement reflects the different orientations of the two States, with Canada as the coastal State, and the United States as the maritime State. Moreover, the perspectives of the two States are dissimilar. Canada sees the Arctic as a local issue, with the Arctic having special characteristics; while the United States is more concerned with global and military considerations. Most critically, the Northwest Passage issue is trumpeted in Canada as a test of sovereignty,[105] with the United States portrayed as indifferent to or challenging Canadian sovereignty. As one author has noted: "it has never taken more than a perception of a United States challenge to Canadian sovereignty [in the Arctic] to bring the issue to the forefront."[106] A 2006 example of this, albeit with a twist, came in the first news conference given by Stephen Harper after his election as Canadian Prime Minister when, in reaction to a largely unnoticed comment by the U.S. Ambassador that the two States disagreed

103 Letter dated 17 December 1973, *supra* note 3, at 279.

104 Commentary–The 1982 United Nations Convention on the Law of the Sea, *supra* note 6, at 18.

105 Regarding the Canadian public's attachment to the Arctic and the Northwest Passage as "symbolic of Canada's destiny" and how this affects Canadian policy, *see* F. Griffiths, *The Shipping News: Canada's Arctic Is Not On Thinning Ice* (2003) 58 INTL J 257, 273–275 and F. Griffiths, *Beyond the Arctic Sublime*, in F. GRIFFITHS (ed.) POLITICS OF THE NORTHWEST PASSAGE (McGill-Queen's University Press, Montreal 1987) 265–268.

106 E. B. ELLIOT-MEISEL, ARCTIC DIPLOMACY: CANADA AND THE UNITED STATES IN THE NORTHWEST PASSAGE (Peter Lang, New York 1998) 3.

respecting Canada's claims to the Northwest Passage,[107] he admonished the United States for not accepting Canada's sovereignty over Arctic waters.[108] The *Toronto Globe and Mail* wrote that Harper's comment seemed to be "designed to refute assertions he will be too cozy with the U.S. administration."[109] Despite all of the above, there has been significant cooperation between Canada and the United States regarding navigation within the Northwest Passage, the most obvious manifestation being the 1988 Arctic Cooperation Agreement.[110]

Over the decades since the Northwest Passage first arose as a bilateral issue, the United States has been largely disinterested in directly challenging Canada's assertions regarding the Northwest Passage. The high-profile 1985 transit by the U.S. Coast Guard ice-breaker *Polar Sea* of the Northwest Passage was not initially intended by the United States to be high profile, or to provoke or test Canada's legal resolve or sovereignty.[111] The Canadian public, however, saw the matter differently and, following the outcry, the Canadian government adopted a number of measures to further assert Canada's historic internal waters claim. The most significant legal measure was the adoption

---

107 The U.S. Ambassador had commented further that the disagreement was "a situation where there is no reason to create a problem that doesn't exist." Royal Society of Canada, *Canada-U.S. Relations: The View from Here*, at <www.rsc.ca/print.php?=Canada-us-relations&page_id=217&lang_id=1> (accessed on 24 April 2007).

In August 2006, Prime Minister Harper made a speech in Iqaluit entitled, Securing Canadian Sovereignty in the Arctic, without directly referencing the United States, at www.pm.gc.ca/eng/media.asp?id=1275 (accessed on 24 April 2007).

108 G. Galloway, *Harper Rebukes U.S. Envoy Over Arctic Dispute*, Toronto Globe and Mail, 27 January 2006, A4. *See also* D. Struck, *Harper Tells U.S. to Drop Arctic Claim*, Washington Post, 27 January 2006, A19.

109 Galloway, *supra* note 108.

110 Agreement on Arctic Cooperation, Ottawa, 11 January 1988, entered into force 11 January 1988, CTS 1988/29, TIAS 11565.

111 This is clear from the diplomatic communications exchanged prior to the passage of the *Polar Sea* through the Northwest Passage. *See* Demarche from the United States to Canada, 21 May 1985, in J. A. Roach and R. W. Smith, (eds.) United States Responses to Excessive Maritime Claims (Martinus Nijhoff, 2nd edition, The Hague 1996) 342–343; Note from Canada to the United States, 11 June 1985, in Roach and Smith, 344–345; Note from the United States to Canada, 24 June 1985, in Roach and Smith, 345–346; and Note from Canada to the United States, 31 July 1985, in Roach and Smith, 346–348.

See also R. Huebert, Steel, Ice and Decision-Making: The Voyage of the Polar Sea and Its Aftermath–The Making of Canadian Northern Foreign Policy (Dalhousie University, Ph.D. thesis, Halifax 1994) 319–320, on file with the author, and C. Kirkey, *Smoothing Troubled Waters: The 1988 Canada–United States Arctic Co-operation Agreement* (1995) 50 Intl J 401, 403. *More generally, see* Chapter Six, section 3.3.1.

of straight baselines.[112] Notwithstanding the measures adopted in 1985, Canada has been reluctant to undertake aggressive actions to support its position regarding the Northwest Passage, lest the United States' disinterest change direction. The Canadian political nightmare scenario is that a strong assertion by Canada that permission to use the Northwest Passage is required by a U.S. vessel results in the United States ignoring the requirement, and a U.S. vessel sails through the Northwest Passage unchallenged. The political fallout in Canada of a failure to protect Arctic sovereignty from the United States would be dire. Even having the means to physically block or otherwise prevent a U.S. vessel intent on disregarding Canada's assertions could result in a situation that could severely strain Canada–United States relations.

The U.S. disinterest regarding the Northwest Passage over the last thirty years has three explanations. First, the United States is unwilling to antagonize its northern neighbor regarding an issue that has shown itself to be of significant political force within Canada.[113] Second, the Northwest Passage is not itself seen as important to U.S. commercial or military interests. The U.S. views its international legal posture regarding the Passage as tied to that of other waterways that the United States believes are important. The concern for precedent has always been at the forefront of U.S. policy concerning the Northwest Passage.[114] Third, an aggressive U.S. international straits agenda in the Northwest Passage would be inconsistent with the U.S. policy of pursuing enhanced North American security.[115] The U.S. position regarding

---

112 Joe Clark, Minister for Foreign Affairs, HC, *Debates*, 10 September 1985, 6462–6464. Regarding the baselines, *see* Territorial Sea Geographical Coordinates (Area 7) Order, *supra* note 1.

113 R. Huebert, *Article 234 and Marine Pollution Jurisdiction in the Arctic*, in A. G. OUDE ELFERINK AND D. R. ROTHWELL (eds.) THE LAW OF THE SEA AND POLAR MARITIME DELIMITATION AND JURISDICTION (Martinus Nijhoff, The Hague 2001) 258 refers to this in the context of the negotiations leading to the 1988 Arctic Cooperation Agreement, *supra* note 110, as detailed in Kirkey, *supra* note 111, at 405–416.

114 *See* Note from the Secretary of State to Embassy of Canada, 14 April 1970, in *Gulf of Maine Pleadings*, Vol. 5, Annex 8 to Reply of the United States, 529–530, para 4 and Elliot-Meisel, *supra* note 106, at 140.

President Reagan is quoted In B. MULRONEY, MEMOIRS (McClelland and Stewart, Toronto 2007) 495 as making this point in a private letter to Prime Minister Mulroney in early 1987:

> I have to say in all candor that we cannot agree to an arrangement that obliges us to seek permission for our vessels to navigate through the Northwest Passage. To do so would adversely affect our legitimate right to freely transit other important areas globally.

See also Chapter Three, section 3.3.

115 Griffiths, *The Shipping News*, *supra* note 105, at 270–271 comments that "an outright US violation of Canada's Arctic sovereignty claim would needlessly diminish US security," and

the Northwest Passage may best be described as benign neglect; the less attention given the Passage and the legal dispute with Canada, the better. A concern for Canada is that, as a result of the effects of climate change on ice conditions[116] and other factors, such as national security and economic developments, the United States may re-evaluate its posture of disinterest and adopt a more aggressive policy regarding the Passage.

Although the Canada-U.S. bilateral international legal dispute regarding the Northwest Passage is narrow, a broad range of related and important international legal and political matters are often attached to or intersect with the Northwest Passage issue. These matters include multilateral Arctic governance;[117] the evolving rights of indigenous peoples of the North and the responsibilities of governments regarding northern indigenous peoples and their way of life;[118] Arctic marine, terrestrial, and atmospheric environmental protection;[119] and species management and preservation respecting, for

---

"The very idea of the Passage as an international strait is being overtaken by altered US security requirements."

R. Huebert, *The Shipping News Part II: How Canada's Arctic Sovereignty Is On Thinning Ice*, (2003) 58 INTL J 295, 305–307 questions, however, whether U.S. homeland security issues have or will make a difference in the U.S. perspective on the Northwest Passage.

116 *See* Chapter Six, section 3.1.

117 *See generally* O. R. YOUNG, CREATING REGIMES: ARCTIC ACCORDS AND INTERNATIONAL GOVERNANCE (Cornell University Press, Ithaca 1998); T. Koivurova and D. L. VanderZwaag, *The Arctic Council at 10 Years: Retrospect and Prospects* (2007) 40 U.B.C. LR 121–194; T. KOIVUROVA, T. JOONA, AND R. SHNORO (eds.) ARCTIC GOVERNANCE (Juridica Lapponica 29) (Oy Sevenprint Ltd, Rovaniemi 2004); and J. Jabour and M. Weber, *Is It Time to Cut the Gordian Knot of Polar Sovereignty?* (2008) 17 RECIEL 27–40.

118 *See generally* M. Nuttall, *Indigenous Peoples, Self-Determination and the Arctic Environment*, in M. NUTTALL AND T. CALLAGHAN (eds.) THE ARCTIC: ENVIRONMENT, PEOPLE, POLICY (Harwood Academic Publishers, Amsterdam 2000) 377–409; M. Nuttall, *Indigenous People's Organisations and Arctic Environmental Co-operation*, in Nuttall and Callaghan, at 621–637; L. Heinämäki, *Environmental Rights Protecting the Way of Life of Arctic Indigenous Peoples: ILO Convention No. 169 and the UN Draft Declaration on Indigenous Peoples*, in Koivurova, Joona and Shnoro, *supra* note 117, at 231–259; T. Koivurova and L. Heinämäki, *The Participation of Indigenous Peoples in International Norm-Making in the Arctic* (2006) 42 POLAR RECORD 101–109; N. LOUKACHEVA, THE ARCTIC PROMISE: LEGAL AND POLITICAL AUTONOMY OF GREENLAND AND NUNAVUT (University of Toronto Press, Toronto 2007) 103–144; and J. Shadian, *Remaking Arctic Governance: The Construction of an Arctic Inuit Policy* (2006) 42 POLAR RECORD 249–259.

119 *See* D. VanderZwaag, R. Huebert, and S. Ferrara, *The Arctic Environmental Protection Strategy, Arctic Council and Multilateral Environmental Initiatives: Tinkering While the Arctic Marine Environmental Totters* (2002) 30 DENVER J INTL L AND POL 131–171; T. KOIVUROVA, ENVIRONMENTAL IMPACT ASSESSMENT IN THE ARCTIC: A STUDY OF INTERNATIONAL LEGAL NORMS (Ashgate, Aldershot 2002); and D. VIDAS (ed.) PROTECTING THE POLAR MARINE ENVIRONMENT: LAW AND POLICY FOR POLLUTION PREVENTION (Cambridge University Press, Cambridge 2000).

example, caribou, whales, and polar bears.[120] All of these matters play a role in the Northwest Passage discussion. However, the international ocean law dispute between Canada and the United States is as regards navigation through the Passage and that will be the focus here.

NORTHWEST PASSAGE

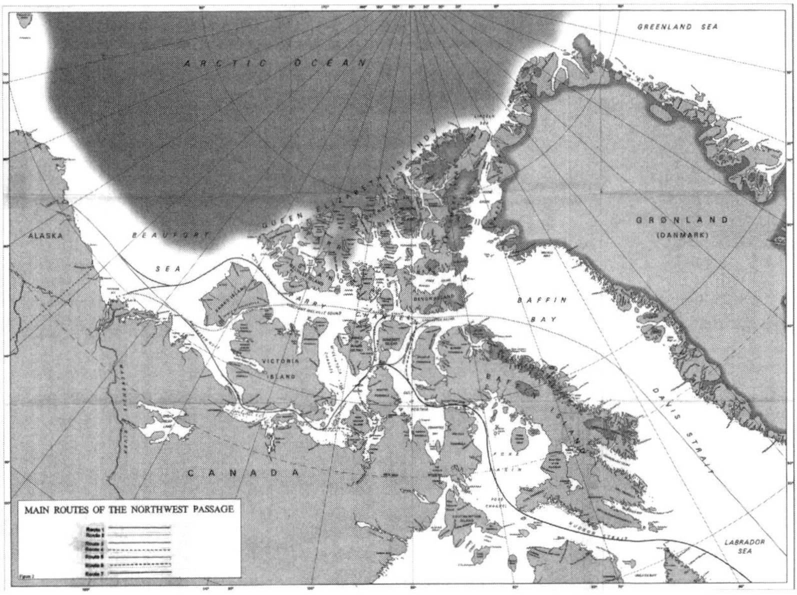

Source: DH Gray

A preliminary matter is one of geographic identification. There is not a single Northwest Passage route. The Canadian Arctic islands allow for a variety of east-west passages. One author has identified five basic routes that could be used for navigation depending on the size of the vessel, icebreaking capability, ice conditions, and the adequacy of navigational information.[121] Three routes appear to have the greatest viability for commercial shipping activity. They are from the Beaufort Sea through M'Clure Strait north of Banks Island and across to Lancaster Sound; from the Beaufort Sea south and east of Banks Island through the Prince of Wales Straits and across to Lancaster

120 *See, for example,* A. Fikkan, G. Osherenko, and A. Arikainen, *Polar Bears: The Importance of Simplicity,* in O. R. YOUNG AND G. OSHERENKO (eds.) POLAR POLITICS: CREATING INTERNATIONAL ENVIRONMENTAL REGIMES (Cornell University, Ithaca 1993) 96–151.

121 *See* Pharand, NORTHWEST PASSAGE, *supra* note 34, at 6 and see 6–21.

Sound; and from the Beaufort Sea south of Banks Island and east hugging the Canadian mainland coast south of Victoria Island and then north through Victoria Strait (between Victoria Island and King William Island) and Peel Sound (between Prince of Wales Island and Somerset Island) and across to Lancaster Sound.[122]

3.1 Ice and Climate Change

The period of hibernation of the Canada-U.S. Northwest Passage dispute that followed 1985, and the flurry of activity and attention respecting the voyage of the *Polar Sea* ended when concern was raised that global climate change could lead to a reduction of ice in the Northwest Passage and turn the Passage into an active shipping route, with consequent concern over challenges to Canadian sovereignty in the Arctic.[123]

The extent, concentration, and thickness of the sea ice in the Northwest Passage and Canadian Arctic waters are the subjects of ongoing study. The trend is one of decreasing ice cover and a lengthening summer shipping season.[124] However, there is doubt about the viability in the foreseeable future of the Northwest Passage for large-scale commercial shipping operations.[125]

---

122 *Id.* 6–15 and *see* K. J. Wilson, J. Falkingham, H. Melling, and R. De Abreu, *Shipping in the Canadian Arctic: Other Possible Climate Change Scenarios*, in GEOSCIENCES AND REMOTE SENSING SYMPOSIUM, 2004, PROCEEDINGS, Vol. 3 (Institute of Electrical and Electronics Engineers, Piscataway, New Jersey 2004) 1853–1856.

123 *See* R. Huebert, *Climate Change and Canadian Sovereignty in the Northwest Passage* (2001) 2 No. 4 ISUMA–CANADIAN JOURNAL OF POLICY RESEARCH 86–94 and R. Huebert, *The Shipping News Part II, supra* note 115, at 295–308. For a spirited rebuttal, *see* Griffiths, *The Shipping News, supra* note 105, at 257–282 and F. Griffiths, *Pathetic Fallacy: That Canada's Arctic Sovereignty Is On Thinning Ice* (2004) Vol. 11, No. 3 CANADIAN FOREIGN POLICY 1–16.

124 See the survey of the science done by I. Kubat, A. Collins, B. Gorman, and W. G. Timco, *A Methodology to Evaluate Canada's Arctic Shipping Regulations*, in PROCEEDINGS OF THE 18TH INTERNATIONAL CONFERENCE ON PORT AND OCEAN ENGINEERING UNDER ARCTIC CONDITIONS (Potsdam, New York, 2005), Vol. 2, 693, 694. *See also* Department of Environment, *Northwest Passage Still Closed for Business*, ENVIROZINE, issue 57, 15 September 2005, at www.ec.gc.ca/EnviroZine/english/issues/57/feature2_2.cfm (accessed on 24 April 2007).

125 *Northwest Passage Still Closed for Business, supra* note 124 and Department of Natural Resources, *Navigating the Northwest Passage Remains Hazardous Despite More Open Water*, (December 2005), at www.nrcan.gc.ca/media/articles/2005/2005art23_e.htm (accessed on 24 April 2007).

National Research Council (NRC), Safe Northern Passage, January 2007, at <www.nrc-cnrc.gc.ca/highlights/2007/0701passage_e.html> (accessed on 24 April 2007) notes:

> A new NRC study reveals that climate change could make it more, not less dangerous, for shipping in the Canadian Arctic. And, even with significant warming in coming

The warming of the Arctic may lead to multi-year ice (ice that is more dense and harder than other sea ice and a significant danger to vessels), breaking free from the Arctic basin icepack and being deposited at the western entrances to the Northwest Passage, creating greater ice problems in the Northwest Passage.[126] The potential for more multi-year ice in Canadian Arctic waters, even during the summer shipping seasons, poses a significant threat to shipping activity. Moreover, annual sea ice conditions are variable, which is expected to continue.[127]

The Northwest Passage, if available, would shorten the vessel traffic route between Asia and Europe through the Panama Canal by 9000 kilometers and avoid the vessel size restrictions of the Canal. As well, less ice in Canada's Arctic waters could encourage more local vessel traffic attached to mining and other activities in the Arctic islands. Increased vessel traffic in the Northwest Passage, whether through-traffic (not visiting a Canadian port) or local-traffic (stopping in a Canadian port), would raise a host of issues for Canada concerning the interests of the local population; vessel-source marine pollution; vessel and navigation safety; law enforcement; and security. Much of the concern expressed about the Northwest Passage and thinning ice has been directed at the government of Canada's lack of presence in the Arctic, the intention being to point out Canada's lack of preparedness and the consequent need for attention to potential vessel traffic increases from all sources.[128] The Canada-U.S. Northwest Passage dispute is a convenient flag to hoist since invoking international sovereignty concerns helps attract attention to the internal Canadian issues of lack of resources and knowledge of the North.

In July 2007, the government of Canada responded to a number of the above concerns by announcing that six to eight patrol vessels, to be part of

---

decades, the research predicts that Canada's legendary Northwest Passage will remain impenetrable to large-scale commercial shipping.

See also S. E. L. Howell and J. J. Yackel, *A Vessel Transit Assessment of Sea Ice Variability in the Western Arctic, 1969–2002: Implications for Ship Navigation* (2004) 30 No. 2 CANADIAN JOURNAL OF REMOTE SENSING 205–215 and E. J. Stewart, S. E. L. Howell, D. Draper, J. Yackel, and A Tivy, *Sea Ice in Canada's Arctic: Implications for Cruise Tourism* (2007) 60 ARCTIC 370–380.

126 Wilson, *et al.*, *supra* note 122, at 1856.

127 *Id.*

128 *See* S. Lalonde, *Increased Traffic through Canadian Arctic Waters: Canada's State of Readiness* (2004) 38 REVUE JURIDIQUE THEMIS 49, 103–124. This was the common ground in Huebert, *Climate Change*, *supra* note 123; Griffiths, *The Shipping News*, *supra* note 105; Huebert, *The Shipping News Part II*, *supra* note 115; and Griffiths, *Pathetic Fallacy*, *supra* note 123.

the Canadian Navy, were to be built that would have the capacity to navigate through the Northwest Passage in the summer months and monitor the approaches year-round.[129] To service these vessels, it was announced that a deep-water docking and refueling facility would be built at Nanisivik. In making the announcement, Prime Minister Harper referred to the importance of Canada defending its Arctic sovereignty and provided the misleading sound bite, "We either use it or lose it."[130] In the February 2008 budget, $720 million was allocated for the purchase of a new polar class icebreaker.[131]

3.2 International Legal Positions

The principal international legal dispute between Canada and the United States respecting the Northwest Passage is the degree of control that Canada can exercise over foreign vessels that navigate the Passage without calling into a Canadian port. In other words, How Canadian is the Northwest Passage? Since the early 1970s, Canada has had in place the Arctic Waters Pollution Prevention Act (AWPPA) that applies ice-specific standards to all vessels that navigate in Canada's Arctic waters.[132] As already noted, Canada's Arctic Waters legislation is tied to Article 234 of the LOS Convention,[133] which permits a coastal State to adopt and enforce for ice-covered areas national laws containing more stringent standards than internationally

---

129 I. Bailey, *Harper Plans Arctic Patrol Fleet*, Toronto Globe and Mail, 10 July 2007, at A-1, 4.

130 *Id.*

It was reported in September 2007 that Canada was going to monitor vessel traffic in the Northwest Passing using underwater listening devices. *Canada to Monitor Water Traffic in Northwest Passage*, CBC News, 24 September 2007, at <www.cbc.ca/canada/story/2007/09/24/technology-passage.html (accessed on 24 September 2007).

131 Department of Finance, The Budget Plan 2008: Responsible Leadership, 26 February 2008, 161, at www.budget.gc.ca/2008/plan/table-eng.asp (accessed on 7 March 2008).

132 Arctic Waters Pollution Prevention Act, St Can 1969–1970, c 47.

133 LOS Convention, *supra* note 19, Art 234:

> Coastal States have the right to adopt and enforce non-discriminatory laws and regulations for the prevention, reduction and control of marine pollution from vessels in ice-covered areas within the limits of the exclusive economic zone, where particularly severe climatic conditions and the presence of ice covering such areas for most of the year create obstructions or exceptional hazards to navigation, and pollution of the marine environment could cause major harm to or irreversible disturbance of the ecological balance. Such laws and regulations shall have due regard to navigation and the protection and preservation of the marine environment based on the best available scientific evidence.

accepted vessel standards.[134] The United States has accepted that Article 234 is part of customary international law.[135] Again, as already noted, Article 234 allows Canada to enact and enforce specific vessel legislation regardless of whether the Northwest Passage is an international strait.[136] McRae has summarized that the Northwest Passage being an international strait, the position of the United States, "would have little impact on Canada's legal authority to regulate commercial shipping."[137] The key point is that regardless of the dispute between Canada and the United States on the legal status of the Northwest Passage, both Canada and the United States recognize Canada as having, significant authority to regulate, for environmental protection purposes, commercial shipping using the Northwest Passage. However, there is uncertainty as to precise extent of a coastal State's authority to interfere with shipping activity under Article 234.[138] Nevertheless, the international legal dispute between Canada and the United States regarding the Passage is primarily about whether Canada can, as an exercise of sovereignty, require a foreign flag vessel to obtain permission to use the Northwest Passage.

3.2.1 Canada's Claim—Historic Internal Waters

Canada's position that the waters within the Arctic archipelago, including the waters of the Northwest Passage, are historic internal waters was made clear in 1973.

---

134 *See* S. Rosenne and A. Yankov, United Nations Convention on the Law of the Sea 1982: A Commentary, Vol. IV (Martinus Nijhoff, Dordrecht 1991) 393, 396 and Chapter Four, section 2.2.2.

135 B. Hoyle, *The United States Government Perspective*, in L. Juda (ed.) The United States without the Law of the Sea Treaty: Opportunities and Costs (Times Press, Wakefield, R.I. 1983) 135. Note also Commentary–The 1982 United Nations Convention on the Law of the Sea, *supra* note 6, at 40 and Chapter Four, sections 2.2.2 and 3.1.

136 *See* D. M. McRae, *The Negotiation of Article 234*, in Griffiths, *supra* note 105, at 110 and Chapter Four, section 2.2.4. *See*, however, M. Byers and S. Lalonde, *Who Controls the Northwest Passage?* (discussion paper manuscript, 2008) 38–39

137 D. McRae, *Arctic Sovereignty? What is at Stake?* (2007) 64 No. 1 Behind the Headlines, 18 and more generally, 17–19. *See also* Lalonde, *supra* note 128, at 96–103.

138 *See* Byers and Lalonde, *supra* note 136, at 50–51. *See also* R. D. Brubaker, The Russian Arctic Straits (Martinus Nijhoff, Leiden 2005) 54–67, who looks at the interpretation of Article 234 and how it has been implemented by Canada, Russia, and the United States.

> Canada . . . claims that the waters of the Canadian Arctic Archipelago are internal waters of Canada, on an historical basis, although they have not been declared as such in any treaty or by any legislation.[139]

Pharand has commented: "This unquestionably constitutes the clearest and most precise statement as to the nature of and basis for Canada's claim over Arctic waters."[140] Pharand refers to comments made in 1969 by Prime Minister Trudeau[141] and in a report from the House of Commons Standing Committee on Indian Affairs and Northern Development,[142] in which history as a basis of claim was noted.[143] Other comments from Prime Minister Trudeau in 1969 referred to the waters between the Arctic islands as "internal waters," noting that, in 1958, the Minister of Northern Affairs had stated that Canada looked upon the islands and waters of the Canadian north "as our own."[144] In 1970, in official communications with the United States as a consequence of the Canadian enactment of the AWPPA[145] and extension of the territorial sea to 12 nautical miles,[146] it was stated that:

> With respect to the waters of the Arctic Archipelago, the position of Canada has always been that these waters are regarded as Canadian.[147]

---

139 Letter dated 17 December 1973, *supra* note 3, at 279.

140 Pharand, CANADA'S ARCTIC WATERS, *supra* note 34 at 112. In 2007, Pharand, *The Arctic Waters*, *supra* note 67, at 11 referred to the above statement as the "first official Canadian claim of internal waters."

141 Pierre Trudeau, Prime Minister, HC, *Debates*, 24 October 1969, 39–40.

142 Report of the Standing Committee Standing Committee on Indian Affairs and Northern Development, HC, *Minutes of Proceedings and Evidence of the Standing Committee on Indian Affairs and Northern Development*, 16 December 1969 (28th Parliament, 2nd Session, 1969), Issue No. 1, 6.

143 Pharand, CANADA'S ARCTIC WATERS, *supra* note 34, at 111.

144 Pierre Trudeau, Prime Minister, HC, *Debates*, 15 May 1969, 8720.
R. D. McConchie and R. S. Reid, *Canadian Foreign Policy and International Straits*, in B. JOHNSON AND M. W. ZACHER (eds.) CANADIAN FOREIGN POLICY AND THE LAW OF THE SEA (University of British Columbia Press, Vancouver 1977) 168 commented that a few days after Trudeau's statement "he obfuscated the government's position by declaring that these waters were not internal." *See also* E. FRANCKX, MARITIME CLAIMS IN THE ARCTIC: CANADIAN AND RUSSIAN PERSPECTIVES (Martinus Nijhoff, Dordrecht 1993) 78.

145 AWPPA, *supra* note 132.

146 Act to amend the Territorial Sea and Fishing Zones Act, St Can 1969–1970, c 68, s 1.

147 Note No. 105 from the Embassy of Canada to the United States Department of State, 16 April 1970, in *Gulf of Maine Pleadings*, Vol. 5, Annex 8 to Reply of the United States, 534 and *Summary of Canadian Note of 16 April Tabled by the Secretary of State for External Affairs in the House*, 17 April 1970, 9 ILM 607, 613.

In 1985, as a consequence of the transit of the Northwest Passage by the *Polar Sea*, Canada put in place straight baselines around the Arctic island archipelago.[148] In announcing the baselines, Minister for Foreign Affairs Joe Clark stated that "these baselines define the outer limit of Canada's historical internal waters."[149] Subsequent government statements have followed this position.[150] The consequence is that the straight baselines delineate the Arctic waters that are historic internal waters, rather than the normal consequence of straight baselines, which is the creation of internal waters.[151] Of final note is the statement in 2001 that:

> Canada's view... is that since... 1880... the waters of the Arctic Archipelago have been Canada's internal waters by virtue of historic title. These waters have been used by the Inuit, now of Canada, since time immemorial.[152]

The U.S. view is that the waters within the Northwest Passage and the Canadian Arctic archipelago are not internal waters of Canada. This position dates back to at least 1964 when Canadian straight baselines for the Arctic, and other areas, were under discussion.[153] Canada reportedly "dropped its claims to the waters of the Arctic archipelago,"[154] although it appears rather

---

148 Territorial Sea Geographical Coordinates (Area 7) Order, *supra* note 1. *See* R. Huebert, *Polar Vision or Tunnel Vision: The Making of Canadian Arctic Waters Policy* (1995) 19 MAR POL 343, 347–348.

149 Clark, *supra* note 112, at 6463.

150 Department of Foreign Affairs, Briefing, 21 May 1987, in (1987) 25 CYIL 406, 406:

> Canada is determined to exercise full sovereignty over the *historic internal waters* of the Arctic archipelago and is prepared to uphold its position before the International Court of Justice if necessary.
>
> These Canadian internal waters have now been delineated by straight baselines that became effective on January 1, 1986. (emphasis in original)

Pharand, *The Arctic Waters*, *supra* note 67, at 12 notes that "not only is this statement crystal clear as to the status of internal waters, but it seems to imply that the legal basis of that status is a historic title exclusively."

151 TSCZC, *supra* note 19, Arts 4, 5 and LOS Convention, *supra* note 19, Arts 7, 8.

152 Department of Foreign Affairs, Paper, 19 March 2001, in (2001) 39 CYIL 486, 488.
In 1880 the Arctic area was transferred to Canada from Great Britain. *See generally* I. L. Head, *Canadian Claims to Territorial Sovereignty in the Arctic Region* (1963) 9 MCGILL LJ 200, 211–212.

153 Department of State, FOREIGN RELATIONS OF THE UNITED STATES (Johnson Administration, 1964–1968), (Washington, 2001), Vol. XII, Document 317, Report Prepared by the Deputy Under Secretary of State for Political Affairs (undated), 678 and Document 321, Memorandum of Conversation, (Ottawa, 6 July 1964) 684–686.

154 Report Prepared by the Deputy Under Secretary, *supra* note 153, at 678.

ARCTIC STRAIGHT BASELINES

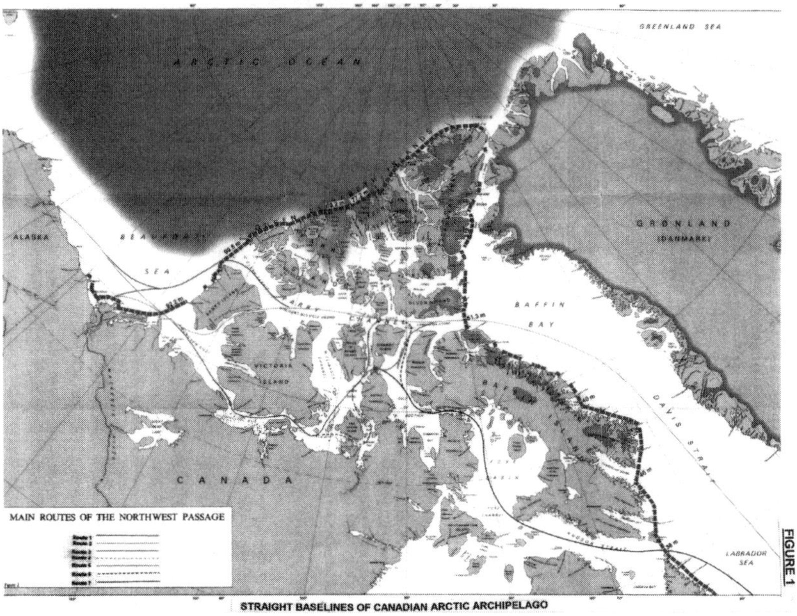

Source: DH Gary drawn for D Pharand, 'The Arctic Waters and the Northwest Passage: A Final Revisit' (2007) 38 ODIL 3, 18.

that Canada elected to defer action respecting the Arctic waters.[155] The U.S. view in 1970 was that:

> We cannot accept the assertion of a Canadian claim that the Arctic waters are internal waters . . . Such acceptance would jeopardize the freedom of navigation essential for United States naval activities worldwide.[156]

In a U.S. communication to Canada in 1985, in anticipation of the voyage of the *Polar Sea* through the Northwest Passage, the disagreement was clearly articulated:

> The United States notes the Canadian statement that the waters of the Arctic archipelago, including the Northwest Passage, are internal waters

155 Memorandum of Conversation, 6 July 1964, *supra* note 153, at 685.

156 Department of State, FOREIGN RELATIONS OF THE UNITED STATES (Nixon-Ford Administrations, 1969–1976), Vol. E-1, Document 367, Information Memorandum for Mr. Kissinger—The White House: Subject—Imminent Canadian Legislation on the Arctic, from T.L. Eliot, Jr., (Washington, 12 March 1970), at www.state.gov/r/pa/ho/frus/nixon/e1/53180.htm (accessed on 7 August 2007).

> of Canada. . . . As the Government of Canada is aware, the United States does not share this view.[157]

In response to the 1985 straight baselines delineating Canada's claimed historic internal waters in the Arctic, it was reported that during bilateral discussions, the United States took the view that "Canada was not justified in stating that all waters between Canadian islands in the Arctic were internal Canadian waters."[158] A 1986 U.S. State Department letter sets out that:

> The United States position is that there is no basis in international law to support the Canadian claim. The United States cannot accept the Canadian claim because to do so would constitute acceptance of full Canadian control of the Northwest Passage and would terminate U.S. navigation rights through the Passage under international law.[159]

The navigation control issue of concern to the United States was that of providing notification of the intended vessel transit of the Northwest Passage or seeking of permission for such travel.[160]

Pharand has undertaken a detailed study of Canada's historic internal waters claim and concluded that "Canada would not succeed in establishing that the waters of the Canadian Arctic Archipelago are historic internal waters."[161] In a 2007 update to this research, he concluded that:

> Canada is not in a position to discharge the heavy burden of proof that it has exercised exclusive jurisdiction over the Arctic waters for a sufficiently long

157 Note to Canada, June 24, 1985, *supra* note 111, at 345.

158 Roach and Smith, *supra* note 111, at 118.

159 Letter from J.W. Dyer, Acting Assistant Secretary of State, Legislative and Intergovernmental Affairs to Senator C. McC. Mathias, Jr., 26 February 1986, in Roach and Smith, *supra* note 111, at 118 and Department of State, United States Responses to Excessive Maritime Claims, LIMITS IN THE SEAS, No. 112 (Washington, 1992) 29.

Note Pharand, *The Arctic Waters*, *supra* note 67, at 12 comments on this wording that the U.S. objection to the Canadian claim of internal waters is not specific to Canada's claim of historic waters, but extends to the claim regardless of its legal basis.

160 Note to Canada, 24 June 1985, *supra* note 111, at 345 and *Responses to Excessive Maritime Claims*, *supra* note 159, at 73.

161 Pharand, CANADA'S ARCTIC WATERS, *supra* note 34, at 125.

period of time and with the acquiescence of foreign states, particularly those affected by its claim.[162]

3.2.2 Possible Alternative Canadian Position

Over the last thirty years, Canada has consistently articulated the view that the waters of the Canadian Arctic, including the Northwest Passage, are historic internal waters. The 1985 deployment of straight baselines around the Arctic islands, however, raises the possibility of a Canadian claim that the waters within the baselines are non-historic internal waters.

The first step in this argument is whether Canada's Arctic straight baselines have been constructed consistent with the relevant international legal criteria and guidelines.[163] Pharand has concluded that Canada's Arctic straight baselines capture the waters of Arctic archipelago as internal waters.[164] His analysis of the geography of the Canadian baselines and their fit with the relevant provisions of the 1982 LOS Convention,[165] the 1958 Territorial Sea and Contiguous Zone Convention,[166] and the 1951 *Anglo-Norwegian Fisheries Case*,[167] concludes that the Canadian straight baselines meet the "flexible" geographic criteria or guidelines of the relevant international law.[168] A contrary view is proffered by Reisman and Westerman, who note that Canada's Arctic baselines utilize "inappropriate basepoints" and that numerous of the lines crossing the bays and inlets of Baffin Island "appear to be impermissible."[169] Beyond geography, Pharand concludes that the validity of the Arctic straight baselines "is reinforced by the longstanding economic interests of the

---

162 Pharand, *The Arctic Waters*, *supra* note 67, at 13.

163 For a review of the various writers who have looked at Canada's Arctic straight baselines, *see* Lalonde, *supra* note 128, at 69–73. *See also* Byers and Lalonde, *supra* note 136, at 23–28.

164 *See* Pharand, *The Arctic Waters*, *supra* note 67, at 28 and Pharand, CANADA'S ARCTIC WATERS, *supra* note 34, at 159–179.

165 LOS Convention, *supra* note 19, Art 7.

166 TSCZC, *supra* note 19, Art 4.

167 *Anglo-Norwegian Fisheries Case*, *supra* note 48, at 131–137.

168 Pharand, CANADA'S ARCTIC WATERS, *supra* note 34, at 178 and *see* Pharand, *The Arctic Waters*, *supra* note 67, at 28.

169 W. M. REISMAN AND G. S. WESTERMAN, STRAIGHT BASELINES IN MARITIME BOUNDARY DELIMITATION (St. Martin's Press, New York 1992) 166, 168 and see 111.

local inhabitants,"[170] that leads to a consolidation of title to the Arctic waters as internal waters.[171] Pharand defines the consolidation of title as involving the history and use of a water area being invoked "as a complementary or subsidiary basis, to solidify or consolidate the title resulting from the primary or main basis,"[172] with the primary basis of title being the effect of the straight baselines.

Acceptance of the above does not resolve whether a right of innocent passage exists within the internal waters landward of straight baselines. Article 8(2) of the LOS Convention and Article 5(2) of the 1958 Convention on the Territorial Sea and Contiguous Zone provide that a right of innocent passage exists in internal waters enclosed by straight baselines, where the waters enclosed had not previously been considered as internal waters.[173] Canada is not a party to the 1958 Territorial Sea Convention and, in 1985, had not yet become a party to the 1982 LOS Convention. Pharand's view is that the international law binding on Canada in 1985 was customary international law as set out in the 1951 *Anglo-Norwegian Fisheries Case*, which provided that no right of innocent passage existed in waters enclosed by straight baselines.[174] He argues that Article 5(2) of the 1958 Convention was not customary international law in 1985, since the wording of the provision was a departure from the customary law that existed in the 1950s and an insufficient number of

---

170 Pharand, *The Arctic Waters*, *supra* note 67, at 21 and *see* Pharand, CANADA'S ARCTIC WATERS, *supra* note 34, at 164.

171 Pharand, CANADA'S ARCTIC WATERS, *supra* note 34, at 139–144, 167–177 and Pharand, *The Arctic Waters*, *supra* note 67, at 23–28.

172 Pharand, CANADA'S ARCTIC WATERS, *supra* note 34, at 140 and Pharand, *The Arctic Waters*, *supra* note 67, at 23.

173 TSCZC, *supra* note 19, Art 5(2) and LOS Convention, *supra* note 19, Art 8(2).
When Article 5(2) was first proposed it was intended to have a narrow scope, as is clear from the following commentary of the International Law Commission.

> The question arose whether in waters which become internal waters when the straight baseline system is applied the right of passage should not be granted in the same way as in the territorial sea. Stated in such general terms, this argument was not approved by the majority of the Commission. The Commission was, however, prepared to recognize that if a State wished to make a fresh delimitation of its territorial sea according to the straight baseline principle, thus including in its internal waters parts of the high seas or of the territorial sea that had previously been waters through which international traffic passed, other nations could not be deprived of the right of passage in those waters.

YEARBOOK OF THE INTERNATIONAL LAW COMMISSION, 1956, Vol. II, 268. *See also* Lalonde, *supra* note 128, at 81–82.

174 Pharand, CANADA'S ARCTIC WATERS, *supra* note 34, at 228–229 and Pharand, *The Arctic Waters*, *supra* note 67, at 43. *See also* Lalonde, *supra* note 128, at 78–79.

States had become a party to the 1958 Convention or applied the straight baseline provisions of the Convention.[175] Pharand has commented that the entry into force of the LOS Convention in 1994, and Canada becoming a party in 2003, does not alter the conclusion that the waters of the Arctic archipelago, including the Northwest Passage, are internal waters of Canada within which no right of innocent passage exists as a result of the 1985 employment of straight baselines.[176] The argument is that if Canada's Arctic straight baselines were redrawn or reconsidered as a result of Canada now being a party to the 1982 LOS Convention, the straight baselines would not have "the effect of enclosing as internal waters areas which had not previously been considered as such,"[177] since pursuant to customary international law in 1985, the waters enclosed by the Arctic baselines were previously considered to be internal waters within which no right of innocent passage existed.[178]

The U.S. view was "that the Canadian straight baseline claim in the Arctic region was not based on principles of international law."[179] The U.S. protested the Canadian measure.[180] The United States takes the view that the Arctic straight baselines are not consistent with the guidelines and criteria found in the relevant international law.[181]

---

175 Pharand, CANADA'S ARCTIC WATERS, *supra* note 34, at 228–229 and Pharand, *The Arctic Waters*, *supra* note 67, at 43. *See also* Lalonde, *supra* note 128, at 78–79 and McRae, *supra* note 137, at 13–14.

Note that if Article 5(2) of the 1958 Territorial Sea Convention was not customary international law in 1985, then Article 8(2) of the LOS Convention was also not customary international law in 1985.

176 Pharand, *The Arctic Waters*, *supra* note 67, at 43–44.

177 LOS Convention, *supra* note 19, Art 8(2).

178 Pharand, *The Arctic Waters*, *supra* note 67, at 44.

179 Roach and Smith, *supra* note 111, at 118.

180 Department of Defense, MARITIME CLAIMS REFERENCE MANUAL (Washington, 2005) 96 notes that protests were made in 1995 and 1996 and see *Responses to Excessive Maritime Claims*, *supra* note 159, at 29. *See* Huebert, *Steel, Ice and Decision-Making*, *supra* note 111, at 323 who states that in 1985 the United States did not want to aggravate relations with Canada and was concerned about unintentionally encouraging Soviet activities in the Northwest Passage. As a result, the United States opted for a low-key response and the giving of little publicity to its communication to Canada about the baselines.

181 *Geographic Note*, *supra* note 4, at 6.

3.2.3 U.S. Claim—International Strait

Although the U.S. position of the Northwest Passage as an international strait may have been asserted during the Canada-U.S. discussions on Arctic baselines in the early 1960s,[182] it most emphatically arose during the *Manhattan* events in 1969 to 1970.[183] Canada's 1970 extension of its territorial sea from three to 12 nautical miles was part of its strategy to attain greater control over the Northwest Passage.[184] As the U.S. explained at the time, a 12-nautical-mile territorial sea was acceptable provided that through an international treaty "freedom of passage through and over international straits" was also accepted.[185] In 1969 to 1970, the United States would not have seen the necessity to assert directly that the Northwest Passage was an international strait such that, pursuant to the 1958 Territorial Sea and Contiguous Zone Convention, a right of suspendable innocent passage applied,[186] since the U.S. view was that with a three-nautical-mile territorial sea a high seas route existed in the Northwest Passage.[187] Presumably in reaction to U.S. comments made in bilateral discussions, Canada forcefully rejected any suggestion that the Northwest Passage was an international strait.[188]

As already noted, during the Third United Nations Conference on the Law of the Sea (UNCLOS III), a central goal for Canada was protection of the Northwest Passage.[189] Canada introduced language, ultimately not accepted,

---

182 *See* Chapter Six, section 3.2.1.

183 *See* Chapter Three, section 3.3.

184 I. L. HEAD AND P. E. TRUDEAU, THE CANADIAN WAY: SHAPING CANADA'S FOREIGN POLICY 1968–1984 (McClelland and Stewart, Toronto 1995) 38.

185 Department of State, Statement on Government of Canada's Bills on Limits of the Territorial Sea, Fisheries and Pollution, 15 April 1970, 9 ILM 605–606.

186 TSCZS, *supra* note 19, Art 14.

187 Note N. C. Howson, *Breaking the Ice: The Canadian - American Dispute over the Arctic's Northwest Passage* (1988) 26 COLUMBIA J TRANSNATIONAL L 337, 365–366 and generally Grunawalt, *supra* note 97, at 448–450.

188 Note No. 105, 16 April 1970, *supra* note 147, at 533 and Summary of Canadian Note of 16 April, *supra* note 147, at 612:

> The Canadian Government is aware of United States interest in ensuring freedom of transit through international straits, but rejects any suggestion that the Northwest Passage is such an international strait. . . . The Northwest Passage has not attained the status of an international strait by customary usage nor has it been defined as such by conventional law.

189 Department of External Affairs, *The Third United Nations Conference on the Law of the Sea* (Ottawa, 1973), 5, 17–18 and R. Hage, *Canada and the Law of the Sea* (1984) 8 MAR POL 2, 5.

that was intended to have the effect of excluding the Northwest Passage from the definition of international straits.[190] The Northwest Passage figured prominently in Canada-U.S. negotiations regarding the ice-covered waters provision (Article 234) of the LOS Convention.[191] The careful language ensured that neither State had to refine their views respecting the status of the Northwest Passage as an international strait to which rights of transit passage applied. In 1975, Canada's Foreign Minister stated that the Northwest Passage was not used for international navigation, was part of Canada's internal waters, and that the LOS Convention regime of transit passage did not apply.[192]

The U.S. position was and remains that, since the Northwest Passage is a waterway that connects one part of the high seas or EEZ from another part of the high seas or EEZ, it is a strait used for international navigation which, pursuant to the 1982 LOS Convention, is subject to the transit passage regime.[193] At the time of the *Polar Sea* events, the United States stated that it "considers the Northwest Passage . . . to be an international strait subject to transit passage."[194] As noted above, it is the U.S. view that "used for navigation" means capable of being used or potential for being used rather than the strait having actually been used for navigation.[195]

The U.S. view on the definition of an international strait is not shared by Canada, which gives effect to the functional criteria and the Passage having

---

190 Draft Article on a Definition of an International Strait, U. N. Doc A/Conf.62/C.2/L.83, 26 August 1974, in UNCLOS III, OFFICIAL RECORDS, Vol. III, 241. *See* McConchie and Reid, *supra* note 144, at 175–176.

191 *See* Chapter Four, sections 2.2.2 and 2.2.4.

192 Allan MacEachen, Minister of External Affairs, HC, *Minutes of Proceedings and Evidence of the Standing Committee on External Affairs and National Defence*, 22 May 1975 (30th Parliament, 1st Session, 1975), Issue No. 24, 6.

193 Commentary—The 1982 United Nations Convention on the Law of the Sea, *supra* note 6, at 18; Roach and Smith, *supra* note 111, at 339; and *Responses to Excessive Maritime Claims*, *supra* note 159, at 29.

In November 2006, the U.S. Ambassador to Canada restated the position. Doug Struck, *Dispute Over NW Passage Revived*, Washington Post, 6 November 2006, A18.

In August 2007, President Bush referred to the Northwest Passage as an "international waterway" and acknowledged that Canada and the United States had a difference of views of the issue. News Conference—President Bush, Prime Minister Harper and President Calderon, Montebello, Quebec, 21 August 2007, WEEKLY COMPILATION OF PRESIDENTIAL DOCUMENTS, 2007, 1091.

194 *Geographic Note*, supra note 4, at 6.

195 *See* Kraska, *supra* note 98, at 275 and U.S. Senate, Executive Report, Declarations and Understandings, *supra* note 97.

not been used as an international waterway.[196] Pharand has commented that the United States' total reliance on geography and dismissal of the functional criterion regarding the definition of a strait used for international navigation appears to be "an isolated interpretation and is completely unsupported by customary international law."[197] Pharand's analysis concludes that, although the geography of the Northwest Passage is that of an international strait, given the scant history of international navigation of the Passage, the Northwest Passage is not a strait used for international navigation within which transit passage rights exist.[198] Pharand allows for the possibility that that increased international shipping through the Northwest Passage not subject to extensive Canadian authority could result in the Northwest Passage becoming a strait used for international navigation.[199]

Regarding the possibility of submarine traffic in the Passage, always a topic of interest, McRae has described it as being an "important qualification" on the above "use" analysis.[200] He well summarizes:

> It is assumed that they occur but it is not clear whether they occur under Canadian authority and with the consent of the Government of Canada or whether they are transit of which Canada knows little.... One assumption is that most submarine transits would have been by US vessels and that they are in some way authorized under defence arrangements between Canada and the United States....[T]here is no solid information about this and there are sufficient conflicting statements by former members of the Canadian military to indicate that this is an area of potential difficulty for the future.[201]

As already noted, if the Northwest Passage is an international strait, Canada would still have "a very wide measure of control over foreign vessels navigating" the Northwest Passage since, as a result of Article 234 of the LOS

196 Note No. 105, 16 April 1970, *supra* note 147, at 533 and Summary of Canadian Note of 16 April, *supra* note 147, at para 7: "The Northwest Passage has not attained the status of an international strait by customary usage nor has it been defined as such by conventional law." *See also* MacEachen, *supra* note 192, at 6.

197 Pharand, *The Arctic Waters*, *supra* note 67, at 36.

198 Pharand, CANADA'S ARCTIC WATERS, *supra* note 34, at 223–225 and Pharand, *The Arctic Waters*, *supra* note 67, at 36–42.

199 Pharand, CANADA'S ARCTIC WATERS, *supra* note 34, at 230 and Pharand, *The Arctic Waters*, *supra* note 67, at 44.

200 McRae, *supra* note 137, at 15.

201 *Id. See also* Byers and Lalonde, *supra* note 136, at 33–35.

Convention, Canada would be entitled to require and enforce against foreign commercial vessels the stringent pollution prevention measures found in the AWPPA.[202]

3.2.4 None of the Above

If the waters of the Northwest Passage are not historic internal waters, as claimed by Canada; if the Passage is not a strait used for international navigation to which a right of transit passage applies, as claimed by the United States; and if the Arctic straight baselines are not drawn consistent with the relevant international law criteria, or the waters enclosed are not internal waters for the purposes of navigation; then within the Northwest Passage there would exist a right of suspendable innocent passage for foreign vessels.[203] This conclusion arises either because the waters are within the territorial sea of Canada or as a result of the operation of Article 8(2) of the LOS Convention or Article 5(2) of the Territorial Sea and Contiguous Zone Convention (as customary international law) that provides for innocent passage rights for waters enclosed by straight baselines. Again, Canada would have significant control over commercial vessels using the Northwest Passage, since the stringent pollution prevention measures found in the AWPPA would apply.[204]

3.2.5 International Adjudication

In 1970, Canada adjusted its acceptance of the compulsory jurisdiction of the International Court to exclude questions regarding, among other things, Canada's legislation as regarding the Arctic waters.[205] In the aftermath of the *Polar Sea* event in 1985, Canada withdrew its 1970 reservation to the compulsory jurisdiction of the International Court as regards the status or

---

202 *See* Lalonde, *supra* note 128, at 103 and, more generally, at 96–103 and McRae, *supra* note 137, at 17–19. *See also* Chapter Four, section 2.2.4.

203 Lalonde, *supra* note 128, at 96–103 and *see* T. L. McDorman, *In the Wake of the Polar Sea: Canadian Jurisdiction and the Northwest Passage* (1986) 10 MAR POL 243, 252.

204 *See* Lalonde, *supra* note 128, at 103 and, more generally, at 96–103 and McRae, *supra* note 137, at 17–18.

205 Declaration Recognizing as Compulsory the Jurisdiction of the Court, April 7, 1970, in International Court, YEARBOOK 1969–1970 (The Hague, 1970) 55–56, 9 ILM 598–599. *See* Chapter Three, section 3.3.

international law applicable to the Northwest Passage[206] with the Foreign Minister asserting that Canada was "confident in our position" and that Canada was "prepared to uphold our position ... [in] Court, if necessary ..."[207] Coincidentally and unrelated to ocean matters or Canada, although undoubtedly known by Canada, in 1985, the United States withdrew its acceptance of the compulsory jurisdiction of the International Court.[208] The result is that neither country can force the other to appear before the International Court respecting Northwest Passage legal issues. As one commentator surmised: "The risk being taken by Canada . . . by withdrawing its 1970 reservation was ... a rather limited one."[209]

Although the LOS Convention contains obligations on States regarding compulsory adjudicative resolution of disputes,[210] the United States is not a party to the Convention and, therefore, is not subject to nor can it make use of the compulsory dispute settlement provisions of Convention. Moreover, the LOS Convention provides that States may elect to shield themselves from compulsory adjudication as regards disputes "involving historic bays or titles."[211] When Canada ratified the LOS Convention, it exercised its option to use this shield.[212] It appears that the United States, when it becomes a party to the Convention, will also take advantage of the shield as regards historic waters.[213] Thus, even if the United States becomes a party to the LOS Convention, the international legal dispute regarding the Northwest Passage is highly unlikely to be subject to the compulsory dispute settlement regime of the LOS Convention.

206 Letter from Ambassador Stephen Lewis to the Secretary-General of the United Nations, 10 September 1985, 24 ILM 1727. *See* Huebert, *Polar Vision, supra* note 148, at 352–353.

207 Clark, *supra* note 112, at 6464. *See also* Huebert, *Polar Vision, supra* note 148, at 349–352.

208 Letter to the Secretary-General of the United Nations from Secretary of State George P. Shultz, October 7, 1985, 24 ILM 1742 and *see* Department of State, CUMULATIVE DIGEST OF THE UNITED STATES PRACTICE IN INTERNATIONAL LAW, 1981–1988 (Washington, 1995) 3329–3338.

209 Franckx, *supra* note 144, at 100.

210 LOS Convention, *supra* note 19, Part XV, Arts 279–299 and, in particular, Art 286.

211 *Id.* Art 298(1)(a)(i). *See generally* Rosenne, *supra* note 46, at 197–200.

212 Declaration Made Upon Ratification, 7 November 2003, 53 LOSB 15 and *see* T. L. McDorman, *Canada Ratifies the 1982 United Nations Convention on the Law of the Sea: At Last* (2004) 35 ODIL 103, 106.

213 U.S. Senate, Executive Report, *supra* note 97.

3.3 Cooperation Respecting the Northwest Passage

Despite all the ink given in the press and by academics to the Northwest Passage issue over the last three decades, there has only been one actual "incident" between Canada and the United States regarding the Northwest Passage and that involved the U.S. Coast Guard vessel *Polar Sea* in 1985. Although the *Polar Sea* event was a U.S. assertion of its perceived navigation rights in the Northwest Passage, there also existed an element of bilateral cooperation respecting the passage of the vessel. The public outcry in Canada over the voyage coupled with the bilateral desire to avoid future such incidents led to the 1988 Arctic Cooperation Agreement.[214] The 1988 Agreement has as its main purpose not the prevention of future U.S. Coast Guard vessel voyages through the Northwest Passage, but the minimization of the public and political sideshow that occurred around the 1985 *Polar Sea* voyage and the creation of a process acceptable to both States to avoid confrontation in the Northwest Passage.

3.3.1 The 1985 *Polar Sea* Event

The proposed passage of the U.S. Coast Guard icebreaker *Polar Sea* through the Northwest Passage in the summer of 1985 was made known to Canadian Coast Guard authorities well in advance.[215] It was Canadian policy not to discourage use of the Northwest Passage, provided rigorous equipment and ship design standards were met. Reportedly, Canada informed the United States that a request for authorization would be required, and the U.S. declined to make such a request.[216] What subsequently occurred was an uncomfortable dance. The United States made it clear that it would not request permission and that the *Polar Sea* would traverse the Northwest Passage. Canada was left trying to find ways to protect its position regarding the Northwest Passage.

In May 1985, the United States formally informed Canada of the impending passage by the *Polar Sea* through the Northwest Passage and invited

214 Arctic Cooperation Agreement, *supra* note 110.

215 Huebert, *Steel, Ice and Decision-Making*, *supra* note 111, at 211–214, 230; Huebert, *Polar Vision*, *supra* note 148, at 344–345; and Kirkey, *supra* note 111, at 403.

216 Pharand, *The Arctic Waters*, *supra* note 67, at 39 and Huebert, *Steel, Ice and Decision-Making*, *supra* note 111, at 232.

Canada to cooperate by having on-board participants.[217] It was noted that "the two countries should agree to disagree on the legal issues and concentrate on practical matters" and that the United States considered the icebreaker's transit as providing a unique opportunity for cooperation that should "not be lost because of possible disagreements over the relevant juridical regime."[218] Canada responded in June 1985 by reiterating its legal position regarding the Northwest Passage and noting that it was "committed to facilitating navigation" through the Northwest Passage and was "prepared to work toward this objective."[219] A further U.S. communication in June made it clear that the United States was not notifying Canada of the transit, but rather was inviting Canadian participation.[220] It was noted that the Coast Guards of the two States had already been engaged regarding the timing and routeing of the transit. Finally, the June communication set out that the:

> United States considers that this transit . . . in no way prejudices the judicial position of either side regarding the Northwest Passage, and it understands that the Government of Canada shares that view.[221]

Reportedly, at this stage, the two sides believed they had achieved an acceptable arrangement regarding the nature and scope of the impending transit of the Northwest Passage by the *Polar Sea*.[222]

In July 1985, Canada sent a further communication to the United States confirming the understanding that the transit was without prejudice to the legal position of either State.[223] It was also communicated that the *Polar Sea* complied with the vessel and equipment standards contained in the AWPPA[224] and that an exemption order under the legislation had been issued for the *Polar Sea*.[225] Finally, the United States was informed that as an exercise

---

217 Demarche to Canada 21 May 1985, *supra* note 111, at 342–343.

218 *Id.* 343.

219 Note to the United States 11 June 1985, *supra* note 111, at 344.

220 Note to Canada 24 June 1985, *supra* note 111, at 345–346.

221 *Id.* 346.

222 Huebert, *Steel, Ice and Decision-Making*, *supra* note 111, at 239 and Huebert, *Polar Vision*, *supra* note 148, at 346.

223 Note to the United States 31 July 1985, *supra* note 111, at 346.

224 AWPPA, *supra* note 132.

225 U.S.C.G.C. Polar Sea Exemption Order, Can Gaz Part II, Vol. 119, SOR/85-722, 1 August 1985, 3437–3438 and *see* Note to the United States, 31 July 1985, *supra* note 111, at 347.

of Canadian sovereignty over the Northwest Passage, "Canada is pleased to consent... [to] the proposed transit."[226]

The *Polar Sea* passed through Lancaster Sound, Barrow Strait, Viscount Melville Sound, and the narrow Prince of Wales Strait, and continued across the Beaufort Sea to Point Barrow in Alaska. Canadian officials were on board during the Canadian part of voyage.[227]

Despite the above legal understanding between the two countries, great public concern was expressed in Canada that the passage of the *Polar Sea* was a violation of Canada's jurisdiction in the Arctic.[228] The focus of attention was that the United States did not and would not request from the Canadian government permission for the *Polar Sea* to transit the Northwest Passage. Dismay was expressed about the Canadian government not "standing up" to the United States and that this failure of resolve would undermine Canada's jurisdictional claims to the waters of the Arctic archipelago. The publicly expressed view from the United States was that they "would have preferred if the dispute had never arisen,"[229] with the U.S. State Department expressing "surprise and disappointment" at the controversy that erupted.[230]

3.3.2 The 1988 Canada-U.S. Arctic Cooperation Agreement

Since 1985, there have been five transits of the Northwest Passage by U.S. Coast Guard icebreakers,[231] the first being the *Polar Star* in October 1988[232]

A newspaper report stated that:

> Lawyers went through appropriate laws with fine-tooth combs and the Canadians took meticulous care over detail, down to the state of every piece of environmental equipment on the vessel.

Northwest Passage not for the Soviets, U.S. Envoy Feels, Toronto Globe and Mail, 2 August 1985, 1.

226 Note to the United States 31 July 1985, *supra* note 111, at 347. Huebert, *Steel, Ice and Decision-Making*, *supra* note 111, at 240–242 reports that the United States was "taken aback" by this unrequested consent as it appeared to be inconsistent with the acceptance of the legal non-prejudice position.

227 Roach and Smith, *supra* note 111, at 348.

228 *See* in detail Huebert, *Steel, Ice and Decision-Making*, *supra* note 111, at 246–271. Elliot-Meisel, *supra* note 106, at 148 noted that "agreeing to disagree on the status of the Passage did not sit well with the Canadian public or in Parliament."

229 *U.S. Voices Regret Over Canada's New Arctic Claim*, Vancouver Sun, 12 September 1985.

230 *Northwest Passage not for the Soviets, U.S. Envoy Feels*, Toronto Globe and Mail, 2 August 1985, 1.

231 Pharand, *The Arctic Waters*, *supra* note 67, at 40 and see Table One at 31–33.

232 See Note to Canada, 10 October 1988 and Note to the United States, 10 October 1988, in Roach and Smith, *supra* note 111, at 351–353, 28 ILM 144–145.

and the most recent being the *Healy* in 2003.[233] These voyages have occasioned little interest or controversy as they were conducted pursuant to the 1988 Arctic Cooperation Agreement.[234]

The Arctic Cooperation Agreement, the product of several years of negotiation and the personal intervention of Prime Minister Mulroney and President Reagan,[235] has resulted in a regularized procedure by which the United States attains the consent of Canada for proposed transits by its Coast Guard icebreakers through the Northwest Passage.[236]

Although *prima facie* it appears that the United States has accepted full Canadian control over navigation of the Northwest Passage, this is not the case. The wording and intent of the 1988 Agreement requires scrutiny. In the Agreement, the United States "pledges that all navigation by U.S. icebreakers within waters claimed by Canada to be internal will be undertaken with the consent of Canada."[237] This wording is embedded in a paragraph that refers to the sharing of knowledge of the marine environment "through research conducted" during the Coast Guard vessel voyages. Attaching consent to scientific research was a key breakthrough in the negotiation of the 1988 Agreement.[238] Although the United States was unwilling to accede to Canada's view of the need for U.S. vessels to obtain permission for transit of the Passage,[239] if a U.S. government vessel were engaged in marine scientific research, then the LOS Convention mandated that consent of the coastal

---

233 *See* Order Exempting the U.S. C.G. Icebreaker Healy from the Application of the Arctic Shipping Pollution Prevention Regulations, Can Gaz Part II, Vol. 137, SOR/2003-247, 18 June 2003, 1929–1932.

234 Arctic Cooperation Agreement, *supra* note 110.
Note, however, regarding the *Polar Star*, A. Gotlieb, The Washington Diaries, 1981–1989 (McClelland and Stewart, Toronto 2006) 596–597.

235 Described in detail in Kirkey, *supra* note 111, at 405–416 and *see* Huebert, *Polar Vision*, *supra* note 148, at 356–359.
Mulroney, *supra* note 114, at 431 indicates that in March 1986 President Reagan assured him that: "Anything we do [in Canadian Arctic waters] will be with your permission." In early 1987 Reagan communicated to Mulroney a different view. See the letter excerpted at *supra* note 114. During the bilateral summit meeting in April 1987, Mulroney reports at 496-499 that Reagan's mind was changed when the uniqueness of the Northwest Passage was stressed and maps presented to show Canada's geographic relationship to the Passage. In achieving the 1988 Agreement, Mulroney at 500 credits that Reagan "was as good as his word."

236 Pharand, *The Arctic Waters*, *supra* note 67, at 40.

237 Arctic Cooperation Agreement, *supra* note 110, Art 3(3).

238 Kirkey, *supra* note 111, at 414–416.

239 *Id.* 408–409.

State was required.[240] Essentially, what the United States agreed was that any U.S. Coast Guard icebreaker transiting the Northwest Passage would be deemed to be conducting marine scientific research and, for that activity, the consent of Canada was necessary. Canada may see the necessary consent under the 1988 Agreement as being for the transit of U.S. icebreakers through the Northwest Passage;[241] whereas, what the United States feels obliged under the 1988 Agreement to seek is consent for the activity of the icebreakers while in transit.

Article 4 of the 1988 Agreement indicates that nothing in the Agreement or any subsequent practice "affects the respective positions" of the United States and Canada regarding the Northwest Passage. Reportedly, this was insisted upon by the United States, which was uncomfortable with the consent wording of Article 3 and sought further assurances that its legal position regarding the Passage was not being compromised.[242] There is no question that both countries accept that the Agreement is without prejudice to their legal positions and that the core of the Agreement is agreeing-to-disagree.[243]

The 1988 Agreement is limited to government icebreakers and does not extend to other government vessels (military) or commercial vessels. The intent of the Agreement was legal neutrality. The United States maintains that it does not recognize the Canadian internal waters claim; whereas Canada maintains that, for icebreaker usage of the Northwest Passage, Canadian consent is needed. Not surprisingly, Canada focused on the consent wording of Article 3, minus the scientific research nuance, as providing much of what Canada was seeking. The Agreement solved an internal political problem within Canada and removed the possibility of a subsequent *Polar Sea* outcry.

---

240 LOS Convention, *supra* note 19, Arts 245, 246(2).

241 Pharand, *The Arctic Waters*, *supra* note 67, at 39–40 refers to the exchange between Canadian Foreign Affairs Minister Joe Clark, who stated that "the United States will undertake to seek Canadian permission before any voyage of an icebreaker" through the Northwest Passage, and U.S. Secretary of State George Shultz's reply, "I agree with what Mr. Clark just said," as being evidence of an implied recognition by the United States of Canada's internal waters claim. However, Pharand makes no mention of the consent being tied to scientific research.

242 Kirkey, *supra* note 111, at 417.

243 *See* Statements of Prime Minister Mulroney and President Reagan, Canada-United States Agreement on Arctic Cooperation, 11 January 1988, on file with the author, and *see* Kirkey, *supra* note 111, at 417–418.

> According to both Canadian and American viewpoints, the general consensus is that both parties managed satisfactorily to fulfil their objectives . . .[244]

The 1988 Arctic Cooperation Agreement has worked well for twenty years.[245] It can be criticized for what it does not contain[246] and for its ambiguity regarding tying Canadian consent to scientific research, which is not readily apparent in the Agreement and can lead to confusion. The 1988 Agreement, however, was a political fix and not a legal fix to accommodate Canada, while not undermining the U.S. legal position. It is an important and instructive example of the cooperative approach that Canada and the United States frequently are able to pursue to circumvent international ocean law disputes.

3.4 Future of the Dispute

The potential for increased navigation in the Northwest Passage occasioned by the implications of global climate change have led to concerns within Canada of foreign challenges to Arctic sovereignty,[247] although there is a contrary opinion of the unlikelihood of such challenges occurring in the immediate future, if at all.[248] A number of writers have made suggestions regarding the future of Canada-U.S. relations respecting the Northwest Passage. Pharand, who starts from the premise that increased shipping through the Passage could lead the Northwest Passage to become a strait used for international navigation with vessels enjoying a right of transit passage,[249] recommends a number of measures be taken by Canada to improve the "capability to exercise effective control over its Arctic waters" and thus prevent the "internationalization" of the Northwest Passage.[250] Almost all commentators

---

244 Kirkey, *supra* note 111, at 420.

245 In August 2007, Prime Minister Harper referred to the 1988 Agreement as having resulted in Canada and the United States being able to manage their disagreement respecting the Northwest Passage. News Conference–President Bush, Prime Minister Harper and President Calderon, *supra* note 193, at 1091.

246 Eliot-Meisel, *supra* note 106, at 154.

247 Huebert, *Climate Change*, *supra* note 123 and Huebert, *The Shipping News Part II*, *supra* note 115.

248 Griffiths, *The Shipping News*, *supra* note 105 and Griffiths, *Pathetic Fallacy*, *supra* note 123.

249 Pharand, *The Arctic Waters*, *supra* note 67, at 44.

250 Pharand acknowledges that many of these recommendations have also been made by others. *Id.* at 51–52.

argue for a greater presence in the Canadian Arctic. The government of Canada has responded with the announcement in July 2007 of the intention to build six to eight patrol vessels for the Arctic.[251] Recommendations that directly engage the United States include that the voluntary reporting system operated by Canada for vessels seeking to enter Canada's Arctic waters [known as the Vessel Traffic Reporting Arctic Canada Traffic Zone (NORDREG)[252]] should be made compulsory, such that vessels intending to enter Canadian Arctic waters be required to give notification and receive authorization.[253] In August 2008, Prime Minister Harper announced the intention to change the relevant regulations to make NORDREG compulsory.[254] Another recommendation is that the 1988 Agreement be terminated and a different agreement involving all U.S. vessels (commercial and government) be negotiated that explicitly recognizes that the Arctic waters are internal waters in exchange for Canada recognizing a right of passage, subject to environmental conditions, by U.S. vessels.[255] Pharand notes that although the 1988 Agreement "has been quite satisfactory," it is not in the long-term interests of Canada.[256] Griffiths similarly suggests extending the 1988 Arctic Cooperation Agreement to cover U.S. commercial and military vessels should shipping become a reality in the Northwest Passage.[257] Griffiths indicates that concerns about homeland security could be the lure

---

251 I. Bailey, *Harper Plans Arctic Patrol Fleet*, Toronto Globe and Mail, 10 July 2007, A-1, 4.

252 Department of Transport, Vessel Traffic Reporting Arctic Canada Traffic Zone (NORDREG), at www.ccg-gcc.gc.ca/cen-arc/mcts-sctm/mcts-services/vtrarctic_e.htm (accessed on 19 July 2007).

253 Pharand, *The Arctic Waters*, *supra* note 67, at 49–50; Griffiths, *The Shipping News*, *supra* note 105, at 272; and Lalonde, *supra* note 128, at 121–123.

Pharand, at 50, notes that according to Transport Canada 99 percent of all vessels entering Canadian Arctic waters comply with the voluntary NORDREG system.

Buyers and Lalonde, *supra* note 136, at 40 refer to Canada's unwillingness to make NORDREG compulsory as "foot-dragging."

254 Canada, PM Announces Government of Canada Will Extend Jurisdiction over Arctic Waters, 27 August 2008 and Steven Chase, *Canada to Widen Arctic Patrols, PM says*, Toronto Globe and Mail, 28 August 2008, A7. Respecting the muted U.S. reaction, *see* Randy Boswell and Andrew Mayeda, *U.S. concerned with new Canadian shipping rules in Arctic*, Canwest News Service, 28 August 2008, at www.dose.ca/news/story.html?id=ddfosf21-1628-4659-aeda-52dfe3635085 (accessed on 1 September 2008).

255 Pharand, *The Arctic Waters*, *supra* note 67, at 51.

256 *Id.* 50–51.

257 Griffiths, *The Shipping News*, *supra* note 105, at 271–271.

that leads to U.S. acceptance of making NORDREG mandatory and modifying the 1988 Arctic Cooperation Agreement.[258]

Buyers and Lalonde argue that U.S. interests in the Northwest Passage have changed and are (or should be) more oriented to continental security,[259] and suggest that Canada should initiate negotiations with the United States and demonstrate that it is in the U.S. national interest to have the Northwest Passage subject to the full force of Canadian domestic law.[260] Former U.S. Ambassador to Canada Paul Cellucci thinks the same way stating that it is in the interest of the United States in the age of terror "for the Northwest Passage to be part of Canada."[261]

Other writers have looked more towards bilateral or multilateral cooperative regime models for vessel traffic management in the Northwest Passage,[262] including the possibility of a Canada-U.S. agreement based loosely on the St. Lawrence Seaway model, whereby both countries undertake regulation of the vessels utilizing the Northwest Passage in a manner that does not compromise the sovereignty or legal position of either State.[263] A U.S. commentator has recently suggested a multilateral approach for vessel activity in the Northwest Passage based on "the Malacca Straits Model," involving intense participation by the International Maritime Organization (IMO).[264] With this particular suggestion, the politics of Arctic sovereignty in Canada would have to be overcome in order to attain such an internationalization of the Northwest Passage and, indeed, this may be a problem even for a bilateral arrangement.

---

258 *Id.*

259 Buyers and Lalonde, *supra* note 136, at 41–44, 52–54.

260 *Id.* 52–54.

261 *Cellucci: Canada Should Control Northwest Passage*, CTV News, 19 August 2007, at <www.ctv.ca/servlet/ArticleNews/print/CTVNews/20070817/qp_cellucci_070819?s_name=&no_ads> (accessed on 13 March 2008).

262 *See* O. Young, *Arctic Shipping: An American Perspective*, in Griffiths, *supra* note 105, 128–132 and, more generally, D. M. Johnston, *The Northwest Passage Revisited* (2002) 33 ODIL 145–164 and C. Lamson and D. L. VanderZwaag, Transit Management in the Northwest Passage: Problems and Prospects (Cambridge University Press, Cambridge 1988).

263 M. Byers, *Sovereignty Will Solve the Northwest Passage Dispute*, Toronto Globe and Mail, 11 August 2007, A-17; B. Flemming, *Northwest Passage: A voyage Canada and the U.S. can take together*, Toronto Globe and Mail, 18 December 2007, A-17; and S. G. Borgerson, *Arctic Meltdown: The Economic and Security Implications of Global Warming* (2008) 87 Foreign Affairs 63, 75–76.

264 Kraska, *supra* note 98, at 279–283.

One international route that Canada has pursued regarding Arctic shipping has been to seek harmonization amongst the various Arctic States of vessel construction and navigation standards. The outcome is the so-called Polar Code adopted by the IMO in 2002 as Guidelines for Ships Operating in Arctic Ice-Covered Waters.[265] Although the original hope was that the Polar Code would be mandatory, objects raised by the United States resulted in the IMO adopting the Polar Code as recommendatory only.[266]

4.0 The Head Harbour Passage

The Head Harbour Passage, within Passamaquoddy Bay, runs between the islands south of Deer Island and Campobello Island (both of which are Canadian) before reaching U.S. waters east of Eastport, Maine, which is located on Moose Island (United States). At its narrowest, Head Harbour Passage is less than one nautical mile wide. It is approximately four nautical miles in length from the northern tip of Campobello Island to the Canada-U.S. maritime boundary east of Eastport. As a result of 1908 and 1910 maritime boundary agreements,[267] there is no question that the waters of the Head Harbour Passage are Canadian as opposed to being waters under the jurisdiction of the United States.

The Head Harbour Passage is the principal navigation route to Eastport, Maine, and has long been used by vessels going to or departing from Eastport and the port at Bayside, New Brunswick, located near St. Andrews at

265 IMO, Guidelines for Ships Operating in Arctic Ice-Covered Waters, Doc MSC/Circular/1056, MEPC/Circular/399, 23 December 2002, at www.imo.org/includes/blastDataonly.asp/data_id%3D6629/1056-MEPC-CIRC399.pdf (accessed on 9 August 2007).

Regarding the background to the Polar Code, *see* L. W. Brigham, *The Emerging International Polar Navigation Code: Bi-Polar Relevance?* in Vidas, *supra* note 119, at 244–262 and Huebert, *Article 234 and Marine Pollution, supra* note 113, at 263–266. For a recent review of the Guidelines, *see* Ø. Jensen, *Arctic Shipping Guidelines: Towards a Legal Regime for Navigation Safety and Environmental Protection?* (2008) 44 POLAR RECORD 107–114.

266 Huebert, *Article 234 and Marine Pollution, supra* note 113, at 263. Brigham, *supra* note 265, at 260 comments: "The IMO's long-term goal would nevertheless be eventually to make the Code a mandatory instrument . . ."

267 Treaty respecting the Demarcation of the International Boundary with Canada, Washington, 11 April 1908, entered into force 4 June 1908, Art 1, 206 Con. TS 377 and Treaty Fixing the Boundary Line in Passamaquoddy Bay, Washington, 21 May 1910, entered into force 20 August 1910, Art 1, USTS 551, in C. I. BEVANS, TREATIES AND OTHER INTERNATIONAL AGREEMENTS OF THE UNITED STATES, 1776–1949, Vol. 12 (U.S. Department of State, 1974) 341. *See* Chapter Five, section 2.2.

PASSAMAQUODDY BAY

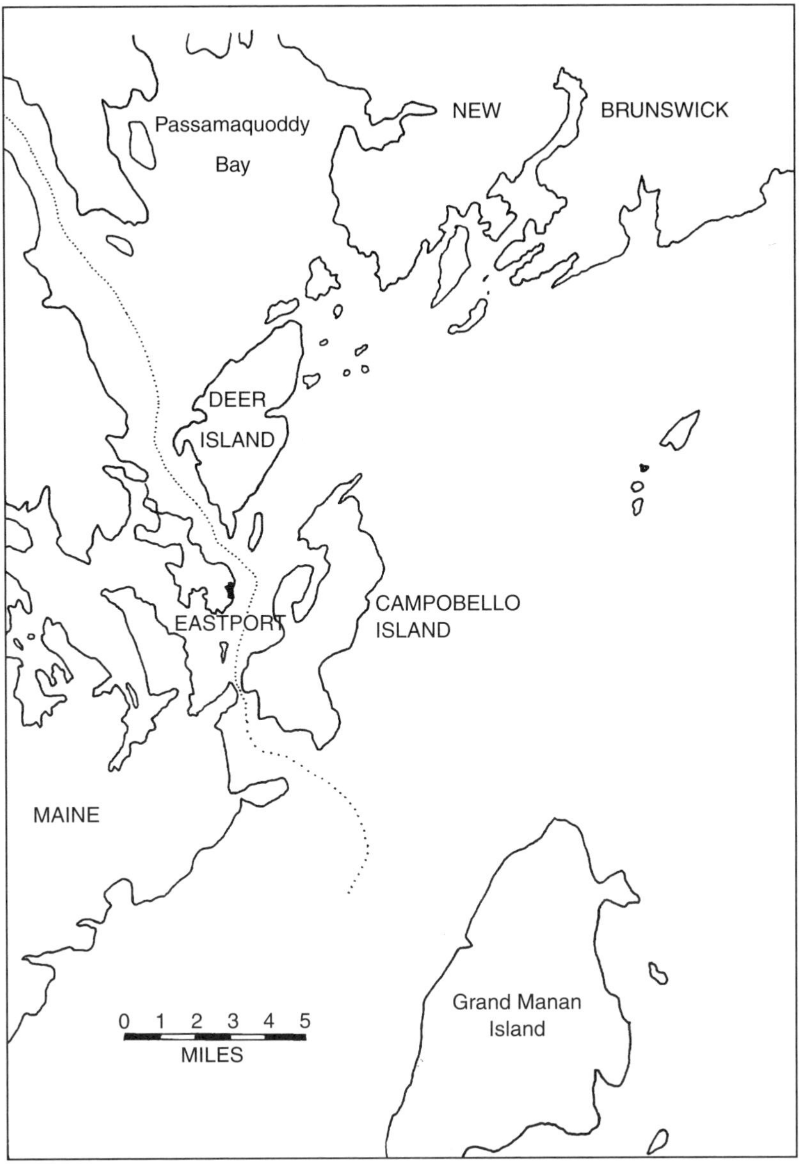

Source: Dalhousie Ocean Studies Programme.

HEAD HARBOUR PASSAGE

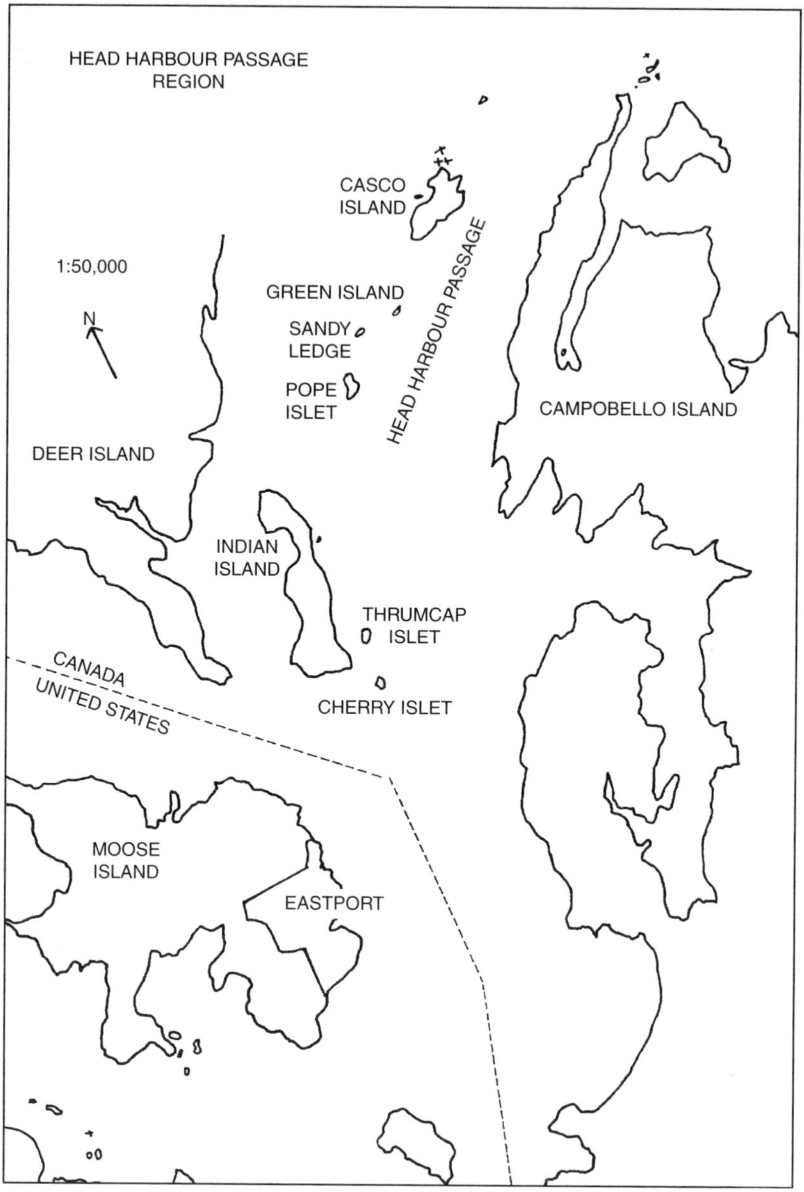

Source: Dalhousie Ocean Studies Programme.

the mouth of the St. Croix River. The estimates of recent yearly commercial traffic are sixty vessels to Bayside and forty vessels to Eastport.[268] The vessel traffic to Eastport has also included U.S. naval and other U.S. government vessels. Canada maintains a vessel traffic separation scheme for the Bay of Fundy designed primarily for vessels destined to and from Saint John, New Brunswick.[269] Vessels heading to the Head Harbour Passage and Passamaquoddy Bay would use the traffic separation scheme.

The United States asserts that the Head Harbour Passage is a strait used for international navigation, through which there exists a right of non-suspendable innocent passage.[270] Canada claims the Bay of Fundy as historic internal waters,[271] and it is presumed that the Bay of Fundy includes the Canadian waters in Passamaquoddy Bay and the Head Harbour Passage.

The Canada-U.S. dispute regarding the Head Harbour Passage resurfaced in 2006 to 2007 as a result of proposals to site liquefied natural gas (LNG) facilities near Eastport, Maine, that would necessitate LNG tanker traffic through the Passage. The dispute had previously arisen in the 1970s and 1980s as a result of a proposed oil refinery near Eastport and consequent proposed oil tanker traffic through the Head Harbour Passage.

4.1 Proposed Tanker Traffic

4.1.1 Eastport Refinery Proposal

In the 1970s, a proposal was made to construct an oil refinery near Eastport that was contingent on oil tanker traffic through the Head Harbour Passage.[272]

---

268 *See* Department of Transport, Proposal: Routeing of Ships, Ship Reporting and Related Matters: Amendment of the Traffic Separation Scheme in the Bay of Fundy and Approaches, para 3.2, at <www.tc.gc.ca/atl/marine/fundyproposal.htm > (accessed on 30 May 2006).

For a more detailed study of vessel traffic patterns, *see* Senes Consulting Limited, *A Study of the Anticipated Impacts on Canada from the Development of Liquefied Natural Gas Terminals on Passamaquoddy Bay* (Ottawa, undated, done for the Government of Canada), section 3.3, Review of Commercial Ship Movements, 3-23 to 3-37, copy on file with the author. This Report is noted in S. McCarthy, *Ottawa unmoved by positive LNG study*, Toronto Globe and Mail, 6 October 2007, B-8 and R. Linke, *LNG ships can 'transit safely' through Head Harbour Passage*, Saint John Telegraph Journal, 5 October 2007, A3.

269 *See* IMO, SHIPS' ROUTEING (London, 9th ed. 2008), Part IX-2.

270 Commentary—The 1982 United Nations Convention on the Law of the Sea, *supra* note 6, at 19.

271 Letter dated 17 December 1973, *supra* note 3, at 279.

272 *See generally* J. E. CARROLL, ENVIRONMENTAL DIPLOMACY: AN EXAMINATION AND A PROSPECTIVE OF CANADIAN-U.S. TRANSBOUNDARY ENVIRONMENTAL RELATIONS

Canada took the view that there was an "unacceptable risk in the transport of a large volume of pollutants" through the Passage[273] and indicated that it was "prepared to regulate, if necessary, to prevent it."[274] More specifically, in a March 1975 *aide-memoire* to the U.S. government, Canada indicated that if the refinery project went ahead, "the Canadian Government would promulgate regulations limiting the amount of oil and/or oil products that may be carried through the waters of Head Harbour Passage."[275] The United States responded:

> The view of the United States Government is that vessels proceeding to or departing from United States ports through the waters of Head Harbour Passage enjoy the right of innocent passage under international law. This right is not subject to unreasonable or arbitrary interference or suspension.[276]

In 1982, Canada adopted a regulation that restricted the amount of oil that could be carried by an oil tanker through the Head Harbour Passage.[277] The regulation was carefully crafted to specifically address the proposed tanker traffic but not the perceived oil needs of the Eastport-area population.[278] The United States publicly protested Canada's regulation and announced that an official protest would be delivered to Canada, taking the view that

---

(University of Michigan Press, Ann Arbor 1983) 62–72; A. L. SPRINGER, THE INTERNATIONAL LAW OF POLLUTION: PROTECTING THE GLOBAL ENVIRONMENT IN A WORLD OF SOVEREIGN STATES (Quorum Books, Westport, Connecticut 1983) 185–200; and J. Spiller and J. Roanowicz, *Effectiveness of Canadian and U.S. Environmental Assessment Processes in Evaluating Transboundary Impacts*, in A. REISER, J. SPILLER, AND D. VANDERZWAAG (eds.) ENVIRONMENTAL DECISIONMAKING IN A TRANSBOUNDARY REGION (Springer-Verlag, New York 1986), at 116–131.

273 Canadian Embassy, Note No. 206 to the United States, 7 June 1973, para 7, copy on file with the author.

274 Department of External Affairs, Letter to Edmund Muskie, 7 November 1979, para 2, copy on file with the author.

275 Canada, Aide-Memoire, 6 March 1975, referenced in Department of State, DIGEST OF UNITED STATES PRACTICE IN INTERNATIONAL LAW, 1975 (Washington, 1976) 432.

276 Aide-Memoire to the Government of Canada, 12 March 1975, cited in *id.* 432.

277 Oil Carriage Limitation Regulations, Can Gaz Part II, Vol. 116, SOR/82-244, 11 February 1982, 892–893. The Regulation was revoked in May 1987 on the grounds that it was *ultra vires* the enabling legislation. Note was made that there was no longer need for the Regulation since the plans to build the facility in Eastport had been abandoned. Oil Carriage Limitation Regulations, revocation, Can Gaz Part II, Vol. 121, SOR/87-268, 7 May 1987, 2077–2078.

278 Carroll, *supra* note 272, at 70–71.

the regulation exceeded Canada's jurisdictional authority.[279] In 1983, the proponent decided not to proceed with the proposed Eastport refinery.

One author has summarized that the disagreements between Canada and the United States were clear: What was the international legal status of the Head Harbour Passage? What was the degree of control that Canada could exercise over vessels using the Head Harbour Passage? Nevertheless, "neither government . . . [was] anxious to explain in detail its position on either question" and neither government fully articulated their positions in public.[280]

4.1.2 The 2006 LNG Proposals

In December 2006, two proposals for the construction of liquefied natural gas (LNG) receiving terminals, pipelines and associated facilities near Eastport, Maine, were received by the U.S. Federal Energy Regulatory Commission (FERC).[281] Both proposals are premised on the transport to the facilities of LNG from tankers that will utilize the Head Harbour Passage.

The proposals were well known prior to their formal submission for approval to FERC. On 26 September 2006, Canadian Prime Minister Harper in answer to a question in the House of Commons about the LNG facilities in Maine commented:

> I gather there are some representatives of that project lobbying around . . . [Parliament] Hill today, so let me be absolutely clear. This government believes that the waters of Passamaquoddy Bay are Canadian waters. We have defended that position for a long time. We oppose the passage of LNG tanker traffic through Head Harbour and we will continue to do so.[282]

On 14 February 2007, Canadian Ambassador to the United States Michael Wilson sent a letter to the chair of FERC regarding the two LNG proposals.[283]

---

279 *See* Carroll, *supra* note 272, at 71 and *U.S. irked by limits on shipping passage*, Montreal Gazette, 20 February 1982.

280 Springer, *supra* note 272, at 187.

281 Federal Energy Regulatory Commission, docket no. CP07-52 to 55 (Downeast LNG) and CP07-35 to 38 (Quoddy Bay LNG). See the website of the Federal Energy Regulatory Commission at www.ferc.gov (accessed on 9 August 2007).

282 Stephen Harper, Prime Minister, HC, *Debates*, 26 September 2006, 3271.

283 Canadian Embassy, Letter from Ambassador Michael Wilson to Joseph T. Kelliher, 14 February 2007, in Saint John Telegraph Journal, 15 February 2007, A8 and available on the FERC website at the Downeast LNG and Quoddy Bay LNG dockets, *supra* note 281.

The letter states the Canadian view that the proposed siting of the terminals and the potential passage of LNG tankers through "environmentally-sensitive and navigationally-challenging marine and coastal areas of the sovereign Canadian waters of Head Harbour Passage" posed an unacceptable risk and that Canada was "prepared to use domestic legal means to . . . prevent such passage from occurring."[284] Reportedly, in August 2007, Prime Minister Harper reiterated in direct talks with President Bush that Canada will not permit tankers through the Head Harbour Passage[285] and, in September 2007, Canada's Minister of Foreign Affairs Maxime Bernier stated that Canada will consider regulations banning tanker traffic from the area.[286]

Although not specifically referencing the above letter from Ambassador Wilson, a 9 March 2007 U.S. State Department letter to U.S. Senator Olympia Snowe commented:

> We have . . . underscored privately to Canadian officials—and asserted publicly as well—that it is our firm position that, though Canada may adopt laws and regulations in respect of safety of navigation and the regulation of maritime traffic, all vessels enjoy a non-suspendable right of innocent passage into and out of Passamaquoddy Bay through Head Harbour Passage.[287]

Based on the position of the government of Canada that LNG tanker traffic would not be permitted to utilize the Head Harbour Passage, New Brunswick requested that the FERC suspend proceeding with the two LNG proposals. In June 2007, FERC decided to continue with its review noting that the projects "can proceed in a timely manner if issues relating to LNG tanker passage through Canadian waters are favorably resolved."[288]

---

284 *Id.* The language is similar to the letter sent regarding the proposed oil refinery almost thirty years earlier. *See* Letter to Edmund Muskie, 7 November 1979, *supra* note 274.

285 R. Linke, *PM to Bush: No Tankers*, Saint John Telegraph Journal, 30 August 2007, A1 and C. Morris, *Possible supertanker ban in the Bay of Fundy strains border relations*, Toronto Globe and Mail, 10 September 2007, A9.

286 C. Morris, *Possible supertanker ban in the Bay of Fundy strains border relations*, Toronto Globe and Mail, 10 September 2007, A9.

287 Department of State, Letter from Jeffrey T. Bergner to Senator Olympia J. Snowe, 9 March 2007, available on the FERC website at the Downeast LNG and Quoddy Bay LNG dockets, *supra* note 281.

288 FERC, Quoddy Bay LNG, LLC and Quoddy Bay Pipeline LLC—Order Denying Motion to Suspend Proceedings, June 1, 2007, 119 FERC 61,226 and Downeast LNG, Inc. and Downeast Pipeline, LLC—Order Denying Motion to Suspend Proceedings, 1 June 2007, 119 FERC 61,228, para 8 of both Orders, available on the website of FERC, *supra* note 281.

4.2 International Legal Positions

4.2.1 U.S. Claim—International Strait

The United States asserts that the waters of the Head Harbour Passage are a strait used for international navigation. The U.S. view is that the Head Harbour Passage meets the wording of Article 45(1)(b) of the LOS Convention as connecting "a part of the high seas or an economic zone and the territorial sea of a foreign State," which gives rise to a right of non-suspendable innocent passage.[289] Article 45(1)(b) creates what is known as a "dead-end" international strait.[290]

Article 45(1)(b) of the LOS Convention replicates Article 16(4) of the 1958 Territorial Sea and Contiguous Zone Convention.[291] Article 16(4) was adopted primarily to address the Strait of Tiran which connects the Red Sea with the Gulf of Aqaba.[292] Four States share the Gulf of Aqaba, namely, Egypt, Saudi Arabia, Israel, and Jordan, with the latter two having coastal areas (ports) only at farthest reaches of the Gulf, and Egypt and Saudi Arabia dominating the entrance of the Gulf of Aqaba and the Strait of Tiran.

4.2.2 Canadian Claim—Historic Internal Waters

Canada's claim regarding the Head Harbour Passage has not been clearly stated. As noted above, in 2006, Prime Minister Harper referred to the area as being "Canadian waters"[293] and in Ambassador Wilson's communication, the phrase was "sovereign Canadian waters."[294] Canada, however, has claimed the Bay of Fundy as historic internal waters,[295] and this claim may extend to include the Head Harbour Passage and the Passamaquoddy Bay. This possibility was enhanced in 1971 when Canada created the Bay of Fundy fishing zone by placing a fisheries closing line across the Bay of Fundy that puts the

---

289 *See* Commentary—The 1982 United Nations Convention on the Law of the Sea, *supra* note 6, at 19.

290 For a graphic view of what the LOS Convention negotiators meant, *see* Nandan and Anderson, *supra* note 36, at 202.

291 *See* Nandan and Anderson, *supra* note 36, at 196.

292 L. Gross, *The Geneva Conference on the Law of the Sea and the Right of Innocent Passage Through the Gulf of Aqaba* (1959) 53 AJIL 564, 593. *See also* Jia, *supra* note 28, at 22.

293 Harper, *supra* note 282, at 3271.

294 Letter of 14 February 2007, *supra* note 283.

295 Letter dated 17 December 1973, *supra* note 3, at 282.

Head Harbour Passage and the Passamaquoddy Bay within the Bay of Fundy Fishing Zone.[296] One writer has noted that:

> [T]he waters of the Bay of Fundy that are considered to be part of Canada's internal waters [based on historic reasons] could be said to be all those waters bounded by a notional straight line drawn across the mouth of the Bay from Brier Island to Machias Seal Island. . . . [T]hese notional lines would presumably follow the so-called fishery closing lines promulgated in 1971 . . .[297]

The historic internal waters claim, as regards the Bay of Fundy generally or the Head Harbour Passage specifically, is complicated by the presence of the U.S. coast as arguably framing part of these waters. Bouchez refers to two categories of "bays enclosed by the territory of more than one State" as being: (1) where two States each have a headland; and (2) where the entry of a bay is within the authority of one State, but the other State borders an inner part of the bay.[298] Based on the second category, it can be argued that it is the claimed waters as a whole that needs to be looked at as being shared and not just the headlands or "natural entrance points." Beyond the geography that may define the waters as shared, there may be a functional consideration respecting whether a bay or water area is shared.[299] Essentially, because of the coasts

---

296 Fishing Zones of Canada (Zone 1, 2 and 3) Order, *supra* note 2.

297 L. L. Herman, *Proof of Offshore Territorial Claims in Canada* (1982) 7 DALHOUSIE LJ 1, 7. B. Johnson, *Canadian Foreign Policy and Fisheries*, in Johnson and Zacher, *supra* note 144, at 68 noted that "External Affairs Minister Sharp claimed . . . that the closing lines were tied to historic Canadian rights . . ." More generally regarding the 1970–1971 fisheries closing lines, *see* Chapter Three, section 3.2.

298 Bouchez, *supra* note 59, at 116.

299 Blum, *supra* note 72, at 270 places considerable weight on functionality.

> [I]t becomes evident that one of the major considerations which permit a given bay to be turned into an historic bay is the fact that by its incorporation into the national domain of the littoral State no harm is done, or is likely to be done, to another State. . . . It is, however, abundantly clear that these considerations do not hold good in those cases where the shores of a bay are possessed by more than one littoral State. In such cases it can hardly be maintained that the bay "is not and cannot be made a roadway from one nation to another". This consideration, which seems to be implicit in all those cases where multinational bays are involved, was given explicit recognition [in *The Washington Award*].

The 1853 *Washington Award*, in J. B. MOORE, HISTORY AND DIGEST OF INTERNATIONAL ARBITRATIONS, Vol. IV (Government Printing Office, 1898) 4342. *The Washington* was a U.S. vessel seized 10 nautical miles from shore for alleged illegal fishing in the Bay of Fundy. The controversy was over the meaning of the word bays in the 1818 Convention on Commerce, London, 20 October 1818, entered into force 30 January 1819, 69 Con. TS 294–297. It was of the two States, the waters are shared, thus making the attitude of both States critical in determining whether the waters are historic internal waters. The 1962 U.N. Secretariat Study commented:

> If all of the bordering States act jointly to claim historic title to a bay, it would seem that in principle what has been said above regarding a claim to historic title by a single State would apply to this group of States.
> The second hypothesis in which a claim to a bay bordered by two or more States might be envisaged arises where only one . . . but not all . . ., claim the area. In this case, it is rather improbable that a historic title to the bay could ever arise in favour of the claiming States. . . . For it must be expected that an attempt to exercise sovereignty over the bay on the part of one . . . [State] would cause immediate and strong opposition on the part of the other riparian State . . .[300]

The United States has made clear its non-acceptance of the Canadian claim of the Bay of Fundy as historic internal waters.

> Canada long has maintained an inchoate claim that the Bay of Fundy constitutes Canadian "historic" or "internal" waters. The United States always has reserved its position in this respect.[301]

---

the opinion of the United Kingdom that the Bay of Fundy was "rightfully claimed by Great Britain as a bay" with this position rejected by the United States. The Umpire did not accept the U.K. position, siding with the United States that the Bay of Fundy was not a bay within the meaning of the 1818 Treaty and, thus, not a British bay. Supporting this view, several points were made:

- The "headlands doctrine" proposed by the United Kingdom was new and had been limited in an 1839 French-British Treaty to only to those bays having mouths less than ten miles;
- The Bay of Fundy has several bays within it and was a "great body of water" with the proper analogy being with the Bay of Biscay and the Bay of Bengal "over which no nation can have the right to assume the sovereignty";
- "One of headlands of the Bay of Fundy is in the United States;" and
- "Ships bound to Passamaquoddy must sail through a large space of it [the Bay of Fundy]."

Regarding the international legal status of the Bay of Fundy generally, *see* G. V. La Forest, *Canadian Inland Waters of the Atlantic Provinces and the Bay of Fundy Incident* (1963) 1 CYIL 149 and T. L. McDorman, *Notes on the Historic Waters Regime and the Bay of Fundy*, in A. Chircop, T. L. McDorman and S. J. Rolston, (eds) The Future of Ocean Regime-Building: Essays in Tribute to Douglas M. Johnston (in press).

300 U. N. Study, *supra* note 41, at 21, paras 147 and 148.

301 Reply of the United States, in *Gulf of Maine Pleadings*, *supra* note 114, Vol. 5, 484, footnote 4.

As noted above, when vessel traffic in the Head Harbour Passage emerged as an issue in the 1970s, the United States informed Canada "that vessels proceeding to or departing from United States ports through the waters of Head Harbour Passage enjoy the right of innocent passage under international law."[302] In 1982, when Canada adopted the regulation that restricted the amount of oil that could be carried on an oil tanker in the waters of the Head Harbour Passage,[303] the United States publicly complained about the regulation and announced that an official protest would be delivered to Canada, taking the view that the regulation exceeded Canada's jurisdictional authority.[304]

4.2.3 Non-Canadian Claim—Non-Innocent Passage

Although no Canadian government document has explicitly suggested it, the Canadian position regarding both oil tankers in the 1970s and 1980, and LNG tankers more recently, is consistent with the view that the voyages of such vessels through the Head Harbour Passage would not be considered as innocent passage. If vessel passage is non-innocent, a coastal State "may take the necessary steps" to prevent the vessel passage.[305] This non-position either accepts the correctness of the U.S. legal position that the Head Harbour Passage is a strait used for international navigation or that the waters are part of Canada's territorial sea, but takes issue with the meaning to be ascribed to when vessel passage is innocent.

Both the 1958 Territorial Sea and Contiguous Zone Convention and the LOS Convention provide that "Passage is innocent so long as it is not prejudicial to the peace, good order or security of the coastal State."[306] However, the LOS Convention also contains Article 19(2), which provides:

> Passage of a foreign ship shall be considered to be prejudicial to the peace, good order or security of the coastal State if in the territorial sea it engages in any of the following activities:
>
> (a) any threat or use of force . . . ;
> (b) any exercise or practice with weapons of any kind;

---

302 Aide-memoire to Canada, 12 March 1975, *supra* note 276, at 432.

303 Oil Carriage Limitation Regulations, *supra* note 277.

304 *See* Carroll, *supra* note 272, at 71 and *U.S. irked by limits on shipping passage*, Montreal Gazette, 20 February 1982.

305 TSCZC, *supra* note 19, Art 16(1) and LOS Convention, *supra* note 19, Art 25(1).

306 TSCZC, *supra* note 19, Art 14(4) and LOS Convention, *supra* note 19, Art 19(1).

(c) any act aimed at collecting information . . .;
(d) any act of propaganda . . .;
(e) the launching, landing or taking on board of aircraft;
(f) the launching, landing or taking on board of any military device;
(g) the loading or unloading of any commodity, currency or person contrary to the customs, fiscal, immigration or sanitary laws and regulations of the coastal State;
(h) any act of willful or serious pollution contrary to this Convention;
(i) any fishing activities;
(j) the carrying out of research or survey activities;
(k) any act aiming at interfering with . . . communication . . . of the coastal State;
(l) any other activity not having a direct bearing on passage.

Churchill and Lowe have commented that Article 19(2) was included in the LOS Convention "in the hope of producing a more objective definition [of innocent passage], allowing coastal States less scope for interpretation and so less opportunity for abuse of their right to prevent non-innocent passage."[307]

Article 19(2) does not refer to navigational hazards, vessel cargoes, or the threat of environmental damage as in themselves making the passage of a vessel non-innocent. Canada had sought to have included in the wording of Article 19(2) that the threat of pollution made vessel passage non-innocent, but was unsuccessful in this regard.[308] It would appear, therefore, that "threat of pollution" by itself does not make passage non-innocent under the LOS Convention wording.

One writer has taken the view that, pursuant to Article 19(2): "it would no longer be possible to deny a right of innocent passage to mammoth oil tankers, nuclear powered vessels etc. unless their behaviour during the passage through the territorial sea fell within one of the categories of prejudicial behaviour listed in Article 19(2)."[309] The United States is of similar view, that Article 19(2) is exhaustive of the situations that can lead to non-innocence.[310] If it is only the vessel "activities" listed in Article 19(2) that

---

307 Churchill and Lowe, *supra* note 7, at 85.

308 *See* External Affairs, *supra* note 189, at 16–17 and Hage, *supra* note 189, at 6.

309 E. D. BROWN, THE INTERNATIONAL LAW OF THE SEA (Dartmouth, Aldershot 1994) 57.

310 United States-U.S.S.R., Uniform Interpretation of Rules of International Law Governing Innocent Passage, 23 September 1989, para 3, 28 ILM 1444–1447 and US Senate, Executive Report, Declarations and Understandings, *supra* note 97, s 3(2)(B).

makes vessel passage non-innocent, then it would appear to be difficult to fit the facts of LNG tanker traffic through the Head Harbour Passage into any of the activities listed. However, the 2000 Report of the ILA Committee on Coastal State Jurisdiction Relating to Marine Pollution indicated that the view that only Article 19(2) activities could deprive a vessel of innocent passage was "too categorical," since the emphasis on activities "leads to the conclusion that something which cannot be regarded as an activity, could in principle never be brought under the heading of 'prejudicial to the peace, good order or security of the coastal State.'"[311] The ILA Report further states:

> Although not explicitly referred to in the 1982 Convention, a coastal State retains in principle a right vested in general international law and based on its sovereignty over the territorial sea, to take and enforce measures to protect its interests.[312]

Moreover, it has been argued that if a "passage is highly risky due to the hazardous nature of the cargo, . . . the coastal State must arguably retain the right to exclude passage . . . subject to the conditions of necessity or proportionality."[313]

Canada has not indicated its views regarding the detailed meaning of when passage is innocent. A 1980 government memorandum reviewing the text of the LOS Convention referred to innocent passage as being defined in detail and "strengthened" by explicit limitations existing on "coastal State powers of environment regulation."[314]

Of interest to the question of innocent passage through the Head Harbour Passage is the concern and action of some countries as regards the transport of hazardous waste and nuclear materials through territorial waters, since the issue is one of cargo and not the activity of the vessel. Some States require either prior notification of intended vessel passage or prior coastal State authorization before vessels carrying such cargoes can enter their territorial waters.[315] The implication of prior notification is that a failure to provide it

---

311 Committee on Coastal State Jurisdiction Relating to Marine Pollution, *Final Report*, in I.L.A., REPORT OF THE SIXTH-NINTH CONFERENCE (London, 2000) 494.

312 *Id.* 495.

313 A. K-J. TAN, VESSEL-SOURCE MARINE POLLUTION: THE LAW AND POLITICS OF INTERNATIONAL REGULATION (Cambridge University Press, Cambridge 2006) 208.

314 Department of Foreign Affairs, Memorandum, 15 July 1980, in (1981) 19 CYIL 328, 329.

315 Summarized from Churchill and Lowe, *supra* note 7, at 92; K. Hakapaa and E. J. Molenaar,

would justify the coastal State to deny the right of innocent passage, while the implication of required prior authorization is that a decision by the coastal State not to provide authorization would render passage by the vessel non-innocent. There is not yet uniformity of State action on this matter.[316]

Whether LNG is a hazardous cargo like nuclear materials or whether what is more important is the increased risk of a cargo causing significant local damage because of navigational hazards is uncertain. The innocent passage wording of the LOS Convention, largely considered to be reflective of customary international law,[317] was "a deliberate choice that favours certainty over context."[318] The innocent passage legal regime provides for the possibility of differences of views between States and, as pointed out by one authority, the regime "appears to be at odds with the preailing preventative and precautionary posture of international . . . environmental policy."[319]

A potential difficulty with Canada adopting the non-innocent passage approach to the Head Harbour Passage rather than relying on historic internal waters is that, if the United States becomes a party to the LOS Convention, the compulsory adjudication provisions of the Convention may become available. Unlike claims of historic waters, the LOS Convention does not provide a shield for States regarding their interpretation and application of the innocent passage wording of the Convention.[320] If the dispute between Canada

---

Innocent Passage–Past and Present (1999) 23 Mar Pol 131, 132; and R. R. Churchill, *The Impact of State Practice on the Jurisdictional Framework Contained in the LOS Convention*, in A. G. Oude Elferink (ed.) Stability and Change in the Law of the Sea: The Role of the LOS Convention (Martinus Nijhoff, Leiden 2005) 111–118. *See also* J. M. Van Dyke, *The Legal Regime Governing Sea Transport of Ultrahazardous Radioactive Materials* (2002) 33 ODIL 77–108.

316 Churchill, *supra* note 315, at 118 summarizes:

> A requirement of prior authorization appears to be contrary to the LOS Convention and so no question of interpretation of the Convention arises. On the other hand, the Convention is arguably unclear and ambiguous about whether a coastal State may require prior notification of the passage of ships carrying hazardous cargoes . . . However, practice is too diverse . . . to amount to an agreed interpretation . . . This diversity of practice also suggests that no rule of customary law has arisen . . .

See also Hakapaa and Molenaar, *supra* note 315, at 144.

317 Uniform Interpretation of Rules Governing Innocent Passage, *supra* note 310, para 1; Churchill and Lowe, *supra* note 7, at 87; and Hakapaa and Molenaar, *supra* note 315, at 143–144.

318 N. Craik, *Presumed Innocent: Navigation Rights and Risk-Based Activities in the Passamaquoddy Bay* (2008) 58 U.N.B. LJ 167, 186.

319 *Id.*

320 LOS Convention, *supra* note 19, Art 298(1)(a)(i). *See* Chapter Six, section 3.2.5.

and the United States existed before the compulsory adjudication provisions of the Convention come into effect for the United States, then the compulsory adjudication provisions are not available.[321] However, the question of when a dispute comes into existence is not necessarily easily determined.[322] If, following U.S. accession to the LOS Convention, Canada enacts and enforces legislation respecting vessel traffic in Head Harbour Passage, the dispute may be said to have arisen at the time of the alleged actual violation of U.S. rights, with the result that compulsory adjudication under the LOS Convention might be available.

4.3 Cooperation and the Future of the Dispute

The positions of Canada and the United States regarding the Head Harbour Passage dispute and the Northwest Passage dispute involve virtually the same international legal issues—historic internal waters and rights of passage through an international strait. A major difference, however, is that unlike within the Northwest Passage, there has long been regular commercial marine traffic through the Head Harbour Passage to both U.S. and Canadian ports. Moreover, for the United States the geography and politics of the disputes are different. The U.S. concern in the Northwest Passage is principally one of global precedent; not so as regards the Head Harbour Passage. Canadian action could result in preventing marine transportation into a U.S. port and this makes the issue simultaneously local to northeastern Maine and national, as regards the protection of U.S. citizens' rights. For Canada, the Head Harbour Passage has yet to and may not generate the national sovereignty response that has accompanied the Northwest Passage issue, although it has been a significant issue within New Brunswick.

Canada and the United States have a history of cooperation regarding passage through the Head Harbour Passage involving vessel traffic services in the waters leading to the Passage and, more recently, regarding an arrangement on pilotage. Nevertheless, only in late 2007 did Canada provide to the

---

321 *See Case Concerning Certain Property (Liechtenstein v. Germany)*, Preliminary Objections, [2005] ICJ Rep. 6, paras 39–52 and S. Rosenne, The Law and Practice of the International Court—1920–2005 (Martinus Nijhoff, Leiden 2006) 562–567.

322 The question of when a dispute arises in the context of jurisdiction of the International Court is discussed in Rosenne, *supra* note 321, at 505–514 and 751–766 and A. Zimmermann, C. Tomuschat, and K. Oellers-Frahm (eds.) The Statute of the International Court of Justice: A Commentary (Oxford University Press, Oxford 2006) 634–636.

United States a copy of the study that was done on the "navigational safety, environmental safety and other impacts" of the LNG traffic through the Head Harbour Passage[323] referred to in the February 2007 letter from Canadian Ambassador Wilson to the chair of the U.S. Federal Energy Regulatory Commission.[324] Given the existing posture of the two States and, in particular, the different political calculus that faces the United States, the cooperative approach to bilateral disputes may be significantly tested if LNG facilities near Eastport, Maine, are approved and construction commences.

5.0 Dixon Entrance, Hecate Strait, and Queen Charlotte Sound

Canada claims that the Dixon Entrance, Hecate Strait, and Queen Charlotte Sound are historic internal waters.[325] The precise delineation of these waters claimed by Canada as historic internal waters has not been articulated. It is assumed, however, that the claimed areas are the waters enclosed by the 1971 fisheries closing lines[326] drawn across the Dixon Entrance and Queen Charlotte Sound in order to create an exclusive Canadian fishing zone.[327]

A few comments about these waters can be made. First, the Canadian historic waters claim to that part of the Dixon Entrance also claimed by the United States is subservient to the maritime boundary delimitation issue.[328]

---

323 Senes Consultants, *supra* note 268.

324 Letter of 14 February 2007, *supra* note 283, at para 2.

325 Letter dated 17 December 1973, *supra* note 3, at 279.

326 Fishing Zones of Canada (Zone 1, 2 and 3) Order, *supra* note 2.

327 Letter dated 17 December 1973, *supra* note 3, at 279 states:

> You should note that these bodies of water [including Dixon Entrance, Hecate Strait and Queen Charlotte Sound] were enclosed in February 1971 as exclusive Canadian fishing zones by "fisheries closing lines" . . . While this legislation makes no claim to sovereignty over these bodies of water, but only claims jurisdiction for fishing purposes and for the prevention of pollution, it does not bar a subsequent claim to full sovereignty on historic or other grounds.

See also Herman, *supra* note 297, at 7.

328 Regarding the maritime boundary issues in the Dixon Entrance, *see* Chapter Five, section 5.1.1.
It appears that some discussions between Canada and the United States regarding the historic waters status of the Dixon Entrance took place in the 1930s and 1940s. *See* Symmons, *supra* note 54, at 23, 28 footnote 56, 30 footnote 66.
More generally, Symmons at 84, footnote 181, indicates that U.S. archival evidence shows that Canada and the United States

Second, one authority has noted that, as regards the Dixon Entrance and Hecate Strait, "the Canadian government since the 1890s has maintained that these are Canadian waters."[329] In 1909, Canada's assertion that the Hecate Strait was under exclusive Canadian authority was set out.[330] Inconsistent with this, the above author acknowledges that U.S. fishing activity had long taken place "in the waters of both Dixon Entrance and Hecate Strait up to three miles from the Canadian shore," and that Canadian customs laws were not enforced in this area.[331] Third, the above author explicitly notes that the claim to Queen Charlotte Sound as historic internal waters emerged in the 1960s and "had no apparent antecedent in British and Canadian practice."[332] Fourth, there has been U.S. opposition dating from the 1960s to the possibility of the use of straight baselines by Canada to enclose the waters of the Dixon Entrance, Hecate Strait, and Queen Charlotte Sound as internal waters[333] and the United States formerly protested the 1971 fisheries closing lines.[334]

---

contemplated *joint action* (by draft agreement) in the 1940s to apply the doctrine of *shared* historic waters to the coast of Alaska and British Columbia, including certain bays, straits, and inlets, with these waters continuing to be "open" to the vessels of "the two countries" and with rights their nationals *then* enjoyed–such as fisheries–continuing. (emphasis in original)

329 L.H.J. Legault, *Maritime Claims*, in R. St. J. Macdonald, G. L. Morris, and D. M. Johnston (eds.) Canadian Perspectives on International Law and Organization (University of Toronto Press, Toronto 1974) 381. *See also* J.-Y. Morin, *The Quiet Revolution: Canadian Approaches to the Law of the Sea*, in R. Zacklin (ed.) The Changing Law of the Sea: Western Hemisphere Perspectives (Sitjhoff, Leiden 1974) 17 and D. Pharand, *The Implications of Canadian Marine and Arctic Legislation for the Development of International Law*, in L. M. Alexander and R. S. Hawkins, (eds.) Canadian—U.S. Maritime Problems (Law of the Sea Institute, Kingston, R.I. 1972) 77.

330 *See* Order-in-Council, 6 July 1909, enclosed in a letter from the Administrator to the Colonial Secretary, 13 July 1909, in Documents of Canada's External Affairs, Vol. I, 1909–1918 (Department of External Affairs, 1967) 400–405.

331 Legault, *supra* note 329, at 381.

332 *Id.* 383, 388. Morin, *supra* note 329, at 17 refers to the waters of the Queen Charlotte Sound as being part of the high seas and Pharand, *Implications of Legislation*, *supra* note 329, at 77 comments that Queen Charlotte Sound had "never been claimed by Canada as historic waters."

333 This Canadian contemplation generated U.S. concern respecting interference with navigational rights and, during the 1960s, with fisheries rights. *See* A. L. Hollick, U.S. Foreign Policy and the Law of the Sea (Princeton University Press, Princeton 1981) 172 and Chapter Three, section 3.2.

334 The State Department issued a Statement specifically on the fisheries closing lines which referred to the Canadian measure as a "unilateral act . . . totally without foundation in international law." Statement on Canadian Fisheries Closing Lines Announcement, *supra* note 5, para 2.

Though the validity of the Canadian claim that the waters of the Dixon Entrance, Hecate Strait, and Queen Charlotte Sound are historic internal waters remains untested, this has not created any significant difficulty between Canada and the United States as compared to the similar situation that has existed as regards the Northwest Passage and the Head Harbour Passage.

6.0 Georgia Strait, Johnstone Strait, Queen Charlotte Strait, and the Inside Passage

Georgia Strait, Johnstone Strait, and the Queen Charlotte Strait are the waterways that separate Vancouver Island from the mainland of British Columbia. The Johnstone Strait and Queen Charlotte Strait are well north of the agreed Canada-United States maritime boundary; whereas the agreed maritime boundary goes through the southern part of the Strait of Georgia.[335] The Georgia Strait is quite wide and leads to the Johnstone Strait, which is about a mile in width at its southern end and two miles in width where it connects to the Queen Charlotte Strait which, where it enters into Queen Charlotte Sound, is about 12 nautical miles in width.[336]

The Inside Passage is the waterway that exists between the numerous islands along the British Columbia coast that are landward of the Hecate Strait and the mainland of British Columbia. The Inside Passage is composed of Fitz Hugh Sound, Finlayson Channel, Princess Royal Channel, Principe Channel, Grenville Channel, and Laredo Sound.

The international legal status of the above waters came into question in 1994 as part of the Canada-U.S. Pacific salmon dispute,[337] when Canada removed an exemption on obtaining a license that had existed for the approximately 300 U.S. salmon vessels going between Alaska and the lower 48 States through these waters.[338] The license requirement, which required the

---

335 Regarding the maritime boundary in the southern Strait of Georgia, *see* Chapter Five, section 2.1.

336 *See* description in *Re Attorney-General of Canada and Attorney-General of British Columbia*, 8 *D.L.R.* (4th) 161 (Supreme Court of Canada) 165.

337 *See* Chapter Seven, section 2.2.2.

338 Department of Fisheries and Oceans, Licence Fee Announced for U.S. Vessels, 9 June 1994. The exemption was set out in Coastal Fisheries Protection Regulations, amendment, Can Gaz Part II, Vol. 119, SOR/85-527, 6 June 1985, 2719–2729, s 13 which replaced s 17 of the Coastal Fisheries Protection Regulations, CRC (1978), c 413, 2911–2919. The exemption

payment of a fee, specifically applied to fishing vessels passing through the waters between Vancouver Island and the mainland of British Columbia (the Georgia Strait, Johnstone Strait, and Queen Charlotte Strait were not explicitly named) and Fitz Hugh Sound, Finlayson Channel, Princess Royal Channel, Principe Channel, Grenville Channel, and Laredo Sound.[339] The United States protested the Canadian licensing measure asserting, among other things, that the license fee was "inconsistent with rights guaranteed to vessels under customary international law as reflected in the 1982 United Nations Convention on the Law of the Sea."[340] The U.S. Congress fulminated in various ways including a proposal to have U.S. Coast Guard vessels accompany U.S. fishing vessels through Canadian waters.[341]

The U.S. view appears to be that the Georgia Strait, Johnstone Strait, and Queen Charlotte Strait are international straits through which, because they separate an island from the mainland and for which there is another route of similar convenience, in this case west of Vancouver Island, there exists a right of innocent passage pursuant to Article 38(1) of the LOS Convention.[342] It has been questioned whether the Georgia and Johnstone Straits meet the geographic criterion for an international strait, given that they are essentially landlocked by the numerous islands within the waters.[343] The Canadian view of these waters is that they are "internal waters at international law."[344]

---

was removed pursuant to Coastal Fisheries Protection Regulations, amendment, Can Gaz Part II, Vol. 128, SOR/94-444, 14 June 1994, 2575–2578. *See generally* T. L. McDorman, *The West Coast Salmon Dispute: A Canadian View of the Breakdown of the 1985 Treaty and the Transit License Measure* (1995) 17 Loyola of Los Angeles Intl and Comp LJ 477, 477–478, 497–498.

339 Coastal Fisheries Protection Regulations, amendment, *supra* note 338.

340 Department of State, Canada Transit Fee, 15 June 1994, as cited and reproduced in part in C. B. Picker, *Fishing for Answers in Canada's Inside Passage: Exploring the Use of the Transit Fee as a Countermeasure* (1996) 21 Yale J Intl L 349, 361.

341 *See* Picker, *supra* note 340, at 362–365.

342 L. M. Alexander, *Exceptions to the Transit Passage Regime: Straits with Routes of 'Similar Convenience'* (1987) 18 ODIL 479, 487–488. Note also Picker, *supra* note 340, at 373.

Alexander, at 487–488, lists several other Canadian waters as being straits formed by an island where there exists a route seaward of the island through the high seas or EEZ, the implication being that the strait in question is subject to innocent passage. All of these waters are in the Gulf of St. Lawrence: Jacques Cartier Passage between Anticosti Island and Quebec; the Northumberland Strait between Prince Edward Island and the mainland; and the Strait of Belle Isle separating the island of Newfoundland from the Canadian mainland.

343 Jia, *supra* note 28, at 67.

344 The Attorney-General of Canada is referenced as having conceded this in *Re A.-G. of Canada and A.-G. of British Columbia*, *supra* note 336, at 168.

WEST COAST WATERS

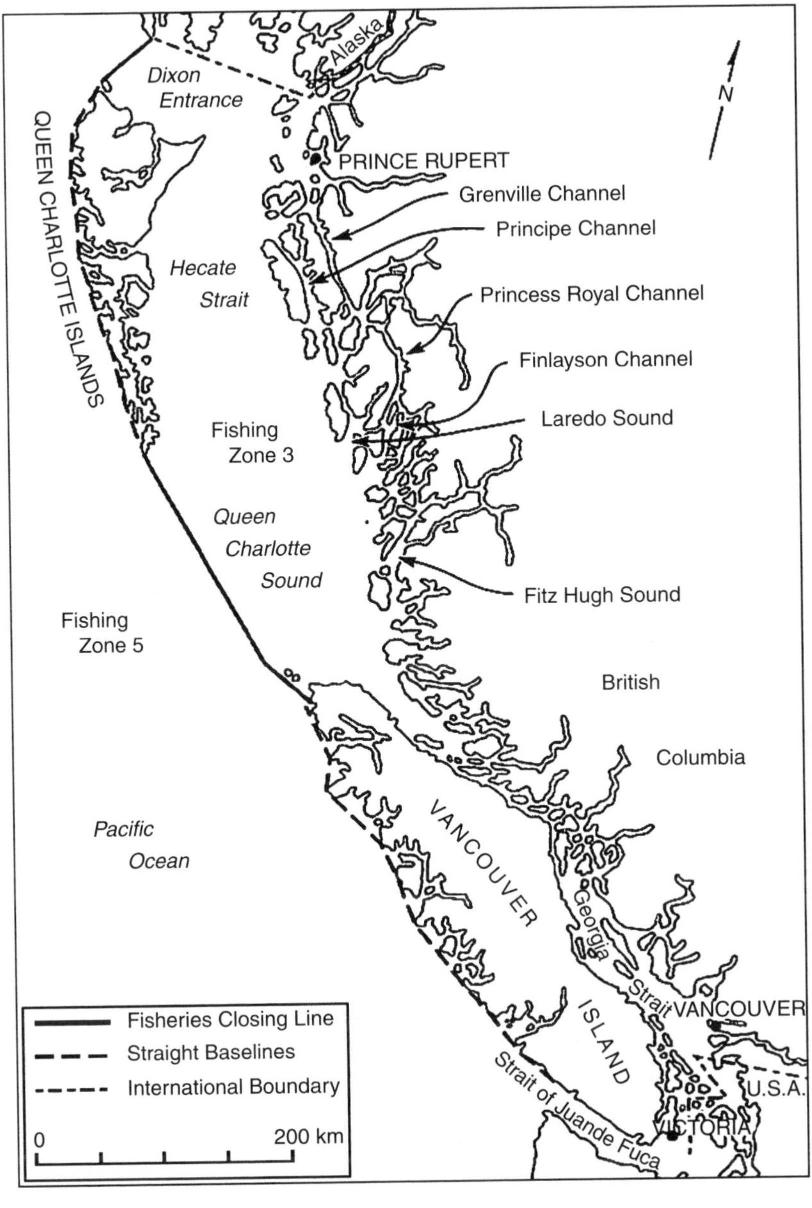

Source: TL McDorman, 'The West Coast Salmon Dispute: A Canadian View of the Breakdown of the 1985 Treaty and the Transit Licence Measure' (1995) 17 Loyola of Los Angeles Intl and Comp LJ 477, 506.

As regards the Inside Passage north of Vancouver Island, based on the geography of the waterway, there seems to be little doubt that these northern British Columbia waters are Canadian internal waters.[345]

In 1994, neither Canada nor the United States detailed their international legal justification for their actions and statements. The enforcement of the license requirement for U.S. vessels, however, was discontinued when the United States undertook a different tact on Pacific salmon discussions.[346]

7.0 Juan de Fuca Strait

The Juan de Fuca Strait between Vancouver Island and the U.S. state of Washington is not an area of significant bilateral dispute. What has arisen occasionally have been Canadian complaints about attempted or actual U.S. regulation of vessels in the Juan de Fuca Strait heading to or from Canadian ports such as Vancouver.

As already discussed, the maritime boundary in the Strait has existed since 1846.[347] That same Treaty provided that "the navigation of the whole of the said channel and Straits south of the forty ninth parallel of north latitude remain free and open to both Parties."[348] Thus, within the Juan de Fuca Strait and adjacent areas covered by Article I, a navigational right exercisable by both Canada and the United States exists as a matter of treaty law. It appears that the waters of the Strait have long been treated by the two States as national as opposed to international waters.[349] Nevertheless, the precise nature of the navigational right and the international legal status of the waters within the Strait are not clear.[350]

This was not an international law case; rather it was a Canadian constitutional law case that decided in favor of British Columbia regarding the ownership of the seabed between Vancouver Island and the mainland of British Columbia.

345 *See* McDorman, *supra* note 338, at 497–503 and Picker, *supra* note 340, at 373.

346 McDorman, *supra* note 338, at 478.

347 Treaty Establishing the Boundary in the Territory on the Northwest Coast of America Lying Westward of the Rocky Mountains, Washington, 15 June 1846, entered into force 5 August 1846, 100 Con. TS 39–42. *See* Chapter Five, section 2.1.

348 *Id.* Art I.

349 *See* J. B. MOORE, A DIGEST OF INTERNATIONAL LAW, Vol. I (Washington, 1906) 658–659 and Jia, *supra* note 28, at 16–17.

350 *See* C. Allen, *The Pacific Northwest Boundary Straits: High Seas or Internal Waters*, February 1995, PACIFIC MARITIME MAGAZINE 20–24 and W. Hettenbach, *Rough Waters in the Strait of Juan de Fuca* (1993) Vol. X No. 8 OCEANS POLICY NEWS 6–7.

The Juan de Fuca Strait may be a "dead-end" international strait, like the Head Harbour Passage, through which a right of non-suspendable innocent passage applies.[351] Or the waterway may be a strait covered by a longstanding international convention and, therefore, outside the scope of the 1982 LOS Convention.[352] It has been reported that:

> At UNCLOS III . . . American delegates . . . indicated that the United States would not insist that the waterway [Juan de Fuca Strait] be characterized as an international strait. This determination probably was because of the regime of passage in the strait is also governed by Article I of the Oregon Treaty . . .[353]

The longstanding U.S. practice within the Straits is that:

> The US has, until very recently, been consistent in permitting vessels bound for Canada to freely navigate waters on the US side of the straits with little or no US regulation, as if they were in innocent passage.[354]

The Canadian view of the Strait is unclear.

In the early 1970s, it was opined that the waters of the Juan de Fuca Strait, even though the width of the Strait varies from nine to seventeen nautical miles, were the historic internal waters of the two countries and that this had never been questioned.[355] The Canadian waters of the Juan de Fuca Strait are not noted in the 1973 listing of Canada's claimed historic waters.[356] Nevertheless, for other Canadian claimed historic waters, the delineation is seen as being the 1971 fisheries closing lines,[357] and there is a fisheries closing line at the mouth of the Juan de Fuca Strait.[358] In a domestic court case, the government of Canada took the view that the waters were internal.[359]

---

351 LOS Convention, *supra* note 19, Art 45.

352 *Id.* Art 35(c).

353 McConchie and Reid, *supra* note 144, at 165.

354 Allen, *supra* note 350, at 24.

355 Morin, *supra* note 329, at 19.

356 Letter dated 17 December 1973, *supra* note 3, at 279.

357 *See* Letter dated 17 December 1973, *supra* note 3, at 279 and Herman, *supra* note 297, at 7. *See also* Chapter Six, sections 4.2.2 and 5.0.

358 Fishing Zones of Canada (Zone 1, 2 and 3) Order, *supra* note 2.

359 The Attorney-General of Canada is referenced as having conceded this in *Re A.-G. of Canada and A.-G. of British Columbia*, *supra* note 336, at 168.

The United States has not asserted an historic claim for its waters in the Juan de Fuca Strait. As a result of the 1989 Proclamation of a 12-nautical-mile territorial sea,[360] all of the U.S. waters in the Strait are territorial seas. Prior to 1989, the U.S. three-nautical-mile limit left pockets of high seas within the Juan de Fuca Strait.

For the most part, questions about the international legal status of and the legal nature of the navigation right within the Juan de Fuca Strait have been happily rendered moot by the 1979 Vessel Traffic Management Agreement for the Juan de Fuca Region.[361] The 1979 Agreement is clear that it is "without prejudice to position of the . . . United States and Canada with respect to the character of, and the nature and extent of coastal State jurisdiction over the applicable and adjacent waters."[362] Reportedly, however, the United States points to the 1979 Agreement as evidence of the character of the Juan de Fuca Strait as an international strait.[363] Nevertheless, to the extent that there may be a disagreement regarding the international legal status of the waters of the Juan de Fuca Strait, the 1979 Agreement is a bilateral, cooperative operational agreement that supersedes the legal issues.

The purpose of the 1979 Agreement was to create "a cooperative system of vessel traffic management" throughout the Juan de Fuca Strait.[364] The impetus for the Agreement was concern on both sides of the border over the commencement of oil tanker traffic from Alaska passing through the Juan de Fuca Strait to U.S. reception facilities in Puget Sound.[365]

---

360 Territorial Sea of the United States, Proclamation 5928 of 27 December 1988, 54 Fed Reg 777, 28 ILM 284.

361 Agreement on Vessel Traffic, *supra* note 11. Regarding the background to the 1979 Agreement, *see* Carroll, *supra* note 272, at 72–75.

362 *Id.* Annex, para 205.1.

363 Hettenbach, *supra* note 350, at 6.

364 Agreement on Vessel Traffic, *supra* note 11, Annex, para 100.1. A good description of the cooperative traffic management service (CVTS) in the Juan de Fuca Strait area is in Department of Commerce, National Oceanic and Atmospheric Administration, UNITED STATES: COASTAL PILOT 7—PACIFIC COAST: CALIFORNIA, OREGON, WASHINGTON, HAWAII, AND PACIFIC ISLANDS (Washington, 2006, 38th edition) 471–476.

365 *See generally* Carroll, *supra* note 272, at 72–79 and W. R. D. Sewell and N. A. Swainson, *West Coast Oil Pollution Policies: Canadian Responses to Risk Assessment*, in O. P. DWIVEDI (ed.) RESOURCES AND THE ENVIRONMENT: POLICY PERSPECTIVES FOR CANADA (McClelland and Stewart, Toronto 1980) 216–229.

Also in response to Canadian concerns of oil tanker traffic from Alaska passing along the West Coast of Canada, the United States included a provision in the Trans-Alaskan Pipeline Authorization Act that "residents of Canada" may make claims to compensation from the

Pursuant to the 1979 Agreement, vessels entering the traffic management area are required to obtain clearance from the appropriate vessel traffic management center.[366] The traffic management centres maintain information on the vessels in the management area and provide navigational information to such vessels.[367] The 1979 Agreement makes it clear that the purpose of the traffic management system is not to "manoeuvre or navigate vessels from the shore" and that the responsibility for safe navigation is with the master of the vessel.[368] The Agreement anticipated that the traffic separation scheme would be submitted jointly to the IMO.[369] In April 1981, the IMO adopted the traffic separation scheme that had been proposed jointly by Canada and the United States for the Juan de Fuca Strait and its approaches. Additional traffic separation schemes were jointly proposed and adopted by the IMO in December 1992 respecting Puget Sound and its approaches and in 2004 respecting Haro Strait, Boundary Bay, and the Strait of Georgia.[370]

Pursuant to the traffic separation scheme, inbound vessels use the U.S. side of the Strait and outbound vessels use the Canadian side. A key legal matter in

---

liability fund established by the legislation "for all damages . . . as the result of discharges of oil" from tankers engaged in transporting oil from Alaska. Trans-Alaskan Pipeline Authorization Act, 87 US Stat. 584, Pub L. 93–153, codified at 43 USC s 1653(c)(1).

In 1977, the United States established a tanker exclusion zone that kept laden tankers from Alaska 100 nautical miles west of the Queen Charlotte Islands and up to 85 nautical miles west of Vancouver Island. Complaints from the industry regarding the costs of complying with the routeing system led to the cancellation of the zone in 1982. Subsequent tripartite discussions led to an interim tanker exclusion zone along the Canadian coast in 1985 that was finalized in 1988. *See* D. Alpen, *Information on the Tanker Exclusion Zone (TEZ) for Canada's West Coast*, in DFO, *Bowie Seamount Ecosystem Overview: Appendices*, Appendix F, (May 1998), para 9, at www.pac-mpo.gc.ca/oceans/Bowie/bowie_appx_e/ htm> (accessed on 21 September 2006). The tanker exclusion zone is approximately 115 nautical miles west of the Queen Charlotte Islands, 73 nautical miles from the northern end of Vancouver Island tapering to 40 nautical miles near the mouth of the Juan de Fuca Strait. *See* Department of Fisheries and Oceans, NOTICE TO MARINERS: ANNUAL EDITION 2006, para 10.2.5, A10-2. The TEZ is not a compulsory routeing system; rather, it is voluntary and only applies to the tankers involved in Alaskan oil carriage. This has been criticized by S. Hawkes and R. M. M'Gonigle, *A Black (and Rising?) Tide: Controlling Maritime Oil Pollution in Canada* (1992) 30 OSGOODE HALL LJ 165, 203–204.

366 Agreement on Vessel Traffic, *supra* note 11, Annex, paras 301.1, 303.1(f).

367 *Id.* Annex, para 303.1.

368 *Id.* Annex, para 206.

369 *Id.* Annex, para 202.1.

370 *See* IMO, New and Amended Existing Traffic Separation Schemes, Doc COLREG.2/Circ.57, 26 May 2006, Annex 2, which was adopted by the Maritime Safety Committee in May 2006 and contains the update traffic separation scheme for the Juan de Fuca Strait and its approaches, at www.imo.org/blastDataOnly.asp/data_id%3D14761/57.pdf (accessed on 9 August 2007). *See also Ships' Routeing, supra* note 269, Part VII–2, 3 and 4.

the 1979 Agreement is the application and enforcement of laws respecting vessels navigating on the U.S. side of the Juan de Fuca Strait headed for Canadian ports and vice versa. The Agreement provides that each State in applying its laws to vessels in its waters "will consider compliance with the requirements of the other Party to be effectively equivalent to material compliance with its own requirements,"[371] but that this does not prevent a State from taking action in regard to a vessel in its waters where "the condition or activities" of a vessel "may pose an actual threat to marine safety or the marine environment."[372]

When the state of Washington sought to impose regulations respecting tanker design, equipment, and operating procedures on all vessels in its waters, even those headed to Canadian ports through the Juan de Fuca Strait, Canada informed the United States and, through an *amicus curia* brief, the U.S. Supreme Court, of its view that, since the Washington state legislation was not based on reciprocity as required by the 1979 Agreement, the legislation would result in the United States not complying with its international legal obligations under the 1979 Agreement.[373] The factual situation is interesting since Canada was arguing against stronger environmental laws applying to vessels relying on the international context, which is the inverse of Canada's usual position *vis à vis* the United States. The U.S. Supreme Court decided that the U.S. federal legislation regarding oil tanker pollution prevention preempted the state of Washington law.[374]

8.0 Conclusion

Of the five geographic areas where Canada-U.S. international ocean law disputes regarding navigation rights exist, the two countries have fully circumvented the legal uncertainty in one area; partially circumvented the legal dispute in another; managed to avoid the problems in a third and fourth; while in the fifth area collision avoidance has yet to activated.

---

371 Agreement on Vessel Traffic, *supra* note 11, Annex, para 204.2.

372 *Id.* Annex, para 204.3.

373 *See* Note No. 0389 to the United States, 7 May 1997, copy on file with the author and *Amicus Curiae* Brief, 22 August 1999, in *United States v. Locke*, U.S. Supreme Court, docket 98–1701 and 98–1706, at <supreme.lp.findlaw.com/supreme_court/briefs/98-1701/98-1701fo11/brief/breif06.html> (accessed on 15 May 2007).

374 *United States v. Locke* (2000), 529 U.S. 89.

The fully circumvented area is the Juan de Fuca Strait, where the international legal uncertainty regarding the status of the waters and the navigation rights that exist has been avoided by the 1979 Vessel Traffic Management Agreement.[375]

Partial circumvention has been accomplished by the two States as regards the Northwest Passage through the 1988 Arctic Cooperation Agreement.[376] Despite the narrow focus of this Agreement, it applies only to Coast Guard ice-breakers, and the ambiguity accepted by both States regarding its meaning, the 1988 Agreement has calmed the waters in the Northwest Passage. Nevertheless, global climate change has raised concerns about Canada's abilities to address any increased vessel traffic in the Passage and has led to a resuscitation of sovereignty rhetoric in Canada-U.S. ocean and Arctic relations. U.S.-flagged commercial vessels or foreign vessels owned by U.S. commercial interests may eventually find it economically beneficial to use the Northwest Passage, and this may result in a serious international ocean law dispute between the two countries regarding the Northwest Passage.

Problems between Canada and the United States have been avoided respecting the navigation rights in the Dixon Entrance, Hecate Strait, Queen Charlotte Sound, Georgia Strait, Johnstone Strait, and Queen Charlotte Strait by benign neglect. The Canadian claims and the U.S. opposition are known, but there have been no recent incidents that have raised the dispute and it is difficult to foresee why either State would upset this situation.

Finally, as regards the Head Harbour Passage, Canada and the United States appear to have staked out divergent views regarding the existence of a passage right. The February 2007 letter from the Canadian Ambassador is worded quite categorically that Canada will use legal means to "prevent" LNG tanker traffic in the Head Harbour Passage.[377] The United States asserts a navigational right through the waters.[378] Collision avoidance, should the LNG projects go ahead in northeastern Maine, is not readily apparent. Note can be made of the wording in the Canadian Ambassador's letter that the LNG facilities and tanker traffic "presents risks . . . Canada cannot accept" and that these are the possible seeds from which collision avoidance may emerge. If Canada can be convinced that the LNG traffic and facilities, as a

375 Agreement on Vessel Traffic, *supra* note 11.

376 Arctic Cooperation Agreement, *supra* note 110.

377 Letter of 14 February 2007, *supra* note 283.

378 Commentary–The 1982 United Nations Convention on the Law of the Sea, *supra* note 6, at 19.

result of careful construction and enhanced navigational safety measures, minimize the "risks," then circumvention of the international legal dispute may be possible. The circumvention would have to protect the international legal position of both States and overcome what might appear to be a reversal of position by Canada and the political fallout this may entail

SEVEN

Fisheries

1.0 Introduction

"Questions concerning fisheries have probably been on the negotiating agenda of Canada and the United States longer than any other issue."[1] A brief review of North American history supports this.

Fisheries matters were central to the 1783 Paris Peace Treaty between the United States and Great Britain that ended the Revolutionary War, with the United States re-acquiring the liberty to fish in all waters adjacent to the then-British colonies.[2] Following the War of 1812, Great Britain and the United States revisited fisheries matters in the 1818 Convention of Commerce, with the United States renouncing fishing rights within three nautical miles of the coasts and bays of the British colonies.[3] The 1800s were subsequently marked by: British and Canadian enforcement efforts regarding alleged illegal U.S. fishing activity; uncertainty regarding the meaning of the 1818 Convention, in particular, the word "bays" that contributed to the allegations of U.S. illicit fishing; short-lived treaties that provided for U.S. fishing rights in

1 H. von Riekhoff, J. H. Sigler and B.W. Tomlin, Canada-U.S. Relations: Policy Environments, Issues, and Prospects (C.D. Howe Institute, Toronto 1979) 95.

2 Definitive Treaty of Peace, Paris 3 September 1783, entered into force 9 April 1794, Art III, 48 Con. TS 487. *See* Historical Introduction in *Gulf of Maine Pleadings*, Vol. 1, Annex to Memorial of the Canada, 184–185 and D. M. Johnston, The International Law of Fisheries (Yale University Press, New Haven 1965) 194–195.

3 Convention of Commerce, London, 20 October 1818, entered into force 30 January 1819, Art I, 69 Con. TS 294. *See* Historical Introduction, *supra* note 2, at 186–187 and Johnston, *supra* note 2, at 195–198.

Canadian/British colonial offshore areas, often tied to reciprocal trading rights;[4] and several arbitrations and court cases.[5]

Although most of the bilateral fisheries action in the 1800s was on the East Coast, in the 1880s, on the West Coast, there were U.S. seizures of Canadian vessels in the fur seal fishery beyond three nautical miles adjacent to Alaska that raised tensions.[6] The United States and Great Britain agreed to arbitrate the dispute.[7] The 1893 *Bering Sea Arbitration Award* found in favor of the British argument that the United States had no authority over fishing activities beyond three nautical miles.[8] The 1800s ended with the 1818 Convention of Commerce being the operative bilateral fisheries agreement; Canada providing *ad hoc* licenses to U.S. vessels to operate in Canadian waters on the East Coast;[9] and on the West Coast, the need for a solution to the decrease of the Alaskan fur seal herd.[10]

The 1910 *North Atlantic Coast Fisheries Case* eased the East Coast Canada-United States fishing problems by, among other things, pronouncing on the meaning of "bays" in the 1818 Convention on Commerce.[11] The Tribunal declined to apply a mechanical approach (a mileage limit on

4 Treaty regarding the North Atlantic Fisheries, Washington, 5 June 1854, entered into force 9 September 1854, Arts I, II, 112 Con. TS 31 and Treaty for the Amicable Settlement of All Causes of Difference, Washington, 8 May 1871, entered into force 17 June 1871, Arts XVIII, XIX, 143 Con. TS 145. *See generally* Historical Introduction, *supra* note 2, at 188–190.

5 *See, for example*, the 1853 *Washington Award*, in J. B. MOORE, HISTORY AND DIGEST OF INTERNATIONAL ARBITRATIONS, Vol. IV (U.S. Government Printing Office, 1898) 4342. *See* Chapter Six, section 4.2.2, footnote 299.

Generally on fisheries relations in 1800s, *see* Historical Introduction, *supra* note 2, at 186–194; J. B. MOORE, DIGEST OF INTERNATIONAL LAW, Vol. I (Washington, 1906) 780–874; Johnston, *supra* note 2, at 196–202; and J. L. Granatstein and N. Hillmer, FOR BETTER OF FOR WORSE: CANADA AND THE UNITED STATES IN THE 1990s (Copp Clark Pitman, Toronto 1991) 10–13, 15, 22–24.

6 Johnston, *supra* note 2, at 206–207; Moore, *Digest*, *supra* note 5, at 895–902; and C. P. R. ROMANO, THE PEACEFUL SETTLEMENT OF INTERNATIONAL ENVIRONMENTAL DISPUTES: A PRAGMATIC APPROACH (Kluwer Law International, The Hague 2000) 135–137.

7 Treaty for submitting to Arbitration the Questions relating to the Seal Fisheries in the Behring Sea, Washington, 29 February 1892, entered into force 7 May 1892, 176 Con. TS 447–453.

8 *Award of the Tribunal of Arbitration (Bering Sea)*, 15 August 1893, in Moore, *Arbitrations*, *supra* note 5, 910–920. *See generally* Johnston, *supra* note 2, at 207–210 and Romano, *supra* note 6, at 138–143.

9 Johnston, *supra* note 2, at 202.

10 Romano, *supra* note 6, at 144–146.

11 *Award of the Tribunal of Arbitration in the Question Relating to the North Atlantic Coast Fisheries*, 7 September 1910, xi RIAA 173.

the mouth of a bay) to the definition of bays.[12] As a result, the Bay of Chaleur, Miramichi Bay, and a number of other bays were determined to be subject to exclusive British control.[13] It is to be noted that, by agreement, the Bay of Fundy was not considered by the Tribunal.[14] The 1910 *Fisheries Arbitration* was implemented through a 1912 treaty which established a Permanent Mixed Fishery Commission to address subsequent fisheries disputes.[15] Recourse to the Commission "was seldom if ever required."[16] On the West Coast, the 1911 Convention for the Preservation and Protection of Fur Seals[17] established a harvesting ban over an extensive area of the North Pacific and eased the concerns that had led to the 1893 *Bering Sea Arbitration*.[18]

L. H. J. Legault, *Maritime Claims*, in R. St. J. Macdonald, G. L. Morris, and D. M. Johnston (eds.) Canadian Perspectives on International Law and Organization (University of Toronto Press, Toronto 1974) 379 writes:

> The decision in the North Atlantic Coast Fisheries Arbitration is of fundamental importance in the history of Canada's maritime claims. It may be seen both as having substantially recognized the principal Canadian claims at issue in the case and as having confirmed the limitations upon them vis-à-vis the United States. And it marked the end of a bitter controversy with the United States over the North Atlantic fisheries (a result which in the long run may have been assisted by the fact that United States fishermen gradually began to lose interest in those fisheries).

See also Historical Introduction, *supra* note 2, at 195, which indicates that with the 1910 *Arbitration* "the old controversies had been largely laid to rest."

12 *North Atlantic Fisheries Arbitration*, *supra* note 11, at 196. *See* Johnston, *supra* note 2, at 202–204.

13 *Id.* 199–200.

14 *Id.* 200.

15 Agreement respecting the North Atlantic Fisheries, Washington, 20 July 1912, entered into force 15 November 1912, 216 Con. TS 314–318.

16 Historical Introduction, *supra* note 2, at 195.

17 Convention respecting Fur Seals in the North Pacific Ocean, Washington, 7 July 1911, entered into force 12 December 1911, 214 Con. TS 80–87.
This Agreement was terminated by Japan in 1941 and replaced in 1957 by the Interim Convention on the Conservation of North Pacific Fur Seals, Washington, 9 February 1957, entered into force 14 October 1957, 314 UNTS 105. The 1957 Convention was amended and extended a number of times, the last being in 1984. The Agreement ceased to operate as of 1985. *See* W. T. Burke, The New International Law of Fisheries (Clarendon Press, Oxford 1994) 278–280 and more generally, E. Hey, The Regime for the Exploitation of Transboundary Marine Fisheries Resources (Martinus Nijhoff, Dordrecht 1989) 249–253.

18 *See* Johnston, *supra* note 2, at 266 and Romano, *supra* note 6, at 146.

West Coast halibut and salmon were significant Canada-U.S. fisheries issues in the first decades of the 1900s, with bilateral accords reached regarding halibut in 1923[19] and Pacific salmon in 1930.[20]

Calmness generally prevailed between Canada and the United States on fisheries matter until the 1960s when fisheries again became a significant bilateral issue. As already noted, Canada's establishment in 1964 of a nine-nautical-mile fishing zone adjacent to the three-nautical-mile territorial sea and the possibility of the use of straight baselines[21] were complained about by the United States.[22] Then came Canada's 12-nautical-mile territorial sea and fisheries closing lines in 1970.[23] This was accompanied by a Canada-U.S. Reciprocal Fisheries Agreement.[24] The Agreement placed on a treaty basis the informal arrangements that had existed in the 1960s, which permitted the continuation of traditional fishing activities in the newly created offshore zones.[25] The scope of the salt water relationship regarding fisheries fundamentally altered in the mid 1970s with the arrival of 200-nautical-mile fishing zones and the modern international law of the sea.

Modern international ocean law and 200-nautical-mile zones have created a number of fisheries issues. First, there are fisheries disputes that arise as a result of overlapping 200-nautical-mile zone claims. The 1984 *Gulf of Maine Case*[26] was propelled by the establishment by Canada and the United States of 200-nautical-mile zones that overlapped in the Gulf of Maine area.[27]

---

19 Convention for the Halibut Fisheries of the Northern Pacific Ocean, Washington, 2 March 1923, entered into force 21 October 1924, 32 LNTS 93. *See* Chapter Seven, section 3.1.

20 Convention for Sockeye Salmon Fishery in the Fraser River System, Washington, 26 May 1930, entered into force 28 July 1937, 184 LNTS 305. *See* Chapter Seven, section 2.1.

21 Territorial Sea and Fishing Zone Act, St Can 1964–1965, c 22, ss 3–5.

22 *See* Chapter Three, section 3.2.

23 Act to amend the Territorial Sea and Fishing Zones Act, St Can 1969–1970, c 68, ss 1, 4 and Fishing Zones of Canada (Zone 1, 2 and 3) Order, Can Gaz Part II, Vol. 105, SOR/71-81, 25 February 1971, 363–364, came into effect on 10 March 1971. *See* Chapter Three, section 3.2.

24 Agreement on Reciprocal Fishing Privileges, Ottawa, 24 April 1970, entered into force 24 April 1970, CTS 1970/11, UST 1283, TIAS 6879.

25 Historical Introduction, *supra* note 2, at 201.

26 *Delimitation of the Maritime Boundary in the Gulf of Maine Area (Canada v. United States)*, [1984] ICJ Rep. 246.

27 Fishery Conservation and Management Act (renamed the Magnuson Fishery Conservation and Management Act), 90 US Stat. 331, Pub L. 265 (1976), codified at 16 USC 1801–1882.

Fishing Zones of Canada (Zones 4 and 5) Order, Can Gaz Part II, Vol. 111, SOR/77-62, 1 January 1977, 115120 replaced by Fishing Zones of Canada (Zones 4 and 5) Order, CRC

The International Court ultimately determined within which areas in the Gulf of Maine Canadians could fish and which areas were under the exclusive jurisdiction of the United States.[28] The claimed 200-nautical-mile zones of Canada and the United States have created numerous areas on the East, West, and Arctic Coasts where there are overlapping claims.[29] The two States have usually adhered to informal arrangements respecting the fishing activities of each side in the overlapping areas that are designed to avoid escalation of problems. These arrangements are based on flag State authority such that neither country will enforce national fishing laws against fishers from the other State within an overlapping claim area. For example, as regards the Dixon Entrance, Canada and the United States exchanged notes in August 1980 reaffirming that each side would observe flag State enforcement respecting fisheries,[30] and, since the early 1970s, the two countries have informally agreed on a policy of flag State enforcement regarding fishing activity within the disputed waters adjacent to Machias Seal Island.[31]

Second, there are disputes that can arise as a result of enforcement action by one State against alleged illegal fishers from another State within its 200-nautical-mile zone. In an impressive display of enforcement capacity, in a single day in August 1979, Canada rounded up nineteen U.S. tuna vessels in Canadian waters on the West Coast.[32] The 1990 Canada-U.S. Fisheries Enforcement Agreement[33] was designed to avoid some of these tensions by making it an offense in each State for its fishers to operate illegally in the

---

(1978), Vol. XVIII, c 1548, 13741–13746 and Fishing Zones of Canada (Zone 6) Order, Can Gaz Part II, Vol. 111, SOR/77-173, 24 February 1977, 652–655, replaced by Fishing Zones of Canada (Zone 6) Order, CRC (1978), c 1549, 13747–13750. Zones 4 and 5 are on the East and West Coasts and zone 6 is in the Arctic.

28 *See* Chapter Five, section 3.0.

29 *See* Chapter Five, section 5.0.

30 Referred to in Department of State, CUMULATIVE DIGEST OF UNITED STATES PRACTICE IN INTERNATIONAL LAW, 1981–1988 (Washington, 1994) 1930. *See* Chapter Five, section 5.1.5.

31 *See* Department of State, DIGEST OF UNITED STATES PRACTICE IN INTERNATIONAL LAW, 1973 (Washington, 1974) 466. *See also* D. Russell, *International Ocean Boundary Issues and Management Arrangements,* in D. VANDERZWAAG (ed.) CANADIAN OCEAN LAW AND POLICY (Butterworths, Toronto 1992) 70 and Chapter Five, section 5.5.2.

32 *See generally* N. P. Rasmussen, *Tuna War: Fishery Jurisdiction in International Law* (1981) U OF ILLINOIS LR 755, 764–765 and Chapter Seven, section 3.2.

33 Agreement on Fisheries Enforcement, Ottawa 26 September 1990, entered into force 16 December 1991, CTS 1991/36, TIAS 11753.

waters of the other State and by having regular bilateral meetings of the enforcement authorities.[34]

Third, there are fisheries disputes that arise because, however much States recognize 200-nautical-mile and ocean boundary constructs, marine living resources do not. Consequently, fishing activity for certain stocks in one State's 200-nautical-mile zone can greatly affect the availability and health of that same stock in the waters of the other State. The 1982 United Nations (U.N.) Convention on the Law of the Sea calls for but does not mandate States to cooperate to manage effectively cross-boundary marine living resources.[35] As already detailed, in the Gulf of Maine area it has only been in the last few years that Canada and the United States have been working together to co-manage a number of stocks that cross the maritime boundary.[36] More generally, over the last few decades, the Atlantic Coast neighborhood has not been the site of significant bilateral cooperation on fisheries management issues. However, on the Pacific Coast, Canada and the United States have fisheries agreements that cover a number of cross-boundary species including halibut,[37] albacore tuna,[38] and hake/whiting.[39]

Another example of the third issue concerns stocks that are either highly migratory or otherwise involves multiple State jurisdictions or the high seas beyond national jurisdiction. Again, harvesting by one State can great affect the availability and health of a stock in the waters of another State and, again, the LOS Convention calls for, but does not mandate, States to cooperate to manage effectively these marine living resources.[40] For these multijurisdiction stocks in the Canada-U.S. neighborhood there

---

34 *See* Chapter Five, section 3.4.3.

35 U. N. Convention on the Law of the Sea, Montego Bay, Jamaica, 10 December 1982, entered into force 16 November 1994, Art 63(1), 1833 UNTS 397.

36 *See* Chapter Five, section 3.4.5.

37 Convention for the Halibut Fishery of the Northern Pacific Ocean and Bering Sea, Ottawa, 2 March 1953, entered into force 28 October 1953, CTS 1953/14, 5 UST 5, TIAS 2900, 222 UNTS 77, as amended by Preservation of Halibut Fishery Protocol, Washington, 29 March 1979, entered into force 15 October 1980, CTS 1980/44, 32 UST 2483, TIAS 9855.

38 Treaty on Pacific Coast Albacore Tuna, Washington, 26 May 1981, entered into force 29 July 1981, CTS 1981/19, 33 UST 615, TIAS 10057, 1274 UNTS 247, as amended by Agreement Amending the Treaty on Pacific Coast, notes exchanged, 21 August 2002 and 10 September 2002, entered into force 28 May 2004, CTS 2004/12.

39 Agreement on Pacific Hake/Whiting, Seattle, 21 November 2003, entered into force 25 June 2008, at <www-comm.pac.dfo-mpo.gc.ca/pages/release/bckgrnd/2003/HakeAgreement_e.htm> (accessed on 5 December 2006).

40 LOS Convention, *supra* note 35, Arts 63(2), 64(1).

exists: the Northwest Atlantic Fisheries Organization (NAFO);[41] the North Atlantic Salmon Conservation Organization (NASCO);[42] the International Commission for the Conservation of Atlantic Tunas (ICCAT);[43] and, albeit a different type of arrangement, the North Pacific Anadromous Fish Stocks Convention.[44] All of these treaties have State parties in addition to Canada and the United States. Finally, there are a number of international fisheries management agreements to which both or either Canada and the United States are party that do not involve neighborhood waters or raise neighborhood issues. An example is the Western and Central Pacific Fisheries Commission (WCPFC) that addresses primarily tuna in the South Pacific.[45]

A fourth set of issues created by modern international ocean law and 200-nautical-mile zones are those specific to Pacific salmon. The issues between Canada and the United States as regards Pacific salmon are not just cooperative management issues about one State overharvesting salmon to the detriment of the other State. There are particular aspects of the salmon provisions in the LOS Convention[46] that create expectations and tensions between a State from whose rivers salmon originate (State-of-origin) and the State in whose 200-nautical-mile zone the salmon may be. It is tension over the interpretation and application of international ocean law that has been at the heart of the Canada-U.S. Pacific salmon dispute. Calm has existed over the last decade, however, as a result of the

41 NAFO is established by the Convention on the Future Multilateral Cooperation in the Northwest Atlantic Fisheries, Ottawa, 24 October 1978, entered into force 1 January 1979, CTS 1979/11.

42 The NASCO was created by the Convention for the Conservation of Salmon in the North Atlantic Ocean, Reykjavik, 2 March 1982, entered into force 1 October 1983, CTS 1983/11, TIAS 10789.

43 The ICCAT was created by the International Convention for Conservation of Atlantic Tunas, Rio de Janeiro, 14 May 1966, entered into force 21 March 1969, 673 UNTS 63.

44 Convention for the Conservation of Anadromous Stocks in the North Pacific Ocean, Moscow, 11 February 1992, entered into force 16 February 1993, CTS 1993/16. The Convention creates the North Pacific Anadromous Fish Commission (NPAFC). *See* Chapter Seven, section 2.4.

45 The WCPFC was established by the Convention on the Conservation and Management of Highly Migratory Fish Stocks in the Western and Central Pacific Ocean, Honolulu, 5 September 2000, entered into force 19 June 2004, 40 ILM 278.

46 LOS Convention, *supra* note 35, Art 66.

1999 Agreement[47] on management and allocation measures completed under the umbrella 1985 Canada-U.S. Pacific Salmon Treaty.[48]

This chapter will first look at Pacific salmon since this has had the highest profile of the recent Canada-U.S. international fisheries disputes. There are two other aspects of the Pacific salmon story that will also be discussed, namely the North Pacific Anadromous Fish Stocks Convention[49] and the 2002 Canada - U.S. Yukon River Salmon Agreement.[50] The West Coast bilateral management agreements for halibut, albacore tuna, and hake/whiting will then be addressed. The nascent Canada-United States bilateral arrangements of specific stocks on the East Coast have been discussed earlier.[51] Although NAFO and the fisheries resources beyond 200 nautical miles adjacent to Atlantic Canada have been a high priority for Canada, this is primarily a matter between Canada and the European Union and not one involving the United States, with the result that it will not been discussed herein.[52] Neither ICCAT nor NASCO have created significant neighborhood issues for Canada and the United States in recent years and, therefore, will also not be discussed herein.

---

47 Exchange of Notes relating to the Pacific Salmon Treaty, Washington, 30 June 1999, entered into force 30 June 1999, CTS 1999/58, Pacific Salmon Commission (PSC), 1999/2000 Fifteenth Annual Report, 111–114, 120–169. The Exchange of Notes references five attachments (A-E):

- Attachment A–New Annex IV of the Pacific Salmon Treaty which has six chapters;
- Attachment B–Management of Northern Boundary Coho;
- Attachment C–Northern Boundary and Transboundary Rivers Restoration and Enhancement Fund and Southern Boundary Restoration and Enhancement Fund;
- Attachment D–Renewed Cooperation on Scientific and Institutional Matters; and
- Attachment E–Habitat and Restoration.

48 Pacific Salmon Treaty, Ottawa, 28 January 1985, entered into force 18 March 1985, CTS 1985/7, TIAS 11091, 1469 UNTS 357.

49 Anadromous Fish Stocks Convention, *supra* note 44.

50 Exchange of Notes under the Pacific Salmon Treaty (Yukon River Agreement), Washington, 4 December 2002, entered into force 4 December 2002, CTS 2002/27, PSC, 2002/2003 Eighteenth Annual Report, 157–167. The Exchange of Notes has three attachments (A-C):

Attachment A–Amendment to Annex I of the Pacific Salmon Treaty;
Attachment B–Amendment to Annex IV of the Pacific Salmon Treaty; and
Attachment C–Restoration and Enhancement Fund.

51 *See* Chapter Five, section 3.4.5.

52 *See generally* Report of the Advisory Panel on Straddling Stocks, *Breaking New Ground: An Action Plan for Rebuilding The Grand Banks Fisheries* (June 2005). *See also* Chapter Two, section 2.4, footnotes 47 and 48.

2.0 Pacific Salmon

2.1 Introduction[53]

The five species of Pacific salmon found along the West Coast of North America are anadromous,[54] beginning life in freshwater rivers or lakes, migrating to the ocean where they feed and mature before returning to their freshwater places of origin. Some salmon from Canadian rivers pass through Alaskan waters on their homeward journey and some salmon from rivers in Washington and Oregon are found in Canadian waters for substantial parts of their oceanic life. Because of these migratory patterns, salmon originating from Canadian rivers may be caught or "intercepted" by fishers in Alaskan waters, and the salmon originating from Washington and Oregon rivers may be caught or "intercepted" by fishers in Canadian waters. This life-cycle poses particular problems for management and international relations. It also results in both Canada and the United States having a special economic-social relationship with the Pacific salmon originating in their rivers and concerns about Pacific salmon from their home rivers being intercepted in the ocean.

In 1930, after years of discussion, the two States concluded the Fraser River Salmon Agreement, which established the International Pacific Salmon Fisheries Commission to manage Fraser River (British Columbia) sockeye salmon.[55] The United States delayed ratification such that the Convention only came into effect in 1937 and the first management measures were adopted only in 1946.[56] The basis of the Agreement was a 50-50 sharing of the sockeye salmon from the Fraser River harvested within the Convention area which included the Fraser River, Juan de Fuca Strait, Strait of Georgia, and Puget Sound. In 1957, pink salmon were included in the sharing and

---

53 Parts of this section are drawn, with modification, from T. L. McDorman, *A Canadian View of the Canada-U.S. Pacific Salmon Treaty: The International Legal Context* (1998) 6 WILLAMETTE J INTL L AND DISPUTE RESOLUTION 79, 80–82 and J. Bond and T. L. McDorman, Canada's Pacific Fisheries Agreements: Halibut, Hake, Tuna and Salmon Outside 200 (manuscript, 2007).

54 The five species are sockeye; chinook; coho; pink; and chum.

55 Fraser River Salmon Agreement, *supra* note 20. *See* M. P. SHEPARD AND A.W. ARGUE, THE 1985 PACIFIC SALMON TREATY: SHARING CONSERVATION BURDENS AND BENEFITS (University of British Columbia Press, Vancouver 2005) 17–21.

56 Shepard and Argue, *supra* note 55, at 18–19.

management apparatus of the 1930 Agreement.[57] Through the 1950s and 1960s, Canada and the United States also attempted to address salmon harvesting outside the Fraser River Convention area.[58]

The Canada and United States special attachment to Pacific salmon manifested itself internationally in the 1952 tripartite North Pacific Fisheries Convention[59] with Japan, which had as its primary purpose the curbing of Japanese fishing of Canada-U.S. -origin Pacific salmon on the high seas.[60] As part of the 1952 Agreement, Japan agreed to abstain from fishing halibut, herring, and salmon in specified areas of the high seas.[61] The abstention principle was: "The most important, and most controversial, feature of the [1952] Convention... [and]... – the first of its kind in the international law of fisheries."[62] Johnston has written that: "The important effect of the Convention... [was]... that Japan... [was]... bound not to exploit the regulated halibut and salmon fisheries on the high seas which... [were]... covered by bilateral treaty..."[63] In 1951, a provisional abstention line was set at approximately 175 degrees west that, while subject to review by the North Pacific Fisheries Commission, remained unaltered.[64] Subsequent amendments to the North Pacific Fisheries Convention and memoranda of understanding resulted in

---

57 Protocol to the Fraser River Salmon Agreement, Ottawa, 28 December 1956, entered into force 3 July 1957, CTS 1957/21, 8 UST 1057, TIAS No. 3867, 290 UNTS 103. *See* Shepard and Argue, *supra* note 55, at 25–28.

58 *See* Shepard and Argue, *supra* note 55, at 28–37.

59 Convention for the High Seas Fisheries of the North Pacific Ocean, Tokyo, 9 May 1952, entered into force 12 June 1953, 205 UNTS 65.

60 For a detailed expose on the background and negotiation of the North Pacific Fisheries Convention, *see* H. N. Scheiber, *Japan, the North Atlantic Triangle, and the Pacific Fisheries: A Perspective on the Origins of Modern Ocean Law, 1930–1953* (2004) 6 San Diego Intl LJ 27, 87–108. *See also* Johnston, *supra* note 2, at 274–275 and Shepard and Argue, *supra* note 55, at 21–25.

61 North Pacific Fisheries Convention, *supra* note 59, Annex, sections I and II. *See* the detailed explanation in Johnston, *supra* note 2, at 275–277. Canada was also subject to the abstention principle as regards salmon harvesting in the high seas area adjacent to Alaska.

62 Johnston, *supra* note 2, at 275 and see 289–297. For a modern view of the abstention principle, *see* Y. Tsuru, *Rethinking the Principle of Abstention: the North Pacific and Beyond* (2004) 28 Mar Pol 541–552.

63 Johnston, *supra* note 2, at 277. The halibut fishery was governed by the 1953 Halibut Convention, *supra* note 37. As regards salmon, there was the 1930 Fraser River Salmon Agreement, *supra* note 20.

64 Burke, *supra* note 17, at 157.

a continuous phasing out of Japanese harvesting of North American origin salmon stocks on the high seas.[65]

Canada and the United States vigorously championed the exceptional status of Pacific salmon (an anadromous species) during the negotiation of the 1982 U.N. Convention on the Law of the Sea (LOS Convention)[66] and succeeded in having Article 66 included in the Treaty. Article 66 sets out that: "States in whose rivers anadromous stocks originate shall have the primary interest in and responsibility for such stocks."[67] This is the State-of-origin principle and is intended to provide the State-of-origin with unique rights and responsibilities regarding salmon from its rivers.

Article 66 distinguishes two situations regarding the realization of the unique rights and responsibilities of the State-of-origin: first, where salmon migrate beyond national jurisdiction to the high seas; second, where salmon migrate into the waters of a neighboring State. In the first case, Article 66 tracks the abstention principle of the 1952 North Pacific Fisheries Convention by providing that no targeted fishing for these anadromous stocks is to take place beyond 200-nautical-mile zones.[68] This prohibition was subject to exceptions in the case of economic dislocation,[69] which was designed to allow for a phasing-out period to accommodate what remained of Japan's high seas salmon fishery.[70] However, enforcement by the State-of-origin on the high seas was only to take place if States agreed.[71] The Article 66 high seas salmon fisheries regulatory regime was based on a suppression of the rights of the high seas fishing States in favor of the rights of the salmon-origin States.[72]

---

65 *See* K. Bryan, *Swimming Upstream: Trying to Enforce the 1992 North Pacific Salmon Treaty* (1995) 28 Cornell Intl LJ 241, 246.

66 *See* Working Paper on the Special Case of Salmon–The Most Important Anadromous Species, U. N. Doc A/Conf.62/C.2/L.81, 23 August 1974, in UNCLOS III, Official Records, Vol. III, 240 and Special Considerations Regarding the Management of Anadromous Species and Highly Migratory Oceanic Fishes: Working Paper Submitted by the United States, U. N. Doc A/AC.138/SC.II/L.20, 2 April 1973. *See also* Chapter Four, section 2.1.1.

67 LOS Convention, *supra* note 35, Art 66(1).

68 *Id.* Art 66(3)(a).

69 *Id.* Art 66(3)(b).

70 Burke, *supra* note 17, at 169.

71 LOS Convention, *supra* note 35, Art 66(3)(d).

72 *See generally* Burke, *supra* note 17, at 166–172.

In the case of the migration of salmon into the waters of a neighboring State, the relevant LOS Convention provisions are:

- Article 66(2), which allows a State-of-origin, after consulting with the neighboring State, to establish total allowable catches (TACs) for salmon originating in its rivers, but this does not carry with it the authority to either prescribe or enforce the TAC in the neighboring State's waters;[73] and
- Article 66(4), which provides that the neighboring State "shall co-operate with the State of origin with regard to the conservation and management of such stocks."

Note must also be made of Article 56(1)(a), which provides that a coastal State has, within its 200-nautical-mile exclusive economic zone (EEZ), "sovereign rights for the purposes of exploring and exploiting, conserving and managing the natural resources, whether living or non-living. . .". Article 56(2) directs that, in exercising rights in the EEZ, States are to "have due regard to the rights and duties of other States." There is a tension between Article 56, which gives exclusive national authority over marine living resources within the 200-nautical-mile zone; and Article 66(1), which gives to the State-of-origin "primary interest and responsibility for" salmon stocks.[74]

2.2 The 1985 Canada—U.S. Pacific Salmon Treaty

2.2.1 Conclusion and Content[75]

In 1971, Canada and the United States commenced formal discussions to revise the 1930 Convention regime for Pacific salmon management.[76] Both countries, having endorsed the State-of-origin principle and the

73 *Id.* 187.

74 For a detailed legal analysis of this tension, *see* McDorman, *A Canadian View*, *supra* note 53, at 81–86, where it is concluded at 85 that: "pursuant to the Law of the Sea Convention, once salmon have left the waters of the state of origin and entered the waters of a neighboring state, that neighboring state can treat the salmon as its own."

75 Parts of this section are drawn, with modification, from McDorman, *A Canadian View*, *supra* note 53, at 87–93.

76 Shepard and Argue, *supra* note 55, at 60 and see at 58–60 regarding the discussions held in the 1960s.

requirement for cooperation in the LOS Convention and elsewhere, sought to implement these approaches. As a result, both countries accepted that the State-of-origin should be able to harvest salmon from its rivers and that the other State should seek to avoid interceptions. However, given that it would be difficult to eliminate all interceptions, it was accepted that there should be an equitable balance of the interceptions of the two countries.[77] The outcome of the bilateral negotiations[78] was the 1985 Pacific Salmon Treaty.[79] The mechanism for cooperation established by the Treaty was the Pacific Salmon Commission.[80] The Commission, composed of an American and a Canadian section with each having four commissioners, was to adopt by consensus quotas and other limitations for the salmon stocks covered by the Treaty. The quotas and other limitations agreed upon by the Commission were to be recommended to the two States, which were to implement them into national law.[81] The Commission was not designed to be nor has it operated as an institution independent from the governments of the two countries.[82]

Annex IV to the Pacific Salmon Treaty outlined management and harvesting arrangements for specific stocks and fisheries to cover the first years of the Treaty regime.[83] The Treaty provided that the Commission was to agree on new arrangements relying on the "principles" set out in the Treaty regarding how the two States were to "conduct its fisheries"[84] and the direction to States on what must be taken into account in fulfilling these principles.[85]

One analysis has concluded that both Canada and the United States achieved their principal objectives in the negotiations. For Canada, this

---

77 *Id.* 60–64.

78 Regarding the negotiations, *see id.* 60–76 and T. C. Jensen, *The United States - Canada Pacific Salmon Interception Treaty: An Historical and Legal Overview* (1986) 16 ENVIRONMENTAL L 363, 373–374.

79 Pacific Salmon Treaty, *supra* note 48.

80 *Id.* Art II. *See* Shepard and Argue, *supra* note 55, at 88–93.

81 *Id.* Art IV(5), (6), (7).

82 Jensen, *supra* note 78, at 401 comments: "[T]he purpose of the Commission is to represent the governments of the United States and Canada in the implementation of the Treaty."

83 Pacific Salmon Treaty, *supra* note 48, Annex IV.
Annex IV contained six chapters respecting: Transboundary Rivers; Northern British Columbia and Southeastern Alaska; Chinook Salmon; Fraser River Sockeye and Pink Salmon; Coho Salmon; and Southern British Columbia—Washington Chum Fisheries. On the specific chapters, *see* Shepard and Argue, *supra* note 55, at 131–137, 147–148, 167–170, 182–183, 189–192, 195.

84 *Id.* Art III(1).

85 *Id.* Art III(3).

involved ending the 1930 Salmon Treaty and thus "regaining control over decisions on conservation, management, and enhancement for the harvest of sockeye and pink salmon" from the Fraser River.[86] For the United States, this involved the attainment of "cooperative management arrangements for limitation of coastwide fisheries in chinook salmon;" limitations on Alaskan interception of Canadian State-of-origin salmon that "were relatively modest;" and the lack of "specific measures to reduce interception fisheries to meet catch sharing (equity) goals."[87]

The heart of the 1985 Treaty is Article III. Article III(1) states that:

> [E]ach Party shall conduct its fisheries . . . so as to:
>
> (a) prevent overfishing and provide for optimum production; and
>
> (b) provide for each Party to receive benefits equivalent to the production of salmon originating in its waters.

Article III(1)(a) is the conservation element of the Pacific Salmon Treaty[88] and is directly related to Article 66(4) of the LOS Convention, which requires cooperation on conservation and management measures.

Article III(1)(b) is referred to as the equity element of the Pacific Salmon Treaty and was the most controversial provision, reportedly having been "consistently opposed" by the United States.[89] Shepard and Argue have taken the view that the equity element in the Treaty arose from the acceptance by Canada and the United States that the State-of-origin had a proprietary interest in its salmon in the waters of the neighboring State that had to be taken into account by the neighboring State.[90] Burke commented that the equity element was "a functional device allowing for the recognition of the dominant position of the State of origin."[91] Jensen summarized that:

> Equity is basically a pragmatic reformulation of the countries' state-of-origin principle for harvest of anadromous fish. In international forums, both countries argued that salmon should only be harvested by

---

86 Shepard and Argue, *supra* note 55, at 198.

87 *Id.* 199.

88 *See id.* 94–96.

89 J. A. Yanagida, *The Pacific Salmon Treaty* (1987) 81 AJIL 577, 588.

90 M. P. Shepard and A. W. Argue, *Ocean Pasturage in the Pacific Salmon Treaty: Fact or Fiction?* (Canadian Industry Report of Fisheries and Aquatic Sciences No. 242, Ottawa February 1998) 8–11, 33–37.

91 Burke, *supra* note 17, at 183.

the country producing the fish. Since Canadian and United States fishers could not, without massive economic disruption, be restructured to eliminate interceptions, the countries devised a principle that theoretically achieves the same effect as the state-of-origin principle. The countries may not get all their own fish back under the equity principle, but both countries will receive benefits commensurate with their production.[92]

The equity element of the Pacific Salmon Treaty was not based directly on any obligation created by Article 66 of the LOS Convention. The equity provision was intended to and does change the balance between the sovereign rights of the neighboring State (as established in Article 56(1)(a) of the LOS Convention) and the primary interest of the State-of-origin (Article 66(1) of the LOS Convention) to favor the State-of-origin. In operational terms, the equity provision does not explicitly prohibit a neighboring State harvesting foreign salmon. Rather, the provision requires there to be a balancing of harvesting and other measures to provide each country with the economic benefits of having been the State-of-origin. Put another way, no legally enforceable ownership right in the salmon that enters a neighboring State waters has been created; rather, the equity provision in the Pacific Salmon Treaty creates a notional ownership right that provides to the State-of-origin a right to "benefits equivalent" to the salmon intercepted.

The equity provision was included in the Pacific Salmon Treaty either because of Canadian insistence (over U.S. objections)[93] or because the equity element was consistent with the long-held position of both the United States and Canada that "salmon should only be harvested by the country producing the fish."[94]

The equity element of the Pacific Salmon Treaty is qualified by the Memorandum of Understanding attached to the Treaty. The Memorandum of Understanding notes that:

> [I]t is anticipated that it will be some time before the Commission can develop programs to implement the provisions of Article III, paragraph 1(b)

92 Jensen, *supra* note 78, at 400.

93 Yanagida, *supra* note 89, at 588. *See also* G. R. Munro and R. L. Stokes, *The Canada—United States Pacific Salmon Treaty*, in D. McRae and G. Munro (eds.) Canadian Oceans Policy: National Strategies and the New Law of the Sea (University of British Columbia Press, Vancouver 1989) 24.

94 Jensen, *supra* note 78, at 400 and Shepard and Argue, *Ocean Pasturage*, *supra* note 90, at 8–10, 34–37.

> in a complete and comprehensive manner. Nevertheless, . . . , the Commission shall ensure that the annual fishery regimes . . . are developed in an equitable manner taking into account the principle outlined in Article III(1)(b).[95]

Thus, the 1985 Treaty left the issue of the operational application of the equity element to be determined by future negotiations. Postponement of full determination and implementation of the equity provision was necessary to secure acceptance of the Treaty.[96]

It is clear that Article III(1)(b) does not necessarily involve a direct fish-for-fish (interception-for-interception) tradeoff since the terminology is that the State-of-origin is to receive "benefits equivalent" to the salmon from its rivers.[97] Canada's view, however, was that the balance in interceptions could be achieved principally through changing fishing patterns.[98] The United States was more willing to consider cash or material contributions to enhancement as means of addressing benefits.[99] Despite the interpretative uncertainties of the "benefits equivalent" wording, in 1985, the hope was that salmon stock abundances would increase such that implementation of Article III(1)(b) would be feasible.[100]

Irrespective of the precision that might be applied to the "benefits equivalent" calculation in the future, central to the working of the Pacific Salmon Treaty was the understanding that U.S. interceptions of Fraser River sockeye (and salmon from other Canadian rivers), mostly by Alaskans, would be matched by Canadian interceptions of coho and chinook originating from U.S. rivers in Washington and Oregon.[101] In 1985, Canada was of the view that there existed "a rough, albeit imperfect, balance" of interceptions.[102]

---

95 Pacific Salmon Treaty, *supra* note 48, Memorandum of Understanding, Part A, para 2.

96 Note Munro and Stokes, *supra* note 93, at 25 and Shepard and Argue, *supra* note 55, at 114.

97 Munro and Stokes, *supra* note 93, at 24 notes that both the United States and Canada understood that "benefits" was to be interpreted as the economic benefits associated with the produced salmon.

98 Shepard and Argue, *supra* note 55, at 117.

99 *Id.*

100 *Id.*

101 Munro and Stokes, *supra* note 93, at 30.

102 G. Munro, T. McDorman, and R. McKelvey, *Transboundary Fishery Resources and the Canada-U.S. Pacific Salmon Treaty* (February 1998), Canadian-American Public Policy (Occasional Paper number 33) 25.

Although the measurement of interceptions is not easily accomplished,[103] the Memorandum of Understanding appears to indicate that unbalanced interceptions or benefits "would be expected" to be corrected by a "phased program to eliminate the inequity."[104]

Also causing uncertainty regarding the application and implementation of the conservation and equity provisions of Article III(1) were the contents of Article III(3) which state that:

> In fulfilling their obligations pursuant to paragraph (1), the parties shall take into account:
>
> (a) the desirability in most cases of reducing interceptions;
> (b) the desirability in most cases of avoiding undue disruption of existing fisheries; and
> (c) annual variations in abundances of the stocks.

There is friction between (1) reducing interceptions and (2) undue disruption of existing fisheries, with the United States placing particular importance on the "avoiding disruption of existing fisheries" wording.[105] This friction is neatly explained as follows:

> Fishers who feel they aren't getting enough fish and want to increase their allocation . . . invoke "equity" as a debating point. Intercepting fishers counter that the treaty also prohibits "undue disruption" of existing fisheries, and therefore, their allocation should not be altered.[106]

Yanagida takes the view that the Treaty expressly requires the parties to "weigh the benefits of reducing interceptions against the costs of economic

---

103 Note D. D. Huppert, *U.S./Canada Salmon Wars: Why the Pacific Salmon Treaty Has Not Brought Peace* (January 1996), New Directions in Marine Affairs, Report No. 1 (School of Marine Affairs, University of Washington, Seattle).

104 Pacific Salmon Treaty, *supra* note 48, Memorandum of Understanding, Part A, para 3:

> In the longer term, if it is determined that one country or the other is deriving substantially greater benefits than those provided from its rivers, it would be expected that the Parties would develop a phased program to eliminate the inequity within a specified time period, taking into account the provisions of Article III, paragraph 3.

105 Shepard and Argue, *supra* note 55, at 115.

106 M. Twitchell, *Implementing the U.S.-Canada Pacific Salmon Treaty: The Struggle to Move from "Fish Wars" to Cooperative Fishery Management* (1989) 20 ODIL 409, 419.

dislocation" and that this undermines the equity element in Article III(1)(b) and qualifies the conservation element in Article III(1)(a).[107]

2.2.2 The 1990s—Renegotiation and Conflict[108]

Serious problems with the Pacific Salmon Treaty were voiced by Canada in 1992 when the various Annex IV management and harvesting arrangements were about to expire and renegotiation was necessary. Canada believed that U.S. interceptions of Canadian salmon had increased dramatically during the late 1980s, while Canadian interception of U.S. salmon had significantly declined due to the weak coho and chinook runs from the northwestern United States. According to Canada, data from the Pacific Salmon Commission revealed that U.S. interceptions had increased from 6 million to 9 million salmon between 1985 to 1992, while Canadian interceptions had decreased from 5 million to 3.5 million salmon.[109] The perceived imbalance was symptomatic of the overall imbalance that Canada felt was taking place under the 1985 Pacific Salmon Treaty.[110] Nevertheless, Washington and Oregon fishers were demanding greater access to plentiful Fraser River salmon and Alaskan fishers were expecting to increase interception of Canadian-origin salmon. Meanwhile, Canada was being pressured to help conserve the weak U.S. chinook and coho salmon runs, thus removing any possibility of balancing interceptions.[111] The Pacific Salmon Treaty was clearly collapsing.[112]

A bedevilment throughout the 1990s was the conflicting interests of Washington, Oregon, and Alaska. Alaska relied on interceptions of

---

107 Yanagida, *supra* note 89, at 591.

108 Parts of this section are drawn, with modification, from McDorman, *A Canadian View*, *supra* note 53, at 96 and T. L. McDorman, *The West Coast Salmon Dispute: A Canadian View of the Breakdown of the 1985 Treaty and the Transit License Measure* (1995) 17 LOYOLA OF LOS ANGELES INTL AND COMPARATIVE LJ 477, 491–492, 494.

A detailed and colorful review of the events of the 1990s from a British Columbia perspective is provided by D. BROWN, SALMON WARS: THE BATTLE FOR THE WEST COAST FISHERY (Harbour Publishing, Vancouver 2005).

109 DFO, Backgrounder, April 1994 and Department of Fisheries and Oceans, Licence Fee Announced for U.S. Vessels, 9 June 1994.

110 Canada, Statement, 3 December 1992, in PSC, 1992/1993 Eighth Annual Report, 8–9.

111 United States, Statement, 3 December 1992, in *id.* 10, 12–14.

112 Brown, *supra* note 108, at 49 refers to the Pacific Salmon Treaty in 1992 as being in a "shambles and the Canadian government vowing to demand repayment of the [U.S.] unauthorized catch."

Canadian-origin salmon within Alaskan waters and saw no need to reduce this effort and little to gain by doing so. Washington and Oregon worried about the recovery of endangered stocks (chinook and coho) and hoped to restrain Canadian interception of these stocks, while at the same time hoping for a larger share of Fraser River stocks.[113] This division of interest was entrenched in the U.S. legislation implementing the Pacific Salmon Treaty, where the four U.S. commissioners on the Commission were to be: an official of the U.S. Government, who is non-voting; a resident of Alaska appointed from a list of nominees established by the Governor of Alaska; a resident of Oregon or Washington appointed from a list of nominees established by the Governors of Oregon and Washington; and an individual appointed from a list of nominees established by the Native American tribes of Idaho, Washington, and Oregon.[114] The legislation also provided that decisions of the U.S. section were to be taken "when there is no dissenting vote."[115]

The legal dispute between Canada and the United States centered on differing views of Article III of the Pacific Salmon Treaty. The Canadian view was that Article III(b) created a legal entitlement for Canada to receive the benefits from the salmon that originated from its rivers and that this had to be accomplished primarily by a reduction of U.S. interceptions.[116] The United States took the view that the balance of interceptions wording in Article III was to be interpreted and applied taking into account, not only the goal of resource conservation, but also the other wording of Article III such as III(3)(b), the avoidance of undue disruption of existing fisheries, and III(3)(a), the desirability of reducing interceptions. In addition, it was the U.S. view that there was no agreed method to measure interception imbalances, such that the balance of interceptions wording in Article III did not have the primacy ascribed to it by Canada.[117]

---

113 *See* Yanagida, *supra* note 89, at 579–588 and Jensen, *supra* note 78, at 384–395.

114 Pacific Salmon Treaty Act of 1985, 99 US Stat. 7, Pub L. 99–5, codified at 16 USC 3631–3644, s 3632(a).

115 *Id.* 16 USC s 3632 (g)(1). The devolution of authority from the U.S. federal government to the local participants, particularly Alaska, was the price paid to obtain domestic support for the Pacific Salmon Treaty. *See* T. Stevens, *United States-Canada Salmon Treaty Negotiations: The Alaskan Perspective* (1986) 16 ENVIRONMENTAL L 423, 429.

For a detailed review of this aspect of the U.S. legislation, *see* E. H. Buck, *The Pacific Salmon Treaty: The 1999 Agreement and Renegotiation of Annex IV*, 30 March 2007 (Congressional Research Service, RL30234) 11–13.

116 D. McRae, *The Negotiation of the 1999 Pacific Salmon Agreement* (2001) 27 CANADA-UNITED STATES LJ 267, 267. *See* Statement of 3 December 1992, *supra* note 110, at 5–6.

117 McRae, *supra* note 116, at 267–268. The U.S. position is noted in D. W. Strangway and

Against this background, the negotiation of new management and harvesting annexes to the Pacific Salmon Treaty was going to be difficult. In 1993, a one-year agreement for Fraser River salmon was concluded.[118] An integral part of the 1993 deal was acceptance that Canada and the United States would negotiate the meaning and implementation of the equity concept detached from the technical negotiations on fisheries arrangements and catch limits.[119] However, in January 1994, Canada postponed scheduled negotiations, citing a lack of U.S. proposals on the equity issue.[120] Efforts to establish 1994 management arrangements under the Pacific Salmon Treaty failed and, in May 1994, Canada broke off negotiations, citing frustration with the inability of the United States to form a united position.[121] From the Canadian perspective, Alaskan fishers were continuing to intercept unacceptable amounts of Canadian-origin salmon.

One measure adopted by Canada, in June 1994, was to require all U.S. commercial fishing vessels utilizing selected "inside water passages" along the British Columbia coast to purchase a license from Canada.[122] Enforcement of the licensing requirement was discontinued soon after it was introduced

---

W. D. Ruckelshaus, *Pacific Salmon: Report to the Prime Minister of Canada and the President of the United States, Fisheries and Oceans Canada,* 12 January 1998, 4, at www.dfo-mpo.gc.ca/communic/reports/pst-tsp/report-rapport_e.htm (accessed on 25 July 2007). *See* U.S. negotiator James Pipkin, *The Stumbling Block in the Salmon Dispute,* Toronto Globe and Mail, 10 November 1997, A-21. *See also* Statement of 3 December 1992, *supra* note 111, at 16 where the United States recognized Canada's high priority on equity but contended that "a numerically simplistic ('bean counting') economic evaluation of production and benefits is not the best way to proceed."

118 PSC, *Letter of Transmittal to Governments Regarding Fishery Regimes for 1993,* 1992/1993 Eighth Annual Report, 127–128.

119 DFO, Canada-U.S. Agreement Reached on Pacific Salmon Harvest, 24 June 1993. *See also* Brown, *supra* note 108, at 52.

120 DFO, Canada Cancels Pacific Salmon Treaty (PST) Negotiations, 20 January 1994.

121 *See* Brown, *supra* note 108, at 55–56.

122 DFO, Licence Fee Announced for U.S. Vessels, 9 June 1994.

What Canada did was remove an exemption for U.S. fishing vessels that existed in Canadian law. *See* Coastal Fisheries Protection Regulations, amendment, Can Gaz Part II, Vol. 128, SOR/94-444, 14 June 1985, 2575–2578, which removed the exemption in Coastal Fisheries Protection Regulations, amendment, Can Gaz Part II, Vol. 119, SOR/85-527, 6 June 1985, 2719–2729, s 13.

See generally McDorman, *Breakdown of the 1985 Treaty, supra* note 108, at 477–478, 495–505 and C. B. Picker, *Fishing for Answers in Canada's Inside Passage: Exploring the Use of the Transit Fee as a Countermeasure* (1996) 21 YALE J INTL L 349, 359–366. *See also* Chapter Six, section 6.0.

in light of both the furious negative reaction in the United States and the intervention into the dispute by Vice President Al Gore.[123]

One Commentator has noted that: "In the years following 1992, a unstated assumption of both parties–that they both abide by conservation measures–allowed the two countries to manage their fisheries."[124] Consistent with this, interim agreements were reached in 1995,[125] 1996,[126] and 1998[127] that placed some limitations on the Fraser River sockeye that could be intercepted by U.S. fishers. Also in 1998, Washington state accepted modest limits on the capture by its fishers of coho salmon bound for the Upper Thompson River in British Columbia.[128] As a general matter, however, Canada and the United States remained deadlocked on the extent of limitations, if any, that were necessary on Alaskan fishers; whether and how interception balance, however it was defined, was to be re-established; and what was meant by "benefits equivalent" and, if determined, how it was to be implemented in a practical manner.

In 1995 to 1996, the two sides agreed on a mediator, Christopher Beebe from New Zealand, to assist regarding the "benefits equivalent" discord.[129] However, he withdrew, seeing no hope for progress since, in the words of U.S. negotiator James Pipkin, "the two countries were simply too far apart."[130] In 1997, a stakeholder process was attempted and two special envoys, one from each country, were appointed to investigate means to resolve the Pacific salmon controversy.[131] Also in 1997 was the blockade of an Alaskan ferry in

123 *See* McDorman, *Breakdown of the 1985 Treaty*, *supra* note 108, at 478, 496.

124 Buck, *supra* note 115, at 2.

125 PSC, *Letter of Transmittal to Governments Regarding Fishery Regimes for 1995*, 1995/96 Eleventh Annual Report, 91–95.

126 PSC, *Letter of Transmittal to Governments Regarding Fishery Regimes for 1996*, 1996/97 Twelfth Annual Report, 97–99.

127 PSC, *Letter of Transmittal to Governments Regarding Fishery Regimes for 1998*, 1998/99 Fourteenth Annual Report, 97–98.

128 DFO, Agreement Reached on Southern Coho and Chinook, 26 June 1998.

129 Agreement on the Establishment of a Mediation Procedure regarding the Pacific Salmon Treaty, Montreal, 11 September 1995, entered into force 11 September 1995, CTS 1995/13, TIAS 12689, 2029 UNTS 307.

130 U.S. Pacific salmon negotiator James Pipkin, testimony before the U.S. House of Representatives Committee on Resources, 12 September 1997, as cited in Brown, *supra* note 108, at 218. Brown, at 218, indicates that Pipkin "flatly rejected" the mediator's proposal and, at 154, states that Pipkin "spurned . . . [the mediator's] . . . proposal . . . calling it a rehash of the Canadian 'theology' on equity."

131 *See* Brown, *supra* note 108, at 159–163, 217–219 and Buck, *supra* note 115, at 9–10.

Prince Rupert, British Columbia, by Canadian fishers, with television cameras capturing and subsequently replaying, throughout North America and the world, the burning of a U.S. flag.[132] In early 1998, the envoys reported that the stakeholder process was a dead-end and that it was up to the two governments to resolve the dispute.[133]

2.2.3 The 1999 Agreement[134]

In June 1999, Canada and the United States reached an agreement that provided a multi-year resolution of the Pacific salmon dispute.[135] The 1999 Agreement did not supersede or replace the 1985 Pacific Salmon Treaty. The 1999 Agreement contains new management arrangements that replaced the expired Annex IV to the 1985 Treaty with a new Annex IV.[136] The 1999 Agreement also contained provisions that created several new obligations for Canada and the United States regarding Pacific salmon.[137]

What made attainment of the 1999 Agreement possible was that Canada and the United States both accepted the importance of conservation and

---

132 Brown, *supra* note 108, at 176–195 relates the story of the blockade and at 190–191 details the flag-burning incident, noting that the individual involved was a dual Canadian-U.S. citizen who almost immediately apologized for the action. At 191, Brown comments that: "The issue of overfishing was buried in the fulminations of US politicians and the groveling apologies of Canadian diplomats."

133 Strangway and Ruckelshaus, *Pacific Salmon: Report*, *supra* note 117. The recommendations of the Strangway-Ruckelshaus Report are in PSC, 1997/1998 Thirteenth Annual Report, 91–92.

134 Parts of this section are drawn, with modification, from T. L. McDorman, *A Canadian View of the 1999 Canada-U.S. Pacific Salmon Agreement: A Positive Turning Point?* (1998) 6 WILLAMETTE J INTL L AND DISPUTE RESOLUTION 99, 104–105.

135 The 1999 Pacific Salmon Agreement, *supra* note 47.
See generally regarding the 1999 Agreement Buck, *supra* note 115, at 13–20; McDorman, *A Canadian View of the 1999 Agreement*, *supra* note 134; and T. L. McDorman, *The 1999 Canada-U.S. Pacific Salmon Agreement: Resolved and Unresolved Issues* (2000) 15 J ENVIRONMENTAL L AND LITIGATION 1–20.

136 The 1999 Pacific Salmon Agreement, *supra* note 47, Attachment A, which renews Annex IV of the 1985 Treaty.

137 *Id.* Attachment C—Northern Boundary and Transboundary Rivers Restoration and Enhancement Fund and Southern Boundary Restoration and Enhancement Fund; Attachment D—Renewed Cooperation on Scientific and Institutional Matters; and Attachment E—Habitat and Restoration. These new obligations are directly tied to the 1985 Treaty such that, if the 1985 Treaty is terminated, then the new obligations in the 1999 Agreement also terminate. The 1999 Agreement, para 8.

sustainability of the Pacific salmon resources.[138] Moreover, as noted by Canada's negotiator:

> What was obvious was that in spite of notorious and difficult public battles over Pacific salmon, there was the potential for a high degree of cooperation at the technical level on both sides of the border.[139]

In Canada's case, adopting conservation as its primary negotiating objective replaced Canada's longstanding goal of attaining an equitable balance of interceptions.[140] In all of the Canadian government publicity trumpeting the completion of the 1999 Agreement no mention was made of the balance of interceptions, although much was made of the predicted reductions in U.S. taking of Canadian-origin salmon.[141] The shift in emphasis to salmon conservation was not unwarranted. Salmon stocks, such as chinook, were in serious need of protection and the only appropriate response was joint – Canada-U.S. action. In the end, the two countries decided that an agreement with the goal of placing some constraints on salmon fishing activity, irrespective of an absolute balance of interceptions, was better for the salmon stocks than no agreement at all.

The Canadian negotiator of the 1999 Agreement has noted that the Agreement "is technically complex," and "a functional arrangement" that "often . . . was drafted by scientists" and, therefore, "written for the people who have to administer it."[142] A number of key elements can be noted.

First, as already noted, the 1999 Agreement replaced the expired Annex IV of the 1985 Treaty with new chapters outlining the management of stocks

---

138 McRae, *supra* note 116, at 270–271.

139 *Id.* 272–273.

140 Buck, *supra* note 115, at 14 notes: "At the heart of the new accord was agreement between the parties to focus on conservation and habitat protection, rather than division of shared salmon stocks." *See generally* McDorman, *A Canadian View of the 1999 Agreement, supra* note 134, at 101–102.

141 DFO, Canada and US Reach A Comprehensive Agreement Under the Pacific Salmon Treaty and Announcement Highlights, 3 June 1999.
Brown, *supra* note 108, at 314 comments that:

> Throughout the process [negotiations with the United States], Canadian negotiators had been determined to minimize or reduce US interceptions, and to provide Canada with harvests or benefits equivalent to its salmonid production. Now in one fell swoop, . . . [the 1999 Agreement] dramatically set back Canada's longstanding goal of realizing "benefits equivalent to the production of salmon originating in its waters."

142 McRae, *supra* note 116, at 273.

and fisheries. The centerpiece of the new fishing arrangements was abundance-based management, described by the negotiators of the 1999 Agreement as a "new conservation-based approach."[143] The idea is that harvest rates for the various salmon stocks were to be set according to the stock's actual abundance, thus avoiding the situation that existed in Annex IV negotiated as part of the 1985 Treaty in which predetermined quantities of salmon (ceilings) could be harvested in a given year.[144] A critical part of abundance-based management was that national shares of the allowable harvest were to be determined as a percentage of or in relation to the actual abundance of the specific stock. It was hoped that with abundance-based management both States would have a sufficient incentive to conserve and enhance stocks in order to increase yields in future years.

Second, as regards the all-important Fraser River salmon, the U.S. share of Fraser River sockeye harvestable in the waters of Washington state was to drop from 22.4 percent in 1999 to 16.5 percent of the TAC in 2002 and remain at that level through the 2010 fishing season.[145] For Fraser River pink salmon, the U.S. harvest in the waters of Washington state were not to exceed 25.7 percent of the TAC.[146] Canada noted that, over the previous years, U.S. interceptions of Fraser River sockeye had been agreed upon at 24.9 and 22 percent,[147] such that the 1999 Agreement on 16.5 percent was announced as being a benefit to Canada. The U.S. interceptions of Fraser River sockeye and pink salmon in Alaskan waters were left out of the equation.

Third, in the 1999 Agreement the United States committed US$140 million for two trust funds, with the interest to be used to restore habitat, improve scientific information, and enhance wild stock production.[148]

---

143 Letter from Donald McRae, Chief Negotiator for Canada, and James Pipkin, Chief Negotiator for the United States, to the Governments of Canada and the United States, 23 June 1999, in PSC, 1999/2000 Fifteenth Annual Report, 109–110, para 7.

144 DFO, Abundance-Based Management Regime, 3 June 1999. *See* McRae, *supra* note 116, at 273–274 and Buck, *supra* note 115, at 13.

145 The 1999 Pacific Salmon Agreement, *supra* note 47, Attachment A, Annex IV, c four, para 2.

146 *Id.* para 2(e).

147 DFO, Highlights of the New Agreement–Fraser River Sockeye and Pink Salmon, 3 June 1999.

148 The 1999 Pacific Salmon Agreement, *supra* note 47, paras 3, 6 and Attachment C—Northern Boundary and Transboundary Rivers Restoration and Enhancement Fund and Southern Boundary Restoration and Enhancement Fund.

The funds are be administered by the Northern Fund Committee and the Southern Fund Committee, composed of equal representatives from each country. Though unstated in the 1999 Agreement, the U.S. financial commitment is related to redressing the imbalance in salmon interceptions that existed throughout the 1990s.[149]

Fourth, a key provision of the 1999 Agreement is paragraph nine, which directs that:

> Compliance with this Agreement shall constitute compliance by our two Governments with their obligations under Article III of the [1985] Treaty.[150]

The desired effect of this paragraph was to stop the wrangling between Canada and the United States as to whether the salmon arrangements in place as a result of the 1999 Agreement resulted in an equitable balance of interceptions.[151]

2.2.4 Post-1999 Agreement

Although the 1999 Agreement cannot be said to have solved all of the Canada-U.S. Pacific salmon problems, there is no question that where there has been disagreement and unhappiness with the new management regime, the discord has not percolated into the press or otherwise become a significant matter between the two States. On the key issue of the balance of salmon interceptions, one commentator writing in 2007 surmised that: "Both parties appear comfortable with the equity achieved under harvest regimes of the 1999 Agreement, and no particular concerns related to overharvesting have arisen."[152]

The Pacific Salmon Commission, largely dysfunctional during the 1990s, has worked well with the Canadian and U.S. sections reaching agreement on two matters directly arising under the 1999 Agreement: the Southern Coho Management Plan in 2002;[153] and rules and procedures for the technical

---

149 *See* McRae, *supra* note 116, at 275 and Buck, *supra* note 115, at 19.

150 The 1999 Pacific Salmon Agreement, *supra* note 47, para 9.

151 *See* McDorman, *A Canadian View of the 1999 Agreement*, *supra* note 134, at 110.

152 Buck, *supra* note 115, at 22.

153 PSC, *Southern Coho Management Plan*, 2001/2002 Seventeenth Annual Report, 143–153 with the notation of the adoption of the Management Plan at 10.

dispute settlement board in 2003.[154] As well, at the recommendation of the Commission, Canada and the United States have formally amended several of the management chapters within Annex IV.[155] One commentator, noting the above successes, has written that: "the 1999 Agreement created a new and much improved paradigm for addressing Pacific salmon issues, permitting U.S. and Canadian participants in the PSC process to work together constructively."[156]

All of the management chapters within Annex IV are to expire in 2008, except for the chapter on Fraser River salmon, which expires in 2010.[157] The fishery regime for chinook salmon has been seen as one of the most difficult of the issues for renegotiation, since many of the chinook runs within the northeast United States are endangered. This species is, therefore, at the center of U.S. attention. However, Canada intercepts Washington and Oregon chinook, within the limits of the 1999 Agreement, as a tacit *quid pro quo* for Alaskan interception of Canadian-origin chinook.[158] A second issue in the renegotiation has been the idea of extending the Pacific Salmon Treaty regime, which has been primarily about harvesting and management issues, to include dealing with habitat protection and development, as encouraged in the 1999 Agreement.[159]

In May 2008, the Pacific Salmon Commission announced that it had reached accord on a new Annex IV which, if accepted and implemented by the two governments, would take effect for the 2009 fishing season and last through to 2018.[160] The 2008 Annex IV tracks closely the overall structure, management philosophy, and emphasis on conservation contained in the 1999 Agreement. Specifically on the contentious issue of chinook, it was agreed that the Alaskan catch of chinook would decrease by 15 percent and the Canadian harvest along the West Coast of Vancouver Island would

---

154 PSC, 2002/2003 Eighteenth Annual Report, 8.

155 *See* Exchange of Diplomatic Notes 26 April 2005 and 17 July 2005, in PSC, 2004/2005 Twentieth Annual Report, 151–170 and Agreement to Amend Annex IV of the Pacific Salmon Treaty, Ottawa, 16 June 2006, at <www.treaty-accord.gc.ca/ViewTreaty.asp?Treaty_ID=105064> (accessed on 25 July 2007).

156 Buck, *supra* note 115, at 25.

157 The 1999 Pacific Salmon Agreement, *supra* note 47, para 8.

158 *See* Buck, *supra* note 115, at 28–29, 38–39.

159 The 1999 Pacific Salmon Agreement, *supra* note 47, Attachment E—Habitat and Restoration and *see* Buck, *supra* note 115, at 29–34.

160 PSC, Letter, 21 May 2008 and attached Annex IV, at www.psc.org (accessed 3 June 2008).

decrease by 30 percent.[161] The United States is to provide to Canada $30 million dollars over two years starting in 2009 with the funds to be used "for a fishery mitigation program designed . . . to reduce effort in [Canada's] commercial salmon troll fishery,"[162] which is located of the West Coast of Vancouver Island. One representative of the trollers association complained that $30 million dollars is a "buyout" and raised issues of "sovereignty" in that "you don't sell your natural resources."[163]

The Commission has worked as it was intended to under the 1985 Pacific Salmon Treaty and has set before the governments of Canada and the United States recommendations regarding all the salmon fisheries except those of the Fraser River. It is expected that the two governments will accept the recommendations of the Commission.

The Canadian position on Pacific salmon has long been the attainment of equity through a balance of interceptions. Despite the wording that the 1999 Agreement and the 2008 Commission recommendations constitutes compliance with Article III of the Pacific Salmon Treaty,[164] the 1999 Agreement, and 2008 recommendations do not implement the equity principle as it was originally understood by Canada. It is clear that Canada has been willing to accept that U.S. funding either directly provided to Canada or directed to Pacific salmon enhancement assists with the meeting of the equity principle. Whether in the Fraser River discussions or at some future time, Canada will return to its earlier posture of a fish-for-fish approach to equity, either with the hope of finally meeting its original expectations for the Pacific Salmon Treaty or as a bargaining position, is not known. Discouraging this is the reality that in the Pacific salmon debate Canada is without significant leverage, since Alaskan interceptions can severely interfere with Canadian-origin salmon, whereas the salmon do not cooperate in giving Canada the opportunity to interfere with Alaskan salmon.

---

161 *Id.*, Annex IV, chapter 3, para 9.

162 *Id.* para 4 and Letter, 21 May 2008, *supra* note 160, para 5.

163 M. Hume, *U.S. salmon payment 'a buyout,'* Toronto Globe and Mail, 23 May 2008, A1, A6 quoting Kathy Scarfo head of the West Coast Trollers Association and *see also* J. Hunter, *Salmon deal sells out fishermen, B.C. trollers say*, Toronto Globe and Mail, 24 May 2008, A14.

164 The 1999 Pacific Salmon Agreement, *supra* note 47, para 9 and Letter, 21 May 2008, *supra* note 160, para 3.

2.3 The 2002 Yukon River Agreement

The Yukon River, which flows into the Pacific Ocean through Alaska and has its headwaters and many tributaries, including the Porcupine River in Canada, has always been the exception in Canada-U.S. Pacific salmon negotiations.

During the negotiations of the 1985 Pacific Salmon Treaty, the Yukon River was not treated like the other transboundary rivers (those that have headwaters in Canada but meet the Pacific Ocean through the United States), primarily at the insistence of the United States.[165] The Yukon River was seen as unique in part because much of the salmon harvesting was subsistence and undertaken by indigenous peoples (First Nations Peoples) and there was a known imbalance in what was harvested in the United States as opposed to in Canada.[166] The two countries agreed to defer detailed discussions of a salmon management regime for the Yukon River and opted in the 1985 Agreement to establish a process for negotiation of the necessary management regime.[167]

Pursuant to the 1985 Pacific Salmon Treaty, the Yukon River Joint Technical Committee was established[168] and commenced work on the tasks assigned by the 1985 Treaty and developing a management regime for Yukon River salmon.[169] In 1995, Canada and the United States formally agreed to interim

---

165 Shepard and Argue, *supra* note 55, at 83–84, 165.

166 *Id.* 83–84, 157, 165–166 and at 166 comment that:

> Postponement of the Yukon issue was a disappointment to Canadian Yukon River fishermen, who felt that Canada's bargaining power with respect to the Yukon was greatly diminished by separating its consideration from all other issues in the coastwide negotiations.

167 *Id.* 84, 166, 170.

See Pacific Salmon Treaty, *supra* note 48, Art VIII and Memorandum of Understanding, Part C. Article VIII(1) provided: "arrangements for conservation, recommendation of escapement targets and approval of enhancement activities in the Yukon River require further development to take into account the unique characteristics of that River."

168 Pacific Salmon Treaty, *supra* note 48, Memorandum of Understanding, Part C, para 2.

169 Yukon River Panel and Yukon River Drainage Fisheries Association, *Yukon River Salmon Agreement Handbook: Information and Reference Materials Pertaining to the Yukon River Salmon Agreement* (Yukon River Panel, 2005) 6.

management arrangements.[170] The interim agreement expired on the last day of 1997[171] as the two countries were unable to agree on harvest limits.[172]

Major declines in the salmon runs on the Yukon River in 1999 corresponded with recommenced negotiations.[173] Agreement on a management regime was reached in March 2001 and was applied provisionally[174] pending the formalized acceptance of the Yukon River Salmon Agreement in late 2002. In an interesting example of advantageous spin, the press release from the Governor of Alaska noted that under the 2002 Agreement, the Alaskan harvest of chinook would be between 74 and 80 percent and that Canada had initially requested 55 percent and that the Alaskan harvest of chum would be between 65 and 71 percent and that Canada had sought 45 percent.[175] The government of Canada press release indicated that the Canadian percentage for chinook would be between 20 and 26 percent, having historically been at 18 percent; and for chum it would be between 29 and 35, having historically been at 19 to 27 percent.[176] On the highly visible issue of resource sharing, both sides could declare negotiating success.

There are a number of features of the 2002 Yukon River Agreement worth noting. First, it is explicitly recognized in the Agreement that "aboriginal fisheries in Yukon have priority over other fisheries in Yukon" and; on the U.S. side, "subsistence fisheries in Alaska have priority over other fisheries in Alaska."[177] Second, the Agreement is simultaneously part of and not part of the 1985 Pacific Salmon Treaty. The role played by the Pacific Salmon Commission under the 1985 Treaty is played by the Yukon River Panel;[178] if the 1985 Pacific Salmon Treaty is terminated, the Yukon River Agreement is

170 Exchange of Notes constituting an Interim Agreement amending Annexes I and IV of the Pacific Salmon Treaty, 3 December 1995, CTS 1995/39, PSC, 1995/1996 Eleventh Annual Report, 117–133.

171 *Id.* para 5.

172 *See* Yukon River Panel, Introduction to the Yukon River Salmon Agreement, at www.yukonriverpanel.com/yrsaintro.htm (accessed on 25 July 2007) at 3.

173 *Yukon River Salmon Agreement Handbook*, *supra* note 169, at 6.

174 Yukon River Agreement, *supra* note 50, final operative paragraph.

175 Alaska, Office of the Governor, Alaska, Canada Agree to Yukon River Salmon Treaty, 4 April 2001, at www.adfg.state.ak.us/news/99-02/4-3gov.php (accessed on 25 July 2007).

176 DFO, International Yukon River Salmon Agreement Signed, 4 December 2002, at www.dfo-mpo.gc.ca/media/newsrel/2002/hq-ac146_e.htm (accessed on 25 July 2007).

177 Yukon River Agreement, *supra* note 50, Attachment B, Chapter 8, s 1(2)(3).

178 *Id.* Attachment B, Chapter 8, ss 13–20 and *Yukon River Salmon Agreement Handbook*, *supra* note 169, at 7.

to continue in force as a separate agreement;[179] and the Yukon River Agreement can be terminated separately from the 1985 Treaty.[180] Third, as with the 1999 Salmon Agreement, there is a Restoration and Enhancement Fund to which the United States (but not Canada) is obligated to contribute.[181]

2.4 North Pacific Anadromous Stocks Convention[182]

The 1993 Anadromous Stocks Convention,[183] a multilateral agreement between Canada, Japan, the Russian Federation, the United States, and Korea, replaced the 1952 North Pacific Fisheries Convention[184] respecting Pacific salmon beyond the 200-nautical-mile zones of Canada and the United States north of 33 degrees north latitude.[185] Consistent with Article 66(3) of the LOS Convention, the Agreement is aimed at ensuring that fishing for anadromous stocks occurs only within 200 nautical miles of the coastline,[186] and, as a consequence, the Convention prohibits directed fishing for these stocks in the North Pacific Ocean.[187] The Anadromous Stocks Convention completes the story of Pacific salmon for Canada and the United States.

The impetus for the 1993 Agreement was that the Russian Federation, having announced in 1988 that high seas fishing for anadromous species originating in its waters would cease by 1992,[188] indicated that it was not

---

179 *Id.* para 8 and *Yukon River Salmon Agreement Handbook*, *supra* note 169, at 7.

180 *Id.* para 9.

181 *Id.* Attachment C, Restoration and Enhancement Fund.
In the 1995 Interim Agreement, *supra* note 170, Attachment A, Yukon River, s 32, the Restoration and Enhancement Fund was directly tied to the equity wording of Article III (1)(b) of the Pacific Salmon Treaty. This connection is not explicit in the 2002 Yukon River Agreement.

182 This section is drawn, with modification, from Bond and McDorman, *supra* note 53.

183 Anadromous Stocks Convention, *supra* note 44.

184 North Pacific Fisheries Convention, *supra* note 58.

185 Anadromous Stocks Convention, *supra* note 44, Art I.

186 *Id.* preamble.

187 *Id.* Art III(1)(a).

188 Burke, *supra* note 17, at 174–175. This announcement by Russia was a "necessary precondition for the development of a new international regime for management and conservation of...anadromous species." V. Zilanov, *Good Cooperation Ensures Good Results*, in North Pacific Anadromous Fish Commission (NPAFC), A DECADE TO REMEMBER: 10TH ANNIVERSARY COMMEMORATIVE ALBUM (Vancouver, 2003) 17.

interested in joining the North Pacific Fisheries Convention.[189] Russia, working with the United States, developed a draft of a new agreement for the conserving North Pacific anadromous stocks.[190] This coalesced with the escalation of concern about alleged high-seas driftnet fishing for salmon and declining catches of salmon in the countries of origin around the North Pacific.[191]

The 1993 Anadromous Stocks Convention, in addition to prohibiting all directed fishing for anadromous fish in the North Pacific Ocean and its adjacent seas,[192] requires that steps be taken to minimize the taking of anadromous fish incidental to other fishing activities[193] and prohibits retaining any anadromous species taken incidentally.[194] These strict measures were a direct response to the high seas driftnet frenzy of 1989 to 1992.[195]

As a result of the prohibition on harvesting salmon in the area subject to the Anadromous Stocks Convention, the Agreement is not a management arrangement. There is no requirement for the determination of TACs or quota allocations. The North Pacific Anadromous Fish Commission (NPAFC), established by the Convention to "promote the conservation of anadromous stocks,"[196] is responsible for making collaborative decisions regarding scientific projects, conservation measures, and enforcement issues.[197]

An interesting aspect of the Anadromous Stocks Convention is its robust enforcement provisions designed to ensure that the Agreement's prohibition on high-seas salmon harvesting is respected. Each party to the Convention is authorized to board and investigate vessels of the other parties if a vessel is reasonably believed to be fishing, either directly or indirectly, for anadromous fish stocks in the Convention area.[198] If onboard

---

189 R. Lauber, *Conception and Early Days of NPAFC*, in *A Decade to Remember*, *supra* note 188, 21.

190 Letter of Submittal from James A. Baker, III to the President regarding the Convention for the Conservation of Anadromous Fish Stocks in the North Pacific Ocean, 14 May 1992, U.S. Senate, Treaty Document 102–30, vi.

191 Zilanov, *supra* note 188, at 17 and *see* Burke, *supra* note 17, at 175.

192 Anadromous Stocks Convention, *supra* note 44, Art II.

193 *Id.* Art III(1)(b).

194 *Id.* Art III(1)(c).

195 *See generally* Burke, *supra* note 17, at 102–107, 117–121.

196 Anadromous Stocks Convention, *supra* note 44, Art VIII(1)(2).

197 *Id.* Art IX.

198 *Id.* Art V(2)(a).

investigation reveals reasonable grounds to believe that such activity is, or was, occurring, the enforcing party has the authority to arrest or seize the vessel and individuals involved. The enforcing party also has the authority to conduct further investigations regarding the vessel and its fishing activity.[199] The Convention does not, however, give parties the ability to prosecute each other's citizens;[200] thus, an enforcing party must deliver detained individuals as soon as the other party is able to accept delivery.[201]

The Anadromous Stocks Convention also contains provisions authorizing action by parties when a vessel of a non-party to the Convention is seen engaging in high-seas fishing for anadromous fish stocks. The parties have committed to drawing such actions to the attention of the vessel's flag State and to encouraging non-party States to adopt laws and regulations that are consistent with the Convention.[202] Parties are also authorized to take action, "consistent with international law and their respective domestic laws," to ensure that vessels of non-party States do not engage in fishing activity prohibited by the Convention.[203]

3.0 Other Fisheries[204]

3.1 Pacific Halibut

Canada-Unitted States agreements regarding Pacific halibut date back to 1923,[205] with the most recent complete text being the 1979 Protocol to the 1953 Halibut Convention.[206] The 1923 Halibut Convention is noteworthy in that it was "the first international attempt at conserving and rebuilding a marine fishery" and, as a result, "has an honored place in the history on

---

199 *Id.* Art V(2)(b).

200 *Id.* Art V(2)(d).

201 *Id.* Art V(2)(b).

202 *Id.* Art IV(2).

203 *Id.* Art IV(4).

204 This section is drawn, with modification, from Bond and McDorman, *supra* note 53.

205 1923 Halibut Convention, *supra* note 19.

206 1979 Halibut Fishery Protocol, *supra* note 37. For a history of the bilateral regulation of the Pacific halibut fishery, *see* F. H. BELL, THE PACIFIC HALIBUT: THE RESOURCE AND THE FISHERY (Alaska Northwest Publishing Company, Anchorage 1981).

international cooperation."[207] Moreover, the 1923 Convention was the first international treaty signed by Canada without an accompanying signature from Great Britain, and is seen as a "significant episode in the development of Canada's autonomy."[208] Finally, the International Fisheries Commission [renamed in 1953 as the International Pacific Halibut Commission (IPHC)], created by the 1923 Convention, was the first international fisheries organization of its kind.[209]

The commercial fishery for Pacific halibut began off the coast of Washington state in 1888. The popularity of the fishery grew rapidly, and by the 1910s, the halibut population was already declining due to overfishing.[210] The declining harvest led to bilateral agreement in 1919 on a draft treaty which, however, was never ratified,[211] and subsequently to the 1923 Convention.

Up to 1979, the approach to halibut management was to have closed seasons, by-catch regulation and controls on the numbers of vessels that Canada and the United States could authorize to engage in the fishery. With the adoption of 200-nautical-mile zones, the 1979 Protocol phased out reciprocal fishing along the coasts of each State, with the fishers from each State confined to harvesting halibut only in their national waters.

The IPHC, composed of three members appointed by each country,[212] has broad authority to study and manage the Pacific halibut fishery and to regulate all halibut found in the Pacific waters of the United States and Canada.[213] The Commission has created ten regulatory areas and one closed area.[214] The IPHC is empowered to: establish open and closed seasons in each area; limit the size of the fish and the quantity of the catch to be taken from each

---

207 Johnston, *supra* note 2, at 372.

208 Bell, *supra* note 206, at 150.
The 1923 Halibut Convention, *supra* note 19, was negotiated and signed by the Canadian Minister of Marine and Fisheries as a representative of the British Crown. *See* C. L. Wiktor, Canadian Treaty Calendar, 1928–1978, Vol. I (Oceana Publication, New York 1982) xii.

209 Johnston, *supra* note 2, at 374.

210 DFO, Halibut–Pacific Region–History of the Fishery, at <www-ops2.pac.dfo-mpo.gc.ca/xnet/content/groundfish/halibut/history.htm> (accessed on 5 December 2006) and see Johnston, *supra* note 2, at 373–374.

211 *See* Bell, *supra* note 206, at 148 and Johnston, *supra* note 2, at 374.

212 1979 Halibut Fishery Protocol, *supra* note 37, Art III(1).

213 *Id.* Art I(3).

214 International Pacific Halibut Commission (IPHC), IPHC Regulatory Areas, at www.iphc.washington.edu/halcom/commerc/regmap.htm (accessed on 4 November 2006).

area; regulate incidental catch; establish the size and character of halibut fishing appliances to be used in any area; and make regulations to aid data collection.[215] The IPHC is responsible for establishing the TAC for the Canada-U.S. commercial halibut fishery. Part of the annual TAC determination is the allocation of the total TAC among each of the areas.

The Halibut Convention has had considerable success in protecting the species. In 2006, the IPHC reported that the "halibut stock is healthy in the central and southern portion of the range,"[216] an area that includes the waters off the coast of British Columbia and the Pacific Coast of the United States. However, in 2008, the IPHC noted that the halibut stock had reached a low point in its population cycle.[217] The total exploitable biomass of Pacific halibut for 2008 was estimated to be 361 million pounds.[218] There has been little serious disagreement over the sharing of halibut stocks.

3.2 Albacore Tuna

As already noted, in August 1979, nineteen U.S. tuna vessels were arrested for fishing without authorization in Canada's Pacific Coast 200-nautical-mile fishing zone.[219] The U.S. vessels were acting consistent with the then-U.S. policy that tuna, and other highly migratory species, were exempt from a coastal State's exclusive authority over fisheries resources within the State's 200-nautical-mile zone.[220] This U.S. policy was reversed in the early 1990s.[221]

---

215 1979 Halibut Fishery Protocol, *supra* note 37, Art III(3).

216 IPHC, News Release: Halibut Commission Completes 2006 Annual Meeting, 23 January 2006, at <www.iphc.washington.edu/halcom/newsrel/2006/nr20060120.htm> (accessed on 5 December 2006).

217 IPHC, News Release: Halibut Commission Completes 2008 Annual Meeting, 22 January 2008, at: <www.iphc.washington.edu/halcom/newsrel/2008/nr20080122.htm> (accessed on 8 May 2008).

218 W. G. Clark and S. E. Hare, *Summary of the 2007 Pacific Halibut Stock Assessment*, at <www.iphc.washington.edu/halcom/research/sa/papers/sa07.bb.pdf> (accessed on 8 May 2008).

219 *See* Rasmussen, *supra* note 32, at 764–765.

220 This U.S. position on highly migratory species is described in W. T. Burke, *Highly Migratory Species in the New Law of the Sea* (1984) 14 ODIL 273, 303–310.

221 Aide-Memoire April 1991 from the U.S. Mission to the United Nations to the Secretary-General of the United Nations, in Department of State, DIGEST OF UNITED STATES PRACTICE IN INTERNATIONAL LAW, 1991–1999 (International Law Institute, Washington, 2005) 1707–1708. *See* C. J. Carr, *Transformations in the Law Governing Highly Migratory Species: 1970 to the Present*, in D. D. CARON AND H. N. SCHEIBER (eds.) BRINGING NEW LAW TO OCEAN WATERS (Martinus Nijhoff, Leiden 2004) 65–69, 75–83.

One of the ramifications of the Canadian seizure of the U.S. tuna vessels was the automatic imposition by the United States of a trade embargo on tuna and tuna products from Canada.[222] Although the trade embargo was lifted in 1980 following assurances that no further tuna vessel seizures would be made,[223] Canada pursued a trade complaint against the United States. Canada successfully argued before a dispute settlement panel of the General Agreement on Tariffs and Trade (GATT) that the U.S. trade embargo, which was tied to the arrest of U.S. fishing vessels, was inconsistent with the trade obligations owed to Canada by the United States under the GATT.[224]

The more productive outcome, however, was the 1981 Canada-United States Albacore Tuna Treaty.[225] The 1981 Treaty was principally a reciprocal fishing rights agreement with no restrictions placed on the number of vessels from either State that could operate in the waters of the other and similarly no restrictions on the amount of albacore tuna that could be taken by these vessels. Visiting vessels were, however, to meet registration and reporting requirements.[226]

Complaints by U.S. fishers that Canadian vessels were "overcrowding" U.S. fishing grounds and that albacore tuna stock migration had resulted in Canadians receiving "disproportionate benefits" under the 1981 Treaty led the United States to initiate negotiations to amend the Treaty.[227] The 2002 Amendment to the 1981 Treaty[228] results in substantial change. Fishing vessels from each State are now only allowed into the other State's waters for a limited amount of time each year, although there remains no restriction

---

222 Fishery Conservation and Management Act, 90 US Stat. 331, Pub L. 94–265, codified at 16 USC 1801–1882, s 1825(a). The operation of this legislation is described in detail in T. L. McDorman, *The GATT Consistency of U.S. Fish Import Embargoes to Stop Driftnet Fishing and Save Whales, Dolphins and Turtles* (1991) 24 GEORGE WASHINGTON J INTL AND ECONOMICS 477, 501–504.

223 Letter of Submittal from Walter J. Stoessel, Jr., to President regarding the Treaty with Canada on Pacific Coast Albacore Tuna Vessels and Port Privileges, 13 June 1981, U.S. Senate, Treaty Document 97–13, v.

224 *United States–Prohibition of Imports of Tuna and Tuna Products from Canada,* (Panel Decision), in GATT, *BISD, 29th Supplement* (Geneva, 1983) 91–109. See McDorman, *supra* note 222, at 511–512, footnote 239.

225 Albacore Tuna Treaty, *supra* note 38.

226 *Id.* Annex A, paras (1), (4).

227 Letter of Submittal from Colin Powell to the President regarding the Agreement Amending the Treaty between the United States and Canada on Pacific Coast Albacore Tuna Vessels and Port Privileges, 9 October 2002, U.S. Senate, Treaty Document 108–1.

228 Albacore Tuna Treaty Amendment, *supra* note 38.

on harvest levels. The time allotments were agreed upon for a three-year period with the 2002 Amendment providing that if a new arrangement were not in place by the end of the third year, the last agreed upon time allocation would carry forward.[229]

The Albacore Tuna Treaty is the only Canada-United States fisheries agreement which creates reciprocal fishing rights for the vessels of each State in the waters of the other.

3.3 Hake/Whiting[230]

Canadian and U.S. scientists, fisheries managers, and fishers have been working together since the 1970s to establish a common TAC for Pacific hake/whiting,[231] with a formal joint scientific assessment process established in 1997.[232] Despite these collaborative efforts, the two countries were not able to agree on how to divide the TAC between them, with the United States generally claiming 80 percent of the TAC and Canada claiming 30 percent.[233] The result was overfishing and a rapidly declining fish stock.[234]

In November 2003, Canada and the United States finalized the Hake/Whiting Agreement.[235] The Agreement applies to all hake/whiting located in the Pacific Coast waters of the United States and Canada, except for the stock found in Puget Sound and the Strait of Georgia. The Agreement provides that the U.S. allocation of the global TAC is to be 73.88 percent and the Canadian allocation 26.12 percent.[236]

The Hake/Whiting Agreement only came into force in June 2008. Prior to its entry into force, the pre-existing mechanisms involving the Stock Assessment

229 *Id.* Annex C, (3),(4),(5),(8).

230 Hake, the Canadian term, and whiting, the U.S. term, refer to the same species of fish.

231 David Balton, Deputy Assistant Secretary of State for Oceans and Fisheries, Comments to the Senate Committee on Foreign Relations, 29 September 2005, at <www.state.gov/g/oes/rls/rm/54128.htm> (accessed on 4 November 2006).

232 DFO, Canada and the United States Sign Treaty to Improve Stewardship of Pacific Hake, at www-comm.pac.dfo-mpo.gc.ca/pages/release/p-releas/2003/nr066_e.htm (accessed on 4 November 2006).

233 Balton, *supra* note 231.

234 T. Helser, I. Stewart, G. Fleischer, and S. Martell, *Stock Assessment of Pacific Hake (Whiting) in U.S. and Canadian Waters in 2006*, 2 February 2006, at www.pcouncil.org/groundfish/gfsafe0406/2006_hake_assessment_FINAL_ENTIRE.pdf (accessed on 5 December 2006).

235 Hake/Whiting Agreement, *supra* note 39.

236 *Id.* Art III (2).

Teams and Stock Assessment Review Panels indicated that their work was being "undertaken in the spirit and intent" of the Hake/Whiting Agreement.[237] Data on 2006 hake/whiting landings suggest that both countries were roughly adhering to the agreed allocation arrangement, despite the fact that the Agreement had not yet entered in force, with the United States harvesting 73.8 percent of total landings and Canada harvesting 26.4 percent.[238]

As the Hake/Whiting Agreement sets out the allocation percentages, the yearly task will be to determine the TAC. This will be undertaken through a complex process involving four distinct but interactive bodies[239] designed to ensure that the input and advice from scientists, fishers, and other interested parties is taken into consideration.

4.0 Conclusion

Thirty years after the adoption by Canada and the United States of 200-nautical-mile fishing zones (and over twenty years since the *Gulf of Maine Case*[240]), there exists a general comfort with their at-sea fisheries relationship, evinced by the general calm that has existed over the last decade. There has been an evolution from a competitive bilateral position between the two States (and their industries) to a cooperative position. The 200-nautical-mile zone was about "removing the foreigners," the projection of national authority, and exclusive national access to fish in the adjacent waters. This fueled rhetoric and expectations of national sovereignty and fishing rights within both Canada and the United States. On the Atlantic Coast in particular, blunting this competitive approach was made more difficult by the differences in philosophy and approach between the two States respecting national fisheries management.[241] Nevertheless, the acquisitive aspects of

---

237 Helser, *et al.*, *supra* note 234, at 17.

238 T. Helser and S. Martell, *Stock Assessment of Pacific Hake (Whiting) in U.S. and Canadian Waters in 2007*, 2 March 2007, at <www.pcouncil.org/groundfish/gfstocks/hake/hake2007 assessment_fuldoc_with_appendices.pdf> (accessed on 20 May 2008).

239 Hake/Whiting Agreement, *supra* note 39, Art II.

240 *Gulf of Maine Case*, *supra* note 26.

241 *See* L. S. PARSONS, MANAGEMENT OF MARINE FISHERIES IN CANADA (National Research Council of Canada, Ottawa 1993) 336; A. L. Springer, *Do Good Fences Make Good Neighbours? The Gulf of Maine Revisited* (1994) 6 INTL ENVIRONMENTAL AFFAIRS 223, 231–232. *See more generally*, D. L. VANDERZWAAG, THE FISH FEUD: THE U.S. AND CANADIAN BOUNDARY DISPUTE (Lexington Books, Toronto 1983) 37–87; G. J. Herbert, *Fisheries Relations in the*

the 200-nautical-mile zone have given way to a cooperative ethic on cross-boundary fisheries matters motivated by the assessment by governing managers and the fishing industries in both countries that without bilateral cooperation there will be a further decline of cross-boundary stocks, an outcome not in the interest of either community. The informal fisheries management arrangements for cross-boundary stocks in the Gulf of Maine[242] and an easing of the tensions regarding lobster harvesting adjacent to Machias Seal Island[243] are evidence of this.

The Pacific salmon dispute also demonstrates this narrative arc. The hot 1990s Pacific salmon issues were fraught with sovereignty rhetoric and the right to fish, both sides claiming the same fish as theirs; in the case of Canada, because of the origin of the salmon, and in the case of the United States, because the salmon was in its waters. Ultimately, the 1999 Pacific Salmon Agreement[244] promoted management and allocation based on the condition of the stocks and conservation. A notable success in this regard has been the Southern Coho Management Plan adopted in 2002.[245]

Also on the Pacific Coast, there have been a number of other important fisheries agreements during the last decade: the 2002 Yukon River Salmon Agreement;[246] the 2003 Hake/Whiting Agreement;[247] and the 2001 Amendment to the 1981 Albacore Tuna Agreement.[248]

Reaching back almost twenty years, note needs to be made of the 1990 Fisheries Enforcement Agreement, which has served as an international model for reducing at-sea tensions regarding cross-border fisheries.[249]

Gulf of Maine: Implications of an Arbitrated Maritime Boundary (1995) 19 Mar Pol 301, 310–311; and DFO, Maritime Region, Transboundary Management Guidance Committee, *Development of a Sharing Allocation Proposal for Transboundary Resources of Cod, Haddock and Yellowtail Flounder on Georges Bank*, (Fisheries Management Regional Report 2002/01, January 2002) 7, Appendix 1, USA and Canadian Management Measures, at www.mar.dfo-mpo.gc.ca/science/tmgc/bacground/FMR%202002_01.pdf (accessed on 5 March 2007).

242 *See* Chapter Five, section 3.4.5.

243 *See* Chapter Five, section 5.5.2.

244 The 1999 Pacific Salmon Agreement, *supra* note 47.

245 Southern Coho Management Plan, *supra* note 153.

246 Yukon River Agreement, *supra* note 50.

247 Hake/Whiting Agreement, *supra* note 39.

248 Albacore Tuna Treaty Amendment, *supra* note 38.

249 Fisheries Enforcement Agreement, *supra* note 33 and *see* Chapter Five, section 3.4.3.

Not all the fisheries issues between Canada and the United States have been resolved such that no future disagreements will occur. The management arrangements under the 1985 Pacific Salmon Treaty are to be renewed between 2008 and 2011[250] and this may reheat the dispute, although few expect or desire a repeat of the 1990s. The May 2008 Pacific Salmon Commission agreed recommendations on all salmon fisheries, but for Fraser River salmon, is a clear indication of an intention to avoid difficulties. The Machias Seal Island fisheries dispute is ultimately tied to the island sovereignty dispute[251] and, as a result, remains one that could flare during any given summer. Nevertheless, in the fish harvesting sector there is a Canada-U.S. ethic of cooperation that should help moderate future disputes

---

250 The 1999 Pacific Salmon Agreement, *supra* note 47, para 8 and *see* Chapter Seven, section 2.2.4.

251 See Chapter Five, section 5.5.1.

EIGHT

Reviewing the Past and Looking to the Future

1.0 Introduction

The primary goal of this work has been to explore both the legal positions of Canada and the United States regarding their international ocean disputes respecting maritime boundaries, navigation rights, and fisheries; and the cooperative and coordination agreements and arrangements that manage the disputes and keep them from being regular irritants in the bilateral relationship.

The Canada-U.S. international ocean law relationship is currently on an even keel. The disputes that exist on maritime boundaries, navigation, and fisheries cause minimal direct friction between the States. The management of the disputes through formal and informal agreements is working well.

This situation may not continue indefinitely. Three prominent features of the early twenty-first century, global climate change, the U.S. attention to national security, and the increasing North American appetite for secure access to and supply of energy resources, may have implications for Canada-U.S. ocean matters. Given the scant Canada-U.S. record of resolving international ocean law disputes, the future of the salt water relationship will most likely be a continuation of dispute management agreements and arrangements, rather than a resolution of the disputes.

2.0 Reviewing the Past

2.1 1970: Different Interests

The current minimal friction on international ocean issues would not have been predicted in 1970. The "landmark year" witnessed significant differences in the views of Canada and the United States respecting national authority over adjacent ocean spaces. Canada was the aggressor seeking to expand the ocean areas under its control; whereas, the United States favored a more restrained approach that took into account historic high-seas freedoms, most specifically that of little-restrained navigation rights. Canada's 1970 Arctic Waters Pollution Prevention Act[1] creating a 100-nautical-mile pollution prevention zone was in reaction to the voyage of the *Manhattan* and the intense domestic pressure focused on Canada's sovereignty in the North. In the case of fisheries zone expansion, the 12-nautical-mile territorial sea, and continental shelf claims, Canada's actions were also in response to domestic pressure. In 1970, the United States was focused on shaping the agenda of the impending multilateral ocean law negotiations and based its reactions to Canadian measures against this background. An important part of the U.S. reaction was the concern of the United States that, if Canada could succeed with adventurist offshore claims without significant U.S. response, other States would feel emboldened to advance similar Canada-like claims in the oceans.[2]

The common narrative is that the Canadian ocean actions of the 1970s reflected the shift of the Trudeau government from a Pearsonian, internationalist foreign policy to one of pursuit of tangible and immediate Canadian interests.[3] Certainly as regards fisheries matters, there was Canadian frustration with the multilateral approach. The Arctic issue, however, arose without much warning. More generally, Canada found itself riding the historic tide of expanding national authority in adjacent ocean waters. The United States, and like-minded partners such as the United Kingdom and the Soviet Union, struggled against this tide. As a result, Canada and the United States had different interests and adopted different approaches to international ocean law issues.

2.2 The 1970s: Disagreement, Discussion, and Disappointment

During the Third United Nations (U.N.) Conference on the Law of the Sea (UNCLOS III), which commenced formally in 1973 and ran until 1982, Canada

1 Arctic Waters Pollution Prevention Act, St Can 1969–1970, c 47.

2 *See* Department of State, FOREIGN RELATIONS IN THE UNITED STATES (Nixon-Ford Administrations, 1969–1976), Vol. E-1, Document 367, Information Memorandum for Mr. Kissinger–The White House: Subject–Imminent Canadian Legislation on the Arctic, from T.L. Eliot, Jr., (Washington, 12 March 1970), at www.state.gov/r/pa/ho/frus/nixon/e1/53180.htm (accessed on 7 August 2007) and Chapter Three, section 3.3.

3 *See, for example,* A. E. Gotlieb, *Canadian Diplomatic Initiatives: The Law of the Sea,* in M. G. FRY (ed.) FREEDOM AND CHANGE: ESSAYS IN HONOUR OF LESTER B. PEARSON (McClelland and Stewart, Toronto 1975) 147–151.

and the United States cooperated infrequently, despite the fact that on a large number of issues they were in general accord. The United States' main concerns, navigation and deep seabed minerals, were not the same as those of Canada. Canada was more interested in the enhancement of offshore authority and, much to the annoyance of the United States, exceptions regarding navigation (e.g., the Arctic, a narrowing of what constituted innocent passage, and the Northwest Passage) and deep seabed mining (*i.e.*, production limitations to protect land producers). Once the U.N. Convention on the Law of the Sea (the LOS Convention)[4] was finalized, the bilateral relationship on the Convention ceased to be a major issue. Canada became as cautious as the United States, and other western industrialized countries, about becoming a party to the Convention.

In the mid 1970s, both Canada and the United States adopted 200-nautical-mile fishing zones. This occasioned a flurry of bilateral activity regarding maritime boundaries and fisheries matters. To date, the only sustained, comprehensive discussions of maritime boundary issues arising from overlapping 200–nautical-mile claims between Canada and the United States took place between 1976 and 1978.[5] These maritime boundary discussions were sidetracked by the urgency of the fisheries problem in the Gulf of Maine.[6] On this issue, the two countries agreed in 1979 to an innovative and comprehensive arrangement for fisheries and the maritime boundary that provided to the fishers of each State an insurance policy against an adverse maritime boundary.[7] The New England fishing communities, however, voiced serious displeasure with the 1979 East Coast Fisheries Agreement and the United States elected to shelve the deal.

Proposed oil tanker traffic into U.S. ports that required the traversing of Canadian waters was an issue on both the East and West Coasts. On the West Coast, oil tanker traffic through the Juan de Fuca Strait led to the two

4 U. N. Convention on the Law of the Sea, Montego Bay, Jamaica, 10 December 1982, entered into force 16 November 1994, 1833 UNTS 397.

5 *See* Chapter Five, section 1.0.

6 *See* Chapter Five, section 3.1.

7 Agreement on East Coast Fishery Resources, Washington, 29 March 1979, U.S. Senate, Executive Document V, 96th Congress, 1st Session (1979), in M. NORDQUIST AND K. R. SIMMONDS (eds.) NEW DIRECTIONS IN THE LAW OF THE SEA, Vol. IX (Oceana Publications, Dobbs Ferry, N.Y. 1980) 178–212 and Agreement to Submit to Binding Dispute Settlement the Delimitation of the Maritime Boundary in the Gulf of Maine, done at Washington, 29 March 1979, U.S. Senate, Executive Document U, 96th Congress, 1st Session, (1979), in Nordquist and Simmonds, 167–177.

States to the 1979 Vessel Traffic Management Agreement.[8] On the East Coast, Canada and the United States were at loggerheads over navigation rights in the Head Harbour Passage in Passamaquoddy Bay. The oil refinery proposal for Eastport, Maine, was shelved by the project proponent in the early 1980s, thus avoiding continued conflict or resolution.[9]

2.3 The 1980s: Calming the Major Issues

Following the demise of the 1979 East Coast Fisheries Agreement, the United States proposed and Canada accepted to adjudicate the location of the maritime boundary in the Gulf of Maine. At stake was the fisheries-rich Georges Bank, of which Canada claimed a large portion and the United States claimed in its entirety. In 1984, a Chamber of the International Court of Justice (International Court) constructed the maritime boundary for the two States in the Gulf of Maine.[10] The Court rejected the boundaries proposed by both States and, relying on the geography of the coasts and geometric methods, constructed a line that crossed the fisheries-rich Georges Bank. The Case resolved the jurisdictional dispute, but left a hangover that made it difficult for either country to engage in necessary discussions on how to cooperatively manage the fishery resources of the area.[11]

Difficulties over enforcement of the maritime boundary *vis à vis* U.S. fishing boats in Canadian waters were placated through the 1990 Fisheries Enforcement Agreement.[12] The 1990 Agreement obligated each State to make it an offense to fish without a permit in the waters of the other State. At the time, this was a novel approach to bilateral fisheries enforcement matters. The 1990 Agreement also mandated regular meetings of the fisheries enforcement agencies from each State to enhance cooperation and reduce misunderstandings.

---

8 Exchange of Notes constituting an Agreement on Vessel Traffic Management for the Juan de Fuca Region, Ottawa, 19 December 1979, entered into force 19 December 1979, CTS 1979/28, 32 UST 377, TIAS 9706, 1221 UNTS 67. *See* Chapter Six, section 7.0.

9 *See* Chapter Six, section 4.1.1.

10 *Delimitation of the Maritime Boundary in the Gulf of Maine Area (Canada v. United States)*, [1984] ICJ Rep. 246.

11 See Chapter Five, section 3.4.5.

12 Agreement on Fisheries Enforcement, Ottawa, 26 September 1990, entered into force 16 December 1991, CTS 1991/36, TIAS 11753. *See* Chapter Five, section 3.4.3.

On the West Coast, the issue was salmon. The decade-long negotiations to modernize the 1930 Fraser River Salmon Agreement[13] climaxed with a 1982 framework accord.[14] However, like the 1979 East Coast Fisheries Agreement, domestic pressure within the United States killed the accord. A revised agreement acceptable within the United States, the Pacific Salmon Treaty,[15] was concluded in 1985. The new Treaty pacified the salmon dispute, albeit as it turned out only temporarily.

And then came the *Polar Sea*. In 1985, the U.S. icebreaker navigated the Northwest Passage. The United States asserted its view that the Passage was an international strait and, as a result, that permission from Canada to use the waterway was not necessary. Canada proclaimed its sovereignty over the Passage and granted the unrequested permission. The Coast Guards of the two States worked together regarding the trip of the vessel and two States agreed-to-disagree on their international legal positions.[16] The government of Canada felt compelled to clarify and enhance its legal claim to the Passage and did so by delineating and unequivocally proclaiming its claim to historic waters in the Arctic.

The 1988 Arctic Cooperation Agreement[17] ensured there would be no repeat of the *Polar Sea* incident. The Agreement, a textbook example of negotiated ambiguity, created a procedure by which the United States attains the consent of Canada for transits of the Northwest Passage by its Coast Guard icebreakers. The United States views the consent as tied to the Coast Guard vessels doing marine scientific research in Canadian waters, as opposed to consent for passing through the Northwest Passage. Moreover, for extra protection, the Agreement stipulates that it, nor any subsequent practice, "affects the respective positions" of either country regarding the international

---

13 Convention for the Sockeye Salmon Fishery in the Fraser River System, Canada-United States, Washington, 26 May 1930, entered into force 28 July 1937, 184 LNTS 305.

14 *See* M. P. SHEPARD AND A. W. ARGUE, THE 1985 PACIFIC SALMON TREATY: SHARING CONSERVATION BURDENS AND BENEFITS (UBC Press, Vancouver 2005) 67–74.

15 Pacific Salmon Treaty, Ottawa, 28 January 1985, entered into force 18 March 1985, CTS 1985/7, TIAS 11091, 1469 UNTS 357.

16 *See* Note from the United States to Canada, 24 June 1985, in J. A. ROACH AND R. W. SMITH, (eds.) UNITED STATES RESPONSES TO EXCESSIVE MARITIME CLAIMS (Martinus Nijhoff, 2nd edition, The Hague 1996) 345–346 and Note from Canada to the United States, 31 July 1985, in Roach and Smith, 346–348. *See more generally* Chapter Six, section 3.3.1.

17 Agreement on Arctic Cooperation, Ottawa, 11 January 1988, entered into force 11 January 1988, CTS 1988/29, TIAS 11565. *See* Chapter Six, section 3.3.2.

legal status of the Northwest Passage.[18] Pursuant to the Arctic agreement-to-disagree, there have been five voyages by U.S. Coast Guard icebreakers through the Northwest Passage, none of which has elicited any notice within Canada or the United States.

There is no question that the 1980s was the decade of results. The *Gulf of Maine Case*, the 1985 Pacific Salmon Treaty, and the 1988 Arctic Cooperation set in place the key components of the bilateral relationship on international ocean matters.

2.4 The 1990s: The Decade of Salmon

The dominate Canada-U.S. international ocean relationship issue in the 1990s was Pacific salmon. The 1985 Pacific Salmon Treaty did three things: (1) created the Pacific Salmon Commission to implement the Treaty; (2) set out principles, factors and considerations to be used by the Commission in determining the allocation of Pacific salmon to the two States; and (3) in appendices to the Treaty, set out for the principal salmon species the allocations that were to exist for the first number of years of the Treaty. It was the task of the Pacific Salmon Commission to renew the appendices to the Treaty. However, the Commission, composed of an equal number of Canadian and U.S. representatives, was unable to reach agreement on new salmon allocation plans to replace the ones that expired in the late 1980s and early 1990s.

What ensued was a decade long struggle on the water, in public debates, and at the negotiating table, with the primary loser being the Pacific salmon stocks that suffered from a lack of a cohesive bilateral management structure and, as a consequence, from overfishing.[19] It is worth noting that an attempt to reach accord involving the stakeholders (fishers from both States) failed,[20] presumably because of the impassioned and uncompromising view of what in their respective views constituted a "fair" allocation. In the end, Canada

---

18 *Id.* Art 4.

19 *See* Chapter Seven, section 2.2.2.

20 D. W. Strangway and W. D. Ruckelshaus, *Pacific Salmon: Report to the Prime Minister of Canada and the President of the United States*, Fisheries and Oceans Canada, 12 January 1998, 4, at www.dfo-mpo.gc.ca/communic/reports/pst-tsp/report-rapport_e.htm (accessed on 25 July 2007). The recommendations of the Strangway-Ruckelshaus Report are in PSC, 1997/1998 Thirteenth Annual Report, 91–92.

and the United States focused on conservation and sustainability of the resource and achieved agreement on new management and allocation plans for Pacific salmon in 1999 that were to last until the 2008, except for Fraser River salmon, which extends until 2010.[21]

2.5 2000-2008: Old Issues, New Shapes

Canada ratified the LOS Convention in 2003. In the same year, the United States Senate Foreign Relations Committee commenced consideration of the Convention and, in 2004, voted unanimously to recommend that the United States become a party to the LOS Convention. The recommendation was not acted upon by the full Senate. In 2007, the Senate Foreign Relations Committee again recommended that the United States become a party to the LOS Convention.[22] Should the U.S. Senate formally endorse this recommendation in 2008, the United States will be the last of the industrialized States to become a party to the "constitution of the oceans."

The United States becoming a party to the LOS Convention will make little difference respecting international ocean law issues with Canada. The legal positions of each State on their various bilateral disputes are already asserted relying on the wording of the Convention and the major areas of dispute, maritime boundaries, historic waters, and international straits, are ones where the Convention provides little clarity. Although the LOS Convention provides for compulsory adjudication of disputes arising respecting the Treaty, a State can exempt itself from certain types of disputes. Canada has already exercised its right to exempt from compulsory adjudication disputes respecting maritime boundaries and historic waters.[23] It is expected that the United States, if it becomes a party, will do the same.[24] Few, if any, of the ocean law disputes between Canada and the United States are outside the exemptions. The United States becoming a party to the

21 Exchange of Notes constituting an Agreement relating to the Pacific Salmon Treaty, Washington, 30 June 1999, entered into force 30 June 1999, CTS 1999/58, PSC, 1999/2000 Fifteenth Annual Report, 111–114, 120–169. *See* Chapter Seven, section 2.2.3.

22 U.S. Senate, Executive Report 110–9, Convention on the Law of the Sea (2007).

23 Declaration Made Upon Ratification, 7 November 2003, 53 LOSB 15.

24 Attached to the Advice and Consent Resolution before the Senate was a declaration outlining the exemptions that were proposed to be attached by the United States to its instrument of accession. Executive Report 110–9, *supra* note 22, Part VIII–Text of Resolution of Advice and Consent to Ratification, s 2, 19.

Convention, however, may be seen as an opportunity to engage in a new round of bilateral discussions on maritime boundaries and navigational matters, including respecting the Northwest Passage.

Progress has been made on a number of bilateral fisheries issues during the last few years. On the West Coast, in 2002, the two States finalized: the West Coast Hake/Whiting Agreement;[25] amendments to the 1981 Albacore Tuna Treaty;[26] and the Yukon River Salmon Agreement.[27] The Pacific Salmon Commission has successfully agreed on recommendations for the replacement of management plans for those stocks where the 1999 Agreement expires in 2008.[28] On the East Coast, twenty years after the *Gulf of Maine Case*, the two sides have adopted an informal process for management and allocation of fisheries stocks in the Gulf of Maine area.[29]

Without U.S. provocation, the international legal status of the Northwest Passage has again become a significant issue in Canada. The concern is that the Passage may, as a result of global climate change, become ice-free for longer periods in the summer and that there may be advantages to commercial shipping in using the Passage to cross between the Pacific to Atlantic Oceans. When asked, the United States continues to assert that the Northwest Passage is an international strait such that the permission of Canada is not required for vessel traffic. Much of the debate in Canada has been about the Canada's lack of presence and knowledge regarding its Arctic waters. The government of Canada has announced several new initiatives regarding vessel monitoring in the Arctic and the building of vessels to patrol the North.[30] The United States has welcomed the announcement of a greater Canadian presence in the Arctic.

---

25 Agreement on Pacific Hake/Whiting, Seattle, 21 November 2003, entered into force 25 June 2008, at <www-comm.pac.dfo-mpo.gc.ca/pages/release/bckgrnd/2003/HakeAgreement_e.htm> (accessed on 5 December 2006).

26 Agreement Amending the Treaty on Pacific Coast Tuna, notes exchanged 21 August 2002 and 10 September 2002, entered into force 28 May 2004, CTS 2004/12. The amendment is of the Treaty on Pacific Coast Albacore Tuna, Washington, 26 May 1981, entered into force 29 July 1981, CTS 1981/19, 33 UST 615, TIAS 10057, 1274 UNTS 247.

27 Exchange of Notes constituting an Agreement under the Pacific Salmon Treaty, Washington, 4 December 2002, entered into force 4 December 2002, CTS 2002/27, PSC, 2002/2003 Eighteenth Annual Report, 157–167.

28 PSC, Letter, 21 May 2008 and attached Annex IV, at www.psc.org (accessed on 3 June 2008).

29 *See* Chapter Five, section 3.4.5.

30 I. Bailey, *Harper Plans Arctic Patrol Fleet*, Toronto Globe and Mail, 10 July 2007, A-1, A-4. It was reported in September 2007 that Canada was going to monitor vessel traffic in the Northwest Passing using underwater listening devices. *Canada to Monitor Water Traffic in*

The stickiest issue in Canada-U.S. international ocean relations at present involves navigation rights through the Head Harbour Passage, the waterway between Maine and New Brunswick. LNG facilities have been proposed for northeastern Maine with the tankers to supply the facilities to go through Canadian waters.[31] This is a sequel to the 1970s dispute regarding oil tankers. Canada has informed the United States that it will not allow LNG tankers through its waters. The United States has long asserted a right of navigation through the Canadian waters. Unless the LNG facility proposals are approved by U.S. authorities and construction commences, the issue is not live. The 1970s oil refinery proposal ultimately was not carried out, and this may be the fate of the LNG proposals.

2.6 Assessing the Past

From a glass half-empty perspective, few of the Canada-U.S. international ocean law disputes have been resolved. With the exception of the Gulf of Maine area, none of the overlapping maritime boundary claims that have resulted from continental shelf and 200-nautical-mile zone claims have been resolved. There is the pesky issue of ownership of Machias Seal Island. Legal differences exist regarding the existence of navigational rights in numerous Canadian waters, most notably the Northwest Passage and the Head Harbour Passage. Respecting fisheries, the 1985 Pacific Salmon Treaty created a process and conflicting principles for determining management and allocation plans that failed in the 1990s, although a better result is anticipated for 2008 and 2010. There have been no formal bilateral discussions aimed at resolving the boundary and navigation disputes for decades.

Even where there are formal and informal agreements that manage disputes, it can be argued that they are incomplete, lack transparency, and, in some cases, are antithetical to a State's best interest. These criticisms have been leveled at, among others: the 1988 Arctic Cooperation Agreement; the Gulf of Maine bilateral fisheries management procedures; and the offshore hydrocarbon development moratoria respecting overlapping areas.

Northwest Passage, CBC News, 24 September 2007, at www.cbc.ca/canada/story /2007/09/24/technology-passage.html (accessed on 24 September 2007). In the February 2008 budget, $720 million was allocated for the purchase of a new polar class icebreaker. Department of Finance, The Budget Plan 2008: Responsible Leadership, 26 February 2008, 161, at www.budget.gc.ca/2008/plan/table-eng.asp (accessed on 7 March 2008).

31 *See* Chapter Six, section 4.1.2.

From a glass have-full perspective, almost all of the Canada-U.S. international ocean law disputes have been managed in a cooperative manner so that the disputes create little ongoing friction. Overlapping offshore claims have been calmed by fisheries enforcement understandings and moratoria on hydrocarbon development. Fisheries disputes have been minimized by the 1990 Fisheries Enforcement Agreement. Respecting navigational issues, there is the 1979 Vessel Traffic Management Agreement for the Juan de Fuca Region and the 1988 Arctic Cooperation Agreement.

The assessment here is that Canada and the United States have an enviable record of finding ways to defuse ocean issues and cooperate on operational matters of importance. The assessment applauds functional cooperation, rather than pointing out the lack of resolution or disregard of legal righteousness.

This positive assessment of cooperation is not to suggest that the Canada-U.S. ocean relationship has always been cordial. Both countries have, on numerous occasions, acted on their perceived international legal rights in a manner seen by the other as aggressive. The U.S. nuclear submarine traffic in the Dixon Entrance[32] and the 1985 *Polar Sea* voyage are examples of U.S. operational assertions of their rights. A Canadian operational assertion of its perceived international legal rights was the arrest in 1979 of U.S. tuna vessels within claimed Canadian waters undertaken at a time when the United States did not recognize Canada's authority to take such enforcement action.[33] And, of course, as regards Pacific salmon both States in the 1970s, 1980s, and 1990s allowed and even encouraged salmon harvesting as an assertion of their perceived rights to the detriment of the other State.

3.0 Looking to the Future

3.1 Differing International Law Positions

Canada and the United States have had and continue to have sharply different views on a large number of international ocean issues. The ocean priorities of the two States are different. In the allocation disputes, fisheries and maritime boundaries, each State responds to the interests of their respective

32 *See* Chapter Five, section 5.1.4.

33 *See* Chapter Seven, section 3.2.

citizenries to a claim of a "fair" share. The navigation and maritime boundary disputes raise sovereignty rhetoric which, particularly in the case of Canada, makes compromise politically risky. For the United States, navigational matters involve multilateral strategic considerations that complicate the bilateral situation. Moreover, although it is convenient to talk of Canada-U.S. international ocean relations and despite the generalizations above, each issue and dispute is separate and involves its own legal, economic, and political dynamic. Finally, there are the ups and downs of the broader Canada – U.S. relationship into which ocean matters fit.

The Canada-U.S. ocean disputes outlined in this work involve or are supported by different views of international law. The two States follow well-prepared scripts when commenting and acting to ensure consistency with their legal positions. It is important to understand that U.S. assertions of their *bona fide* legal position are not bullying; Canadian assertions are not petulance.

The strength or weakness of international legal support for a position is helpful in legitimizing it both within government and the public. It can be important in negotiations and, of course, in evaluation of the option of adjudication. Ultimately, however, the strength or weakness of an international legal position is only one factor, albeit often an important one, in bilateral discussions.

3.2 The Twenty-First Century Factors: Security, Environment, and Energy

Security, environment, and energy are not new influences on the Canada-U.S. international ocean relationship. For example, it was energy concerns, particularly the exploring of different options for transporting oil from Alaska to the lower forty-eight states, that spurred the 1969 to 1970 voyages of the *Manhattan* through the Northwest Passage. In the next few decades, these factors may take on increasing importance in the manner in which the two States view their bilateral ocean disputes and relationship. However, for all of the factors, it is difficult to assess whether their increased influence will encourage or discourage resolution or continued management of Canada-U.S. international ocean law disputes.

Although security concerns respecting vessel traffic through the Northwest Passage are raised as a reason for greater Canadian control over the Passage, as yet, the United States does not have a level of concern on security that has led to a change of position on the legal status of the Passage. Moreover, though the U.S. security concern in the last few years has shifted to its own waters, the United States also sees its ocean security as tied to freedom of navigation, which may include continuing to proclaim navigational rights in straits, such as the Northwest Passage, that the United States perceives to be international.

Global climate change has spurred debate and concern about the consequences of the opening of the Northwest Passage to increased vessel traffic. The call in Canada has been for greater assertions by Canada of its international legal position that the Arctic waters are subject to absolute Canadian authority. The United States, however, may see the opening of the Arctic as a shipping opportunity and be motivated to assert more aggressively its position that navigation rights exist in Canada's Arctic waters. Both States share concerns about the environment of the region and the safe navigation of vessels. Article 234 of the LOS Convention and the Arctic Waters Pollution Prevention Act, accepted by the United States, gives Canada significant, though not unlimited, scope to legislate and enforce protection of the Arctic environment and safe navigation.[34] The United States and Canada disagree whether there is a need for greater Canadian authority over passing vessels, in particular whether there is a legal necessity for vessels to obtain permission to utilize Canada's Arctic waters.

The reduction of fish stocks puts increased pressure on Canada and the United States to cooperatively manage cross-boundary fish stocks. At the same time, the reduction of harvesting opportunities puts pressure on the two States to protect the existing catches of their nationals. It is clear, however, that the urgency for conservation led the United States and Canada to overcome differing views on legal principles and complete the 1999 Pacific Salmon Agreement.

Both Canada and the United States have an interest in reliable supplies of energy resources. This may encourage the two States to reach an agreement in the Beaufort Sea to allow for hydrocarbon exploration.[35] The need for energy may also lead the two States to pursue their maximal positions and thus be unwilling to make the necessary compromises to obtain an agreement. Offshore hydrocarbon activity in the Beaufort Sea, like many other areas offshore Canada and the United States, raises considerable environmental opposition.

---

34 *See* Chapter Four, sections 2.2.2 and 2.2.4.

35 *See* Chapter Five, section 5.4.

The Head Harbour Passage might become a captive of the energy factor. Should one of the LNG facility proposals in the United States proceed to construction, the energy factor may result in a hardening of the U.S. resolve respecting the dispute. Canada has already staked out its position based on environmental considerations.

3.3 Dispute Resolution *versus* Dispute Management

The question for the future is whether Canada and the United States can find ways to resolve any or all of their international ocean law disputes or whether there will be a continuation of the past practices of managing the disputes.

3.3.1 Dispute Resolution

Resolution of international legal disputes can arise as a result of one of the following:

- *Capitulation*—One State concedes its position to that of the other.
- *Compromise*—Both States accept a less-than-optimal position.
- *Adjudication*—Use of international third-party dispute settlement eliminates a dispute.

As already noted, there is little opportunity for either Canada or the United States to force the other into international adjudication, hence to utilize international adjudication, the only option is for the two countries to agree to do so. The 1984 *Gulf of Maine Case* stands as the sole recent example of the two States using international adjudication regarding an ocean matter. It is unnecessary to replay the factors that led the two States to the International Court or to analyze the results. What can be pointed out is that international adjudication is costly (both in dollars and energy), can be divisive, is often unpredictable and may inhibit subsequent cooperation. For Canada and the United States to invest in international adjudication regarding an ocean issue, one of the following must be true of the matter in dispute: negotiation has been unsuccessful; it causes significant annoyance in the relationship; it is important to both States (although not so important that it affects either State's vital economic or political interests); the relevant stakeholders, however defined, are willing to gamble on adjudication; the legal positions of both sides are credible; and an adjudicative outcome will resolve the principal issue in dispute. The overlooked factor in some situations is that one or both States may see adjudication as an option to overcome a weak or untenable negotiating position. In this situation, better that an adjudicative tribunal make a ruling against a State, then the State compromise in negotiation.

One dispute that might fit the above considerations is the Dixon Entrance A-B Line dispute.[36] It is conceivable that the Machias Seal Island sovereignty dispute would also lend itself to adjudication.[37] Both of these disputes involve interpretations of historic documents and events. Moreover, the possibility of the international adjudication of these two disputes has already arisen between Canada and the United States.[38] Nevertheless, although these disputes are perceived as candidates for adjudication, neither Canada nor the United States have expressed such an interest in the last few decades. Beyond these two disputes, it is highly unlikely that in the immediate future Canada and the United States will seek or accept the adjudicative option for any of the other bilateral ocean law disputes.

The capitulation of a legal position is rare in international ocean disputes, whether the issues involved are maritime boundaries, fisheries, or navigation. The strength of legal argument for one State does not usually result in the other State backtracking. It is, therefore, highly unlikely that in the immediate future any of the Canada-U.S. ocean disputes referred to in this work will be resolved by one of the States reversing its long-held legal posture. To expect or advocate capitulation by either State on the principal Canada-U.S. ocean issues (*i.e.*, the Northwest Passage, the Head Harbour Passage, Pacific salmon, and the Beaufort Sea maritime boundary) is unrealistic.

A negotiated compromise can overcome a dispute. Canada and the United States have few modern examples of compromise agreements that fully resolve an ocean law dispute. The bilateral fisheries agreements involving halibut, tuna, and hake/whiting may be cited as examples, although these are really accords that address resource allocations and management rather than differences of international legal position. Maritime boundary agreements resolve overlapping claim disputes usually through the States compromising

---

36 *See* Chapter Five, sections 5.1.1 and 6.0.

37 *See* Chapter Five, section 5.5.1.

38 *See* Department of State, DIGEST OF UNITED STATES PRACTICE IN INTERNATIONAL LAW, 1973 (Washington, 1974) 465–466 and Aide-Memoire from Embassy of Canada to the Department of State, 4 January 1974, in *Gulf of Maine Pleadings*, Vol. 5, Annex 18 to Reply of the United States, 552–553.

on their asserted positions. However, it was 1925 when Canada and the United States last completed such an agreement[39] and the 1970s when the last detailed talks on maritime boundaries took place. The Canada-U.S. navigation issues do not lend themselves easily to compromise, since either a navigation right exists (the U.S. posture) or it does not (the Canadian view). The two most promising bilateral disputes for a compromise agreement are the Beaufort Sea maritime boundary and the overlapping claims dispute seaward of the Gulf of Maine boundary.[40] In the case of the latter, attention, if not resolution, will be necessary prior to Canada making its submission to the Commission on the Limits of the Continental Shelf regarding the outer limit of its continental margin beyond 200 nautical miles on the Atlantic Coast. Reaching of an agreement may be a bit easier since there is little awareness of the existence of the dispute. The Beaufort Sea maritime boundary is at the other extreme. It has long been seen as the bilateral boundary dispute of most urgency, given the need for certainty in order to pursue the potential hydrocarbon resources in the area. It is this urgency and high profile that may allow the two States to find an acceptable compromise. Here also, attention will have to be given by the States to the maritime boundary prior to Canada or the United States makng their submission to the Commission on the Limits of the Continental Shelf regarding the outer limits of the continental shelf in the Arctic Ocean.

It is occasionally mooted that the linking of differing issues should be pursued between Canada and the United States as a means to achieve the necessary compromise for resolution. The two States linked the fisheries and maritime boundary issues in the Gulf of Maine only to have the fisheries agreement rejected in favor of gambling on adjudicating the maritime boundary. Linking the various maritime boundary disputes in a comprehensive deal was discussed in the 1970s, although Canada made it clear that no trade-offs of Atlantic and Pacific regions would be undertaken. It has been suggested that the Beaufort Sea be linked to the Northwest Passage, with the U.S. yielding to Canada on the Passage and Canada yielding to the United States regarding the Beaufort Sea.[41] One can envision various linkage

---

39 Treaty regarding the Demarcation of the Boundary between the United States and Canada, Washington, 24 February 1925, entered into force 17 July 1925, Art. 3, 43 LNTS 239.

40 *See* Chapter Five, section 5.3.

41 K. M. Shusterich, *International Jurisdictional Issues in the Arctic Ocean*, in W. E. WESTERMEYER AND K. M. SHUSTERICH (eds.) UNITED STATES ARCTIC INTERESTS: THE 1980s AND 1990s (Springer-Verlag, New York 1984) 253.

scenarios, however, Canada and the United States have not regularly engaged in linkage negotiating preferring to view each dispute on its own merits.

3.3.2 Dispute Management

Given the undistinguished record of Canada and the United States resolving their international ocean law disputes, the more likely outlook for the future is a continuation of the management of disputes through formal and informal agreements and arrangements. This will allow both States to continue to assert their international legal positions, yet functionally and operationally ensures that both States cooperate.

It can be expected that the international legal positions of Canada and the United States respecting Pacific salmon (State-of-origin for Canada; coastal State authority for the United States), will remain as it was in the late 1990s as secondary to conservation of the resource. In the 1999 Agreement, the two States buried their disagreement over international legal principles with ambiguous language on respect for each State's position and crafted an allocation and management arrangement that focused primarily on conservation, and this has been repeated in the 2008 recommendations of the Pacific Salmon Commission to replace the 1999 Agreement.

It has been argued by various commentators that safety, environmental, and security considerations should lead Canada and the United States to find a resolution of their international legal dispute on the status of and navigational rights within the Northwest Passage and that this is becoming more critical because of global climate change and U.S. security concerns. There have been suggestions to internationalize the Northwest Passage or establish a bilateral agreement or arrangement whereby the United States obtains from Canada unimpeded navigational rights in the Passage and the United States recognizes Canada's legal position as superior. Each of these scenarios would entail either Canada or the United States recanting its international legal position. The two States may indeed heed the calls and enter into such a resolutive agreement. However, history is against it. A more likely future is a management arrangement that operationally provides for safety, environmental, and the security monitoring and control of vessels in the Northwest Passage and which allows Canada and the United States to maintain their international legal positions. The 1988 Arctic Cooperation Agreement already accomplishes this as regards U.S. Coast Guard icebreakers. U.S. government vessels engaging in marine scientific research as the basis for seeking consent is not easily transferable to U.S.-flagged commercial vessels; thus, some other manner of respecting the legal positions of both States is necessary. Canada's proposed increased presence and capacity in the Arctic may create an opportunity either formally or informally. One possibility concerns the proposed deepwater port to be constructed by Canada along the Northwest Passage. Ports are internal waters over which the port State has absolute sovereignty including the right to require consent for entry. A Canada-U.S. treaty, akin to the 1988 Arctic Cooperation Agreement, through which all U.S.-flagged vessels using the Northwest Passage would be required to seek the consent of Canada to enter the new port, whether or not the vessel elected to use the privilege, may bury the international legal dispute and enhance the functional and operational needs to control and monitor commercial vessels in the passage.

Regarding the Beaufort Sea maritime boundary dispute, if a negotiated line cannot be achieved, the obvious alternative that has already been mooted by Canada and the United States is some type of joint development or bilateral sharing arrangement for the hydrocarbon resources of the disputed area. Typically, such joint arrangements suspend the resolution of the maritime boundary until a future date. However, joint hydrocarbon development agreements are not easily negotiated or implemented.

4.0 Conclusion

Fisheries, maritime boundaries and navigational rights have been staples of the Canada-U.S. international ocean law relationship since the 1700s. The 200-nautical-mile zone eased some of the historic problems, such as disputes over near-shore fishing. However, it exacerbated or created maritime boundary and other fishery issues. Moreover, navigation disputes in waters such as the Northwest Passage have remained problematic.

Over three decades of conflict, rhetoric, collaboration, negotiation, and litigation have shaped the modern Canada-U.S. salt water relationship. The record is bereft of resolved disputes, but fulsome regarding cooperative agreements and arrangements that circumvent and manage the disputes. It is because of these cooperative agreements and arrangements that ocean matters, which once dominated the Canada-U.S. bilateral agenda as recently as the 1980s, now are seen as minor issues. Where the relationship is composed of one party sensitive respecting its engagement with and reception by the other; and the other party neglectful, although not malevolent, towards its neighbor largely as a result of a global agenda and responsibilities; this is not a bad situation.

Selected Bibliography and Government Documents

GOVERNMENT DOCUMENTS

Canada

i) Department documents

Coast Guard

—"Canada-US Relations," at www.ccc-gcc.ca/ia-ai/Canada_usa_e.htm (accessed on 14 May 2007).

Department of Finance

—"The Budget Plan 2008: Responsible Leadership," February 26, 2008, at www.budget.gc.ca/2008/plan/table-eng.asp (accessed on 7 March 2008).

Department of Fisheries and Oceans/Department of Fisheries

—"Canada-U.S. Agreement Reached on Pacific Salmon Harvest," 24 June 1993.

—"Canada and the United States Sign Treaty to Improve Stewardship of Pacific Hake," at www-comm.pac.dfo-mpo.gc.ca/pages/release/p-releas/2003/nr066_e.htm (accessed on 4 November 2006).

—"Licence Fee Announced for U.S. Vessels," 9 June 1994.

—Maritime Region, Transboundary Management Guidance Committee, *Development of a Sharing Allocation Proposal for Transboundary Resources of Cod, Haddock and Yellowtail Flounder on Georges Bank*, (Fisheries Management Regional Report 2002/01, January 2002), at www.mar.dfo-mpo.gc.ca/science/tmgc/bacground/FMR%202002_01.pdf (accessed on 5 March 2007).

—*Notice to Mariners: Annual Edition 2006.*

—*Overview of Current Governance in the Bay of Fundy/Gulf of Maine: Transboundary Collaborative Arrangements and Initiatives* (May 2006).

Department of Foreign Affairs and International Trade/Department of Foreign Affairs/Department of External Affairs

—"Briefing," 21 May 1987 in (1987) 25 CYIL 406.

—"Letter to Edmund Muskie," 7 November 1979, copy on file with the author.

—"Letter," 17 December 1973 in (1974) 12 CYIL 277.

—"Joint Report by Chief Negotiators of Canada—U.S. Maritime Boundaries and Related Resource Issues," 21 October 1977, attached to the Department of External

Affairs document is the "Joint Report of Ambassador Cadieux and Ambassador Cutler to the Governments of Canada and the United States: Negotiations on Maritime Boundaries and Related Resource Issues," all reprinted in Canada, *Minutes of Proceedings of the Standing Committee on Fisheries*, 11 April 1978, (30th Parliament, 3rd Session, 1977–1978), Issue no. 15, appendix.

—"Memorandum," 15 July 1980 in (1981) 19 CYIL 328.

—"Memorandum," 6 August 1987 in (1988) 26 CYIL 320.

—"Memorandum - Canada Ratification Practice," April 2002 in (2002) 40 CYIL 490.

—"Paper," 19 March 2001 in (2001) 39 CYIL 486.

—"Some Examples of Current Issues of International Law of Particular Importance to Canada," October, 1986, at p. 16 cited in D Russell, "International Ocean Boundary Issues and Management Arrangements" in D VanderZwaag (ed) *Canadian Ocean Law and Policy* (Butterworths, Toronto 1992), at p. 494.

—*The Third United Nations Conference on the Law of the Sea* (Ottawa, 1973).

Department of Natural Resources

—"Georges Bank Moratorium Extended," 22 December 1999, in Can Gaz Part I, Vol. 134, 29 January 2000, at pp. 274–276.

—*Georges Bank Review Panel Report* (June 1999).

Department of Transport

—"Vessel Traffic Reporting Arctic CanadaTraffic Zone (NORDREG)," at www.ccg-gcc.gc.ca/cen-arc/mcts-sctm/mcts-services/vtrarctic_e.htm (accessed on 19 July 2007).

ii) House of Commons

D.R. Bollivar, Associate Director, International Fisheries Branch, Department of Fisheries and Environment, *Minutes of Proceedings and Evidence of the Standing Committee on Fisheries and Forestry*, 23 February 1979, (30th Parliament, 4th Session, 1978–1979), Issue no. 6.

Joe Clark, Minister for External Affairs, *Debates*, 10 September 1985, at pp. 6462–6464.

Lorne Clark, Deputy Negotiator for Maritime Boundaries Canada/U.S., *Minutes of Proceedings and Evidence of the Standing Committee on Fisheries and Forestry*, 11 April 1978 (30th Parliament, 3rd Session, 1977–1978), Issue no. 15.

Jack Davis, Minister of Fisheries and Forestry, *Debates*, 18 December 1970, at pp. 2189–2190.

J. J. Greene, Minister of Energy, Mines and Natural Resources, *Debates*, 9 March 1970, at pp. 4570.

Alvin Hamilton, Minister of Northern Affairs and Natural Resources, *Debates*, 25 July 1958, at pp. 2682–2683

B. G. Hankey, Secretary, Negotiations for Maritime Boundaries Canada/U.S., House of Commons, *Minutes of Proceedings and Evidence of the Standing Committee on Fisheries*, 11 April 1978, (30th Parliament, 3rd Session, 1977–1978), Issue no. 15.

Stephen Harper, Prime Minister, *Debates*, 26 September 2006, at p. 3271.

Allan MacEachen, Minister of External Affairs, *Minutes of Proceedings and Evidence of the Standing Committee on External Affairs and National Defence*, 22 May 1975 (30th Parliament, 1st Session, 1975), Issue no. 24.

L. B. Pearson, Prime Minister, *Debates*, 4 June 1963, at p. 621.

Mitchell Sharp, Minister of External Affairs, *Debates*, 16 April 1970, at p. 5951.

—*Debates*, 17 April 1970, at pp. 6014–6015.

Brian Tobin, Minister of Fisheries and Oceans, *Debates*, 11 May 1994, at pp. 4213–4214.

Pierre Trudeau, Prime Minister, *Debates*, 15 May 1969, at p. 8720.

—*Debates*, 24 October 1969, at pp. 39–40.

Erik Wang, Director, Legal Operations Division, Department of External Affairs, *Minutes of Proceedings and Evidence of the Standing Committee on External Affairs and National Defence*, 27 April 1978 (30th Parliament, 3rd Session, 1977–1978), Issue no. 16.

iii) Communications with the United States

1969 "Diplomatic Note No. 366," 1 December 1969, in *Case Concerning Delimitation of the Maritime Boundary in the Gulf of Maine Area (Canada/United States), ICJ Pleadings, Oral Arguments, Documents*, Vol. 1, Annex 44 to Memorial of Canada, at p. 390.

1970 "Note No. 105 from the Embassy of Canada to the United States Department of State," 16 April 1970, in *Case Concerning Delimitation of the Maritime Boundary in the Gulf of Maine Area (Canada/United States), ICJ Pleadings, Oral Arguments, Documents*, Vol. 5, Annex 8 to Reply of the United States, at p. 534.

"Summary of Canadian Note of April 16 Tabled by the Secretary of State for External Affairs in the House April 17," in (1970) 9 ILM 607.

1973 "Note No. 206 to the United States," 7 June 1973, copy on file with the author.

1974 "Aide-Memoire from Embassy of Canada to the Department of State," 4 January 1974, in *Case Concerning Delimitation of the Maritime Boundary in the Gulf of Maine Area (Canada/United States), ICJ Pleadings, Oral Arguments, Documents*, Vol. 5, Annex 18 to Reply of the United States, at pp. 552–553.

1976 "Diplomatic Note No. 626," 22 December 1976, in *Case Concerning Delimitation of the Maritime Boundary in the Gulf of Maine Area (Canada/United States), ICJ Pleadings, Oral Arguments, Documents*, Vol. 1, Annex 46 to Memorial of Canada, at pp. 430–433.

1977 "Diplomatic Note No. 221," 26 May 1977, in *Case Concerning Delimitation of the Maritime Boundary in the Gulf of Maine Area (Canada/United States), ICJ Pleadings, Oral Arguments, Documents*, Vol. 1, Annex 54 to Memorial of Canada, at pp. 444–448.

"Diplomatic Note No. GNT-067," 3 November 1977, in *Case Concerning Delimitation of the Maritime Boundary in the Gulf of Maine Area (Canada/United States), ICJ Pleadings, Oral Arguments, Documents*, Vol. 1, Annex 59 to Memorial of Canada, at pp. 452–454.

1983 "Diplomatic Note No. 021," 17 January 1983, in *Case Concerning Delimitation of the Maritime Boundary in the Gulf of Maine Area (Canada/United States), ICJ*

Pleadings, Oral Arguments, Documents, Vol. 5, Annex 22 to Reply of Canada, at pp. 350–351.

1985 "Note from Canada to the United States," 11 June 1985, in part in JA Roach and RW Smith, *United States Responses to Excessive Maritime Claims* (Martinus Nijhoff, 2nd edition, The Hague 1996), at pp. 344–345.

"Note from Canada to the United States," 31 July 1985, in JA Roach and RW Smith, *United States Responses to Excessive Maritime Claims* (Martinus Nijhoff, 2nd edition, The Hague 1996), at pp. 346–348.

1997 "Note No. 0389 to the United States," 7 May 1997, copy on file with the author

2007 "Letter from Ambassador Michael Wilson to Joseph T. Kelliher," 14 February 2007, in *Saint John Telegraph Journal*, 15 February 2007, at p. A8.

iv) Miscellaneous

"*Amicus Curiae* Brief," 22 August 1999, in *United States v. Locke*, U.S. Supreme Court, docket 98-1701 and 98-1706, at <supreme.lp.findlaw.com/supreme_court/briefs/98-1701/98-1701fo11/brief/breif06.html> (accessed on 15 May 2007).

"Declaration Recognizing as Compulsory the Jurisdiction of the Court," 7 April 1970, in ICJ, *Yearbook 1969–1970* (The Hague, 1970), at pp. 55–56, 9 ILM 598.

"Declaration Made Upon Ratification," 7 November 2003, in 53 LOSB p. 15.

"Historical Introduction" in *Case Concerning Delimitation of the Maritime Boundary in the Gulf of Maine Area (Canada/United States), ICJ Pleadings, Oral Arguments, Documents*, Vol. 1, Annex to Memorial of the Canada, at pp. 181–201.

"Letter from Ambassador Stephen Lewis to the Secretary-General of the United Nations," 10 September 1985, 24 ILM 1727.

A.J. MacEachen, Canadian Minister of External Affairs, "Statement," 6 December 1982, in UNCLOS III, *Official Records*, Vol. XVII, at pp. 14–16.

Order-in-Council, 6 July 1909, enclosed in letter from the Administrator to the Colonial Secretary, 13 July 1909, in *Documents of Canada's External Affairs*, Vol. I, 1909–1918 (Department of External Affairs, 1967), at pp. 400–405.

Prime Minister Harper, "Securing Canadian Sovereignty in the Arctic," at www.pm.gc.ca/eng/media.asp?id=1275 (accessed on 24 April 2007).

Securing an Open Society: Canada's National Security Policy (Ottawa, 2004).

"Statement," 3 December 1992, in PSC, 1992/1993 Eighth Annual Report, at pp. 8–9.

"Working Paper on the Special Case of Salmon—The Most Important Anadromous Species," U.N. Doc. A/Conf.62/C.2/L.81, 23 August 1974, in UNCLOS III, *Official Records*, Vol. III, at p. 240.

United States

i) Presidential Statements

President G. Bush, "Statement on Outer Continental Shelf Oil and Gas Development," 26 June 1990, in *Public Papers of George Bush 1990* (Government Printing Office, 1991), at pp. 869–870.

President G. W. Bush, "Statement on Advancing U.S. Interests in the World's Oceans," 15 May 2007, 46 ILM 890.

President Clinton, "Memorandum on Withdrawal of Certain Areas of the United States Outer Continental Shelf from Leasing Deposition," 12 June 1998, in *Public Papers of William J. Clinton, 1998* (Government Printing Office, 1999), at p. 945.

President Nixon, "Statement—United States Policy for the Seabed," 23 May 1970, in SH Lay, R Churchill and M Nordquist (eds) *New Directions in the Law of the Sea*, Vol II (Oceana Publications, Dobbs Ferry, N.Y. 1973), at pp. 751–752.

President Reagan, "Statement" and "White House Fact Sheet," 29 January 1982, in *Department of State Bulletin*, March 1982, Vol. 82, No. 2060, at pp. 54–55.

—"Statement," 9 July 1982, reprinted in *Department of State Bulletin*, August 1982, Vol. 82, No. 2065, at p. 71.

—"Statement - U.S. Oceans Policy," 10 March 1983, 22 ILM 464.

ii) Department Documents

Coast Guard

—"Office on Law Enforcement," at <www.uscg.mil/hq/g-o/g-opl/Welcome.htm> (accessed on 13 July 2007).

Department of Defence

—*Maritime Claims Reference Manual* (Washington, 2005).

Department of State

—*Cumulative Digest of United States Practice in International Law, 1981–1988* (Washington, 1994).

—*Digest of United States Practice in International Law, 1973* (Washington, 1974).

—*Digest of United States Practice in International Law, 1974* (Washington,1975).

—*Digest of United States Practice in International Law, 1975* (Washington, 1976).

—*Digest of United States Practice in International Law, 1991–1999* (Washington: International Law Institute, 2005).

—*Foreign Relations of the United States* (Johnson Administration, 1964–1968), (Washington, 2001), Vol. XII, Document 317, "Report Prepared by the Deputy Under Secretary of State for Political Affairs" (undated), at p. 678.

—Document 321, "Memorandum of Conversation," (Ottawa, 6 July 1964), at pp. 684–686.

—Document 325, "Telegram from the Department of State to the Mission to the United Nations," (Washington, 9 December 1964), at pp. 693–694.

—*Foreign Relations of the United States* (Nixon-Ford Administrations, 1969–1976), Vol. E-1, Document 367, "Information Memorandum for Mr. Kissinger—The White House: Subject—Imminent Canadian Legislation on the Arctic," from T.L. Eliot, Jr., (Washington, 12 March 1970), at www.state.gov/r/pa/ho/frus/nixon/e1/53180.htm (accessed on 7 August 2007).

—Document 369, "Memorandum for the President," prepared by U.A. Johnson (21 March 1970), at www.state.gov/r/pa/ho/frus/nixon/e1/53185.htmat (accessed on 7 August 2007).

—*Geographic Note*, No. 2, 31 January 1986.

—Public Notice 320, 12 February 1970, 35 Fed Reg 3301.

—"Summary of Provisions of Draft 'United Nations Convention on the International Seabed Area'," prepared by John R. Stevenson, Legal Adviser, 3 August 1970, in SH Lay, R Churchill and M Nordquist (eds) *New Directions in the Law of the Sea*, Vol II (Oceana Publications, Dobbs Ferry, N.Y. 1973), at pp. 753–768.

—"United States Responses to Excessive Maritime Claims," *Limits in the Seas*, No. 112 (Washington, 1992).

Department of Interior

—Gary M. Edson, Donald L. Olson and Andrew J. Petty, "Georges Bank Petroleum Exploration: Atlantic Outer Continental Shelf" (OCS Report MMS 2000-031, May 2000), at <www.gomr.mms.gov/PDFs/2000/2000-031.pdf> (accessed on 19 April 2007).

Fish and Wildlife Service

—*Maine Coastal Islands National Wildlife Refuge: Final Comprehensive Conservation Plan* (April 2005), at p. 3–76 at <library.fws.gov/CCPs/MaineIslands/ccp_final.pdf> (accessed on 6 December 2007).

iii) Treaty Documents

1979 Agreement between Canada and the United States on East Coast Fishery Resources, done at Washington 29 March 1979, United States, Senate, Executive Document V, 96th Congress, 1st Session (1979), in M Nordquist and KR Simmonds (eds) *New Directions in the Law of the Sea*, Vol. IX (Oceans Publications, Dobbs Ferry, N.Y. 1980), at pp. 178–212.

Agreement between Canada and the United States to Submit to Binding Dispute Settlement the Delimitation of the Maritime Boundary in the Gulf of Maine, done at Washington 29 March 1979, United States, Senate, Executive Document U, 96th Congress, 1st Session, (1979).

1981 "Letter of Submittal from Walter J. Stoessel, Jr., to President regarding the Treaty with Canada on Pacific Coast Albacore Tuna Vessels and Port Privileges," 13 June 1981, U.S. Senate, Treaty Document 97-13.

Senate, Executive Report No. 5, 97th Congress, 1st Session, "Maritime Boundary Settlement with Canada.".

1992 "Letter of Submittal from James A. Baker, III to the President regarding the Convention for the Conservation of Anadromous Fish Stocks in the North Pacific Ocean, 14 May 1992," U.S. Senate, Treaty Document 102-30.

1993 "Standing Rules of the Senate" in *Treaties and Other International Agreements: The Role of the United States Senate*, Senate Part 103-53, (November 1993), Rule XXX—Proceedings on Treaties.

1994 President Clinton, "Message from the President of the United States transmitting United Nations Convention on the Law of the Sea, with Annexes, done at Montego Bay, December 10, 1982 (the Convention) and the Agreement Relating to the Implementation of Part XI of the United Nations Convention on the Law of the Sea of December 10, 1982, adopted at New York, July 28, 1994 (the Agreement) and signed by the United States, subject to ratification, on July 29, 1994," Senate, Treaty Document 39, 103d Congress, 2d Session IV (1994), 34 ILM 1393.

2002 "Letter of Submittal from Colin Powell to the President regarding the Agreement Amending the Treaty between the United States and Canada on Pacific Coast Albacore Tuna Vessels and Port Privileges," 9 October 2002, U.S. Senate, Treaty Document 108-1.

2004 Senate Executive Report 108-110, Part VII—Text of Resolution of Advice and Consent to Ratification, at 16-21 (2004) (S. Cong. Rec. S2712-S2716 (March 11, 2004).

2007 United States, Senate, Executive Report 110-9, Part VIII—Text of Resolution of Advice and Consent to Ratification, at 19–24 (2007).

iv) Communications with Canada

1966 "Note from the Department of State to the Embassy of Canada," 29 November 1966, in *Case Concerning Delimitation of the Maritime Boundary in the Gulf of Maine Area (Canada/United States), ICJ Pleadings, Oral Arguments, Documents*, Vol. 4, Annex 34 to Counter-Memorial of the United States, at p. 472.

1967 "Note from the United States Department of State to the Embassy of Canada," 1 November 1967, in *Case Concerning Delimitation of the Maritime Boundary in the Gulf of Maine Area (Canada/United States), ICJ Pleadings, Oral Arguments, Documents*, Vol. 4, Annex 34 to Counter-Memorial of the United States, at pp. 473–474.

1969 "Note from the Secretary of State to Embassy of Canada," 25 April 1969, in *Case Concerning Delimitation of the Maritime Boundary in the Gulf of Maine Area (Canada/United States), ICJ Pleadings, Oral Arguments, Documents*, Vol. 5, Annex 4 to Reply of the United States, at pp. 503–504.

"Note from the Department of State to the Canadian Embassy," 5 November 1969, in *Case Concerning Delimitation of the Maritime Boundary in the Gulf of Maine Area (Canada/United States), ICJ Pleadings, Oral Arguments, Documents*, Vol. 2, Annex 56 to Memorial of the United States, at pp. 356–357.

1970 "Note from the Secretary of State to Embassy of Canada," 14 April 1970, in *Case Concerning Delimitation of the Maritime Boundary in the Gulf of Maine Area (Canada/United States), ICJ Pleadings, Oral Arguments, Documents*, Vol. 5, Annex 8 to Reply of the United States, at pp. 529–530.

"Department of State Statement on Government of Canada's Bills on Limits of the Territorial Sea, Fisheries and Pollution," 15 April 1970, 9 ILM 605.

"Note from the Secretary of State to Embassy of Canada," 5 May 1970, in *Case Concerning Delimitation of the Maritime Boundary in the Gulf of Maine Area (Canada/United States), ICJ Pleadings, Oral Arguments, Documents*, Vol. 5, Annex 8 to Reply of the United States, at pp. 529–530 and 535–537.

"Statement on Canadian Fisheries Closing Lines Announcement," 18 December 1970, in SH Lay, R Churchill and M Nordquist (eds) *New Directions in the Law of the Sea*, Vol I (Oceana Publications, Dobbs Ferry, N.Y. 1973), at p. 74.

1975 "Aide-Memoire to the Government of Canada," 12 March 1975, cited in Department of State, *Digest of United States Practice in International Law, 1975*, (Washington, 1976), at p. 432.

1976 "Diplomatic Note No. 103," 20 May 1976, in *Case Concerning Delimitation of the Maritime Boundary in the Gulf of Maine Area (Canada/United States), ICJ Pleadings, Oral Arguments, Documents*, Vol. 1, Annex 32 to Memorial of Canada, at pp. 410–411.

1977 "Note from the Department of State to the Embassy of Canada," 16 February 1977, in *Case Concerning Delimitation of the Maritime Boundary in the Gulf of Maine Area (Canada/United States), ICJ Pleadings, Oral Arguments, Documents*, Vol. 2, Annex 66 to Memorial of the United States, at pp. 378–379.

1978 "Note from the Department of State to the Embassy of Canada," 3 February 1978, in *Case Concerning Delimitation of the Maritime Boundary in the Gulf of Maine Area (Canada/United States), ICJ Pleadings, Oral Arguments, Documents*, Vol. 2, Annex 70 to Memorial of the United States, at pp. 385–386.

"Note from the Department of State to the Embassy of Canada," 20 September 1978, in *Case Concerning Delimitation of the Maritime Boundary in the Gulf of Maine Area (Canada/United States), ICJ Pleadings, Oral Arguments, Documents*, Vol. 2, Annex 74 to Memorial of the United States, at pp. 396–397.

1979 "Note from the Department of State to the Embassy of Canada," 15 February 1979, in *Case Concerning Delimitation of the Maritime Boundary in the Gulf of Maine Area (Canada/United States), ICJ Pleadings, Oral Arguments, Documents*, Vol. 2, Annex 74 to Memorial of the United States, at pp. 397–398.

1983 "Diplomatic Note No. 49," 23 February 1983, in *Case Concerning Delimitation of the Maritime Boundary in the Gulf of Maine Area (Canada/United States), ICJ Pleadings, Oral Arguments, Documents*, Vol. 5, Annex 22 to Reply of Canada, at pp. 351–352.

1985 "*Demarche* from the United States to Canada," 21 May 1985, in JA Roach and RW Smith, *United States Responses to Excessive Maritime Claims* (Martinus Nijhoff, 2nd edition, The Hague 1996), at pp. 342–343.

"Note from the United States to Canada," 24 June 1985, in JA Roach and RW Smith, *United States Responses to Excessive Maritime Claims* (Martinus Nijhoff, 2nd edition, The Hague 1996), at pp. 345–346.

1994 Department of State, "Canada Transit Fee," 15 June 1994, as cited and reproduced in CB Picker, "Fishing for Answers in Canada's Inside Passage: Exploring the Use of the Transit Fee as a Countermeasure" (1996) 21 Yale J Intl L 349, at p. 361.

v) Miscellaneous

Mark B. Feldman, "Testimony before the U.S. Senate Foreign Relations Committee," 18 March 1981, in *Department of State Bulletin*, May 1981, Vol. 81, No. 2050, at p. 23.

James L. Malone, "Statement," 30 April 1982, in UNCLOS III, *Official Records*, Vol. XVI, at pp. 154 and 155–156.

John D. Negroponte, "Current Developments in the U.S. Oceans Policy" in *Department of State Bulletin*, September 1986, Vol. 84, No. 2114, at p. 86.

"News Conference—President Bush, Prime Minister Harper and President Calderon, Montebello, Quebec," 21 August 2007, *Weekly Compilation of Presidential Documents*, 2007, at p. 1091.

United States, "Aide-Memoire April 1991 from the U.S. Mission to the United Nations to the Secretary-General of the United Nations," in Department of State, *Digest of United States Practice in International Law, 1991–1999* (Washington: International Law Institute, 2005), at pp. 1707–1708.

—"Changes Suggested by the Delegation of the United States," UN Doc A/Conf.62/WG.21/Infrormal Paper 18, 10 March 1982, in R Platzoder (ed) *Third United Nations Conference on the Law of the Sea Documents*, Vol. VI (Oceana Publications, Dobbs Ferry, N.Y. 1984) at pp. 278–303 and Vol. VIII (Oceana Publications, Dobbs Ferry, N.Y. 1985) at pp. 304–337.

—"Delegation Report from the Seabed Committee, Geneva, July 2-August 24, 1973," in MH Nordquist and C Park (eds) *Reports of the United States Delegation to the Third United Nations Conference on the Law of the Sea* (Law of the Sea Institute, Honolulu 1983), at pp. 45–46.

—"Delegation Report of Third Session, 1975," in MH Nordquist and C Park (eds) *Reports of the United States Delegation to the Third United Nations Conference on the Law of the Sea* (Law of the Sea Institute, Honolulu 1983), at p. 94.

—"Letter to the Secretary-General of the United Nations from Secretary of State George P. Shultz," 7 October 1985, 24 ILM 1742.

—"Reply of the United States," in *Case Concerning Delimitation of the Maritime Boundary in the Gulf of Maine Area (Canada/United States), ICJ Pleadings, Oral Arguments, Documents*, Vol. V, at pp. 373–496.

—"Special Considerations Regarding the Management of Anadromous Species and Highly Migratory Oceanic Fishes: Working Paper Submitted by the United States," UN Doc A/AC.138/SC.II/L.20, 2 April 1973.

—"Statement," 3 December 1992, in PSC, 1992/1993 Eighth Annual Report, at pp. 10 and 12–14.

BOOKS

Lewis M. Alexander (ed.) *The Law of the Sea: The United Nations and Ocean Management* (Law of the Sea Institute, Kingston, R.I. 1971).

Lewis M. Alexander and R.S. Hawkins (eds.) *Canadian-U.S. Maritime Problems* (Law of the Sea Institute, Kingston, R.I. 1972).

R.C. Amacher and R.J. Sweeney (eds.) *The Law of the Sea: U.S. Interests and Alternatives* (American Enterprise Institute for Public Policy Research, Washington 1976).

Salvatore Arico and Charlotte Salpin, *Bioprospecting of Genetic Resources in the Deep Seabed: Scientific, Legal and Policy Aspects* (United Nations University, Yokohama 2005).

F. Heward Bell, *The Pacific Halibut: The Resource and the Fishery* (Alaska Northwest Publishing Company, Anchorage 1981).

F. Berkes, R. Huebert, H. Fast, M. Manseau, and A. Diduck (eds.) *Breaking Ice: Renewable Resources and Ocean Management in the Canadian North* (University of Calgary Press, Calgary 2005).

L. M. Bloomfield and Gerald F. Fitzgerald, *Boundary Waters Problems of Canada and the United States* (Carswell, Toronto 1958).

Yehuda Z. Blum, *Historic Titles in International Law* (Martinus Nijhoff, The Hague 1965).

Philippe Boisson, *Safety at Sea: Policies, Regulations and International Law* (Bureau Veritas, Paris 1999).

L.J. Bouchez, *The Regime of Bays in International Law* (A.Y. Sythoff, Leyden 1964).

Patricia Birnie and Alan E. Boyle, *International Law and the Environment* (Oxford University Press, 2nd ed., Oxford 2002).

Dennis Brown, *Salmon Wars: The Battle for the West Coast Fishery* (Harbour Publishing, Vancouver 2005).

E.D. Brown, *The International Law of the Sea* (Dartmouth, Aldershot 1994).

R. Douglas Brubaker, The *Russian Arctic Straits* (Martinus Nijhoff, Leiden 2005).

William T. Burke, *The New International Law of Fisheries* (Clarendon Press, Oxford 1994).

Barry Buzan, *Seabed Politics* (Praeger Publishers, New York 1976).

Bruce Calderbank, Alex M. MacLeod, T.L. McDorman, and David H. Gray, *Canada's Offshore: Jurisdiction, Rights, and Management* (Trafford Publishing, 3rd edition, Victoria 2006).

D. Carment, F. O. Hampson, and N. Hillmer (eds.) *Canada Among Nations, 2004: Setting Priorities Straight* (McGill-Queen's University Press, Montreal 2005).

Chi Carmody, Yuji Iwasawa, and Sylvia Rhodes (eds.) *Trilateral Perspectives on International Legal Issues: Conflict and Coherence* (American Society of International Law, Washington 2003).

David D. Caron and Harry N. Scheiber (eds.) *Bringing New Law to Ocean Waters* (Martinus Nijhoff, Leiden 2004).

John E. Carroll, *Environmental Diplomacy: An Examination and a Prospective of Canadian-U.S. Transboundary Environmental Relations* (University of Michigan Press, Ann Arbor 1983).

Jonathan I. Charney and Lewis M. Alexander (eds.) *International Maritime Boundaries*, Volume I (Martinus Nijhoff, Boston 1993).

R.R. Churchill and A. V. Lowe, *The Law of the Sea* (Manchester University Press, 3rd edition, Manchester 1999).

Stephen Clarkson, *Canada and the Reagan Challenge: Crisis and Adjustment, 1981-1985* (James Lorimer and Company, Toronto 1985).

H. George Classen, *Thrust and Counterthrust: The Genesis of the Canada—United States Boundary* (Longmans Canada, Don Mills, Ontario 1965).

David A. Colson and Robert W. Smith (eds.) *International Maritime Boundaries*, Volume V (Martinus Nijhoff, Leiden 2005).

Adrian Cook, *The Alabama Claims: American Politics and Anglo-American Relations, 1865-1872* (Cornell University Press, London 1975).

Andrew F. Cooper and Dane Rowlands (eds.) *Canada Among Nations, 2006: Minorities and Priorities* (McGill-Queen's University Press, Montreal 2006).

Charles F. Doran, *Forgotten Partnership: U.S.-Canadian Relations Today* (The Johns Hopkins University Press, Baltimore 1984).

O.P. Dwivedi (ed.) *Resources and the Environment: Policy Perspectives for Canada* (McClelland and Stewart, Toronto 1980).

Elizabeth B. Elliot-Meisel, *Arctic Diplomacy: Canada and the United States in the Northwest Passage* (Peter Lang, New York 1998).

A.B. Fox, A.O. Hero, Jr., and J. S. Nye, Jr. (eds) *Canada and the United States: Transnational and Transgovernmental Relations* (Columbia University Press, New York 1976).

Erik Franckx, *Maritime Claims in the Arctic: Canadian and Russian Perspectives* (Martinus Nijhoff, Dordrecht 1993).

David Freestone, R. Barnes, and D.M. Ong (eds.) *The Law of the Sea: Progress and Prospects* (Oxford University Press, Oxford 2006).

Michael G. Fry (ed.) *Freedom and Change: Essays in Honour of Lester B. Pearson* (McClelland and Stewart, Toronto 1975), at pp. 147–151.

George V. Galdorisi and Kevin R. Vienna, *Beyond the Law of the Sea: New Directions for U.S. Oceans Policy* (Praeger, Westport, Connecticut 1997).

F.V. Garcia Amador, *Latin America and the Law of the Sea* (University of Rhode Island, Law of the Sea Institute, Kingston, R.I. 1972).

Terrence D. Gill and W. P. Heere (eds.) *Reflections on Principles and Practice of International Law* (Martinus Nijhoff, The Hague 2000).

Allan Gotlieb, *The Washington Diaries, 1981–1989* (McClelland and Stewart, Toronto 2006).

J.L. Granatstein and Norman Hillmer, *For Better of For Worse: Canada and the United States in the 1990s* (Copp Clark Pitman, Toronto 1991).

David Greer and Brian Harvey, *Blue Genes: Sharing and Conserving the World's Aquatic Biodiversity* (Earthscan, London 2004).

Franklyn Griffiths (ed.) *Politics of the Northwest Passage* (McGill-Queen's University Press, Montreal 1987).

Michael Harris, *Lament for an Ocean* (McClelland and Stewart, Toronto 1998).

Ivan L. Head and Pierre Elliott Trudeau, *The Canadian Way: Shaping Canada's Foreign Policy 1968-1984* (McClelland and Stewart, Toronto 1995).

Ellen Hey, *The Regime for the Exploitation of Transboundary Marine Fisheries Resources* (Martinus Nijhoff, Dordrecht 1989).

Ann L. Hollick, *U.S. Foreign Policy and the Law of the Sea* (Princeton University Press, Princeton 1981).

Rob Huebert, *Steel, Ice and Decision-Making: The Voyage of the Polar Sea and Its Aftermath—The Making of Canadian Northern Foreign Policy* (Dalhousie University, Halifax Ph.D. thesis, 1994).

International Law Association, *Report of the Sixth-Ninth Conference* (London, 2000).

International Law Association, *Report of the Seventy-First Conference* (London, 2004).

Bing Bing Jia, *The Regime of Straits in International Law* (Clarendon Press, Oxford 1998).

Barbara Johnson and Mark W. Zacher (ed.), *Canadian Foreign Policy and the Law of the Sea* (University of British Columbia Press, Vancouver 1977).

Douglas M. Johnston, *Canada and the New International Law of the Sea* (University of Toronto Press, Toronto 1985).

—*The International Law of Fisheries* (Yale University Press, New Haven 1965).

—*The Theory and History of Ocean Boundary-Making* (McGill-Queen's University Press, Montreal 1988).

Douglas M. Johnston and Norman G. Letalik (eds.) *The Law of the Sea and Ocean Industry: New Opportunities and Restraints* (Law of the Sea Institute, Honolulu 1984).

Douglas M. Johnston and Mark J. Valencia, *Pacific Ocean Boundary Problems: Status and Solutions* (Martinus Nijhoff, Dordrecht 1991).

Lawrence Juda, *International Law and Ocean Use Management: The Evolution of Ocean Governance* (Routledge, New York 1996).

—*Ocean Space Rights: Developing U.S. Policy* (Praeger Publishers, New York 1975).

—(ed.) *The United States without the Law of the Sea Treaty: Opportunities and Costs* (Times Press, Wakefield, R.I. 1983).

Stuart B. Kaye, *The Torres Strait* (Martinus Nijhoff, The Hague 1997).

Timo Koivurova, *Environmental Impact Assessment in the Arctic: A Study of International Legal Norms* (Ashgate, Aldershot 2002).

Timo Koivurova, Tanja Joona, and Reija Shnoro (eds.) *Arctic Governance* (Juridica Lapponica 29) (Oy Sevenprint Ltd, Rovaniemi 2004).

Robert Kolb, *Case Law on Equitable Maritime Delimitation* (Martinus Nijhoff, The Hague 2003).

Cynthia Lamson and David L. VanderZwaag, *Transit Management in the Northwest Passage: Problems and Prospects* (Cambridge University Press, Cambridge 1988).

David Kenneth Leary, *International Law and the Genetic Resources of the Deep Sea* (Martinus Nijhoff, Leiden 2006).

Peter M. Leitner, *Reforming the Law of the Sea Treaty: Opportunities Missed, Precedents Set and U.S. Sovereignty Threatened* (University Press of America, New York 1996).

R.M. Logan, *Canada, the United States, and the Third Law of the Sea Conference* (Canadian-American Committee, Montreal and Washington 1974).

Natalia Loukacheva, *The Arctic Promise: Legal and Political Autonomy of Greenland and Nunavut* (University of Toronto Press, Toronto 2007).

Ronald St. J. Macdonald, Gerald L. Morris, and Douglas M. Johnston (eds.) *Canadian Perspectives on International Law and Organization* (University of Toronto Press, Toronto 1974).

J. McCabe, *The San Juan Boundary Question* (University of Toronto Press, Toronto 1964).

Donald McRae and Gordon Munro (eds.) *Canadian Oceans Policy: National Strategies and the New Law of the Sea* (University of British Columbia Press, Vancouver 1989).

Edward L. Miles, *Global Ocean Politics: The Decision Process at the Third United Nations Conference on the Law of the Sea 1973-1982* (Martinus Nijhoff, The Hague 1998).

James B. Morell, *The Law of the Sea: An Historical Analysis of the 1982 Treaty and Its Rejection by the United States* (McFarland and Company, London 1992).

Brian Mulroney, *Memoirs* (McClelland and Stewart, Toronto 2007).

John F. Murphy, *The United States and the Rule of Law in International Affairs* (Cambridge University Press, Cambridge 2004).

Satya N. Nandan and Shabtai Rosenne (eds.) *United Nations Convention on the Law of the Sea, 1982: A Commentary*, Vol. II, (Martinus Nijhoff, Dordrecht 1993).

Myron H. Nordquist (ed.) *United Nations Convention on the Law of the Sea, 1982: A Commentary*, Vol. I (Martinus Nijhoff, Dordrecht 1985).

Myron H. Nordquist and John Norton Moore (eds.) *Entry into Force of the Law of the Sea Convention* (Martinus Nijhoff, The Hague 1995).

Myron H. Nordquist, John Norton Moore, and Tomas H. Heidar (eds.) *Legal and Scientific Aspects of Continental Shelf Limits* (Martinus Nijhoff, Leiden 2004).

M. Nuttal and T. Callaghan (eds.) *The Arctic: Environment, People, Policy* (Harwood Academic Publishers, Amsterdam 2000).

Alex G. Oude Elferink (ed.) *Stability and Change in the Law of the Sea: The Role of the LOS Convention* (Martinus Nijhoff, Leiden 2005).

A.G. Oude Elferink and D.R. Rothwell (eds.) *The Law of the Sea and Polar Maritime Delimitation and Jurisdiction* (Martinus Nijhoff, The Hague 2001).

Bernard H. Oxman, David Caron, and C. Buredi (eds.) *Law of the Sea: U.S. Policy Dilemma* (Institute for Contemporary Studies Press, San Francisco 1983).

Z. Oya Ozcayir, *Port State Control* (Lloyd's of London Press, London 2001).

L.S. Parsons, *Management of Marine Fisheries in Canada* (National Research Council of Canada, Ottawa 1993).

Peter Bautista Payoyo, *Cries of the Sea: World Inequality, Sustainable Development and the Common Heritage of Humanity* (Martinus Nijhoff, The Hague 1997).

Norman Penlington, *The Alaska Boundary Dispute: A Critical Reappraisal* (McGraw-Hill Ryerson, Toronto 1972).

Donat Pharand, *Canada's Arctic Waters in International Law* (Cambridge University Press, Cambridge 1988).

—*Northwest Passage: Arctic Straits* (Martinus Nijhoff, Dordrecht 1984)

Donat Pharand and U. Leanza (eds.) *The Continental Shelf and the Exclusive Economic Zone: Delimitation and Legal Regime* (Martinis Nijhoff, Dordrecht 1993).

G. Pontecorvo (ed.) *The New Order of the Oceans: The Advent of a Managed Environment* (Columbia University Press, New York 1986).

D.P. O'Connell, *The International Law of the Sea*, Vol. I (edited by I. A. Shearer) (Clarendon Press, Oxford 1982).

Victor Prescott and Clive Schofield, *The Maritime Political Boundaries of the World* (Martinus Nijhoff, 2nd ed., Leiden 2005).

A. Reiser, J. Spiller, and D. VanderZwaag (eds.) *Environmental Decisionmaking in a Transboundary Region* (Springer-Verlag, New York 1986).

W. Michael Reisman and Gayl S. Westerman, *Straight Baselines in Maritime Boundary Delimitation* (St. Martin's Press, New York 1992).

Elizabeth Riddell-Dixon, *Canada and the International Seabed: Domestic Determinants and External Constraints* (McGill-Queen's University Press, Montreal 1989).

J. Ashley Roach and Robert W. Smith, *United States Responses to Excessive Maritime Claims* (Martinus Nijhoff, 2nd ed, The Hague 1996).

Cesare P.R. Romano, *The Peaceful Settlement of International Environmental Disputes: A Pragmatic Approach* (Kluwer Law International, The Hague 2000).

Shabtai Rosenne, *The Law and Practice of the International Court—1920–2005* (Martinus Nijhoff, Leiden 2006).

Shabtai Rosenne and Alexander Yankov, *United Nations Convention on the Law of the Sea 1982: A Commentary*, Vol. IV (Martinus Nijhoff, Dordrecht 1991).

Donald R. Rothwell, *Maritime Boundaries and Resource Development: Options for the Beaufort Sea* (Canadian Institute of Resources Law, Calgary 1988).

Donald R. Rothwell and David L. VanderZwaag (eds.) *Towards Principled Oceans Governance: Australian and Canadian Approaches and Challenges* (Routledge, New York 2006).

Oscar Schachter, *International Law in Theory and Practice* (Martinus Nijhoff, Dordrecht 1991).

Harry N. Scheiber (ed.) *Law of the Sea: The Common Heritage and Emerging Challenges* (Martinus Nijhoff, The Hague 2000).

Markus G. Schmidt, *Common Heritage or Common Burden? The United States Position on the Development of a Regime for Deep Sea-Bed Mining in the Law of the Sea Convention* (Clarendon Press, Oxford 1989).

M.P. Shepard and A.W. Argue, *The 1985 Pacific Salmon Treaty: Sharing Conservation Burdens and Benefits* (University of British Columbia Press, Vancouver 2005).

—"Ocean Pasturage in the Pacific Salmon Treaty: Fact or Fiction?" (Canadian Industry Report of Fisheries and Aquatic Sciences No. 242, Ottawa February 1998).

Allen L. Springer, *The International Law of Pollution: Protecting the Global Environment in a World of Sovereign States* (Quorum Books, Westport, Connecticut 1983).

Olav Schram Stokke (ed.) *Governing High Seas Fisheries: The Interplay of Global and Regional Regimes* (Oxford University Press, Oxford 2001).

Reginald C. Stuart, *Dispersed Relations: Americans and Canadians in Upper North America* (The Johns Hopkins University Press, Baltimore 2007).

Clive R. Symmons, *Historic Waters in the Law of the Sea: A Modern Re-appraisal* (Martinus Nijhoff, Leiden 2008).

Alan Khee-Jin Tan, *Vessel-Source Marine Pollution: The Law and Politics of International Regulation* (Cambridge University Press, Cambridge 2006).

Yoshifumi Tanaka, *Predictability and Flexibility in the Law of Maritime Delimitation* (Hart Publishing, Oxford 2006).

S.J. Tangredi (ed.) *Globalization and Maritime Power* (National Defense University Press, Washington, D.C. 2002).

Tullio Treves (ed.) *The Law of the Sea: The European Union and Its Member States* (Martinus Nijhoff, The Hague 1997).

Scott C. Truver, *The Strait of Gibraltar and the Mediterranean* (Sijthoff and Noordhoff, Alphen aan den Rijn 1980).

David L. VanderZwaag (ed.) *Canadian Ocean Law and Policy* (Butterworths, Toronto 1992).

—*The Fish Feud: The U.S. and Canadian Boundary Dispute* (Lexington Books, Toronto 1983).

Gibran Van Ert, *Using International Law in Canadian Courts* (Kluwer Law International, The Hague 2002).

Harald von Riekhoff, John H. Sigler, and Brian W. Tomlin, *Canada-U.S. Relations: Policy Environments, Issues, and Prospects* (C.D. Howe Institute, Toronto 1979).

Davor Vidas (ed.) *Protecting the Polar Marine Environment* (Cambridge University Press, Cambridge 2000).

Davor Vidas and Willy Ostreng (eds.) *Order of the Oceans at the Turn of the Century* (Kluwer Law International, The Hague 1999).

Jennifer Welsh, *At Home in the World: Canada's Global Vision for the 21st Century* (Harper Collins, Toronto 2005).

W.E. Westermeyer and K. M. Shusterich, *United States Arctic Interests: The 1980s and 1990s* (Springer-Verlag, New York 1984).

Christian L. Wiktor, *Canadian Treaty Calendar, 1928–1978*, Vol. I (Oceana Publication, New York 1982).

Oran R. Young, *Creating Regimes: Arctic Accords and International Governance* (Cornell University Press, Ithaca 1998).

Oran R. Young and Gail Osherenko (eds.) *Polar Politics: Creating International Environmental Regimes* (Cornell University, Ithaca 1993).

Ralph Zacklin (ed.) *The Changing Law of the Sea: Western Hemisphere Perspectives* (Sitjhoff, Leiden 1974).

A. Zimmermann, C. Tomuschat and K. Oellers-Frahm (eds.) *The Statute of the International Court of Justice: A Commentary* (Oxford University Press, Oxford 2006).

ARTICLES/BOOK CHAPTERS

Lewis M. Alexander, "Exceptions to the Transit Passage Regime: Straits with Routes of 'Similar Convenience'" (1987) 18 *Ocean Development and International Law* 479.

—"The Nature of Offshore Boundaries," in L.M. Alexander and R.S. Hawkins (eds.) *Canadian—U.S. Maritime Problems* (Law of the Sea Institute, Kingston, R.I. 1972) 56–62.

G.W. Alexandrowicz, "Canadian Approaches to the Seabed Regime" in R. St. J. Macdonald, G.L. Morris and D.M. Johnston (eds.) *Canadian Perspectives on International Law and Organization* (University of Toronto Press, Toronto 1974) 410–433.

Craig Allen, "The Pacific Northwest Boundary Straits: High Seas or Internal Waters" February 1995 *Pacific Maritime Magazine* 20.

David Anderson, "Development in Maritime Boundary Law and Practice" in D. A. Colson and R. W. Smith (eds.) *International Maritime Boundaries*, Volume V (Martinus Nijhoff, Boston 2005) 3199–3222.

Camille M. Antinori, "The Bering Sea: A Maritime Delimitation Dispute between the United States and the Soviet Union" (1987) 18 *Ocean Development and International Law* 1.

Caitlyn L. Antrim, "Mineral Resources of Stateless Space: Lessons from the Deep Seabed" (2005) 59 No. 1 *Journal of International Affairs* 55.

G. B. Ayles, L. Amos, L. Bell, K. Bill, L. Harwood, and M. Papst, "Constraints and Opportunities for the Development of Commercial Fisheries in the Canadian Beaufort Sea," powerpoint presentation prepared for the Coastal Zone Canada 2006 Conference, held in Tuktoyaktuk, August 2006, available at www.czc06.ca/images/PDF/1-2-B%20Ayles.pdf (accessed on 16 August 2007).

David A. Balton, "The Bering Sea Doughnut Hole Convention: Regional Solution, Global Implications" in Olav Schram Stokke (ed.) *Governing High Seas Fisheries: The Interplay of Global and Regional Regimes* (Oxford University Press, Oxford 2001) 143–177.

Doug Bandow, "Don't Resurrect the Law of the Sea Treaty" No. 552 *Policy Analysis* (13 October 2005, Cato Institute, Washington).

— "UNCLOS III: A Flawed Treaty," (1982) 19 *San Diego Law Review* 475.

David J. Bederman, "The Old Isolation and the New Law of the Sea: Reflections on Advice and Consent for UNCLOS" (2008) 49 *Harvard International Law Journal (Online)* 21, at <www.harvardilj.org/online/126> (accessed on 8 March 2008).

J. Alan Beesley, "International Political Context of the LOS Negotiations" in Lawrence Juda (ed.) *The United States without the Law of the Sea Treaty: Opportunities and Costs* (Times Press, Wakefield, R.I. 1983) 11–22.

Richard B. Bilder, "The Canadian Arctic Waters Pollution Prevention Act" in L.M. Alexander (ed.) *The Law of the Sea: The United Nations and Ocean Management* (Law of the Sea Institute, Kingston, R.I. 1971) 204–223.

Scott G. Borgerson, "Arctic Meltdown: The Economic and Security Implications of Global Warming" (2008) 87 *Foreign Affairs* 63.

Elizabeth Mann Borgese, "The New International Economic Order and the Law of the Sea" (1977) 14 *San Diego Law Review* 584.

C.B. Bourne and D.M. McRae, "Maritime Jurisdiction in the Dixon Entrance: The Alaska Boundary Re-examined" (1976) 14 *Canadian Yearbook of International Law* 175.

Lawson W. Brigham, "The Emerging International Polar Navigation Code: Bi-Polar Relevance?" in Davor Vidas (ed.) *Protecting the Polar Marine Environment* (Cambridge University Press, Cambridge, 2000) 244–262.

Marjorie Ann Browne, "The Law of the Sea Convention and U.S. Policy," 12 May 2006 (Congressional Research Service Issue Brief, IB95010).

— "The U.N. Law of the Sea Convention and the United States: Developments Since October 2003," 27 January 2006 (Congressional Research Service Report, RS21890).

Kelly Bryan, "Swimming Upstream: Trying to Enforce the 1992 North Pacific Salmon Treaty" (1995) 28 *Cornell International Law Journal* 241.

Eugene H. Buck, "The Pacific Salmon Treaty: The 1999 Agreement and Renegotiation of Annex IV," 30 March 2007 (Congressional Research Service, RL30234).

W. Scott Burke and Frank S. Brokaw, "Ideology and The Law of the Sea" in B. Oxman, D. Caron, and C. Buredi (eds.) *Law of the Sea: U.S. Policy Dilemma* (Institute for Contemporary Studies Press, San Francisco 1983) 43-58.

William T. Burke, "Highly Migratory Species in the New Law of the Sea" (1984) 14 *Ocean Development and International Law* 273.

Barry Buzan, "Canada and the Law of the Sea" (1982) 11 *Ocean Development and International Law* 149.

Barry G. Buzan and Danford W. Middlemiss, "Canadian Foreign Policy and the Exploitation of the Seabed" in B. Johnson and M.W. Zacher (eds.) *Canadian Foreign Policy and the Law of the Sea* (University of British Columbia Press, Vancouver 1977) 1–51.

Michael Byers and Suzanne Lalonde, "Who Controls the Northwest Passage?" (discussion paper manuscript, 2008).

Christopher J. Carr, "Transformations in the Law Governing Highly Migratory Species: 1970 to the Present" in D.D. Caron and H. N. Scheiber (eds.) *Bringing New Law to Ocean Waters* (Martinus Nijhoff, Leiden 2004) 55–94.

Anthony T. Charles, "The Atlantic Groundfishery: Roots of Collapse" (1995) 18 *Dalhousie Law Journal* 65.

Jonathan I. Charney, "Progress in International Maritime Boundary Delimitation Law" (1994) 84 *American Journal of International Law* 227.

Robin R. Churchill, "The Impact of State Practice on the Jurisdictional Framework Contained in the LOS Convention" in A. G. Oude Elferink (ed.) *Stability and Change in the Law of the Sea: The Role of the LOS Convention* (Martinus Nijhoff, Leiden 2005) 91–143.

— "Maritime Delimitation in the Jan Mayen Area" (1985) 9 *Marine Policy* 16.

Robin R. Churchill and Geir Ulfstein, "Autonomous Institutional Arrangements in Multilateral Environmental Agreements: A Little-Noticed Phenomenon in International Law" (2000) 94 *American Journal of International Law* 623.

Thomas A. Clingan, Jr., "Third-Party Imitations of Canadian Legislation and the Implications for International Law Development" in L.M. Alexander and G.R.S.

Hawkins (eds.) *Canadian—U.S. Maritime Problems* (Law of the Sea Institute, Kingston, R.I. 1972) 68–74.

— "The United States and the Law of the Sea Conference," in G. Pontecorvo (ed.) *The New Order of the Oceans: The Advent of a Managed Environment* (Columbia University Press, New York 1986) 219–237.

Maxell Cohen, "The Regime of Boundary Waters—The Canadian-United States Experience" (1975) Vol. III *Recueil des Cours* 219.

David A. Colson, "The Delimitation of the Outer Continental Shelf between Neighboring States" (2003) 97 *American Journal of International Law* 91.

Beverly Cook, "Lobster Boat Diplomacy: The Canada-US Grey Zone" (2005) 29 *Marine Policy* 385.

Neil Craik, "Presumed Innocent: Navigation Rights and Risk-Based Activities in the Passamaquoddy Bay" (2008) 58 *U.N.B. Law Journal* 167.

Donald G. Crosby, "The UNCLOS III Definition of the Continental Shelf: Application to the Canadian Offshore" in D.M. Johnston and N.G. Letalik (eds.) *The Law of the Sea and Ocean Industry: New Opportunities and Restraints* (Law of the Sea Institute, Honolulu 1984) 473–486.

V.D. Degan, "Internal Waters" (1986) 17 *Netherlands Yearbook of International Law* 3.

A.L.C. de Mestral and L.H.J. Legault, "Multilateral Negotiation - Canada and the Law of the Sea Conference" (1979) 35 *International Journal* 47.

John A. Duff, "A Note on the United States and the Law of the Sea: Looking Back and Moving Forward" (2004) 35 *Ocean Development and International Law* 195.

William Edeson, "The International Plan of Action on Illegal, Unreported and Unregulated Fishing: The Legal Context of a Non-Legally Binding Instrument" (2001) 16 *International Journal of Marine and Coastal Law* 603.

Mark B. Feldman and David Colson, "The Maritime Boundaries of the United States" (1981) 75 *American Journal of International Law* 729.

Edward Feege and Scott C. Turver, "Homeland Security: Implications for the Coast Guard" in S.J. Tangredi (ed.) *Globalization and Maritime Power* (National Defense University Press, Washington 2002) 441–454.

Anne Fikkan, Gail Osherenko, and Alexander Arikainen, "Polar Bears: The Importance of Simplicity" in O. R. Young and G. Osherenko (eds.) *Polar Politics: Creating International Environmental Regimes* (Cornell University, Ithaca 1993) 96–151.

Francesco Francioni, "The Status of the Gulf of Sirte in International Law" (1984) 11 *Syracuse Journal of International Law and Commerce* 311.

L. F. E. Goldie, "Historic Bays in International Law–An Impressionistic Overview" (1984) 11 *Syracuse Journal of International Law and Commerce* 211.

Montserrat Gorina-Ysern and Captain Joseph H. Jones, "International Law of the Sea, Access and Benefit Sharing Agreements, and the Use of Biotechnology in the Development, Patenting and Commercialization of Marine Natural Products as Therapeutic Agents" (2006) 20 *Ocean Yearbook* 221.

A. E. Gotlieb, "Canadian Diplomatic Initiatives: The Law of the Sea" in M.G. Fry (ed.) *Freedom and Change: Essays in Honour of Lester B. Pearson* (McClelland and Stewart, Toronto 1975) 136–151.

Allan Gotlieb and Charles Dalfen, "National Jurisdiction and International Responsibility: New Canadian Approaches to International Law" (1973) 67 *American Journal of International Law* 229.

David H. Gray, "Canada"s Unresolved Maritime Boundaries" (1994) Vol. 48 No. 2 *Geomatica* 131 and reprinted in (1997) Vol. 5, No. 3 *Boundary and Security Bulletin* 60 (University of Durham, International Boundaries Research Unit).

Franklyn Griffiths, "Beyond the Arctic Sublime" in F. Griffiths (ed.) *Politics of the Northwest Passage* (McGill-Queen's University Press, Montreal 1987) 241–268.

— "Pathetic Fallacy: That Canada's Arctic Sovereignty Is On Thinning Ice" (2004) Vol. 11, No. 3 *Canadian Foreign Policy* 1.

— "The Shipping News: Canada's Arctic Is Not On Thinning Ice" (2003) 58 *International Journal* 257.

Leo Gross, "The Geneva Conference on the Law of the Sea and the Right of Innocent Passage Through the Gulf of Aqaba" (1959) 53 *American Journal of International Law* 564.

Richard J. Grunawalt, "United States Policy on International Straits" (1987) 18 *Ocean Development and International Law* 445.

Robert Hage, "Canada and the Law of the Sea" (1984) 8 *Marine Policy* 2.

K. Hakapaa and E. J. Molenaar, "Innocent Passage—Past and Present" (1999) 23 *Marine Policy* 131.

Joanna Harrington, "The Role for Parliament in Treaty-Making" in O. E. Fitzgerald (ed.) *The Globalized Rule of Law: Relationships between International and Domestic Law* (Irwin Law, Toronto 2006) 159–199.

Suzanne Hawkes and R. Michael M'Gonigle, "A Black (and Rising?) Tide: Controlling Maritime Oil Pollution in Canada" (1992) 30 *Osgoode Hall Law Journal* 165.

Ivan L. Head, "Canadian Claims to Territorial Sovereignty in the Arctic Region" (1963) 9 *McGill Law Journal* 200.

Glen J. Herbert, "Fisheries Relations in the Gulf of Maine: Implications of an Arbitrated Maritime Boundary" (1995) 19 *Marine Policy* 301.

Lawrence L. Herman, "Proof of Offshore Territorial Claims in Canada" (1982) 7 *Dalhousie Law Journal* 1.

Hartmut Hesse and Nicolaos L. Charalambous, "New Security Measures for the International Shipping Community" (2004) 3 *World Maritime University (WMU) Journal of Maritime Affairs* 123.

Wayne Hettenbach, "Rough Waters in the Strait of Juan de Fuca" (1993) Vol. X, No. 8 *Oceans Policy News*, p. 6.

John Higginbotham and Jeff Heynen, "Managing Through Networks: The State of Canada-US Relations" in D. Carment, F.O. Hampson and N. Hillmer (eds.) *Canada Among Nations, 2004: Setting Priorities Straight* (McGill-Queen's University Press, Montreal 2005) 123–140.

Ann L. Hollick, "Canadian-American Relations: Law of the Sea" in A. B. Fox, A. O. Hero, Jr., and J. S. Nye, Jr. (eds.) *Canada and the United States: Transnational and Transgovernmental Relations* (Columbia University Press, New York 1976) 162–187.

S. E. L. Howell and J. J. Yackel, "A Vessel Transit Assessment of Sea Ice Variability in the Western Arctic, 1969–2002: Implications for Ship Navigation" (2004) Vol. 30, No. 2 *Canadian Journal of Remote Sensing* 205.

Nicholas C. Howson, "Breaking the Ice: The Canadian—American Dispute over the Arctic's Northwest Passage" (1988) 26 *Columbia Journal of Transnational Law* 337.

Brian Hoyle, "The United States Government Perspective" in L. Juda (ed.) *The United States without the Law of the Sea Treaty: Opportunities and Costs* (Times Press, Wakefield, R.I. 1983) 133–137.

Rob Huebert, "Article 234 and Marine Pollution Jurisdiction in the Arctic" in A. G. Oude Elferink and D.R. Rothwell (eds.) *The Law of the Sea and Polar Maritime Delimitation and Jurisdiction* (Martinus Nijhoff, The Hague 2001) 249–267.

— "Canada and the Law of the Sea Convention" (1996–97) 52 *International Journal* 69.

— "Climate Change and Canadian Sovereignty in the Northwest Passage" (2001) Vol. 2, No. 4 *Isuma—Canadian Journal of Policy Research* 86.

— "Polar Vision or Tunnel Vision: The Making of Canadian Arctic Waters Policy" (1995) 19 *Marine Policy* 343.

— "The Return of the Vikings: The Canadian–Danish Dispute over Hans Island—New Challenges for the Control of the Canadian North" in F. Berkes, R. Huebert, H. Fast, M. Manseau, and A. Diduck (eds.) *Breaking Ice: Renewable Resources and Ocean Management in the Canadian North* (University of Calgary Press, Calgary 2005) 319–336.

— "The Shipping News Part II: How Canada's Arctic Sovereignty Is On Thinning Ice" (2003) 58 *International Journal* 295.

Daniel D. Huppert, "U.S./Canada Salmon Wars: Why the Pacific Salmon Treaty Has Not Brought Peace" (January 1996), *New Directions in Marine Affairs*, Report No. 1 (School of Marine Affairs, University of Washington, Seattle).

International Law Association Committee on Coastal State Jurisdiction Relating to Marine Pollution, "Final Report," in I.L.A., *Report of the Sixth-Ninth Conference* (London 2000) 443–500.

—Committee on Legal Issues of the Outer Continental Shelf, "Report," in I.L.A., *Report of the Seventy-First Conference* (London 2004) 773–819.

Julia Jabour and Melissa Weber, "Is It Time to Cut the Gordian Knot of Polar Sovereignty?" (2008) 17 *Review of European Community and International Environmental Law* 27.

Øystein Jensen, "Arctic Shipping Guidelines: Towards a Legal Regime for Navigation Safety and Environmental Protection?" (2008) 44 *Polar Record* 107.

Thomas C. Jensen, "The United States-Canada Pacific Salmon Interception Treaty: An Historical and Legal Overview" (1986) 16 *Environmental Law* 363.

Joseph T. Jockel and Joel J. Sokolsky, "Renewing NORAD—Now If Not Forever" (July/August, 2006) Vol. 27, No. 6 *Policy Options* 53.

Barbara Johnson, "Canadian Foreign Policy and Fisheries" in B. Johnson and M. W. Zacher (eds.) *Canadian Foreign Policy and the Law of the Sea* (University of British Columbia Press, Vancouver 1977) 52–99.

Constance Johnson and Alex G. Oude Elferink, "Submissions to the Commission on the Limits of the Continental Shelf in Cases of Unresolved Land and Maritime Disputes: The Significance of Article 76(10) of the Convention on the Law of the Sea" in D. Freestone, R. Barnes and D.M. Ong (eds.) *The Law of the Sea: Progress and Prospects* (Oxford University Press, Oxford 2006) 161–179.

Douglas M. Johnston, "The Challenge of International Ocean Governance: Institutional, Ethical and Conceptual Dilemmas" in D. R. Rothwell and D. L. VanderZwaag (eds.) *Towards Principled Oceans Governance: Australian and Canadian Approaches and Challenges* (Routledge, New York 2006) 349–399.

— "The Northwest Passage Revisited" (2002) 33 *Ocean Development and International Law* 145.

— "Recent Canadian Marine Legislation: An Historical Perspective" in L.M. Alexander and G. R. S. Hawkins (eds.) *Canadian—U.S. Maritime Problems* (Law of the Sea Institute, Kingston, R.I. 1972) 63–67.

F. J. E. Jordan, "The International Joint Commission and Canada–United States Boundary Relations" in R. St. J. Macdonald, G.L. Morris and D.M. Johnston (eds.) *Canadian Perspectives on International Law and Organization* (University of Toronto Press, Toronto 1974) 522–543.

Christopher C. Joyner, "On the Borderline? Canadian Activism in the Grand Banks" in O. S. Stokke (ed.) *Governing High Seas Fisheries: The Interplay of Global and Regional Regimes* (Oxford University Press, Oxford 2001) 207–233.

Stuart Kaye, "The South Australian Historic Bays: An Assessment" (1995) 17 *Adelaide Law Review* 269.

Lee Kimball, "Turning Points in the Future of Deep Seabed Mining" (1986) 17 *Ocean Development and International Law* 367.

Christopher Kirkey, "Smoothing Troubled Waters: The 1988 Canada–United States Arctic Co-operation Agreement" (1995) 50 *International Journal* 401.

Philippe Kirsch and Douglas Fraser, "The Law of the Sea Preparatory Commission after Six Years: Review and Prospects" (1988) 26 *Canadian Yearbook of International Law* 119.

John Kirton and Don Munton, "The *Manhattan* Voyages and Their Aftermath" in F. Griffiths (ed.) *Politics of the Northwest Passage* (McGill-Queen's University Press, Montreal 1987) 67–97.

Tommy T. B. Koh, "A Constitution for the Oceans" in M. H. Nordquist (ed.) *United Nations Convention on the Law of the Sea, 1982: A Commentary*, Vol. I (Martinus Nijhoff, Dordrecht 1985) 11–16.

Timo Koivurova and Leena Heinämäki, "The Participation of Indigenous Peoples in International Norm-Making in the Arctic" (2006) 42 *Polar Record* 101.

Timo Koivurova and David L. VanderZwaag, "The Arctic Council at 10 Years: Retrospect and Prospects" (2007) 40 *U.B.C. Law Review* 121.

James Kraska, "The Law of the Sea Convention and the Northwest Passage" (2007) 22 *International Journal of Marine and Coastal Law* 257.

I. Kubat, A. Collins, B. Gorman, and W. G. Timco, "A Methodology to Evaluate Canada's Arctic Shipping Regulations" in *Proceedings of the 18th International Conference on*

Port and Ocean Engineering under Arctic Conditions (Potsdam, New York, 2005), Vol. 2, 781–791.

Louise de La Fayette, "Access to Ports in International Law" (1996) 11 *International Journal of Marine and Coastal Law* 1.

— "The Role of the United Nations in International Ocean Governance" in D. Freestone, R. Barnes and D.M. Ong (eds.) *The Law of the Sea: Progress and Prospects* (Oxford University Press, Oxford 2006) 63–74.

Suzanne Lalonde, "Increased Traffic through Canadian Arctic Waters: Canada's State of Readiness" (2004) 38 *Revue Juridique Themis* 49.

Rick Lauber, "Conception and Early Days of NPAFC" in North Pacific Anadromous Fish Commission, *A Decade to Remember: 10th Anniversary Commemorative Album* (Vancouver, 2003) 21–22.

John W. Lavers and Iain S. Stewart, "Fisheries Surveillance and Enforcement" in D. VanderZwaag (ed.) *Canadian Ocean Law and Policy* (Butterworths, Toronto, 1992) 173–189.

Karin L. Lawson, "Delimiting Continental Shelf Boundaries in the Arctic: The United States—Canada Beaufort Sea Boundary" (1981) 22 *Virginia Journal of International Law* 222.

Leonard Legault, "Canadian Arctic Waters Pollution Prevention Legislation" in L.M. Alexander (ed.) *The Law of the Sea: The United Nations and Ocean Management* (Law of the Sea Institute, Kingston, R.I. 1971) 294–300.

— "Maritime Claims" in R. St. J. Macdonald, G. L. Morris, and D. M. Johnston (eds.) *Canadian Perspectives on International Law and Organization* (University of Toronto Press, Toronto 1974) 377–397.

Leonard Legault and Blair Hankey, "Method, Oppositeness and Adjacency, and Proportionality in Maritime Boundary Delimitation" in J.I. Charney and L.M. Alexander (eds.) *International Maritime Boundaries*, Vol. I (Martinus Nijhoff, Boston 1993) 203–241.

James L. Malone, "Who Needs the Sea Treaty?" (1984) 54 *Foreign Policy* 44.

Joan Marshall, "Defining Maritime Boundaries: 'The Murky Hand of History's Oversight' in the Gulf of Maine" (2004) 48 *The Canadian Geographer* 266.

R. Michael M'Gonigle, and Mark W. Zacher, "Canadian Foreign Policy and the Control of Marine Pollution" in B. Johnson and M.W. Zacher (eds.) *Canadian Foreign Policy and the Law of the Sea* (University of British Columbia Press, Vancouver 1977) 100–157.

Roger McConchie and Robert S. Reid, "Canadian Foreign Policy and International Straits" in B. Johnson and M.W. Zacher (eds.) *Canadian Foreign Policy and the Law of the Sea* (University of British Columbia Press, Vancouver 1977) 158–201.

T. L. McDorman, "Canada Ratifies the 1982 United Nations Convention on the Law of the Sea: At Last" (2004) 35 *Ocean Development and International Law* 103.

—"Canada and Whaling: An Analysis of Article 65 of the Law of the Sea Convention" (1998) 29 *Ocean Development and International Law* 179.

—"Canada's Aggressive Fisheries Actions: Will They Improve the Climate For International Agreements" (1995) Vol. 2, No. 3 *Canadian Foreign Policy* 5.

—"The 1999 Canada-United States Pacific Salmon Agreement: Resolved and Unresolved Issues" (2000) 15 *Journal of Environmental Law and Litigation* 1.

—"A Canadian Perspective on the Continued Non-Ratification of the Convention on the Law of the Sea by the United States" (2005) 43 *Canadian Yearbook of International Law* 393.

—"A Canadian View of the Canada-United States Pacific Salmon Treaty: The International Legal Context (I)" (1998) 6 *Willamette Journal of International Law and Dispute Resolution* 79.

—"The GATT Consistency of U.S. Fish Import Embargoes to Stop Driftnet Fishing and Save Whales, Dolphins and Turtles" (1991) 24 *George Washington Journal of International Law and Economics* 477.

—"An Overview of International Fisheries Disputes and the International Tribunal for the Law of the Sea (ITLOS)" (2002) 40 *Canadian Yearbook of International Law* 119.

—"Port State Enforcement: A Comment on Article 218 of the 1982 Law of the Sea Convention" (1997) 28 *Journal of Maritime Law and Commerce* 305.

—"The Role of the Commission on the Limits of the Continental Shelf: A Technical Body in a Political World" (2002) 17 *International Journal of Marine and Coastal Law* 301.

—"In the Wake of the *Polar Sea*: Canadian Jurisdiction and the Northwest Passage" (1986) 10 *Marine Policy* 243.

—"The West Coast Salmon Dispute: A Canadian View of the Breakdown of the 1985 Treaty and the Transit License Measure" (1995) 17 *Loyola of Los Angeles International and Comparative Law Journal* 477.

—"Will Canada Ratify the Law of the Sea Convention?" (1988) 25 *San Diego Law Review* 535.

T. L. McDorman, P. M. Saunders, and D. L. VanderZwaag, "The Gulf of Maine Boundary: Dropping Anchor or Setting A Course?" (1985) 9 *Marine Policy* 90.

Richard J. McLaughlin, "Foreign Access to Shared Marine Genetic Materials: Management Options for a Quasi-Fugacious Resource" (2003) 34 *Ocean Development and International Law* 297.

Donald McRae, "Arctic Sovereignty? What is at Stake?" (2007) Vol. 64, No. 1 *Behind the Headlines*.

—"Canada and the Delimitation of Maritime Boundaries" in D. McRae and G. Munro (eds.) *Canadian Oceans Policy: National Strategies and the New Law of the Sea* (University of British Columbia Press, Vancouver 1989), 145–164.

—"Delimitation Problems of Canada (First Part)" in D. Pharand and U. Leanza (eds.) *The Continental Shelf and the Exclusive Economic Zone: Delimitation and Legal Regime* (Martinis Nijhoff, Dordrecht 1993) 159–169.

—"The Negotiation of Article 234" in F. Griffiths (ed.) *Politics of the Northwest Passage* (McGill-Queen's University Press, Montreal 1987) 98–114.

—"The Negotiation of the 1999 Pacific Salmon Agreement" (2001) 27 *Canada–United States Law Journal* 267.

Karin Mickelson, "Rereading *Trail Smelter*" (1993) 31 *Canadian Yearbook of International Law* 219.

John Norton Moore, "The Regime of Straits and the Third United Nations Conference on the Law of the Sea" (1980) 74 *American Journal of International Law* 77.

Jacques-Yvan Morin, "The Quiet Revolution: Canadian Approaches to the Law of the Sea" in R. Zacklin (ed.) *The Changing Law of the Sea: Western Hemisphere Perspectives* (Sitjhoff, Leiden 1974) 11–31.

Gordon R. Munro and Robert L. Stokes, "The Canada- United States Pacific Salmon Treaty" in D. McRae and G. Munro (eds.) *Canadian Oceans Policy: National Strategies and the New Law of the Sea* (University of British Columbia Press, Vancouver 1989) 17–35.

Gordon Munro, T. McDorman and Robert McKelvey, "Transboundary Fishery Resources and the Canada-United States Pacific Salmon Treaty," (February 1998) *Canadian-American Public Policy* (Occasional Paper Number 33).

Satya Nandan, "Administering the Mineral Resources of the Deep Seabed" in D. Freestone, R. Barnes, and D.M. Ong (eds.) *The Law of the Sea: Progress and Prospects* (Oxford University Press, Oxford 2006) 75–92.

S. N. Nandan and D. H. Anderson, "Straits Used for International Navigation: A Commentary on Part III of the United Nations Convention on the Law of the Sea 1982" (1989) 60 *British Year Book of International Law* 159.

G. David Nied, "International Adjudication: Settlement of the United States—Canada Maritime Boundary Dispute" (1982) 23 *Harvard International Law Journal* 138.

John E. Noyes, "U.S. Policy and the United Nations Convention on the Law of the Sea" (2007) 37 *George Washington International Law Review* 621.

Mark Nuttal, "Indigenous People's Organisations and Arctic Environmental Co-operation" in M. Nuttal and T. Callaghan (eds.) *The Arctic: Environment, People, Policy* (Harwood Academic Publishers, Amsterdam 2000) 621–637.

—"Indigenous Peoples, Self-Determination and the Arctic Environment" in M. Nuttal and T. Callaghan (eds.) *The Arctic: Environment, People, Policy* (HarwoodAcademic Publishers, Amsterdam 2000) 377–409.

David M. Ong, "The 1979 and 1990 Malaysia-Thailand Joint Development Agreements: A Model for International Legal Co-operation in Common Offshore Petroleum Deposits" (1999) 14 *International Journal of Marine and Coastal Law* 207.

—"The New Timor Sea Arrangement 2001: Is Joint Development of Common Oil and Gas Deposits Mandated under International Law?" (2002) 17 *International Journal of Marine and Coastal Law* 79.

Robert E. Osgood, "U.S. Security Interests and the Law of the Sea" in R. C. Amacher and R. J. Sweeney (eds.) *The Law of the Sea: U.S. Interests and Alternatives* (American Enterprise Institute for Public Policy Research, Washington 1976) 11–35.

Alex G. Oude Elferink, "Arctic Maritime Delimitations: The Preponderance of Similarities with Other Regions" in D.R. Rothwell (ed.) *The Law of the Sea and Polar Maritime Delimitation and Jurisdiction* (Martinus Nijhoff, The Hague 2001) 179–199.

—"Does Undisputed Title to a Maritime Zone Always Exclude its Delimitation: The Grey Area Issue" (1998) 13 *International Journal of Marine and Coastal Law* 143.

—"Submissions of Coastal States to the CLCS in Cases of Unresolved Land or Maritime Disputes" in M. H. Nordquist, J.N. Moore and T.H. Heidar (eds.) *Legal and Scientific Aspects of Continental Shelf Limits* (Martinus Nijhoff, Leiden 2004) 263–285.

Bernard H. Oxman, "The 1994 Agreement and the Convention" (1994) 88 *American Journal of International Law* 687.

—"The 1994 Agreement Relating to the Implementation of Part XI of the UN Convention on the Law of the Sea" in D. Vidas and W. Ostreng (eds.) *Order of the Oceans at the Turn of the Century* (Kluwer Law International, The Hague 1999) 15–35.

—"From Cooperation to Conflict: The Soviet Union & the United States at the Third U.N. Conference on the Law of the Sea," 1984 Donald L. McKernan Lecture in Marine Affairs, (University of Washington Press, Seattle 1985).

—"The Territorial Imperative: A Siren Song at Sea" (2006) 100 *American Journal of International Law* 830.

Irini Papanicolopulu, "A Note on Maritime Delimitation in a Multizonal Context: The Case of the Mediterranean" (2007) 38 *Ocean Development and International Law* 381.

Donat Pharand, "The Arctic Waters and The Northwest Passage: A Final Revisit" (2007) 38 *Ocean Development and International Law* 3.

—"The Implications of Canadian Marine and Arctic Legislation for the Development of International Law" in L.M. Alexander and G.R.S. Hawkins (eds.) *Canadian—U.S. Maritime Problems* (Law of the Sea Institute, Kingston, R.I. 1972) 75–81.

Colin B. Picker, "Fishing for Answers in Canada's Inside Passage: Exploring the Use of the Transit Fee as a Countermeasure" (1996) 21 *Yale Journal of International Law* 349.

A. H. E. Popp, "Legal Aspects of International Oil Spills in the Canada/U.S. Context" (1992) 18 *Canada—United States Law Journal* 309.

Emily J. Pudden and David L. VanderZwaag, "Canada—USA Bilateral Fisheries Management in the Gulf of Maine: Under the Radar Screen" (2007), 16 *Review of European Community and International Environmental Law* 36.

N. Peter Rasmussen, "Tuna War: Fishery Jurisdiction in International Law" (1981) *University of Illinois Law Review* 755.

Leigh Ratiner, "The Law of the Sea: A Crossroads for American Foreign Policy" (1982) 60 *Foreign Affairs* 1006.

—"United Nations Ocean Policy: An Analysis" (1971) 2 *Journal of Maritime Law and Commerce* 225.

Elliot L. Richardson, "Law of the Sea: Navigation and Other Traditional National Security Concerns" (1982) 19 *San Diego Law Review* 553.

Sang-Myon Rhee, "The Application of Equitable Principles to Resolve the United States—Canada Dispute Over East Coast Fishery" (1980) 21 *Harvard International Law Journal* 667.

J. Ashley Roach, Robert W. Smith and Tom Malionek, "Cuba-United States" in D.A. Colson and R.W. Smith (eds.) *International Maritime Boundaries*, Volume V (Martinus Nijhoff, Leiden 2005) 3555–3557.

Davis R. Robinson, "The Convergence of Law and Diplomacy in United States—Canada Relations: The Precedent of the *Gulf of Maine* Case" (2000) 26 *Canada—United States Law Journal* 37.

Shabtai Rosenne, "Historic Waters in the Third United Nations Conference on the Law of the Sea" in T.D. Gill and W.P. Heere (eds.) *Reflections on Principles and Practice of International Law* (Martinus Nijhoff, The Hague 2000) 191–203.

Dawn Russell, "International Ocean Boundary Issues and Management Arrangements" in D. VanderZwaag (ed) *Canadian Ocean Law and Policy* (Butterworths, Toronto 1992) 463–507.

Dawn Russell, David VanderZwaag, Emily Pudden, and Thea Lowry, "Fisheries and Shellfish Sanitation," in Canada, Department of Fisheries and Oceans, *Overview of Current Governance in the Bay of Fundy/Gulf of Maine: Transboundary Collaborative Arrangements and Initiatives* (May 2006).

Charlotte Salpin and Vaelntina Germani, "Patenting of Research Results Related to Genetic Resources from Areas beyond National Jurisdiction: The Crossroads of the Law of the Sea and Intellectual Property Law" (2007) 16 *Review of European Community and International Environmental Law* 12.

Christopher Sands, "The Rising Importance of Third-Country Issues in Canada's Relations with the United States" in A. F. Cooper and D. Rowlands (eds.) *Canada Among Nations, 2006: Minorities and Priorities* (McGill-Queen's University Press, Montreal 2006) 125–144.

Phillip M. Saunders, "Jurisdiction and Principle in the Implementation of the Law of the Sea: The Case of Straddling Stocks" in C. Carmody, Y. Iwasawa and S. Rhodes (eds.) *Trilateral Perspectives on International Legal Issues: Conflict and Coherence* (American Society of International Law, Washington 2003), 377–401.

William L. Schachte, Jr., "The Unvarnished Truth: The Debate on the Law of the Sea Convention" (2008) Vol. 61, No. 2 *Naval War College Review* 119.

Harry N. Scheiber, "Japan, the North Atlantic Triangle, and the Pacific Fisheries: A Perspective on the Origins of Modern Ocean Law, 1930–1953" (2004) 6 *San Diego International Law Journal* 27.

William E. Schrank, "The Newfoundland Fishery: Ten Years After the Moratorium" (2005) 29 *Marine Policy* 407.

Shirley V. Scott, "The LOS Convention as a Constitutional Regime for the Oceans" in A. G. Oude Elferink (ed.) *Stability and Change in the Law of the Sea: The Role of the LOS Convention* (Martinus Nijhoff, Leiden 2005) 9–38.

W.R.D. Sewell and N.A. Swainson, "West Coast Oil Pollution Policies: Canadian Responses to Risk Assessment" in O.P. Dwivedi (ed.) *Resources and the Environment: Policy Perspectives for Canada* (McClelland and Stewart, Toronto 1980) 216–242.

Jessica Shadian, "Remaking Arctic Governance: The Construction of an Arctic Inuit Policy" (2006) 42 *Polar Record* 249.

Kurt M. Shusterich, "International Jurisdictional Issues in the Arctic Ocean" in W.E. Westermeyer and K.M. Shusterich (eds.) *United States Arctic Interests: The 1980s and 1990s* (Springer-Verlag, New York 1984) 240–267.

Yann-huei Song, "Declarations and Statements with Respect to the 1982 UNCLOS: Potential Legal Disputes between the United States and China after U.S. Accession to the Convention" (2005) 36 *Ocean Development and International Law* 261.

Judith Spiller and John Roanowicz, "Effectiveness of Canadian and U.S. Environmental Assessment Processes in Evaluating Transboundary Impacts" in A. Reiser, J. Spiller and D. VanderZwaag (eds.) *Environmental Decisionmaking in a Transboundary Region* (Springer-Verlag, New York 1986) 109–139.

Allen L. Springer, "Do Good Fences Make Good Neighbours? The Gulf of Maine Revisited" (1994) 6 *International Environmental Affairs* 223.

Ted Stevens, "United States-Canada Salmon Treaty Negotiations: The Alaskan Perspective" (1986) 16 *Environmental Law* 423.

E. J. Stewart, S. E. L. Howell, D. Draper, J. Yackel and A. Tivy, "Sea Ice in Canada's Arctic: Implications for Cruise Tourism" (2007) 60 *Arctic* 370.

Clive R. Symmons, "The Irish Partial Submission to the Commission on the Limits of the Continental Shelf in 2005: A Precedent for Future Such Submissions in the Light of the 'Disputed Areas' Procedures of the Commission" (2006) 37 *Ocean Development and International Law* 299.

G. D. Taylor, "The Collapse of the Northern Cod Fishery: A Historical Perspective" (1995) 18 *Dalhousie Law Journal* 13.

Tullio Treves, "The Agreement Completing the UN Law of the Sea Convention: Formal and Procedural Aspects" in M.H. Nordquist and J.N. Moore (eds.) *Entry into Force of the Law of the Sea Convention* (Martinus Nijhoff, The Hague 1995) 99–118.

—"The General Assembly and the Meeting of States Parties in the Implementation of the LOS Convention" in A. G. Oude Elferink (ed.) *Stability and Change in the Law of the Sea: The Role of the LOS Convention* (Martinus Nijhoff, Leiden 2005) 55–74.

Michael Tsimplis, "Alien Species Stay Home: The International Convention for the Control and Management of Ships' Ballast Water and Sediments 2004" (2005) 20 *International Journal of Marine and Coastal Law* 411.

Yasuko Tsuru, "Rethinking the Principle of Abstention: The North Pacific and Beyond" (2004) 28 *Marine Policy* 541.

Marilyn Twitchell, "Implementing the U.S. - Canada Pacific Salmon Treaty: The Struggle to Move from 'Fish Wars' to Cooperative Fishery Management" (1989) 20 *Ocean Development and International Law Journal* 409.

Peter J. Usher, "Inivialuit Use of the Beaufort Sea and Its Resources, 1960–2000" (2002) 55, Sup. 1 *Arctic* 18.

Eduardo Valencia-Ospina, "The Use of Chambers of the International Court of Justice" in V. Lowe and M. Fitzmaurice (eds.) *Fifty Years of the International Court: Essays in Honour of Sir Robert Jennings* (Cambridge University Press, Cambridge 1996) 503–527.

David VanderZwaag, "The Management of Straddling Stocks: Stilling the Troubled Waters of the Grand Banks" in D. VanderZwaag (ed.) *Canadian Ocean Law and Policy* (Butterworths, Toronto 1992) 115–139.

—"Transbounday Challenges and Cooperation in the Gulf of Maine Region: Riding a Restless Sea Toward Misty Shores" in H. N. Scheiber (ed.) *Law of the Sea: The Common Heritage and Emerging Challenges* (Martinus Nijhoff, The Hague 2000) 265–286.

David VanderZwaag, Rob Huebert and Stacey Ferrara, "The Arctic Environmental Protection Strategy, Arctic Council and Multilateral Environmental Initiatives: Tinkering While the Arctic Marine Environmental Totters" (2002) 30 *Denver Journal of International Law and Policy* 131.

Jon M. Van Dyke, "The Legal Regime Governing Sea Transport of Ultrahazardous Radioactive Materials" (2002) 33 *Ocean Development and International Law* 77.

Marjo Vierros and Charlotte Salpin, "Evaluating and Enhancing the Implementation of the Marine and Coastal Programme of Work of the Convention on Biological Diversity" (2005) 19 *Ocean Yearbook* 232.

Erik B. Wang, "Canada-United States Fisheries and Maritime Boundary Negotiations: Diplomacy in Deep Water" (1981) Vol. 38, No. 6 *Behind the Headlines.*

S. L. Waters, "Non-Consumptive Utilisation of Marine Mammals in Canada: International and National Regulation" in D. VanderZwaag (ed.) *Canadian Ocean Law and Policy* (Butterworths, Toronto 1992) 141–172.

Jill Wherrett, "Bill C-8: Canada-Yukon Oil and Gas Accord Implementation Act" (Canada, Library of Parliament, 1998, LS-297E), available at <dsp-psd.pwgsc.gc.ca/Collection-R/LoPBdP/LS/361/c8-e.htm> (accessed on 9 April 2007).

K. J. Wilson, J. Falkingham, H. Melling, and R. De Abreu, "Shipping in the Canadian Arctic: Other Possible Climate Change Scenarios" in *Geoscience and Remote Sensing Symposium, 2004, Proceedings*, Vol. 3 (Institute of Electrical and Electronics Engineers, Piscataway, New Jersey 2004) 1853–156.

Rudiger Wolfrum, "Germany and the Law of the Sea" in T. Treves (ed.) *The Law of the Sea: The European Union and Its Member States* (Martinus Nijhoff, The Hague 1997) 199–224.

Patricia K. Wouters, "Allocation of the Non-Navigational Use of International Watercourses: Efforts at Codification and the Experience of Canada and the United States" (1992) 30 *Canadian Yearbook of International Law* 43.

Joy A. Yanagida, "The Pacific Salmon Treaty" (1987) 81 *American Journal of International Law* 577.

Oran Young, "Arctic Shipping: An American Perspective" in F. Griffiths (ed.) *Politics of the Northwest Passage* (McGill-Queen's University Press, Montreal 1987) 115–133.

Vyacheslav Zilanov, "Good Cooperation Ensures Good Results" in North Pacific Anadromous Fish Commission, *A Decade to Remember: 10th Anniversary Commemorative Album* (Vancouver, 2003) 17–18.

MISCELLANEOUS

Douglas Alpen, "Information on the Tanker Exclusion Zone (TEZ) for Canada's West Coast," in Canada, Department of Fisheries and Oceans, *Bowie Seamount Ecosystem Overview: Appendices*, Appendix F, (May 1998), at www.pac-mpo.gc.ca/oceans/Bowie/bowie_appx_e/htm> (last visited 21 September 2006).

Richard R. Baxter and Morton J. Horwitz, "Opinion in Support of Sovereignty of the United States of America over Machias Seal Island and North Rock," submitted to the Marine Resources Commission, State of Maine, 1 March 1975, on file with the author.

British Columbia, *Submission of British Columbia on West Coast Maritime Boundaries between Canada and the United States* (1977), on file with the author.

William Clark and Steven Hare, International Pacific Halibut Commission, "Summary of the 2005 Pacific Halibut Stock Assessment," at <www.iphc.washington.edu/halcom/research/sa/papers/sa05.sum.pdf> (accessed on 5 December 2006).

International Boundary Commission, *Joint Report Upon the Survey and Demarcation of the Boundary Between the United States and Canada* (U.S. Government Printing Office, 1921).

Joint Report Upon the Survey and Demarcation of the Boundary between the United States and Canada from the Source of the St. Croix River to the Atlantic Ocean (U.S. Government Printing Office, 1934).

Joint Report Upon the Survey and Demarcation of the Boundary between the United States and Canada from Tongass Passage to Mount St. Elias (U.S. Government Printing Office, 1952).

"Juridical Regime of Historic Waters, Including Historic Bays," Study prepared by the U.N. Secretariat, UN Doc A/CN.4/143, 9 March 1962, reprinted in *Yearbook of the International Law Commission, 1962*, Vol. II (New York, 1964).

Report of the Advisory Panel on Straddling Stocks, "Breaking New Ground: An Action Plan for Rebuilding The Grand Banks Fisheries," (June 2005).

Report of the United Nations Conference on Environment and Development, UN Doc A/Conf.151/26, 12 August 1992, Annex II, Agenda 21.

Senes Consulting Limited, "A Study of the Anticipated Impacts on Canada from the Development of Liquified Natural Gas Terminals on Passamaquoddy Bay" (Ottawa, undated, done for the Government of Canada), on file with the author.

David W. Strangway and William D. Ruckelshaus, "Pacific Salmon: Report to the Prime Minister of Canada and the President of the United States, Fisheries and Oceans Canada," 12 January 1988, at www.dfo-mpo.gc.ca/communic/reports/pst-tsp/report-rapport_e.htm (accessed on 25 July 2007).

Third United Nations Conference on the Law of the Sea (UNCLOS III), *Official Records*, Vols. III, XVI, XVII.

"US and Canada Collaborate on Bird Sanctuary Management despite Sovereignty Dispute" (Summer, 2007) Vol. 1 No. 2 *Gulf of Maine Times*, available at www.gulfofmaine.org/times/summer97/index.html (accessed on 6 December 2007).

Yukon River Panel and Yukon River Drainage Fisheries Association, *Yukon River Salmon Agreement Handbook: Information and Reference Materials Pertaining to the Yukon River Salmon Agreement* (Yukon River Panel, 2005).

Index